D0590765

Good Housekeeping

FOOD
ENCYCLOPEDIA

First published in the United Kingdom in 2009 by
Collins & Brown
10 Southcombe Street
London
W14 0RA

An imprint of Anova Books Company Ltd

The Good Housekeeping website is
www.allaboutyou/goodhousekeeping

ISBN 978-1-84340-413-2

A CIP catalogue for this book is available from the British Library.

10 9 8 7 6 5 4 3 2 1

Repro by Rival Colour Ltd, UK
Printed and bound by 1010 Printing International Ltd, China

This book can be ordered direct from the publisher at
www.anovabooks.com.

Good Housekeeping

FOOD
ENCYCLOPEDIA

COLLINS & BROWN

Contents

Foreword

Good cooking starts with good ingredients, but with such a dazzling array in shops and markets, it can be tricky to know what to buy and how to prepare it. Deli counters and specialist food shops are a feast for the senses: piles of plump, oozing cheeses – a mix of the familiar and the unusual – cured meats of every description, herbs and spices that tempt you to experiment. Meat counters and butchers sell anything from familiar racks of lamb and pork chops to forgotten nose-to-tail cuts that are a gift to the frugal cook. Fish counters no longer sell just cod, haddock, monkfish and plaice but give space to ever more exotic fish such as tilapia and megrim. If you're an experienced cook, the culinary opportunities are endless and exciting – but if you're a novice it can be baffling.

For more than 80 years, Good Housekeeping has been giving inspirational, failsafe advice on how to cook, underpinned by an expert understanding of ingredients. An essential addition to your bookshelf, this encyclopaedia is an invaluable work of reference, whatever your level of cooking expertise. Ingredients are explained and beautifully photographed, techniques are made clear with step-by-step instructions, and there's a collection of classic, foolproof, tried-and-tested recipes at the end of the book to inspire you.

Karen

Karen Barnes
Head of the Good Housekeeping Institute
Good Housekeeping

Dairy, cheese and eggs

Milk

Cow

Milk is a highly nutritious food, and cow's milk is a major source of both protein and calcium. It is usually pasteurised and sometimes homogenised. In pasteurisation, the milk is briefly heated to a high temperature to sterilise it and destroy natural bacteria without making it taste as though it has been cooked. Homogenisation breaks down the globules of fat so that they remain in solution, in order to keep the cream from separating and rising to the top; this makes the milk more digestible. Unpasteurised milk is available and is preferred by some for its creamy richness. However, it carries a health risk and should be avoided by those vulnerable to infection, such as pregnant women, the elderly and people whose immune systems are compromised. Jersey or Channel Island milk is the richest and creamiest, with 4.8 per cent fat content. Ordinary full-fat (whole) milk has around 3.25–3.8 per cent fat; 1 and 2 per cent fat are commonly found levels for semi-skimmed; and skimmed has almost all the cream removed. UHT or long-life milk is homogenised then briefly heated to an ultra-high temperature, which keeps it fresh for months. Once opened, it should be treated as fresh milk. Its flavour is altered by the heat treatment.

TO USE Drink hot or cold or mix with other drinks; pour on cereals; a basic ingredient in sauces, soups, batters, pancakes and desserts.

Goat and sheep

The milk of goats and sheep has long been an important part of the human diet – indeed more people in the world consume goat's milk than that of cows. Goats and sheep have been domesticated for longer than cattle; goats were being 'farmed' 9,000 years ago. Goat's milk is naturally homogenised (the small globules of cream are evenly distributed in the milk) and has less lactose (the natural sugar in milk) than cow's milk. It is easier to digest and less allergenic. Those with a lactose intolerance, or children suffering from asthma, eczema and skin disorders, can try replacing cow's milk with goat's milk. It contains more of the minerals manganese, potassium and copper as well as vitamins A and D, but less folic acid than cow's milk.

Sheep's milk is rich, with a slightly sweet taste. It is higher in total solids than cow's or goat's milk, and is high in calcium and zinc. It will keep for up to four months in the freezer.

TO USE Drink cold; pour on cereals, or substitute for cow's milk in cooking.

Condensed

Pasteurised, homogenised cow's milk is processed to become condensed milk by boiling it until it has reduced to about a third of its original volume. Heat causes the natural sugars to caramelise, creating a sweeter flavour, but often sugar is also added to act as a preservative. Condensed milk is thick and viscous and the colour slightly darker than that of fresh milk. In Asia and parts of Europe, condensed milk is added to tea or, in Vietnam, to coffee. It is also spread on bread. Canned condensed milk has a long shelf life and will last for years if unopened. Once opened, keep in the fridge and use within a few days.

TO USE In fudge and sauces; the main ingredient for dulce de leche toffee sauce (originally from Latin America); use for pies, cheesecakes and desserts.

Evaporated

To produce evaporated milk, unhomogenised milk is boiled until it has just half its original volume. It is then homogenised, canned and sterilised. It has a pouring consistency and is thinner than condensed milk, but it has a similar colour. The process alters the taste, making it stronger in flavour than fresh milk. Evaporated milk can be used in the same way as fresh by mixing it with an equal amount of water. It has a long shelf life and will last for years in its can if unopened. Once opened, keep in the fridge and use within a few days.

TO USE Pour over desserts instead of cream; in sauces and desserts; in coffee.

Dried/powdered

Powdered milk is made from skimmed milk using a process called spray-drying. After drying it is packaged in cans or jars to protect the powder from moisture, air and light. It needs to be reconstituted in a little cold water before being made up to the required volume. The flavour is different from (and inferior to) that of fresh, but the difference is not noticeable if used in cooked foods. Baby-formula manufacturers and commercial sweet factories use dried whole milk. Powdered milk keeps well for months, but should be treated as fresh milk once reconstituted. Mix well to dissolve any lumps. Convenience is the main advantage of powdered milk over any other kind. Few people would claim to enjoy its flavour more than they enjoy the flavour of fresh.

TO USE Reconstituted, it can be used for cooking or for drinks. The addition of flavourings, such as chocolate powder, will disguise the taste if necessary. Used for machine breadmaking.

Buttermilk

The liquid left over after churning cream into butter is called buttermilk. Commercially produced, cultured buttermilk is pasteurised and homogenised. The presence of lactic acid, formed during fermentation, acts as a natural preservative, and buttermilk will keep well in the fridge or freezer. It is composed of water, mineral salts, protein and milk sugar and has a thickened texture and sour flavour. As it does not contain any cream, it is lower in fat and calories than ordinary milk, but higher in potassium, vitamin B^{12} and calcium. It is also easier to digest. Buttermilk is often used to make pancakes in the US, and its tangy flavour goes well in the batter used for fried chicken.

TO USE As a drink; in baking, to add flavour and, when combined with bicarbonate of soda, to act as a raising agent for soda bread and scones.

Cream

Single and double cream

Cream, the fat globules in milk, is one of the richest and most luxurious of foodstuffs, capable of enhancing the texture and body of any dish to which it is added. At one time, cream was left to separate from the milk and collect at the top, when it was simply 'creamed off'; nowadays the process is a mechanical one. Cream is classified according to its fat content, which also determines its use, and most is pasteurised. Single cream (around 18 per cent fat) cannot be whipped, but it is excellent for pouring. Whipping cream and double cream can be whipped until thick: whipping cream has the lower fat content of the two (around 38 per cent as opposed to 48 per cent in double), and gives a lighter result. Extra-thick cream has been homogenised, so is not suitable for whipping – use as a rich spooning cream. Cream may curdle when heated; if you are using it in cooking, do not let the mixture reach boiling point after cream has been added. Double cream is the best to use in cooking, as it is less likely to curdle. All creams have a short shelf life and should be kept in the fridge.

TO USE In its various types, to add to sauces, soups, savoury and sweet dishes; a main ingredient in ice creams and other desserts; as a topping for fruit, cakes, puddings and breakfast cereals; added to drinks.

Clotted cream

This very rich cream (fat content 55 per cent) is a speciality of south-west England and is often called Cornish or Devonshire cream. Traditionally the milk was put in shallow pans until the cream had risen to the top, heated to about 82°C and cooked for 30 minutes, then left to cool overnight. Today it is produced in factories by scalding and cooking the cream until it forms a thick yellow crust, which is then skimmed off. Clotted cream is a close relation of the Near Eastern kaymak, which is believed to have been brought to Cornwall by Phoenician traders more than 2,000 years ago. Clotted cream has a distinctive 'cooked' taste, keeps for much longer than ordinary cream and is too thick to pour.

TO USE Main ingredient of a cream tea, served with scones and jam; in ice cream; as a dessert topping.

Aerosol cream

Aerosol cream has a recognisably creamy and slightly sweet taste. Cream that has been treated at an ultra-high temperature to preserve it (UHT cream) is whipped and packed into aerosol containers with stabilisers and up to 13 per cent added sugar. A gas propellant is added to expel the cream under high pressure when the container's nozzle is opened. To serve, simply shake the can and turn upside down; press the nozzle and the cream shoots out as a foam. Aerosol cream should be used just before serving as it does not hold its shape for long periods and quickly melts; it is not suitable for decoration. Keep in the fridge once opened and use within a few days. Aerosol cream is a convenience product only, and should not be regarded as a substitute for home-made whipped cream.

TO USE To top desserts or drinks.

Crème fraîche

As its name suggests, crème fraîche is a French ingredient and the best comes from a strictly controlled area of Normandy, Isigny-sur-Mer. It is made by leaving fresh cream from pasteurised cow's milk to mature and ferment through the action of natural bacteria. The process thickens the cream slightly and gives it a deliciously rich, slightly sharp taste. Crème fraîche adds a slight tang to savoury dishes and acts as a thickener. A great advantage of cooking with crème fraîche is that it does not curdle like most other creams. It keeps better than fresh cream, too – ten to 14 days in the fridge – although it will become thicker as time passes. Half-fat crème fraîche, containing additives such as thickeners and stabilisers, is also available. You can make your own crème fraîche at home by gently heating together double cream with soured cream or buttermilk, then leaving the mixture in a warm place until thick.

TO USE Mixed with sugar and vanilla as a filling for crêpes; on desserts and breakfast cereals; in sweet and savoury dishes.

Soured cream

Traditionally, soured cream (also called sour cream) was made by allowing fresh cream to sour naturally. Today it is produced under more controlled conditions, by inoculating pasteurised and homogenised single cream with starter cultures of bacteria to convert the lactose (the natural sugar in milk) into lactic acid. The cream is kept warm to encourage the growth of the bacteria until it is sour and thick. Then it is re-pasteurised to halt the souring process. It has around 18 per cent fat and a sharp, tangy taste. Soured cream cannot be whipped. It will curdle if boiled, and should be brought to room temperature before adding to a hot liquid. A traditional and widely loved ingredient in the cuisines of Eastern and Central Europe, it is used both as an ingredient and as a topping. It is an essential last-minute addition to Hungarian goulash, and a favoured topping for blini, Russian buckwheat pancakes.

TO USE Add to sweet and savoury dishes; use in salad dressings; as a garnish alongside meat dishes or as a topping for soups; mix with snipped chives or spring onions and serve with jacket potatoes.

Panna da cucina

This UHT (ultra-high temperature) treated long-life cream is a staple in Italian cooking – particularly in sauces. Sold in waxed cartons, it is twice as thick as whipping cream. Panna da cucina needs to be stirred well before using, as it may separate; thin with a little milk if necessary.

Other varieties include smetana or smietana, which is used in a similar way in Central and Eastern European countries. Sometimes referred to as 'sour cream', it is actually a mixture of soured and fresh cream and has a milder taste than soured cream alone.

TO USE Excellent blended into sauces, especially those used for pasta dishes, soups and anything savoury. Use in place of soured cream on canapés or with fresh fruit.

Yogurt

Basic yogurts

Yogurt is a fermented milk product made by introducing harmless bacteria into either whole or skimmed milk. It has a tangy flavour and may be smooth or set and silky in texture. Cow's milk is the most common type, but milk from goats, ewes, mares, camels, yaks and water buffalo can be used, with changes in taste and cooking properties according to the animal source. Yogurt is easier to digest than milk and is said to have a beneficial effect on the digestive system. 'Live' yogurt has not been pasteurised or sterilised after the bacteria have been added, so they are still active. Bio yogurt is made with bacteria that survive in the digestive system, where they aid digestion and boost the immune system. Natural yogurt contains no colour, preservatives, stabilisers or thickeners. Greek yogurt is made from cow's or ewe's milk and has a thick, creamy consistency and higher fat content. Set yogurt is made in the container in which it is sold. Some yogurts have fruit or additional flavourings added to them. When cooking with yogurt, take care not to overheat it or it will curdle; adding a little cornflour blended with a little water can help to stabilise it.

TO USE In sweet or savoury dishes; on breakfast cereals; spooned on to desserts; in salad dressings; as a meat tenderiser in a marinade.

Frozen

Frozen yogurt is a popular lower-fat alternative to ice cream. Once flavourings have been added to the basic yogurt, it is then made in the same way as ice cream. You can do this at home, as long as you remember that yogurt is slower both to freeze and to melt than ice cream. When the yogurt is commercially made, freezing for the second time kills off beneficial bacteria, so frozen yogurt is not suitable for those with a lactose intolerance. It generally contains gelatine (so it is not suitable for vegetarians), sweeteners and added flavourings and colours. Fat-free and sugar-free versions are available. Store in the freezer.

TO USE As a topping oras an accompaniment to desserts, with fresh fruit and nuts, or on its own.

Drinks

The benefits of drinking fermented milk have long been recognised. Lassi is a popular drink in India, made with diluted natural yogurt that is either sweetened with sugar or flavoured with salt or spices. Chaach, also from India, is sweetened and flavoured with lemon, mint and ginger. Ayran is the Turkish and Arabic name for a yogurt drink seasoned with salt and mint, or cucumber.

It is only recently that the practice has become widespread outside certain areas of Europe and the East. Modern yogurt drinks are often specially formulated with added probiotics (which replenish the 'good' bacteria in the gut) and sometimes prebiotics (which 'feed' the good bacteria). Both may be beneficial in helping to maintain a healthy digestive tract and immune system. There is some scientific evidence to suggest that they help lower cholesterol, and prebiotics encourage the body's absorption of calcium. Store chilled in the fridge.

TO USE As a cold drink. Probiotic yogurt drinks can be added to cereals and porridge.

Non-dairy milks and products

There are many alternatives to dairy products. They are suitable for vegetarians, vegans and people with a lactose intolerance, and for those who have an allergic reaction to animal products, or those wanting to reduce their fat and/or cholesterol intake. Some of these substitutes contain very little protein, but they do provide carbohydrates and may be enriched with extra calcium and essential vitamins. Available in major supermarkets, health-food stores or via the Internet, they are sold under brand names or 'own label' brands. Check the list of ingredients carefully, particularly for butter substitutes, as they may contain lactose, whey or casein, which are all animal products. The most common alternatives are:

Soya products

Made from soya beans, soya milk is probably the most common dairy-product alternative. It is sweeter and darker than cow's milk, with a distinctive flavour that some people find hard to get used to. There are subtle differences between the brands, however, so it's worth trying several until you find one you like. Soya milk has almost as much protein as dairy milk, but less fat and no cholesterol. It is sold as long-life or fresh, sweetened or unsweetened, sometimes with added chocolate or fruit flavourings. Add carefully to tea or coffee, as it may curdle slightly, but it's a straight replacement for dairy milk in sauces and any sweet or savoury recipe. Soya yogurts, desserts and ice cream are widely available. Soya cream is a good substitute for single cream, and will even whip a little if well chilled. Soya cream cheese tastes similar to cow's milk cream cheeses and can be used in their place; and the hard soya cheese is a good replacement in cooked dishes.

Rice milk

Free of lactose, dairy, nuts, eggs, wheat and gluten, rice milk is not as thick as soya or dairy milks and has a translucent appearance. It is sold plain or flavoured with chocolate or vanilla. Rice milk is good for drinking, pouring on to cereals and, because it is slightly sweet, for desserts and sweet dishes. It is not recommended for savoury dishes. Manufacturers generally recommend that it should not be boiled. Rice milk is used to make other dairy substitutes such as coffee creamers and ice cream.

It has less protein than soya or almond milk and is readily available in different-sized cartons, and it can also be made at home. Shake well before using.

Almond milk

Thick and creamy, with a smooth consistency and nutty taste, almond milk is not widely available, but it's easy to make your own by blending blanched almonds with a little water, a little vanilla extract and raw honey. Beaten to a smooth consistency, it can be used as a butter substitute. Drink cold, pour on to cereals, add flavourings and/or fruit to make milkshakes or smoothies, or use in sweet recipes or for baking. Add sparingly to soups and sauces at the end of cooking and heat gently. Shake well before using. Should be avoided by anyone with a nut allergy.

Oat milk

Smooth and mild, oat milk has a less pronounced flavour than soya milk and no aftertaste, but has a hint of oat flakes or porridge. Darker than cow's milk, reflecting the colour of the oats, it is a versatile, low fat alternative. Oat milk can be added to tea, coffee and other hot beverages once they are no longer at boiling point. Drink cold from the fridge, pour on to cereals, add to cheese sauces and other savoury dishes. Chill well before serving and shake well just before using.

Non-dairy spreads

There are many branded spreads available, made from milk alternatives or various oils – sunflower and olive being the most popular. Dairy-free spreads or coconut oil can be used to replace butter when making cakes or pastry, although the flavour will not be as good. Substitute olive or nut oil for butter when frying and sautéing.

Other alternatives

Branded alternatives to dairy creams, which can be used as toppings or for serving with desserts, are sold in supermarkets and food stores.

Coconut milk is available canned. It has a creamy flavour that is not suitable for all uses: serve as a drink, or add to curries and sweet dishes.

As a substitute for buttermilk, add 1 tablespoon of white vinegar or lemon juice to a cup of soya milk and mix well. It has a similar flavour and will work well in recipes where buttermilk is called for, such as scones.

Butter and other fats

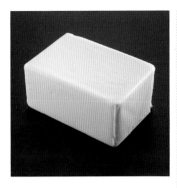  

Butter

Butter is made by churning cream until the fat forms a solid mass that can be gathered, washed and shaped. The remaining liquid is the buttermilk, which can be used separately. Butter is about 80 per cent fat. It stays firm if kept cold, but softens when warm and melts when heated. While most butter is made from cow's milk, it can also be made from goat, sheep, yak and water buffalo milk. The flavour of the butter will differ according to the animal (goat's butter has a nutty, salty taste, for example) and to the animal's diet. Salted butter has 1 per cent or more salt added, but unsalted is the one to use for baking or cooking. Many people believe that the very best butters come from Normandy, in northern France, and some of them now have worldwide distribution. Butter contains vitamins A and D but it is extremely high in calories. Eat, in moderation, as part of a well-balanced diet. It will keep (tightly covered) for several weeks in the fridge and can be frozen.

TO USE Spread on bread, scones, teacakes and crumpets. Adds flavour and richness to cakes, pastry, biscuits, sauces, casseroles, stews and soups. Flavoured butters can be used to top steaks, fish or vegetables.

Clarified

This pure butter is made by heating butter gently so that the fat rises to the top, along with a thin froth of whey, while most of the water, salt and casein (protein solids) remain at the bottom. Skim off the froth with a spoon, then pour off the clear butter, leaving behind the white solids at the bottom. You can also pour the butter through muslin to make sure that all impurities are removed. All the things that you pour away (especially the whey) make unclarified butter burn. Without them, the butter has a higher smoking point. Clarified butter is an invaluable fat in frying and baking. When heated, ordinary butter burns quickly and, if left too long on the heat, acquires an unpleasant flavour. This can be avoided by frying in half butter and half oil, but it is much more effective to use clarified butter.

Ghee, which is much used in Indian cookery, is clarified butter that has been cooked a little longer to develop a pleasant, nutty taste. It will keep for several weeks in the fridge, or longer in the freezer.

TO USE For frying, especially Ghee (see above) in Indian cooking; for baking, particularly in cake mixtures such as Genoese sponge.

Butter substitutes

There are several alternatives to butter for people with allergies or health concerns, or who need, or prefer, to follow a dairy-free diet. Hard margarine, made from various mixtures of animal and vegetable fats and oils blended with milk, is fortified to have the same levels of vitamins as butter, and is also high in saturated fat. The softer types, which tend to be easier to spread, are labelled as 'polyunsaturated'. Spreads made using a single oil or blend of oils, including sunflower, olive, vegetable and/or soya bean are often labelled 'low-fat spread'. Some substitutes are manufactured to look and taste like butter. Margarines and spreads will keep in the fridge for several weeks.

TO USE In many of the same ways as butter: for spreading on bread, toast, teacakes and crumpets; for topping vegetables. Hard margarine works better in cooking and baking than the softer margarines and low-fat spreads.

Other hard cooking fats

There are three types of fat: saturated, polyunsaturated and monounsaturated.

Saturated fats contain a high proportion of saturated fatty acids, which encourage the body to produce cholesterol. They tend to be solid at room temperature. Most saturated fats are found in meat and dairy products, and in coconut oil and hydrolysed vegetable oils.

Polyunsaturated fats contain a high proportion of polyunsaturated fatty acids, which are thought to reduce cholesterol, and are sometimes known as the 'healthy fats'. Usually liquid at room temperature, they include the essential fatty acids omega-3 and omega-6, which cannot be made by the body. Good sources are fish oils and oily fish, nuts, seeds and the oils and margarines made from them.

Monounsaturated fats are believed to help reduce the risk of heart disease. They are found in olives, olive oil, groundnut oil, nuts and avocados.

Margarine

Originally made from beef fat and skimmed milk as a substitute for butter, margarine is now made from vegetable oils. These oils have generally undergone a process of hydrogenation, which hardens them, but this has the effect of transforming polyunsaturated fats into saturated fats. In general, the harder the margarine at room temperature, the more saturated fat it contains; if soft enough to be spreadable, it will have a higher proportion of polyunsaturated fats. The most frequently used vegetable oils are sunflower, soya and corn oil; some margarines are made from a blend of oils. Margarines can be used much like butter, but the taste is not as creamy or as rich. Soft margarine is best in cakes or for use as a spread; hard margarine is better for pastry-making; both can be used for frying. Usually sold in plastic tubs.

Shortening

This is an expression for any fat used in pastry-making that makes the mixture 'short' or crisp and light. Butter, dripping, lard, margarine, suet and nut oils all come under this heading. Fats differ in their shortening powers. Generally speaking, the more workable the fat, the greater its shortening power: thus lard is good for the purpose, but oils lack workability and must therefore be used differently to get good results.

Lard

Found between the flesh and skin of pigs, and around the internal organs. Lard is white and bland, and high in saturated fats, which is the chief reason for its decline in popularity as a frying fat – its main attribute being that it does not splutter when heated and has a high smoking point. At one time, it was a popular spread on bread in Britain, and is still used as such in some parts of Europe, particularly Spain, and the US. Today, lard is mainly used for making pastry, mixed with butter or margarine, to provide both 'shortness' and good flavour.

Suet

Traditional suet is the hard fat from around the kidneys and loins in beef and mutton; it can be bought from the butcher. However, ready-shredded suet is most commonly used today and is sold in packets in supermarkets and food stores, in both beef and vegetarian versions. It is used in suet puddings, both sweet and savoury – steak and kidney, bacon pudding, spotted Dick, steamed jam pudding – as well as Christmas pudding, and in the mincemeat for mince pies. It adds flavour, but not a 'meaty' taste, to the finished dish. As suet has a high melting point, it keeps the structure of suet pastry intact even after the dough has begun to set, leaving hundreds of tiny air holes, so that the resulting pastry is light and smoothly textured, not heavy or stodgy as might be expected.

Goose fat

Regarded as something of a delicacy and excellent for roasting potatoes, goose fat has long been used as a cooking fat in parts of Europe. It has a rich, silky texture and savoury flavour, and a lower proportion of saturated fats than butter and lard. Although fairly solid when kept in the fridge, it becomes liquid at room temperature. Goose fat can be cooked at a high temperature without smoking: it can be used for frying, in stuffings, and instead of suet or lard in pastry and dumplings. If roasting a goose at home, preserve the fat by straining through muslin into sterilised jars and storing it in the fridge, where it will keep for up to six months. Commercially produced goose fat is widely available in supermarkets and food stores.

Dripping

The fat that drips from roasted joints of meat, especially beef, is used to make dripping. It is collected, then clarified to form a solid fat that is sold in blocks. Once used as a spread on bread, it is now generally used for roasting potatoes or to rub over a joint to keep it moist during cooking. Available in supermarkets, from butchers, food stores and on the Internet.

Fresh cheeses

Boursin

This hugely popular fresh cream cheese was created in 1957 by François Boursin, a French cheesemaker, and was the first flavoured fresh cheese to be sold in France. Made from pasteurised, cultured cow's milk and cream, Boursin is known as a triple crème cheese and has a minimum fat content of 75 per cent. There is also a lighter version with 41 per cent fat and, therefore, fewer calories. The most familiar Boursin is flavoured with garlic and herbs; others are rolled in crushed peppercorns, or contain herbs, nuts or raisins. Boursin has been certified kosher by the Orthodox Union. Even though it is wrapped in foil to keep it fresh, Boursin has a relatively short shelf life.

TO USE As a spread; a garnish for grilled meats; in a stuffing or pasta sauce; as a topping for jacket potatoes. To accompany a dry white wine, or a fruity red.

Cottage cheese

This dieter's friend has a soft texture. The large curds of skimmed cow's milk are slowly heated to make them firm and dense. Then the whey is drained off and the curds washed several times before being left to cool. Once cool, the resulting curd cheese is finished with the addition of a little cream. This process, combined with the high moisture content of cottage cheese, gives it its soft texture. Cottage cheese is low in fat: no more than 4 per cent and much less than that in low-fat and non-fat versions. It is also high in protein. Usually sold in tubs, cottage cheese sometimes contains added fruit or herbs such as chives. As it has poor keeping qualities it should be eaten soon after opening.

TO USE In baking and desserts, including cheesecakes; in salads; in a stuffing for vegetables.

Cream cheese

The bagel's dream partner, cream cheese is made from a mixture of cream and pasteurised milk that is firmed by the introduction of lactic acid. It has a mildly acid flavour, a rather granular texture, and a buttery consistency that makes it easy to spread. The fat content varies from type to type and from brand to brand. Philadelphia is the most famous brand. Some companies make it in large tubs, with customers buying as much as they need. There are many varieties to choose from, sometimes with added herbs or garlic. Cream cheese should be eaten shortly after opening or within a day or two of purchase if bought from a large tub.

TO USE As a spread, particularly in bagels with smoked salmon; in baking and desserts, and as a frosting for cakes; sauces and savoury dishes; in dips.

Feta

This soft, unpressed fresh Greek cheese has been awarded a Protected Designation of Origin by the EU. As a result, only cheese made from 70 per cent sheep's milk in a defined geographical area in and around Greece can bear the name. Feta is a pure-white rindless cheese, made in rectangular blocks using animal rennet, and stored in brine, where it will keep almost indefinitely. It has a sharp, salty taste and a crumbly texture. Other countries produce a similar cheese, which can be made from sheep's, goat's or cow's milk, or a combination of all three, and must be identified as coming from that country – for example, Danish feta.

Yarra Valley Pyramid is an Australian feta made from goat's milk and has a creamy, lemony, slightly salty taste. **Beyaz Peynir** originates in Turkey and is made from sheep's milk using a vegetarian rennet.

TO USE In salads; as a stuffing for pastries, pies or edible flowers; sprinkled on to stews.

Fromage frais

A soft cheese produced from skimmed cow's milk and rennet, fromage frais originated in France but is now made in other countries. During the cheesemaking process the curds are stirred to give the cheese a yogurt-like consistency. Sometimes it is enriched with cream, which increases its fat content, and often it is sold flavoured with fruit. Fromage frais has a light, fresh, clean taste and a smooth, creamy texture; its consistency varies from runny to very thick, depending on the fat content. Some varieties are quite rich and sold in very small pots. Fromage frais should be kept in the fridge and eaten soon after opening.

Fromage blanc is similar, but has a lower fat content.

TO USE An alternative to cream; in sauces or stuffings; as a dessert either on its own, with fresh fruit, or as an ingredient, for example in the French dessert coeur à la crème.

Goat's curd

Goat's curd cheese is an increasingly popular ingredient in cooking, and for eating on its own as you would eat any soft fresh cheese. Made mostly in English-speaking countries (especially Australia and the UK), it is usually lightly salted and has a fresh, tangy, mildly goaty flavour. Goat's curd can be eaten for breakfast with honey or cinnamon sprinkled on top, or as a simple dessert with fruit or nuts. It can serve as an alternative to cream cheese for spreading on toast or in cheesecake. It is also a tangy accompaniment for savoury dishes, including grilled or roast meat, quiches, grains and soufflés. Prolonged heating will curdle it, so add to cooked dishes just before serving.

TO USE For breakfast; as a dessert cheese with fresh fruit or nuts; in cheesecakes; to accompany savoury dishes.

Halloumi

This Cypriot cheese is like no other cheese in taste, consistency or cooking properties. A traditional semi-hard sheep's milk cheese flavoured with shreds of mint, it has a milky, salty taste and a creamy-white rubbery texture. It is sometimes made with goat's milk, and increasingly with cow's milk. Chopped mint is kneaded into moulded curds, which are then rolled out like pastry and cut into bars. Halloumi can be eaten soon after making, or left to ripen for a month. Soaking in brine during manufacture makes it a robust cheese that keeps well. It has a higher melting point than other cheeses, so it retains its shape when cooked. And it is always served cooked, usually by grilling, griddling or frying until the exterior is browned and slightly crisped. It is often found in the cuisines of Middle Eastern countries – cubed and grilled on skewers with slices of vegetables and served with pitta bread and hummus. It also has a natural affinity with red, ripe tomatoes and crisp cucumber.

TO USE Slice and pan-fry, griddle or grill; in stuffings for vegetables.

Le Roulé

The distinctive green swirl of garlic and herbs makes this soft French cheese instantly recognisable. Le Roulé was introduced in 1980 by Fromagerie Triballat and is made from cow's milk with added salt and a starter culture, without rennet, so it is suitable for vegetarians. The herbs, garlic and other seasonings are spread over the top of the cheese, which is then hand-rolled into a log shape and sliced. It has a smooth creamy texture and a piquant taste. A low-fat version is available. Use soon after opening.

TO USE As a spread or part of a cheeseboard; in sauces for pasta and other dishes; in dips; in quiche. To accompany dessert wine.

Mascarpone

Though technically not a cheese, as it is made from matured cream, mascarpone is often described as a cream cheese. It is made in the Lombardy region of Italy in much the same way as yogurt. A culture is added to the cream that has been skimmed off the milk, usually cow's milk, used in the production of other cheeses, such as Parmesan. The cream is heated, then allowed to mature and thicken for a few days. Mascarpone has a soft texture, a creamy, mild flavour, and a fat content of 75 per cent. Mascarpone is sold in small containers and does not keep well once opened.

TO USE Serve as an alternative to cream with fresh fruit; as a cake filling or topping; in cheesecakes; in sauces to thicken and enrich them; as a dessert mixed with chocolate and alcohol – most famously tiramisu.

Mozzarella

Soft and delicate mozzarella might have been invented to partner tomatoes, so beautifully do the two ingredients combine whether in salad, pizza, or lasagne. The cheese is traditionally made from buffalo milk but is now often made with cow's milk, and it is valued for its smooth texture. It originally came from the area around Naples. Now it's made all over Italy as well as in other countries, although the best is either made in Italy or to an Italian recipe. The pasteurised milk is curdled and the curd stretched, cut and formed into small balls, which are kept fresh through storage in their own water or whey. Older mozzarella, sold in blocks, is inclined to be rubbery but melts to form an elastic, stringy and chewy cheese, which is one of the characteristic ingredients in a pizza topping. Look for bocconcini, small balls sold in tubs; treece, plaits of mozzarella; or the smoked version. Mozzarella should be stored in its own whey or water in the fridge to keep it moist and used within a few days of opening.

TO USE Young mozzarella in salads; older mozzarella in pizzas, lasagnes and pasta bakes; to top meat or chicken with thin slices before grilling.

Paneer

A semi-soft cheese, paneer is also known as panir or peymir, popular in the Indian subcontinent and the Near East. It is commercially made from whole cow's milk: the milk is curdled, then the curds are tied in cloth; then, unusually for a fresh cheese, they're placed under pressure to solidify. The pressed curd is then cut into slabs. It can be made at home by adding lemon juice or vinegar to warmed milk, which curdles and separates. Paneer is rich in nutrients and is a versatile ingredient, and in India it is an important source of protein for vegetarians. It keeps its shape when cooked and soaks up other flavours, making it a perfect companion to rich, spicy foods.

TO USE In Indian savoury and sweet dishes, such as mattar panir (with green peas and spices).

Perroche

An English goat's cheese from Herefordshire, Perroche is made with unpasteurised fresh goat's milk. After a long coagulation period to develop firm curds, it is drained under its own weight, given a quick wash in brine, and wrapped. The small, stark-white rounds have a light, bright, lemony and goaty flavour which is nicely balanced by the slightly salty tang. It has a moist, mousse-like but substantial texture. Sold plain, or rolled in chopped fresh herbs. Suitable for vegetarians.

TO USE As part of a cheeseboard; as a dessert cheese. In cooking, grills well. To accompany Sauvignon Blanc wine.

Quark

This moist white cheese is believed to date from the Iron Age. Quark has a clean, acidic flavour and a soft, slightly granular texture. It is made by the action of lactic acid on skimmed or whole milk, and it may also include added cream. In the original version rennet is not used, but some Eastern European manufacturers add a small amount of rennet to make the curd thicker. Some types have a very low fat content, less than 1 per cent, which makes it a healthy alternative to cream cheese and some other fresh cheeses. Quark is sold in pots, either plain or flavoured with herbs, spices or fruit. It is not a long-lasting cheese and should be kept in the fridge. The name, which is German, means 'curd'.

TO USE In sandwiches; in salads; for cheesecakes; toppings for tarts, cakes and pies.

Ricotta

A soft, moist, unripened Italian cheese traditionally made from the cow's or sheep's whey left over from producing other cheeses. The whey is fermented, then boiled to form a second batch of curds. (Ricotta means 'recooked' in Italian.) Sometimes whey from goat's or buffalo's milk is used. Low in fat and mild in flavour, fresh ricotta is unsalted, crumbly, moist and delicious. Dried ricotta is salted, heavily pressed and dried. Ricotta may be thought of as the Italian equivalent of cottage cheese, but they are different in that cottage cheese has a high moisture content and a little added cream. The various regions of Italy produce their own versions of ricotta. Keep covered in the fridge for no more than a few days.

TO USE As a dessert cheese with fresh fruit; to stuff pasta, such as ravioli, or stir into a sauce; in desserts and sweet pastries. To accompany dessert wine.

Rigotte

Originally Rigotte de Condrieu (to use its full name) was exclusively made from the whey of unpasteurised goat's milk. Today it is also made from cow's milk. It originated in the Lyonnais region of France and is named after the town of Condrieu, a winemaking centre in the northern Rhône Valley. The whey is left over from producing other cheeses, but it is not recooked during the manufacturing process, unlike the whey used in ricotta. It is formed into small round cheeses. After maturing for three weeks, the cheese is a pale orange colour, covered with a soft, blooming rind, finely textured, and with a delicate honeyed taste. It is sold in small round portions. Rigotte is also available marinated in aromatic oil and flavoured with peppers and herbs. Keep in the fridge and use as fresh as possible.

TO USE As part of a cheeseboard; in salads; can be grilled. To accompany dessert wine.

More about fresh cheeses

What is a fresh cheese?

A fresh cheese can be made from any type of milk and should have no visible rind or mould. It is soft and light in texture with a high moisture content. The taste tends to be slightly acidic. Although often used for cooking, fresh cheese can also be served as a table cheese. All have a relatively short shelf life. A slightly bitter smell and greyish-brown mould mean the cheese has gone off.

The cheesemaking process

The milk is warmed and a starter culture added. For lactic cheeses such as fromage frais, this is enough. For most, rennet is stirred in and the milk is left for a few hours to coagulate. The curd is placed in cloth bags or perforated containers and left to drain slowly so that it retains much of the whey; this is what gives it its high moisture content. Fresh cheeses are usually left to drain without any added pressure, although there are exceptions, such as paneer and dried ricotta. Once enough whey has drained off, the cheese is mixed or sprinkled with salt; then it's ready. Often there is no maturing or ripening period, and fresh cheese is sold and eaten within a few days of being made.

The different types

Some fresh cheeses are made from the whey left over from cheesemaking, so they are known as whey cheeses; ricotta is an example. For travelling herdsmen and shepherds and their families, whey cheeses were an economical way of using a precious food source, as whey contains about a third of the protein in milk. Once the whey has boiled, small solid particles float to the top. They're scooped off and put into basket moulds to drain until solid enough to stick together.

Stretched curd cheeses such as mozzarella have an elastic, stringy texture. Once the young curd has been heated in the whey, it is stretched or kneaded, then formed into balls or plaited before being sealed in hot water.

How to store and serve fresh cheese

It seems obvious, but fresh cheese should be bought just before it is needed. Store in the fridge, away from the freezer compartment. Bring to room temperature, if serving as part of a cheeseboard.

Fresh, light, crisp white wines such as Sauvignon or Chenin Blanc go well with fresh cheese.

Other varieties include

From England: **Cerney** is a vegetarian goat's milk cheese, dusted with oak ash and salt; made in Gloucestershire. **Sussex Slipcote**, named after the county in which it is produced, is a vegetarian sheep's milk cheese, light and creamy, which is matured for ten days. **Vulscombe** from Devon is made from goat's milk; it has a fresh lemony taste.

From Scotland: **Caboc**, from the Ross and Cromarty region, is a traditional vegetarian cow's milk cheese that dates back to the 15th century – shaped like a log and coated in oatmeal, it has a rich, smooth, buttery texture. **Crowdie** is similar to cottage cheese, but with a finer texture, and is sometimes rolled in oats and crushed peppercorns.

From Wales: **Pant ys Gawn**, from Monmouthshire, is a modern vegetarian goat's milk cheese that has a fresh citrus flavour with a hint of herbs.

From Spain: **Cuajada**, made with sheep's and goat's milk, is sold in pots and used instead of yogurt to serve with honey and fruit.

From Italy: **Burrata** is a variant of mozzarella that is shaped like a pouch and has cream inside. It must be eaten in one sitting because the cream pours out in a thick, rich flow once it's opened.

From Finland: **Juustoleipä** is made from cow's and reindeer milk and is creamy under a toasted surface; it's usually eaten as a dessert with cream and jam.

From Hungary: **Liptoi** (or Liptauer), made from a mixture of sheep's and cow's milk, is a spiced white cheese sold in pots.

From Romania: **Brinza** is a ewe's milk cheese with a crumbly texture similar to that of feta.

From Mexico: **Queso blanco**, a cow's milk cheese, is a cross between mozzarella and cottage cheese and a good cooking cheese.

From New Zealand: **Hipi iti** (which means 'little sheep' in Maori) has a sweet caramel taste from the ewe's milk and is packed in herb-infused oil.

Vegetarian rennet

The traditional rennet used to separate milk into firm curds and liquid whey comes from the stomach lining of a young calf. Its effect was probably discovered by travelling herdsmen who carried milk in sacks made from the stomach of a young animal. Cheeses suitable for vegetarians are made using a non-animal rennet substitute from either the bacteria *Bacillus subtilis* or *Bacillus prodigiosum*, the fungus *Mucor miehei*, or certain plants, such as cardoon. Some traditional cheeses have always been made using natural rennets including fig juice, melon, wild thistle and safflower.

Soft white cheeses

Brie

One of the world's most popular and most imitated cheeses. This unpressed farm cheese was originally produced at least 800 years ago in the north of France, from whole cow's milk. It is flat and round with a white, bloomy, edible rind, a smooth, creamy texture, and a subtle flavour with a slight mushroomy aroma. Brie can be bought whole or in wedge-shaped portions. There are many variations, with Brie-style cheeses made in several countries.

Somerset Brie is a creamy, mild-tasting cheese, which comes from Britain.
Pencarreg, also from Britain, is an organic vegetarian Brie-style cheese
Jindi, from Australia, has a rich, buttery texture and sweet taste.
Cape Wickham is an Australian soft, creamy wheel-shaped cheese with a velvety soft rind.
Aorangi, from New Zealand, has a smooth buttery texture with a soft fluffy rind.
Brie de Meaux and **Brie de Melun**, both made in the original area around Paris and both protected by an *appellation d'origine contrôlée*, are especially rich, creamy and finely flavoured.

TO USE As part of a cheeseboard; in sandwiches; in salads; baked or melted into sauces. To accompany champagne or Burgundy wines.

Camembert

Another of France's world-famous unpressed cheeses is Camembert, created at the end of the 18th century in the Normandy town after which it is named. Made from unpasteurised cow's milk, it has a bloomy, edible rind, creamy texture and a taste of wild mushrooms. The cheese is usually sold in a round wooden box. Camembert is at its best when it starts to soften and the inside begins to turn from white to creamy yellow; when overripe, it develops an unpleasant smell. Camembert has inspired some excellent variations and imitators.

Coeur de Camembert au Calvados is a semi-ripe cheese dipped in Normandy's renowned apple brandy, then coated in fresh breadcrumbs and walnuts.
Pithiviers au Foin and **Olivet au Foin** are Camembert-style cheeses whose rinds are rolled in wisps of hay or grass.
Olivet Cendré is cured for three months in vine wood ash and has a spicy aroma.
Cooleeney, is an Irish full-flavoured cheese with a fresh, grassy aroma.

TO USE Serve with bread or fruit; bake gently. To accompany red Bordeaux wine or Beaujolais.

Caprice des Dieux

Caprice des Dieux comes from the Champagne region of France and was first manufactured in 1956 by the large Bongrain creamery (which also produces Saint Agur, see page 60). Made from cow's milk and enriched with cream, it has a pure white rind, a smooth velvety texture and a mildly creamy taste. It is a relatively young cheese, matured for just two weeks, with a tender interior that melts in the mouth. Sold in its distinctive oval cardboard box, Caprice des Dieux is one of France's bestselling cheeses. And its popularity is beginning to spread around the world.

TO USE As part of a cheeseboard; with French bread or fresh fruits; in a salad. To accompany light red or white wines.

Capricorn

This creamy goat's cheese is produced in Somerset, in the south-west corner of the UK. Selected cultures are added to pasteurised goat's milk with a vegetarian rennet to form the curds. Lightly dusted with salt, the cheese is left to mature for ten days, after which it is wrapped and the ripening process continues. When young the cheese is mild and crumbly, with a slightly nutty flavour. As it ripens, from the outside towards the centre, the curd becomes softer and creamier and the flavour deepens. It is suitable for those who are lactose-intolerant.

TO USE When younger and firmer, crumble into salads; grill. When mature, serve as part of a cheeseboard. To accompany dry white wine.

Chaource

Chaource is named after the village in the Champagne-Ardenne region of France where it was first made; it carries the *appellation d'origine contrôlée* stamp to show that its production is restricted to a particular area and governed by quality criteria. Made from cow's milk, the cheese has a creamy texture and delicate, nutty flavour with a mushroom aroma. When young, it tastes piquant and sharp. As it ages, it becomes very creamy, almost liquid, and melts in the mouth. Ripening and maturing takes two to four weeks. Though available all year, Chaource is at its best when made during the early spring months as the new grass is emerging. Sold in cylindrical shapes of different sizes.

TO USE Serve cubed as an appetiser with champagne or port; with seeded breads; when very ripe it can be eaten with a spoon. To accompany crisp white wine.

Coulommiers

A soft and creamy French cow's milk cheese that is very like Brie, but has a slightly lower fat content and milder flavour. Some claim it is a predecessor of Brie, and it comes from the same region (the Ile-de-France). Coulommiers has a soft, bloomy white rind and is the colour of fresh churned butter, with a supple texture that tastes mild and mushroomy when young and becomes tangy with age. At its peak, it simply melts in the mouth. It may leave behind a sweet almond aftertaste or, when produced in the spring, a hint of herbs. Coulommiers is traditionally about 12cm (5in) in diameter.

TO USE As part of a cheeseboard; in salads. To accompany Sauvignon Blanc wine.

Gratte-Paille

Gratte-paille was invented in the 1970s in Seine-et-Marne in France, and the name comes from the words meaning 'scratch', and 'straw'. This is in reference to the straw mats on which it ripens. The cheese is made from unpasteurised cow's milk enriched with fresh cream. It has a natural white rind, a buttery texture, and a faintly mushroomy flavour. Hand-moulded into brick shapes, it is matured and ripened over three weeks, and as it matures the rind becomes dry and reddish.

TO USE As part of a cheeseboard; as a dessert cheese; cooked with chicken and vegetables in pastries. To accompany red Bordeaux wine.

Saint Albray

This soft cheese is produced at the foot of the French Pyrenees from pasteurised cow's milk and matured for two weeks. Similar to Camembert, but not as strong, it is a moist cheese with a creamy texture and a distinctively perfumed taste. Despite its creamy consistency, Saint Albray holds its shape well and slices easily. Available in different sizes, it makes an impressive centrepiece at a party.

TO USE As part of a cheeseboard; cubed and served as an appetiser; in salads; with bread. To accompany Pinot Noir or Chianti.

Vignotte

From the Champagne-Ardenne region in France. This is a triple crème farmhouse cheese, meaning it is enriched with cream and has a minimum fat content of 75 per cent. (Dieters may care to choose something different.) Made from cow's milk, Vignotte has a white rind, a light, firm texture and a creamy, lemony and slightly salty flavour. It softens as it matures and, when fully ripe, melts in the mouth. Highly prized among soft cheeses for its versatility, Vignotte is made in various sizes.

TO USE As part of a cheeseboard; with fresh fruit; in salads; in savoury pastries and tarts; grilled. To accompany champagne or dry white wine.

More about soft white cheeses

What is a soft white cheese?

A typical soft white cheese has a creamy, runny texture and a bloomy *Penicillium* mould on the soft rind. It may be mild and buttery or rich and savoury with a mushroomy or earthy aroma, and can be made with skimmed or whole milk, sometimes enriched with cream. Most soft white cheeses – and certainly the best known – come from France. But excellent versions are now being produced around the world. The use of bacteria and moulds in the ripening process may cause health problems for the young, the elderly, pregnant women and people with a compromised immune system, so soft cheeses are best avoided by these groups.

The cheesemaking process

Soft cheese is made by coagulating milk with rennet. Adding a starter culture (warm or slightly sour milk from the previous evening's milking) just before the rennet ensures a clean, acid flavour. When the curd forms, it is ladled into perforated moulds to allow the whey to drain off. This takes place in rooms with a high humidity to ensure that the curd doesn't lose too much moisture. Once drained, the cheese is turned out of the moulds and left to mature.

The combination of the high moisture in the cheese and the high humidity in the room encourages the growth of the *Penicillium* fungus on the rind. This helps break down the curds, ripening the cheese from the outside in, softening the cheese and adding to the flavour, as well as preventing the interior from drying out.

Some cheesemakers introduce the mould by dusting or spraying the rinds of the ripening cheeses with a specific bacterium.

The different types

Soft white cheeses with a long shelf life have been treated to prevent them from becoming too runny. They usually have a milder taste and an springy texture. Those made with milk enriched with cream will not have a great depth of flavour, but will melt in the mouth, leaving a buttery or ice-creamy aftertaste. A double crème cheese has a fat content of 60 per cent, a triple crème 75 per cent. These cheeses are not for those who try to watch every calorie.

How to store and serve soft white cheese

Store in the warmest part of the fridge, away from the freezer compartment, wrapped in foil, waxed or greaseproof paper. Store pungent cheeses in a plastic box away from other cheeses. When ripe, the rind will change from pure white to a more mottled colour. The cheese should yield to gentle thumb pressure and have a slightly runny texture. If it develops a strong smell of ammonia it means the cheese is beginning to ferment or has been kept too damp. Bring to room temperature at least an hour before eating.

Good with full-bodied white or a light red wine.

Other varieties include

From England: **Bath** is an unpasteurised cow's milk cheese from Somerset, a modern cheese based on an old recipe; mild and tart when young, it has an oozy texture when aged. Also from Somerset is **Emlett**, made from ewe's milk; firm when young, ageing to a creamy texture with sweet acidity and a yeasty aroma. **Bosworth**, made in Staffordshire from goat's milk, has a firmer texture than most soft cheeses but a melting fudge-like bite. **Finn**, made with unpasteurised cow's milk in Herefordshire, is the only triple crème cheese made in England, and good for cooking as well as eating. **Flower Marie**, made in East Sussex from ewe's milk and vegetarian rennet, has a thin rind with a pink tint and a lemony-fresh flavour.

From France: Modern varieties include **Bougon**, a goat's milk cheese from the Poitou-Charentes region, which has a taste likened to a blend of tarragon, thyme and white wine. **Brillat-Savarin** is a triple crème cow's milk cheese with a thicker crust as it ages. **Butte**, from the Ile-de-France region, is an enriched cow's milk cheese with a salty, bitter tang and a reddish rind as it ripens. **Pavé d'Affinois** is a creamy, vegetarian cow's milk cheese from the Lyonnais region, with a taste similar to Brie as it ages. Traditional soft cheeses include **Dreux à la Feuille** from the Ile-de-France region, which is wrapped in a chestnut leaf that gives the cheese a nutty, aromatic taste, and **Gaperon** from the Auvergne, made with skimmed cow's milk. The curds are mixed with garlic and peppercorns, tied with raffia and dried.

From Spain: **Queso del Montsec** from Catalonia is a modern cheese made from goat's milk, coated with wood ash. It has a dense grainy texture and a strong, herbaceous spicy finish.

Natural-rind Cheeses

Banon

Also known as Banon à la Feuille, in reference to the chestnut leaf (feuille) in which it's always wrapped. This French cheese dates back to the Gallo-Roman period and is named after the market town in northern Provence where it was first produced. It carries the *appellation d'origine contrôlée* designation. Banon is made from unpasteurised goat's milk with a small amount of cow's milk added. It is hand-moulded into small rounds, wrapped in chestnut leaves, and tied with raffia or straw. The leaves ripen with the cheese, giving it a full, woody and fruity flavour. It is a creamy cheese, white, slightly crumbly and pungent. As it ripens, a small amount of edible blue mould develops. Best eaten soon after fully ripe.

Fromage fort du Mont Ventoux is produced by putting an unwrapped young Banon cheese in an earthenware crock, adding salt, pepper and vinegar or the local eau-de-vie, then leaving it to ferment in a cool cellar, stirring occasionally. The longer it is left, the stronger it becomes.

TO USE As part of a cheeseboard; with fresh fruit. To accompany sweet dessert wine.

Chabichou du Poitou

Also known as Chabi, this soft goat's milk cheese is made in the area around Poitou south of the Loire Valley. It dates back to the 8th century and is believed to have been introduced by the Saracens. The farmhouse variety has a grey rind with red streaks, whereas the dairy variety has a white rind. Both are small, cylindrical or slightly cone-shaped cheeses, with a strong 'goaty' smell and flavour. The cheese has a sweet, delicate taste, slightly acidic and salty at the finish, and a velvety rind. Its soft, even texture becomes dry, dense and smooth with a distinct layer next to the rind as it matures, and the rind then takes on a blue-grey mould. Chabichou du Poitou can be eaten fresh (at three weeks), ripe (six weeks) or dry (two months). Spring, summer and autumn cheeses are best. Their size makes these a particularly good choice for using in goat's cheese salad.

TO USE As part of a cheeseboard; as a dessert cheese; in salads; sliced and grilled. To accompany white or red Loire wine.

Crottin de Chavignol

A crottin is a small cylindrical goat's cheese, and may be made anywhere. But this famous *appellation d'origine contrôlée* name may only be applied to cheeses produced around the village of Chavignol, near the even more famous wine town of Sancerre. The milk may be pasteurised or unpasteurised, and it is kept in its moulds for just a brief time before being transferred to straw mats or trays for maturing. Crottin can be eaten very young, after around 12 days of maturing; it will have a downy-white rind perhaps with a hint of blue, a light and open texture, and a mild but unmistakeably goaty flavour. With further ageing, up to four months, the rind darkens to grey, deep blue and sometimes black. The interior becomes hard and crumbly, and flavour and aroma intensify. Crottin is a popular cheese for cooking, usually grilled or baked and served with salad; a single cheese is a good serving size. Best spring to autumn.

TO USE As part of a cheeseboard; in salads; as a starter; grilled or baked. To accompany Sauvignon Blanc from the region of production.

Mâconnais

Also known as chevreton de Mâcon, this *appellation d'origine contrôlée* cheese is produced in the Burgundy region of France. It is usually made from goat's milk, but sometimes cow's milk is used, depending on the season. When young, Mâconnais is light in colour, with a fresh, milky flavour and a faint smell of herbs. As it matures, over three to four weeks, it develops an ivory-coloured rind that turns brown. The soft texture becomes dry and crumbly, and the distinctive taste becomes stronger and saltier. This cheese is at its best in the summer months.

TO USE As part of a cheeseboard. To accompany Chablis, white or red Mâcon, or Beaujolais.

Perail

This traditional farmhouse cheese is made in small, thin discs from ewe's milk in the Aveyron district of south-west France. Perail is the colour of pale straw, with a pinkish tinge. It has a soft, delicate rind with a nutty, almost barnyard aroma and a sweet taste, with hints of the rich, florally abundant land the sheep graze on. The smooth texture is like thick cream and melts easily. La Perail au Lou Perac has the scent of meadow and hay.

TO USE As part of a cheeseboard; in savoury dishes. To accompany champagne or beer.

Poivre d'Âne

Also known as pebre d'ai, this rich creamy cheese is named after the French herb (also known as *sarriette* or in Provence as *pebre d'ai* and in English as savory). Savory grows abundantly in the meadows around the alps of High Provence, where the cheese is made. The milk is a mixture of unpasteurised cow's, ewe's and goat's milk, and the herb – said to be an aphrodisiac – is added to the well-drained curd, so the little discs of finished cheese have a brilliant green scattering of *sarriette* throughout. Ripening can take from less than two weeks to up to a month. This is a similar cheese to Banon: the rind is white with a hint of blue or yellow, the texture soft and slightly damp, with a peppery bite. Good between spring and autumn, although some say the best cheese is produced in autumn.

TO USE As part of a cheeseboard; in salads. To accompany white or rosé wine.

Pouligny-Saint-Pierre

Named after the small town in the Brenne Valley in central France where it originated, this *appellation d'origine contrôlée* cheese is made from goat's milk, flavoured by the heather and herbs of the rich pasturelands where they graze. The curd is carefully ladled into perforated pyramid-shaped moulds and left to drain for several days. It is then removed from the moulds, salted, and dried on willow trellises. After four weeks the rind develops a dry, naturally blue mould. If left longer, the rind's colour will deepen and the mould will spread. Pouligny-Saint-Pierre has a fine, creamy texture that is moist and soft, and a complexity of flavours that turn to a sweet nuttiness in the mouth. The early spring cheeses are particularly creamy. Its distinctive shape has earned it its nickname: 'the Eiffel Tower'.

TO USE As part of a cheeseboard. To accompany dry white or rosé wines.

Saint Marcellin

Originally Saint Marcellin was made exclusively from goat's milk; today, cow's milk is usually used. The name comes from the village in the Dauphiné region of France where production has been recorded since the 13th century. The young wheels of cheese are so tender that they are packed into individual terracotta pots for protection and that is how they are sold. It is a supple cheese with a soft rind that carries a slight white to cream-coloured mould. When young, the texture is creamy with a slight mushroomy aroma. As it ages it becomes firmer and saltier; and its complex nutty, fruity flavour changes from sweet to slightly acidic as it matures. At its best in the summer, eaten in its creamy state when the cheese clings to the knife.

TO USE As part of a cheeseboard; as a snack or starter; in savoury dishes. To accompany white and light red wines.

Valençay

This soft goat's milk cheese, *appellation d'origine contrôlée* designated, is made in central France, and named after the town around which production is centred. Valençay is shaped like a pyramid with the top cut off. Legend has it that Napoleon, returning from his disastrous campaign in Egypt, stopped at the local château and was offered the cheese. Offended by its resemblance to a pyramid, he drew his sword and chopped off the top. It is also possible, however, that the shape was established long before Napoleon's time. The curd is put into a mould and allowed to drain, then removed, coated with salted charcoal ashes, and left to ripen for three weeks. When young, the cheese can be seen through the ash; as it ripens, the colours merge and blue-grey moulds appear. The texture is smooth and white with a nutty flavour, and the cheese does not have a goaty smell. Best spring to autumn.

TO USE As part of a cheeseboard; in salads; as a starter. To accompany light, crisp wines.

More about natural-rind cheeses

What is a natural-rind cheese?

Although traditionally natural-rind cheeses were made from goat's or ewe's milk, today they may also be made from cow's milk or a mixture of all three. They have a slightly wrinkled, cream-coloured rind when young. As they dry out, the wrinkles become more obvious and the rind grows a blue-grey mould. When young, natural-rind cheeses have a fresh, almost fruity taste that holds a hint of goat or sheep. As the cheese ages, the flavours become richer, stronger and more nutty.

The cheesemaking process

Many natural-rind cheeses are made using upasteurised (raw) milk. The initial process is much the same as for fresh cheeses, but after the milk has coagulated, the curd is placed in cloth bags or perforated containers and left to drain for longer and in a drier atmosphere. Once the curds are firm, the cheeses are taken out of the moulds and salted and, at this stage, are sometimes covered with charcoal or wood ash. They are then left to mature and ripen in a ventilated, humid cellar. Natural bacteria take root on the cheese, and a mould, which starts as a discrete hue on the surface, gradually covers the cheese in blotches. Some varieties, such as Banon, are wrapped in leaves to encourage a mould to grow. The cheese must be kept dry so that it will mature and ripen successfully. That can take from ten days to four or even six weeks.

The different types

The methods used by the cheesemaker to encourage the natural moulds will influence the flavour and texture of the cheese. Wrapping the cheese in leaves imparts a fresh vegetable flavour and a distinct taste that comes from the yeast produced on and under the leaves. If the uncovered cheeses are left to ripen for a long time, the natural greyish-blue moulds will deepen to a dark grey colour, almost black, as the cheese dries out. The flavour becomes more pungent, and some people prefer cheese such as crottin de Chavignol when they are older and drier.

How to store and serve natural-rind cheese

Store in the warmest part of the fridge, away from the freezer compartment. Natural-rind cheeses have a long shelf life: usually a couple of weeks. Keep the cheese well wrapped in waxed or greaseproof paper to allow it to breathe. It's important to keep it dry, as a natural-rind cheese will lose its sharp, clean taste if it becomes damp. If mould appears on a cut surface, just trim it off and serve as usual.

Bring the cheese to room temperature before serving, and brush off any excess mould from the bought cheese before taking it to the table. Most natural rinds are edible, but they can be hard or gritty and don't add anything to the flavour of the cheese. Some people like them and many others do not. If in doubt, cut the rind off.

Dry, fruity white wines like Alsace, Anjou and Sancerre go well with these cheeses; chilled rosé also makes a good accompaniment.

Other varieties include

From France: **Arômes au gêne de marc**, produced in the Lyonnais region, is a traditional, unpasteurised farmhouse cow's and goat's milk cheese cured in vats of fermenting grape skins and pips; it has a strong, bittersweet, yeasty taste and aroma. **Sancerre**, made from goat's milk in the Loire Valley, is similar to crottin de Chavignol, with a fresh white-wine fruitiness when young, and a strong, nutty, goaty taste when aged. **Cabécou de Rocamadour** comes from the Midi-Pyrénées and is a mixture of ewe's and goat's milk – good for baking and grilling as well as eating. **Picodon de l'Ardèche** and **Picodon de la Drôme** are goat's milk cheeses from the Rhône-Alpes region with a pale ivory to soft white or pale blue-grey rind and aromatic compact interior, also sold in jars of local olive oil and herbs. **Selles-sur-Cher** is made with goat's milk using a method that has been followed for centuries; the charcoal covering is a subtle blue, the interior snowy-white, with a pronounced nutty flavour. **Tomme de Romans** is made from cow's milk and has a slightly sour, grassy flavour with a nutty finish; it is traditionally sold in wooden trays lined with straw.

From Spain: **Peñamellera**, from Asturias on the country's north coast, can be made from cow's, goat's or ewe's milk, or a combination; it has a yellowish-orange crust and a dense interior, with a few irregular holes and a mellow, vaguely nutty taste.

Washed-rind cheeses

Ardrahan

This is an award-winning semi-soft cheese from Country Cork in south-west Ireland, made using traditional methods and whole milk from the family farm's herd of Friesian cows. Vegetarian rennet is added, and the cheese is left to mature for up to eight weeks. Its edible, moist, full-bodied rind turns a deep yellow, and the centre develops a buttery texture and a nutty flavour that leaves a pleasant aftertaste. Adrahan is a versatile, distinctive and characterful cheese with a pungent, lingering aroma. When ready, the wheel-shaped cheese is wrapped in wax-coated paper and boxed. The small cheese has a shelf life of eight weeks, the large one 16 weeks.

TO USE As part of a cheeseboard; as an appetiser, cubed and served with Irish whiskey; in toasted sandwiches, melted on to baked potatoes and in other savoury dishes. To accompany full-bodied red wines.

Chaumes

Pasteurised cow's milk from south-west France is used by Fromageries des Chaumes, one France's largest cheesemaking companies, to produce this dense, mellow cheese. The production method is based on a traditional process used by Trappist monks. The soft, bright tangerine-orange rind develops after the crust has been washed several times and brushed with bacteria. Maturing takes four weeks, and produces cheese with a smooth, supple and quite rubbery texture. The taste is nutty, almost meaty, the aroma is mild, and the cheese feels rich and creamy on the tongue. Chaumes is best eaten within two weeks. A variety made in the Dordogne has a golden-yellow rind and creamy, solid consistency and is sold in boxes.

TO USE As part of a cheeseboard; spread on crusty French bread; grilled; baked in gratins or other savoury dishes. To accompany full-bodied red wines.

Epoisses de Bourgogne

Described by French gastronomic philosopher Brillat-Savarin as the 'king of cheeses', this *appellation d'origine contrôlée* cheese is produced on a single farm in Burgundy, France. It was originally made by Cistercian monks, but production petered out during the Second World War. It was revived by Robert and Simone Berthaut in 1956, and their family has been making the cheese ever since. Well-chilled evening cow's milk is mixed with warm morning milk and traditional rennet is added. The cheese is regularly washed by hand during the ripening process with a mixture of salt water and a gradually increasing proportion of high-proof Marc de Bourgogne (a brandy distilled from the pressed grapes used in making the local wine). A small brush is used to spread the bacteria evenly over the rind. The resulting cheese is uncompromisingly pungent, with a russet-coloured, smooth rind, a fine texture, and a tangy, fruity alcoholic flavour. The cheese has a yeasty tang when young and a strong meaty taste when older. Made and eaten all year.

TO USE As part of a cheeseboard; with fruit; in salads; grilled; in sauces and baked dishes. To accompany red or white burgundy.

  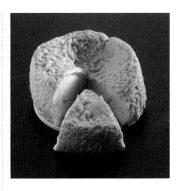

Gubbeen

This Irish cheese was first made in 1979 by a husband-and-wife team in County Cork and has established itself since then as one of the pre-eminent modern Irish cheeses. A mixed herd of cows feed on grass made lush by Ireland's heavy rainfall. Their milk is pasteurised before cheesemaking and cultured with animal rennet, and the curds are packed into circular moulds 15cm (6in) in diameter and 5cm (2in) high. After turning out of the moulds they are aged for around two months, with regular turning. The washing liquid is unusual, containing not just brine but a solution replicating the population of micro-flora found growing naturally on the cheese's rind. Gubbeen is pale yellow in colour with a few small holes in the paste. Soft but firm, it has a mellow, nutty flavour and a good finish.

TO USE As part of a cheeseboard or on its own as a dessert cheese. To accompany crusty bread and an aromatic white wine, or soda bread and a pint of Guinness.

Gris de Lille

Also known as puant de Lille or puant macéré (*puant* means 'stinking'), this is an unpasteurised cow's milk cheese from the Nord-Pas-de-Calais region of France. It is a soft, slab-shaped cheese; regularly washed with brine and/or beer, it is matured for three months. Gris de Lille has a sticky, pinkish-grey rind and a soft, slightly elastic texture. The aroma is very pungent, with a distinct farmyard influence – which is how the locals prefer it! Gris de Lille is best in the spring, autumn and winter.

TO USE As a table cheese; in salads; as a snack. To accompany champagne, or full-bodied red wines.

Langres

An *appellation d'origine contrôlée* French cheese, made from the milk of cows that graze on the plateaus around Langres in the Champagne region. Its history can be traced back to the 18th century, and traditional methods are still used, including a long ripening period in a humid cellar. The brown-red rind is created by regular washing in brine coloured with annatto, a natural orange-red food colouring. When washed with Marc de Champagne (a brandy distilled from the pressed grapes used for champagne-making), it is sold as Langres au marc. Langres has a strong, penetrating aroma; the texture is firm and supple, and melts in the mouth to release a complex mix of flavours. After further maturing, the texture becomes creamier and the flavour spicy. If matured for just 15 days, it is sold as petit Langres. It is best in the summer.

Rouy is the commercially made version of Langres, hexagonal- or square-shaped. It is milder but still pungent, and has a creamy texture and nutty aroma.

TO USE As part of a cheeseboard; in salads. To accompany champagne or brandy.

Limburger

This soft cheese, made from whole cow's milk, originated in Belgium but is now also produced in Germany and the US. Limburger was first produced by Trappist monks and named after the province where it was created. It has a legendarily strong aroma, but removing the rind reduces the smell. The curd is cut up, heated, formed into rectangular moulds and salted. It's then left to ripen in high humidity conditions for two weeks, and at a lower temperature for two months. After initial washing it is bathed several times a day with a brine of salt water and bacteria and turned regularly. The smooth, sticky, reddish-brown rind has deep ridges; the yellow soft-ripened interior has a mild, slightly spicy, piquant taste with a llingering finish.

TO USE Traditionally, sliced and served on rye or pumpernickel bread; with fruit, cold meats and in salads. To accompany ice-cold beer or Riesling.

Munster

A soft, unpressed cheese made from cow's milk in the Alsace region of France, with an orange-red rind, a soft, creamy texture, tangy taste and a highly pungent smell. It carries the *appellation d'origine contrôlée* designation. It was originally created by Irish monks who settled in Alsace in the 7th century, and the traditional process is still used in the farmhouse versions. Made from unpasteurised milk, the cheese is formed in cylindrical moulds. It is rubbed by hand with a solution of rock salt and water, then aged outside for a week before being transferred to caves where it is washed and brushed every other day. Maturing takes two to three months, and summer and autumn are the best seasons. Creamery-produced Munster is made using pasteurised milk and is available all year.

Münster, is the German version, which is made from pasteurised cow's milk.
Muenster, the American variety, is much milder; it has a smooth texture and an orange rind, and is also available flavoured with caraway or aniseed.

TO USE As part of a cheeseboard; good for grilling or melting. To accompany Gewürztraminer wine, full-bodied reds, or cold beer.

Nantais

A romantic story lies behind this cheese from the Loire Valley in France. It is said to have been created by a priest from Nantes who was fleeing the French Revolution. Hence the cheese is often referred to as curé Nantais. For many years it was produced on local farms but is now made commercially, using cow's milk and adapting traditional methods. Also known as le petit Breton or le fromage du curé, the cheese is washed several times during ripening, giving it its pronounced taste. The cheese is enclosed in an orange-coloured smooth rind; the paste is soft and yellow with small holes.

TO USE As part of a cheeseboard; as an appetiser. To accompany Muscadet.

Ogleshield

This award-winning cheese was created in the late 1990s, and in two stages. First it was a hard cheese called Shield, made by two visiting cheesemakers at the Somerset farm of renowned Cheddar-maker James Montgomery. The idea of washing the rind came later, at the Neal's Yard Dairy in London. The dairy's cheese maturer who did the work was named William Oglethorpe, and lent part of his name to the cheese that is now produced. Ogleshield is made using unpasteurised milk from Jersey cows and animal rennet. It is formed into large disks and at the end of maturation has a creamy texture with a few small holes, and a mellow, fruity and nutty flavour with wine-like notes. Ogleshield is similar in character to raclette (see page 41) and can be used in the same way.

TO USE As part of a cheeseboard; for melting on toast or boiled new potatoes. To accompany a well-hopped ale or a fruity Alsace white wine such as Pinot Gris.

Serra da Estrela

Taking its name from the highest and coldest region in Portugal, this ewe's milk cheese has a long history. Serra da Estrela cheese was originally made by the mountain shepherds. It has a protected designation of origin similar to the French *appellation d'origine contrôlée*, specifying that only cheeses from a designated area that fulfil certain conditions can bear the name. Serra da Estrela is still handmade – even the curds are broken up by hand – with a maturing and ageing period of 30–40 days. It has a leathery rind and soft, almost spreadable, slightly gooey interior, with a mildly herby perfume from the rich grazing the sheep enjoy on their mountain pastures, and a burnt toffee flavour on the finish. As it ages, the texture becomes harder and slightly chewier.

TO USE As part of a cheeseboard; traditionally, scooped out of the rind and eaten with dense, rough bread. To accompany spicy red wines.

Soumaintrain

This pungent cow's milk cheese originated in the Yonne, the northern area of Burgundy which is also the home of Chablis. The milk may be pasteurised but is traditionally unpasteurised, and the curds are packed into small round moulds with minimal pressing. Frequent rubbing with brine during maturation makes the rind turn deep orange, while the fine-textured interior ages from a mild, lemony flavour to a strong, spicier tang with a creamier texture and a robustly sweet and salty flavour. Soumaintrain is usually aged for between six and ten weeks, and gains steadily in strength the longer it is kept.

TO USE As part of a cheeseboard. To accompany white Burgundy, especially Chablis.

Stinking Bishop

Once made by Cistercian monks in the village of Dymock in Gloucestershire, Stinking Bishop is now produced by a small farmhouse operation in the same village, using pasteurised milk from the Gloucester breed of cattle. It is the washing of the wheels of cheese in perry – made from the Stinking Bishop variety of pear grown on the border with Herefordshire – that gives the cheese its name and its pungent and spirited aroma. It has a sticky orange rind, with a texture that varies from firm to soft and creamy depending on the season, and a full, nutty flavour with fruity overtones. It is not as strong as its name suggests, but some mail-order companies won't sell it during the summer months. Suitable for vegetarians.

TO USE On its own as a dessert cheese; as a snack with warm crusty bread. To accompany dessert wine.

Vacherin

Produced on the French–Swiss border, this seasonal cheese has a sweet, nutty flavour and a buttery, runny texture. The Swiss version, vacherin du Mont d'Or, is made with pasteurised cow's milk, while the French version, vacherin du Haut-Doubs, is made from unpasteurised. *Appellation d'origine contrôlée* designated, it has a strict production period and is available only during the autumn and winter months. Shaped in cloth-lined moulds, and washed with brine for at least three weeks, the cheese is wrapped with strips of spruce bark and packed in a shallow spruce box, which gives it a piney fragrance. The undulating crust is tinged pink, and the texture is soft, aromatic, velvety and meltingly rich. This seasonal delicacy is at its best when fully ripe and runny.

TO USE As an appetiser – just lift off the top and spoon out; baked with fresh herbs and/or garlic and served with bread or small vegetables to dip; as a dessert cheese. To accompany Beaujolais Nouveau, Jura wines, champagne.

Vieux Boulogne

Poor old Vieux Boulogne achieved a certain notoriety in 2004 when scientists in the UK named it 'the world's smelliest cheese'. (It even beat Epoisses de Bourgogne, see page 32.) Vieux Boulogne is made from unpasteurised cow's milk in the Nord-Pas-de-Calais, near Boulogne; the milk comes from cows that feed on salty grass near the sea, and this may give the cheese some of its salty undertones. During the maturation period the rind is washed regularly with beer, and the deep barnyard perfume comes from micro-organisms created by the interaction between bacteria in the beer and enzymes in the milk. Vieux Boulogne's infamous odour is largely skin-deep: the paste is comparatively mild on the palate, with a creamy and supple texture.

TO USE As part of a cheeseboard. To accompany French beer or a light red wine such as Beaujolais.

More about washed-rind cheeses

What is a washed-rind cheese?

Washed-rind cheeses have an orange-brown sticky rind, with an interior that ranges from soft and runny to supple and elastic. Most notably, they have a spicy, piquant taste and a pungent, yeasty, almost meaty, aroma – so strong that they were once banned on French public transport. They come mainly from Europe – northern France, Belgium and Germany – and more recently from Ireland. Many are sold in small wooden boxes, originally designed to protect them during transportation.

Origins

The original recipe for washed-rind cheese is believed to have been developed by the Cistercian monks to augment their limited diet and add some variety. Initially the cheese was for their own consumption only, but later it was made available to local people, along with the recipe. Production then moved outside the monasteries.

The cheesemaking process

Washed-rind cheeses are made from pasteurised as well as raw milk. Once the rennet has been added and the curds formed, they are scooped into moulds and left to drain before being shaped and moved to a cave, cellar or maturing rooms with a high humidity. During the maturing period (which lasts on average from one to six months, but can be shorter or longer), the cheeses are regularly washed with, or dunked in, a mixture of water, salt and bacterial cultures. The red cultures used give the rind its distinctive orangey-brown colour. Annatto, a natural red-orange colouring from a South American plant, is often included.

The washing process is almost always carried out by hand. To encourage the bacteria to spread evenly over the cheese, rather than gathering in clusters, the brine is spread using a small brush or, traditionally, a cloth dipped in the brine; this is known as 'smear-ripening'. Sometimes the wash includes alcohol (as in Stinking Bishop, washed with perry made from local pears). Alcohol may also be added to the final wash, as in Epoisses de Bourgogne. The cheese ripens from the outside inwards, and the surface bacteria react with the paste to give the cheese its distinctive smell and taste.

How to store and serve washed-rind cheese

Store in the warmest part of the fridge, away from the freezer compartment. When storing pungent cheeses, double-wrap them and place in an airtight container in foil, waxed or greaseproof paper, separate from other cheeses. They have a long shelf life, but a dull brown rind is an indication that the cheese has been kept too long, or has been allowed to dry out. If you notice the cheese cracking, wrap it in clingfilm to retain the moisture. If there is a strong ammonia-like smell coming from the cheese, leave it uncovered for a few hours. If the smell has gone, rewrap it and put back in the fridge; if it hasn't, discard the cheese. If the cheese is stored at too high a temperature, the rind will dry out and the cheese will become hard, bitter and inedible. Remove the cheese from the fridge an hour before eating.

The larger cheeses, such as Langres, which have a sunken top (*fontaine* or *cuvette*), make an ideal centrepiece for a party table: pour champagne or Marc de Bourgogne into the *fontaine* and serve with spoons for guests to help themselves. Beer, spicy white wines or robust reds go well with washed-rind cheeses.

Other varieties include

From France: **Baguette Laonnaise** is a loaf-shaped cheese made from cow's milk, and has a pungent, spicy taste and a sticky orange-brown rind. Burgundy's **Cîteaux** (Abbaye de Cîteaux) is made from cow's milk; it is milder than other washed-rind cheeses and has a fine crust. **Mamirolle**, from the Franche-Comté region, is a good grilling cheese with a semi-hard texture and sweet flavour.

From Belgium: **Brusselse kaas** (or fromage de Bruxelles), a cow's milk cheese, is smooth and sharp, with a citrus flavour and strong, salty bite. **Plateau de Herve** is a lightly pressed cow's milk cheese with a pale yellow interior and creamy consistency. **Postel** was created by the monks at the Abbey of Postel, who began making it again in the 1960s using milk from their own herd of cows; it has a distinctive and memorable flavour.

From Austria: **Mondseer** has a deep orange-coloured rind covered with a powdery white mould. The interior is open-textured with a few irregular holes, and has a sweet–sour taste and a slightly spicy aroma.

Semi-soft cheeses

Bel Paese

This famous cheese came originally from the Lombardy region of Italy; it is a trade name for a rich creamery cheese created by Galbani in the early part of the 20th century. Now, however, it is made under licence around the world. Bel Paese (beautiful country) takes its name from the title of an 1875 book by Abbot Stoppani; it is sold in discs in a distinctive wrapping featuring the head of a priest and a map of Italy. It was inspired by French cheeses, notably Port Salut and Saint-Paulin. Made from whole cow's milk, this rich and creamy cheese is surface-ripened for six to eight weeks. It has a thin, shiny rind, milky, buttery aroma and ivory-coloured interior. It is mild when young but the flavour becomes more pronounced with age.

TO USE As part of a cheeseboard; with fresh pears; as a topping for pizzas, grilled or melted into savoury dishes. To accompany soft, fruity red wine.

Caciocavallo

One of the oldest cheeses of the south of Italy, and one of the most amusingly named: caciocavallo means 'cheese on horseback.' It has a protected designation of origin. Originally made using mare's milk, it now uses cow's milk and sometimes a mixture of cow's and ewe's. The compressed curd is fermented in hot whey and then sliced and covered with hot water to give it further elasticity. After that it is stretched and shaped by hand. The distinctive gourd shape comes from the drying method: the cheeses are hung in pairs, tied at the neck by a cord. The rind is shiny yellow, the flavour mild and slightly salty, the aroma delicate. Caciocavallo has a firm, smooth texture when young (three months is the usual minimum); as it ages (for up to two years), it becomes pungent and granular. Similar to another, smaller Italian cheese called cacietto.

TO USE When young, as a dessert cheese. When older, in cooking – especially pasta dishes – and for grating. Caciocavallo and cacietto are both good melting cheeses. To accompany Italian wines.

Danbo

A very popular cheese in Denmark, Danbo has a distinctive ageing process: the rectangular blocks of curd are coated with bacteria which are then washed off at the end of the ageing cycle. The ageing period lasts between six weeks and five months. Danbo's paste is pale yellow and elastic, with a few small holes. It has a firm texture and mildly sweet, nutlike flavour. As the cheese ages, the taste gets sharper. Sometimes it is sold coated in red or yellow wax. Variations include one with caraway seeds added, a low-fat variety and a vegetarian option, made using vegetarian rennet.

TO USE As an appetiser; at breakfast with cold meats and bread; as a snack; in sandwiches. In cooking, particularly grilled. To accompany Danish beer.

Edam

This world-famous Dutch cheese is easily identified by its slightly flattened ball shape and distinctive coating of red wax (although this is used only on cheeses that are exported). Dating back to the Middle Ages, Edam was once made with whole cow's milk, but now semi-skimmed milk is used. The texture of the deep yellow interior is firm and springy and the flavour mild. It is comparatively low in calories and may be flavoured with herbs, peppercorns or cumin. The standard cheese is available in various sizes and sold in wedge-shaped portions. A longer-matured version, which is drier and firmer, is sold wrapped in black wax. Edam is sometimes referred to as a semi-hard cheese.

TO USE A good all-purpose cheese: as part of a cheeseboard; as a snack; in sandwiches; for cooking. To accompany dark beer, Pinot Noir or red Bordeaux wine.

Fontina

Many commercially produced versions of this great cheese, including Fontal, are made around the world. But the genuine article, Fontina Val d'Aosta, comes from the Italian Alps near the French and Swiss borders, where it has been produced for centuries. It is made using unpasteurised cow's milk, aged for three months and sold in wheels. The tough brown rind encloses a mildly flavoured dark yellow interior, with a soft, slightly rubbery texture pitted with small holes. Fontina has a delicate, nutty taste, with a hint of honey, but when cooked, the flavour is earthy with a fresh melting acidity.

TO USE As a dessert cheese; in cooking, an excellent melting cheese, used to make fonduta (the Piedmont dish similar to fondue, which also contains truffles). To accompany local red or white wines.

Gräddost

A firm-textured cheese from Sweden created at the beginning of the 20th century. The rich pasteurised milk of local cows is used to make this cheese, and this is what gives it its distinctive flavour. Formed into cylinder shapes, it is aged in caves for seven months and then bathed in pure glacial water. Gräddost has a satiny, ivory paste with evenly distributed holes; it is mild and very creamy with a little fruitiness and a tangy bite. Gräddost is sometimes referred to as semi-hard.

TO USE As part of a cheeseboard; as an appetiser; as a snack; in sandwiches. To accompany Chenin Blanc or Sauvignon Blanc wine.

Havarti

Named after the farm where Hanne Nielsen first made it in the 1800s, this traditional semi-soft cheese is now produced in factories both in its native Denmark and around the world. Made from pasteurised cow's milk, it is aged for three months, during which time its thin rind is periodically washed. It has a yellow paste dotted with irregular holes, and a soft, loose texture. The mild, sweet taste has a slightly acidic tang when young, but becomes sharper and saltier, with hints of hazelnut, as it ages. An enriched version with added cream is soft and luxurious in the mouth. It may also be smoked or mixed with other flavourings such as caraway seeds, fruits, herbs or spices. Havarti is usually sold foil-wrapped.

TO USE As part of a cheeseboard; with fresh fruits; sliced, grilled, melted in snacks and sandwiches. To accompany white wine (Chardonnay or Sauvignon Blanc) or a red from Bordeaux or Rioja.

Livarot

Made in and around the village of that name in the Calvados region of Normandy, Livarot is possibly one of the oldest French cheeses. Most of today's Livarot comes from industrial creameries using pasteurised cow's milk, but there are also farmhouse versions using unpasteurised milk, some of which have been washed in Calvados. A distinctive feature of the cheese is the five narrow strips of rush leaves tied around each cylinder to keep it from collapsing during ripening. (Some industrial dairies use bands of green paper.) This has earned it the nickname 'the colonel' after the badge of rank in the French army. Ripening can take up to three months in warm, humid cellars; the resulting reddish-brown rind is slightly sticky, the paste golden yellow, with a full, perfumed, piquant and spicy flavour. The odour is strong, but the cheese is worth it.

Petit Livarot is a smaller version.

TO USE As an appetiser with crusty French bread; as a dessert cheese with fresh fruits. To accompany Calvados, French cider, or full-bodied red wines.

Milleens

This award-winning farmhouse cheese has been made by the Steele family since 1976 on the Beara peninsula, County Cork, in south-west Ireland. The unpasteurised milk of Friesian cows, which graze on the slopes of the Miskish mountains, is used with a vegetarian rennet to produce this round, delicate cheese. It has a peachy, sometimes bright-orange washed rind; the paste matures from semi-firm to almost fluid, with a herbaceous tang that lingers on the palate, and a farmyard aroma. The discs are matured on the farm for two to three weeks before being packed into wooden boxes and shipped to retail outlets. Some shops sell Milleens immediately, others leave it to mature for a further four to six weeks, resulting in a strong, complex and savoury flavour.

TO USE As part of a cheeseboard. To accompany a soft red Burgundy.

Pont l'Evêque

A noble French soft cheese that dates back to the 13th century, Pont l'Evêque is named after the town in Normandy around which it is made. Pont l'Evêque has *appellation d'origine contrôlée* status and is mostly factory-made, but unpasteurised farmhouse versions are available. It is a mould-ripened cheese made with whole cow's milk. The curd is drained on a straw mat, which creates ridges on the crust, then packed into small square moulds. When firm, the cheeses are dried standing on edge and turned frequently to avoid sagging. Occasional washing with brine stops the natural mould from growing too much. The rind can develop a reddish tinge as it ripens, and the texture is firm yet soft and supple, with small holes. It has a piquant taste with a hint of sweetness, and a tangy smell. Sold in wooden boxes.

TO USE Serve as a dessert cheese. To accompany cider, Pinot Noir or Saint-Emilion wines.

Provolone

This southern Italian cheese is made from unpasteurised cow's milk and moulded by hand into a variety of shapes and sizes, including cones or pear-shapes, rounds like a melon, and cylinders. Sometimes called a semi-hard cheese, it is closely related to caciocavallo. Provolone is a traditional creamy, stretched-curd cheese, with a yellowish rind, a soft, smooth texture and a flavour that varies from mild to strong, depending on how long it has been matured.

Dolce, matured for two to three months, is a mild-tasting variety.
Piccante, aged for six months up to two years, is darker with small holes and a sharper, saltier taste. There is also a smoked variety.
Provolone Lombardo, a similar cheese, comes from the regions of Brescia and Cremona.

TO USE An all-purpose cheese, depending on its age. Young, as part of a cheeseboard or a dessert cheese; older, it is excellent for cooking and grating. To accompany regional wines.

Raclette

Raclette has been known for over 400 years. The cheese is common to Savoie in France and the canton of Valais in Switzerland, and is often referred to as semi-hard. Matured for four to seven months, raclette has a rough, grey-brown rind, a golden paste with a few small holes, and a mild flavour somewhat similar to that of Gruyère. There are many local Swiss varieties. Raclette is primarily a melting cheese, used to make an informal dish which also bears the name raclette. When heated it becomes nutty, sweet and slightly fruity. Traditionally it is toasted over an open fire or in a special grill-like appliance. As the cheese melts, it is scraped off on to a hot plate (the name comes from *racler*, 'to scrape') and is eaten with baked potatoes, pickled white onions and gherkins. The cheese would also go well with other vegetables.

TO USE For cooking. To accompany hot beverages or white wine.

Reblochon

This surface-ripened semi-soft French cheese from the Haute Savoie and Savoie regions has been made since the 13th century and has *appellation d'origine contrôlée* status. The cheese is made using whole unpasteurised milk, and there are two different types: reblochon *fermier*, identified by a green casein tag on the edge of the cheese, which is made on farms in the Thônes valley; and reblochon *fruitier*, with a red tag, which is made in factories and farmers' co-ops further afield. The thicker, richer milk from the second milking is used while still warm, and the cheese is aged in cellars or caves, turned every two days and washed with whey to speed the ageing process. It has a pinkish-white rind, creamy texture, nutty aftertaste and strong herbal aroma, but becomes bitter when overripe. Reblochon is one of the greatest of France's many great cheeses. It is at its best in the summer.

TO USE As part of a cheeseboard; an appetiser; in cooking for melting or in tartiflette (oven baked with sliced potatoes and bacon). To accompany Savoie white wines or fruity reds.

Ricotta mustia

Traditionally, this Sardinian speciality is made from the whey of milk left over after production of the island's famous sheep's milk cheese, pecorino Sardo. The whey is filtered and supplemented by a small amount of sheep's milk and salt. The whey is heated and stirred, then brought to a higher heat without stirring so that the curds can rise. They are poured into moulds to drain and cool, then wrapped in cloth, pressed for four to five hours, salted and finally smoked over wood and herbs for a few hours. The smoke gives the cheese a light amber colour, but does not penetrate far into it, so its flavour is fairly mild and subtle.

TO USE To stuff pasta, such as ravioli, or stir into a sauce; with toast as a snack or dessert cheese. To accompany Sardinian white wine.

Rollot

Rollot has been made in France at least since the 17th century, when it was said to have been served to King Louis XIV (who loved it so much he made it a 'royal cheese'). It has its origins in the north-eastern town of the same name in Picardie, and is produced from pasteurised or unpasteurised cow's milk with a minimum of around four weeks of ageing. Regular washing builds up the orange colour, and the soft, creamy paste intensifies in flavour and aroma with longer ageing (up to six weeks or so). Rollot is made either in round or in heart-shaped moulds. The latter shape is sometimes called *coeur* (heart) *de Rollot*. Rollot has fairly good melting properties and can be baked in slices on top of quiches or tarts, or grilled on toast.

TO USE As part of a cheeseboard; grill or bake. To accompany an Alsace wine such as Gewurztraminer.

Saint-Nectaire

Produced in the Auvergne since the 17th century, Saint-Nectaire is made from unpasteurised milk from the Salers cows that graze on its lush pasturelands. The unique character of that milk is essential to the flavour of Saint-Nectaire, which has been long established as one of France's pre-eminent cheeses. *Appellation d'origine contrôlée* designated, the farmhouse version can be identified by its green label. The curd is pressed into moulds by hand, then the cheese is removed, salted and wrapped in cloth. It is pressed again before being aged in cool, damp cellars for a minimum of three weeks. The cheese is disc-shaped and the bloomy rind has a white, yellow and red mould; the supple texture has tiny holes and melts in the mouth, releasing a nutty, fruity flavour with a touch of salt and spices. The maturing process gives Saint-Nectaire an unmistakeably pungent smell of mushrooms, damp cellars and rye straw – on which it is stored during the ripening process. Best in summer and autumn.

TO USE As part of a cheeseboard. To accompany light, fruity reds, such as Beaujolais.

Saint-Paulin

Saint-Paulin is a wheel-shaped cheese originally made by the monks of Port du Salut in Brittany. It is sometimes sold as Port Salut, and is now made in creameries in other parts of France. Versions are also made in other countries. Saint Paulin was the first French cheese to be produced using pasteurised milk. Sometimes referred to as semi-hard, it is a pressed, uncooked cheese with a thin washed rind that is smooth and leathery. Usually creamy yellow in colour, sometimes graduating to bright orange, it has a very mild and delicate flavour and should be eaten while slightly soft. Although creamy and buttery, it is firm enough to slice.

TO USE As part of a cheeseboard or as a dessert cheese. To accompany light, fruity wine.

San Simon

A popular smoked cow's milk cheese from Galicia in the north-west of Spain. This remote region has an ancient history of successful cheesemaking, due to its mild, wet climate and lush green pastures on which the cows graze. The curd is put into the pear-shaped moulds for a day, and the cheese is then removed and immersed in hot whey. Two weeks after leaving the moulds, the cheeses are gently smoked. The result is a supple, open consistency and attractive reddish-brown, thin rind. The creamy, buttery cheese has a smoky flavour, which ages from mild to piquant. San Simon is made both on farms and in creameries.

Bufones (dunce caps), is a smaller version available.

TO USE As part of a cheeseboard or as a dessert cheese; paired with fresh fruit, fruit pies or tarts. To accompany Spanish wines.

Scamorza

Scamorza is usually made from cow's milk, sometimes from ewe's or goat's milk, or a mixture of both. Scamorza is a close relative of mozzarella and resembles provolone. Once exclusive to Puglia in southern Italy, it is now produced in creameries across the country. It is a stretched-curd cheese, in which the fresh curd is left to mature in its own whey for several hours. The cheese is formed into round shapes, tied with string about one-third from the top, then hung to dry, creating its distinctive 'money-bag' shape. Ageing is brief: between 6 and 15 days. The smoked version has a light brown skin and woody aroma, and is slightly rounder. Scamorza has a rubbery texture, is drier than mozzarella, and has a bland, rather milky taste.

TO USE As a dessert cheese; in salads. As a substitute for mozzarella in pasta dishes; as a stuffing for meat or vegetables. To accompany light white wines.

Stracchino

The name stracchino is given both to a semi-soft cheese and to a family of soft, square-shaped Italian cheeses (including Gorgonzola and Taleggio) that have been made in Lombardy since the 12th century. Stracchino is a derivative of the word *stracco*, which means 'tired'. The cheeses were originally made in autumn from the milk of cows migrating south to avoid the winter cold; the journey made their milk thin or 'tired'. Today it is made from pasteurised whole cow's milk mixed with the previous evening's milking. It is best eaten young, when it has a soft, creamy texture and mild, delicate flavour. Fresh stracchino is also known as crescenza.

TO USE As a dessert cheese. Melted into risottos, on cooked vegetables or pizzas; baked. To accompany regional wines.

Taleggio

This soft, mould-ripened Italian cheese takes its name from the Taleggio valley in Lombardy, and its history goes back to the 11th century. It can bear the name only if made in a restricted area around the valley. The fermentation of curds in high-humidity rooms produces the unique springy texture of Taleggio. The cheese is shaped into squares, washed in brine, and matured for 25–50 days in conditions similar to that found in caves. The result is a thin and bloomy rose-grey rind with a white, soft paste. The cheese has a delicate, slightly sour taste and an aroma reminiscent of almonds, which becomes more pungent with age.

TO USE As part of a cheeseboard or a dessert cheese; in cooking – it melts into an appetising creamy sauce. To accompany young, light red wines.

Tomme de Savoie

The word *tomme* is a used for medium-sized drums of cheese, and it is applied to a number of French cheeses. Tomme de Savoie is possibly the best of them, and certainly the most famous. It originated as a farmhouse cheese using semi-skimmed milk from the family cows, and that method continues today. The curds are stirred and broken up into fine pieces, and pressed in cloth-lined moulds. After salting and drying, it is matured in caves for at least six weeks (sometimes several months) and builds up thick, greyish-brown rind. Tomme de Savoie has an attractively nutty, grassy flavour which intensifies considerably in older cheeses. Its creamy but firm texture makes it suitable for melting, and it can be used in the rustic *aligot*, a traditional dish of the Auvergne combining mashed potatoes, garlic, milk and melted cheese.

TO USE As part of a cheeseboard; grill or bake. To accompany a fruity Alsace wine such as Riesling.

Waterloo

Waterloo is made by artisanal cheese makers in Berkshire, England. It was given its name because the Duke of Wellington's dairy herd formerly provided the milk used in making it. The cow's milk is unpasteurised, and the rennet is vegetarian. Waterloo is a washed-curd cheese: during the curdling phase, some of the whey is drained off and water is added in its place. This gives a milder, gentler flavour to the finished cheese. When optimally ripe, Waterloo is soft under the rind but still quite firm at the centre. It has a nicely salty tang, and its soft creaminess balanced by gentle acidity goes particularly well with a crisp pear or apple.

TO USE As part of a cheeseboard. To accompany dry cider or a crisp white wine with good acidity, such as Chenin Blanc.

Wigmore

This award-winning cheese comes from the same dairy as Waterloo. It too uses vegetarian rennet, but the milk is unpasteurised sheep's milk rather than cow's milk. Like Waterloo, Wigmore is a washed-curd cheese: some of the whey is drained off and the curds are rinsed with water, giving a milder flavour and very smooth texture to the final cheese. It develops soft white and grey moulds on the rind, and is aged for around four weeks. When the cheese is young the texture is somewhat crumbly. With age, it becomes meltingly smooth.

TO USE As part of a cheeseboard. To accompany a fairly young and fruity Merlot or Cabernet Sauvignon wine.

More about semi-soft cheeses

What is a semi-soft cheese?

Semi-soft cheeses vary widely in appearance, but tend to have a firm but springy interior, although some have a soft white bloomy rind with an interior that's creamier and slightly runny. The cheeses have a round, full-bodied flavour that is not too strong, and often the taste is reminiscent of the herbs, flowers or grass of the pastures grazed by the cows, goats or sheep whose milk was used in making them. Sometimes these cheeses are linked with semi-hard cheeses, which can be cut into cubes, sliced and grated.

The cheesemaking process

The curd is cut using a special knife in order to release some of the whey before it is placed into moulds to drain off further. To speed up the draining, the curds may be lightly pressed with weights. After a couple of days, the cheese is turned out of its mould and given a brine wash to seal the rind. It is then placed in cellars or ripening rooms. Natural moulds will start to grow on the surface of the cheese, but these are frequently brushed off, gradually building up a leathery rind. Depending on the cheesemaker and the type of cheese, these rinds vary: sometimes pale in colour and so fine the rind is barely distinguishable from the interior; sometimes pale yellow rind like that on reblochon, or orange-brown as on raclette; and sometimes thick grey-brown and leathery, like the rind on tomme de Savoie. Some varieties, most notably Edam are wrapped in a wax coating. Maturing and ageing varies from a matter of days up to two years.

The different types

Cheeses that are intended to be eaten within a few days are pressed very lightly at the curd stage. To keep a rind from growing, the cheese is wrapped in plastic, then put in the ripening rooms; or it will be treated to produce a soft white bloomy rind. Semi-soft cheeses may go through a similar process as washed-rind cheeses to produce a pungent aromatic coating.

How to store and serve semi-soft cheese

Store in the warmest part of the fridge, away from the freezer compartment. Most varieties will keep for several weeks wrapped in foil or waxed paper and stored in an airtight container in the fridge. If a mould does appear, simply cut it away; the rest is good to eat. If there is a strong ammonia-like smell from the cheese, however, it should be discarded. Remove semi-soft cheese from the fridge an hour before serving, to allow it to come to room temperature so that its full flavour and texture can develop.

Full-bodied white wines or light, fruity reds go well with semi-soft cheeses.

Other varieties include

From England: **Loddiswell** is a modern vegetarian goat's milk cheese from Devon, with a brownish-orange rind and sweet almond taste with a sherbet-like zing.

From Ireland: **Croghan** is a vegetarian goat's milk cheese made in County Wexford and available from spring to autumn, has a brown-pink to terracotta leathery rind, a flavour of grass and hay and an aromatic finish. **Durrus** is a vegetarian cow's milk cheese from West Cork; buttery, mild and slightly acidic with complex flavours including caramel toffee, apples, a hint of smoke and a nutty creaminess. **Orla**, from County Cork, is a sheep's milk cheese; supple and semi-soft when young but ageing to sharp and salty with a burnt-sugar flavour.

From Italy: **Caciotta di Urbino** (sometimes spelled Casciotta) can be made with cow's, goat's or ewe's milk (or a mixture) and has a moist texture and sweet flavour with undertones of grass, nuts and wild flowers; it is produced from early spring to late summer. **Raschera** is a square cow's milk cheese, sometimes with sheep's or goat's milk added, which is sweet and fresh in the spring and summer, and more solid and vibrant in the winter.

From France: **Aisy cendré**, a cow's milk cheese from Burgundy coated in ash, has a white, salty, chalky centre and earthy-tasting outer layer (brush off the ash before serving). **Fromage corse** is a sheep's and goat's milk cheese from Corsica, a centuries-old, genuinely local product whose supple, almost runny paste has small holes and a flavour of maquis and wild herbs; **le Fium'Orbo** is a farmhouse version of the same cheese. **Morbier**, a cow's milk cheese from the Franche-Comté region, has a horizontal band of ash and salt in its centre, separating two layers of an elastic, springy cheese with a flavour of nuts and fruit and an aroma of fresh hay. **Murol**, from the Auvergne, is a cow's milk cheese with a thin, smooth rind, a creamy paste with a flavour of fresh milk, and a nutty aroma. **Ossau-Iraty-Brebis Pyrénées** (appellation d'origine contrôlée) is a traditional farmhouse sheep's milk cheese with a nutty, robust taste, produced during the summer. **Pavé d'Auge**, from Normandy, is a cow's milk cheese with a reddish rind, supple, creamy paste and spicy flavour.

From Germany: **Bruder Basil** from Bavaria is a modern cow's milk cheese with a smooth, firm, yellow interior with small holes and a pleasantly smoky taste that's also good for grilling. **Butterkäse**, made with cow's milk, has a golden-to-red-coloured natural rind and a buttery taste and colour.

From Belgium: **Passendale**, from Flanders, is a mild, creamy cow's milk cheese with a white mould, which looks like a loaf of bread (named after the Flemish village previously called Passchendaele).

From Denmark: Made from a traditional recipe, **Esrom** is a mild, buttery cow's milk cheese with many small holes that develops a fuller, more robust flavour as it ages.

From Sweden: **Hushållsost**, a cow's milk cheese, has a history going back over 700 years; it has a pale straw-coloured open texture and small irregular holes, and the flavour is mild and creamy with a lemony finish.

From Norway: Invented in Sweden, but now made in Norway, **Ridder** is similar to Saint-Paulin, with an elastic texture and sweet–savoury taste.

From Romania: **Telemea** is a ewe's milk cheese with a creamy texture and tangy bite, sometimes with added cumin seeds.

From America: **Colby** is a washed-curd cheese (the curds are rinsed in fresh water to remove any excess whey or lactose) that has a sweet, mild flavour.

From Australia: **King River Gold** is produced from cow's milk on a farm in Victoria; it has a pinkish-orange mouldy rind, a smooth dense paste with small holes, and a slightly sharp, grassy finish.

From New Zealand: **Port Nicholson** is a vegetarian cow's milk cheese, similar to Port Salut, with a sweet–sour, slightly smoked aroma, and is also an excellent grilling and melting cheese.

How to choose cheese

The best place to buy cheese is a specialist cheese shop, and many have an online ordering service. However, many supermarkets have a fresh-cheese counter offering a reasonably good variety of farmhouse and factory-made cheeses. Ask to taste the cheese before you buy, as artisan cheeses vary within, as well as across, varieties: some cheeses differ according to the time of year, and certain varieties are seasonal.

Ask about the age of the cheese, as it is important to know its stage of maturity so that it can be served at its peak. Some, such as Camembert, ripen and change texture as they age, becoming softer and runnier. Others can be bought young and will continue to ripen at home.

Avoid any cheese that has a strong ammonia odour; if in doubt check with the seller. Hard or semi-hard cheese that has beads of moisture on the surface, or a dry, cracked rind, should be rejected. Semi-soft cheeses should yield to gentle pressure and any powdery bloom on the rind should be evenly coloured and slightly moist.

Once you have chosen, make sure the cheese is freshly sliced to your requirements. Buy only as much as you need (even if it's just a sliver) for consumption within a few days. Refrigeration will dry out the cheese once you get it home.

If buying pre-packed cheese, check that it does not look sweaty or excessively runny and that it is within the life of its date stamp. If the date is many weeks ahead, it may mean that the cheese is immature, but this may not matter if you intend to serve the cheese at this immature stage or to store it for using when mature.

Buying online is an option if you don't have access to a good cheese shop. The variety of cheeses is wide and any reputable supplier will supply the cheese with full care and storage instructions.

Hard cheeses

Appenzeller

Swiss Appenzeller takes its name from the town of Appenzell, close to the Austrian border. It has a long history, traced back to the 8th century and the cheese can now only carry the name if made in a strictly defined production area around Appenzell. The milk comes from cows that graze on meadow grasses and herbs, in 70 village dairies. Skimmed and full-fat milk are mixed together. During the three to six month maturing period the wheels of cheese are regularly washed in a mixture of wine and herbs, imparting a unique aromatic flavour. The pebbled, brownish rind covers a golden-yellow interior that is peppered with small holes; the texture is firm but elastic, with a herbaceous, nutty flavour, smooth, milky finish, and a pungent, farmyard aroma. A low-fat version is available.

TO USE As part of a cheeseboard; in cooking, especially in a fondue. To accompany Merlot or Alsace white wine.

Asiago

A long-established Italian cheese, named after a town in the northern province of Vicenza. At one time Asiago was made with ewe's milk, but cow's milk has been used since the 16th century and it now carries a *denominazione di origine protetta* label (similar to the French *appellation d'origine contrôlée*). There are two types of Asiago: fresh and aged. Fresh Asiago is made from whole milk and aged for 20 days. It has a firm, elastic crust and a light-coloured interior dotted with large holes. The flavour is sweet and delicate, with a touch of acidity, and it has a buttery aroma. Aged Asiago is made from skimmed milk and left to mature for six to 18 months. The crust is smoother, and the interior is straw-coloured with a crumbly texture and chewy consistency. The piquant flavour gets sharper with age and has an aroma of chestnuts.

TO USE Fresh, as a dessert cheese; in sandwiches; as a snack; in salads. Aged, grated into soups, pasta and sauces. To accompany red wine.

Caerphilly

A Welsh cheese, Caerphilly is named after the Glamorgan village where it was originally produced in the early 19th century, although the bulk of it is now made in south-west England. Made using whole cow's milk, the cheese is eaten in its 'green' state, when about ten days old. Caerphilly is soft and white, with a creamy, milky flavour; it has a fresh, lemony, notably salty taste and a very pleasantly crumbly texture. Farmhouse production died out during the Second World War, when milk was transferred to Cheddar manufacture and the factories began producing their own version of Caerphilly. The original is now being made again in Wales on small family farms. It is aged there for longer, tending to be dry in the middle and creamy around the edges.

TO USE As part of a cheeseboard; as a snack; with fruit. Baked or grilled. To accompany Zinfandel wine.

Cheddar

Perhaps the most popular of hard English cheeses, Cheddar takes its name from the town of Cheddar in Somerset. It is now made worldwide, and the name has come to describe a technique of cheesemaking rather than one particular cheese. The drained curds are cut into blocks and squeezed together to extract even more whey to produce a hard cheese. Cheddar is traditionally made from unpasteurised cow's milk. English farmhouse Cheddar is made with whole milk from a single herd of cows and allowed to mature longer to produce a richer and more mellow flavour. Young Cheddar is pale in colour, with a milky, nutty smell and a rich, sweet taste. As it matures, the cheese acquires a deeper flavour and a more intense colour. Smoked versions, including applewood and charnwood, are available.

TO USE As part of a cheeseboard; in sandwiches; in salads. In cooking for its good melting and grating properties. To accompany cider or beer, red wine or port.

Comté

This French cheese takes its name from the mountainous Franche-Comté region where it is made. It is a cooked, pressed cheese that has been produced since the time of Charlemagne and was the first *appellation d'origine contrôlée* cheese in France. Ninety-five per cent of the milk used to make Comté comes from Montbéliardes cows kept on family farms on the Jura plateau, and production is based on traditional methods. The cheese is matured in cellars, where the rounds sit on spruce boards for four to 24 months. The rind is grey-brown and pebbled, the interior ivory-coloured with small holes and a complex, deeply nutty flavour. The taste can vary according to the season of the milk and the diet of the cows. Sold in wheels wrapped either with a green band – Comté extra – or a brown one. Comté is a traditional cheese for fondues, and has excellent melting properties for all types of cooking.

TO USE As an appetiser; part of a cheeseboard; in salads. Cooked in sauces and savoury dishes. To accompany regional Jura wines.

Cornish Yarg

Cornish Yarg is based on a 17th-century recipe, but it was first produced in 1983 by a couple called Allan and Jenny Gray, who created its rustic name by reversing their surname. This award-winning cheese is now made exclusively at a dairy in Cornwall using pasteurised milk from their own and their neighbours' herds. Made by hand in round, open vats using a vegetarian rennet, the curds are pressed into moulds and brined before being wrapped in nettle leaves. The nettles attract natural moulds and impart a delicate, slightly mushroomy taste. The finished cheese, which is matured for between three weeks and two months, has an attractive lacy pattern of blue and green leaves. It is creamy under the rind and crumbly at the core; when young it has a fresh, slightly tangy taste that becomes more musty with age. A wild garlic variety is available.

TO USE As part of a cheeseboard; in sandwiches; in salads. Melted on to bruschetta or baked potatoes. To accompany fine red wine.

Doolin

This award-winning vegetarian cow's milk cheese from County Clare, Ireland, is very similar to Gouda in style. Wheel-shaped, it has a smooth, hard, golden-yellow waxed rind, a fine, grainy texture, and a buttery flavour. There are three versions, sold at different stages of the maturing process: young Doolin is sold after two months' ageing; mature Doolin is identifiable by its more distinctive fruity character; vintage Doolin has been matured for 18 months and has a strong nutty flavour with a tangy finish.

TO USE When young as part of a cheeseboard; in sandwiches; in salads; as a snack. Older, as a dessert cheese or in cooking, for its good grating and melting properties. To accompany Guinness.

Emmental

A cooked, pressed Swiss cheese, Emmental originally came from the Emmen valley near Bern, where it was first made in the 13th century. It is now produced in France and Germany, as well as other countries around the world, but a genuine Swiss example will always have 'Switzerland' stamped in red on the rind. Made from unpasteurised cow's milk, it has a hard, thin rind and is deep yellow in colour, with a mild, fruity and sweet taste and characteristic large holes or 'eyes'. The aroma is sweet, with tones of freshly cut hay. If left longer to mature (more than four months and up to 18), it develops a chewy density and a much fuller, nuttier flavour.

TO USE As part of a cheeseboard; in salads; as a snack. Cooked in fondue or added to savoury dishes. To accompany light white wines or a Syrah/Shiraz red.

Garrotxa

This is a contemporary Spanish cheese, created in the late 1980s by a group of cheesemakers who adapted an old recipe and applied modern methods to its manufacture. Produced in the volcanic Garrotxa area of Catalonia in north-west Spain, it uses local goat's milk (usually unpasteurised), and has a short ripening period of one to two months. The thin crust is rubbed with oil to give it its natural dark, bloomy colour, which makes a startling contrast to the pure white interior; the texture is close and crumbly with a moist sweetness and light goaty flavour, and there is a hint of herbs in the taste. Garrotxa is at its best when eaten young.

TO USE As a dessert cheese or as part of mixed tapas. To accompany Spanish sherries or wines.

Double Gloucester

This is a pressed English cheese, made in large rounds from whole cow's milk. It is mentioned in records as far back as the 8th century. Double Gloucester ranges from pale to deep red-orange in colour, the colour coming (in modern times) from a natural vegetable dye called annatto (see page 317). Matured for three to four months, it has a smooth, flaky texture with a rich buttery taste. Double Gloucester has a nutty character from the full-cream milk of both evening and morning milking sessions that is used in its production. A vegetarian variety is also available. Single Gloucester is made from partly skimmed milk and is lighter and more crumbly.

Double Worcester is a version of Double Gloucester, made in Worcestershire. Matured for five to seven months, it has a firm, flaky texture, orange interior and citrus flavour.

TO USE As part of a cheeseboard; in salads. For cooking, in savoury dishes. To accompany red wine.

Gjetöst

First made in the Gudbrandsdalen valley in Norway over 130 years ago, Gjetöst, a unique rindless whey cheese, has a distinctive brown colour and sweet taste. It is made from a combination of milk, cream and whey, slowly cooked until the natural sugars caramelise. The cheese is then cooled and moulded into blocks. It has a smooth, fudge-like texture and a sweet caramel taste with just a hint of sourness.

Ekte Gjetöst is one of two types sold under brand names. The traditional cheese is made solely from goat's milk and whey.
Ski Queen, is the other, and is made from a mixture of goat's and cow's milk and whey, and is slightly sweeter than the original.
Mysöst, is the name most commonly used for Gjetöst when it is principally made with cow's milk.

TO USE Serve for breakfast in wafer-thin slices with toast or Norwegian flatbread; as part of a cheeseboard or with slices of rich fruit cake. In cooking for its good melting properties. To accompany light, fruity white wines.

Gouda

This popular Dutch cheese is a wheel-shaped cow's milk cheese, called after the city of that name in South Holland, and is similar to Edam. When young, the flavour is milky, even bland. It has a compact, slightly elastic, creamy texture and a yellow wax coating. When aged, Gouda develops a sweet, caramel-like intensity with a stronger, more assertive and interesting flavour. Mature Gouda (18 months plus) is coated in black wax. Gouda is now made in other countries and is produced in various sizes. Note: in the Dutch name, the letters ou rhyme with *cow*, not with *moo*.

Coolea is an Irish version of Gouda made by a couple of Dutch descent in the hills of County Cork and named after the nearby town. The wild herbs growing in the grazing meadows give it a richer, fruitier flavour than Dutch Gouda. Mature Coolea, aged for over six months, is extremely piquant and has a fresh aftertaste.

TO USE As part of a cheeseboard; as a dessert cheese with fruit; as a snack. In cooking – grated and used in sauces and fondues. To accompany light, fruity wines.

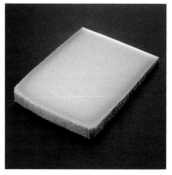

Grana Padano

Grana is the generic name for a group of Italian hard cheeses. The history of the cheese can be traced back to 1000AD, when it was valued highly because it kept well and was easy to transport. Grana cheeses are all made in much the same way, using partially skimmed cow's milk followed by an initial ripening of six to 12 months and then further ripening for 18 or 24 months. The smooth, natural rind is hard and thick, the pale yellow interior grainy and crumbly, with small holes and a delicate fragrance. Padano is made in an area around the Po Valley and in the province of Trentino, often using traditional methods with veal rennet. It melts in the mouth with a sweet, intense flavour that strengthens with age.

TO USE As a dessert cheese with fresh fruit. Excellent for grating to use in cooking. It freezes well. To accompany regional wines.

Gruyère

The most famous of Swiss cheeses, Gruyère is named after the village where it was first made in the 12th century. It is now also produced in France, Italy and other parts of Europe. Within Switzerland, the use of the name is strictly controlled and Gruyère made there has the name Switzerland stamped in red on the face of its broad wheels. Unpasteurised cow's milk is used in the process and, although most is produced in creameries, some is still made in small village dairies. Ripening takes between three and ten months, and the longer it is left, the better the cheese. The natural rust-coloured brown rind is hard and dry and the interior pale yellow, with a dense, compact texture dotted irregularly with pea-sized holes. Gruyère has a distinctive and fairly sweet taste – at first fruity, then more earthy and nutty.

TO USE As part of a cheeseboard; in salads; as a snack. An excellent cooking cheese – in sauces, gratins, soups and fondues. To accompany fruity white wine.

Idiazabal

Idiazabal is a full-fat, uncooked cheese made with unpasteurised milk from Latxa sheep in the Basque region of Spain, high in the Pyrenees. Most Idiazabal is made commercially, but there are still some small local farms producing their own versions. The cheese is matured for a minimum of two months but not more than six, and the natural rind is smooth and hard, and ringed with marks from the wooden moulds in which it is drained. The interior is pale yellow-to-amber in colour, with a compact texture and a few pinprick holes; it is dry, not crumbly, feeling pleasantly moist in the mouth, slightly acidic and salty. When the cheese is smoked, the interior takes on a brownish colour, a drier, stronger, nutty taste, and a smoky aroma. It is usually cylindrical, although sometimes moulded into cone or octagonal shapes.

TO USE Serve with membrillo (quince paste), apples, grilled meat; in salads. Melted on toast, into sauces and savoury dishes. To accompany oaky Rioja wine or Spanish cider.

Jarlsberg

This large, wheel-shaped Norwegian cheese was first produced in the 1830s. Production was discontinued in the early 20th century but it recommenced in 1956, when the recipe was recreated combining the old traditions with modern technology. The name comes from the county where the original version was made. Jarlsberg is a semi-hard cheese with a yellow wax rind, made from pasteurised cow's milk and usually sold in wedges. Produced commercially in creameries, it has a thick rind and semi-firm interior, which is smooth and buttery-rich with large, round holes; the mild, sweet flavour leaves a nutty aftertaste. The selection of the bacteria used to produce the wide-eyed holes and sweet flavouring is a closely guarded secret. Low-fat, smoked and special reserve versions are available. The latter is ripened for 12 months, and has a stronger, more complex flavour and aroma.

TO USE As part of a cheeseboard; in sandwiches. In cooking, in fondues, sauces and soufflés. To accompany light, fresh white wines, beer or aquavit (a traditional Scandinavian spirit).

Kefalotiri

Kefalotiri can be a sheep's or goat's milk cheese, or sometimes a mixture of the two, and has been made throughout Greece and the Greek islands for centuries. It is also produced in Cyprus and throughout the Middle East. Once heated and curdled, it is packed into moulds that resemble a hat (*kefalo*, hence the name) and left to mature for three to four months. It has a natural rind, close-textured, creamy interior with a scattering of small holes, a sharp, rather salty flavour and a definite nutty aroma. The colour of the interior varies from white to golden yellow depending on the mix of milk and the season. The Cypriot version is harder, with an ivory-coloured interior, a mushroomy flavour and a stronger, more fudge-like aroma.

TO USE On a meze platter. In cooking in classic Greek dishes – pastitsio, moussaka – grated on to pasta and casseroles, grilled or fried. To accompany light white wines or ouzo (a traditional Greek aniseed-flavoured spirit).

Leerdammer

This is a trademark name for the generic cheese *maasdam*. It is named after the city of Leerdam in Utrecht in Holland, where development of the cheese began in the 1970s before being launched on the market in 1984. It is made from pasteurised cow's milk and is suitable for vegetarians. Leerdammer is aged for three to 12 months, during which time this boulder-shaped cheese develops its characteristic yellow rind. The interior is firm but not hard, with an open texture and large holes. It is creamy white, and has a sweet and nutty flavour that becomes more pronounced with age. A low-fat version is available. Often sold in wedges.

TO USE As an appetiser; as a snack; in sandwiches; at breakfast with cold meats and bread. In cooking, can be baked, grilled and melts well. To accompany beer or light white wines.

Mahón

Made on the Spanish island of Menorca for centuries, Mahón was awarded the *denominacion de origen* (denomination of origin) in 1985. Originally it was made with sheep's milk but now uses cow's milk or a mixture of the two: usually pasteurised, sometimes unpasteurised. The cheese is chiefly produced in creameries, although there are also traditional farmhouse examples. Mahón is a square cheese with rounded corners, a smooth, yellow, oily rind, and a firm texture dotted with small holes. Its distinctive taste is slightly acidic and salty, qualities that grow stronger and more piquant with age. The cheese can be matured for two to three months but it can also be left for up to two years for semi-cured or aged varieties. The rind is rubbed with oil or paprika gives it an aroma of fresh peaches.

TO USE Traditional appetiser with fresh rosemary and olive oil; with membrillo (quince paste). In cooking, grated over pasta and vegetable dishes. To accompany sherry or an oaky white wine.

Manchego

A pressed, uncooked cheese made from whole ewe's milk and produced in the La Mancha region of central Spain. Manchego is rich and creamy, with a wax-coated rind, a nutty, caramel flavour and small, irregular holes. It is sold at different stages of ripening: *fresco* is ripened for just two weeks, and is bone-white with a rich buttery flavour; *curado* is left for three to six months and is semi-firm, with a sweet flavour; *viejo* is aged for up to a year, giving it an ivory colour, firm texture, and a sharp, slightly peppery flavour. The distinctive pattern on the sides of the cheese came originally from the plaited straw baskets in which the curds were pressed; today, the pattern is replicated using less romantic (but perfectly effective) metal cylindrical moulds. Smoked and rosemary-flavoured varieties are available.

TO USE Serve as part of tapas; with figs, dates or membrillo. In cooking, good melting and grating cheese when older. To accompany sherry, Rioja or Cava.

Parmigiano Reggiano

Parmesan is the best-known of the grana group of cheeses. It is a cooked, pressed cheese with a distinctive flavour that sharpens with age. Only the genuine Parmesan cheese, made between April and November, by a unique method in one region of northern Italy, carries the name Parmigiano Reggiano. The curd is broken up, heated, packed into a large mould the shape of a millstone, and matured for at least two years. When it is ripe, the crust is almost black and the interior is a pale straw colour, full of tiny holes. It has a profoundly complex flavour, nutty and salty, with a granular melt-in-the-mouth texture. *Stravecchio* has been aged for three years, *Stravecchione* for four, the best for up to seven years. Sold whole or in wedges, preferably cut with a traditional parmesan knife. Ready-grated Parmesan is a pale shadow (often no more tasty than sawdust) of the great cheese in all its glory; avoid it.

TO USE Serve as an appetiser, with figs or pears; as the centrepiece (or only occupant) of a cheeseboard; in salads. Baked, melted or grated; add the scraped rind to soups, stock or sauces. To accompany Prosecco or Lambrusco.

Pecorino

This cooked, pressed Italian cheese is made from sheep's milk and pressed into large cylinders to give it its familiar drum shape. Pecorino, like Parmesan, is a grana cheese with a granular texture, popularly used in cooking and for grating over pasta and other savoury dishes. It has a hard rind, pale straw-to-dark-brown colour, and an excellent sharp, pungent and salty flavour. Many types of pecorino are produced all over Italy, some only between the months of November and late June.

Pecorino Romano and **pecorino Sardo** (from Sardinia) are left to mature for several months to become hard and develop a fruity tang.
Pecorino Siciliano (from Sicily) is similar, but it matures more quickly and has, if anything, a stronger flavour.

TO USE When young, as an appetiser; with fresh fruit; in salads. When mature, in cooking, grated, melted or baked. To accompany sparkling wines.

Wensleydale

This pressed cheese from England's Yorkshire Dales is based on an 11th-century recipe created by Cistercian monks. It is made using milk from cows that graze on the limestone pastures of Upper Wensleydale, imparting the unique flavour of the grass to the cheese. The curds are finely cut and lightly pressed, giving a high moisture content and crumbly, flaky texture. Ripened for only three weeks, Wensleydale has a white interior and a mild, slightly sweet flavour with a honeyed finish. Mature Wensleydale has been ripened for up to six months, extra-mature for up to nine months; although the flavour deepens, it is not acidic. A smoked version is available, as are varieties mixed with fruits, spices or herbs. There is also a blue Wensleydale.

TO USE As part of a cheeseboard; traditionally eaten with apple pie or fruit cake. Melted into soups, on toast; grilled; used in cheesecake. To accompany cider, port or light red wines.

White Stilton

English white Stilton is made in the same way as its more famous brother, blue Stilton, except that no mould is added to the vat with the milk and rennet, and it is sold young – at about three weeks of age. The history of Stilton dates back hundreds of years and the name is now protected by law, with only a limited number of dairies licensed to make it in three counties: Derbyshire, Leicestershire and Nottinghamshire. White Stilton has a crumbly texture with a tangy flavour and a mild, fresh aftertaste. There are a number of varieties available blended with citrus or vine fruits or spices.

TO USE As part of a cheeseboard; crumbled on to bread, toast or crackers; served with fresh fruits or figs as a dessert cheese. To accompany tawny port, dessert wines, sweet dark sherry or full-bodied red wines.

More about hard cheeses

What is a hard cheese?

A hard cheese has a thick rind, which is often waxed, oiled or cloth-bound. The texture is generally firm and dense, although some, such as Cheshire, can be more open and granular. The colour of the cheese will vary according to the season and the milk used: cow's milk is often a creamy yellow, sheep's and goat's milk are usually much whiter. Hard cheese is primarily a cow's milk cheese and is frequently used in cooking, as it has good grating and melting properties.

The cheesemaking process

Once the curd is formed, it is cut into small pieces so that it will lose more whey during the next stage. The curds are then gently heated to force out more moisture before being drained again. The curd is salted and may be cut again before being put into large perforated moulds and pressed to release any remaining whey. At this stage, once the salt has been absorbed, most traditional British hard cheeses are wrapped in a linen cloth, sealed with lard and left to mature in cellars or ripening rooms for some weeks, or, in the case of a good farmhouse Cheddar, for years. Others, notably those made by many European cheesemakers, are soaked in a brine overnight to seal the rind before being left to mature, some for a few months (Garrotxa), others for two years or more (Parmigiano Reggiano). These cheeses may be washed in a brine, or a mixture of wine and herbs, towards the end of the maturing period, or brushed with oil to harden the rind.

The different types

Light pressing will produce a softer, crumbly-textured cheese, such as Caerphilly. Rindless hard cheeses are pressed into shape before being wrapped in a special plastic that prevents the cheese developing either moulds or a rind, then left to mature. These cheeses will mature faster than cloth-wrapped cheeses and have a softer texture. To produce a coloured cheese, such as Red Leicester, natural plant colours such as annatto are added to the milk.

How to store and serve hard cheese

Store in the warmest part of the fridge, away from the freezer compartment. If you do not have the original wrapping, wrap any leftover cheese in greaseproof or waxed paper and store in the fridge in a lidded container. Hard cheeses have a long shelf life; if a mould has grown on a cut surface, cut it off and use the remainder of the cheese. Hard cheeses can be frozen, but the texture will be more crumbly once thawed; grated cheese can be added while still frozen to hot sauces and soups. Remove hard cheese from the fridge up to two hours before serving to bring it to room temperature. Special knives for cutting hard cheeses cleanly are widely available.

The stronger the cheese, the more robust a wine required to accompany it. Serve a mild cheese with light, fruity reds, an extra-strong one with a fortified wine such as port.

Other varieties include

From England: **Berkswell**, from the West Midlands, is a modern vegetarian sheep's milk cheese with a russet-red rind that shows the marks of the basket mould in which it is made; it is dense and nutty, with a complex mix of flavours and a prickly tang. **Cheshire** is one of the oldest English cheeses and some small producers are once again making it in the traditional way, using unpasteurised cow's milk, so it is moist, mellow and slightly salty with a crumbly texture; red (annatto-coloured) and blue Cheshire are also available. **Derby**, from the county of Derbyshire, is a traditional, cylindrical-shaped cow's milk cheese, with a natural rind, a softer, flakier curd than a Cheddar and a melted-butter taste (**Sage Derby** is flavoured with sage leaves). **Coquetdale** is a farmhouse cow's milk cheese made in Northumberland and ripened in local caves. It has a leathery, yellowish-grey mould, a soft, supple interior with a mix of sweet–savoury flavours, and a nutty finish. **Curworthy**, a hand-made vegetarian cow's milk cheese from Devon, is based on a 17th-century recipe. It has a creamy interior with an open texture and a buttery taste in a firm chocolate-coloured rind. **Duddleswell**, an unpasteurised ewe's milk cheese from East Sussex, has a firm, almost flaky texture with a sweet caramel flavour and a hint of Brazil nuts and fresh hay. **Hereford Hop** from Gloucestershire is a vegetarian cheese made from cow's milk and coated in local hops that give it its unusual rind; mellow, sweet and buttery with a slightly yeasty taste. **Lancashire**, named after the county it comes from, is a traditional cow's milk cheese with a pale gold, thin, natural rind. When young it is moist and crumbly; with age, it becomes harder and the flavour intensifies. **Malvern**, from Worcestershire, is a modern vegetarian ewe's milk cheese which is firm and dry, yet dense and creamy in the mouth with a sweet butterscotch taste and a hint of thyme. **Northumberland**, a vegetarian farmhouse cow's milk cheese made using a washed-curd recipe, is moist and firm, with a sweetly fruity flavour and a tart bite. **Red Leicester**, a traditional creamery cow's milk cheese, has a firm body and close, flaky texture with a delicately sweet flavour. It is good for grilling and grating. **Ribblesdale goat** from North Yorkshire is an unpasteurised vegetarian goat's milk cheese (first made in the early 1980s) with a distinctive white rind and interior, and a taste of chicory, almonds and a trace of wild herbs; Ribblesdale is also made with cow's milk. **Swaledale**, also from North Yorkshire, is made from either ewe's or cow's milk and matured in humid cellars, where it gets its blue-grey mould and moist, fresh, slightly acidic flavour; flavoured varieties include chives and garlic, mint, and one soaked in Old Peculier, an ale brewed in the area by the Theakston brewery. **Tala**, from Cornwall, is a modern unpasteurised vegetarian sheep's milk cheese, creamy and full-bodied, with a sweet, aromatic burnt-caramel taste and a suggestion of lanolin and rosemary.

From Scotland: **Cairnsmore** is a modern sheep's milk cheese made in Dumfries and Galloway from spring to early autumn; it has a mouldy rind, firm texture, and a nutty, sweet caramel-and-burnt-toffee taste.

From Wales: **Acorn** is a modern ewe's milk cheese made in Cardiganshire; it has a firm yet crumbly texture, a crème-caramel taste, and a citrus finish.

From France: **Abbaye de Belloc**, made in the Pays Basque from unpasteurised sheep's milk and shaped into a flat wheel, has a crusty, brownish rind with a firm, dense, rich and creamy texture and a burnt-caramel taste. **Beaufort** (*appellation d'origine contrôlée*), from the Savoie region, is a cow's milk cheese dating from the days of the Roman Empire, with a slightly rough rind and sweet herbaceous flavour. **Cantal**, from the Auvergne region and another of France's oldest cheeses, is moist, open-textured and springy when young (*jeune*), with the sweetness of raw milk, and more Cheddar-like when aged (*vieux*), with a tangy butter taste. **Mimolette Française** (or Boule de Lille) from Flanders is basically an Edam-type cheese with a deep orange colour. When young it is firm, compact and slightly oily, with a subtle fruity aroma and mellow nutty taste; aged, it is fruity and very tangy.

From Italy: **Montiaso** is a traditional unpasteurised cow's milk cheese, sometimes with added ewe's milk, which is firm with small holes and a creamy, rich taste with a hint of pineapple.

From Spain: **Castellano**, a ewe's milk cheese from Castilla y Léon in north-central Spain, may be made with either pasteurised or unpasteurised milk. It has a pale-brown rind with zigzag marks from the hoops that hold it during the draining process. It has a crème-caramel taste, with fresh acidity and a hint of salt.

From Holland: **Maasdam** is a modern creamery cow's milk cheese with a smooth, natural rind that may be waxed, and a sweet, buttery, somewhat fruity flavour; it makes an excellent breakfast cheese.

From Denmark: **Samso**, a traditional cow's milk cheese, looks like a pale Emmental with a supple texture and irregular-sized holes. When young, it has a mild, buttery quality that develops a sweet–sour pungency as it ages, and a hazelnut flavour.

From Poland: **Oszczypek** is a smoked, unpasteurised ewe's milk cheese made for generations by shepherds living in the Tatra mountains of southern Poland. It is oval-shaped, and the colour of the rind varies from pale lemon to chocolate-brown depending on how long it was smoked. The taste is distinctive and slightly salty.

From America: **Dry Jack**, a cow's milk cheese, has a natural rind which is hand-rubbed with oil, cocoa and pepper to give it a chocolate-icing look. The deep yellow interior is hard, sweet and fruity, with a taste of wine.

Cooking with cheese

When cooking with cheese, remember that too fierce a heat can make it stringy. It should melt rather than bubble hard and should not be allowed to boil once it has been added to a sauce. Hard cheeses can be grated, but softer cheeses are best sliced, shredded or crumbled before adding to a recipe. If a recipe specifies a particular type of cheese, it is because its individual flavour and texture are considered the best one for that particular dish. Substituting another variety will inevitably alter the taste and possibly the texture of the final dish. If necessary, however, some cheeses can be used as substitutes for each other. Simply look for similar characteristics and strengths. And remember: it is sometimes better to make a substitution of a good-quality cheese than use a poor example of the 'right' cheese.

Blue cheeses

Bavarian Blue

This is a recent invention from Germany. Pasteurised whole cow's milk is used in its production, sometimes with the addition of extra cream; the result is rich and soft. Made in small wheel shapes, Bavarian blue has a very creamy, ivory-coloured paste with splotches of blue mould rather than the traditional veins of a blue cheese. It is mild and supple, with a spicy, slightly sour flavour. Bavarian Blue's softness makes it a very spreadable cheese.

TO USE As part of a cheeseboard; with fresh fruit; as a snack with French bread or crackers; crumbled into salads. To accompany a red wine, such as Barolo.

Cambozola

This is the trademark name for a German blue cheese that was created in the 1970s and is produced in the Bavarian Alps. It is a soft triple crème cheese made in large wheels and resembling a combination of two famous cheeses: Camembert and Gorgonzola. (Hence the name, which combines those two.) There is a bloomy Camembert-like mould on the thick, smooth white rind, and a blue Gorgonzola-like mould inside. Cambozola has a rich and creamy consistency and a spicy, sweet–sour taste, with a light bite coming from the blue. It is a mild cheese, and very spreadable.

TO USE As part of a cheeseboard; as a snack; crumbled into salads. In cooking, blended into soups and pasta sauces. To accompany Sauvignon Blanc or Chardonnay, or a Merlot.

Danish blue

Invented in the early 20th century by a Danish cheesemaker looking for an alternative to Roquefort, this popular blue cheese is also known as Danablu. It is made in factories using pasteurised cow's milk that is cooked to ensure a smooth curd and clear taste, and aged for eight to 12 weeks. Danish blue has no rind, a white interior, blue-mould veining, and irregularly distributed holes. The flavour is milder than that of Roquefort, but sharp and salty. In texture it is rich and creamy but it can be crumbly and it cuts easily. It's wheel-shaped, and sold in a distinctive blue wrapping, either as wedges or as a whole cheese.

TO USE As part of a cheeseboard; with fresh fruit; as a snack; crumbled into salads. In cooking, blended into soups and sauces; in dips and dressings. To accompany a robust red wine, such as Cabernet.

Dolcelatte

A mild Italian cheese whose name means 'sweet milk' – and the name is apt. This is the commercial name for a factory-made Gorgonzola, but it is slightly softer and creamier than the original. It was created by Galbani, the famous cheesemaking company. Made from the curd of only one milking from a cow, the wheel-shaped cheese has a soft, creamy texture that melts in the mouth – a bit like ice cream – and a mild, spicy flavour. Ageing and maturing takes two to three months, and the fat content is higher than average for a blue cheese: about 50 per cent. Similar cheeses include Dolceverde and Torta Gaudenzio.

Dolcelatte Torta is a natural-rind blue cheese, also made from cow's milk, comprising layers of Mascarpone alternating with layers of Dolcelatte cheese. It is sometimes known as Gorgonzola Torta. It is exceedingly rich.

TO USE Serve as an appetiser with figs and Parma ham; in salad dressings. Melted into pasta sauces, and cooked in quiches. To accompany Danish beer, light red or white wines.

Gorgonzola

This creamy-textured Italian cheese is one of the oldest blue cheeses in the world. The original name, Stracchino Verde, was changed in 1955 to that of the village near Milan where it was first made. *Denominazione di origine protetta* (similar to the French *appellation d'origine contrôlée*), Gorgonzola is made in a controlled area by some 40 dairies. Traditionally ripened in cold, draughty caves, it is now aged in controlled storage areas. There are two styles: *dolce* (also called *nuovo*) is soft, creamy and smelly, aged for three to five months; *naturale* or *picante*, aged for about a year, is more crumbly, firmer in texture, and stronger in flavour. Gorgonzola is wrapped in gold foil to keep it moist

Mycella, known as Danish Gorgonzola, is a semi-soft, full-fat cow's milk cheese with blue-green veins and a milder flavour.

TO USE As part of a cheeseboard; as a dessert cheese with pears; in salads, dips and dressings. In cooking – add to soups, pasta sauces, risottos. To accompany robust red wines.

Roquefort

This famous and enduringly popular blue French cheese is made from unpasteurised ewe's milk from one breed of sheep, the Lacaune. It has been produced and then matured in the cool, damp limestone caves of Cambalou for over 2,000 years. The special conditions these caves offer are crucial to the development of the uniquely crumbly and creamy texture and strong, salty, sharp flavour that distinguishes Roquefort from other blue cheeses. The final stages of the ageing process can take up to three months. Its production is strictly controlled and the red Lacaune sheep on the label denotes that it is the genuine article. It takes 4.5 litres (8 pints/1 gallon) of milk to produce just 1kg (2¼lb) of the cheese, which explains why it is expensive, but because it is so rich a small portion is sufficient. The mould that gives Roquefort its colour and flavour, *Penicillium roqueforti*, was first isolated in the local caves and is now used in manufacturing blue cheeses all over the world.

TO USE As part of a cheeseboard; with nuts and figs; in salads, dressings and dips. Melt into pasta sauces, soups, and other savoury dishes. To accompany Muscat, Sauternes or port.

Saint Agur

The modern cheese was developed in 1988 by the large Bongrain creamery and is made with pasteurised milk from cows that graze in the mountainous Auvergne region of central France. It is enriched with extra cream and aged in cellars for 60 days to yield a rindless cheese, smooth and creamy, with splodges of blue mould. The taste begins as subtle, mild and spicy, and gets stronger and spicier as the cheese ages. Moist on the tongue, with a rich melt-in-the-mouth quality, Saint Agur is sold in octagonal shapes or wedges, often wrapped in foil to prevent further moulding.

TO USE As part of a cheeseboard; served with pears; as a snack; in salads. Melted into sauces, risottos, or on top of grilled meats. To accompany full-bodied red wines.

Shropshire Blue

The name of this cow's milk blue cheese is misleading. Shropshire Blue originated in Scotland in the 1970s, production was later transferred to Leicestershire. An orange-coloured, semi-hard blue cheese, it has a flavour resembling a cross between two other great English cheeses – Stilton and blue Cheshire – but it is perhaps closer to that of Stilton, as the production process is similar. The distinctive orange colour comes from annatto – a natural food colouring from a South American plant, see page 317 – added to the milk. It has a slightly tangy aroma, a creamy, crumbly texture and a good flavour – less nutty but sometimes stronger than Stilton. There is a hint of caramel in the flavour that contrasts with the sharp taste of the blue mould. Shropshire blue can take up to 12 weeks to mature.

TO USE As part of a cheeseboard; as a snack; in salads. In cooking, melt and whisk into crème fraîche for a warm salad dressing. To accompany dessert wine or port.

Stilton

One of Britain's favourite cheeses, and the nation's original contribution to the club of world-class blue cheeses. Cheese can only be labelled as Stilton if it is produced in Nottinghamshire, Derbyshire or Leicestershire, and to a particular recipe. It is made from full-cream cow's milk with no applied pressure, forming its own crust. Stilton is semi-hard, with a very creamy, firm texture, a strong, tangy flavour, and blue-green veining. The veining is caused by a mould that in most cases is a natural growth throughout the curd, accelerated by using stainless-steel skewers to pierce the cheese. The veins of mould should be evenly distributed throughout. The rind is a dull, drab colour, well crinkled and regular, and free from cracks. Stilton is at its best when fully ripe: four to five months after it has been made. Sold in wedges as well as a whole cheese.

TO USE As part of a cheeseboard; as a dessert cheese; in salad dressings. Melted into soups and sauces. Traditionally served with port.

More about blue cheeses

What is a blue cheese?

Blue cheese is the name given to a cow's, sheep's and/or goat's milk cheese that has a blue or blue-green mould running through it. The famous ones have been around for a very long time: the Roman author Pliny referred to a blue cheese, probably Roquefort, in the AD 2nd century, and the monks of St Gall offered Roquefort to the Emperor Charlemagne in the 9th century.

As it is mould-ripened, there is a danger of listeria contamination, so blue cheeses should be avoided by pregnant women, children, the elderly and anyone vulnerable to infection.

Origins

Tradition says that blue cheese came about accidentally when cheese was inadvertently left in a cave and became streaked with a bluish-green mould; our ancestors decided they liked the flavour.

The cheesemaking process

The distinctive veining and taste in a blue cheese come from a bacterium, usually *Penicillium roqueforti* or *Penicillium glaucum*. At one time, the cheese was left to develop these moulds where they occurred naturally – usually in limestone caves. Today, most blue cheeses are either injected with the mould, such as Roquefort, or it is mixed into the curd, as with Gorgonzola. In larger and harder cheeses, copper or stainless steel needles are used to stab the cheese so that the mould penetrates through to its interior. The mould grows between the curd granules, giving the cheese its marbled appearance.

During the injection process, the cheese is kept turning to produce the crumb-like texture. Injecting also introduces air into the cheese, causing the high acid content and strong flavour to develop. Ageing averages three months, during which the cheese becomes more solid and consistent in texture.

Quality control

Although temperature and humidity in factory-produced cheeses are now mechanically controlled, most older varieties of blue cheeses are still aged in the original caves, where the conditions are maintained by natural ventilating faults in the rock. For some, such as Roquefort, this is a condition of bearing the name, carried by the Protected Designation of Origin from the European Union. In France, the *appellation d'origine contrôlée*, and in Italy the *denominazione di origine protetta*, carry the same weight. The titles are awarded to cheeses made only in certain regions or areas, and they offer a guarantee to the buyer that the cheese is genuine.

The different types

Blue cheeses vary in pungency and strength; no two are the same, from the mild Cambozola to the piquant Saint Agur. Some of the cheeses have been around for centuries, whereas others from Australia, America and Ireland are just beginning to make an appearance on the cheeseboard. All blue cheeses grow more pungent with age or mishandling, and are best used within a few days of purchase.

How to store and serve blue cheese

Store in the warmest part of the fridge, away from the freezer compartment. Wrap in waxed or greaseproof paper, then in a lidded container away from other foods, to prevent the spread of the mould spores. Before serving, bring the cheese to room temperature in its wrapping, and, if offering it with other cheeses, use two knives so that there is a separate one for the blue cheese.

Serve milder blues with a light fruity white or a rosé wine; more piquant varieties need a robust, spicy red, or a sweet dessert wine.

Other varieties include

From England: **Dorset blue vinny** is a hard, low-fat cow's milk cheese with a dry texture (*vinny* is old English for veining). **Blue Wensleydale** is the original double-crème Wensleydale, left to mature until it becomes blue; it is considered to be one of the best English blue cheeses after Stilton.

From Scotland: **Lanark Blue**, a hand-made creamy-white unpasteurised ewe's milk cheese made using vegetarian rennet.

From Ireland: **Blue Rathgore**, a semi-soft goat's milk cheese from Antrim, is moist and crumbly with a spicy taste. **Cashel Blue**, made from cow's milk, is firm and tangy when young, spicier and creamier when older.

From France: **Bleu d'Auvergne** is a rich, sharp cheese made from whole cow's milk. **Bleu des Causses** is a sheep's milk cheese similar to Roquefort. **Olivet bleu**, a soft cheese made with unpasteurised cow's milk, tastes like a mild Camembert. **Fourme d'Ambert**, an ancient cow's milk cheese from the Auvergne, has a rounded flavour and pungent after-taste. **Bleu de Bresse**, a cow's milk cheese, is creamy and relatively mild.

From Australia: **Gippsland Blue**, a cow's milk cheese with a runny texture and astringent flavour.

From America: **Maytag Blue**, a hand-made semi-hard cow's milk cheese.

Eggs

Hen

There is a wide range of hens' eggs available, produced by different farming methods, including organic, free-range and barn eggs, and eggs from caged hens. Eggs are graded into four categories according to weight: very large, large, medium and small. They are full of protein and the yolk also contains fat. When cooking with eggs, it is important to use the correct size for a recipe. There is no intrinsic difference in flavour or nutritional value between white or brown eggs.

TO USE Boiled, scrambled, poached, coddled, fried, as an omelette and baked. An essential ingredient for many recipes, including cakes and sauces; to add richness and flavour to a dish and to bind ingredients together.

Duck

Larger and richer (higher in fat) than hens' eggs, duck eggs have a smooth shell which is stronger and less porous. The yolk is a deep yellow and proportionately larger than a hens' egg, and the whites are more gelatinous. Duck eggs should be eaten by the use-by date, like any egg, but you may have to ask about this because the eggs are often sold loose rather than in labelled boxes like hens' eggs.

TO USE Cook in the same way as hens' eggs and use in cakes and puddings, but not in meringues or any dessert that is cooked for only a short time or at a low temperature.

Quail

Much smaller than hens' eggs, and with attractively speckled shells, quails' eggs are often used as a garnish (sometimes in their shells or half-shells) or canapé. They have a light texture pale yolk, and can be soft-boiled in 1–2 minutes. Their shells are very thin, almost crumbly, and this makes them maddeningly laborious to peel. Find them in supermarkets, fishmongers or butchers. A common way of serving them is hard-boiled, fully peeled, with a dish of coarse salt for dipping.

TO USE Soft- or hard-boiled as an appetiser or garnish; in salads; to accompany meats and seafood; as a topping.

Bantam

Bantam eggs are much creamier than hens', with a denser yolk and less white. The shells can be different colours, from very pale through to light brown and blue, and are sometimes speckled. The bantam is a breed of small hen, and therefore its eggs are smaller. As a general rule, you will need two to three bantam eggs for one hen's egg.

TO USE Cook in the same way as hens' eggs and use in cakes and puddings.

Guinea fowl

The eggs of guinea fowl have a thicker shell than hens' eggs, and a rich, flavoursome yolk that is deep yellow in colour. They are considered by many people to be superior in flavour to hens' eggs, but they are rarely sold outside areas where the birds are farm-raised.

TO USE Can be used in much the same way as hens' eggs, especially for baking, where they add a rich yellow colour to the mixture.

Pigeon

This small white egg is larger than a quail's egg but slightly smaller than that of a guinea fowl. It is popular in French and Chinese cuisine: in France, pigeon egg is often poached in a well-flavoured consommé, whereas in China it will be par-boiled, then peeled and simmered in a spicy sauce, or hard-boiled and served with soy sauce for dipping. Because of their small size, pigeon eggs are best suited to cooking whole.

TO USE Boil; poach; fry.

Turkey

Larger and richer than hens' eggs, turkey eggs are particularly vulnerable to salmonella and should be cooked thoroughly. Turkey eggs are not easily available, as the birds do not lay many eggs over the year, and they are expensive to produce commercially. Most are bought direct from the farm. When soft-boiling, a turkey egg will take about 7 minutes. Store them for up to four days.

TO USE Cook in the same way as hens' eggs; they add extra richness to cakes and puddings, but should not be used in any dessert that is cooked for only a short time or at a low temperature.

Goose

A goose egg weighs about the same as three hens' eggs. They have a slightly stronger taste and make excellent scrambled egg and omelettes. Allow about 7 minutes for a soft-boiled egg. Goose eggs should be eaten by the use-by date, like all eggs, and you may have to ask what it is because the eggs are often sold loose rather than in labelled cartons.

TO USE Cook in the same way as hens' eggs; they are also good for desserts and baking.

Ostrich

With a distinctively light flavour and texture, an ostrich egg is 24 times the size of a hen's egg and will take 2 hours to hard-boil. Available from late spring to summer.

TO USE Good for soufflés and meringues – but only if you are cooking for a large crowd or a small army: one egg will make 100 meringues!

Other eggs

Pheasant

The shell of the pheasant egg is khaki in colour and a little larger than a quail's egg. It has a large yolk, and soft-boiling takes 3 minutes. The eggs are only available in early spring for six to eight weeks.

Emu

As the bird that hatches it is very large, this egg is equivalent in weight to 12 hens' eggs. Emu eggs have a mild flavour and a pale yellow yolk. They can be used in the same way as hens' eggs, but will take up to 1¾ hours to boil. When used in recipes, the egg will need weighing (50g of emu egg = 1 hen's egg). Emu eggs will keep in the fridge for up to two months. Usually available from winter through to spring.

Coloured hens

It may surprise some people to know that hens' eggs don't just come in white, pale brown or speckled: the colour varies according to the breed of hen. Burford Browns lay an egg with a dark brown shell that is thicker and harder than that of other breeds; the egg has a denser texture, and a larger than average deep-yellow yolk. The Old Cotswold Legbar egg is even more spectacular, coming in a variety of pastel colours, including turquoise, blue, olive, pink and peach. Silver Grey Dorkings lay eggs with a white shell that has a pinkish tinge.

Pickled eggs

These are shelled, hard-boiled eggs – usually hens' but sometimes ducks' or quails' – soaked in a mixture of vinegar, salt and spices for about six weeks. When pickled eggs are made commercially, distilled malt vinegar is used. At home, you can use wine or cider vinegar for a more refined flavour. Spices used include peppercorns, mustard seeds mace or chillies. Eaten as a snack, often with relishes.

Thousand-year-old eggs

Despite the name, the eggs (sometimes called 'century eggs') have been preserved for 'just' 100 days. Usually duck eggs, they are coated in a mixture of salt, ashes, garden lime and black tea, covered with earth and left for 100 days. When washed and cracked open, the white will have turned a translucent brown with a gelatinous texture; the yolk will be green. Thousand-year-old eggs are part of Chinese cuisine, and are usually found in Oriental food stores. Serve with pickled vegetables.

Salted eggs

Whole uncooked duck eggs are covered in a solution of water and salt and left in a cool place for three weeks. The white will be slightly cloudy and still runny; the yolks a bright yellow-orange and quite firm. The eggs are boiled for 20 minutes before serving. Available in Chinese and Asian food stores and supermarkets. Slice and serve as an accompaniment to rice dishes.

Separating eggs

1 Crack the egg more carefully than usual: right in the middle to make a break between the two halves that is just wide enough to get your thumbnail into.

2 Holding the egg over a bowl with the large end pointing down, carefully lift off the smaller end. Some of the white will drip and slide into the bowl while the yolk sits in the large end of the shell.

3 Carefully slide the yolk into the smaller end, then back into the large end to allow the remaining white to drop into the bowl. Take care not to break the yolk; even a speck can stop the whites from whisking up.

More about eggs

Eggs are a concentrated source of protein and vitamins, including vitamins A, B2 and D, as well as iron. They are not high in calories, but they are relatively high in cholesterol and for many years certain people were advised to limit their intake. It is now thought, however, that this dietary cholesterol does not have a marked effect on the cholesterol in our blood. As long as you eat a healthy, balanced diet there should be no reason to limit the number of eggs you eat.

Egg production

A number of different farming methods are used to produce eggs. Battery production – keeping large numbers of hens in restricted conditions – has increasingly come under attack for the intensive methods used, but it is still how the majority of eggs sold in the UK are produced. Barn eggs come from hens living indoors with space for them to move around freely. Free-range eggs are produced by hens that have daylight access to open pasture where they can forage. Organic eggs are from free-range hens that roam organic land and are fed an organic diet. Eggs are also available from hens fed particular diets, such as grain only. The hen's diet will affect the colour and nutritional content of the yolk. Hens fed with a diet that includes flaxseeds will have eggs with higher levels of omega-3 essential fats.

Storing eggs

When buying eggs, check the use-by date and never buy cracked or damaged eggs, because they may have been contaminated by dirt or bacteria. Store eggs in the fridge, pointed-end down to centre the yolk within the white, away from other foods, as the porous shells can absorb strong odours. To check for freshness, place an uncooked egg in a bowl of water; if it stays on the bottom, it is fresh; if it tilts, it is older and better fried or scrambled, rather than boiled; if it floats to the top, it is likely to be stale.

Yolks, covered with water, can be stored in the fridge for two to three days; keep whites in a covered container for up to seven days. Whites and yolks can also be frozen; freeze yolks lightly whisked with a pinch of sugar so that they can be used in either savoury or sweet recipes.

Safety first

Eggs are susceptible to salmonella, which can cause serious food poisoning. Cooking until white and yolk are solid will destroy the bacteria, but raw or lightly cooked eggs may contain salmonella and should be avoided by the very young, the elderly, pregnant women and anyone with an immune-deficiency disease. This includes all the recipes that use raw or lightly cooked eggs, including mayonnaise, cold soufflés, meringues, ice creams and sorbets, tiramisu, lemon curd and scrambled eggs.

Follow basic hygiene rules when handling eggs, as there may be bacteria inside the shell as well as on the outside. These can be spread very easily to other foods, and anything you might touch, including the fridge handle, may be contaminated. Always wash your hands thoroughly after handling eggs, and clean any handles, worktops, dishes or utensils you've touched.

Since 1998 the lion quality mark with a 'best before' date has been stamped on to egg shells and boxes in Britain to show that the eggs have been produced to the highest standards of food safety.

If eating eggs from other fowl, such as pigeon eggs that probably come from a breeder, it would be advisable to cook them well to avoid any risk of salmonella poisoning. And some eggs shouldn't be eaten for environmental or legal reasons, including those of wild birds and turtles.

Cooking with eggs

Apart from being a useful fast food, eggs are an invaluable and versatile ingredient in the kitchen. In addition to being poached, fried, baked, boiled, scrambled or turned into an omelette, eggs are used to lighten soufflés and cakes; thicken mousses; bind stuffings; set baked custards; glaze pastry and breads; and emulsify sauces and dressings, such as hollandaise and mayonnaise. When air is whisked into egg whites they dramatically increase in volume, giving soufflés, meringues and whisked cakes their characteristic light and airy texture.

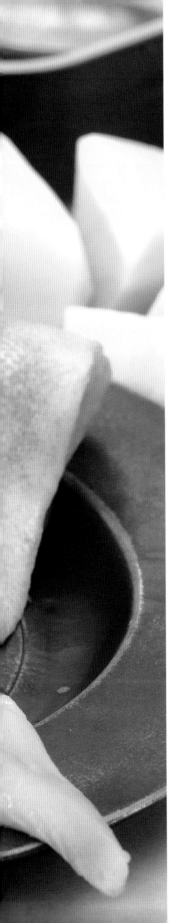

Fish

All about fish

There are fewer types of freshwater fish than sea fish, which has many subcategories.

Freshwater fish These fish, which live in freshwater rivers and lakes, are rarely caught commercially, although some, such as trout and salmon, are farmed. Freshwater fish may have oily or white flesh, and their taste and texture varies greatly according to the particular type.

Round white fish This large group of sea fish all have a 'round' body and eyes on either side of the head (as opposed to flat fish – see below). The flesh is usually firm and white, although the flavour and texture varies according to the different kinds.

Flat fish Usually found on or around the seabed, these fish have a distinctive flat shape with a dark underside, and both eyes on their upper side. The flesh is white and delicate.

Oily fish These fish usually swim in shoals near to the surface of the sea. They contain highly nutritious oils and essential fatty acids including omega-3, which are dispersed throughout the flesh. They have a firm texture and a rich flavour.

Migratory fish Several species, including salmon, trout and eels, travel every year from salt sea water to fresh water, or vice versa, to spawn. Having spawned, the fish return to their original habitat.

Exotic fish Living in tropical waters, exotic fish often have strikingly coloured skins, and usually have delicate or mildly flavoured white flesh.

Deep-sea fish Because these fish live deep in the sea, they are rarely found close to shore. Most have firm, meaty flesh.

How to buy and store fish

Fresh fish Fish should be evaluated with both your eyes and your nose. Whole fish should have bright eyes standing proud of the head rather than sunk into it, glossy, taut skins, tight-fitting scales, and bright pink or red gills. Fillets and steaks should show no signs of dryness or discoloration, and you should avoid any that look wet, shiny or slimy. The smell of truly fresh fish is, somewhat surprisingly, not a 'fishy' smell. It is a fresh sea smell or, in fact, hardly any smell at all – and you shouldn't be able to detect it until you get quite close to the fish.

Fish is always best eaten fresh. So store it in the fridge when you get home, and cook it that day.

Frozen fish

Fish sold frozen is usually snap-frozen shortly after it is caught, and is generally of good quality. It is usually prepared as fillets and is used in processed products, such as fish fingers and fishcakes. Many types of fish and processed foods can be cooked directly from frozen. Frozen fish should be thawed according to the pack instructions and cooked as for fresh fish.

How to freeze and thaw fish

Fish can be frozen whole or in fillets, cutlets or steaks. Freeze as soon as possible after purchase.

- Gut and clean the fish. Pat dry on kitchen paper, then snip off any sharp fins or spikes.
- Wrap fish or fillets individually in clingfilm or a freezer bag, making sure the wrapping is airtight. Label with the date and store in the freezer. Use within two to three months.
- To thaw, place the fish in the fridge until completely thawed. This may take 24 hours for a large fish.
- Do not refreeze thawed raw fish. You can, however, freeze it again after you have cooked it.

Preparing and cooking

All fish need to be gutted and cleaned before cooking (except whitebait and red mullet). Those with tough scales should have the scales removed. Small to medium-sized fish can be cooked whole, whereas medium-large fish may be filleted or cut into steaks or chunks. Fillets and steaks may be cooked with the skin on or off, but skin should be removed before cutting the flesh into chunks or cubes. For detailed instructions on cleaning, scaling and filleting fish, see pages 92–3.

Different fish suit different cooking techniques. The main techniques are below. For simple methods, such as steaming, pan-frying, searing, grilling and baking, the fish can be marinated briefly, for example with lemon or lime juice. Fish cooks very quickly, and overcooking will ruin it.

Poach Most fish can be poached whole or in pieces such as fillets. The most common poaching liquids are water, court bouillon (a cooking liquor made with water, vinegar, lemon juice and white wine) or milk, just deep enough to cover the fish. Bring to a bare simmer, then cook gently until the flesh is just cooked through and flakes easily.

Stir-fry This method is best suited to pieces of firm fish such as monkfish or for shellfish such as prawns or squid. Toss the prepared fish or shellfish in a little oil with spices and aromatics in a wok for 1–2 minutes until just cooked through. Prawns are cooked when they turn pink. Do not overcook them.

Pan-fry Use this method for fish fillets and steaks, and for smaller fish such as small red mullet. Heat a little oil in a frying pan, then cook the fish for a few minutes on each side until just cooked through.

Sear Use for firm-fleshed fish such as tuna or for shellfish such as scallops. Heat a little oil in a frying pan until very hot, then cook briefly for about 1 minute on each side, to give it a flavourful crust on the outside while the centre remains tender.

Deep-fry Use for whole small fish such as whitebait, fillets, pieces or strips of fish, or shellfish. Prepare the fish and a coating (which can be batter, seasoned flour, or flour, egg and breadcrumbs). Heat vegetable oil in a deep-fryer to 180°C, or until a cube of bread browns in 40 seconds. Coat the fish, then carefully lower into the oil a few pieces at a time and cook until crisp and golden. Remove using a slotted spoon. Drain on kitchen paper. **Note** Do not add too much fish to the oil at one time. This will cause the temperature to drop and impair the final result

Grill This is best suited to whole small to medium fish such as sardines, flat fish on the bone, thick fillets or steaks, or shellfish. Marinate the fish, or season and brush with oil, then grill on both sides until just cooked through.

Griddle Use for dense fish such as tuna. Marinate in oil and lemon juice or brush with oil. Preheat the griddle for 3 minutes or until smoking. Reduce the heat slightly, then griddle until the fish is cooked through and has brown griddle lines on the outside.

Bake Whole fish such as salmon or larger pieces of fish are suitable for baking. Cooking times will vary according to the size of fish: allow 30–40 minutes for a whole salmon; 20–25 minutes for whole trout; and about 15 minutes for trout or salmon fillets. Preheat the oven to 190°C (170°C fan oven) mark 5. Score the fish skin with a sharp knife, squeeze over lemon juice and season, then bake until just cooked through. To check if the fish is done, slip a knife into the flesh; when cooked the flesh will be opaque.

Braise Best suited to fish fillets, pieces of fish and shellfish such as prawns. Prepare a tomato sauce, then add the prepared fish or shellfish. Spoon the sauce over to cover and simmer gently for 5–10 minutes until just cooked through. Shellfish will need only a few minutes.

Steam Suitable fish for steaming include whole fish, such as mackerel; fish fillets or pieces; and shellfish. Season and/or marinate the fish or shellfish, then put into a dish that will fit into a bamboo steamer. Put the steamer into a pan or wok over boiling water. Steam for 10–15 minutes until firm and just cooked through. Shellfish will require just a few minutes.

Environmentally-friendly seafood

Although fish and shellfish are one of the most delicious ingredients to cook, and a valuable source of healthy protein, it is important to consider the state of the world's fish stocks before buying. The environmental sustainability of wild caught seafood encompasses a variety of issues and depends on a number of factors: level of exploitation, biological characteristics of the species, management measures in place to protect the stock and marine environment, and the impact of the fishing gear on target and non-target fish species, marine organisms and the marine environment. When buying fish, consumers should be aware of breeding seasons and how to avoid them, depleted stocks and declining species. For the reasons given above the following fish are considered unsustainable at current fishing levels: torsk, ling, eel, whitebait, orange roughy, shark and parrotfish, ray, skate. Attempts are being made to rebuild depleted stocks so the ratings are likely to change. The Marine Conservation Society (MCS) provides free comprehensive sustainability information and ratings to help consumers make informed buying choices. Look out for the Marine Stewardship Council's (MSC) logo on fish and shellfish. This indicates that they have been caught sustainably.

Round white sea fish

1. Whiting
2. Haddock fillet
3. Bream
4. Gurnard fillet
5. Gurnard
6. Coley fillet
7. Hake
8. Bass fillet
9. Bass
10. Pollack
11. Red mullet
12. Red mullet fillet
13. Cod fillet
14. Grey mullet

Round white sea fish

❶ Whiting

Whiting is one of the smallest members of the cod family, and measures about 40.5cm (16in) long. Also known as merling, it is narrow in shape with silvery skin and very tender, delicately flavoured flesh. Whiting is found throughout Atlantic waters and is usually sold whole. Less expensive than cod, it is good cooked with garlic, tomatoes and dill or a citrus sauce.

TO USE Pan-fry or grill whole fish. Fillets deep-fried, braised, added to soups or poached.

❷ Haddock

This member of the cod family is similarly over-fished. Found on both sides of the North Atlantic, it is smaller than cod, growing to about 1m (3ft 3in) in length, with a distinctive dark streak along its back and two large, dark marks above the gills. Haddock has tender, well-flavoured white flesh, and is usually sold as fillets. Pair with butter and garlic, or tomatoes and herbs, or add to fish pies.

TO USE Batter and deep-fry, braise in well-flavoured sauces, poach, bake or roast. Avoid overcooking, as the flesh easily becomes dry or watery.

❸ Bream

There are numerous varieties in this large family of fish, including gilthead bream, red bream, black bream, porgy and dentex. The gilthead is generally regarded as having the best flavour. Many are found in the Mediterranean and Atlantic, although red bream is found in northern European waters, and porgy is found in North American coastal waters. With a rounded body tapering to a narrow tail and with a fairly small head, bream range in colour from dark grey to rosy and red. Most have tender, well-flavoured flesh and are sold whole or in fillets; larger fish (up to 60cm/24in) can feed a tableful, but most fish are suitable for one or two servings. They are good cooked with basil and tomatoes.

TO USE Preparation, see page 92. Scale whole fish and slash several times on both sides to ensure even cooking. Bake, grill, braise or pan-fry.

❹❺ Gurnard

There are several varieties of gurnard, including red, yellow, tub and grey; red and tub are usually considered the best for cooking. Gurnard can grow to 75cm (30in) long, and are mostly found in the northern Atlantic and Mediterranean. Also known as sea robin, piper and gurnet, it has a large head of striking ugliness and a narrow, tapering body. Gurnard is a bony fish with firm white flesh, which has a mild taste. It is still in plentiful supply. Good with tomatoes and garlic, sage or rosemary.

TO USE Bake, grill, poach; in soups.

❻ Coley

Also known as coalfish, saithe or pollock in the US, coley is found on both sides of the North Atlantic. It is a long, tapering fish – reaching about 1m (3ft 3in) – dark grey in colour with a silvery underbelly and with firm, greyish flesh. With a fairly mild flavour, coley goes well with Asian flavourings such as ginger, garlic, chilli and soy sauce, and with creamy or tomato sauces. Coley is also frequently cooked in pies, made into fishcakes or added to soups. Although not as good as cod or haddock, it is in good supply and therefore provides a more sustainable alternative to those two threatened species.

TO USE Best eaten extremely fresh. Bake, braise, grill, fry or add to soups, casseroles and fish pies.

❼ Hake

Found in the Atlantic, Pacific and Mediterranean, hake is a member of the cod family, and similarly over-fished. These dark grey fish with a pale underbelly have a long slender body and grow to between 1kg (2¼lb) and 5kg (11lb) in weight. Their flesh is white and fragile with a delicate flavour, and should be cooked with care. Hake is usually available as steaks and cutlets and goes well with garlic and white wine, tomatoes and paprika. It is particularly popular in Spain.

TO USE Poach, braise, bake or fry.

Hoki

Also known as blue grenadier, hoki is related to hake and is found in the coastal waters of Australia and New Zealand. It has large eyes and a pointed tail, with a long, tapering body; it can grow to between 60cm (24in) and 1.2m (4ft) long. It has blue-green skin and a silver underbelly. The flesh is white, firm and flaky with a mild flavour. It is usually sold as fillets, loins or pieces. Hoki suits flavours such as tomatoes and garlic, or spicy marinades.

TO USE Suited to most cooking methods; good fried, braised, added to fish pies or grilled as kebabs.

❽❾ Bass

Sea bass can grow to a fairly large size, up to 5kg (11lb), but are also caught when relatively small (around 500g/1lb 2oz). They are found in coastal waters around the UK and Mediterranean, and sometimes in saltwater lakes and river estuaries. The fish is shaped like a salmon, with dark blue-grey skin and a white or yellowish underbelly. The flesh is firm but tender, with a fine flavour. Stocks have been depleted by over-fishing, and it is now commercially farmed, although farmed fish is generally considered to be inferior to wild. Sea bass is sold whole or as fillets and goes well with Asian and Mediterranean flavours.

TO USE Preparation, see page 92. Whole fish should be scaled. Bake, steam or poach. Smaller bass and fillets can be grilled or pan-fried.

⑩ Pollack

Also known as greenfish, green cod and lythe, pollack is a member of the cod family. Found in the North Atlantic, it is greenish-brown in colour and can grow to a large size, weighing up to 9kg (20lb). Pollack has firm, white, flavoursome flesh. Although usually considered inferior to cod and haddock in flavour, its abundance and lower price make it a good alternative. Pollack is usually sold as fillets or cutlets. It goes well with Indian spices such as cumin, coriander and turmeric as well as Mediterranean flavours.

TO USE Braise, bake or add to soups, casseroles and fish pies.

Torsk

Also known as tusk, torsk is found in North Atlantic waters. It has brownish skin and a pale underbelly, and grows to about 51cm (20in) long. The flesh is firm and white, and suits flavours such as garlic, lemon, wine and dill.

TO USE Batter and deep-fry, braise in well-flavoured sauces, poach, bake or roast. Avoid overcooking, as the flesh easily becomes dry or watery.

⑪ ⑫ Red mullet

A completely different species from grey mullet, red mullet is smaller and rarely over 30cm (12in) long, with a striking pinkish colour and a rounded head. The scales are thick and protect a soft, delicate skin which is easily damaged. Although fairly bony,

red mullet is of excellent quality, with meaty, firm flesh which flakes easily and has a strong flavour. It is usually sold whole and suits Mediterranean dishes with white wine, garlic, lemon and herbs. It is also good grilled or barbecued with lemon. The liver of the red mullet is delicious, although very small. Finger-length mullet can be cooked without gutting.

TO USE Scale whole fish before cooking. Grill, pan-fry, bake or braise.

⑬ Cod

Once plentiful, cod has been over-fished and stocks have dropped to dangerously low levels. It is found in the cold waters of the North Atlantic, and can grow to a very large size, although most weigh in at around 3–8kg (6½–17½lb). Cod has speckle-spotted beige-brown skin and a paler underbelly, with tender, flaky white flesh, which is usually available as steaks or fillets. Cod suits simple flavourings such as butter and lemon, or sauces such as parsley or a creamy cheese sauce, as well as Mediterranean flavours.

TO USE Batter and deep-fry, braise in sauces, poach, grill, bake or roast. Avoid overcooking, as the flesh easily becomes dry or watery.

Ling

A relative of cod, ling is found in deep northern waters near Iceland, Scandinavia and the British Isles. It has a long, tapering body resembling an eel, and can grow to a substantial size – sometimes up to 2m (6½ft) long. Ling has pinkish-brown skin and firm, well-flavoured flesh. It is usually available as fillets or cutlets, and goes well with Mediterranean-style flavours such as garlic, tomatoes, thyme, olives, lemon.

TO USE Pan-fry, braise, or add to soups, casseroles and fish pies.

Pouting

Found in the eastern Atlantic and western Mediterranean waters, pouting is also known as pout. This small member of the cod family is brownish-silver with a rounded body and narrow tail, and grows to about 25.5cm (10in) long. The fish is bony and the fillets are very small. It is best eaten extremely fresh. Pouting's mild-tasting flesh is good with stronger flavours such as tomatoes and garlic.

TO USE Add the flesh to soups or braised dishes; in fishcakes.

⑭ Grey mullet

There are several species of grey mullet. The one most commonly sold in the UK is fairly large, growing to a weight of 3.5kg (7¾lb). Grey mullet is an olive-grey colour and has a long, sleek shape with a pointed head. The fish may have a slightly muddy flavour, as it feeds on the mud of estuaries and the seabed, so must be rinsed well under water. Sold either as whole fish or in fillets, it goes well with white wine, garlic, lemon and herby marinades. The roe of grey mullet is prized in southern France and in Italy, where it is salted and pressed into a dense mass, then used in pasta sauces and canapés.

TO USE Scale whole fish before cooking. Grill, pan-fry, bake or braise.

Wrasse

Found in Atlantic and Mediterranean waters, wrasse is a large family of fish with numerous varieties. They grow to about 40.5cm (16in) long, and range in colour from brown and speckled or spotted to blue, green, orange and gold. Wrasse has rather coarse, mild flesh and is best cooked with flavourings such as garlic, bacon and tomatoes.

TO USE Add to soups and stews.

Oily and migratory fish

1 Sea trout
2 Herring
3 Eel
4 Sardine
5 Whitebait
6 Salmon
7 Sprat
8 Anchovy
9 Mackerel
10 Tuna steak

Oily and migratory fish

① Sea trout

Also known as salmon trout, sea trout are a migratory relative of the common brown trout – they live in the sea and return to freshwater rivers to spawn. With a silvery, dark-specked skin and dark pink, fine-flavoured flesh, sea trout tends to be smaller than salmon, growing only to about 3kg (6½lb) in weight. They suit flavourings similar to those used for salmon, but it's best to avoid overpowering flavours that could mask the delicate taste of the flesh. Use with lemon and garlic marinades, fragrant herbs such as dill and fennel, and Mediterranean flavours.

TO USE Very fresh sea trout can be served raw – as sushi and sashimi, or marinated in vinegar or lemon juice with other flavourings, or prepared as for as gravadlax (see page 125). Whole sea trout is best baked or poached in court bouillon; steaks and fillets can be grilled, baked, poached, pan-fried or steamed. Add to mousses, terrines and fishcakes; cubed, threaded on to skewers and grilled.

② Herring

These relatively small, narrow, shoaling fish are plentiful in the North Atlantic and North Sea and grow to about 30.5cm (12in) long. They have a slender shape, bluish skin and a pale, silvery underbelly. The flesh is firm and rich, with many tiny bones. Usually sold whole, herring are best eaten extremely fresh. They are good coated with oatmeal and fried with bacon, or suit sharp flavourings such as lemon and gooseberry, and piquant flavours such as horseradish.

TO USE Slash the skin on both sides. Grill, barbecue or pan-fry and serve with a squeeze of lemon juice. Small herrings can be boned and marinated for a few days in an acidic mixture such as lemon juice or vinegar, and eaten raw.

③ Eel

A migratory fish, the snake-like eel lives in freshwater rivers but returns to the sea to spawn and die. There are approximately 600 species, including the conger and moray, and they can range in length from 5cm (2in) to just under 3m (9ft 10in) long. The common river eel is usually a dark green-black colour, and the flesh is pale and well flavoured. Tiny elvers (baby eels) are occasionally available at a very high cost, and are considered a delicacy. Eels do not keep well so they are always sold live; but you can usually ask your fishmonger to kill and prepare it for you. They go well with piquant flavours such as horseradish and mustard, but are also good cooked with tomatoes, garlic and wine. Jellied eels are a classic English dish.

TO USE Cut eels into short lengths and fry, stew, jelly (see page 125), or add to pies. Elvers can be dipped in milk, coated in seasoned flour and deep-fried, stewed or sautéed.

④ Sardine

These small, silvery, shoaling fish are found in the Atlantic and Mediterranean. They vary in size, with the average fish about 10cm (4in) long. Sardines have a firm, richly flavoured flesh, and are best eaten extremely fresh. They go well with citrus flavours such as lemon and orange, and with tomatoes. But they are particularly tasty when simply brushed with oil (optionally flavoured with garlic, marjoram or thyme) and then barbecued. They have a multitude of fine bones which can sometimes be eaten but may be pulled off the meat with great care.

TO USE Allow 3–5 sardines per serving. Cook whole, or fillet, and grill, barbecue or pan-fry and serve with a squeeze of lemon juice. Add the flesh to pasta sauces.

Pilchard

Pilchards are adult sardines, found in the same waters. As a general rule, if the fish is over 10cm (4in) long it is classified as a pilchard. Although they are sometimes available fresh, they are more often processed and sold canned, often in tomato sauce. Like sardines, pilchards suit citrus flavours such as lemon and orange, as well as tomatoes, and are a favourite fish for barbecuing, brushed with a herb-and-garlic-flavoured oil.

TO USE Cook whole, or fillet, and grill, barbecue or pan-fry and serve with a squeeze of lemon juice. Add the flesh to pasta sauces.

⑤ Whitebait

Fish sold as whitebait are the young of various fish – usually sprats and herring. Found in waters throughout the world, from Australia and New Zealand to China and the UK, these tiny silver fish are usually no longer than 5–6.5cm (2–2½in). Whitebait has limited uses: it is almost always coated in flour and deep-fried, and served with lemon wedges for squeezing. The whole fish is usually eaten because the bones are so soft, but some people prefer to pinch the head off first.

TO USE Cook whole – ungutted and with the heads on. Dip in milk, then coat in seasoned flour (perhaps spiced with cayenne pepper) and deep-fry until crisp.

⑥ Salmon

This noble migratory fish is found in both the Atlantic and Pacific but returns to freshwater rivers to spawn. It is large and silvery in appearance, with a dark-speckled back. The flesh is rich and pink with a firm yet tender texture and a mild flavour. Salmon vary in size according to variety and age, and can grow to about 3–7kg (6½–15½lb). Farmed salmon – which is the type we usually buy – tends to have paler and fattier flesh with a slightly inferior flavour to the darker-fleshed wild salmon. Available whole and as steaks and fillets, salmon is a versatile fish in the kitchen. Combine with zesty lemon and garlic marinades, Asian flavours such as soy sauce, ginger, garlic and chilli, fragrant herbs such as dill and fennel, and Mediterranean flavours such as tomato, garlic and thyme. Grilled fish goes well with fresh-tasting salsas, such as tomato, chilli, lime and fresh coriander. Salmon also takes well to home curing, either in acidic marinades or dry cures.

TO USE Very fresh salmon can be served raw – either as sushi or sashimi, or marinated in vinegar or lemon juice with other flavourings, or cured as for gravadlax (see page 125). Whole salmon is best baked or poached in court bouillon; steaks and fillets can be grilled, baked, poached, pan-fried or steamed. Add to mousses, terrines and fishcakes; cubed, threaded on to skewers and grilled.

❼ Sprat

Found in temperate waters of the north-eastern Atlantic and Baltic, this small, silvery fish is similar in appearance to a small herring or sardine. It has firm, rich and oily flesh, and is best eaten extremely fresh. Sprats go well with sharp flavours such as lemon juice, and piquant flavours such as mustard. Sometimes they are small enough to eat whole, head included – although some people don't like doing this. If you're frying them, coat them in seasoned flour first to give a nice crunch to the skin.

TO USE Allow 3–5 sprats per serving. Cook whole, or fillet, and grill, barbecue or pan-fry and serve with a squeeze of lemon juice. Add the flesh to pasta sauces.

❽ Anchovy

Found in the Mediterranean, Black Sea, Atlantic and Pacific, anchovies are small, slender and silvery shoaling fish. They are particularly popular in the Mediterranean and usually measure about 9cm (3½in) long. The flesh is firm and rich, and goes well with sharp flavours such as lemon. Because they are best eaten as soon as possible after being caught, they are rarely found fresh outside the areas in which they are fished. They are always sold whole, so you will need to clean and fillet them yourself. Making marinated anchovies is worth the trouble.

TO USE Grill or pan-fry fillets; marinate in lemon juice, olive oil, garlic, and eat raw.

❾ Mackerel

This shoaling fish is found in the North Atlantic, North Sea and Mediterranean. Mackerel is elegantly shaped, round and strikingly beautiful. It has steely blue skin with blue-black, wavy stripes and a pale underbelly, and can vary greatly in size; the average fish weighs about 450g (1lb). The flesh is a beige-pink and has a meaty texture and rich flavour. Mackerel are in plentiful supply and inexpensive, and are excellent in terms of price:quality ratio. They are usually sold whole and are best eaten very fresh. Serve well seasoned with pepper and grilled, with just a squeeze of lemon juice, or accompany with a sharp and piquant sauce such as gooseberry, cranberry, rhubarb, mustard or horseradish. They also take well to being presented en escabeche: cooked with onions, garlic, lemon and wine, then chilled with their cooking juices and served cold or at room temperature.

TO USE Whole fish and fillets can be grilled, baked, pan-fried or braised.

Bluefish

A medium-sized fish found in the Mediterranean and North Atlantic, bluefish is round in shape with bluish skin and a pale underbelly. It has firm, white flesh with a mild flavour, similar to mackerel, although with a slightly more delicate texture. Bluefish is usually available whole or as cutlets. Lemon and piquant flavours such as mustard and paprika go well with it.

TO USE Grill, bake, pan-fry or poach.

❿ Tuna

These large fish migrate in a yearly pattern and can be found in the waters of the Bahamas and Caribbean, Norway, Newfoundland and the Mediterranean. Related to the mackerel, tuna can grow to a very large size, weighing anything from about 1kg (2¼lb) to a gargantuan 675kg (1,500lb). They have a pointed mouth and a round body tapering to a narrow tail. There are numerous varieties of tuna, including skipjack, bonito, albacore, big-eye and the highly regarded bluefin. Tuna is usually sold cut into steaks; the flesh is meaty with a dark pinkish-red colour. Serve it with fresh, spicy salsas, or marinated in garlic, lemon juice and herbs, or with Asian flavours such as ginger, chilli and fresh coriander. **Notes** The larger varieties, especially bluefin, are over-fished. Pollutants (including mercury) are contained in the flesh, so medical authorities caution against eating too much, especially in the case of pregnant women and children.

TO USE Cook briefly over a high heat to prevent the flesh overcooking and becoming greyish and dry and so that the flesh remains pink and moist in the centre; chargrill or barbecue; cube and grill on skewers. Very fresh tuna can be eaten raw, marinated with spices and lemon juice or vinegar, or in sushi and sashimi.

Exotic and deep-sea fish

1. John Dory
2. Monkfish fillet
3. Red snapper
4. Barracuda
5. Pomfret
6. Swordfish steak
7. Tilapia fillet
8. Parrotfish

Exotic and deep-sea fish

❶ John Dory

This is an excellent fish found in the Pacific, Atlantic and Mediterranean, with sludgy grey-brown skin and a single dark spot in the centre of its body. It can grow to 65cm (25½in) long. Although John Dory is a strange-looking fish, the white flesh is highly regarded, with a fine flavour and a firm texture. It is usually bought whole, and this entails a good deal of waste as the fillets make up a relatively small proportion of the fish. Cook with Mediterranean ingredients such as garlic, tomatoes, peppers and herbs, as well as lighter flavours such as white wine and lemon.

TO USE Whole fish may be baked, braised, steamed or poached. Fillets may be grilled, baked, braised, pan-fried, steamed or poached.

❷ Monkfish

Also known as anglerfish, monkfish is found in the Mediterranean and Atlantic. It has grey-black skin, a large head, which is exceptionally unattractive, and a body that tapers dramatically to a narrow tail. In many places the fish is never displayed with its head on, although you will see it that way in France and other places where the appearance of the head is recognised as a key indicator of freshness. Only the firm white tail meat is eaten. It has a sweet flavour a little like lobster. A whole tail can weigh up to 3kg (6½lb), although 1kg (2¼lb) is more common. The tails are usually sold skinned but the tough pink membrane may still be present and should be removed before cooking. Monkfish goes well with robust herbs such as rosemary, sage and oregano, and bacon or pancetta, and also takes well to marinating in olive oil, lemon juice and garlic. Unfortunately, it is over-fished.

TO USE Cut away any remaining membrane. Grill, roast, bake, pan-fry,

stir-fry or poach. When baking the whole tail, flavour with herbs or aromatics and tie with string.

❸ Snapper

The snapper is found in tropical and subtropical waters. There are approximately 250 different varieties, the best known of which is probably the brightly coloured red snapper, with its rounded shape, pointed nose, tapering tail and orange-pink skin. Other varieties range from orange and pink to grey and blue-green. All have white, mildly flavoured flesh. Although usually sold whole, snappers can also be bought as fillets or steaks. A whole fish should be enough to feed two people. Snapper goes well with Creole and Caribbean spicing such as thyme, oregano and cayenne, as well as South-east Asian flavours.

TO USE Scale whole fish. Grill, bake, pan-fry, poach or steam.

❹ Barracuda

Also known as sea pike and becune, the long, slender barracuda inhabits warm waters throughout the world. It has fierce-looking teeth and the skin ranges in colour from dark brown and grey to green with a pale underbelly. It can grow to 2m (6½ft) long. Barracuda has pale, firm, meaty and well-flavoured flesh that goes well with spices and aromatics. It is usually sold as steaks and fillets.

TO USE Grill, bake, pan-fry or poach.

Orange roughy

Also known as sea perch, orange roughy is found in deep waters around New Zealand and Iceland. It is a medium-sized fish growing to about 60cm (24in) long. Its head is large, and the skin is red while the fish is alive but yellow-orange once caught. The flesh is firm and white

with a mild, fairly sweet flavour. Usually sold as fillets. Orange roughy suits Mediterranean-style flavours such as garlic, tomatoes and lemon.

TO USE Pan-fry, bake, poach, steam; add to soups and stews.

❺ Pomfret

Also known as butterfish, this silvery-grey tropical fish with a pale underbelly and oval shape is found in the Indian, Pacific and Atlantic oceans. They can vary in size according to variety, with smaller specimens weighing about 450g (1lb) and the largest growing up to 6kg (13¼lb). Pomfret has firm, meaty flesh that goes well with spices. It is particularly popular in Indian, Chinese and South-east Asian cuisines, and can be sold whole or as fillets. Cook with Chinese flavourings such as ginger, spring onions, soy sauce and sesame oil.

TO USE Grill, steam or pan-fry.

Mahi mahi

Also known as dolphin fish, dorade and lampuka, mahi mahi inhabits warm and tropical waters around the world, including the Mediterranean, around Hawaii, Central and South America and the Caribbean. Mahi mahi has silvery skin in hues of blue and yellow, a large, blunt-faced head, and a narrow body tapering to a forked tail. Once the fish dies, the skin turns a silvery grey-yellow. The fish grows to a fairly large size but rarely more than 15kg (33lb), and is usually sold as fillets or steaks. Its meaty flesh goes well with lime and garlic, and with Asian flavourings.

TO USE Prepare as for gravadlax (see page 125) and serve raw. Grill, barbecue, or bake in pies.

Flying fish

These elegant fish inhabit tropical waters, including those around the Caribbean, and the warmer waters of the Pacific and Atlantic. There are approximately 50 varieties, with enlarged, wing-like pectoral fins. Flying fish are best eaten very fresh and are available whole or as fillets. They are considered the national fish of Barbados, where they are cooked with thyme, chilli, garlic, tomatoes and hot pepper sauce, and served with cou-cou (a cornmeal porridge).

TO USE Bake, braise or pan-fry.

❻ Swordfish

A long, sword-like upper jaw is the distinguishing feature of the swordfish. Living in deep waters around the world, but particularly common in the Mediterranean, swordfish can grow to 150kg (330lb). The skin is grey in colour, and the flesh pale and firm with a very dense, meaty texture. Swordfish is usually sold as steaks and goes well with Mediterranean-style flavours such as garlic, lemon and capers, but also suits spices such as chilli, Tabasco and paprika. It is important to keep its meaty flesh moist during cooking. The health note on tuna (page 79) also applies to swordfish.

TO USE Grill, bake or pan-fry. Marinade or baste frequently to prevent the flesh from drying out.

Shark

The numerous varieties of shark range from fairly small to extremely large, weighing up to 4,000kg (8,800lb), and they swim in waters throughout the world. The most common varieties sold include dogfish, tope, porbeagle and blue shark. Shark is known as a cartilaginous fish because its skeleton is made of cartilage rather than bone. With a firm, meaty texture and a distinctive taste, shark goes well with spices and strong, aromatic flavourings such as teriyaki sauce, garlic, ginger, chilli and soy sauce. It is usually available as steaks, fillets and loins. The health note on tuna (page 79) also applies to shark.

TO USE Braise, grill or pan-fry. Marinade or baste frequently to prevent the flesh from drying out.

Marlin

Similar to swordfish, with an elongated upper jaw, marlin is found in warm seas throughout the world. It is long and slender in shape with a forked tail, and can grow to more than 2m (6½ft) long and weigh upwards of 120kg (264lb). Usually sold as loins or steaks, the flesh is pinkish in colour with a firm texture but a milder and blander taste than swordfish. Marlin goes well with Mediterranean-style ingredients or spicy flavourings.

TO USE Grill, bake or pan-fry. Marinade or baste frequently to prevent the flesh from drying out.

Sailfish

Similar in appearance to both marlin and swordfish, sailfish has the same elongated upper jaw, and is another inhabitant of warm seas and oceans throughout the world. The skin is blue-grey in colour, and the sailfish has a large, blue dorsal fin that unfurls along the entire length of its back. They are large, growing to about 1.5m (5ft) in their first year, but rarely exceed more than 3m (9ft 10in) long when fully grown. Sailfish has firm, meaty flesh, which is usually available as steaks or fillets. It goes well with Mediterranean flavours.

TO USE Grill, bake or pan-fry. Marinade or baste frequently to prevent the flesh from drying out.

❼ Tilapia

Tilapia are found in tropical seas and warm rivers such as the Nile, and are also widely farmed, particularly in Africa and South-east Asia. The colourings range from pinkish-red to grey and the flesh is white with a firm texture and mild flavour. Tilapia may be sold whole or as fillets. They go well with garlic and chilli, and with Thai flavours such as coconut, chilli, lime juice and fresh coriander.

TO USE Grill, bake or pan-fry.

Pompano

There are around 20 varieties of pompano, most with silvery skin and a forked tail; they can grow to between 45.5cm (18in) and 90cm (3ft) depending on the species. Native to warm seas throughout the world, including the Mediterranean and Caribbean, they are also farmed. The average weight is about 900g (2lb). Pompano has firm, rich-tasting, oily flesh with a slightly stronger flavour than mackerel. It is sold whole or as fillets and is good served with spices such as cayenne, paprika, garlic and thyme and citrus flavours.

TO USE Grill, barbecue or bake.

❽ Parrotfish

These beautiful fish are found in tropical and subtropical waters such as the Red Sea and the Indian and Pacific Oceans. They have a parrot-like beak and brightly coloured skins, ranging from blue-green, red and pink, to violet and grow to 40.5cm (16in) long. Parrotfish have firm, pale but rather bland flesh that goes well with spices and aromatics. They are usually sold whole to show off their decorative appearance, but may also be filleted. Use Caribbean-style seasonings such as thyme, cayenne or hot pepper sauce and garlic.

TO USE Steam, poach, braise or bake.

Flat sea fish

1. Lemon sole
2. Brill fillet
3. Halibut
4. Turbot
5. Plaice
6. Skate wing
7. Dover sole
8. Witch fillet

Flat sea fish

① Lemon sole

Lemon sole is found in the Atlantic, North Sea and around the coast of New Zealand. Lemon sole is unrelated to Dover sole and is not as highly regarded – although it still makes very good eating. Larger than Dover sole, lemon sole weighs between 350g (12oz) and 1.5kg (3¼lb), although it is roughly similar in shape. With a dark brown-grey skin and pale underside, lemon sole has soft white flesh with a mild, fairly sweet flavour. Cook with lemon and herbs such as parsley.

TO USE Preparation, see page 93. Lightly grill or pan-fry in butter. Fillets may be coated and deep-fried.

Dab

Also known as sand dab, these fish are found in the Atlantic and northern European waters. Dabs are oval in shape and grow to about 35.5cm (14in) in length. They have coarse, pale brown skin and a pale underside, and the flesh is white with a mild flavour. Dabs are best eaten extremely fresh and are available whole or as fillets. Their mild flesh is best enlivened with flavourings such as garlic, lemon and fresh herbs such as thyme.

TO USE Preparation, see page 93. Pan-fry, grill, steam, poach or bake.

② Brill

Found in the Atlantic, Mediterranean and Baltic seas, brill has brown-grey skin and a pale underside. The flesh is fine, with a similar taste and texture to turbot but not as firm. Brill grows to between 51cm (20in) and 75cm (30in) long and is usually sold whole. It can be treated in the same way as turbot, although it's not as well suited to cutting up into strips, and also goes well with fragrant herbs such as basil, fennel and rosemary, lemon and garlic. Slightly less expensive than turbot, it is regarded by some as being every bit as good. Stocks in some areas are under threat from over-fishing.

TO USE Preparation, see page 93. Grill, bake, poach or pan-fry.

③ Halibut

Inhabiting the deep, cold waters of the North Atlantic, halibut are the largest of the flatfish and can weigh between 1.5kg (3¼lb) for young halibut and 15kg (33lb) or more for mature fish. Halibut has green-brown skin and extremely firm, dense white flesh of excellent flavour. Small young halibut may be sold whole, whereas larger fish are sold as fillets or steaks. Halibut is expensive, and goes well with subtle flavourings such as garlic, lemon and white wine.

A related fish is Greenland halibut, much smaller than its noble family member, and it has softer flesh and an oily texture. It is usually sold smoked and sliced.

TO USE Bake, braise or poach. The flesh can dry out easily, so cook with plenty of liquid and baste regularly. Very fresh raw fish can be marinated and served as ceviche (cubed and marinated in lime and lemon juice, garlic, onions, chillies and fresh coriander, and eaten raw) or used in sushi and sashimi.

④ Turbot

Turbot is usually regarded as the finest of the larger flat fish, and indeed as one of the best fish of any type. It is found in the North Atlantic, Mediterranean, Baltic and Black seas, and is also farmed quite successfully; the farmed variety is the ethical choice, as wild stocks are under threat. These diamond-shaped fish have dark brownish-grey skin studded with distinctive bony protuberances and a pale underside. They can grow to almost 1m (3ft 3in) long. Turbot is always very expensive. The flesh is creamy-white and very firm, with a fine flavour. Small fish may be sold whole; larger fish are usually sold as fillets or steaks. Turbot is especially well suited to poaching in white wine, and may be served with a creamy sauce such as hollandaise. Its firm flesh also makes it suitable for cutting into strips and sautéing or coating in in a batter and frying.

TO USE Preparation, see page 93. Grill, poach or pan-fry, and take particular care not to overcook.

⑤ Plaice

Found in the Atlantic and North Sea, plaice are diamond-shaped with distinctive orange spots on a green-brown skin and a pale underside. The flesh is soft and white and has a mild flavour. Plaice is sold whole or as fillets. As the fillets are very thin, care must be taken not to overcook them, as this will destroy their delicate texture. They must also be handled with care when turning, because the soft flesh breaks up all too easily. Plaice is good served with chive or parsley butter, and is also an excellent choice for deep-drying in batter.

TO USE Preparation, see page 93. Grill, pan-fry, steam or coat and deep-fry.

Flounder

Found in oceans around the world, including the North Atlantic and Pacific, flounder are similar in appearance to plaice, growing to about 30.5cm (12in) long with a dark green to grey-brown skin and pale underside. The flesh is white with a fairly mild flavour, which is not as highly regarded as plaice. Flounder is best eaten extremely fresh and is good served with browned butter, herb butter or a creamy sauce.

TO USE Preparation, see page 93. Grill, pan-fry, steam or coat and deep-fry; use in fishcakes, terrines and fish balls.

Megrim

Found in European waters, megrim has a tough, grey-brown skin and a pale underside. It is oval in shape and grows to between 25.5cm (10in) and 51cm (20in) long. The flesh is white, fairly dry and mildly flavoured and is often described as bland. Best eaten extremely fresh, megrim is sold whole or as fillets and is good served with browned butter and capers, spicy Thai or Chinese flavours, or a creamy sauce.

TO USE Preparation, see page 93. Grill, pan-fry, steam, coat and deep-fry, or use in fishcakes.

❻ Skate

Found in most of the world's oceans around the world, skate is a bottom-dwelling cartilaginous fish that is related to shark. It is bluish-grey in colour and shaped like an elongated diamond with a long tail, and normally grows to no more than 1m (3ft 3in) long, although some varieties can reach 2m (6½ft). Usually it is only the 'wings' or side parts of the skate that are eaten, although you will occasionally also find skate 'knobs', pieces cut from the tail, and the small 'cheeks', which are a delicacy that fishermen often save for themselves. The wings are usually sold already cut from the body, skinned on both sides or left with just the pale underskin on one side. The wings are divided into two fillets by a sheet of thick cartilaginous fibres which are edible but unpleasantly crunchy. Skate is best eaten extremely fresh; avoid any that has a strong smell of ammonia. The flesh has a firm texture and delicate flavour, and is easy to eat off the 'bone'. Larger wings tend not to have such a fine flavour. It is

classically served with capers and browned butter, but also goes well with creamy mustard sauces. Unfortunately, skate has been over-fished and stocks are under severe threat.

TO USE Wash well, then grill, pan-fry or poach.

Ray

Similar to skate and sold in the same way, ray wings are often called skate wings when sold. Once skinned, there is little difference in appearance, but the flavour may not be as fine as that of skate.

TO USE Wash well, then grill, pan-fry or poach.

❼ Dover sole

Caught in the English Channel and Atlantic, oval-shaped Dover sole is one of the best sea fish, as well as one of the most expensive, and is also one of the most versatile for cooks. It has a pale brown skin, with a pale underside and a narrow tail; the skin, unlike those of other soles, cannot be eaten and must be removed before cooking either on or off the bone. The flesh is firm and almost meaty, and well flavoured. Dover sole varies in weight from 200g (7oz) to 1kg (2¼lb) and is sold whole or as fillets. Cook with lemon and herbs such as parsley and tarragon.

Other types of sole include Atlantic sand sole, French sétau, and Dakar or Moroccan sole. These go well with Mediterranean flavours such as garlic, oregano, basil and tomatoes.

TO USE Preparation, see page 93. All soles are best cooked simply: lightly grilled or pan-fried in butter. Fillets may be coated and deep-fried. Sole may also be used raw in sushi and sashimi.

❽ Witch

Mostly caught off the south-west coast of England and in the north-western Atlantic, witch is similar in shape and appearance to Dover sole. Also known as Torbay sole, witch grows to about 25.5cm (10in) long and has a brownish-grey skin. Its soft, white, mildly flavoured flesh is similar in taste and texture to lemon sole and goes well with similar flavourings, such as lemon, parsley and tarragon.

TO USE Best eaten very fresh, witch gives the best flavour when cooked on the bone. Best cooked simply: lightly grilled or pan-fried in butter. Fillets may be coated and deep-fried. It may also be used raw in sushi and sashimi.

Freshwater fish

1 Trout 3 Carp

2 Catfish 4 Pike

Freshwater fish

❶ Trout

There are two main types of freshwater trout: brown and rainbow. Brown trout is found in rivers and lakes throughout the world, although it was originally native to Europe and Asia. It has a golden-brown skin and flaky, fine-flavoured, creamy-white flesh. It is considered superior to the silvery green-brown rainbow trout, which is predominantly farmed and has pale pink flesh. (Wild rainbow trout can be fine quality, however.) Although they can grow to a larger size, most trout weigh about 1kg (2¼lb). Brown trout is less easily available, and both types of trout are usually sold whole and filleted. They are good with browned butter and almonds, fresh herbs and lemon.

TO USE Grill, bake, pan-fry, poach or steam. (See also sea trout, page 78)

Grayling

Related to the salmon, this silvery fish with a green-brown back has firm, white flesh, similar to that of brown trout. It grows to between 250g (9oz) and 900g (2lb) and mostly lives in freshwater lakes and streams in Europe. Grayling is rarely found on the fishmonger's slab or at the supermarket; you are more likely to obtain freshly caught whole fish from a line fisherman. It goes well with butter, white wine, garlic and lemon.

TO USE Grill, pan-fry, bake, poach or steam.

Whitefish

A relative of the salmon, whitefish is found in American and northern European lakes. It has pale, silvery skin, and it grows to about 45.5cm (18in) long. Its firm, white flesh goes well with fresh, zesty salsas, lemon and garlic. It is also often smoked.

TO USE Grill, pan-fry, bake, poach or steam.

Shad

Different fish called shad are found in Europe and the US. It is related to the herring and spawns in fresh water. Shad can weigh between 1.5kg (3¼lb) and 3.5kg (7¾lb). It has blue-grey skin with a silver belly, and its flesh has a very good flavour, although it contains many tiny bones. Shad tastes good cooked with butter, and is traditionally served with a little vinegar sprinkled over it at the table. The finest shad of all is that found in the eastern USA. It is caught only during a brief period in the spring. The flesh is pale beige, delicate in flavour, and one of the great seasonal delicacies of the USA. The shad roe, fried in butter and served with nothing more than a squeeze of lemon juice, is even more highly prized.

TO USE Scale, then bake or grill.

Bream

Freshwater bream, with its green-brown skin, is less highly regarded than sea bream. It is found in rivers throughout Europe and is also farmed, and can grow to 51cm (20in) long. The flesh is soft and white with a bland flavour; it can sometimes be muddy tasting and contains many small bones. The sharp scales need to be removed before cooking. Bream suits strong flavours such as spices, especially ginger, and garlic.

TO USE Scale carefully, then soak in acidulated water (1 tbsp lemon juice stirred into 1 litre/1¾ pints cold water) for at least 1 hour. Use in stews and braised dishes.

❷ Catfish

Also known as wolf fish, this long, dark grey fish with a flat head has distinctive barbels that resemble the whiskers of a cat. There are many different species, which can be small or grow to an enormous size, and are found in rivers throughout the world. When cooked, the flesh turns from pink to white and has a firm, meaty texture with very few small bones. Catfish is usually sold as fillets or cutlets, sometimes under the name of rock salmon or rock turbot. It is widely farmed. Catfish suits strong flavours such as tomatoes, herbs and spices.

Basa fillets are taken from the Vietnamese catfish: a species native to the Mekong river delta. They go well with spicy flavourings such as Cajun seasoning, or Vietnamese recipes such as ca kho (cooked in a spiced caramel sauce).

TO USE Skin catfish, then bake, grill, pan-fry, coat and deep-fry or add to stews and soups.

Gudgeon

Found in European rivers and lakes, gudgeon is a small white fish that grows to less than 20.5cm (8in) long and is related to the carp. The flesh is delicate and well flavoured, and tastes best when cooked with just butter, salt and black pepper.

TO USE Soak in salted water for at least 1 hour to remove impurities, then grill, pan-fry or coat in flour and deep-fry.

Char

A relative of the salmon, char is native to Arctic waters and is found in mountain lakes in Europe and Canada as well as being farmed. It usually grows to between 900g (2lb) and 2.5kg (5½lb), and has blue-green skin with a reddish belly and firm, white or pink, sweet flesh. It is available whole or as fillets and is good with simple flavourings such as butter, garlic and lemon, although it also suits more robust ingredients such as chilli and Cajun spices.

TO USE Scale, then bake, pan-fry or steam, or pot with butter.

❸ Carp

The river fish, carp, is also extensively farmed, and it is found throughout the world. It is particularly popular in Jewish and Chinese cooking, and is often a central part of the Christmas feast in Eastern European countries. Carp has sweet, firm flesh, although it can taste muddy, and it has quite a few bones. Growing to between 30.5cm (12in) and 60cm (24in), it is usually sold whole, but sometimes as fillets. In Eastern European recipes it is often cooked with peppers, sour cream and paprika, or with fruits, or a piquant sauce such as horseradish. In Ashkenazi Jewish cooking it is one of the traditional fish used to make gefilte fish. And in Chinese cooking it may be paired with traditional flavourings such as ginger, spring onion and rice wine.

TO USE Scale, then soak in salted water for 3–4 hours to remove any muddy flavour from the flesh. Braise, poach or stuff and bake.

❹ Pike

Also known as freshwater shark and water wolf, these vicious-looking, flat-nosed fish with sharp teeth are found in lakes and streams in Europe and the US, and can grow to 18kg (40lb) in weight. The skin is greyish or olive-green in colour and the flesh has a good flavour although quite dry and full of small bones. Pike is available whole or as steaks. In Ashkenazi Jewish cooking it is another of the traditional fish used to make gefilte fish. One of its variants, called sandre (pike-perch), is particularly popular in France, where it is often stuffed with breadcrumbs, onions, tomatoes and herbs or made into quenelles (poached fishcakes) or mousses.

TO USE If the fish appears muddy, soak in cold water for a few hours before cooking. Use to make quenelles or stuffing, poach or bake.

Perch

Also known as darter, perch is found in European lakes, rivers and ponds, as well as in parts of the US. Growing to between 500g (1lb 2oz) and 2.5kg (5½lb), it has a greenish skin and golden underbelly, and the flesh is mild and white with a slightly coarse texture. Perch is popular in Italian and Chinese cuisine. It is best eaten extremely fresh, and should be prepared and cooked the day it is caught. It is good cooked with wine, onions and paprika.

TO USE Scale, then grill, pan-fry, poach or coat in flour and deep-fry.

Sturgeon

The beluga sturgeon is found mainly in the Caspian and Black Sea, and is best known for caviar, its roe. The common sturgeon is sometimes found in British coastal waters. These large fish, growing to between 2m (6½ft) and 5.5m (18ft) in length, live in the sea but return to fresh water to spawn, which is where they are caught. Sturgeon has dark skin, a bony head and snout, and trailing barbels. The flesh is firm, meaty and white. As stocks of most species of sturgeon are diminishing, it is rarely available to buy. When available it is usually sold as steaks. It suits strong flavours such as tomatoes, garlic, capers and fresh herbs.

TO USE Poach, bake or roast.

Roach

Native to Europe and Western Asia and related to the carp, roach grow to 35.5cm (14in) long. It has a silvery green-blue skin with red-tinged gills and white, firm flesh that contains a large number of small bones. Roach

is not considered among the most distinguished of freshwater fish and is often valued more for the sport of catching it than for its gastronomic appeal. Cook it with butter, spices, fresh herbs and lemon.

TO USE Soak in salted water for 2–3 hours to remove any muddy flavour before cooking. Grill or pan-fry.

Barbel

Native to Britain and inhabiting fast-flowing rivers in Europe, the barbel gains its name from the two pairs of barbels (like long whiskers) hanging from each side of its mouth. It grows to between 25.5cm (10in) and 90cm (36in) long, and has a brown back, yellow sides and a pale underbelly. The flesh is rather bland, and contains many small bones. Barbel is a popular dish in France, where it is often cooked in red wine.

TO USE Grill, poach, braise or add to stews. Barbel suits strong, robust accompanying flavours.

Tench

A relative of the minnow, tench inhabits slow-moving rivers and lakes in Europe and Asia. It weighs between 500g (1lb 2oz) and 2kg (4½lb), and it has coppery-green skin. The flesh is rather bland, tending towards muddiness, and not regarded as a delicacy, but it can be enlivened with strong flavourings such as garlic, tomatoes and paprika.

TO USE Scale, then soak in salted water for several hours to remove any muddiness from the flesh. Bake, pan-fry or add to stews. Tench suits strong, robust flavours.

Cleaning and boning round fish

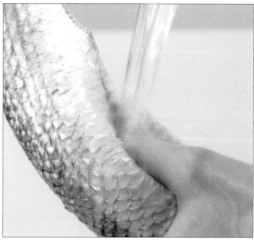

1 Cut off the fins with scissors. Using the blunt edge of a knife, scrape the fish from tail to head and rinse off the loose scales. (The scaled fish should feel smooth.)

2 Insert a sharp knife at the hole towards the rear of the stomach and slit the skin up to the gills. Ease out the entrails. Use scissors to snip out anything that remains. With the knife, cut along the vein under the backbone. Wash the cavity under running water.

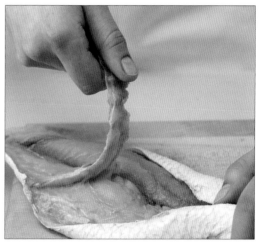

3 Working from the belly side of the fish, cut along one side of the backbone, then remove as many fine bones as possible and separate the backbone from the flesh.

4 Turn the fish over and repeat on the other side of the backbone. Carefully snip the backbone with scissors, then remove.

Skinning flat fish

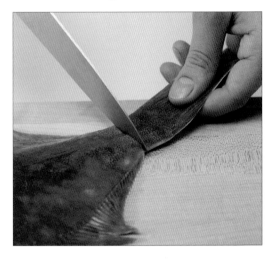

1 Skin thick-skinned fish, such as sole, by hand. Make a nick down to the backbone where the body meets the tail.

2 Lift the skin until you have enough to grip on to. Holding the tail in one hand, pull on the flap in the direction of the head.

3 Thinner-skinned fish can be filleted first, then skinned using a knife. Put the fillet on a board with the skin down and the tail towards you. Make a nick in the tail flesh, just deep enough to cut through to the skin, and lift the little flap of flesh with the knife.

4 Hold the knife on the skin at a very shallow angle, almost parallel to the work surface, and work it between flesh and skin to remove the skin in a single piece.

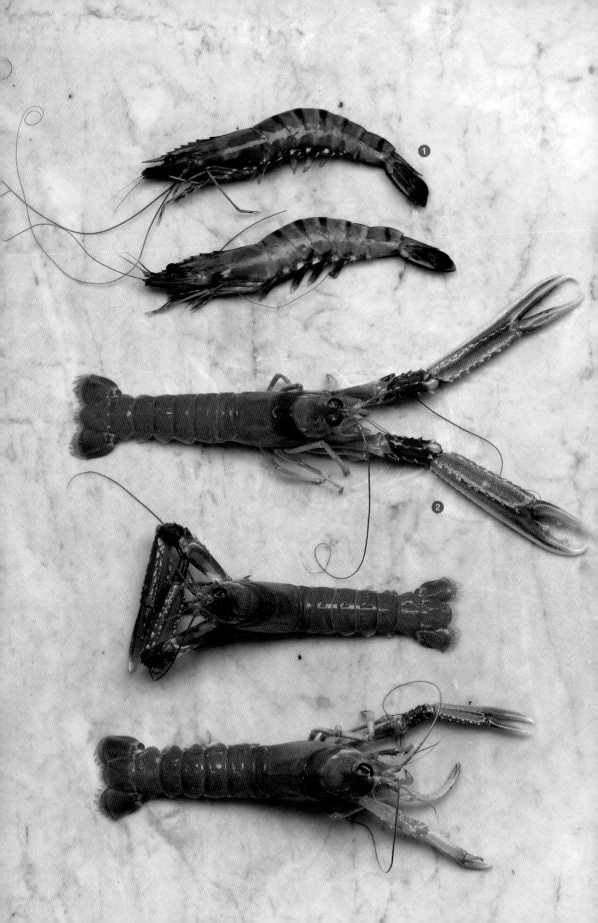

Prawns and small crustacea

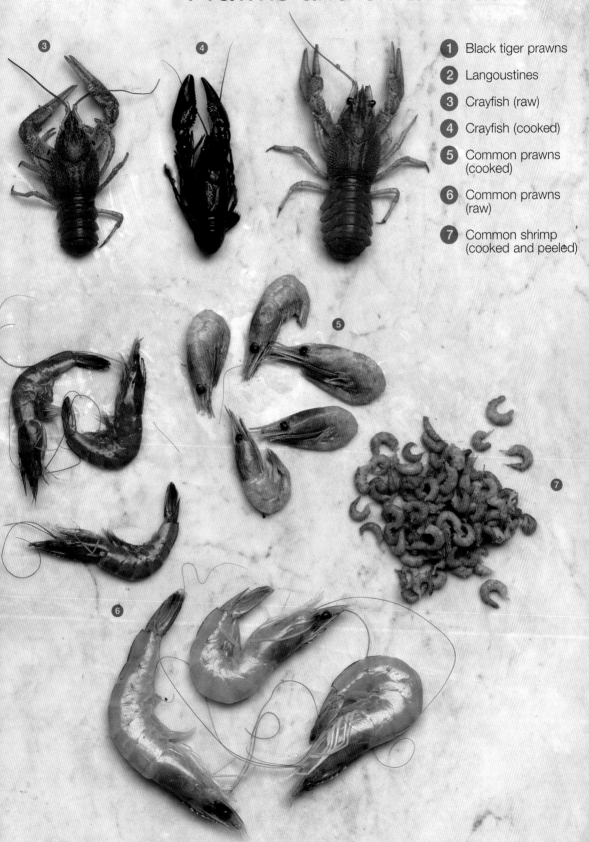

1. Black tiger prawns
2. Langoustines
3. Crayfish (raw)
4. Crayfish (cooked)
5. Common prawns (cooked)
6. Common prawns (raw)
7. Common shrimp (cooked and peeled)

Prawns and small crustacea

❶ Tiger prawn

Known as jumbo shrimp in the US, tiger prawns are the largest variety of prawn found in the warm, temperate waters of the Indian and Pacific oceans. Most of those sold today are farmed, and there are a number of concerns about the environmental and economic impact of this large industry. They can grow to an enormous size – sometimes up to 30.5cm (12in) long. A translucent grey colour with dark stripes when raw, the prawns turn pink on cooking and have tender, juicy flesh. They are sold either raw or cooked, peeled or unpeeled, and sometimes partially shelled with just the tail left on. Prawns go well with a variety of flavour combinations: Mediterranean flavours such as garlic and tomato; South-east Asian flavours such as chilli, ginger, garlic, kaffir lime leaves, lemongrass and coconut milk; and Indian flavours such as cumin, coriander and turmeric.

TO USE Preparation, see page 98. Raw prawns should be deveined, and can be peeled or cooked in the shell: grill, barbecue, stir-fry, pan-fry, braise, coat and deep-fry; add to fish stews and curries. Cooked prawns can be eaten cold in salads, or added to dishes until just warmed through.

Gulf shrimp

These bright red or greyish-pink prawns come from the Gulf of Mexico, and can grow to up to 40–50g (1½–2oz) in weight. They have outstandingly juicy, sweet flesh, but are less commonly found now than farmed shrimp, which are much less expensive. They go well with South-east Asian and Indian-style spices, or simple, zesty marinades.

TO USE Preparation, see page 98. Raw prawns should be deveined, and can be shelled or cooked in the shell. Pan-fry, stir-fry, grill or boil; add to other prawn dishes such as fish stews and curries.

Japanese prawn

Also known as kuruma prawns, these large prawns are found throughout the Indo-Pacific and Red Sea and can grow to up to 23cm (9in) long. They have yellow tails flecked with blue-black, and pale brown bodies. The flesh is tender and juicy, with a fine sweet flavour.

TO USE Preparation, see page 98. Raw prawns should be deveined, and can be peeled or cooked in the shell. Pan-fry, grill or braise; coat and deep-fry; add to other prawn dishes such as stews and curries.

❷ Langoustine

Pink-shelled langoustines are a relative of the lobster. They are sometimes referred to as Norwegian lobster, although they are much smaller and have narrow bodies and long, slender claws. They are also sometimes referred to as Dublin Bay prawns when found in the waters off the coast of Ireland, where they are widely fished. Langoustines are an excellent shellfish, with tender flesh that is sweet and succulent. They are found along the coasts of the Atlantic, Mediterranean and Adriatic. They do not store well once caught so are often frozen at sea. They go well with Mediterranean flavours such as tomatoes, garlic, white wine and fresh herbs.

TO USE Poach, grill or add to recipes such as paella and risotto.

Scampi

Scampi is the Italian word for langoustine and is also the term commonly used for a particular preparation of langoustines. The tail meat is peeled and separated from the head, and is most often breadcrumbed and deep-fried, then served with mayonnaise, aioli or tomato ketchup. The term is used more loosely in some countries to mean any dish based on peeled shrimp or prawn tail. If you are buying pre-prepared scampi, make sure it has not been manufactured from minced, re-formed fish.

TO USE Prepare and cook whole as for langoustine, or coat in egg and breadcrumbs and deep-fry the tail meat.

③ ④ Crayfish

These freshwater crustaceans are rather like miniature lobsters and can grow to 10cm (4in) long. There are numerous of different species of varying colours found in the streams and ponds of Europe, the US and Africa. Once cooked, they turn bright red and are valued for their tail and claw meat, which is similar to that of lobster. They are good made into creamy bisques, cooked in butter and served with lemon, or poached and served cold with mayonnaise.

TO USE Preparation, see page 98. Poach, or add to soups and sauces. Keep the shells for making stock.

⑤ ⑥ Common prawn

Found in the deep waters of the Atlantic and Mediterranean, these coldwater prawns are a translucent brownish colour when alive, and turn an opaque red-pink when cooked. They can grow to up to 10cm (4in) long and have a tender texture and very good, sweet flavour that goes well with garlic, tomatoes and spices or with a cold sauce such as mayonnaise.

TO USE Preparation, see page 98. Larger raw prawns should be deveined, and can be peeled or cooked in the shell: pan-fry, grill or braise; add to other prawn dishes such as stews and curries. Cooked prawns can be eaten cold in salads or with mayonnaise, or added to dishes until just warmed through.

Mediterranean prawn

Also known as king prawns, these are found in the Mediterranean and can grow to up to 20.5cm (8in) long. They generally have a reddish hue when alive, and a pinkish colour when cooked, with a tender, juicy texture and sweet flavour. Mediterranean flavours such as garlic, tomatoes and lemon are particularly good partners for these prawns.

TO USE Preparation, see page 98. Cooked prawns can be eaten cold in salads or with mayonnaise, or added to dishes until just warmed through. Raw prawns should be deveined, and can be peeled or cooked in the shell: pan-fry, grill or braise; add to Mediterranean-style fish stews and other prawn dishes.

Deep-sea prawn

Found in the cold waters of the North Sea, deep-sea prawns can grow to up to 12.5cm (5in) long. These translucent pink prawns turn an opaque pink when cooked and have a juicy texture and sweet flavour. They are usually sold cooked and peeled. Serve with spices, garlic and tomatoes, or a zesty mayonnaise.

TO USE Serve cold in salads, with mayonnaise, in sandwiches; tossed into prawn dishes such as curries and fish stews at the last minute to warm through.

⑦ Common shrimp

Also known as brown shrimp, these small shrimp inhabit coastal waters from the North Sea to the Mediterranean. Common shrimp grow to up to 5–6.5cm (2–2½in) long. They have translucent greyish bodies that turn an opaque pinkish colour when cooked and the flesh has a fine, strong flavour. The smallest shrimps need only to have the heads removed before eating. Because they are so small, these tasty shrimps are best served as an appetiser rather than as a main course. One of the best recipes is potted shrimp: put whole, peeled shrimp into a container and cover with clarified butter.

TO USE As potted shrimp; can also be boiled and served cold with mayonnaise or pan-fried.

Crawfish

This variety of lobster is also known as rock lobster, spiny lobster and southern lobster and generally grows to between 5cm (2in) and 15cm (6in) long. It is found in European and US coastal waters, the south Atlantic and around South-east Asia. Crawfish has a rough, spiny shell that varies in colour according to its origin; unlike other lobsters it does not have heavy claws. Once cooked, crawfish turn pinkish red and the white meat is similar to that of lobster, although with a milder flavour. Crawfish is valued for its tail meat and is a common ingredient in Creole cooking, flavoured with cayenne, garlic, lemon and parsley.

TO USE Preparation, see lobster, page 104. Raw crawfish can be boiled or grilled. Cooked crawfish can be served cold in salads or with mayonnaise; add to soups, pasta fillings and sauces, and Asian-style dishes such as soups and stir-fries.

Peeling and butterflying prawns

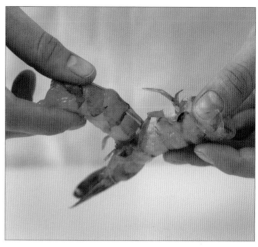

1 To shell prawns, pull off the head and put to one side. Using pointed scissors, cut through the soft shell on the belly side.

2 Prise the shell off, leaving the tail attached. (Add the shell to the head; it can be used later for making stock.)

3 Using a small sharp knife, make a shallow cut along the length of the back of the prawn. Using the point of the knife, carefully remove and discard the black vein (the intestinal tract) that runs along the back of the prawn.

4 To 'butterfly' the prawn, cut halfway through the flesh lengthways from the head end to the base of the tail, and open up the prawn.

All about shellfish

Shellfish fall into the following categories:

Crustacea

A large family of shellfish, crustacea are characterised by an external skeleton and jointed limbs. They include crabs, lobsters and shrimps.

Molluscs

These are a highly diverse group of shellfish including bivalve, gastropods and cephalopods:

Bivalves With a hinged, two-piece external shell, this group of shellfish includes mussels and oysters.
Gastropods These have snail-like shells and include whelks, winkles, conch, abalone and limpets.
Cephalopods These creatures are classed as shellfish, although most do not have an obviously external skeleton and have a modified body that includes tentacles or arms, such as squid, cuttlefish and octopus. The 'shell' is in the form of a hard, transparent internal quill.

Buying shellfish

Shellfish have seasons and although some are available all year-round, others are harder to find. Weather conditions can affect availability and therefore cost. When buying crustaceans they should smell sweet and fresh and be moist. Crabs, lobsters and langoustines are best when sold live for home cooking and should feel heavy for their size. When buying molluscs, look for those with shells that are smooth and shiny. The shells of oysters, scallops, clams and mussels should be shut, or should close when tapped. Some shellfish are always sold live. This includes all the bivalves except scallops, which are sometimes removed from their shells and cleaned. Live crabs, lobsters and crayfish should display plenty of movement, with snapping claws or pincers. When buying pre-cooked shellfish, such as langoustines, prawns and crab, buy from a reputable supplier. Use all shellfish on the day of purchase.

Frozen shellfish

Frozen shellfish – such as prawns and scallops – is sold either raw or cooked. Shellfish can be cooked from frozen.

Preparing and cooking shellfish

Stir-fry This method is best suited to pieces of firm shellfish prawns or squid. Toss the prepared fish in a little oil with spices and aromatics in a wok for 1–2 minutes until just cooked through. Prawns are cooked when they turn pink. Do not overcook them.
Sear Use for firm-fleshed shellfish such as such as scallops. Heat a little oil in a frying pan until very hot, then cook briefly for about 1 minute on each side, to give it a flavourful crust on the outside while the centre remains tender.
Deep-fry Use for all shellfish. Prepare the fish and a coating (which can be batter, seasoned flour, or flour, egg and breadcrumbs). Heat vegetable oil in a deep-fryer to 180°C, or until a cube of bread browns in 40 seconds. Coat the shellfish, then carefully lower into the oil a few pieces at a time and cook until crisp and golden. Remove using a slotted spoon. Drain on kitchen paper.
Grill Marinate the shellfish, or season and brush with oil, then grill on both sides until just cooked through.
Braise Best suited to shellfish such as prawns. Prepare a tomato sauce, then add the prepared shellfish. Spoon the sauce over to cover and simmer gently for 5–10 minutes until just cooked through. Shellfish will need only a few minutes.
Steam Season and/or marinate the shellfish, then put into a dish that will fit into a bamboo steamer. Put the steamer into a pan or wok over boiling water. Steam for 10–15 minutes until firm and just cooked through. Shellfish will require just a few minutes.

Crabs and lobsters

1 Blue swimmer crab
2 Green mud crab
3 Kingsize common crab
4 Common crab
5 Soft-shell crab
6 Canadian lobster
7 Spider crab
8 European lobster

Crabs and lobsters

❶ Blue swimmer crab

These small crabs are strikingly beautiful, with dark blue-grey or blue-green bodies and bright blue claws, Native to the Atlantic Ocean from Canada down to South America, they can grow to up to 20.5cm (8in) in diameter and have sweet, well-flavoured meat which is best picked out and eaten by hand. The flavourings for common crab are also suitable for blue crab.

TO USE Preparation, see page 105. Boil raw crabs. Serve cooked crabmeat with mayonnaise or serve in salads, toss into stir-fries, soups or crab cakes.

❷ Green mud crab

Found throughout the world, this crab has a dark shell and an extra pair of legs shaped like paddles. The green mud crab is a type of swimming crab, of which there are numerous varieties, including the green-shelled shore crab and reddish-brown velvet crab. They all have sweet and tender flesh. The flavourings for common crab are also suitable for swimming crab.

TO USE Preparation, see page 105. Boil raw crabs. Serve cooked crabmeat with mayonnaise or serve in salads, toss into stir-fries, soups or crab cakes. Shore crabs can be eaten as for soft-shell crabs: deep-fried and eaten whole.

❸❹ Common crab

Also known as brown crab, the common crab is found on the coasts of the Atlantic and Mediterranean. It is reddish-brown in colour and grows to up to 20.5–25.5cm (8–10in) in diameter with four pairs of hairy legs and heavy front claws. The flesh is firm, sweet and well flavoured, and nearly the equal of lobster flesh (but much more difficult to extract from the shell). Common crab is available cooked or live, but it is preferable to buy a live crab and cook it at home to ensure it is perfectly fresh. Crab is good served simply with a squeeze of lemon or lime juice and a tangy mayonnaise, but also suits spicy flavours such as cayenne, paprika and Thai- and Chinese-style flavourings such as garlic, ginger and chilli.

TO USE Preparation, see page 105. Boil raw crabs. Serve cooked crabmeat with mayonnaise; lightly dress the white meat with white wine vinegar, seasoning and a little cayenne pepper, and the brown meat with a little dry mustard, fresh brown breadcrumbs, lemon juice, chopped parsley and seasoning, to serve with a salad; toss into stir-fries, soups or crab cakes.

❺ Soft-shell crab

This seasonal delicacy is popular in the US and a classic ingredient in cuisine from New Orleans. Soft-shell crabs are blue crabs caught shortly after they have shed their shell and before they are able to grow a new one. The 'shell' that remains is no thicker and little harder than paper, so the whole crab can be eaten, shell and all. Soft-shell crabs are always sold live at the fishmongers, and killed either by the fishmonger or the customer at home. They do not store well so are frequently sold frozen if destined for markets far from the region of production, and they are best early in the season because the shell grows harder as the season progresses. They go well with garlic, herbs and lemon, but are also good enough to eat with nothing more than salt, pepper, and a squeeze of lemon juice.

TO USE Coat with seasoned flour and pan-fry or deep-fry, and eat whole.

❻ Canadian lobster

Also known as American lobster, these lobsters are found in the western Atlantic, and in the USA are called Maine lobsters if caught off the coast of that New England state. They are similar in appearance and size to the European lobster although when alive they tend to be brown in colour and with more rounded claws. Canadian lobster turns bright red when cooked. Inside, the flesh is tender, sweet and well flavoured. They are available live or cooked, although it is preferable to buy live lobsters to cook at home. Serve cooked lobster with melted butter and lemon or make the flesh into dishes such as bisque or stew.

TO USE Preparation, see page 104. Cooked lobster can be served cold in salads or with mayonnaise; add to soups, pasta fillings and sauces, and Asian-style dishes such as soups and stir-fries. Raw lobster can be boiled or grilled.

❼ Spider crab

Spider crabs are found in European waters. They grow to about 20.5cm (8in) in diameter and have a spiny shell and long, hairy legs that give the appearance of a spider. When alive, they are purple-brown in colour, turning bright red when cooked. The flesh is sweet, and flavourings for common crab are also suitable for spider crab.

TO USE Preparation, see page 105. Boil raw crabs. Serve cooked crabmeat with mayonnaise or serve in salads, toss into stir-fries, soups or crab cakes.

Snow crab

Also known as queen crab, these pinkish-brown, long-legged crabs are found in the north Pacific and grow to about 15cm (6in) in diameter. The flesh is sweet, tender and well flavoured, but is more often available canned or frozen than fresh. The flavourings for common crab are also suitable for snow crab.

TO USE Preparation, see page 105. Boil raw crabs. Serve cooked crabmeat with mayonnaise or serve in salads, toss into stir-fries, soups or crab cakes.

King crab

Also known as stone crab, these imposingly large crabs can grow to 1m (3 ft 3in) in diameter at full maturity. They inhabit cold seas, originally the waters off Alaska, although they are now being farmed in Norway. King crabs have spiny, reddish shells and long, spindly, spiky legs. The meat – concentrated mainly in the legs – is sweet and well flavoured, and is often sold canned although it is sometimes possible to find the legs being sold frozen. The flavourings for common crab are also suitable for king crab.

TO USE Preparation, see page 105. Boil raw crabs. Serve cooked crabmeat with mayonnaise or serve in salads, toss into stir-fries, soups or crab cakes.

Dungeness crab

These excellent crabs are also known as California crab, but are named after the port city of Dungeness in the state of Washington on the Pacific coast of the USA. Dungeness crab can grow to up to 20.5cm (8in) in diameter. The flesh is a pale greyish colour with a sweet flavour and is comparable to that of the common crab; there is a relatively high proportion of meat to shell, found more in the legs and claws than in the body. The flavourings for common crab are also suitable for Dungeness crab.

TO USE Preparation, see page 105. Boil raw crabs. Serve cooked crabmeat with mayonnaise or serve in salads, toss into stir-fries, soups or crab cakes.

❽ European lobster

Found around the British Isles, Norway and France, these are often considered to have the best flavour of all lobsters. They can grow to up to 3.9–5kg (8½–11lb) in weight, although sizes of around 500g (1lb 2oz) are more common. They are dark blue-black when alive and turn bright red when cooked. The flesh is tender, sweet and white. Although lobster can be bought live or cooked, it is preferable to buy it live and cook it yourself at home to ensure absolute freshness. A classic lobster dish is lobster thermidor, where the meat is removed and chopped, then replaced in the half shells, covered with a cream, wine and mustard sauce, and grilled. It is also used to make lobster bisque, a rich and creamy soup containing chunks of the white meat. Lobster also suits a much simpler preparation: steaming or boiling with flavourings such as melted butter and lemon to let its sweet, distinctive flavour shine through. This approach is also the easiest by far.

TO USE Preparation, see page 104. Cooked lobster can be served cold in salads or with mayonnaise; add to soups, pasta fillings and sauces, and Asian-style dishes such as soups and stir-fries. Raw lobster can be boiled, steamed or grilled.

Slipper lobster

There are numerous types of this flattened, warm-water crustacean, which has long spindly legs and more closely resembles a crab than a lobster. They can grow to 18cm (7in) long and have a smaller tail than European and Canadian lobsters. The meat inside is tender and particularly sweet and flavoursome, but there is not a great deal of it. Use for lobster bisque or serve steamed or grilled with melted butter and lemon.

TO USE Preparation, see page 104. Cooked lobster can be served cold in salads or with mayonnaise; add to soups, pasta fillings and sauces and Asian-style dishes such as soups and stir-fries. Raw lobster can be boiled or grilled.

Preparing and cooking lobsters

To kill a lobster humanely before cooking, put it on a chopping board and hold the body firmly. Take a large cook's knife and plunge it straight down into the lobster's head, right between or just below the eyes. (It is inhumane to plunge it into boiling water or to put it into cold water and then bring it up to the boil.)

1 If you are going to split the raw lobster for grilling or baking, cut the freshly killed lobster right through the head, then cut all the way down the length of the tail to split it in two.

2 Remove the head sac, which lies just behind the eyes, and discard. If you wish, you can remove the black coral (tomalley) and the green intestine, which lie inside the back of the shell just behind the head sac, or they may be left in place for cooking.

3 If you want the tail meat in one piece, split the head to where the tail begins, then use scissors to cut through the soft shell of the belly, down to the tail.

4 Pull the tail meat out with your fingers. Clean the head as in step 2. Cut off the claws and spiny legs. Crack the claws with a hammer or lobster cracker and remove the meat. Save the shells to make stock.

Preparing and cooking crabs

1 Live crabs must be humanely killed before cooking. Put the crab on a board, with the belly facing up. Take a large cook's knife and plunge it straight down into the crab's head, right between or just below the eyes.

2 Put the crab in a pan of boiling water and cook for 5 minutes per 450g (1lb). Alternatively, steam for 8 minutes per 450g (1lb). To serve whole, simply set on the table with crackers and crab picks for diners to use themselves.

3 To remove the cooked meat for a recipe, put the crab on a board, with the belly facing up. Twist off the legs and claws. Lift off and discard the 'apron' (tail) – long and pointed in a male, short and broad in a female.

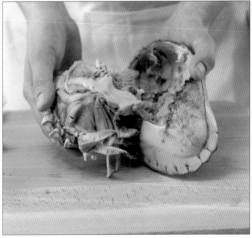

4 Pull the body out of the shell. Remove and discard the feathery gills and grey stomach sac. Cut the body into pieces and pick out the meat. Scrape the brown meat from the shell, keeping it separate from the white meat. If there is roe in a female, keep that separate, too. Crack the claws with the back of a large knife, and pull out the meat in a single piece. Cut through the shells of the legs with scissors. Pull off the shell halves to expose the meat and remove.

Oysters and other bivalves and molluscs

1 Winkles

2 Green-shell mussels

3 Mussels

4 Cockles

5 Razor clams

6 Vongole clams

7 Native oyster

8 Venus clams

9 Queen scallops

10 Oyster

Oysters and other bivalves and molluscs

❶ Winkle

These small molluscs grow to about 4cm (1½in) long and have coiled shells, usually green-brown or black in colour, resembling a pointed snail. Inside is a small nugget of slightly chewy flesh. They may be sold live or cooked. They are highly valued in France, where they are often served as part of a plateau de fruits de mer.

TO USE Cooked winkles can be eaten as they are. Rinse live winkles well, then leave to stand in salted water for several hours to purge away any sand or impurities. Boil in salted water for about 5 minutes, then drain. Pick the flesh gently from the shell using a pin, first removing the tiny plate at the opening.

❷ ❸ Mussel

This thin-shelled bivalve usually has a blue-black shell, although it may be brown or green. The shell is rounded at one end and pointed at the other. Inside, the flesh is tender, smooth and sweet tasting. Mussels are found in seas all over the world, and they are also widely cultivated; nearly all of those sold in markets are farmed. They are always sold live, and the ease of cultivation makes them the cheapest of common shellfish. Mussels are often served steamed in wine with garlic, shallots and fresh herbs, sometimes finished with a little cream. They can also be opened, topped with aromatic seasonings and breadcrumbs, and baked or grilled on the half-shell.

TO USE Preparation and cooking, see page 111. Steam, stuff and bake or grill, or add cooked mussels to salads, paellas, pasta sauces and fish stews.

❹ Cockle

Found around the world, these bivalves have two small, rounded ribbed shells that are hinged on one side. The cockle shell usually grows between 2.5cm (1in) and 4cm (1½in) in diameter. Inside is a small nugget of tender flesh. There are numerous varieties, varying in colour from pinkish brown and beige to dark blue. Cockles go well with garlic, shallots and white wine and can be added to seafood pasta dishes. They can also be eaten raw.

TO USE Soak in cold water for 2–3 hours to purge of sand. Steam or add to soups, stews and other seafood dishes such as risotto.

❺ ❻ ❽ Clam

Clams are found in oceans throughout the world, and they are also cultivated. There are many varieties, of different colours and sizes, from the tiny vongole, reddish-pink Venus clams, yellow-brown carpetshell clams to brown cherrystone and prairie clams, which grow to about 7.5cm (3in) in diameter. The creamy-beige soft-shell clams (also known as long-neck or steamer clams) grow to 15cm (6in) in diameter, and there are also pale brown razor clams with a long shell, up to 16cm (6¼in), resembling a cut-throat razor. Clams suit Mediterranean-style ingredients such as garlic, tomatoes, lemon and wine. Larger, tougher-fleshed clams are more suitable for chopping and using in creamy chowders.

TO USE Preparation and cooking, see page 111. Steam or add to soups, stews and sauces. Larger clams can be grilled or baked. Small clams may be eaten raw.

❼ ❿ Oyster

There are numerous varieties of this bivalve, many of which are farmed. Oysters have a distinctive, craggy, hard shell with a slightly whorled pattern. The shell is jointed on one side and difficult to prise open; the best way is to use a specialised oyster knife, and the process requires both skill and strength. The oyster flesh is soft and slippery and has a salty, marine flavour that many people love and others hate. The taste is an acquired one, and even people who don't appreciate their first oyster often find that a second, third or fourth one makes them see what a delicacy these greatest of bivalves can be. The types listed below represent just a small sample of the wide variety found in the oyster family.

Native oyster With a rounded shell, which may be grey-green or pale brown in colour, the native oyster is highly regarded and is found in the UK, Ireland, Belgium and France. In France, where oyster farming is a major industry, this type has several different names (including plates and Belons), and is classified by the location of the farm and by size.

Eastern oyster Also known as the Atlantic oyster, the Eastern oyster has mildly flavoured flesh.

Geiger oyster Also known as the Pacific oyster, these oysters have a relatively large, elongated shell and are widely cultivated. They are popular for cooking, as they have slightly coarser flesh than some other varieties.

Portuguese oyster These oysters are found particularly in Portugal, Spain and Morocco, but are also now cultivated in other countries. With a craggy grey-brown shell, Portuguese oysters have a slightly coarse-textured flesh and are considered to be inferior to native

oysters, although they are still good. They may also be called Portugaise.
Sydney rock oyster This oyster is farmed extensively in Australia around New South Wales. It has a good flavour and texture.

TO USE Preparation, see page 110. Eat raw and live with a squeeze of lemon juice or a little vinaigrette. To cook, steam, then drizzle with a little cream and a sprinkling of grated Parmesan; grill; add to pies; coat in breadcrumbs or batter and deep-fry.

Whelk

Larger than winkles, and with a similar but greyish, pointed, spiral shell, whelks can grow to up to 10cm (4in) in length and contain chewy flesh which has a good flavour and is high in protein. Whelks are traditionally eaten with black pepper and vinegar in the UK. They may be sold live or cooked. In France, where they are called bulot, they are often served as part of a plateau de fruits de mer.

TO USE Cooked whelks can be eaten as they are, or the flesh added to salads, sauces and other fish dishes. Rinse live whelks well, then leave to stand in salted water for several hours to purge away any sand or impurities. Boil in salted water for about 10 minutes. Pick the flesh from the shell using a pin.

Limpet

Not available commercially, conical, grey-shelled limpets can be found growing on rocks on seashores throughout the world. The cooked flesh tends to be quite chewy with a mild flavour. They can be collected from the rocks, although it is important to avoid areas where the sea is polluted.

TO USE When collecting, find limpet-covered rocks that are washed daily by the tide and are situated away from towns. Use a knife to prise the limpet away from the rock. Soak in salted cold water for 2–3 hours to purge the limpet of sand, then steam as for mussels and clams (see page 111), or add to soups, stews and other seafood dishes such as risotto.

Conch

This large mollusc, related to the whelk, is found in the warm waters of the Atlantic and Caribbean. The conch has a decorative, spiral-shaped shell. Inside, the flesh is pink and well flavoured, although it can be tough. The flesh is usually sold out of the shell. Lime or lemon juice, garlic, chilli and herbs make a good marinade for conch before eating raw or cooking.

TO USE Beat the flesh with a meat mallet or a rolling pin to tenderise, then marinate and eat raw or add to soups or chowders.

Abalone

Also known as ormer and sea ear, this large mollusc is found in warm waters off the coast of California, the Channel Islands, Australia, Japan, China and the Mediterranean. It is considered an endangered species in many of its habitats. Abalone varies in size from 10cm (4in) to 20.5cm (8in). It has a decorative shell, and the flesh inside is sweet and juicy, rather like that of a scallop, although it can be tough. Marinate with lime or lemon juice, garlic, chilli and herbs before cooking or eating raw.

TO USE Remove the flesh from the shell, then beat with a meat mallet or rolling pin to tenderise. Slice, marinate and eat raw, or pan-fry briefly. Overcooking will make the meat tough.

9 ## Scallop

This beautiful bivalve has two fan-shaped shells with a hinge on one side, and is found on seabeds throughout the Atlantic, Pacific and Mediterranean. There are hundreds of species, with shells varying in colour from brown to orange and pink, but the two best known are the common (king) scallop and the smaller queen (or bay) scallop. All have a thick disk of pale creamy-white flesh with a pink or orange coral (roe). Once cooked, the flesh turns opaque; it has a juicy texture and sweet, mild flavour. Scallops can be marinated briefly in oil flavoured with garlic and lemon juice and then griddled. They are also good flavoured with a hint of chilli, lime juice and fresh herbs. Be careful not to mask their flavour by using excessively strong flavours, and do not overcook them: their delicate flesh turns tough and rubbery with prolonged cooking.

TO USE Preparation, see page 110. Bake, steam, grill, sear, pan-fry or coat and deep-fry. Cook very briefly and avoid overcooking.

Opening scallops

1 Hold the scallop with the flat half of the shell facing up. Firmly ease a very sharp small knife between the shells at a point close to the hinge.

2 Keeping the knife angled towards the flat shell, cut all along the shell surface until the two shells can be separated easily. Cut along the bottom of

the rounded shell to release its contents. Cut loose the round white meat and the grey/orange coral and discard everything else.

3 Rinse off any grit, cut the coral from the round meat, and cut the little scrap of muscle from the edge of the meat.

Opening oysters

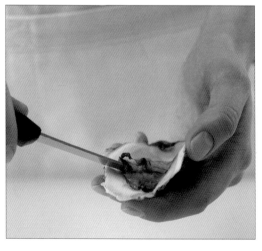

1 Hold the oyster in one hand with the flat half of the shell facing up, using a towel to protect your hand. Insert an oyster knife in the hinge and twist.

2 When the upper shell comes off, scrape off any shell and cut under the oyster to release it from the shell, holding it level to retain the juices.

Cooking mussels

1 Scrape off the fibres (beards) attached to the shells. Rinse under the cold tap or scrub if sandy. Rap barnacles sharply with a metal spoon, then scrape off. Discard any open mussels that don't shut when sharply tapped.

2 Melt 25g (1oz) butter in a pan. Fry 2 chopped shallots and a handful of parsley for 2 minutes or until soft. Pour in 1cm (½in) dry white wine.

3 Add the mussels and cover tightly. Steam for 5–10 minutes until the shells open. Immediately take the pan away from the heat.

4 Using a slotted spoon, remove the mussels from the pan and discard any that haven't opened. Boil the cooking liquid rapidly to reduce. Pour over the mussels and serve immediately.

Cooking clams

1 To cook, rinse or lightly scrub the clams. Place in a large bowl of cold salted water (2 tbsp salt per 1 litre/1¾ pints water). Leave to stand for a few hours to allow the clams to open and release any sand and grit.

2 Cook as for mussels, then use according to the recipe.

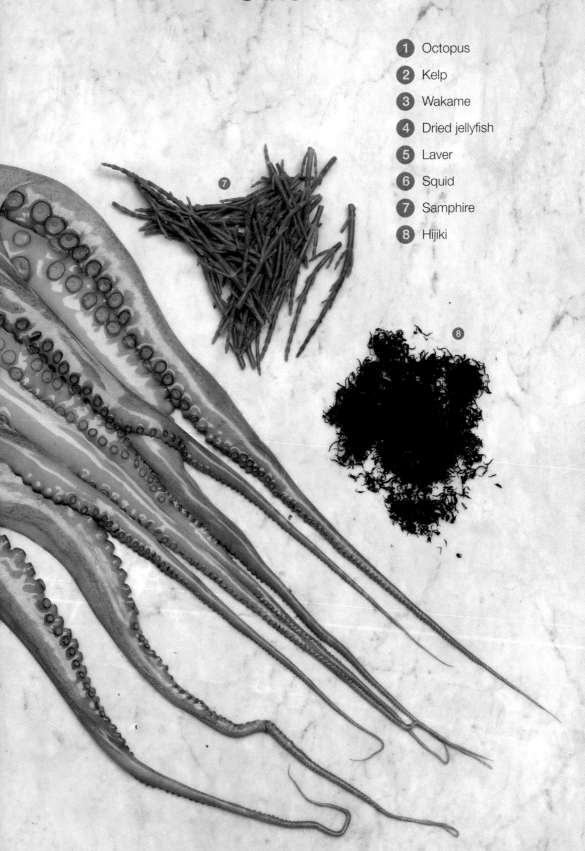

Other foods of the sea

1 Octopus
2 Kelp
3 Wakame
4 Dried jellyfish
5 Laver
6 Squid
7 Samphire
8 Hijiki

Other foods of the sea

❶ Octopus

The third major cephalopod differs from squid and cuttlefish in having no internal 'shell'. Octopuses have rounded heads and eight suckered tentacles, and can range in size from baby octopuses little bigger than a walnut to gigantic – up to 4m (13ft) long. Smaller octopuses have a better taste and texture, being sweet and firm, rather than tough and chewy. Octopus tends to be a mauvish brown-grey in colour, although this may vary also. Small octopuses are usually sold whole, whereas larger specimens are usually sold prepared and cut into smaller pieces. They are good cooked with garlic, tomatoes and red wine.

TO USE Preparation, see page 117. Rinse and pound the tentacles and body with a rolling pin or meat mallet to tenderise. Very small specimens can be cooked whole, fried either with or without a batter or flour coating. For larger specimens, cut the tentacles into pieces and slice the body into rings, or leave whole for stuffing. Braise, stew or add to soups. Most octopus benefits from long, slow cooking to achieve tender results.

❷❸❺❽ Seaweed

Numerous varieties of these green, purple, brown and black sea vegetables grow variously in the sea and on shore. Enjoyed in both the East and West, they are particularly valued for their nutritional and health-giving benefits.

Arame The fine black strips of this seaweed have a mild flavour and a crisp bite. To use, soak in cold water, then add to salads, stir-fries and Asian-style soups.
Dulse This Atlantic seaweed has known popularity in the US and northern Europe, particularly Ireland. Dulse grows in red-brown 'strips'. It

has a salty, tangy flavour and can be eaten cold in salads or added to dishes such as mashed potato. Soak in cold water, then simmer for about 45 minutes until tender.
Hijiki A mild, sweetly flavoured Japanese seaweed made up of fine brown strands that are often available dried. To use, soak in cold water and add to Asian-style soups.
Kelp This is also known as kombu. It is a brown seaweed and is particularly common in Japanese cooking as a flavouring for soups and stocks. It is said that adding a strip of kelp to the cooking water of beans and pulses will help to soften them.
Laver Commonly found around the British Isles, laver is featured in much regional cooking (especially in Wales and Scotland). This salty, strongly flavoured seaweed may be soaked, then simmered slowly to make a black purée for spreading on toast. It is also mixed with oatmeal and fried into round cakes (laverbread) for serving at breakfast.
Nori A type of seaweed favoured in Japan. The shiny black sheets of dried nori are made by chopping the seaweed, then flattening it on to frames and leaving it to dry. Nori sheets are traditionally rolled around sushi rice and fillings to make sushi, or toasted over a flame and crumbled over food as a garnish.
Wakame Dark green and with a tender bite, wakame is mildly flavoured and usually sold dried, in which form it takes on a brownish colour. To use, soak in cold water, then add to salads and Asian-style soups such as Japanese miso.

❹ Dried Jellyfish

Lightly salted and dried in the sun, this creamy, translucent, dried jellyfish is regarded as a delicacy in Chinese cooking. When soaked and reconstituted it has little flavour, but has a gelatinous texture with a definite bite. Dried jellyfish is added to braised dishes and stir-fries, and is eaten as a snack in some countries of south-east Asia.

TO USE Soak and shred, then add to Chinese-style dishes such as soups.

❻ Squid

This is the most commonly available member of the group of shellfish known as cephalopods, which have a transparent quill inside the body instead of an external shell or skeleton. There are approximately 300 different varieties of squid, found in waters throughout the world. The squid has a long, slender body and ten tentacles, and the commonest specimens sold commercially can vary in size from about 5cm (2in) to about 25.5cm (10in) long. The colour can vary from pale and translucent to pinkish brown-grey, and the flesh turns an opaque white when cooked; as long as it is not overcooked, it is very tender and has a sweet, mild flavour. Squid can be marinated in chilli, olive oil and garlic, then quickly griddled or pan-fried. Tender rings of cooked squid make a tasty addition to a seafood salad, and a popular way to eat them all over the world is coated in batter and quickly fried.

Squid ink is frequently used in Mediterranean cooking. The black ink contained in the body can be cooked with the squid. It is also used to flavour seafood dishes such as risotto and pasta.

TO USE Preparation, see page 116. Cut the tentacles into pieces and either slice the body into rings, or keep whole and stuff. Pan-fry, deep-fry, grill, poach or stew; add to seafood dishes such as paella. Squid should be cooked very briefly to ensure the flesh is tender rather than rubbery. Alternatively, it can be simmered slowly for a long time to achieve the same results.

Cuttlefish

Part of the same family of shellfish (cephalopods) as squid and octopus, cuttlefish has a rounded, almost bell-shaped body with a ruffled underside and ten tentacles. Cuttlefish vary greatly in size, with smaller varieties only about 5cm (2in) long and larger ones with bodies up to about 25.5cm (10in) long. Colours vary from shades of pinkish-brown to grey. Inside is a single long oval 'shell', known as the cuttlebone. Found in the Mediterranean, and widely used in the region's cooking, it is similar in taste and texture to squid although sometimes tougher, and is good prepared and cooked in similar ways. The ink is even more highly prized and widely used than squid ink – and also more abundant. Try not to break the ink sac during preparation, as it can stain everything in sight.

TO USE Preparation, see page 110. Cut the tentacles into pieces and either slice the body into rings, or keep whole and stuff. Pan-fry, deep-fry, grill, poach or stew; add to seafood dishes such as paella. Cuttlefish should be cooked very briefly to ensure the flesh is tender rather than rubbery. Alternatively, it can be simmered slowly for a long time to achieve the same results.

Sea urchin

These spiky, spherical creatures, purple or greenish-black, grow to about 6.5cm (2½in) in diameter. Stepped on at the beach, they are a menace. Carefully handled in the kitchen, they make an unusual seafood delicacy which is particularly enjoyed in Japan but also eaten in France, Italy and Spain. Only the orange coral inside, salty and soft, is eaten – and usually eaten raw, although it may be added to cooked dishes. When buying, look for urchins with firm spines and a tightly closed mouth. Great care should be taken when preparing sea urchins because the spines are very sharp and poisonous. The coral is eaten as it is, made into sushi (in Japan), or added to sauces or soups.

TO USE Wear protective gloves and/or wrap the urchin in several layers of tea towel to protect your skin from the spines, then carefully cut a hole in the top of the urchin using a pair of sharp scissors or a sharp knife. Scoop out the coral with a teaspoon and eat raw, or add to sauces or Japanese-style soups.

➐ Samphire

This delicious, fleshy, bright green plant is a sea plant that appears to grow as 'shoots'. The best variety for eating is the marsh samphire found growing on salt marshes. Its strong, salty flavour and firm, crunchy texture make it a tasty accompaniment to fish.

TO USE Wash well in cold water, then steam for about 3 minutes until just tender. Serve drizzled with melted butter, or stir-fry briefly in a little oil and season with pepper – but no salt, as the plant packs its own salty tang.

Sea cucumber

Also known as trepang or sea slug, these cucumber-shaped creatures live on the sea floor throughout the world and are considered a delicacy in Asia. There are numerous varieties of varying size and colour, all of which have a gelatinous texture. They can be eaten as sashimi or cooked in Chinese dishes such as braised abalone with sea cucumber. They are definitely an acquired taste.

TO USE Slice and eat raw as sashimi, or use in traditional Chinese recipes.

Preparing squid and cuttlefish

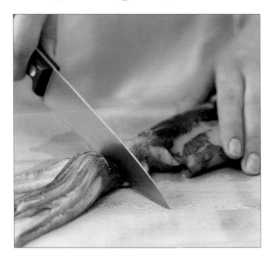

1 If you want to save the ink for using in a recipe, position the head over a bowl and cut open the ink sac so that the ink can drain into it. Set aside. Cut off the tentacles just behind the 'beak' (mouth).

2 Pull out the beak and clean the tentacles well, scraping off as many of the plastic-like rings from the suckers as you can.

3 Reach inside the body and pull out the internal organs, including the plastic-like 'pen' (in squid) or cuttle bone (in cuttlefish).

4 Scrape and pull off the loose, slippery skin covering the body. Rinse the body thoroughly to remove all internal organs, sand and other debris.

5 Detach the 'wings' and set aside, then cut up the tentacles and body as required in your recipe. Generally speaking, the longer the squid or cuttlefish is going to be cooked, the larger the pieces should be.

Preparing octopus

1 Cut off the tentacles just behind the 'beak' (mouth).

2 Pull out the beak and clean the tentacles well, removing as many of the plastic-like rings from the suckers as you can.

3 Turn the body inside out to expose the sac containing the internal organs. Pull out the sac and rub, scrape and pull off the loose, slippery skin covering the body. Rinse the body thoroughly to remove all internal organs, sand and other debris.

4 Rinse well. Cut up the tentacles and body as required in your recipe.

Smoked fish and shellfish

1 Smoked haddock
2 Smoked prawns
3 Smoked oysters
4 Kipper
5 Smoked trout
6 Smoked salmon
7 Smoked mussels
8 Smoked scallops
9 Smoked mackerel
10 Smoked halibut
11 Smoked eel
12 Buckling

Smoked fish and shellfish

Smoking was traditionally used as a preserving method, but now it is appreciated more for its flavour. There are two main methods of smoking fish: hot and cold. In both methods the fish is first salted or soaked in brine before it is smoked over wood, or sometimes tea. Different woods will impart their own unique flavour.

Hot smoking The salted fish is smoked at a high temperature (75–85°C) which cooks the flesh as well as curing it. It can be eaten as it is in cold dishes such as salads or pâtés, or warmed through before serving.

Cold smoking The salted fish is smoked at a lower temperature, typically around 35°C or less, to cure the fish while leaving the flesh raw. Most cold-smoked fish requires further cooking, although a few (such as smoked salmon and trout) are eaten raw.

❶ Smoked haddock

Cold-smoked haddock is available as fillets, and may be pale or dyed a bright yellow colour. Haddock has a tender, succulent texture and a salty, smoky taste. Choose the paler, undyed fillets where possible. This is the classic fish to use with kedgeree and can also be grilled or poached and served with a mustard sauce.

TO USE Remove the skin, then grill, poach or add to dishes such as kedgeree or fish pie.

❷❸❼❽ Smoked shellfish

There are numerous types of smoked shellfish, including oysters, scallops, mussels and prawns. All are lightly salted and smoked, giving (when done carefully) tender flesh and a salty and sweetly smoky flavour. Smoked oysters add a rich dimension to a pie of beef braised in wine. Smoked shellfish make flavourful canapés.

TO USE Serve in salads, as hors d'oeuvres or as part of a mixed cold fish platter.

❹ Kipper

Golden-brown kippers are whole herrings that have been split, gutted and cold-smoked, usually over oak. They're often sold in pairs, and when buying you should look out for the paler kippers rather than the darker red-brown ones (which may have been coloured artificially). Although traditionally sold as whole fish, they are also often available as fillets (which are easier to handle both in cooking and in eating). Kippers have a rich, salty, smoky and fishy flavour with a tender texture. They are fairly bony fish, but the finer bones can usually be eaten safely. They are a classic British breakfast dish, often served with a poached egg, but are also excellent in pâtés and pastes.

TO USE Grill, poach, or put in a jug, pour over boiling water and leave to stand for about 10 minutes.

❺ Smoked trout

Both cold- and hot-smoked trout are widely available. Cold-smoked sea trout is similar in colour, appearance and flavour to smoked salmon. It is usually sold thinly sliced and vacuum-packed. Hot-smoked trout has a pale pink colour and is usually sold as skinless fillets; the texture is tender and the flavour salty. Smoked trout can be served in the same ways as smoked salmon.

TO USE Serve cold-smoked trout raw in thin slices with a squeeze of lemon juice, either in salads, with brown bread and butter, or in sandwiches or bagels with cream cheese. Serve with scrambled eggs; toss into creamy pasta sauces. Serve hot-smoked fillets as an appetiser, in salads, or puréed in mousses and pâtés.

❻ Smoked salmon

Smoked salmon is most commonly cold-smoked, using oak in the smoking process. It is usually sold cut into paper-thin slices, although whole sides of smoked salmon can be bought for slicing at home. It is best to slice the fish shortly before serving, as it begins to dry out from the moment of slicing; slices wrapped in air-tight packaging escape the drying process until they're opened. The pink-orange flesh should have a moist and tender texture, with a salty, smoky and fishy flavour. The best smoked salmon is generally thought to come from Scotland, but Irish and Norwegian are also of high quality. This versatile fish is added to sandwiches, sauces, flans, as canapés and tossed into creamy pasta sauces. It is also a classic accompaniment to scrambled eggs for breakfast. The trimmings are sometimes sold by smokehouses at a lower price, and are useful for cooking and for making pâtés.

Hot-smoked salmon is usually sold in fillets, and is a paler pink-orange than cold-smoked salmon. Its texture is similar to that of cooked unsmoked salmon, but with a slightly sweet, smoky, salty and more fishy flavour.

TO USE Serve cold-smoked salmon raw in slices or flakes with a squeeze of lemon juice, either in salads, with brown bread and butter, or in sandwiches or bagels with cream cheese. Serve with scrambled eggs; toss into creamy pasta sauces. Serve hot-smoked salmon cold in salads; add to pâtés, mousses and terrines; warm through; add to fish pies and other dishes.

⑨ Smoked mackerel

Most often sold as hot-smoked fillets, smoked mackerel is widely available either plain or coated in crushed peppercorns. The flesh is a pale pinkish-brown with a tender yet firm, rich, meaty texture and strong, salty, smoky and fishy flavour. Lemon juice or horseradish are classic accompaniments. It makes particularly successful pâtés and fish pastes, especially when mixed with chopped onion and lemon juice.

TO USE Peel off the skin, checking for bones, then serve cold in salads or purée in pâtés. Alternatively, flake into hot dishes such as kedgeree and warm through.

⑩ Smoked halibut

This is Greenland halibut, not the larger and more expensive kind. Sold in thin slices rather like smoked salmon, smoked halibut is a pale creamy white colour and has tender, oily flesh with a delicate flavour.

TO USE Serve as it is in salads or as an hors d'oeuvre.

⑪ Smoked eel

Hot-smoked eel has a rich, dense, oily texture. It has a shiny black skin and pinkish-beige flesh with an excellent flavour, and goes particularly well with piquant accompaniments such as horseradish.

TO USE Peel off the skin, then add to salads; mash or purée into pâté.

⑫ Buckling

Buckling are hot-smoked herring. They are golden brown and have a strong smoky and gamey flavour. Eat within a day of buying.

TO USE Serve cold with brown bread and butter or in salads; mash into a pâté or paste; grill.

Bloater

These are ungutted herring that have been lightly salted and cold-smoked. Smoking the fish with the guts still inside causes them to swell slightly, giving the appearance of a bloated herring. They have a strong, smoky, fishy flavour and make a classic English fish paste. Eat within a day of buying.

TO USE Fry or grill and serve hot, or leave to cool and mash with butter and lemon juice to make bloater paste. The guts should not be eaten.

Preserved seafood

1. Shrimp paste
2. Rollmops
3. Pickled herring
4. Dried cuttlefish
5. Salt cod
6. Pickled cockles
7. Dried shrimp
8. Bonito flakes
9. Dried squid
10. Jellied eel
11. Gravadlax

Preserved seafood

Traditionally used as ways to preserve fish, salting, pickling in vinegar and drying all impart distinctive tastes and textures to fish and shellfish. That's why they are still used now, even when their original function has largely been eliminated by refrigeration and freezing. Fish may be dry-salted, or soaked in brine, and salt is also used to preserve most fish that is pickled or dried.

❶ Shrimp paste

Shrimp paste is used throughout South-east Asia as a flavouring ingredient. There are numerous varieties with different names in different countries, including *blachan, terasi* and *kapi*. All are made from salted, dried shrimp that have been pounded and then left to ferment. Shrimp paste has a strong, pungent aroma that mellows with cooking and adds a distinctive flavour to dishes such as stir-fried noodles.

TO USE Heat over a flame or fry before adding to South-east Asian-style dishes.

❷❸ Pickled herring

There are numerous varieties of pickled herring, which are particularly enjoyed in northern Europe and Scandinavia. Most of them are preserved in a similar way by marinating in vinegar, salt and spices. Some of the more common varieties include:

Bismarck herring Split, gutted herrings marinated in white wine vinegar with spices.
Maajtes herring Skinned fillets from female herring that are cured in salt, sugar and spices.
Rollmops Rolled herring fillets pickled in sweet white wine vinegar with thinly sliced onions and spices.

TO USE Serve all the above as hors d'oeuvres or with rye bread or sour cream.

❹❾ Dried squid and cuttlefish

Strips of pale grey-brown, salted, dried squid and cuttlefish are eaten as a snack in China and Japan. They have a dry, chewy texture, a salty, slightly sweet flavour, and an assertively fishy aroma.

TO USE Serve as a snack with drinks.

❺ Salt cod

Also known as bacalao, salt cod is an ancient dish which is still highly prized in some countries. It is prepared either by dry-salting or by soaking the filleted fish in brine, then drying it until nearly all the water has evaporated. Salt cod is hard, greyish-creamy white and woody in appearance; it is a common ingredient in many cuisines from Portugal and Spain to the Caribbean. Once reconstituted, it retains much of its salty flavour and has a slightly chewy texture. For the home cook, the key to success with salt cod is to remember how strong and salty its flavour is – and to balance that with milder, sweeter flavours. Tomato sauces particularly complement the flavour and texture of salt cod: it can be baked, for instance, with potatoes, rosemary, garlic and olives in a rich sauce of tomatoes and olive oil. Another top-class approach is exemplified by the French *brandade de morue*, salt cod puréed with olive oil, milk and/or cream and sometimes garlic for flavouring. Although it may seem obvious, it is best to make sure: never add salt to any salt cod dish.

TO USE Soak for 24 hours, changing the water regularly to remove as much salt as possible, then drain and remove any bones and skin. Cook in well-flavoured sauces such as tomato, or mix with mashed potato to make fishcakes.

Dried scallop

Dried scallops are made from the white muscle of the scallop. They resemble small, squat, creamy-beige cylinders and have an extraordinarily pungent aroma and salty flavour. They are used – as a flavouring rather than main ingredient – in Chinese cooking, especially Cantonese and Hong Kong cuisines. They are hugely expensive.

TO USE Shred and use as a garnish or seasoning sprinkled over dishes such as Chinese *congee* (rice porridge), stir-fries and braised dishes.

⑥ Pickled shellfish

Mussels, winkles and cockles are all commonly available in jars, preserved in vinegar and flavoured with spices. Sharp in flavour, they tend to be slightly chewier than the freshly cooked fish. Prawns and shrimp are also sold in brine, usually a fairly mild one.

TO USE Drain and serve cold as part of a selection of hors d'oeuvres or a cold fish platter, or add to salads.

⑦ Dried Shrimp

Tiny salted, dried shrimp are widely used in South-east Asian cooking. They have a pungent and distinctive aroma, and are usually added to dishes as a condiment, flavouring or garnish. In Thai cooking they are a classic ingredient of stir-fries such as pad Thai (fried noodles).

TO USE Soak in cold water to reconstitute, then pound into a paste and use to flavour dishes such as stir-fries, soups and curries.

⑧ Bonito flakes

Used in Japanese cooking, these small, salty fish flakes are shavings from smoked, dried, fermented bonito tuna. Pale brown in colour, they have a salty, fishy flavour and are generally used as a seasoning, particularly to flavour dashi (the stock used to make miso broth).

TO USE Sprinkle over soups as a seasoning; use to flavour dashi.

Bombay duck

An Indian delicacy, these salty pieces of fish are made from the dried fillets of the small, transparent bummaloe fish. Pale brown and woody in appearance, Bombay duck has a very strong, pungent smell and salty flavour.

TO USE Bake or fry and serve as an appetiser or crumble over Indian food as a garnish.

Shark's fin

The salted, sun-dried fin of various species of shark is highly regarded in Chinese cuisine. When dried it has a coarse, almost stringy and hairy texture and a creamy yellow colour, but when soaked, reconstituted and cooked, it takes on a gelatinous texture, but has little flavour. In China it is made into a soup. Sharks of all types are under threat from human exploitation, and eating shark's fin is difficult if not impossible to justify.

TO USE Add to Chinese-style dishes such as shark's fin soup.

⑩ Jellied eel

A traditional dish from London's East End, and one of those that tends to divide the world into true fans and true opponents. The dish is made by boiling sections of eel in vinegar with herbs, then leaving the fish to cool and set in the liquid, which turns to jelly. The eel is served with some of the jelly.

TO USE Serve cold with bread and butter.

⑪ Gravadlax

A Swedish delicacy, also known as gravlax. This is made from raw salmon fillet that is cured with salt, sugar, dill and peppercorns. It has a tender texture rather like smoked salmon and a sweet, sharp and fragrant flavour, and is traditionally served with a sauce of mustard, sugar, vinegar, oil, and more dill. The name literally means 'buried salmon' or 'salmon in a hole', and refers to the original method of preparing the fish by burying it in a hole in the ground.

TO USE Serve thinly sliced as an appetiser with brown bread and butter, as an hors d'oeuvre or in salads.

Fish roe

The eggs contained in the ovaries of certain fish are considered a great delicacy in many cuisines around the world. They are sold fresh, salted or smoked, depending on the variety. These eggs or roes can look and taste very different, and may be eaten as they are or used to make other dishes such as pâtés.

Botargo

This type of roe is considered a great delicacy in Italy (where it's called bottarga) and other parts of the Mediterranean. Botargo is made from the salted, pressed, dried roe of the female grey mullet (and sometimes tuna), which is removed from the fish still in its sac. Once dried, the flattened sausage-shaped roe is coated in a thin layer of wax to protect and seal it. The end result is a salty, distinctively flavoured roe with a very firm texture and a dark red colour.

TO USE Thinly slice and serve as an appetiser or hors d'oeuvre with a little lemon juice; grate over pasta.

Tarama

Regarded as a delicacy in Greece, tarama is made from smoked cod's roe and is a dark orange-red colour. Tarama is the main ingredient in the Greek dip taramasalata. It has a firm texture and a distinctive salty, slightly smoky and fishy flavour.

TO USE In dips such as taramasalata.

Soft cod's roe

Less common than the hard, smoked cod's roe, soft cod's roe is available fresh or canned. With an almost wobbly texture, the fresh roe is a pink-cream colour. When cooked, the roe turns creamy-white but the texture remains soft. It has a mild flavour.

TO USE Fresh roe should be cleaned well, then sliced, pan-fried and served on toast, dipped in batter, or poached and puréed in pâtés.

Herring roe

Also known as milts, herring roe is the bag of seminal fluid of the male fish. It is pink-cream in colour when fresh, creamy white when cooked, with a soft texture and a mild flavour.

TO USE Fresh roe should be cleaned well, then sliced, pan-fried and served on toast, dipped in batter, or poached and puréed in pâtés.

Caviar

The tiny, shiny, salty eggs of the sturgeon are one of the most highly regarded and expensive of delicacies. The tiny balls explode in the mouth with a salty, fishy flavour. Colour can vary according to variety and may be greyish, brown or golden. Varieties include beluga caviar from the large beluga sturgeon, which are light grey in colour; smaller sevruga and osetra; and the cheaper mandarin caviar from the Chinese white sturgeon. The eggs are lightly salted to cure them, and most are then pasteurised and should be kept chilled. Just a small amount is needed to add flavour to canapés or as a garnish to fish dishes. Wild sturgeon stocks in the Caspian Sea are under threat from over-fishing (often illegal). The best hope may be sturgeon farming, which has had success in the US and Europe.

TO USE Serve in small quantities on toast, crackers or blini; use to top canapés or as a garnish.

Mock caviar

There are numerous roes on the market that try to provide an alternative to caviar taken from sturgeon, at a fraction of the price. Mock caviars vary in colour from black to red, orange and pale gold.

Lumpfish roe Also known as mock or Danish caviar, these tiny, salty eggs are widely available and much cheaper than true caviar. The eggs are dyed either black or bright red.

Salmon roe These larger, translucent, shiny pinkish-orange eggs are the roe of the salmon and have a mild, salty flavour. Keta is a name given to the eggs of the Pacific salmon. Salmon roe is one of the more expensive caviar alternatives, but it is also one of the best.

Sea trout roe These small golden eggs have a similar salty taste and texture to lumpfish roe.

Whitefish roe A golden mock caviar taken from the female whitefish, with a salty taste and 'exploding' texture.

Herring roe Not actually a type of roe or fish egg at all, this product is made from herring that has been processed and dyed black to resemble the tiny black salty balls of true caviar and other mock caviars. Though similar in appearance and with a salty, fishy flavour, it has a different texture – more gelatinous to the bite than the tender, exploding quality that is unique to caviar.

TO USE Serve in small quantities on toast, crackers or blini with sour cream; to top canapés or as a garnish.

Canned fish and shellfish

A number of common canned varieties make useful storecupboard standbys, as fish is convenient for making into quick meals.

Anchovy

Tiny, pinkish brown anchovy fillets are salted and then preserved in oil, either in cans or in glass jars. They have a firm, quite smooth texture and strongly salty, piquant flavour. Once opened, the anchovies should be stored in the fridge. As long as they remain covered by oil, they can be kept for a week. They are often used in small amounts to add flavour to dishes or to top pizzas or the flan pissaladière.

TO USE Drain, then crush or finely chop. Use as a seasoning for stews, sauces, pasta dishes and dressings; mash with butter to make anchovy butter. Lay strips on pizzas and pissaladière; add to salads.

Sardine

Whole sardines are gutted, with their heads and tails removed, then canned in oil or tomato sauce. Canning softens the bones, making them edible. Once opened, store in the fridge for up to two days.

TO USE Drain sardines in oil. Serve on toast, mash to make pâté, or add to pasta sauces.

Pilchard

These fish, which are mature sardines, are usually canned in tomato sauce. Pilchards are canned in the same way as sardines, resulting in soft, edible bones. Once opened, store in the fridge and use within two days.

TO USE Serve on toast, or add to pasta sauces.

Mackerel

Skinned mackerel fillets are canned in oil, brine or a sauce such as tomato or mustard. They have a firm, meaty texture. Once opened, store in the fridge and use within two days.

TO USE Drain mackerel in oil or brine. Serve on toast, or add to pasta sauces.

Salmon

Canned salmon is soft and slightly gelatinous. Although it still contains its bones, these are softened by the canning process, making them edible and a good source of calcium. Once opened, store in the fridge and use within two days.

TO USE Drain and use in fishcakes, pies, mousses, soufflés and sandwiches.

Tuna

Canned in oil, brine or spring water and available as chunks or steaks, canned tuna has a different texture to fresh. It is pinkish-grey in colour, with a dry and firm texture, and the fish flakes easily. Once opened, store in the fridge and use within two days.

TO USE Drain. Can be mixed with mayonnaise to use in sandwiches; in salads; added to sauces.

Crab

Crab is available as canned white meat, which may be in shreds or chunks. It has a salty, sweet flavour and flaky texture, and makes a convenient alternative to fresh crabmeat. Once opened, store in the fridge and use within two days.

TO USE Drain. Use to make crab cakes; add to pasta salads, sauces, bisques and Asian-style broths; use in sandwich fillings or to top canapés.

Oyster

Canned oysters are inferior in texture and flavour to fresh oysters, but are useful for cooking if fresh are unavailable. Canned smoked oysters make good snacks with drinks. Once opened, store in the fridge and use within a day.

TO USE Drain and use for oyster stuffing or add to sauces and soups, and just warm through.

Mussel

Canned mussels have a soft texture and the flavour is not as good as fresh. They are a reasonable alternative to fresh when added to dishes.

TO USE Drain and use in dishes such as fish soups and stews, risotto and paella.

Clam

Canned clams are usually the tiny Italian vongole variety. They have a salty, slightly sweet flavour and a chewy texture. Once opened, store in the fridge and use within two days.

TO USE Drain and add to salads, pasta sauces, soups and chowders.

Poultry and game birds

All about poultry and game birds

Poultry describes birds that have been domesticated and farmed, such as chicken and turkey, whereas game birds live in the wild and are hunted for food. Originally, all birds were wild game birds. By far the greatest proportion of what we eat today is farmed – the distant descendants of wild birds.

Poultry and farmed game birds are available all year round, but true game birds are available only seasonally – usually in autumn and winter, and not during their breeding season in spring and early summer. Some farmed birds, such as turkeys and geese, still have some degree of seasonality due to their traditional role in celebration meals such as Christmas and Thanksgiving.

Chicken is probably the most widely eaten of all poultry and suits most cooking methods: grilling, pan-frying, deep-frying, stir-frying, steaming, poaching, braising, casseroling, baking and roasting. Game birds such as pheasant tend to have drier flesh and are better suited to moist methods of cooking such as braising and pot-roasting.

Breeding and rearing

How poultry is bred and reared has a significant effect on its health and welfare, and on taste and texture. The issues arise mainly in connection with chickens and turkeys, as these are often for intensively reared. Other birds, such as ducks and geese, are usually farmed in a more humane way because they do not adapt well to intensive rearing.

Selective breeding and intensive rearing methods have changed the way chicken and turkey are farmed in recent decades. Scientific advances have led to a huge increase in production, with a drop in the price paid by consumers. For centuries, chicken was a luxury. Now it is one of the cheapest forms of animal protein. But this has had serious consequences for both birds and consumers.

The greatest changes are in maturation and in housing. Intensively reared chickens have been bred to take just six weeks to become fully grown (about 2kg/4½lb) and ready for slaughter. A naturally reared chicken will reach that weight in about 14 weeks. The shorter lifespan of intensively reared birds can result in health problems such as weak, under-developed legs that are not strong enough to carry the bird's weighty, ever-growing body. With thousands of birds packed into a single shed, regular use of antibiotics and other chemicals is essential to protect the flock from disease and infection. Traces of these chemicals will remain in the poultry flesh and end up on the consumer's plate.

Dubious hygiene is a natural part of intensive rearing. Excrement-filled sheds containing dead birds cannot be cleaned adequately until the flock is removed for slaughter. Disease and bacterial infection such as salmonella spread quickly, and as these infections remain in the meat after slaughter they pose risks for the consumer.

There are two main alternatives to intensively reared birds, which offer a more ethical, healthy – although more expensive – choice to the consumer:

Free-range Different countries have their own definitions of free-range rearing, but broadly speaking the birds must be able, for a significant part of their lives, to roam and feed freely without being constrained in cages or other restrictive enclosures. They are usually shut up in sheds at night to protect them from predators such as foxes. In the UK there are three categories of free-range bird: free range, traditional free range, and free range – total freedom. The last category is regarded as the best, and these birds are likely to cost more than the other two.

Organic Different countries have their own guidelines, but generally these birds are not intensively reared and are bred without artificial intervention, using methods designed to prevent harm to the surrounding environment and wildlife. Like free-range chickens, organic chickens are not kept in restricted enclosures but are allowed to move freely. They are allowed to feed on organic pasture and are fed at least 80 per cent organic, non-GM (genetically modified) feed. Synthetic medicines and pesticides are avoided wherever possible.

How to buy and store poultry

As a general rule, healthy and content animals will have a better flavour and texture than those that have been intensively reared. They almost always cost more, but the extra money buys far better quality. Intensively reared birds sometimes have so little flavour that they require heavy seasoning, and the texture of their meat is soft and watery.

Most poultry and game birds from the butcher or supermarket are sold already plucked, drawn, and ready for the oven. Look for birds with no signs of damage or blemishes. If the birds are not wrapped in plastic, check that they smell pleasant. Generally, the larger the bird, the greater proportion of meat to bone there will be – and therefore better value.

Some whole birds are bought with a packet of giblets (neck, liver, heart and crop) tucked inside the carcass. Remove and store them in a sealed container in the fridge, to use within a day. Put the bird in a shallow dish, cover with clingfilm and store in the fridge. Use within two days, or according to the 'use by' date on its label. Poultry from the supermarket can be left in its original packaging.

How to freeze and thaw poultry

Fresh chicken and poultry can be frozen successfully and safely. Be sure to follow the guidelines below:

- Always freeze poultry before its 'use by' date, preferably on the day of purchase.
- Follow any freezing or thawing instructions given.
- Wrap portions in individual freezer bags, seal tightly, and label with the date of freezing. They can be stored in the freezer for up to three months.
- To thaw, put the poultry in a dish (to catch dripping juices) and leave overnight in the fridge until completely thawed, then cook within 24 hours.
- Do not re-freeze thawed poultry. You can, however, freeze it again after you have cooked it.

For larger whole birds such as turkey and geese, you will need to allow more thawing time:

- Remove the bird from its packaging and put it in a large dish to catch any juices. Cover and put in the fridge, checking and emptying the dish regularly.
- Follow the instructions on packaged birds for thawing times, or use the following as a guide:

2kg (4½lb) bird	20–24 hours
3kg (6½lb) bird	30–36 hours
4kg (8lb 13oz) bird	40–48 hours
5kg (11lb) bird	50–60 hours

Before you start cooking, check carefully that the bird is thoroughly thawed:

- Put your hand inside the cavity to check that there are no ice crystals.
- Pierce the thickest part of the meat with a fork. If you feel ice crystals, thaw for a little longer.

How to buy and store game birds

Game birds are best eaten young. The feathers are a good guide, as young birds tend to have soft, even feathers. Young pheasants and partridges tend to have long, V-shaped wing feathers, whereas in older birds the same feathers tend to be rounded. Also look for a plump breast, smooth legs and pliable spurs. Look for birds that have not been extensively damaged by shot: telltale signs are red/black entrance wounds on the breast and/or broken legs.

Game birds are traditionally hung for several days to deepen their gamey flavour and tenderise the flesh – an unhung bird will be tough and tasteless. Most game from a butcher or supermarket will have been hung, but if you have a freshly shot bird, hang it yourself in a cool, airy place (see below).

A prepared bird can be stored in the fridge for one to two days. But birds that have been significantly damaged by shot will not keep as well, so cook as soon as possible.

Hanging times for birds	
Duck	2–3 days
Goose	2–9 days
Grouse	2–4 days
Partridge	3–5 days
Pheasant	3–10 days
Wood pigeon	Requires no hanging
Woodcock	3–5 days

Food safety

Raw or undercooked poultry may contain bacteria that can cause food poisoning, so it is essential to store, handle and cook poultry appropriately.

Safe storing Always store as described earlier. Ensure that no juices can escape on to other foods. Cover and make sure it does not touch other foods.
Safe handling Always wash your hands (and the tap) immediately after handling raw poultry to avoid spreading bacteria. If the poultry has been in the sink for any reason, wash the sink well – splashing water can carry raw juices on to nearby surfaces. Thoroughly scrub chopping boards, knives and other utensils used for preparing raw poultry, and never use the same equipment for preparing other ingredients without thoroughly cleaning first in plenty of washing-up liquid and hot water.
Safe cooking Always check that chicken and turkey are thoroughly cooked before serving. Be sure that:

- The meat is piping hot all the way through.
- When you cut into the thickest part of the meat, there is no sign of pinkness.
- When you pierce the thickest part of the thigh of a roasted bird, the juices run clear.

Cooking poultry and game

When preparing poultry, follow the safety guidelines above, and check the preparation techniques on pages 140–3. While chicken and turkey must be thoroughly cooked, duck and game birds become dry and tough if overcooked: there should still be a trace of pinkness in the flesh and juices.

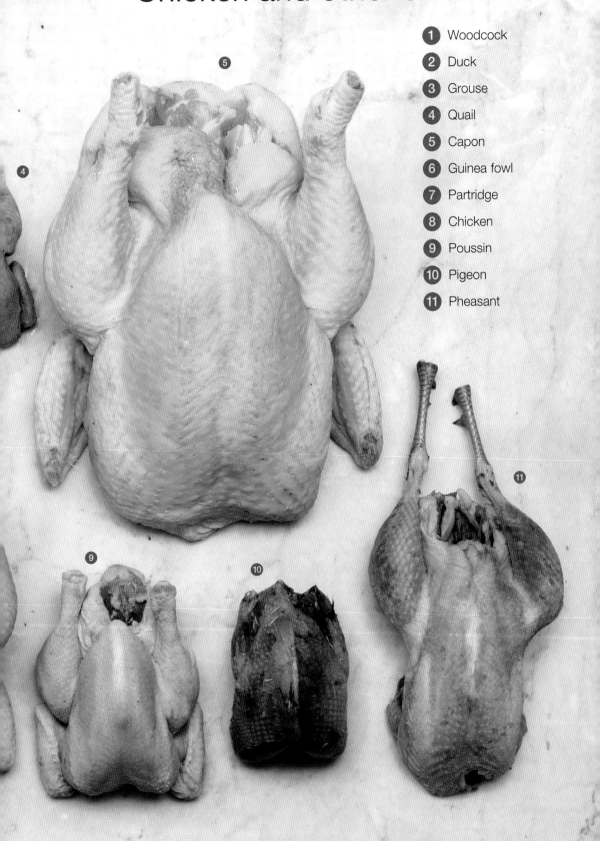

Chicken and other small birds

1 Woodcock
2 Duck
3 Grouse
4 Quail
5 Capon
6 Guinea fowl
7 Partridge
8 Chicken
9 Poussin
10 Pigeon
11 Pheasant

Chicken and other small birds

❶ Woodcock

These long-beaked birds rarely found on sale. Richly flavoured, they are at their best when still young. Look for birds with soft, downy feathers under their wings, supple feet and short, round spurs. They are usually cooked with their heads and guts intact, which brings out their full flavour. They go well with bacon, wine and herbs such as thyme and marjoram. They are often served on a piece of hot toast, which absorbs the juices. Do not overcook: there should be a trace of pink at the centre of the breast.

TO USE Bard with strips of bacon and roast, or braise, grill or barbecue.

❷ Duck

Domesticated duck has rich, dark, meaty flesh. It can also be very fatty, so it is often served with sharp-tasting sauces such as orange or pomegranate. There are many breeds available for eating, including the British Aylesbury, the American Long Island, and the French Rouen, Nantes and Barbary. Duck is available as whole birds for roasting, and in leg and breast portions. The breasts are often cut off the bird for separate cooking, but the legs also have an excellent flavour. Some cooks like to buy a whole duck and joint it, cooking breast and leg separately. Whole ducks look large because they have a large cavity and carcass. They don't feed as many people as the size might suggest.

Some breeds are much fattier than others: as a general rule, the larger the bird the fattier it will be. Some fat may be in the cavity, and should be pulled out before cooking. Most of the fat is under the skin and will melt out during cooking. Save it and use for roasting root vegetables.

TO USE Roast whole birds; portions can be pan-fried, braised, casseroled or cut into strips and stir-fried. When cooking duck, allow the fat to drain away, either by roasting at a high temperature or by initially frying portions skin side down.

Wild Duck

The most common type of wild duck is the mallard. It has a particularly good flavour, rich but not overpowering, and is far leaner than its domesticated counterpart. Wild ducks do not provide a great deal of meat: one duck will feed two, but not amply. They go particularly well with fruity sauces, and with gravy made by deglazing the roasting tin with sweet or medium-sweet wine, stock and aromatics and boiling to concentrate the flavour.

TO USE Brush with oil and roast.

❸ Grouse

The grouse sold in the UK are native to Scotland, where the annual hunting season begins on 12 August. This highly prized, usually very expensive game bird has dark flesh and a rich, gamey flavour. Grouse is best eaten young, so look for birds with soft, downy breast feathers, pointed flight feathers and rounded spurs. They go well with fruity sauces and gravies, such as those flavoured with redcurrant jelly, and herbs such as rosemary, thyme and oregano. Young grouse is at its best when roasted until slightly pink.

TO USE Roast or grill young birds. Braise or casserole older birds.

❹ Quail

Native to the Middle East, and once prevalent throughout Europe, this small, pretty bird used to be considered a game bird, although it is now widely domesticated and available all year round from supermarkets and butchers. It is usually sold ready for the oven. Quail has a mild flavour that is less gamey than other birds, and a tender texture, but can easily become dry if overcooked. They go well with bacon, with spicy flavours such as paprika, and herbs such as sage. They make a good choice when seeking something elegant and unusual.

TO USE Bard with strips of bacon and roast; spatchcock and grill; pot-roast, casserole or braise.

❺ Capon

Strictly speaking, capons are cocks that have been castrated when young, then fattened up. The practice is no longer legal in the UK but the term is still used for larger birds weighing about 2.7–3.6kg (6–8lb). A capon will feed six to eight people, and it can be cooked in the same way as chicken (but for longer).

TO USE Whole birds can be roasted, casseroled or pot-roasted. Portions can be pan-fried, coated and deep-fried, baked, braised, casseroled, poached or steamed.

❻ Guinea Fowl

Originally a game bird native to Africa, the guinea fowl has been domesticated in Europe for at least 500 years. With darker flesh than chicken and a slightly gamey flavour, it can be used in most chicken or pheasant recipes and suits robust flavours such as shallots, bacon and red wine. Look for birds with a plump breast and smooth-skinned legs. Guinea fowl are not as full-breasted as chickens; one bird will feed two to four people.

TO USE Bard with strips of bacon and roast; spatchcock; braise, casserole.

❼ Partridge

There are two main varieties of this small game bird: red-legged and grey-legged. Both have pale flesh with a delicate flavour and fine texture, although the flavour of grey-legged birds is usually more highly regarded. The best age for eating partridge is between two and four months old. Good indicators of a young bird are: the legs and feet will be yellowish rather than bluish; the beak will be supple and the wing feathers pointed rather than rounded. Partridge goes well with bacon, shallots, cabbage and herbs such as bay leaves, but also suits fruity flavours such as grapes and pears.

TO USE Bard young birds with bacon, and roast; braise, pot-roast or stew older birds.

❽ Chicken

Chicken is the most widely available of domesticated birds. The breast is fine-textured, lean and white. Leg meat is darker, looser in texture and more flavoursome. Breast and leg cook at different speeds, the breast reaching perfection faster than the leg. There are numerous different types of chicken on the market, including:

Corn-fed These chickens are fed on corn rather than standard chicken feed, and have bright yellow flesh and, often, an improved flavour. They weigh about 2kg (4½lb).
Roasting Usually young birds, chickens for roasting are tender and weigh about 2kg (4½lb).
Boiling These birds are usually about 18 months old, and have tougher flesh that is better suited to long, slow cooking such as stewing, poaching, casseroling or pot-roasting. They usually weigh around 2.5–3kg (5½–6½lb).

Chicken is available both fresh and frozen. Whole, oven-ready birds (sometimes containing the giblets) are available for roasting, for cooking whole or for jointing at home. Portions – including breast on the bone, breast fillets, leg, thigh and wing – are available, as well as diced chicken and mini fillets. Chicken can also be bought roasted whole or in slices.

Some classic chicken dishes from around the world include coq au vin, the French chicken stew made with red wine, mushrooms and baby onions; roast chicken with 40 cloves of garlic; Indonesian chicken satay served with spicy peanut sauce; southern fried chicken from the US; and the Italian tomato and garlic stew, chicken cacciatore. Chicken is also a great in stir-fries, curries, tagines, risotto, paella, pilaff and fajitas, and marinated and grilled on skewers.

TO USE Whole birds can be roasted, casseroled or pot-roasted, or spatchcocked (split through the back and flattened out) and grilled or barbecued. Portions can be pan-fried, coated and deep-fried, grilled, steamed, baked, braised, casseroled or cut into strips and stir-fried.

❾ Poussin

Also known as spring chicken, poussin is a young chicken. The small, tender birds are usually four to eight weeks old, and weigh only about 450g (1lb). The flesh has a mild flavour. Poussin is usually sold whole, ready for the oven, and one bird will feed one person. A double poussin is a slightly older bird of about twice the size, suitable for two. They can be cooked in the same way as chicken.

TO USE Whole poussin can be roasted or spatchcocked and grilled; portions can be pan-fried, grilled or barbecued.

❿ Pigeon

Young farmed pigeon are known as squab. Relatively rare outside France, they are small, fine in flavour, and invariably very expensive. The wild version, often called wood pigeon, is much more common and usually the cheapest of the game birds. It has very dark meat with a full flavour. Available fresh or frozen, usually plucked and ready for the oven. Look for birds that have supple feet with no scales. They go well with onions, mushrooms, bacon and red wine and are particularly good braised. In Morocco, pigeon flesh is cooked in a filo pie with dried apricots and almonds. In England, it can be combined with beef to make a rich game pie. When roasting or grilling pigeon, take care not to overcook it.

TO USE For young birds, bard with strips of bacon and roast or split in half and grill; braise or stew older birds, or add them to pies.

⓫ Pheasant

Often sold in a pair (brace), with one male (cock) and one female (hen), pheasant has fairly pale flesh with a mildly gamey flavour. The hens are slightly smaller but are regarded as having the better flavour. When buying, look for birds with downy feathers under the wings and pointed wing feathers, and cocks with short spurs. Pheasant is normally quite a lean bird, and the flesh tends towards dryness, so needs care when roasting not to overcook it. Unless you have a very young bird, pheasant is better suited to moist cooking methods such as braising and pot-roasting. They are good cooked with bacon, white wine or sherry, and herbs such as thyme.

TO USE Young birds may be barded with bacon and roasted; braise, pot-roast or casserole older birds.

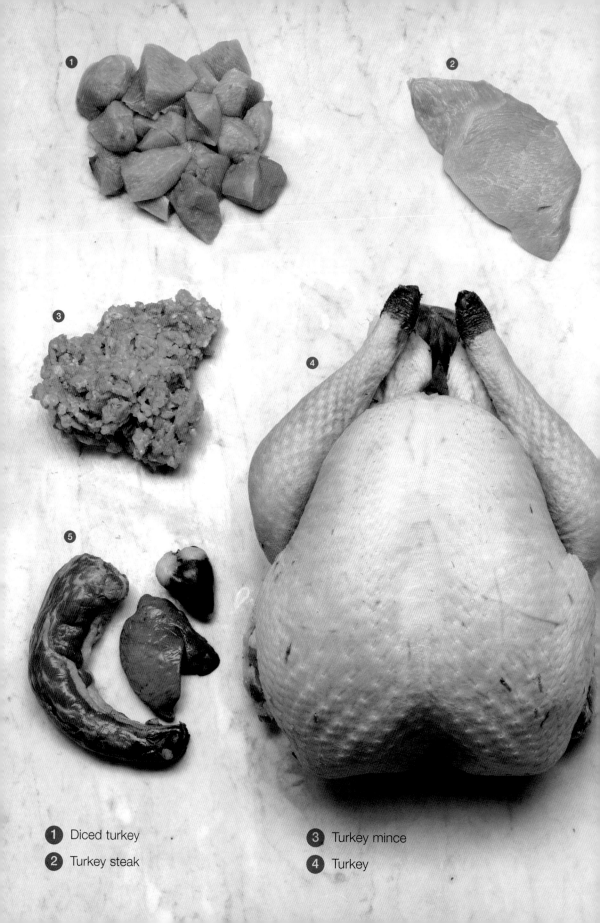

1 Diced turkey

2 Turkey steak

3 Turkey mince

4 Turkey

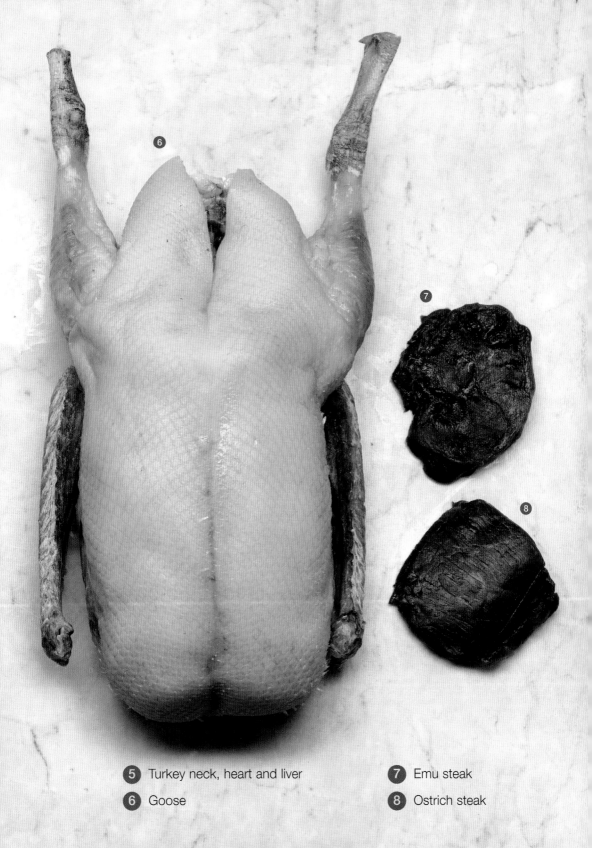

5 Turkey neck, heart and liver

6 Goose

7 Emu steak

8 Ostrich steak

Larger poultry and birds

① ② ③ ④ ⑤ Turkey

Native to America and still seen living in the wild in the USA, turkey is now widely domesticated and is the popular choice for roasting at Thanksgiving, Christmas and Easter. It will feed a large number of people. Turkey has lean, pale meat but is drier and coarser than chicken. There are numerous different varieties of turkey, which include the general groups of white, bronze and wild birds. White-feathered turkeys are the most widely available and are generally produced using intensive rearing methods. Bronze birds have dark feathers and a plump breast with good flavour, and they are usually reared non-intensively. Wild turkeys, not widely available, are smaller than their domesticated counterparts and have a much stronger and gamier flavour.

Whole turkeys weighing upwards of 2kg (4½lb) are easily found in the shops, particularly during the holiday seasons, and are available both fresh and frozen. They are usually ready for the oven and may have a small bag of giblets (neck, heart and liver) in the cavity for making gravy. Turkey's relatively low cost and very low fat content have made it a popular bird for selling as a part-boned breast, breast slices or steaks, escalopes, drumsticks, wings, thighs, chops cut from the thigh, cubed and minced (ground), as well as in products such as burgers, sausages and roasted or smoked turkey. This versatile bird can be used in most recipes that call for chicken

Classic accompaniments to roast turkey are cranberry sauce, chestnut stuffing, bread sauce and white wine gravy.

TO USE Roast whole birds and part-boned breasts. For cuts: grill, barbecue, pan-fry, stir-fry, roast, stew or braise, curry; use minced meat in burgers, patties, meatloaves, meatballs and sauces.

⑥ Goose

Originally a game bird, the goose has been successfully domesticated since Roman times. It does not adapt well to modern intensive methods of rearing, so it is not as widely available as chicken or turkey – and is much more expensive. There is also a degree of seasonality, with geese most often sold for the Christmas and Easter table. The flesh is dark, rich, meaty and fatty, so it suits sharp and acidic accompaniments such as apple or gooseberry sauce or sweet-and-sour red cabbage.

Goose is most often bought whole for roasting, although goose legs are a traditional addition to the classic French bean stew cassoulet. Look for a young goose that is less than a year old with a yellow, hair-free bill and supple feet. Yellow feet indicate a young bird – they gradually turn red as the bird ages – and the fat should be pale. (Older geese will have dark yellow fat.) A bird labelled 'green goose' is less than three to four months old, whereas a 'gosling' is less than six months old.

There are a number of different varieties including the popular Canada goose, which is usually around 2.5–3kg (5½–6½lb) in weight, the similar greylag and smaller pinkfoot, both of which are well flavoured, and the still smaller variety, whitefront. Like ducks, geese have a large cavity and large carcass, so even a large bird will not feed as many people as a turkey of comparable size.

TO USE Remove any fat from inside the bird, then prick the skin, rub with salt and roast on a rack set inside a roasting tin to allow the fat to drain away. Try to collect the fat and use it, as you would duck fat, for roasting potatoes. The best way to collect the fat is to spoon it out of the roasting tin regularly during cooking.

⑦ Emu

This enormous bird is indigenous to Australia and common in most of the mainland there. It is smaller than the ostrich, growing up to 2m (6½ft) in height. Its feathers are soft, and it is unable to fly. Originally hunted as a game bird, today they are domesticated and reared for their meat not just in Australia but also in other parts of the world, including Europe. The meat is dark and lean, with less fat than chicken and turkey. It has a distinct gamey flavour that some liken to venison, although in texture it is slightly softer than beef. Emu is available as fillet, steaks, cubed and minced, as well as in products such as sausages, patties and jerky. It is also smoked. Emu goes well in dishes that usually use beef, such as chilli con carne and Bolognese sauce.

TO USE Grill, barbecue, pan-fry, braise or roast; minced in burgers, meatballs, meatloaves and sauces.

⑧ Ostrich

The ostrich is the largest living bird species. Native to Africa, where it has been eaten for thousands of years, it is now widely farmed throughout the world, including North America and Europe. The meat is very dark and lean, and is often likened to beef. Ostrich has a strong flavour, even stronger than beef, although its texture is finer. It is promoted as a healthy meat because of its very low fat and low cholesterol content. It is available as fillet, slices, steaks and minced, and in products such as burgers and jerky. Ostrich goes well in recipes that would usually use beef, such as goulash, peppered steak, meatloaf, cottage pie and Chinese-style stir-fries.

TO USE Grill, barbecue, pan-fry, braise or roast; minced in burgers, meatballs, meatloaves and sauces.

Roasting times for poultry and game birds

Chicken	Preheat oven to 200°C (180°C fan oven) mark 6	Allow 20 mins per 450g (1lb)
Duck	Preheat oven to 200°C (180°C fan oven) mark 6	Allow 20 mins per 450g (1lb)
Goose	Preheat oven to 220°C (200°C fan oven) mark 7	Allow 35 minutes per 1kg (2¼lb)
Grouse	Preheat oven to 200°C (180°C fan oven) mark 6	Allow about 40 minutes total roasting time
Guinea fowl	Preheat oven to 200°C (180°C fan oven) mark 6	Allow 35 minutes per 1kg (2¼lb), plus 15 minutes
Ostrich	Preheat oven to 150°C (130°C fan oven) mark 2	Allow 45 minutes per 1kg (2¼lb), plus 20 minutes
Partridge	Preheat oven to 200°C (180°C fan oven) mark 6	Allow about 40 minutes total roasting time
Pheasant	Preheat oven to 230°C (210°C fan oven) mark 8	Roast for 10 minutes, then reduce the temperature to 200°C (180°C fan oven) mark 6 and roast for a further 30–50 minutes
Pigeon	Preheat oven to 200°C (180°C fan oven) mark 6	Allow 20–30 minutes total roasting time
Poussin	Preheat oven to 200°C (180°C fan oven) mark 6	Allow 25–40 minutes total roasting time
Quail	Preheat oven to 220°C (200°C fan oven) mark 7	Allow about 25 minutes total roasting time
Turkey	Preheat oven to 180°C (160°C fan oven) mark 4	Allow 45 minutes per 1kg (2¼lb), plus 20 minutes
Woodcock	Preheat oven to 190°C (170°C fan oven) mark 5	Allow 15–25 minutes total roasting time

Quantities for roasting

Chicken	A 2kg (4½lb) bird will serve about 5 people
Duck	When buying a whole bird, allow 450g (1lb) per person
Goose	A 4.5kg (10lb) goose will serve 6–8 people
Grouse	Allow 1 bird per person
Guinea fowl	1 bird will serve 2–4 people
Partridge	Allow 1 bird per person
Pheasant	1 bird will serve 2–3 people
Pigeon	Allow 1 bird per person
Poussin	Allow 1 bird per person
Quail	Allow 2 birds per person
Turkey	A 3.5kg (7¾lb) turkey will serve about 10 people
Woodcock	Allow 1 bird per person

Cleaning and trussing

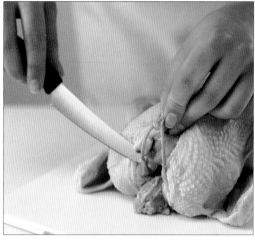

1 Before stuffing a bird for roasting, clean it thoroughly. Put the bird in the sink and pull out any loose fat with your fingers. Then run cold water through the cavity and dry the bird well using kitchen paper.

2 Trussing poultry before roasting gives it a neater shape for serving at the table. Cut the wishbone out by pulling back the flap of skin at the neck end. Run a sharp knife along the inside of the bone on both sides. Use poultry shears to snip the tip of the bone from the breastbone, and pull away. Snip or pull out the two ends.

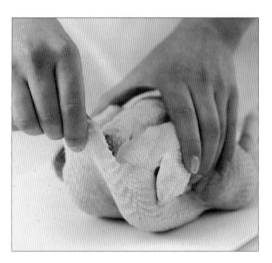

3 Put the wing tips under the breast and fold the neck flap on to the back of the bird. Thread a trussing needle and use it to secure the neck flap.

4 Push a metal skewer through the legs, at the joint between thigh and drumstick. Twist some string around both ends of the skewer and pull firmly to tighten. Turn the bird over. Bring the string over the ends of the drumsticks, pull tight and tie to secure the legs in place.

Jointing

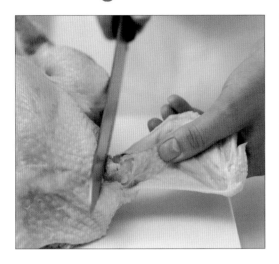

1 Using a sharp meat knife with a curved blade, cut out the wishbone and remove the wings in a single piece. Remove the wing tips.

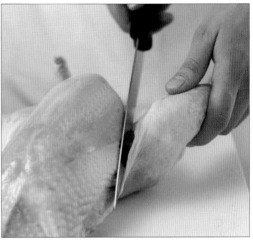

2 With the tail pointing towards you and breast side up, pull one leg away and cut through the skin between leg and breast. Pull the leg down until you crack the joint between the thigh bone and ribcage. Cut through that joint, then cut through the remaining leg meat. Repeat on the other side.

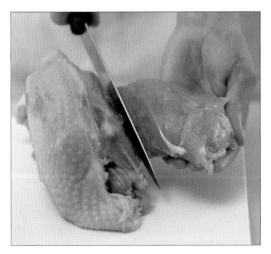

3 To remove the breast without any bone, make a cut along the length of the breastbone. Gently teasing the flesh away from the ribs with the knife, work the blade down between the flesh and ribs of one breast and cut it off neatly. (Always cut in, towards the bone.) Repeat on the other side.

4 To remove the breast with the bone in, make a cut along the full length of the breastbone. Using poultry shears, cut through the breastbone, then cut through the ribcage following the outline of the breast meat. Repeat on the other side. Trim off any flaps of skin or fat.

Spatchcocking

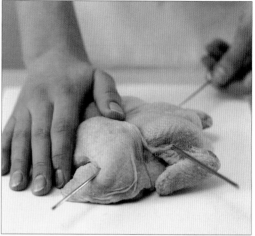

1 Hold the bird on a board, breast down. Cut through one side of the backbone with poultry shears. Repeat on other side and remove the backbone.

2 Turn the bird over, press down until you hear the breastbone crack. Thread skewers through the legs and breasts.

Cutting escalopes

1 Cut or pull out the long strip of flesh lying on the inside of the breast fillet. (It can be used for stir-fries, stuffings, etc.) Pressing the breast firmly on to the chopping board with the flat of one hand, carve a thin slice from underneath the breast using a sharp knife. Remove that slice, then repeat until the breast meat is too small to slice.

2 To make escalopes, put the slices of chicken between two sheets of clingfilm or greaseproof paper and pound them with a meat mallet until they are about 3mm (⅛in) thick.

Roasting a chicken

1 Make incisions all over the chicken except the breast. Loosen the breast skin. Crush 3 garlic cloves and slip under the skin with lemon slices, mustard and herbs. Squeeze the juice from 1 lemon and set aside.

2 Put the lemon halves in the cavity. Put the chicken in a roasting tin. Spoon 2 tbsp lemon juice into the cavity and pour the remaining juice over. Chill for a few hours. Take out of the fridge 30 minutes before cooking.

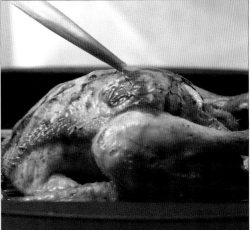

3 Preheat the oven to 200°C (180°C fan oven) mark 6. Put the chicken, breast down, on a rack in the roasting tin. Add 1 sliced onion, 2 garlic cloves and 4 tbsp each stock and wine.

4 Roast for 20 minutes, then turn and roast for 35 minutes or until the juices run clear when the leg is pierced. Baste now and then, adding a little more wine if needed.

5 Put the chicken on a large plate and cover loosely with foil. Spoon off as much fat as possible, leaving behind the juices in the tin. Put the tin over a medium-high heat, add 250ml (9fl oz) each of stock and wine, and scrape up the sediment from the tin. Simmer for 5 minutes to make gravy. Strain before serving.

Meat and game

All about meat and game

The term 'meat' describes the edible flesh of a wide range of animals: commonly farmed animals, namely cattle (beef and veal), pig (pork) and sheep (lamb and mutton); game such as wild pig (boar) and deer (venison); and more unusual 'new meats' such as alligator and llama. All are good sources of protein and other nutrients such as iron and B vitamins, but some can also be high in fats, particularly saturated fats, which everyone should aim to limit for health reasons.

Each animal is divided into different cuts, all of which have their own characteristic flavour and texture. Cuts from parts of the animal that have worked hardest contain the toughest muscle tissue, and usually require long, slow cooking. Cuts from parts that have worked the least are usually more tender and suit quicker cooking.

Rearing

Different meats are reared in different ways. Some, such as pigs, are often reared using modern intensive methods, where the animals may be subjected to inhumane conditions and be treated routinely with medicines and chemicals. Others, such as sheep, can only be reared using more traditional methods of grazing on open pastures. As a general rule, animals that have been allowed to grow naturally and lead healthy, happy lives in humane conditions will have a better flavour and texture than intensively reared animals. What benefits the animal also benefits the person who eats it. Wherever possible, buy the best-reared meat that you can.

There are two main alternatives to intensively reared meat: free-range and organic. Meat bought from the supermarket will be labelled; if you buy from a butcher, ask how the meat has been reared.

Free-range Different countries have their own guidelines as to what constitutes free-range rearing, but broadly speaking the animals are allowed to roam and graze freely. All lamb is free-range.

Organic Different countries have their own guidelines, but, broadly speaking, these animals are not intensively reared and are bred without artificial intervention. They are allowed to feed on organic pasture and are fed at least 80 per cent organic, non-GM (genetically modified) feed. Synthetic medicines and pesticides are avoided wherever possible.

How to buy meat

If buying meat for a specific recipe, make sure that you choose the right cut. For example, if you want beef for a speedy stir-fry, you will need a tender, quick-cooking cut such as sirloin. A tougher cut such as shin, which requires long, slow, moist cooking, would be wholly unsuitable. You will find a description of the different cuts and how to use them on the following pages.

When buying meat, always check it carefully first: it should look and smell fresh. The flesh should look moist but not watery, and pink or red according to variety (mature beef will be dark red). Fat should be pale, creamy and firm – avoid meat where the fat is yellowing, crumbly or waxy.

Look for meat that has been well cut and neatly trimmed. You need smaller quantities when buying cuts of meat off the bone: allow 100–150g (3½–5oz) per person. For meat on the bone, allow slightly more, anything from 175–350g (6–12oz) per person depending on the cut. Cuts that appear cheap do not always offer the best value. If they contain lots of bone, gristle, sinew and fat, the waste-matter may make these cuts cost more per ounce of meat than some more expensive cuts.

How to store meat

Meat should be wrapped and stored in the fridge, placed in a dish so that if any juices escape they cannot drip and contaminate other foods. Do not allow the meat to touch any other foods. Raw meat can generally be stored for three to five days, although offal and minced or processed meat such as sausages can deteriorate more quickly and should be used within two days. Meat that is bought sealed in a pack can be stored unopened, making sure that it is eaten before the use-by date.

Cooked meats such as ham and cured sausages should be wrapped and stored in the fridge, on the shelf above raw meat. Use within four to five days.

How to freeze and thaw meat

Meat can be successfully and safely frozen, but be sure to follow the guidelines below:

- Always freeze meat before its 'use-by' date, preferably on the day of purchase.
- Follow any freezing or thawing instructions given.
- Wrap portions in individual freezer bags, seal tightly and label with the date of freezing. They can be stored in the freezer for up to three months.
- To thaw, put the meat in a dish to catch any juices and put in the fridge until completely thawed. Use within two days.

• Do not refreeze raw meat that has thawed. You can, however, freeze dishes made from thawed meat that you have then cooked.

Food safety

Although raw meat does not carry the same food-poisoning risks as poultry, it may still contain bacteria that can cause food poisoning.

Safe handling Always wash your hands immediately after handling raw meat to avoid spreading bacteria. Scrub chopping boards, knives and other utensils used for preparing raw meat with plenty of washing-up liquid and hot water, and never use the same boards and utensils for preparing other ingredients without thoroughly cleaning them first. Keep separate boards for handling raw meat.

Safe cooking Cook meat thoroughly to kill any bacteria. Whole joints of certain meats or cuts such as lamb chops and steaks are safe to eat slightly undercooked or rare, as long as the outside has been thoroughly cooked at high heat (leaving the flesh pink in the centre), but others, such as pork, burgers, sausages, rolled joints and kebabs, must be cooked thoroughly. When cooking food for reheating later, cool it and chill (or freeze) as quickly as possible, as warm food encourages the growth of bacteria.

Preparing and cooking meat

Check the guidelines for preparation techniques on pages 152–5, 164–5 and 170–1. Different cuts of meat suit different cooking techniques:

Grill Best suited to cuts such as steaks, chops, cutlets, cubed meat made into kebabs, and minced products such as burgers and sausages. Season or marinate the cut, then cook under a preheated grill.

Griddle Best suited to cuts such as steaks, chops and cutlets. Preheat the griddle for about 3 minutes or until smoking hot, then brush the meat with oil and cook for a few minutes on each side until cooked to your liking.

Stir-fry Best suited to tender cuts such as fillet that have no excess fat or sinew. Slice the meat into strips no thicker than 5mm (¼in). Heat a wok or large heavy pan until hot, then add oil to coat the inside. Add the meat and stir-fry, moving the pan contents constantly. Remove, then cook the remaining ingredients. Return the meat to the pan to warm through.

Pan-fry Best suited to cuts such as steaks, chops and cutlets. Preheat a frying pan and season the meat. Add enough oil to coat the base of the pan,

then add the meat and brown on one side, not moving it for at least 1 minute, before turning to cook on the other side.

Braise and pot-roast Suited to tougher cuts that require long, slow cooking. Preheat the oven to 170°C (150°C fan oven) mark 3. Heat some oil in a large, flameproof casserole and brown the meat all over, working in batches if necessary. Remove from the pan and fry onions and garlic for a few minutes until beginning to colour, then return the meat to the pan with tomatoes or vegetables, and wine or stock. Stir well and season, then cover and cook in the oven for 2 hours or until tender.

Roast Suited to larger and more tender joints of meat. Different cuts need different treatment, but the following tips should ensure perfect results:

• Bring the meat to room temperature before cooking. This may take several hours.
• Cook on a wire rack or a bed of vegetables so that the fat can drip off.
• Roast fat side up.
• Check the pan juices regularly to make sure they are not drying out; add a little water if necessary.
• Once cooked, cover the meat with foil and allow to rest for 20 minutes before carving.

Roasting times for meat

Beef: rare
Preheat oven to 170°C (150°C fan oven) mark 3
allow 12–15 minutes per 450g (1lb) meat

Beef: medium-rare
Preheat oven to 170°C (150°C fan oven) mark 3
allow 15–18 minutes per 450g (1lb) meat

Beef: well done
Preheat oven to 170°C (150°C fan oven) mark 3
allow 20–25 minutes per 450g (1lb) meat

Lamb: rare
Preheat oven to 180°C (160°C fan oven) mark 4
allow 15–20 minutes per 450g (1lb) meat

Lamb: well done
Preheat oven to 180°C (160°C fan oven) mark 4
allow 20–25 minutes per 450g (1lb) meat

Pork: medium-rare
Preheat oven to 190°C (170°C fan oven) mark 5
allow 20–25 minutes per 450g (1lb) meat

Pork: well done
Preheat oven to 190°C (170°C fan oven) mark 5
allow 25–30 minutes per 450g (1lb) meat

Beef cuts

1. Topside
2. Fillet
3. Rump
4. Silverside
5. T-bone steak
6. Sirloin
7. Entrecote
8. Skirt
9. Fore rib
10. Flank

11 Thin rib

12 Chuck steak

13 Blade steak

14 Thick rib

15 Brisket

16 Neck

17 Shin

18 Mince

Beef

① Topside

Cut from the inside of the hind leg, this is a very lean cut with a fine grain and little marbling of fat. It is sold off the bone and rolled into a joint, and is often barded (tied with a layer of fat around the outside) to keep the beef moist during cooking. It is good used in recipes such as steak and kidney pie, boeuf bourguignon and braised beef with beer and mustard. It can be roasted, although it is not as tender as a rib roast, sirloin or fillet.

TO USE Braise, pot-roast or roast; cubed in pies.

② Fillet

The most tender of all cuts of beef, this long, lean, tapering piece of meat is taken from underneath the sirloin section of backbone. The fillet muscle gets almost no exercise, making it very tender, and it has a good flavour. It suits quicker cooking techniques. Chateaubriand is the steak cut from the centre of the fillet; it can also be roasted in one piece. As well as making excellent individual steaks, fillet steak is cooked in pastry for beef Wellington; raw fillet is thinly sliced for carpaccio, and is finely chopped and seasoned for steak tartare.

TO USE Roast; wrap in pastry and bake; cut into steaks and pan-fry or griddle; cut into strips and stir-fry; finely shred and serve raw as steak tartare or slice thinly for carpaccio.

③ Rump

A large, lean and relatively tender cut, rump is taken from the saddle just in front of the leg. It is usually sliced for steaks, although it may also be sold as a very large roasting joint known as a baron of beef; the joint contains both sides of the rump with the back part of the sirloin attached, and weighs between 45kg (100lb) and 90kg (200lb). Although a highly regarded cut, rump is not quite as tender as sirloin, and much less tender than fillet.

TO USE Grill, griddle, pan-fry or braise steaks. Roast when sold as baron of beef. Braise in a single piece for casseroles.

④ Silverside

Taken from the outside thigh of the hind leg, this cut is traditionally salted for boiling as salt beef. It is also sold unsalted for roasting, but because it is lean it requires frequent basting during cooking; even with basting, it is much less tender than the prime roasting cuts. Silverside suits slow, moist cooking methods such as poaching and pot-roasting. It is traditionally boiled with onions, carrots, bay leaves and pearl barley.

TO USE Braise, pot-roast or roast. Boil and press salted silverside.

⑤ ⑥ ⑦ Sirloin

This very tender joint is the saddle between the forerib and rump – a highly regarded cut from the back of the carcass. When sold as a joint it may be either on the bone or boned and rolled – with or without the fillet. It is also sliced into steaks, including: entrecote, sirloin, T-bone, which is cut across the sirloin and includes the bone, and the larger porterhouse, which includes both sirloin and rib. This is a prime cut for roasting or grilling. It goes well with robust flavours such as garlic, shallot, mushroom and red wine, and herbs such as thyme.

TO USE Roast on the bone or roll; pan-fry, grill or griddle steaks.

⑧ Skirt

Cut from the belly, this is a well flavoured, fairly tough cut that is lean but with quite a coarse texture. It usually requires long, slow cooking, but can also be marinated and used for stir-frying.

TO USE Stew, braise or pot-roast.

⑨ Fore rib

Also known as best rib, this cut is taken from the top of the carcass, next to the sirloin. Sold either on the bone or boned and rolled, it is one of the most expensive cuts of beef: a traditional roasting cut providing lean, tender meat. A good butcher will 'chine' the joint for you, cutting through the ribs where they meet the backbone to make carving easier. It is good rubbed with herbs and spices or mustard before roasting.

TO USE Roast.

Prime rib

Cut from below the fore rib, prime rib, also known as wing rib, is one of the largest roasting joints and one of the most expensive cuts. Look for joints with a large central 'eye' of meat and a good layer of fat on the outside. Prime rib should be chined, and it may also be boned and sliced and sold as rib-eye steak, for frying or grilling. Some people regard rib-eye steak as superior to all others. For roasting, use simple seasoning such as black pepper or garlic and mustard, and serve with Yorkshire puddings and gravy.

TO USE Roast. Pan-fry or grill steaks.

⑩ Thick flank

Cut from the front of the thigh of the hind leg, thick flank is usually sold in thick slices. It is a lean, fibrous cut that requires long, slow cooking to tenderise. Cook in beer or wine with onions, vegetables, potatoes and herbs such as thyme and bay leaves.

TO USE Stew, braise or pot-roast.

Thin flank

Cut towards the belly, this cut can be fatty. Many cooks use long, slow cooking to make it tender. It is often made into mince, rather than sold as a piece. When trimmed of fat and sliced thinly across the grain, it can be marinated and used in Chinese-style stir-fries. Although chewier than the more expensive cuts, the flavour is excellent and the cost economical.

TO USE Stew or braise. Slice thinly and stir-fry.

⑪ Thin rib

Cut from the forequarter, behind the thick rib, thin rib is usually sold boned and rolled. Tomatoes and garlic or red wine and mushrooms are good flavourings. It may be bought, on request, with the bones left in.

TO USE Braise or pot-roast.

⑫ ⑬ Chuck and blade

Taken from the top forequarter, this is a lean cut with a good flavour and a subtle marbling of fat through the meat. Usually sold off the bone as chuck, blade or braising steak, the cuts are the best of the stewing steaks and need long, slow cooking. With long marinating in a mixture of acidic ingredients such as vinegar, plus oil, chuck can be used as a grilling steak. Although not as tender as the prime cuts, the flavour is good.

TO USE Braise, stew or use in pies. Marinate and grill as steak.

⑭ Thick rib

Also known as top rib, thick rib is cut from the forequarter, just above the brisket. Usually boned and rolled, it may also be cut into steaks. Thick rib goes well with tomatoes and garlic, or red wine and mushrooms.

TO USE Braise or pot-roast.

⑮ Brisket

Cut from the lower side of the shoulder, brisket may be sold on the bone or (more commonly) boned and rolled. It tends to be rather fatty but it has a good flavour and firm texture, and it is an inexpensive cut. Brisket requires long, slow cooking to achieve tender results and can be cooked in stock with bacon, leeks, root vegetables and herbs such as thyme and bay. It is sometimes sold salted and spiced.

TO USE Stew, braise or pot-roast. It is good eaten cold.

⑯ Neck

Neck is lean and flavourful, and is one of the most inexpensive cuts of beef. It is invariably rather tough, so it requires long, slow, moist cooking and benefits from robust flavours. Neck is usually sold as stewing steak or mince. Clod is a similar cut, lying between the neck and shin, and is used in the same way.

TO USE Stew or braise.

⑰ Shin

Shin is cut from the foreleg, and is sold with or without the bone. The cut is tough and requires long, slow cooking, but its excellent flavour compensates for the toughness. The high proportion of connective tissue running through the meat gives it a distinctive texture which is highly prized by many cooks. It is high in gelatine, so is also suitable for adding to brawn – made from jellied cow's or calf's head. (More traditionally, brawn is made from jellied pig's head.) A classic dish for braised shin of beef is with bacon, red wine, onions, celery, tomatoes, carrots and a bouquet garni. It may also be poached in water and served with a dipping sauce such as soy sauce seasoned with garlic, ginger, spring onion and chilli, or with an Italian-style salsa verde.

TO USE Stew, poach or casserole; use to make stock, soup or brawn.

Leg

Cut from the back legs of the carcass, leg is similar to shin in taste and texture. It has a good flavour, but it requires long, slow cooking to tenderise both the meat itself and the sinews and connective tissue. It is good cooked in red wine or beer, with robust flavourings such as garlic, onions, thyme and bay leaves.

TO USE Stew, casserole; use to make stock, soup or brawn.

⑱ Mince

This inexpensive and versatile form of meat is used in a wide variety of dishes. Mince is made from various parts of the animal, usually the cheaper cuts. Not all minced beef is equal: it may vary enormously in quality. The best place to buy it is from a trusted butcher, whom you can ask to mince beef to order. You can also ask for particular types of mince, such as very low fat (best for sauces and stuffings) or some fat (which is best for burgers). If buying from a supermarket, check the label for fat content. Darker, evenly coloured mince will usually have a lower proportion of fat than paler mince or mince visibly streaked with white fat. If mincing meat at home, use neck, thin flank or braising steak.

TO USE Add to meat sauces; use in lasagne, moussaka and cottage pie; to fill stuffed vegetables; for burgers, patties, meatloaf and meatballs.

Boning

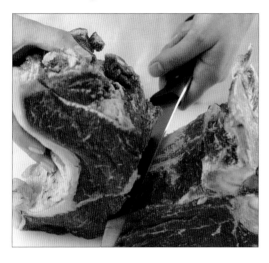

The joints you are mostly likely to want to bone are rib and sirloin, to make them easier to slice when cooked; they can also be rolled. The principle for preparing both joints is the same.

1 Put the joint on your chopping board with the bone facing down and the shorter vertebral bones facing upwards.

2 Use a long, sharp knife to make a thin cut all the way along the length of the spine. Cut towards the bone, working the knife between bone and meat until you reach the ribs.

3 Lift the meat in one hand and cut between the ribs and meat, cutting towards the bone, to remove the meat in a single piece. Trim off the cartilage and fat.

Trimming

1 Cut off the excess fat to leave a thickness of about 5mm (¼in). This isn't necessary for very lean cuts.

2 Trim away any stray pieces of meat or sinew left by the butcher. If the joint has a covering of fat, you can lightly score it – taking care not to cut into the meat – to help the fat drain away during cooking.

Tying

Tie the joint if you are using a boned and rolled joint, or if you have boned the joint and want to roast it using the bones as a 'roasting rack'.

1 Tie a piece of string around the length of the joint, securing it to the bones if you are using them. If you are cooking a boned and rolled joint, turn it 90 degrees, then tie another piece in the same way.

2 Starting at one end of the joint, loop string around the meat and tie it securely and firmly. Cut it off and make another loop about 5cm (2in) from the first.

3 Continue tying the joint in this way along the whole length of the joint until neatly and firmly secured.

Barding

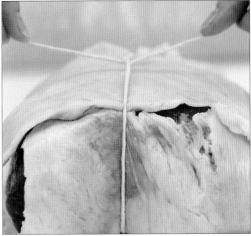

Lean joints of meat can be barded – wrapped in a thin layer of fat to moisten the meat during cooking. If the butcher hasn't done this for you, it's easy to do at home. You will need string and 3–4 sheets of pork fat, preferably back fat, large enough to cover the whole joint, dried herbs, ground black pepper.

1 Season the meat with freshly ground black pepper and dried herbs if you like. Wrap the sheets of fat around the joint so that both the sides and ends are covered.

2 Tie a piece of string around the length of the joint. Turn it 90 degrees, then tie another piece in the same way, so that the fat is held in place.

3 Starting at one end, loop string around the meat, tie it securely and cut off. Make another loop about 5cm (2in) from the first. Continue along the length of the joint.

Larding

Threading narrow strips of fat through beef fillet is another way of guaranteeing juiciness. The fat is threaded through the joint using a larding needle.

1 Cut long strips of pork fat, preferably back fat, which will fit easily into the larding needle. Chill well or freeze.

2 Push the needle right through the joint, so that the tip sticks out at least 5cm (2in) through the other side.

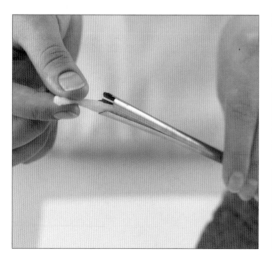

3 Take a strip of fat, place it in the hollow of the larding needle, and feed it into the tip. When the fat can't go in any further, press down on the joint and pull the needle out. The fat should stay inside.

4 Repeat at 2.5cm (1in) intervals on all sides of the joint.

Tenderising steak

Some cuts of steak benefit from tenderising. There are two ways to do it: by pounding or scoring.

1 **To pound**, lay the steaks in a single layer on a large piece of clingfilm or waxed paper. Lay another sheet on top of the slices and pound gently with a rolling pin, small frying pan or the flat side of a meat mallet.

2 **Scoring** is especially useful for cuts that have long, tough fibres, such as flank. It allows a marinade to penetrate more deeply into the meat. Lay the steak on the chopping board and, using a long, very sharp knife, make shallow cuts in one direction across the whole surface.

3 Make another set of cuts at a 45 degree angle to the first. Now turn the meat over and repeat on the other side.

Mincing

If you don't have a mincer you can mince meat using a food processor or a knife.

1 **Using a food processor** Cut the meat into chunks about 2.5cm (1in) square. Put a handful of meat into the food processor and pulse for a few seconds at a time. Stop when the meat is just starting to form a ball on the sides of the bowl. Remove and set aside, and repeat with the remaining meat.

2 **Using a knife** This is an old-fashioned method but a really excellent one. Trim off all fat and sinews, and cut the meat into thin pieces. Chop with two large, heavy knives or cleavers, using a decisive hammer action, until the meat is coarsely minced.

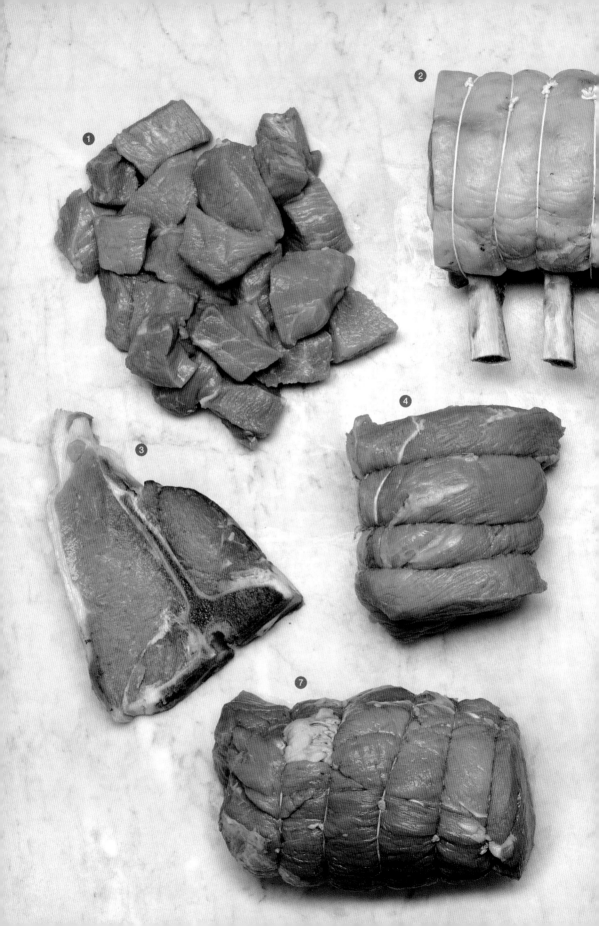

Veal cuts

1 Diced shoulder   6 Loin

2 Best end   7 Leg

3 Loin chop   8 Cutlet

4 Rolled breast   9 Mince

5 Fillet   10 Knuckle

Veal

❶ Shoulder

Also known as chuck or oyster, this economical cut is sold on the bone, or off the bone for stuffing and rolling. It has a fuller flavour than some of the more expensive cuts of veal, and is particularly tasty braised or pot-roasted; for example, with garlic, mushrooms, tomatoes, rosemary and red wine.

TO USE Roast; cut into chunks for stewing, braising or adding to pie fillings.

❷ Best end

Also known as rack this is the ribs cut from the back of the animal, between the shoulder and loin. Best end is sold on the bone for roasting. It is a moist and tender cut. The tender 'eye' of the cut may be removed and sliced, then sold as cutlets. If you are roasting on the bone, ask the butcher to chine it: this means separating the ribs from the backbone to make carving easier. Boned best end can be stuffed with spinach, garlic and breadcrumbs, for example, before it is rolled and roasted.

TO USE Roast on or off the bone; pan-fry cutlets.

❸❻ Loin

This cut corresponds roughly to the sirloin on a beef carcass, being taken from the back of the animal between the hindquarters and ribs. Loin is a tender cut with full flavour; it may be sold whole for roasting or sliced into chops or medallions. The whole boned piece may be stuffed – for example with a pancetta and sage stuffing – and rolled into a joint. Medallions are taken off the bone. Chops are left on it, as with a lamb loin chop. Veal loin always requires careful attention to timing, as it is a lean cut and can easily overcook. Loin chops are particularly well suited to quick cooking methods, and benefit from marinating, for example, in lemon juice and rosemary or thyme, before pan-frying or grilling.

TO USE Stuff, roll and roast a whole piece; pan-fry or grill chops and cutlets; pan-fry medallions.

❹ Rolled breast

Cut from the underside of the carcass, this is an economical cut with excellent flavour and a rich, varied texture from the contrasting layers of meat, cartilage and fat. Breast is the fattest part of a veal carcass – although nothing like as fatty as mature beef. It is often sold boned, stuffed – for example, with prosciutto, capers, Parmesan cheese, garlic, herbs and breadcrumbs – then rolled ready for roasting. Breast of veal benefits from braising with pronounced flavours such as white wine with herbs and tomatoes. With careful attention to timing and a moderate oven, it can also be roasted.

TO USE Roast on the bone; stuff and roll, braise or stew.

❺ Fillet

Cut from the top end of the hind leg, the fillet weighs about 225–350g (8–12oz) and is one of the most expensive cuts, because it is ultra-tender with a delicate flavour. It is sold either as a large piece for roasting or in slices and medallions. Saltimbocca (meaning 'jumps in the mouth') is a classic Italian dish in which thinly sliced fillet is rolled with fresh sage leaves and slices of prosciutto, then cooked in butter.

TO USE Roast a whole piece. Pan-fry slices and medallions.

Rump

A tender cut taken from the top of the carcass towards the hindquarters, rump is usually sliced into escalopes or medallions and can be cooked in the same way as leg escalopes.

TO USE Pan-fry or grill.

Flank

A tough cut taken from the underside of the carcass, flank requires long, slow cooking to achieve tender results. But the flavour is good, and the cut is relatively inexpensive. Lemon, garlic, mushrooms and thyme are complementary flavours for cooking with veal flank.

TO USE Stew or casserole.

⑦ Leg

A large, lean and tender joint, leg (which means the hind leg) may be sold on the bone as a roasting joint, although it is more often sold boned for stuffing or thinly sliced into escalopes. Cut along the grain, escalopes are taken from the prime muscle of the leg, the topside. They are one of the most popular ways to eat veal, either rolled around a filling such as blue cheese and breadcrumbs or coated in egg and breadcrumbs and quickly pan-fried. Leg can also be pot-roasted with garlic and rosemary, but care must be taken with timing or the joint will end up dry and stringy.

TO USE Roast on the bone; stuff and roll, braise or pot-roast; pan-fry escalopes.

⑧ Cutlet

Sliced from the loin and sometimes pounded with a meat mallet to make them thinner and larger, cutlets are an expensive cut. They are very tender and suit quick cooking methods such as grilling and pan-frying. Cutlets go well with a sauce of garlic, capers, lemon and white wine, or a creamy sauce such as sour cream and mushrooms. They can also be fried simply and served with nothing more than a squeeze of lemon juice. Take care not to overcook: this will leave you with dry, stringy (and very expensive) meat.

TO USE Pan-fry, grill or griddle.

⑨ Mince

Pale pink veal mince is sometimes available from butchers, but you will more commonly need to mince the meat yourself or ask your butcher to do it for you. It has a mild flavour and is most often combined with other minced meats such as pork and beef.

TO USE Add to sauces or use in meatloaf and lasagne; as fillings for stuffing vegetables, such as peppers and aubergines.

⑩ Knuckle

The knuckle is cut from the shin, the bony lower end of the hind leg; it is usually sawn crossways through the bone into thick slices. It is classically cooked in the Italian stew osso buco, which is flavoured with white wine, tomatoes, garlic and bay leaves and served with a simple risotto flavoured with saffron (alla Milanese).

TO USE Stew, casserole or braise.

Middle neck

A flavoursome but not particularly tender cut, middle neck is usually sliced into cutlets. It requires long, slow and moist cooking, such as braising or stewing, for tender results.

TO USE Braise, stew or casserole.

Neck

This bony, rather tough but flavoursome cut needs long and slow cooking, such as casseroling. It also makes a an excellent contribution to stocks and soups.

TO USE Stew, casserole or use in stock; mince or finely chop for pies.

Pie veal

Also referred to as diced veal, pie veal consists of trimmings from shoulder, breast, neck and knuckle. The meat is generally tough but well flavoured and requires long, slow cooking. Classic pie-filling combinations include: veal and ham; veal and mushroom; and Venetian pie, which combines veal with tomatoes, Parmesan cheese, garlic and oregano.

TO USE Add to pie fillings and casseroles.

Lamb cuts

1. Chump chop
2. Neck fillet
3. Saddle
4. Double loin chop
5. Middle neck
6. Leg steak
7. Leg
8. Rack
9. Mince
10. Loin
11. Noisette
12. Scrag end
13. Breast
14. Shoulder
15. Shank

Lamb

❶ Chump chop

Cut from between the leg and the loin, these tender chops have a small bone in the centre. As there are only two chump chops from each animal, they may be even more expensive than loin chops.

TO USE Grill, pan-fry or braise with garlic, thyme and potatoes.

❷❺⓬ Scrag end and middle neck

Usually grouped together, these two cuts come from the bony end of the neck and are tough but flavoursome and often quite fatty. They suit long, slow cooking to achieve tender results and are good stewed with, for example, red wine, tomatoes, red peppers, paprika and thyme. The 'eye' of meat from the middle neck may be sold separately as fillet of lamb, and it is a cut worth seeking out. It contains a fair bit of connective tissue and some fat, but the flavour is strong and the texture good. Cut into chunks, the neck fillet makes a good and economical alternative to shoulder in lamb stews.

TO USE Stew or casserole. Fillet of lamb may be grilled, pan-fried or braised.

❸ Saddle

Also known as double loin of lamb, saddle consists of both loins with a good covering of fat to baste and protect the meat during cooking. It may be sold boned or unboned, and makes a very large and impressive joint for dinner parties, weighing about 3.6kg (8lb). Saddle is good when flavoured with rosemary and garlic, the natural accompaniments to lamb, and if boned it can be stuffed before rolling and cooking.

TO USE Roast.

❹ Double loin chop

Cut from across the saddle, these large, double-sided chops are also known as butterfly chops or Barnsley chops. Tomatoes, red wine, garlic and herbs complement the flavour of the chops when braising.

TO USE Grill, pan-fry or braise.

❻ Leg steak

Cut from the top end of the leg, these tender, juicy steaks have a small bone in the centre and suit quick, simple cooking such as grilling and pan-frying. They are also sold boned. Good flavourings include lemon and thyme or mint, or Moroccan-style spicing such as cumin, garlic and cayenne. They are not quite as tender as loin, and they can be just as expensive, but they are also leaner and produce less waste because the bone is smaller.

TO USE Grill, pan-fry or braise.

❼ Leg

One of the most popular joints for roasting, leg is often divided into two: the fillet end and the shank end. Either piece may be cooked on the bone, and a popular method is to pierce the flesh and stuff the slits with rosemary and garlic. Leg can also be boned and stuffed – for example, with garlic, sage and lemon rind – then rolled before it is roasted. If you are buying a leg from your butcher, ask him to make sure the H-bone has been removed. This will make carving much easier.

TO USE Roast, braise or casserole; cut into pieces to stew; marinate cubes with cumin, garlic, lemon juice and olive oil and thread on to skewers and grill.

❽ Rack

Also known as best end of neck, this rib joint is taken from between the middle neck and the loin. The rack consists of six to eight chops with a long bone and a relatively small section of eye meat. It may be roasted as a single joint for two to three people. When two racks are tied together, they are called a guard of honour (see page 165) or a crown roast. These joints can be cooked with a herb crust containing garlic, mustard, thyme and rosemary. Rack can also be sliced into individual ribs and either fried or grilled (lamb cutlets) or used in the classic recipes Lancashire hotpot and Irish stew. The rib chops may also be boned and rolled to form noisettes (see page 165), which can be served with mint sauce or a red wine sauce flavoured with rosemary and redcurrant jelly.

TO USE Roast, or slice into cutlets and stew or grill. Noisettes may be pan-fried or grilled.

❾ Mince

Made from numerous parts of the animal, but usually the tougher or scrappier cuts, lamb mince can vary enormously in quality. Look for mince with a low proportion of fat. Darker, evenly coloured meat will usually have a lower proportion of fat than paler mince or mince visibly streaked with white fat.

TO USE Add to meat sauces such as Bolognese; use in dishes such as lasagne, moussaka and shepherd's pie; as fillings for stuffed vegetables such as peppers and aubergines; in burgers, patties, meatloaf, meatballs, kofta and kebabs.

⑩ Loin

This is one side of the saddle; it is a very tender cut of lamb and a prime cut for roasting or grilling. It is usually divided into two cuts: the loin end near the ribs and the chump end near the tail. It may be cut into chops, roasted in a whole piece – seasoned or coated, for example, with a herb and mustard crust – or boned and stuffed; for example, with a breadcrumb, apricot and pine nut filling. The eye meat is the main attraction of loin chops, and sometimes the fatty end is trimmed or even cut off completely. If you're roasting the loin, however, the fat should be left on and tied around the eye.

TO USE Roast the whole piece, either on or off the bone; stuff and roll. Pan-fry or grill chops.

⑪ Noisette

Made from the boned 'eye' of loin tied into a neat round and then sliced (see page 165), this is an expensive but very tender, flavoursome cut. Noisettes can also be made from boned best end of neck (rack). Serve noisettes with a fruity redcurrant sauce or jelly, or with a French-style sauce of fresh herbs, garlic and white wine.

TO USE Pan-fry, grill or griddle.

⑬ Breast

Taken from the belly, breast is a long, thin cut that tends to be fatty. It is extremely inexpensive, however, and with sufficient care it can be turned into a very good dish. Breast can be boned, stuffed and rolled into a joint. Garlic, lemon, rosemary and sultanas or dried apricots combined with breadcrumbs make a flavoursome stuffing. It can also be braised, left to cool, cut into riblets and then coated with a savoury breadcrumb mixture before grilling or frying to crispness.

TO USE Roast; trim well, removing as much fat as possible, and braise.

⑭ Shoulder

Although it is fatty and somewhat scrappy because of the many different muscles it contains, shoulder is a juicy and tender roasting joint with excellent flavour – and is much less expensive than loin and leg. It can be cooked on the bone, or boned, stuffed and rolled. The meat can also be cut from the bone and cubed or minced. Complementary flavours for shoulder include: lemon, garlic and thyme; Middle Eastern spices such as harissa paste or cumin, coriander, cinnamon and ginger. It is the standard cut for lamb kebabs and one of the principal cuts for French lamb stews.

TO USE Roast on the bone or bone, stuff and roll; or bone and cube for kebabs, stews, tagines and casseroles.

⑮ Shank

Taken from the lower part of the hind leg, the shank is usually cooked on the bone and served as a generous individual portion. It suits long, slow cooking and is classically braised with, for example, tomatoes, red wine, garlic and thyme. There is also a shank that comes from the lower part of the shoulder, which is not as large or as finely textured as the hind leg shank but has excellent flavour and a good texture after long, slow cooking.

TO USE Braise, casserole or pot-roast.

Rack of lamb

A rack of lamb comprises the seven or eight cutlets, chops from the neck end, served as a joint. It is one of the tastiest and most impressive lamb joints, and easy to prepare. You can cook it just as it comes from the butcher, or as a French-style rack.

1 If necessary, pull off the papery outer membrane from the fat side of the rack. Trim away the excess fat. Look for a long strip of cartilage on one end of the rack and cut it out if it is there.

Do the same with a long strip of sinew running the length of the rack under the ribs.

2 Make a cut right down to the bone across the fat side of the rack about 2.5–5cm (1–2in) from the tips of the bones. Place the knife in that cut and, holding the knife almost parallel to the ribs, slice off the meat as a single piece to expose the ends of the bones.

3 Insert the knife between one pair of bared ribs at the point of the initial cut. Push through it to cut the meat between the ribs. Continue in the same way with the other ribs. Slice down on both sides of each rib to remove the strips of meat.

4 Turn the rack bone side up and scrape off the papery membranes from the backs of the ribs. This will leave the top parts of the bones clean.

Guard of honour

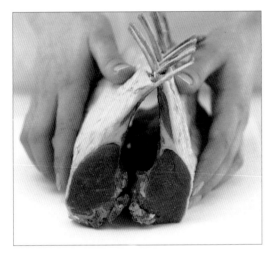

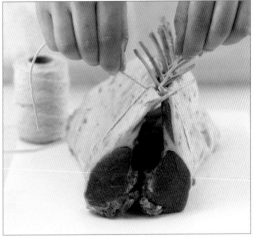

1 Prepare the racks as described for rack of lamb. Place with the bases pressed together and the exposed end-bones interlocking.

2 Using a piece of string, tie the joint vertically between every two ribs. Roast as it is, or stuff the space between the two racks and cook in a preheated oven at 220°C (200°C fan oven) mark 7 for 30–35 minutes.

Noisettes of lamb

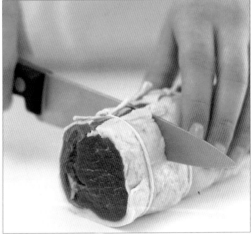

Loin of lamb can be boned, rolled and sliced to make noisettes (usually with a layer of fat on the meat), both delicious and elegant. Buy them ready prepared or ask the butcher to do it – or try this simple version.

1 Use a thin-bladed knife to scrape and cut along the backbone until the tenderloin falls away. Remove and save for a stir-fry.

2 Turn the loin around and cut between the backbone and eye meat, always cutting towards the bone. Remove the meat in a single piece and trim the excess fat.

3 Roll the flat apron of fat around the eye and tie it securely with string at 2.5cm (1in) intervals.

4 Slice the loin about 2.5cm (1in) thick. Grill (for 8–12 minutes) or pan-fry (for 6–10 minutes).

Pork cuts

1. Chump
2. Chump chop
3. Loin chop
4. Loin
5. Shoulder steak
6. Blade bone
7. Leg

8	Tenderloin	**11**	Leg fillet
9	Spare rib	**12**	Belly
10	Hand and spring	**13**	Knuckle

Pork

❶ Chump

Cut from the hindquarters, this joint can be cooked whole to feed two to four people, but ask your butcher to saw through the chine bone (backbone) for ease of carving. Thyme, rosemary or sage go well with roasted chump.

TO USE Roast.

❷ Chump chop

Cut from between the loin and leg, chump chops are large with a good flavour. They may be sold on or off the bone. Caraway is a complementary spice that goes well with chump chops.

TO USE Snip the fat at regular intervals around the chop to prevent it from curling. Grill, pan-fry, braise or casserole.

❸ Loin chop

Cut from the hindloin, these large, chunky chops are tender and well flavoured; some are sold with the kidney left in. They are good flavoured with mustard and sage, or served with fruity braised red cabbage. If the rind is left on, it should turn to crackling when the chop is grilled. Very fatty chops may have the rind taken off and the fat trimmed.

TO USE Snip the fat and rind at regular intervals around the chop to prevent it from curling up during cooking. Grill, pan-fry, braise or casserole; slice the meat into strips and stir-fry.

❹ Loin

Taken from the back of the carcass, loin is divided into hind loin and foreloin, and is sold both boned and unboned. Hind loin contains the tenderloin and kidney; foreloin comes from the rib end. Both are quite lean with a good but mild flavour, and the hind loin is considered by many to be the best cut of pork. Two unboned foreloins of pork can be tied to make a crown roast that would serve about ten people. Boned loin can be stuffed with apple and sage before rolling and roasting. The eye of the loin, the choicest part, is very lean. The fat lies in a strip which can vary in thickness from around 5mm (¼in) to 2.5cm (1in), and which is usually sold with the rind (skin) attached. The rind will turn to crackling if left on the joint. Ask the butcher to score the rind to make it easier to serve the crackling.

TO USE Roast on the bone; bone, stuff and roll.

❺ Shoulder steak

Cut from the shoulder, these steaks have a sweet flavour and tender, succulent texture. Because the shoulder contains several sections of separate muscles joined by connective tissue, the steaks must be cut fairly thickly. The rind (skin) should ideally be removed before cooking. Shoulder steaks are also suitable for cutting into strips and stir-frying, for example, with ginger and black bean sauce.

TO USE Grill, pan-fry or braise with, for example, bay, caraway and cider; cut into strips and stir-fry.

❻ Blade bone

Cut from the neck end of the shoulder and sold off the bone, this is a fatty joint that can be cooked whole or cut into cubes for grilling or braising. It has a fine flavour and is usually one of the less expensive cuts, often used for sausage making. Caribbean, Chinese or Mediterranean flavourings are suitable for braising blade of pork. Cubes can be marinated with lemon juice and herbs such as thyme or oregano or with spices such as coriander and then grilled on skewers.

TO USE Whole: roast, pot-roast or braise; cut into cubes, thread on to skewers and grill, or casserole.

❼ Leg

The whole hind leg weighs between 4.5kg (10lb) and 6.8kg (15lb), and makes an enormous and impressive joint for roasting. But it is more commonly divided into two: the knuckle end and the fillet end. The fillet end is the more highly regarded, as the knuckle end contains more bone relative to the amount of meat, but both are flavoursome, tender, and relatively lean. Ask the butcher to score the rind to make it easier to serve the crackling. The leg is also sold boned, cut into smaller sections and rolled, giving joints about 1–2kg (2¼–4½lb) in weight. Leg can also be diced and used in recipes such as sweet-and-sour pork or pork and mushroom pie.

TO USE Roast and serve with apple sauce; cut into cubes and braise.

⑧ Tenderloin

Lean, tender and succulent, this is a relatively small cut taken from the hind loin, just beneath the backbone. It corresponds to the fillet of beef. A single tenderloin usually provides enough meat for two, but some are larger and can feed more. Tenderloin can be split lengthways and stuffed – for example, with mushrooms and thyme – or sliced into medallions, cubes or strips. Its tenderness and leanness make it an excellent (if expensive) cut to use in pork stir-fries.

TO USE Cut off the fine membrane that covers the tenderloin. Split, stuff and roast basting regularly. Pan-fry or grill medallions; pan-fry or braise cubes; stir-fry strips.

⑨ Spare rib

These are the long rib bones that are cut from the belly. The rind and excess fat are removed and the ribs separated. They contain very little meat, but their flavour is excellent and they are popular around the world. Spare ribs are particularly good cooked with Chinese-style flavourings such as five-spice powder, soy sauce and honey, but also suit barbecue sauce or Caribbean-style spices such as jerk seasoning.

TO USE Marinate, then roast or barbecue.

⑩ Hand and spring

Taken from the lower part of the forequarter, this is a large joint that is often divided into two: the hand and shank. These cuts contain a lot of sinew and connective tissue so should be well trimmed, but they have a good flavour and can be tender. They are best cooked slowly in pot-roasts or casseroles flavoured with, for example, garlic, juniper, sage and white wine. The hand, which has plenty of rind for crackling, can also be roasted at a low temperature after first cooking at a high temperature for 30 minutes.

TO USE Pot-roast, casserole or braise; cut into cubes and stew; roast. For crispy crackling, score the skin into narrow strips and rub with salt before roasting.

Rolled shoulder

This relatively inexpensive cut is one of the prime choices for a roast of pork. It is very large (around 4kg/9lb) and can be bought either as a single piece or in shorter sections for smaller groups of people. The colour is quite dark, indicating the well exercised nature of the muscles in the shoulder, and the flavour is deeply 'porky'. Get the butcher to score the rind (skin), and coat the flesh with a mixture of dried herbs, finely chopped garlic, and salt and pepper a few hours before cooking. Shoulder can also have the skin removed before rolling, making it suitable for braising, and can be cut into large chunks for a stew.

TO USE Roast, braise or casserole; cut into cubes and stew. For crisp crackling, score the skin deeply into narrow strips and rub well with salt before roasting.

⑪ Leg fillet

Taken from the top of the leg, this prime roasting joint is tender with a good flavour. The meat may also be sliced into steaks or escalopes or cubed and used for recipes such as Greek *souvlakia* (marinated pork skewers flavoured with oregano, bay and red wine or lemon juice).

TO USE Roast on the bone or bone, stuff – for example, with an apricot and sage stuffing – and roll. Grill, pan-fry or braise steaks or escalopes.

⑫ Belly

A long, thin, flat cut with sheets of meat separated by layers of fat. Belly may have a high proportion of fat, and is usually sold with the ribs removed ready for stuffing, rolling and roasting. Suitable stuffings include pancetta and sage. However, it is also suitable for roasting unboned. The best cut is the thicker part of the belly, as it is leaner and sometimes more tender. If you are roasting belly, ask the butcher to score the rind deeply to make it easier to crisp up and serve the crackling. Belly can be sliced or chopped into pieces to make rich, filling casseroles and stews, and is also good for mincing and/or using to make sausages.

TO USE Roast whole or as a rolled joint. For crispy crackling, score the skin into narrow strips and rub with salt before roasting. Grill or fry slices; add pieces to casseroles and stews.

⑬ Knuckle

Taken from the lower part of the forequarter, this joint offers a very economical option: it is inexpensive but has plenty of meat on it and an excellent flavour. It should be well trimmed of excess fat and connective tissue, and is usually given long, slow cooking such as braising. But it can also produce a delicious joint with plenty of crisp crackling when roasted. The meat is chewier than other roasting joints such as loin, so slice it very thinly for serving. Braised knuckle suits Chinese-style flavourings such as garlic, star anise, cinnamon, soy sauce and rice wine. It can also be poached and served as 'white-cooked pork', with a spicy and aromatic Chinese dipping sauce.

TO USE Bone, stuff, roll and roast; pot-roast, braise or casserole; cut into cubes and stew.

Removing the tenderloin

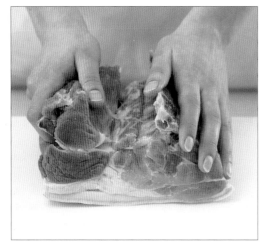

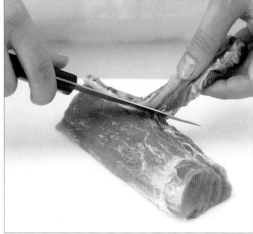

1 Place the loin skin side down and locate the long rounded strip of tenderloin meat. Make a cut along the edge of the tenderloin closest to the backbone. Take care not to cut into the meat. Work the knife between meat and bone until you can pull away the tenderloin.

2 Cut off the thin strip of meat connected to the main section and save it for stock, if you like.

3 Using a sharp small knife, make a cut at the thick end of the tenderloin just underneath the thick, silvery membrane covering it on one side.

4 Taking care not to cut the meat, cut and pull off the membrane in long strips. Make sure every bit of membrane comes away. Trim away any loose scraps of meat, and tidy the ends if they look at all ragged.

Trimming and rolling loin of pork

1 Using a long, thin-bladed knife, cut a long slit into the fat from the rib end just below the rind (skin), taking off as little fat as you can. Work the knife into the fat to remove the rind in single sheet. Trim off all but 5mm (¼in) of fat.

2 Turn the loin around and place the knife flat on the ribs. Following the line of the ribs, and always cutting towards the bone, cut through the meat until you reach the vertebrae.

3 Use a small, sharp knife to scrape the pieces of meat connecting the loin to the underlying bones, and remove the meat. Trim off any ragged scraps.

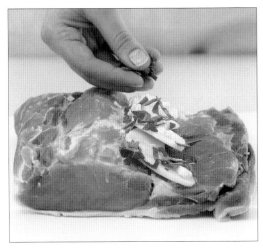

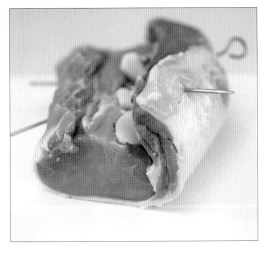

4 If you want a fully trimmed loin that doesn't need rolling, cut off the flap meat from the eye. Trim away any visible fat and sinews. The loin may be rolled with or without stuffing. To stuff, shape the stuffing into a thin sheet or cylinder. Lay the loin with the fat side down on the chopping board, and put the stuffing on the line where the eye meets the flap meat.

5 Fold the flap of meat over the eye of loin and secure with skewers. Tie the loin with string every 5cm (2in) and remove the skewers.

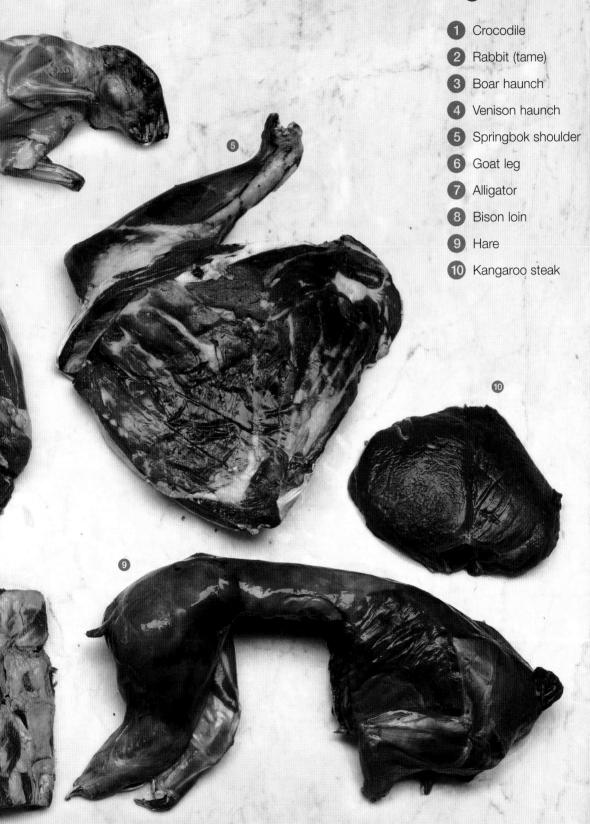

Other meats and game

1 Crocodile

2 Rabbit (tame)

3 Boar haunch

4 Venison haunch

5 Springbok shoulder

6 Goat leg

7 Alligator

8 Bison loin

9 Hare

10 Kangaroo steak

Other meats and game

① Crocodile

Found in Africa, Asia, America and Australia, these large reptiles live in freshwater rivers, lakes and wetlands. Crocodile is particularly popular in Australia, where it is farmed. It has a pale colour, mild flavour and tender, flaky texture rather like a combination of chicken, pork and fish. It is available as fillets and steaks and can be cooked in the same ways as chicken portions, for example marinated with garlic, chilli and lemon juice and grilled, or cubed and marinated with ginger, soy sauce, garlic and lime juice, then grilled on skewers and served with a spicy peanut sauce (like chicken satay). It can also be baked or braised with tomatoes, white wine, garlic and herbs.

TO USE Grill, pan-fry, braise or casserole.

② Rabbit

Originally hunted in the wild, rabbit is now widely farmed. Wild and farmed rabbit are strikingly different: farmed rabbit has pale and tender meat while the wild animals usually have flesh which is darker and much tougher. Farmed rabbit is often likened to chicken in flavour and texture. The meat is low in fat and cholesterol, making it a healthy option. Rabbit can be bought whole, or cut into pieces, and can be cooked with garlic or shallots, tomatoes, wine, mushrooms and oregano. Young, tender rabbit can be treated in all the ways you would treat chicken, including roasting, grilling and sautéing. Because the meat is lean, however, it should be basted with oil and not overcooked. The liver and kidneys of farmed rabbit are tiny but delicious.

TO USE Wild: braise, casserole, stew or add to pie fillings. Farmed: grill, sauté, roast.

③ Boar

A type of wild pig, from which modern domesticated pigs are descended, boar is found throughout Europe and Asia, and is now also farmed. The meat is much darker and more strongly flavoured than pork (because the meat is not bled before cooking as it is for pork). The flesh is also leaner and must be cooked carefully to keep it from drying out. Boar is sold in various cuts, for example mince and processed into products such as sausages and burgers. It goes well with robust flavourings such as thyme, rosemary, sage, juniper, garlic and red wine.

TO USE Roast tender cuts; braise, stew or casserole tougher cuts or use in pie fillings. Use in sauces, or make into patties, meatballs and meatloaves. Sausages and burgers can be grilled or pan-fried.

④ Venison

The term venison is used to describe the meat from fallow, red and roe deer. The meat is dark red and lean, with a fine texture and a fairly strong flavour. Meat from older deer has a better flavour but requires long, slow cooking to achieve tender results. The meat from younger animals can be cooked more quickly. Young animals have white fat, whereas that of older animals tends to be more yellow. Venison is sold as joints and smaller cuts, cubed, minced and processed into products such as sausages and jerky. Venison suits fruity sauces such as cherry, blueberry and redcurrant, as well as earthier flavours such as mushrooms, marjoram and red wine.

TO USE To keep venison meat moist and tender, marinate and then baste regularly during cooking. For smaller cuts taken from the saddle, loin or fillet, pan-fry or grill. Roast larger joints such as saddle, leg or haunch. Otherwise braise, casserole, stew or add to pie fillings.

⑤ Springbok

A type of antelope, springbok is found in south and south-west Africa where it is hunted as game. Springbok is a low-fat red meat with tender and juicy flesh and a strong flavour, similar to that of venison. It is available in specialist shops as steaks or haunch and suits similar cooking methods to venison, such as braising in red wine with garlic and thyme or oregano. Best cooked medium-rare.

TO USE Pan-fry, grill or griddle steaks, medium-rare. Braise, casserole or stew haunch.

⑥ Goat

Full-flavoured goat's meat appears in Mediterranean cooking as well as dishes from the Caribbean, the Middle East and other parts of the world. Goat is not commonly found, but it is worth buying if you come across it. Like goat's cheese, the meat has a distinctive and pungent aroma. The meat of young goats (kids) is tender, juicy and lean, and can be cooked more quickly, but generally goat's meat is best suited to long, slow cooking such as stewing. Classic goat recipes include Jamaican goat curry, jerked leg of goat, Greek kid with *avgolemono* (egg and lemon sauce), and Filipino *kalderetta* (spicy goat stew).

TO USE Braise, stew or casserole. Roast or barbecue young goat.

⑦ Alligator

Once eaten from the wild, alligator is now successfully farmed and its meat is particularly enjoyed in the southern states of the US and in Cajun cooking. The meat is pale and mildly flavoured, with a flaky, tender texture similar to a combination of chicken, pork and fish. Alligator can be cooked in similar ways to chicken and veal, such as marinated with garlic, lemon and marjoram, then grilled. It can also be added to jambalaya (a spicy Creole rice dish, similar to paella), or cooked with lemon and white wine. It is most often available frozen, either on or off the bone.

TO USE Grill, pan-fry, braise or casserole.

❽ Bison

Also known as American buffalo, the bison can grow to 2m (6½ft) tall with a huge head and forequarters. Bison meat is like slightly tough beef and can be cooked in similar ways. It is lower in fat and cholesterol than beef, and is farmed in the USA. A cross-breed with domestic cattle, known as beefalo, has also been produced.

TO USE Roast, grill, pan-fry, braise, casserole or stew.

❾ Hare

Similar in appearance to rabbit, but much larger and with longer ears, hare has darker, more strongly flavoured flesh. As hare is unsuited to farming, only wild are available. Young hare (leveret) is best, and can be roasted, as saddle of hare. Older hare can be potted or casseroled and requires long, slow cooking to achieve tender results. A traditional English recipe is for jugged hare, which is marinated in wine and juniper berries, then cooked_for a long time in a tightly covered earthenware jug or casserole.

TO USE Roast young hare; braise, casserole or stew older hare, or add to pie fillings.

❿ Kangaroo

Native to Australia and a traditional part of the aboriginal diet, kangaroo is a dark, lean meat with a fine texture and a rich, strong flavour. It is very low in fat (2 per cent) compared to other red meats. But that leanness means that care must be taken when cooking to keep the meat from drying out: it is usually best when cooked no more than medium-rare. Kangaroo is available as steaks and slices. Popular recipes include roast medallions wrapped in prosciutto, chilli kangaroo stir-fry (similar to chilli beef), and kangaroo-tail soup (similar to oxtail soup).

TO USE Roast, grill, pan-fry, braise, casserole or stir-fry.

Buffalo

In Africa, these large bovine animals are hunted in the wild and their meat is cut into strips, salted and spiced, dried and smoked to make biltong, a dark, chewy dried meat (see page 194). Asian water buffalo are found both in the wild and as domesticated animals. The meat is similar to beef in flavour and texture, but it tends to be tougher. Available in similar cuts to beef, buffalo can be cooked in the same ways: roasted as a joint; pan-fried or grilled as steaks; cubed and stewed with garlic, red wine and tomatoes; or minced and made into burgers, meatloaves, meatballs and Bolognese-style sauce to serve with pasta.

TO USE Roast, grill, pan-fry, braise, casserole or stew.

Llama

Growing from 1.6–1.8m (just over 5ft to around 6ft) tall, these animals were originally native to North America. Today, they are found throughout South America, where they are used as pack animals and bred for their wool and meat. The meat is low in fat and quite dark, with a flavour similar to beef and lamb. Best eaten young, it is available as cutlets, chops and legs, and is also processed into products such as burgers. Older animals are usually dried and made into jerky. Llama goes well with flavourings such as tomatoes, red wine, oregano, thyme, rosemary and garlic.

TO USE Roast joints such as legs; pan-fry, grill or griddle cutlets and chops.

Snail

A delicacy appreciated particularly by the French, snails are usually purged by starving for several days to remove any toxins from their digestive tracts, then boiled and served in garlic butter. You can collect your own from the garden and do the purging and cooking yourself. Mostly, however, they are farmed and sold ready-prepared, needing nothing more than heating through with butter.

TO USE Purge for at least three days, rinsing regularly with water, then feed on carrots for about one day until their excrement appears orange. Boil until just tender, about 5 minutes, then serve with garlic butter.

Offal

1. Lamb's liver
2. Goose liver
3. Oxtail
4. Lamb's heart
5. Lamb's kidneys
6. Lamb sweetbreads
7. Tripe
8. Lights (lungs)
9. Pig's liver
10. Calf's kidney
11. Ox tongue
12. Pig's trotter
13. Lamb's brain
14. Ox kidney
15. Calf's liver
16. Chicken liver

Offal

① ② ⑨ ⑮ ⑯ Liver

With a colour ranging from pale cream to dark purple-brown and a smooth surface, liver has a smooth, dense texture and distinctive flavour. It is a rich source of iron. There are numerous types of liver available, both from birds and beasts.

Chicken, duck and turkey livers are generally similar in appearance and taste, although duck and turkey are richer in flavour (and often in colour) than chicken. These livers are often made into smooth pâtés, but they can also be sautéed in butter and/or oil for use in salads or for serving on their own. Goose liver tends to be larger and paler, and is highly prized – especially in the form of foie gras. This probably originated in France, which is still the main market for it. Foie gras is produced by intensive feeding of geese to make their livers grow to several times the normal size. The practice is condemned by many advocates for the humane treatment of animals. Foie gras can also come from ducks fed in the same way.

Of the animal livers, calf's liver is by far the most highly regarded and most expensive. It has a mild and delicate flavour and texture, and is usually quickly pan-fried to preserve its tenderness and juiciness. Calf's liver is often served alongside bacon, the saltiness of which makes a good partner for its creamy texture. Lamb's liver is also fairly mild, although stronger in flavour than calf's. Pig's and ox liver tend to be quite strongly flavoured and with a coarser texture; pig's liver is often used to make pâtés.

TO USE Soak in milk to mellow the flavour (optional), then pat dry. Pan-fry with bacon; grill; add to braised dishes such as liver with onions and Marsala, casseroles or pie fillings such as bacon and mushroom; use in pâtés. Be careful not to overcook any form of liver, as this will make it tough.

③ Oxtail

Oxtail is one of the toughest and most flavourful parts of the beef carcass. It is usually sold jointed, which produces chunks ranging in size from around 2cm (¾in) to 7.5cm (3in) in diameter. Larger pieces are suitable for casseroles, whereas smaller pieces are better for making stocks and soups. Oxtail contains a modest amount of meat and often plenty of firm white fat, although the fat can be trimmed before cooking. It also releases generous amounts of gelatine, which helps to enrich dishes. It suits long, slow, moist methods of cooking until the meat falls off the bone. Classic recipes are oxtail soup and oxtail stew with red wine, onions and root vegetables.

TO USE Braise, stew, casserole or make into soup.

④ Heart

Lamb's hearts are the most commonly available and have a tender texture and a mild flavour. Pig's and ox hearts are larger and coarser. All suit long, slow cooking to achieve tender results. Lamb's hearts can be stuffed with apples, spices and cider.

TO USE Rinse, trim away any fat and tubes, then snip inside the cavity wall. Soak in salted water for 1 hour, then rinse and slice or stuff. Braise, casserole or stew.

⑤ ⑩ ⑭ Kidney

With a dark purple-brown colour and smooth surface, kidneys have a smooth, dense texture and distinctive flavour. Veal kidneys are the palest in colour and have a sweet, mild flavour; they are always very expensive, and since most go to the restaurant trade, they are hard to find in most butchers. Lamb's kidneys are smaller, and have a distinctive 'lamby' taste. Much cheaper than veal

kidneys, they are good in dishes such as devilled kidneys spiced with Worcestershire sauce and cayenne pepper. Pig's and ox kidneys have a stronger flavour and coarser texture and are better suited to long, slow cooking methods. Ox kidney is added to the traditional English dish, steak and kidney pudding.

TO USE Remove the membrane, slice in half lengthways and snip out the white cores and tubes using sharp-pointed kitchen scissors. Grill, pan-fry, or add to casseroles, stews or in fillings for pies and savoury puddings.

⑥ Sweetbreads

Usually taken from young animals, sweetbreads are the thymus and pancreas of calves and lambs. They are a pale, pinkish colour with a tender texture. Sweetbreads require precooking in stock or water and can then be pan-fried, roasted or braised. Creamy sauces and sautéed mushrooms are classic partners.

TO USE Soak in lightly salted water, then rinse, blanch and remove the outer membrane. Pan-fry, roast or braise.

⑦ Tripe

The stomach lining of the cow, thick, creamy-coloured tripe may be smooth (from the first stomach) or with a honeycomb texture (from the second). Both have the same distinctive taste, which some people love and others can't even smell without being put off. Tripe is sold bleached and par-boiled and suits slow cooking to achieve tender results. Some tripe is cooked for so long at the par-boiling stage, however, that it needs relatively little final cooking. The traditional English recipe for tripe is to cook it with milk and onions, and then to thicken the milk to make a sauce. This is one of the blander approaches to tripe. The meat is used with more assertive flavourings in Mediterranean, Eastern European and Cajun cuisines to make dishes such as Italian *trippa alla Romana* (cooked with onion, garlic, tomato, pecorino cheese and mint), the French *tripes à la mode de Caen* (with aromatic vegetables, garlic and wine), Chinese tripe with black beans and chilli, and Cajun tripe cooked with tomatoes, peppers, garlic and Creole seasoning.

TO USE Casserole or stew.

8 Lights

Not widely eaten, lights are the lungs of sheep, calves, deer and pigs. They are among the traditional offal used in Scottish haggis.

TO USE Add to pâtés and faggots (see page 191).

11 Tongue

When cooked, tongue has a coarse texture and distinctive flavour. Ox tongue is the most widely available. Lambs' tongues are sometimes sold, especially by butchers catering for Middle Eastern communities. Pig's and calf's tongues, however, are more often sold with the head of the animals. Ox and lambs' tongues are sold fresh or brined. Ox tongue is often sold pressed and served cold, cut into thin slices. It can also be served hot, with a sharp mustard-based sauce to cut through its richness. Sweet-and-sour tongue is a classic Jewish recipe.

TO USE Soak fresh tongue for about 2 hours, and brined tongue for 3–4 hours for lamb or overnight for ox. Boil with spices until tender, then drain and peel away the thick outer skin. Press ox tongue and serve cold in thin slices. Lambs' tongues may also be casseroled.

12 Trotter

Pig's feet may be used as an ingredient in stocks or brawn, releasing plenty of gelatine for a good set. They may also be eaten as a dish in themselves, in particular in the classic African–American dish of pickled pig's feet, as well as in other rustic stews and casseroles. Trotters are awkward to eat because they have little meat, which needs to be picked out from between the bones; they are often eaten more as a snack food than a meat dish in their own right. But they are also used in some top-quality French restaurants as a kind of casing for other ingredients. In this case the trotters are cooked until soft, boned, and then rolled with a filling that may include other meats, wild mushrooms and complex seasonings.

TO USE Boil to make stock; boil with vinegar and spices; or boil, then grill or bake.

Chitterlings

Chitterlings are pigs' intestines, sometimes used for sausage casings but also eaten as a dish, most often in the USA and France. They are usually sold (where they are sold at all) ready-cleaned and par-boiled. Their flavour is very strong, and finds one of its greatest uses in the French andouillettes (see page 187). It is fair to say that chitterlings in any form are an acquired taste.

TO USE Clean well and use as sausage casings; finely chop as part of the sausage filling; blanch and grill, pan-fry or stew.

13 Brain

Usually taken from the heads of lambs and calves, brains are pale grey-pink when raw and pale creamy white when cooked, with a tender texture. They are usually sold in 'sets', and one set is sufficient for one portion. Because brains have such a soft texture, they are often coated in flour and cooked over a high heat to give them a crisp texture on the outside.

TO USE Rinse, soak in cold water for 1–2 hours, then cut away any arteries or membranes. Par-boil the brains for 5–15 minutes, depending on size, then refresh in cold water and slice. Pan-fry or braise.

Bovine Spongiform Encephalopathy

More commonly known as BSE, or mad cow disease, bovine spongiform encephalopathy is a fatal neurodegenerative disease found in cattle. It is thought to have arisen as a result of feeding ground-up sheep carcasses infected with a similar disease that affects sheep – scrapie – to cattle. Cattle in the UK have been the most widely affected and any animals suspected of having the disease are slaughtered. It is widely believed that the disease can be transferred to humans who eat the brain and spinal cords of infected carcasses; it presents itself in the form of new variant Creuzfeldt-Jacob disease (vCJD). As a result, high-risk products are banned from sale in the UK.

Gammon and ham

1. Middle gammon
2. Gammon knuckle
3. Bacon bacon
4. Streaky bacon
5. Cooked ham
6. Lardo
7. Pancetta
8. Prosciutto de San Daniele
9. Jamón serrano
10. Speck
11. Prosciutto cotto
12. Prosciutto crudo

Gammon and ham

① ② Gammon

Gammon is cut from the hind leg and hindquarters of the pig. Like bacon it is cured with dry salt or brine, or a mixture of salt, sugar and seasonings, and may be smoked or unsmoked. Cuts include:

Knuckle Cut from the end of the gammon, gammon knuckle is usually sold with the bone in. To use, boil or par-boil and bake; trim, cube and stew; or make soup such as split pea and ham; casserole or braise with, for example, Puy lentils, onions and bay leaf.

Middle A prime cut taken from the centre of the leg, middle gammon may be sold on the bone, or boned and rolled. To use, boil, braise, or par-boil and bake in recipes such as honey-mustard roast gammon.

Steak Usually about 1cm (½in) thick, gammon steaks are cut from boned middle gammon. Grill or pan-fry and serve with a sweet–sharp sauce such as apple.

③ ④ ⑥ ⑦ ⑩ Bacon

Usually cut from the back and sides of the pig and sold as rashers, like gammon, bacon is cured with dry salt, brine or a mixture of salt, sugar and seasonings. It may be unsmoked (sometimes referred to as green bacon) or smoked. Smoked bacon tends to have a golden rind, whereas unsmoked bacon is paler, with white fat and a creamy-coloured rind. Both should have moist, pink flesh. Varieties include:

Back bacon This is cut from the back of the loin (see page 168), and therefore has the loin's structure of a very lean 'eye' of meat with a strip of fat along one side. The leanest type of bacon (as long as the fat is removed), back bacon may be cut as rashers or as thicker slices. Sometimes back bacon is sold in the form of the eye alone, with the fat removed. Grill, pan-fry or bake.

Lardo This extremely fatty Italian product is best described as cured pork fat with a tiny trace of meat attached to it. Lardo is predominantly creamy white in appearance and is almost always cured with other seasonings as well as salt. It can be pan-fried at the start of recipes to flavour the dish, but Italians usually serve the best lardo (Tuscany's lardo di Colonnata) in thin slices on toast.

Pancetta This is the Italian version of streaky bacon. It may be smoked or unsmoked, and is almost always cured with garlic and other seasonings. Sold in strips or round slices cut from a roll, it can be used in the same way as streaky bacon.

Speck From the Tyrol region near the Swiss–German border, this fatty bacon is cut from the belly, flavoured with herbs and spices and smoked over beech wood, giving it a distinctive flavour. Pan-fry at the beginning of a recipe to flavour sauces, soups and casseroles.

Streaky bacon A fattier bacon made from boned belly (see page 169), and therefore streaked with pink flesh and white fat. Streaky bacon is best suited to grilling or wrapping around poultry or game birds for roasting, and for use in dishes where bacon is used as a seasoning and a source of fat for body and flavour (such as pulses or casseroles).

⑤ ⑪ Ham eaten cooked

Ham is the upper hind leg of the pig, cured and matured. The taste and texture of different hams varies greatly depending on a number of factors: the age and breed of the pig; the feed it has been given; the method of curing; whether it has been smoked and the smoking materials used; and how long the ham has been allowed to mature. Curing may involve dry-salting, soaking in brine or, in many commercial hams, injecting the ham with brine.

Hams that are eaten cooked are available pre-cooked and uncooked. Cooked hams may be sold whole, or sliced. Varieties include:

Belfast ham Also known as Ulster roll, this dry-cured ham from Northern Ireland is smoked over peat, giving it a distinctive flavour. It is usually boneless.

Bradenham ham This traditional English ham is cured with dry salt, then soaked in molasses for a month and matured for several months before it is smoked. It has a distinctive black skin and red meat with a fairly sweet flavour. As Bradenham ham is quite salty, uncooked hams should be soaked for at least three days in several changes of cold water before they are cooked.

Cumberland ham This traditional English ham is made with lower-shank meat from Middle White pigs, though originally the ham came from Cumberland pigs (hence its name). It is cured with dry salt, saltpetre and brown sugar or treacle, then matured for about two months. Cumberland ham is usually unsmoked, but you will occasionally find varieties smoked over juniper wood.

Jambon de Paris Also known as jambon blanc, this boneless French ham is cured in brine.

Kentucky ham This American ham is made from Hampshire pigs fattened on acorns, beans and clover. After dry-salting, it is smoked over corn cobs, hickory, applewood or sassafras and matured for 12 months. It has a dry texture and a delicate flavour.

Prosciutto cotto Italian cooked ham, cured in brine and usually flavoured with herbs and spices.

Suffolk ham This traditional English ham is not widely available today. Suffolk ham is brined, then pickled in a mixture of beer and sugar or honey, or molasses. It has a golden skin and sweet flavour.

Virginia ham An American ham made from razorback pigs fed on peanuts and peaches. Virginia ham is cured with dry salt, then basted with molasses and black pepper before being matured for about a year. It may be smoked or unsmoked. Smoked hams are usually hung over hickory or applewood. Virginia hams have a sweet flavour and moist texture.

Wiltshire ham Cured in brine and sweetened with brown sugar to give a mild flavour and moist meat.

York ham A traditional English ham cured with dry salt, then lightly smoked over oak. It is a pale ham with a light and delicate flavour.

TO USE If bought uncooked, traditionally cured hams should be soaked for 12 hours in cold water to remove some of the salt. Drain, then simmer in fresh water – allow 20 minutes per 450g (1lb), plus 20 minutes extra. Drain, skin, glaze and bake. Cooked ham should be thinly sliced and can be served hot, or cold as part of a selection of cold cuts, in salads, sandwiches or snipped into sauces and other dishes such as risotto, omelettes or baked eggs.

8 9 12 Ham eaten raw

Like hams for cooking, raw hams are taken from the upper hind leg of the pig and are cured and usually air-dried. They do not need to be cooked and are usually sliced very thinly and eaten raw. With a brownish-pink or red colour, most raw hams have a distinctively chewy texture. They are sold either sliced and pre-packed or cut off the bone just before sale. Varieties include:

Bayonne ham Originally from the Pyrenees region of France, but now produced all over the country, this distinctively flavoured ham is cured with dry salt, then smoked and air-dried.

Jamón Ibérico This greatest of the Spanish hams is made from Iberian pigs (a distinct breed, sometimes called pata negra) fattened on acorns. The method of production is similar to that used for jamón serrano, but the meat is flecked with fine traces of this breed's distinctively creamy fat. Production is strictly governed by EU laws specifying the place and method of feeding and curing, and the minimum ageing period is two years. This accounts for the very high prices.

Jamón serrano The name means 'mountain ham', in reference to the hilly regions where Spain's best-known hams are aged. The ham is cured with dry salt and air-dried for about six months, giving it a sweet flavour and pink-red colour. Jamón serrano comes from several different areas, and there are regional variants in curing and flavouring.

Mainz ham This German ham is cured in brine, then soaked in brandy and smoked for a long period. The flavour is unusual and very strong.

Prosciutto di San Daniele Another of the most highly regarded Italian hams, San Daniele comes from the Friuli region and is made from pigs fattened on acorns. The ham is dry-cured with salt and then air-dried. It has a sweet, more pronounced flavour than Parma ham and a slightly darker colour.

Prosciutto di Parma A classic Italian ham from the province of Parma in the Emilia-Romagna region, Parma ham is made from pigs fattened on whey. The ham is cured with dry salt, then air-dried for at least a year giving it a sweet and mild flavour. It is regarded as one of the best raw hams.

Westphalian ham The best known of the German hams, Westphalian ham is cured with dry salt and juniper berries, then smoked over ash or beech wood to give it a distinctive smoky flavour.

TO USE Eat raw hams as they are, as part of a selection of cold cuts or antipasti; use in salads or sandwiches; add to hot dishes such as pasta and risotto.

Sausages for cooking

1. Salsicce
2. Merguez
3. Lincolnshire
4. Cumberland
5. Salchicha
6. Bratwurst
7. Luganeghe
8. Cotechino
9. Saveloy
10. Chipolata
11. Bordeaux
12. Toulouse

Sausages for cooking

Links

This generic term is used to describe a traditional style of sausage-making. As the long tube of casing gets filled with meat, it is twisted at intervals to create a string of short-length sausages. Links may be made from pork, beef, veal, venison or a mixture of the meats, and they can be flavoured with a wide array of herbs, spices and aromatics.

TO USE Grill, pan-fry or braise with, for example, onions and wine.

❶ Salsicce

Salsicce is the Italian word for sausages, and there are numerous different local and regional recipes. Salsicce are usually made from pork and flavoured with garlic. In salsicce e fagioli the sausage is cooked with white beans flavoured with garlic and herbs.

TO USE Grill, pan-fry or poach.

❷ Merguez

This spicy red sausage from Algeria is made from lamb or beef, and sometimes from goat. Flavoured with sweet pepper and chilli, it is often served with couscous. Sun-dried merguez are sometimes used to flavour tagines.

TO USE Grill, or add to tagines.

❸ Lincolnshire sausage

A traditional thick English sausage. Lincolnshire sausage contains pork and is flavoured with sage and thyme. They are made from coarsely ground meat, which gives them a fairly open and chunky texture.

TO USE Grill, pan-fry or braise as for links.

❹ Cumberland sausage

These distinctive English sausage are traditionally sold coiled into a round, rather than twisted into links. They are made from coarsely ground pork and seasoned with black pepper, and have a chunky texture.

TO USE Grill or pan-fry.

❺ Salchicha

The salchicha is Spain's cooking sausage, and is usually made from chopped lean pork and pork fat, seasoned with salt and black pepper.

TO USE Grill or pan-fry.

❻ Bratwurst

A German sausage made from pork or veal flavoured with salt, pepper and mace. Bratwurst has a fine texture and a pale colour, similar to that of frankfurters (see page 190), and it may be smoked or unsmoked. Accompaniments vary according to region – for example, in Thuringer in central Germany bratwurst is served with hot mustard in a roll (brotchen), whereas in Frankonia, east of the Rhine, it is served with sauerkraut or potato salad but without mustard. In the city of Nuremberg it is eaten with sauerkraut or potato salad and horseradish.

TO USE Grill, pan-fry or braise in beer.

❼ Luganeghe

These long, thin sausages are made from pork and are popular in northern Italy. They are sold as strands, rather than being twisted into links, and are usually bought by the length rather than the weight. They may be grilled, boiled or cooked in riso e luganeghe, the classic risotto-like dish of the Veneto.

TO USE Grill or boil.

8 Cotechino

A large Italian sausage that is usually sold whole. Cotechino is made from a number of different pork cuts, including cooked skin (which gives it a rich texture) and flavoured with white wine and spices. Available both fresh and cured, it is usually boiled and served with beans, lentils, soft polenta or mashed potato, as part of *bollito misto* (mixed boiled meats) or served with *mostarda di frutta* (mustard fruit pickles). A close relative of cotechino is Zampone, which has the same type of stuffing but uses a boned pig's trotter as a casing.

TO USE Boil.

9 Saveloy

A large smoked English sausage with a distinctive bright red skin. Saveloys are usually made from pork and beef, and usually also contain lights (lungs). They have a fine texture, closer to that of a frankfurter than a traditional breakfast sausage. Saveloys are traditionally sold in fish and chip shops, sometimes battered.

TO USE Deep-fry, grill or pan-fry.

10 Chipolata

Often eaten at breakfast, these slender pork sausages have a fine texture and are usually sold in links.

TO USE Grill or pan-fry.

11 Bordeaux

Bordeaux sausage is a fairly small sausage, French in origin, it is highly seasoned with herbs, and often with garlic and wine, and has a rich, savoury flavour.

TO USE Grill, pan-fry or braise.

12 Toulouse sausage

A coarse pork sausage from south-west France, Toulouse sausage also contains smoked bacon and white wine. It is highly seasoned and flavoured with garlic and herbs, and is one of the key ingredients in the bean stew *cassoulet*. It can also be eaten on its own, with potato salad and mustard.

TO USE Grill, pan-fry, braise or add to casseroles (in particular, cassoulet).

Andouillettes

These French sausages are made from pork, chitterlings (pig's intestines) and tripe, and flavoured with pepper, wine and onions. The mixture is not finely chopped or minced, but has a quite chunky texture, and is stuffed inside chitterlings. Andouillettes have a lumpy appearance and a strong, earthy flavour; like all forms of chitterlings, they are an acquired taste. Some versions are smoked, although they are most often unsmoked. They are traditionally eaten with potatoes and a little Dijon mustard.

Andouilles are a larger version of andouillettes. They are usually eaten cold rather than hot.

TO USE Grill, pan-fry or braise in white wine.

Cooked sausages

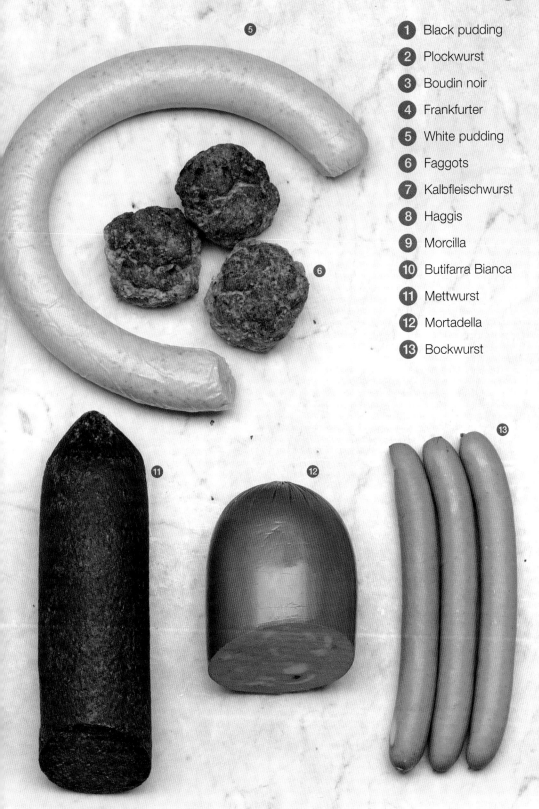

1. Black pudding
2. Plockwurst
3. Boudin noir
4. Frankfurter
5. White pudding
6. Faggots
7. Kalbfleischwurst
8. Haggis
9. Morcilla
10. Butifarra Bianca
11. Mettwurst
12. Mortadella
13. Bockwurst

Cooked sausages

❶❸❾ Blood sausage

There are numerous types of blood sausage, all specialities of their region or country of origin. They are usually made by cooking pig's or cattle blood with a filler such as fat, oatmeal or bread until it is thick enough to congeal when cooled. Common varieties include:

Black pudding The classic British blood sausage that is most often served as part of the traditional breakfast fry-up. Black pudding is made from blood, fat, cereal, onions and spices. Usually formed into a U-shaped sausage, black pudding is dark brown or black in colour and is cut into slices and fried.

Boudin noir The French blood sausage, boudin noir, is made from pig's blood, pork fat, cream, onions and spices. Sold already poached, it is traditionally grilled or sliced and pan-fried and served with potatoes and sometimes apple. There are a number of regional variations made with different proportions of ingredients and seasonings.

Morcilla There are many variations of morcilla, a blood sausage from Spain. The basic sausage is usually made from pig's blood, pork fat, onions and seasoning. Variations may include rice, breadcrumbs, pine nuts and almonds. It is usually highly seasoned and quite strongly flavoured. It is a classic addition to the white bean stew, *fabada*.

Blutwurst Germany's blood sausage also contains pork rind, bacon fat, allspice and marjoram. It is usually sliced and fried, but may also be eaten cold.

Butifarra negra Similar to Spanish morcilla, butifarra negra is ready-poached. It can be sliced and fried or grilled.

Zungenwurst A variation of German blutwurst, zungenwurst is made with the addition of pickled ox tongue.

❺❿⓭ White sausage

As with blood sausage, there are numerous types of white sausage, all a speciality of their country of origin. All have a pale, whitish colour, but their fillings can vary considerably.

White pudding Traditionally, white pudding contains offal such as brains, lights (lungs), tongue and heart and also ingredients such as pearl barley, suet, leeks, rusks, milk and seasoning. It is sold ready-cooked, and can be poached, grilled or fried to warm through.

Boudin blanc This French white sausage is made from pork and typically includes liver and heart as well as milk. It is usually grilled or fried. There is a similar Cajun boudin blanc, from the southern American state of Louisiana, which often uses rice instead of milk. It has a less delicate taste and texture and is usually simmered or braised.

Boudin rouge Not strictly a white pudding, this Cajun sausage is similar to boudin blanc, but with the addition of blood.

Bockwurst A delicately flavoured German sausage. Bockwurst is made from finely chopped pork and veal mixed with milk, eggs, parsley and chives. There is also a smoked version. Bockwurst is usually poached, although it may also be grilled.

Butifarra bianca A comparatively mild Spanish pork sausage seasoned with garlic and spices. Butifarra bianca is boiled and air-dried, and is usually eaten cold without further cooking.

Weisswurst A traditional Bavarian sausage made from finely minced veal and bacon, weisswurst is usually flavoured with spices and parsley. It is poached and eaten without the skin, with a sweet mustard.

❹ Frankfurter

A classic, lightly smoked German sausage made from very finely minced pork and salted bacon fat, frankfurters are smooth and slim, with a uniform texture and pinkish-beige colour. They are the standard sausage used to make hot dogs. American-style frankfurters are usually made from a mixture of pork and beef, but sometimes (for kosher hot dogs) from beef only. Frankfurters are usually sold in vacuum packs, in jars or canned.

TO USE Poach to warm through.

❷ Plockwurst

This dry-cured German sausage is also known as cervelat. It is made from beef and pork, and has a fairly high fat content; the fat may be a combination of small flecks and larger chunks, or just evenly distributed flecks. Plockwurst is pinkish-brown in colour. Mildly flavoured and with a fairly soft texture, it is a popular choice for sandwiches made with dense, chewy, pumpernickel or rye breads. Pfeffer plockwurst is a square sausage coated with coarsely ground black pepper.

TO USE Eat cold as a spread; slice or pan-fry.

⑦ Kalbfleischwurst

Kalbfleisch means veal in German, but this large sausage may contain not just veal but beef and cured pork (and turkey in some cases). The meats are ground to a fine texture and sometimes have pistachio nuts mixed in, as in the Italian mortadella. Kalbfleischwurst has a mild flavour and is usually sold thinly sliced for serving as part of a selection of cold meats.

TO USE Eat cold as a spread; slice or pan-fry.

⑧ Haggis

This large, rounded Scottish sausage is made from diced sheep's or venison offal, which includes liver, heart and lights (lungs). Oatmeal, onions, suet and spices are also added, and the mixture is packed into a sheep's stomach or plastic wrapping. It is traditionally eaten at celebrations for Burns' night (25 January), served with 'bashed neeps and tatties' (mashed swede and potatoes). Cooked haggis just needs reheating. It is also frequently sold fresh.

TO USE Boil fresh haggis; pre-cooked haggis can often be wrapped in foil and baked (check the instructions on the packaging).

⑥ Faggots

A type of sausage traditionally enjoyed in the north of England and Wales. Faggots are small balls made from finely chopped pork offal, onion, breadcrumbs and seasoning. After shaping they may be wrapped in caul (the thin, lacy membrane of fat from the lower portion of the intestine). Faggots are sold cooked and ready for reheating.

TO USE Pan-fry, poach or bake and serve with gravy.

⑪ Mettwurst

Made from finely ground pork and beef, this German smoked sausage has a smooth, quite soft texture and a strong flavour. Similar sausages include the holsteiner, which has a firmer texture, and teewurst, made from a mixture of pork and bacon.

TO USE Eat cold as a spread; slice or pan-fry.

⑫ Mortadella

A large Italian sausage traditionally from Bologna, mortadella is made from finely minced pork, ham and pork fat seasoned with white pepper and garlic, and is sometimes studded with pale green pistachio nuts. It has a smooth texture and a pale pink colour flecked with white fat, and is sold ready-cooked. Though usually eaten cold, it can also be heated for serving in pasta sauces.

TO USE Thinly slice and serve as antipasti as part of a plate of mixed cold cuts.

Crépinette

This French sausage is made from finely chopped pork and pork offal, pressed into a flattened sausage shape and wrapped in caul (the thin, lacy membrane of fat from the lower portion of the intestine). Crépinette is sometimes also made from other minced meats, including lamb, veal or poultry. It is sold cooked, ready for reheating – usually by sautéing in butter.

TO USE Pan-fry.

Cured sausages and other meat

1. Biltong
2. Salami
3. Bresaola
4. Katenrauchwurst
5. Pepperoni
6. Pastrami
7. Fuet
8. Kabanos
9. Salf beef
10. Salchichón
11. Chorizo
12. Coppa crudo
13. Knoblauchwurst
14. Corned beef

Cured sausages and other meat

➊ Biltong

A speciality of South Africa, biltong is made from strips of dried meat – most often beef or game – and it can last for years. Biltong was developed by Dutch settlers as a method of preserving meat in the days before fridges and freezers. It is usually salted and spiced or smoked. Its appearance is rather like dark brown leather, but while it is very hard and chewy, it has a good flavour. Usually eaten as a snack, it can also be sliced thinly or grated and added to salads, creamy spreads and breads or muffins.

TO USE Eat raw as a snack, or slice thinly or grate.

➋ Salami

Salami is the Italian term for salt cured sausages, but there are numerous different types from countries throughout Europe, all with their own distinctive tastes and textures. They are usually made from a mixture of lean meat and a relatively high proportion of fat, together with spices, aromatics and other flavourings. They are most commonly made with pork, although beef and veal are also used. Salami may be air-dried, smoked or pickled to produce a firm sausage for slicing. Varieties include:

Italian There are countless different varieties of Italian salami – mostly regional specialities – which vary in flavour from quite mild to highly spiced with a definite peppery bite. Some of these include: large salame fiorentino; large, coarsely textured salame di Cremona; long, thin, peppery salame milanese; salame genovese, made from a mixture of pork and veal; large, square-shaped salame romano, studded with peppercorns; garlicky salame toscano; and salame dei cacciatori, made from wild boar. Within each

variety there are numerous variations, each one the product of individual or local practice.

Danish Containing quite a large proportion of fat, this bright red salami speckled with white is made from a mixture of pork, beef, veal and pork fat. It has a mildly smoky flavour and a fine, soft texture.

Hungarian These sausages are typically flavoured with paprika and lightly smoked.

TO USE Slice thinly and serve as an hors d'oeuvre; part of a plate of mixed cold cuts; in sandwiches and salads; as a snack on bread; snipped over pizza.

➌ Bresaola

An Italian speciality made from salted beef that is then air-dried and matured for several months. Bresaola has a rich dark red colour, a similar texture to prosciutto (page 182), and a sweet, musty aroma. Made in Valtellina in Lombardy, it is protected with a PGI (protected geographical indication) and similar products sold outside of Valtellina will be labelled as beef prosciutto rather than bresaola.

TO USE Slice thinly and marinate in olive oil, lemon juice and black pepper, and serve as antipasti.

Culatello

This most highly regarded (and expensive) cured meat of Parma is produced in the Zibello area in particular. This sausage is made from the 'fillet' of prosciutto, which is seasoned and salted, then stuffed into a pig's bladder and tied to produce a pear-shaped piece weighing between 3kg (6½lb) and 5kg (11lb). It is then air-dried for 8–12 months. When sliced, it is similar in appearance to prosciutto (see page 182), with – many people would say – an even finer flavour.

TO USE Slice thinly and serve raw as antipasti, or as part of a plate of mixed cold cuts.

➍ Katenrauchwurst

This chunky German sausage is made from coarsely chopped pork wrapped in a casing. It undergoes a lengthy smoking, which gives it a firm texture, dark colour and a fairly strong flavour that goes well with rye bread.

TO USE Slice thinly and serve raw as an hors d'oeuvre; as part of a plate of mixed cold cuts; as a snack on bread.

➎ Pepperoni

A long, narrow cured sausage from Italy, pepperoni is made from a mixture of coarsely chopped pork and beef, flavoured with spices and red pepper. It has a peppery bite, is chewy in texture and has a red-brown colour that deepens with cooking.

TO USE Thinly slice and scatter over pizza before baking; eat uncooked as a snack.

⑥ Pastrami

Popular in the US, this spiced beef is made from brisket that has been cured with dry salt and spices, then smoked. It is classically served as a sandwich using rye bread and is a favourite in Jewish delis. The best pastrami has a lining of fat along one side, which adds succulence.

TO USE Slice thinly and serve cold or warm. Usually eaten in a sandwich with mustard but can also be served in slices with potatoes and pickles.

⑦ Fuet

A long and narrow cured sausage from Catalonia in Spain, fuet may be sold as a long sausage or bent into a long U-shape. It is made from pork meat stuffed inside a natural casing and has a firm texture. Inside the flesh is dark red, marbled with white fat. Fuet made in the Osona region of Catalonia is known as fuet de Vic, after the capital of Osona.

TO USE Slice thinly and serve raw as an hors d'oeuvre; as part of a plate of mixed cold cuts; as a snack on bread.

⑧ Kabanos

A long, narrow sausage from Poland, kabanos has a firm texture and may be eaten raw or cooked. Kabanos tends to be strongly spiced and is usually smoked.

TO USE Eat as a snack; pan-fry or braise.

⑨ Salt beef

Made from brined brisket (see page 151) flavoured with spices and seasoning, salt beef may be raw or cooked. The cooked version is a favourite of the US deli counter and it is typically served on rye bread with mustard.

TO USE Boil raw salt beef and serve hot. For cold, cooked salt beef, slice thinly and use in salads and sandwiches or as part of a selection of cold cuts.

⑪ Salchichón

A cured smoked sausage from Spain, salchichón is made from pork flavoured with spices. It has dark red flesh speckled with white fat and a firm texture similar to a hard salami. It often includes peppercorns.

TO USE Slice thinly and serve as an hors d'oeuvre; as a snack on bread.

⑫ Chorizo

This popular Spanish sausage is made from minced pork and pimiento, giving it a distinctive red colour. It has a relatively coarse texture, sometimes with large chunks of fat embedded in the meat, and a hot, spicy flavour. There are numerous variations, available both raw and cooked, smoked and unsmoked. A version is also eaten in Mexico. Although usually made with pork, it may contain other meats such as goat. In Portugal a comparable sausage is called chouriço, and has as many variants as its more famous Spanish cousin.

TO USE Pan-fry, grill or add to dishes such as paella, stews and casseroles, particularly those that contain beans.

⑩ Coppa crudo

A salted, dried sausage from Italy, coppa crudo is made from the neck or shoulder of pork packed into a natural casing. It has a slightly lumpy, irregular triangular shape with a firm texture, and the flesh inside is dark red with streaks of white fat. Coppa crudo is similar in taste and texture to prosciutto (see page 182).

TO USE Slice thinly and serve raw as antipasti, an hors d'oeuvre; as part of a plate of mixed cold cuts or in sandwiches.

⑪ Knoblauchwurst

This hot-dog style of sausage from Germany is usually made from beef and is always well flavoured with garlic (*Knoblauch* is the German word for garlic).

TO USE Poach or grill.

⑭ Corned beef

Made from salted compressed beef, corned beef gains its name from the 'corns' of salt used during its processing. With a pinkish-brown colour flecked with white fat, it has a fairly tender texture. Corned beef is sold canned. (In the US, the term 'corned beef' refers to salt beef or pickled beef.)

TO USE Slice and use cold in sandwiches or salads; chop and use in recipes such as corned beef hash; coat in batter and fry to make fritters.

Fruit

Citrus fruits

Valencia orange

The Valencia variety of orange is important around the world because of its abundant crop. Valencia oranges have thin, smooth skins, sweet–sharp, juicy, pale-coloured flesh, and few or no pips. Excellent for juicing, they may also be eaten as a dessert fruit: peeled and eaten raw, or sliced into fruit salads. The flesh and grated zest can be used in both sweet and savoury recipes, such as the classic French dish duck à l'orange, crêpes Suzette, sorbets and cakes. The zest can also be pared off in strips and used whole as a flavouring or cut into thin shreds as a decoration; it can also be caramelised in a sugar syrup.

TO USE Preparation, see page 204. For juicing; raw as a dessert fruit or snack; in salads or sorbets; the flesh, juice and grated zest for flavouring sweet and savoury dishes; the julienned zest (cut into matchstick strips) for decorating desserts or for caramelising.

Navel orange

One of the most popular of the sweet oranges, navel oranges are favoured for their sweet, intense flavour, lack of pips and thick, easy-to-peel skins. They are distinctive in appearance, with a slight bulge at the stem end, embedded into which is a 'baby fruit' (the navel), which is usually discarded along with the peel (but can sometimes be eaten, at least in part). Navels make a good dessert fruit, peeled and eaten raw, or used in both sweet and savoury dishes.

TO USE Preparation, see page 204. For juicing; raw as a dessert fruit or snack; in salads or sorbets; the flesh, juice and grated zest for flavouring sweet and savoury dishes.

Blonde orange

These sweet, pale-skinned oranges include the commonly found Jaffa (or Shamouti) orange, and the less common Salustiana. The fruits are of a good size with a slightly oval shape and a thick, easy-to-peel skin; the flesh inside is sweet and juicy and contains few or no pips. They are available in winter.

TO USE Preparation, see page 204. For juicing; raw as a dessert fruit or snack; in salads or sorbets; the flesh, juice and grated zest for flavouring sweet and savoury dishes.

Blood orange

Grown mostly in the Mediterranean, blood oranges are so named for the dramatic colour of their flesh. The skin is usually flushed a reddish-orange, and the flesh can vary (sometimes within a single fruit) from reddish-gold to an intense ruby red. Blood oranges have an intense flavour, making them a good dessert orange or juicer, and their zest can be used in both sweet and savoury dishes. Blood oranges are an essential ingredient of sauce maltaise, an orange-flavoured mayonnaise. Available in January and February.

TO USE Preparation, see page 204. For juicing; raw as a dessert fruit or snack; in salads or sorbets; the flesh, juice and grated zest for flavouring sweet and savoury dishes.

Seville orange

Available only for a short season in January and February, this bitter orange is grown in Spain, with most of the crop being exported to the UK for making marmalade. Seville oranges are favoured not only for their bitter flavour but for their aromatic zest, which is very different in fragrance and taste to that of sweet oranges. They are unsuitable for eating raw, but may be used to make jams and jellies. The fruit is sometimes crystallised, and the white blossom distilled to make orange flower water. The oil from the skin is used commercially to flavour liqueurs such as Cointreau and Grand Marnier.

TO USE For making marmalade: pare and slice the zest, squeeze the flesh and retain the pith.

Lemon

Lemons may be the single most versatile and useful foodstuff on earth, lending their inimitable lift to almost any dish. The skin may be smooth or knobbly, depending on the variety. The juice is sharp and vitamin-C-rich. The outer part of the rind, the zest, is packed (like all citrus fruits) with tiny cells of aromatic volatile oil; it can be grated and used in savoury dishes, desserts and baking. Lemon juice is a classic accompaniment for seafood. It can be brushed on to the cut surfaces of fruit such as avocados that oxidise when exposed to the air, or to acidulate water to preserve the whiteness of vegetables such as celeriac during cooking. Classic lemon dishes include tart au citron (lemon tart), lemon meringue pie and lemon sorbet.

Fresh lemon leaves can be used like bay leaves to impart their scented, zesty fragrance to foods, or threaded on to skewers with meat, fish or vegetables.

TO USE Finely grate the zest; halve and squeeze the juice, or slice or wedge the unpeeled fruit. The grated zest and juice to flavour savouries, desserts, baking and preserves; in marinades, dressings, mayonnaise and sauces; in sorbets; the juice as a souring agent, and to halt oxidisation; slices and wedges as a garnish. (see also bottled fruits, page 237)

Citron

Resembling a very large, knobbly lemon, these fruits have a thick, tough rind; the flesh is not very juicy with either a sour or sweet, slightly lemony flavour. The rind has a distinctive aroma, and it is for this that the fruit is used – almost exclusively for the manufacture of candied peel. The flesh may be used to make marmalade, and in Corsica it is used to make the liqueur cedratine.

A variety of citron, known as *etrog* (the Hebrew word for citron), is in great demand in the Jewish community around the festival of Sukkot, in which the fruit represents one of the four species of plant in the rabbinic tradition.

TO USE For making marmalade: pare and slice the zest, squeeze the flesh and retain the pith.

Lime

Smaller and rounder than lemons, limes are bright green tropical fruit. They have thin, smooth skins and distinctively flavoured, sour, astringent juice. There are several varieties, including the key lime, Tahitian or Persian lime (known as Bearrs lime in the US), and sweet lime, which has a less astringent flavour. Limes can generally be used in the same ways as lemons, although their juice is somewhat more tart. They are widely used in the cuisines of South-east Asia, India, Mexico, South America and the Caribbean. Lime juice is squeezed over salsas or used to add a sour edge to Thai green curries and stir-fries. It is used in marinades for fish, meat and poultry, or combined with sugar and water as a drink. Lime is an essential ingredient in dishes such as key lime pie, South American or Mexican ceviche, and the Brazilian cocktail caipirinha.

TO USE Finely grate the zest; halve and squeeze the juice, or slice or wedge the unpeeled fruit. The grated zest and juice to flavour savouries, desserts, baking and preserves; in marinades, dressings, mayonnaise and sauces; the juice as a souring agent; the slices as a garnish or with drinks; the wedges to serve with poultry and seafood.
(see also bottled fruits, page 237)

Grapefruit

One of the larger citrus fruits, grapefruits generally have bright yellow skin. The flesh can vary in colour from pale yellow through pinkish blushes to ruby red. The paler-fleshed fruits usually have a much more bitter–sour flavour, whereas the rosier-hued varieties tend to be sweeter. The sweetest of all is the bright green-skinned Sweetie.

TO USE Preparation, see page 204. For juicing; the segments added to savoury dishes and salads; in marmalade. To serve as a light first course or breakfast dish: halve the fruit crossways, then slice between the membranes of each segment with a curved serrated knife to loosen the flesh. Serve with a teaspoon and sugar for sprinkling.

Clementine

The clementine originated in Algeria at the beginning of the 20th century. It is the smallest of the tangerine family, with thin, bright orange peel. Clementines have a distinctive sweet–sharp, intensely flavoured aromatic flesh with no pips, but they are slightly more difficult to peel than the other, looser-skinned tangerines. Coming into season in autumn, they make a popular Christmas fruit and are at their best when eaten raw, peeled and divided into segments. Their small size makes them good for peeling and bottling in syrup or alcohol. They can also be added to a mixed fruit marmalade.

TO USE Peel. Raw as a dessert fruit or snack; in salads or sorbets; for bottling; in a mixed-fruit marmalade. (see also crystallised fruit, page 237, bottled fruits, page 237)

Satsuma

Smaller and slightly flatter in shape oranges, satsumas are large tangerines that were developed in Japan in the 16th century and have achieved worldwide popularity for several reasons. Their loose, almost 'baggy' skin makes them easy to peel. They have a sweet, slightly tart flavour that is less acidic than many other tangerines, and they contain few pips. They make a good snack fruit, particularly for children, who favour their easy-peeling skin and their sweet flesh.

TO USE Peel. Raw as a dessert fruit or snack; in salads or sorbets.

Mandarins and tangerines

The names 'mandarin' and 'tangerine' do not designate a specific variety of fruit, but are used as a generic term for the whole family of small, slightly flat, loose-skinned orange citrus fruits with fibrous strands of pith under the skin. Many fruits described as tangerines and mandarins are actually hybrids of mandarins and other types of citrus fruits.

Usually light in colour and small with a mild level of acidity and a good sweet flavour, they are best eaten raw as a dessert fruit. Because of their delicate flavour they are not well suited to cooking.

Ortanique

Also known as honey tangerine for its sweet flavour, the ortanique is a mandarin–orange hybrid. It is sometimes known as a tangor. Ortaniques were discovered in Jamaica early in the 20th century and are believed to be a chance cross (a random cross-fertilisation rather than a deliberate cultivar). They have juicy flesh with a distinctive acid–sweet flavour and few or no pips. The skin is mustard-yellow to orange in colour, marked with brown specks, and is harder than most mandarins, although easy to peel. Ortaniques are widely grown in Jamaica, and although they are also grown in the Mediterranean, these specimens tend to have thicker skins, and sometimes pips. Ortaniques can be used in the same way as sweet oranges.

TO USE Preparation, see page 204. For juicing; raw as a dessert fruit or snack; in salads or sorbets; the flesh and grated zest for flavouring sweet and savoury dishes.

Minneola

A mandarin–grapefruit hybrid, and thus a member of the tangelo family. Bright orange minneolas are about the size of an orange but with a distinctive bulge at the stalk end. They have a fairly thick skin and are easy to peel, revealing a seedless fruit with an intense, fairly sharp flavour and juicy flesh. Minneolas are eaten as a dessert fruit – peeled and eaten raw – and should be treated in the same way as sweet oranges.

TO USE For juicing; raw as a dessert fruit or snack; the flesh and grated zest for flavouring sweet and savoury dishes.

Ugli fruit

Another mandarin–grapefruit hybrid, like the minneola. The large ugli fruit can grow to more than 15cm (6in) in diameter and bears little resemblance to either of its parent fruits. It has a thick, baggy, yellowish-green rind, which is easy to peel away from the juicy segmented fruit inside. The flesh has a sweet, scented, honey flavour. Ugli fruits are usually eaten as a dessert fruit, peeled and divided into segments, or cut in half and served like a grapefruit.

TO USE Preparation, see page 204. For juicing; raw as a dessert fruit; halved and segmented as for grapefruit.

Pomelo

Also known as pummelo and shaddock, the pomelo is the largest of the citrus fruits, sometimes growing up to 30.5cm (12in) in diameter. The thick, dimpled, yellowish or greenish rind can be peeled away easily to reveal the pale or pinkish segments of flesh inside. Often quite dry in texture, the fruit has an intriguing sweet–sharp flavour. Thought to be a native of Malaysia and Indonesia, the pomelo is usually eaten raw as a fruit, and may also be used in Asian-style salads. In parts of China, the peel is parboiled and cooked as a vegetable.

TO USE Preparation, see page 204. As a dessert fruit; the segments used in salads.

Kumquat

The small, oval kumquat, which is rarely more than 3cm (1¼in) in diameter, resembles a tiny orange. However, it has a different structure from citrus fruit and belongs to its own botanical genus: *Fortunella*. The kumquat's thin, soft rind is not pithy like that of other citrus fruits and is edible, so the whole fruit can be eaten: flesh and rind together. The taste is quite bitter, though some varieties are sweeter than others. The raw fruit may be eaten whole or sliced and added to fruit salads. It is also used as a garnish, candied, added to marmalades, or sliced into sweet tarts.

Kumquat hybrids include the limequat and cintrangequat.

TO USE Rinse and slice, halve or leave whole. As a dessert fruit; in salads; as a garnish; candied; in marmalades.
(see also crystallised fruit, page 237, bottled fruits, page 237)

Tangelo

Bright orange tangelos are mandarin–grapefruit hybrids, which may have occurred accidentally in nature but were first created scientifically in the late 19th century. They have the same bulbous stalk end as minneolas and can range from the size of an orange to as large as a grapefruit. All have a loose, easy-to-peel skin and exceptionally juicy flesh with an intensely tart flavour. Tangelos are usually eaten as a dessert fruit: peeled and eaten raw.

Orlando tangelos are an early-maturing, slightly larger variety, with a sweet flavour.

TO USE Peel. As a dessert fruit.

Zesting citrus fruits

1 For finely grated zest, wash and thoroughly dry the fruit. Use a fine grater or zester to scrape over the surface of the fruit so that just the zest is removed and none of the white pith. Continue until you have removed as much as you need.

2 For thin shreds, wash and dry the fruit. Using a vegetable peeler, cut away the zest (the coloured outer layer of skin), leaving the bitter white pith attached to the fruit. Continue until you have removed as much zest as you need. Stack the slices of zest on a chopping board and shred or dice as required, using a sharp knife.

Segmenting citrus fruits

1 Using a sharp knife, cut off a slice at both ends of the fruit, then cut off the peel, just inside the white pith.

2 Hold the fruit over a bowl to catch the juice and cut between the segments just inside the membrane to release the flesh. Continue until all the segments are removed. Squeeze the juice from the membrane into the bowl.

More about citrus fruits

The citrus family is one of the more diverse, varying greatly in size, flavour profile and culinary uses. Family members are native to an area stretching from East Asia to Australia, but their common feature is their scented, oily, bitter skin lined with white pith and the juicy, segmented flesh inside. Within each segment, the flesh is divided up into tiny sacs (vesicles) filled with juice.

No one knows when citrus fruits were first cultivated, but they are thought to have grown for more than 20 million years. References appear in ancient texts dating back to 800BC. The citron was the first to arrive in Europe, providing the family with its generic title *Citrus*. Oranges and lemons followed some time in the 1st century AD, and by the 12th century, some of the fruits were being widely cultivated in the Arab world. After Columbus introduced citrus fruits to the New World, they spread quickly and are now central to the fruit industry in Florida and California.

More about oranges

There are many varieties of orange, which divide into two main species: sweet and bitter. Sweet oranges can be juiced or peeled and eaten as they are; bitter oranges are cooked, mostly in marmalade.

Seville (see page 199) is the main variety of bitter orange but other sweet varieties include:

Sugar oranges An unusual variety, found mainly in Brazil, North America and Italy. They are almost devoid of acid, giving them an insipid flavour.
Pera oranges An important crop in Brazil and very good for juicing.

Citrus hybrids

There are many crosses between different varieties of citrus fruits, each of which produces a unique fruit. The most common fruits have been described individually on pages 201–203; other hybrids include:

Temple orange A mandarin–orange hybrid that is easy to peel and has aromatic flesh with a tart, tangy and sweet flavour.
King orange A mandarin–orange hybrid that is dark orange and easy to peel, with a sweet flavour.
Bergamot orange Thought to be a bitter orange–Palestinian sweet lime hybrid, the bergamot orange has now been assigned its own species. The flesh is very bitter, but the rind is used to make bergamot oil, the flavouring used in Earl Grey tea.
Calamondin orange A miniature fruit, grown as a decorative houseplant, the Calamondin orange is thought to be a mandarin–kumquat hybrid.

How to buy and store citrus fruits

As a general rule choose citrus fruits that feel heavy for their size, as this indicates they contain plenty of juice. If the leaves are still attached, look for those that are green and fresh-looking. Avoid fruits with damaged skins. If buying pre-packed fruits, check for soft spots or mould, as these will quickly taint other fruits in the pack. Store at room temperature.

When buying satsumas or tangerines, don't worry if the skins feel 'baggy'. This isn't necessarily a sign of age or poor quality, but a characteristic of the variety. Loose-skinned fruits are a good choice for children because they are easier to peel than tighter-skinned varieties such as clementines.

When buying limes, look for ones with a tinge of yellow, and which give a little when squeezed.

Oranges, lemons and limes are frequently sold with a waxed skin, to prolong the life of the fruit by preventing it from drying out so quickly. If you want to use the rind either for flavouring or garnishing, it's best to buy unwaxed fruits.

Citrus products

As well as the fresh fruits, there are a number of citrus products that are widely available.

Candied peel Made by simmering the peel in sugar syrup until tender. You can find chopped mixed peel in most supermarkets. In specialist shops and delicatessens you can find larger slices of peel – generally orange, lemon and citron – which often have a better flavour than the chopped variety. Both are used in cakes, desserts and mincemeat. (see also page 237)
Canned citrus fruits Mandarin and grapefruit segments canned in juice make a good storecupboard standby and can be served on their own, or used in desserts such as trifle.
Marmalade Orange marmalade is probably the best-known variety, but you will find marmalades made from most citrus fruits, including grapefruit and lime, as well as blends of citrus fruits.
Fruit curds Lemon and orange curds are widely available and are spread on toast, scones and other baked goods in place of jam, or stirred into crème fraîche or yogurt to serve with desserts. You may also find grapefruit and lime curd.
Lemon and lime juice The flavour of these ready-squeezed juices tends to be inferior to that of freshly squeezed fruits, and they often contain preservatives.

Apples

Braeburn

This popular apple was first cultivated in New Zealand in the 1950s, after being discovered growing in an orchard there. Braeburn is now a widely available dessert apple with a green, red-flushed, vertically streaked skin, and white, crisp, juicy flesh that has a fresh and balanced flavour – neither too sweet or too sharp. Thought to be a cross between Lady Hamilton and Granny Smith, it has good keeping properties and can be eaten both raw and cooked. It is well suited to baking in dishes such as crumbles, cobblers, cakes and pies.

TO USE Preparation, see page 209. For juicing; raw as a dessert fruit or snack; in salads; cooked in desserts and cakes.

Cox's Orange Pippin

This is an exceptionally well-flavoured dessert apple that is widely available, Cox's is a small–medium fruit with a greenish skin flushed with red, usually with a brown russeted area around the stalk. It has crisp, white, juicy flesh with an intense sweet–sharp flavour. Cox's is the best of the Pippin family (defined since the 16th century as a hard, late-ripening and long-keeping apple with an acid flavour).

Other pippins include the Ribston Pippin, from which the Cox's Orange Pippin was developed, and the Sturmer Pippin.

TO USE Preparation, see page 209. For juicing; raw as a dessert fruit or snack; in salads; cooked in desserts and cakes, and savouries.

Golden Delicious

The ubiquitous supermarket dessert apple, due to its heavy cropping and good keeping properties, this pale yellow, slightly elongated and tapering fruit originated in the US at the turn of the 20th century. The cream-coloured flesh has a crisp, juicy texture and mild flavour. When grown in cooler climates, which allows acidity to develop, the apple can be of good quality, but frequently, when grown in warmer areas, the flesh is bland and 'flabby' and makes for a disappointing apple. On cooking, the flesh retains its shape, making it a good choice for tarts or other dishes where the look of the fruit is important.

TO USE Preparation, see page 209. For juicing; raw as a dessert fruit or snack; in salads; cooked in pastries.

Pink Lady

The Pink Lady has, as the name suggests, a distinctive pink blush to its skin. It is one of the best known of the modern apples, with a sweet and mild flavour. An Australian cross between Lady Williams and Golden Delicious, it is produced with careful control over quality in both flavour and colour, and any apples not achieving the specified standard are sold as Cripps Pink rather than Pink Lady. The apple is widely grown in both northern and southern hemispheres but needs a long, hot growing season to ripen fully. It has a long shelf life.

TO USE Preparation, see page 209. For juicing; raw as a dessert fruit or snack; in salads.

Granny Smith

This fairly large dessert apple is distinctive for its bright green skin, which turns a yellowish-green as it ripens. Usually sold underripe, it has a bright white, crunchy flesh and a particularly sharp flavour. It was discovered in the 1860s in Australia by Mrs Mary Smith (the original 'granny Smith') and enjoyed a huge popularity until more recently, when bi-coloured, sweeter apples have climbed into public favour. Granny Smiths can be eaten raw, but due to their sharp flavour, and because they retain their shape, they are also well-suited to cooking. Many French chefs regard them as the perfect apple for making tarte tatin.

TO USE Preparation, see page 209. For juicing; raw as a dessert fruit or snack; in salads; cooked in desserts and savouries.

Gala

A widely grown and popular supermarket dessert apple, the Gala originated in New Zealand and is a cross between Kidd's Orange Red and Golden Delicious. It has a yellow skin, blushed all over with red-orange, which intensifies with age, indicating that a paler apple is new season, and a darker apple has either been left to mature on the tree, or has been maturing in cold storage for some time. The flesh is faintly yellow, sweet and juicy, making it a good eating apple.

Royal Gala are similar, but have an entirely red skin.

TO USE Preparation, see page 209. For juicing; raw as a dessert fruit or snack; in salads.

Fuji

Fuji apples were first bred in the 1940s in Japan, and are a cross between Red Delicious and the lesser-known Ralls Genet. The skin has flecks, streaks or a broad covering of pink (sometimes delicate and sometimes deep) on a base of pale yellow. Their flesh is sweet, crisp and juicy, with less acidity than some other varieties, and they are usually fairly large. The Fuji's sweetness has helped it attain wide popularity, and the variety is now extensively grown not only in Japan but in the US and China. Although usually eaten raw, Fuji can be used in baked dishes such as apple tarts.

TO USE Preparation, see page 209. Raw as a dessert fruit or snack; in salads; cooked in desserts.

Egremont Russet

The most widely available of all russet apples, the medium-sized Egremont dates from the Victorian era. It has a rough, porous, dull-golden skin that allows moisture in the fruit to evaporate as the apple grows, giving the flesh a dense, slightly dry texture that is moist rather than juicy. It has a sweet, distinctively nutty flavour, balanced with a good degree of sharpness. While other apples available in supermarkets have shiny skins, the Egremont Russet's skin feels more like very fine sandpaper. It tastes much better than it feels.

TO USE Preparation, see page 209. Raw as a dessert fruit or snack; in salads; cooked in desserts.

Bramley's Seedling

The best known of the cooking apples. Bramley's Seedling is a large, bright-green apple with a flattish shape and an almost waxy skin. The flesh is coarse and white with a very sour but intense flavour, and when cooked it breaks down to a mushy pulp. Bramleys are unsuitable for eating raw but are excellent for cooking when a softer texture is required. Standard approaches include stuffing them with butter, brown sugar and dried fruit and baking whole, and using in desserts such as crumbles and pies. Bramleys always need to be sweetened. And because they do not hold their shape, they are unsuitable for French-style apple tarts.

TO USE Preparation, see page 209. Cooked in desserts.

More about apples

The large, sweet apples we know today are a far cry from their ancient ancestors, which were small and sour, rather like the wild crab apple. Originating in central Asia and grown for millennia, they can be found in references dating back to antiquity, and they have been revered through the centuries as having various qualities: in the Bible the apple is referred to as the fruit of knowledge and the Romans believed they were an aphrodisiac.

Today apples are one of the most commonly enjoyed fruits and can be divided into two categories: dessert and cooking. Dessert apples have sweet flesh, which makes them suitable for eating raw. Cooking apples have a much sharper, sourer flavour that is better suited to cooking with added sugar. Dessert apples can also be cooked, and their firmer flesh tends to retain its shape when cooked, unlike cooking apples, which generally turn to pulp.

How to buy and store apples

Different apples come into season at different times of the year, with the early cropping varieties becoming available from late summer and early autumn. However, varieties with good keeping properties are available from cold storage all year round. Choose unblemished apples with no bruises, broken skin or holes from insects or grubs. They should be firm, not wrinkled or soft. A fragrant smell is a good indicator, although colour has little to do with flavour and more to do with variety. Note, however, that an apple should have the appropriate colour for its variety.

For short-term storage, keep apples at room temperature or in the fridge. For longer-term storage of home-grown fruit, use only apples in perfect condition. Wrap in newspaper and store in a single layer in wooden trays in a cool, dry, dark place.

How to prepare apples

Raw apples are usually eaten whole or can be quartered and cored or sliced. For cooking, apples are often better peeled using a vegetable peeler or a small, sharp knife. Once cut, the exposed flesh quickly starts to oxidise and turn brown. If preparing ahead, or if the apple is to be exposed to the air, brush with lemon juice or drop into acidulated water – made with 1 tbsp lemon juice and 1 litre (1¾ pints) cold water – to prevent the flesh discolouring.

Culinary uses for apples

A natural partner for cheese, raw dessert apples are also a good addition to savoury salads as well as fruity salads. They are also good for cooking; because they retain their shape when cooked, they are particularly well suited to dishes where the apples are exposed to view such as the classic French tarte aux pommes or the upside-down tart, tarte tatin. Both dessert and cooking apples are used in pies, crumbles, cobblers and cakes, and are a classic filling for the Austrian strudel – frequently paired with the complementary flavours of cinnamon and raisins. They can be peeled, sliced and stewed in a little water with sugar to taste, or baked whole, stuffed with sugar, butter and dried fruit.

The sharp apple taste complements many other fruits, such as blackberries, and helps cut the richness of fatty meats such as pork, duck and goose.

Apples are commonly used in preserves such as chutneys, and their high pectin content aids setting for sweet jams and jellies. They can also be cored, sliced into rings, brushed with lemon juice and then dried to preserve them.

Other varieties include

There are more than 7,000 named varieties of apple, but only a handful of these are available in most shops and supermarkets. However, many can be found at farmer's markets when they are in season. Some of the more popular varieties include:

Blenheim orange Mainly a cooking apple, this old English variety is large and slightly flat in shape with a dull red-yellow skin. It has a well-flavoured, acidic flesh that cooks to a pulp, making it ideal for apple charlotte and crumbles.

Cider apples Distinct from eating and cooking apples, cider apples are inedibly sour and bitter.

Orleans Reinette An 18th-century variety of the old French Reinette, this highly regarded apple has an intensely sweet, aromatic flesh and an orange-speckled russet skin with a slightly rough texture.

Spartan Originally from Canada, Spartan is a cross between McIntosh and Newton's Pippin and has a highly fragrant aroma and flavour, and a juicy texture.

Worcester Pearmain Available in early autumn, this green and red apple has a good tart flavour and crisp flesh. It is the best-known of the group of pearmain apples, whose name has been recorded as far back as 1204. Worcester Pearmain does not keep well and is best eaten soon after picking.

(see also dried apples, page 236)

Pears

Conference

This extremely popular variety is one of the most widely grown of the commercial pears. Conference is an elegantly shaped variety, long and green and marked with dark golden russeting. It's equally good for eating and cooking, with creamy-white flesh and a sweet and juicy flavour. The slightly grainy texture is tender to the bite. Conference pears keep relatively well and this makes them a popular supermarket variety.

TO USE Peel, chop or slice. For juicing; raw as a dessert fruit or snack; in salads; cooked in desserts.

Comice

Considered by many to be one of the best pears, this noble French variety carries the full name of Doyenné du Comice, meaning 'top of the show'. Rounded and squat in shape, it has a relatively thick, yellow-green skin with golden-brown russeting, while the flesh inside is creamy-white with a tender bite and a sweet, richly aromatic flavour. Comice pears are best eaten raw, and are especially good for serving with cheese.

TO USE Peel, chop or slice. For juicing; raw as a dessert fruit or snack; in salads; to serve with cheese.

Asian pear

Also known as Nashi pear. There are several varieties of Asian pear, all of which have the same characteristic round shape – like an apple rather than a pear – and golden-russeted skin. Inside, the flesh is white and juicy with a mild, sweet flavour and crisp granular texture that is much crunchier than a 'classic' pear. They may be cooked but are at their best eaten raw or in fruit salads. Asian pears differ from European varieties in being ready to eat when still hard; choose hard specimens with no blemishes.

TO USE Peel, chop or slice. For juicing; raw as a dessert fruit or snack; in salads.

More about pears

The ancients revered pears as a superior fruit to apples and cultivated them as such: Greek authors wrote about growing and cultivating pears as early as 300BC. Pears are related to the apple, and have a longer shape with a bulbous base and varying length of neck. The ripe flesh is softer and juicier, with an almost grainy texture and sweet, perfumed, delicate flavour. Their skin is more fragile and varies in colour from yellow-gold through bronze and green to a few red-blushed varieties.

How to buy and store pears
Pears are in season during the autumn, but available from cold storage throughout winter and spring. Look for unblemished fruits without bruises or broken skin. A perfectly ripe pear should give slightly at the stem end, but should be firm, not soft. Pears are usually picked underripe and continue to ripen off the tree. If your pears are hard, leave at room temperature until ripe. They pass from being perfect for eating to overripe very quickly, so eat ripe pears as soon as possible, or store in the fridge to preserve them for longer. The exception here is Asian pears, which should be hard.

Culinary uses for pears
Pears can be eaten raw or cooked. For eating raw, they are eaten whole or can be quartered and cored or sliced. To cook, they are best peeled using a vegetable peeler or small, sharp knife, and the core removed through the base. Poach them whole in syrup, wine or port, with spices such as cinnamon, ginger or star anise, or fragrant flavourings such as vanilla. Or cook in tarts, pies, crumbles, cakes and sorbets. Pears have a natural affinity with chocolate, and classic desserts include poires Belle Hélène (cooked pears served with chocolate sauce and vanilla ice cream), and pear and chocolate tart. They also go very well with salty cheeses such as Stilton, Parmesan and pecorino, and make a good addition to savoury salads using these ingredients. To preserve pears, bottle them in syrup, wine or brandy, make into chutneys to serve with cheese and cold meats, or slice into thin wedges or rings and dry.

Other varieties include
There are about 1,000 varieties of pear and, like apples, only a handful of these are available in most shops and supermarkets, although farmers markets usually have a good choice of pears in season. Less common varieties include:

Anjou A fairly round pear with yellowish-green skin speckled with russet. It has very soft, juicy flesh with a slightly grainy texture and sweet flavour. Eat raw or cooked.

Williams Known as Bartlett in the US, these golden pears are speckled with russet and have a sweet, musky flesh. There are also green and red varieties. All are good eaten raw or cooked.

Winter Nellis A roundish pear with a yellow-green skin and dark gold russeting. This variety is becoming less common. The flesh is juicy and sweet with a distinctive, spicy flavour and soft texture. Suitable for cooking or eating raw.
(see also dried pears, page 236)

Avocado pear
Native to Mexico, this isn't a pear but merely pear-shaped, and it is eaten as a vegetable rather than a fruit. Appearance varies according to variety, of which there are four main types. Hass, which has the best flavour, has a rough, knobbly, purple-black skin and yellowish flesh. Fuerte and Ettinger are a longer pear-shape, with shiny dark skin and blander flesh. Nabal are similar but with a rounder shape.

Inside, the mild-tasting flesh is buttery and smooth when ripe and can be mashed into dips such as guacamole; chopped and added to salsas; sliced into salads; or eaten straight out of the skin with a dressing as an appetiser. They may also be blended into soups or smoothies. In Mexico they are sometimes eaten with sugar, as a fruit. They are rarely cooked, as heat ruins both flavour and texture.

When choosing, look for undamaged fruits that give slightly when gently squeezed in the palm of the hand, but avoid very soft fruits, as they will be overripe. Harder avocados can be ripened at home at room temperature.

TO USE Cut the fruit lengthways around the large, round stone in the centre, then twist apart. Tap a sharp knife blade into the centre of the stone, then twist the blade to lift it out. Avocado flesh turns brown on exposure to air, so prepare just before use. To store half an avocado, brush the cut surface with lemon juice and press clingfilm on to the surface, then store in the fridge. Chop or slice the flesh as recquired. Use in salsas and salads; as guacamole; as an appetiser: fill the indentation with vinaigrette or salad such as prawn mayonnaise.

Quince

Quinces are related to apples and pears. These slightly lumpy yellow fruits may be apple- or pear-shaped and although the raw fruit has a fragrant scent, its hard, sour white flesh is sharp and inedible until cooked, when it turns pink. Unripe fruits have a downy skin, which becomes smooth as the fruit ripens. They may be cooked in pies and tarts, but are high in pectin and are therefore also good in preserves such as quince jelly, quince cheese, and the Spanish *membrillo* – a type of quince paste, which is traditionally served with cheese. Quinces are often paired with game, and cooked in spiced meat dishes in Moroccan and Persian cuisine.

TO USE For making jelly, there is no need to peel or core; chop and simmer in water until tender. To roast with meats, peel, core and quarter or cut into wedges and add to the roast. In dessert pies and tarts; in jellies and preserves; in spicy meat dishes; to serve with game.

Japonica

A cultivated quince originating in Japan – hence its name – the Japonica quince has a rounded, lumpy shape and yellow skin, and grows to 3–4cm (1¼–1½in) in diameter. The flesh is less heavily scented than ordinary quinces, but has a pleasant aroma and can be used in exactly the same way in preserves and desserts, or in meat and game dishes. Like quinces, they are rich in pectin and therefore have good setting properties for jams and jellies.

TO USE For making jelly, there is no need to peel or core; chop and simmer in water until tender. To roast with meats, peel, core and quarter or cut into wedges and add to the roast. In dessert pies and tarts; in jellies and preserves; in spicy meat dishes; to serve with game.

Medlar

Native to Persia (Iran), the medlar is related to the rose and apple families. The fruits resemble large golden-brown rosehips that are open at one end, revealing five seed cases. The fruit is hard and green when ripe, with a sharp–sour flavour, but does not become edible until it has bletted (become soft and overripe). When ready to eat, the flesh browns and softens and becomes sweet and sticky, rather like dates, but with a slightly more astringent flavour. They are rarely sold commercially and are most likely to be found around the Mediterranean, but they can also be grown in the UK.

TO USE Rinse. Chop to make jellies and preserves. As a dessert fruit: eat raw, halve and spoon out the flesh.

Stone fruits

Plum

There are thousands of varieties of plum, and they can vary in colour and size from tiny blue-black wild sloes (see page 218), to golden-yellow mirabelles and large purple-red Victoria plums. What they have in common is a smooth skin and juicy, sweet translucent flesh with a sour to pleasantly tart bite.

Usually available from late summer into autumn, plums can be eaten raw or cooked, and are good in tarts, pies, crumbles, cobblers and preserves. They can also be poached, baked or stewed, or used in fools and ices. When choosing plums, look for unblemished fruits that are plump and firm, but give slightly when gently squeezed.

TO USE Cut in half and twist the two halves to open the fruit. Remove the stone. For juicing; raw as a dessert fruit or snack; in ices; cooked in desserts and cakes.
(see also bottled fruits, page 237)

Greengage

This small, green-skinned plum is considered to have the best and sweetest flavour of all plums, with juicy, translucent yellow flesh. It was developed in the Loire Valley in France at the beginning of the 16th century and was named after the queen, Reine Claude, which is the name still used in France today. It is thought to have gained its English name after Sir William Gage brought some trees to England in 1724. It is best eaten raw, poached, cut in half and baked, or displayed in a fruit tart, but can be used in the same way as any other plum – in pies, crumbles, preserves, fools and ices.

Greengages are in season from late summer into autumn. When the fruit is fully ripe, the skin begins to take on a golden hue and the plump fruit will give slightly when gently squeezed.

Golden-gage is a yellow-skinned variety of greengage.

TO USE Cut in half and twist the two halves to open the fruit. Remove the stone. For juicing; raw as a dessert fruit or snack; poached in light syrup or baked; cooked in desserts and cakes.

Peach

Peaches are native to China, and there are two types of this wonderful stone fruit: clingstone and freestone. The names refer to the ease with which the stone can be pulled from the flesh. Most peaches are rounded, but some are flatter and almost cushion-shaped, such as the doughnut peach. All have the same velvet-like fuzzy skin, which ranges from yellow-orange to red blushed. The flesh inside may be yellow or white, with (when ripe) a tender, juicy texture and sweet, fragrant flavour.

Peaches are in season during the summer. Look for unblemished fruits that give slightly when gently squeezed. Avoid green or bruised specimens and eat within a few days of purchase. The skin can be peeled if preferred. Eat raw or cooked – either poached, baked, filled and grilled, in pies, crumbles or cobblers, or bottled in syrup, liqueur or brandy.

TO USE To peel, see page 215. Cut in half and twist the two halves to open the fruit. Remove the stone. For juicing or smoothies; raw as a dessert fruit or snack; in salads and ices; cooked in desserts.
(see also dried peaches, page 236)

Nectarine

This summertime treasure is a variety of peach rather than a cross between a peach and a plum. The smooth-skinned nectarine has a darker, orange-red skin and flesh that can be white, yellow or pinkish with a slightly tarter flavour than the peach. Like peaches (see page 213), nectarines are either clingstone or freestone. Nectarines are often favoured over peaches for eating fresh because of their smooth skin, which does not require peeling. Although they may be cooked in the same way as peaches, they are considered to be better eaten raw, and are good in fruit salads or used to decorate desserts and fresh fruit tarts. Look for unblemished fruit that gives slightly when gently squeezed. Nectarines will ripen at room temperature but should be eaten within a few days when ripe.

TO USE Cut in half and twist the two halves to open the fruit. Remove the stone. For juicing or smoothies; raw as a dessert fruit or snack; in salads and ices; cooked in desserts.

Apricot

Related to the plum, peach, cherry and almond, the small yellow -orange and pink-blushed apricot has a velvety skin. It can be rather bland in flavour and mealy-textured when raw, but it becomes soft and intensely flavoured with a sweet–sharp taste when cooked.

Apricots are available in mid-summer. Choose ripe fruits with a deep colour, as the apricot does not ripen off the tree. The skin should be smooth and unblemished – avoid pale or green fruits. Bake, poach, add to tarts and pies, make into jam, or stir the cooked fruit into fools or mousses. The kernel of the stone has a distinctive almond flavour and is used to flavour amaretto liqueur and biscuits.

TO USE Cut in half and twist the two halves to open the fruit. Remove the stone. As a dessert fruit; cooked in desserts; in preserves.
(see also dried apricots, page 236, crystallised fruit, page 237)

Cherry

The smallest of the stone fruits, cherries can be divided into three main groups: sweet, sour and sweet–sour. Sweet cherries are good for eating raw and may have crisp or soft flesh depending on the variety, whereas sour cherries are too tart to eat raw and are best for cooking. Sweet–sour cherries can be eaten either raw or cooked.

Cherries are available in summer. Look for plump, shiny, unblemished fruits with green, flexible stalks, as this is a sign of freshness. Eat raw or use to decorate desserts and cakes such as Black Forest gateau. Cook in pies or desserts such as clafoutis, the classic French batter pudding, bottle in brandy or liqueur, or make into preserves.

TO USE Preparation, see page 215. Raw as a dessert fruit or snack; in salads and ices; as a decoration; cooked in desserts; bottled or in preserves.
(see also dried cherries, page 236, glacé cherries, page 237, and bottled fruits, page 237)

Pitting cherries

1 To eat raw, cherries need only to be stemmed and washed. If your recipe requires you to remove the stones, a cherry stoner will do this neatly, but it is important to take care to position the fruit correctly on the cherry stoner.

2 First, pull off the stems from the cherries, and then wash the fruits gently and pat dry on kitchen paper.

3 Put each cherry on the stoner with the stem end facing up. Close the stoner and gently press the handles together so that the metal rod pushes through the fruit, pressing out the stone.

4 Alternatively, if you do not have a cherry stoner, cut the cherries in half and remove the stones with the tip of a small, pointed knife.

Peeling peaches

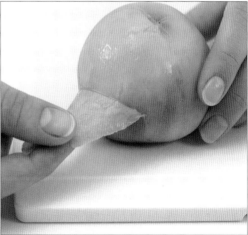

1 Peaches can be peeled before being used in desserts. Put in a bowl of boiling water for 15 seconds–1 minute (depending on ripeness). Don't leave in the water for too long, as heat will soften the flesh. Put in a bowl of cold water.

2 Work a knife between the skin and flesh to loosen the skin, then gently pull to remove. Rub the flesh with lemon juice.

Berries and currants

Gooseberry

Particularly popular in Britain, gooseberries are small fruits that are a relative of the blackcurrant. They may be round or oval with either smooth or hairy skins, and can range in colour from green through to yellow-white and red. Although there are sweeter dessert varieties that can be eaten raw, most gooseberries are sour to the point of inedibility, and should be cooked with the addition of sugar. Their sharp, astringent flavour can be used in savoury and sweet dishes. More commonly, however, they are used to make desserts such as pies, crumbles, puddings, fools and preserves.

Gooseberries are in season in summer. Look for firm, unblemished fruits with no bruising and use within a few days of purchase.

TO USE Remove the stems and flower ends using scissors or a sharp knife. Cook in a little water with sugar. Sweeter varieties as a dessert fruit; cooked in pies and desserts; in preserves; as a sauce to serve with oily fish such as mackerel and rich meats such as roast pork.

Cranberry

Related to the bilberry and blueberry, cranberries are hard, bright-red berries which have a tart, sour flavour. They can be eaten only when cooked – or, if uncooked, with a great deal of added sugar. Cranberries contain a large amount of pectin, making them particularly good for use in preserves such as cranberry jelly. They can also be made into cranberry sauce, the classic accompaniment for a Christmas or Thanksgiving turkey; the sauce can also be served with oily fish. Cranberries can be added to desserts such as tarts, pies, muffins and cakes.

Cranberries are available in winter. Look for shiny, firm berries and avoid any that are squashy. (Traditionally, ripe cranberries were tested by seeing if they would bounce when dropped.) Fresh berries will keep for many weeks due to their high content of benzoic acid, a natural preservative. Out of season, they are available frozen.

TO USE Rinse. In cooked desserts; in cakes; as a preserve; as a sauce to accompany rich meats and fish. (see also dried cranberries, page 236)

Blackberry

These plump, dark blue-black berries are a relative of the rose and raspberry, and grow wild as well as being cultivated. They have a mild, sweet flavour and can be eaten raw or cooked. Cooked blackberries pair well with the sharp flavour of apples and are used in pies and crumbles as well as jams and jellies.

Blackberries are in season during the late summer and early autumn. Pick or buy shiny, plump berries and avoid any that are green or squashy. They do not keep well, so use on the day of purchase.

Dewberries are a smaller relative of the blackberry, with a blue-grey colour and subtler flavour. Use in the same way as blackberries.

TO USE Rinse and remove any stalks. In smoothies; as a dessert fruit, cooked or raw; in ices; in cakes; as a preserve.

Blueberry

These small blue-black berries with a subtle bloom grow wild but are now widely cultivated. They have a sweet, mild taste with a certain sharpness and look attractive when used to decorate desserts such as cheesecakes. They can be eaten raw or cooked in pies, muffins and cakes, or made into jam.

Look for firm, plump berries with that distinctive white bloom and avoid any that are squashy or shrivelled. Store in the fridge and use within a few days of purchase. They need little or no preparation.

Bilberries are also known as whortleberries and huckleberries, these are smaller than blueberries but can be used in the same way.

TO USE Rinse. In smoothies; as a dessert fruit, cooked or raw; as decoration; in cakes; as a preserve. (see also dried blueberries, page 236)

Raspberry

Related to the rose, raspberries are usually a deep pinkish red in colour, although there are also yellow, white and black varieties. Soft and delicate in texture, they are wonderfully juicy and have an intense, sharp and perfumed flavour. Raspberries are best eaten raw (with cream and sugar if you wish), or used to top, fill or decorate cakes and desserts. The raw berries can be crushed, sieved and sweetened to make a coulis (a thin purée) for drizzling over desserts and ice cream, or they can be made into jam.

Raspberries are available in summer. Look for fruits that are plump, with a good colour, and avoid any that are squashy or have specks of mould. Check the underside of the punnet for juice, as this will indicate whether the berries are overripe or have been crushed in transport and storage. Handle them with extreme care, as their fragile exterior is easily damaged. Store them in the fridge and use within a day or so of purchase. Raspberries are best used without washing.

TO USE Best unwashed; remove any remaining hulls. In smoothies; as a dessert fruit, cooked or raw; in ices and cakes; as a preserve.

Strawberry

Probably the most popular of the summer fruits, and with good reason. The fleshy red strawberry grows around a firm pale hull, and the surface of the berry is covered with tiny seeds. Although many cultivated strawberries can be bland, a good strawberry has an intense, fragrant flavour and sweet, firm, juicy flesh. Eat raw with cream, or use to top, fill and decorate cakes, tarts and desserts, or blend and sieve to make a coulis. Strawberries can also be cooked in pies or made into jam.

Look for plump, shiny strawberries with green hulls and avoid soft or squashed fruit. (Check the base of the punnet for juice seeping out, as this will indicate that the berries are overripe or crushed.)

Tiny wild strawberries are less widely available and are always expensive unless you pick your own, but they have a memorably sweet flavour.

TO USE Hull and rinse. In smoothies; as a dessert fruit; in ices, cakes and preserves.

Other berries

There are a number of less common berries that it's worth looking out for or growing yourself at home.

Mulberry

Similar in appearance to blackberries, these sweet, juicy berries grow on large dome-headed trees. There are two main varieties: black and white. The black have a sharp, intense flavour with dark red juice. The white (which are actually slightly pink) have a sweeter, milder taste.

Eat raw as for other berries, add to ices, make into jams, use to flavour vinegars and vodka, or make into a sauce for richly flavoured meat and game such as lamb and poultry.

Choose plump, firm fruits. Be careful of the dark red juice, which will stain.

TO USE Rinse carefully by placing in a colander and dipping in cold water. In smoothies; as a dessert fruit; in ices, preserves and sauces.

Cloudberry

Similar in appearance to raspberries, cloudberries are a rich orange-tinged yellow and have an intensely sweet flavour. They grow in the cooler climates of Scandinavia, Siberia and Canada. In northern North America cloudberries are known as baked apple berries, or sometimes bakeapple.

Cloudberries are rarely cultivated and hard to find outside their native regions. Though most often used for jam, they can be used in desserts and fruit soups.

TO USE Rinse. In desserts and fruit soups; in preserves.

Loganberry

This is a hybrid of the raspberry and American blackberry. The berries are large, slightly hairy, wine-coloured, with a sharp flavour similar to that of the raspberry. They require plenty of sugar. Use to make jams, ice cream, fools and fruity sauces.

TO USE Hull and rinse. In desserts and ices; preserves and sauces.

Youngberry

A blackberry–dewberry hybrid, similar to the loganberry but with a sweeter flavour.

TO USE Hull and rinse. In jams, jellies, pies, ice creams.

Tayberry

A blackberry–raspberry hybrid, larger than loganberries, with a distinctive, elongated shape and a much sweeter flavour. Use in the same way.

TO USE Hull and rinse. In desserts and ices; preserves and sauces.

Boysenberry

A raspberry–youngberry hybrid resembling large red-purple blackberries. They have an intense flavour, sweeter than a loganberry, and are good in jam.

TO USE Hull and rinse. In smoothies and preserves.

Wild and hedgerow fruits

Several exclusively wild fruits are worth hunting in hedgerows and woods. Most appear in the autumn .

Crab apple This small, sour apple is the forebear of the modern apple and can be found growing wild in hedgerows. Inedibly astringent raw, it is excellent in sweet fruit jellies. Wash and chop before use.

Elderberry The fruit of the elder tree, both berries and flowers can be found all over the countryside in spring and summer. The flowers can be used to make a fragrant cordial or wine, and the berries in wine, jellies, crumbles, pies and similar desserts.

Pick berries or flowers from trees growing away from the road to avoid pollution. Rinse before use.

Rosehip The bright red seed pods of the rose, which appear after the flowers have died off, are rich in vitamin C and can be turned into jellies or syrup. Rinse and use as recipe.

Haw The dark-red fruits of the hawthorn tree have a bitter taste but can be combined with other fruits to make sweet jellies, or made into fruit sauces for meat and game. Rinse and use as recipe.

Rowanberry The orange-red fruits of the mountain ash can be combined with other hedgerow fruits and made into jelly to serve with meat or game. Rinse and use as recipe.

Sloe The fruit of the blackthorn tree, this small, hard blue-black wild plum is unpalatably astringent when raw. However, the berries are good in jams and jellies, and can be used to make sloe gin: prick the washed fruit all over; macerate 450g (1lb) of sloes with 75–125g (3–4oz) sugar in one 50cl bottle of gin for about three months; strain and bottle.

Huckleberry and tangleberry Wild cousins of blueberries. Huckleberries have a tougher skin, hard seeds and a sharper flavour. They can be used in the same way as blueberries. Tangleberries have a purplish colour and sweeter flavour.

Blackcurrant

These small, round purple-black fruits have a pale golden-green flesh and an intense, sharp flavour and are usually cooked and sweetened, although they can be used raw if naturally sweet enough. They are a classic ingredient in summer pudding, but are good used in tarts, pies, jams, ice creams and sorbets where their flavour shines through.

Blackcurrants are available in summer and are usually sold on the stem. Look for plump, glossy blackcurrants, avoiding any that are withered, dusty, soft or squashed.

TO USE Rinse; to remove the currants from the stem, strip the stalk through the tines of a fork. In smoothies; as a dessert fruit, cooked or raw; in ices, cakes and preserves.

Redcurrant

These bright red, jewel-like fruits are almost translucent and have a slightly sweeter, less intense flavour than blackcurrants, although their taste is still sharp. Because of their attractive appearance, they are often used to decorate desserts and can also be used in jellies and syrups. Redcurrant jelly is a classic accompaniment to meat and game, and the main ingredient of Cumberland sauce.

Redcurrants are available in summer and usually sold on the stem. Look for plump, glossy redcurrants, avoiding any that are withered, dusty, soft or squashed.

TO USE Rinse; to remove the currants from the stem, strip the stalk through the tines of a fork. As a dessert fruit; in ices; as a decoration; in preserves and sauces to serve with meat.

Whitecurrant

The least common of all the currants, the whitecurrant is a translucent pale white-cream colour and is a variant of several redcurrant species. Whitecurrants have the mildest, least tart flavour and can be eaten raw, or used in the same way as black- and redcurrants.

Available in summer and usually sold on the stem, look for plump, glossy whitecurrants, avoiding any that are withered, dusty, soft or squashed.

TO USE Rinse; to remove the currants from the stem, strip the stalk through the tines of a fork. As a dessert fruit; as a decoration; in preserves.

Melons

Cantaloupe

Named after the Italian town of Cantalupo near Rome, this fairly small melon has green skin marked with a distinctive golden pattern and with segments marked out by greenish 'ribs.' Its pale orange flesh has a sweet, almost perfumed flavour.

Cantaloupe is served in wedges or the flesh scooped into balls or cut into pieces and added to fruit salads. Serve with Parma ham or prosciutto as an appetiser.

The season for cantaloupe melon is summer. Look for firm, heavy fruits with a sweetly perfumed aroma, as this will indicate ripeness. Avoid any with a musky aroma. If storing in the fridge, wrap tightly in clingfilm, as the aroma of melon is pervasive and can affect other foods.

Charentais One of the best-regarded varieties of cantaloupe, this melon has a yellow-green skin, orange flesh, and a particularly sweet, fragrant taste. Charentais are sometimes known as Cavaillon, after the main growing area in the south of France.

TO USE Preparation, see page 222. Small melons can be halved and served between two people. For juicing and in smoothies; as an appetiser; in desserts and salads.

Galia

The smallish, round Galia melon is a relative of the cantaloupe with a golden, netted skin and bright green flesh. Sweet and juicy, it has a mild flavour and relatively soft texture. It can be served as for cantaloupe.

Galia melon is in season during the summer. Look for fruits with a golden skin. The skin turns from green to gold as the fruit ripens, so this is a good indicator. They are pleasantly scented; avoid any that smell musky.

TO USE Preparation, see page 222. Small melons can be halved and served between two people. For juicing and in smoothies; as an appetiser; in desserts and salads.

Piel de sapo

The name is Spanish for 'toad skin', which describes the bumpy, waxy, mottled green skin of this oval-shaped melon. The flesh is pale yellow-green, juicy and sweet. Serve as for cantaloupe.

Piel de sapo is in season during the summer. When ripe the skin becomes streaked with gold; as it is thick-skinned, the ripe melon will not be particularly aromatic, but it should feel heavy and should give slightly, if gently pressed at the end opposite the stem.

TO USE Preparation, see page 222. For juicing and in smoothies; as an appetiser; in desserts and salads.

Ogen

A hybrid from Israel, the Ogen melon is named after the kibbutz in which it was developed. It has a lightly netted golden skin marked with green stripes and sweet, juicy flesh. Serve as for cantaloupe.

Ogen melons are in season during the summer. Look for heavy fruits with a sweet fragrance, avoiding any with a musky aroma. The skin turns from green to golden as the fruit ripens, so use this as an indicator.

TO USE Preparation, see page 222. Small melons can be halved and served between two people. For juicing and in smoothies; as an appetiser; in desserts and salads.

Honeydew

This medium-sized melon is shaped rather like a rugby ball with the fruit tapering to a point at each end. The bright yellow skin of the honeydew melon is smooth but slightly ridged, and the flesh inside is pale green with a sweet, mild flavour. Serve as for cantaloupe.

Honeydew melon is available in late autumn and winter. Look for heavy fruits. Scent is not always the best test of ripeness with honeydew melons; gently press the end opposite the stem. It should give slightly when ripe.

TO USE Preparation, see page 222. For juicing and in smoothies; as an appetiser; in desserts and salads.

Watermelon

These large melons are native to Africa. They can be round or oval in shape, growing up to 12kg (26½lb) in weight, with a dark-green or striped green-and-yellow smooth skin. Inside, the flesh is a striking pinkish-red studded with small black (or sometimes white) seeds. The flesh has a sweet flavour and an abundance of refreshingly sweet juice, while the texture is crisper than those of most other summer melons. Eating watermelon from a slice or wedge held in one's hands is a fairly messy business, and spitting out the seeds is an essential summertime ritual in many places.

TO USE Cut into wedges and pick out the seeds using the tip of a small, pointed knife, then cut away from the skin and cut into chunks. For juicing (the seeds can be left in) and in smoothies; raw as a dessert fruit or snack; in sweet and savoury salads.

Seeding, balling and slicing melons

1 Halve the melon by cutting horizontally through the middle.

2 Use a spoon to scoop out the seeds and fibres, and pull or cut out any that remain.

3 **Balling** Using a melon baller, cut into the flesh close to the hollow left by the seeds and scoop out a ball. Continue around the perimeter of the hollow until you have come full circle. Keep scooping until you have scooped out all of the soft flesh. (Avoid the harder flesh just under the skin.)

4 **Slicing** Cut each seeded half into slices of the required thickness. Trim off the skin in a single piece, taking care to remove the harder flesh just under the skin (the knife will meet more resistance here than when it meets the softer flesh).

Figs and grapes

Fig

These small fruits are shaped like a squat pear with a pinched neck at the stem. They vary in colour from purple and black to green and gold, with the sweet, honeyish, tender flesh inside ranging from pale pink to a deeper red and studded with tiny seeds. Skin and flesh are both edible.

Figs are in season in autumn. Look for soft, unblemished fruits with a whiteish bloom and eat within a day or two of purchase.

TO USE To eat raw, rinse and snip off the woody stem to eat the fruit whole; or halve, quarter or cut into wedges, almost to the base, and press gently into a flower shape; can be served this way as a starter with Parma ham or with crème fraîche for a simple dessert. To cook, poach in syrup or sprinkle with sugar and bake.
(see also dried figs, page 236, and bottled fruit, page 237)

Grape

There are many varieties of this vine fruit, ranging in colour from pale green and golden-yellow to red, purple and bluish-black, with seeds and without. Grapes may be grown for wine, for drying into sultanas and raisins, or as dessert fruit. Popular dessert varieties with a sweet, juicy, translucent flesh include the scented Muscat, which may be golden, red or black; sweet green Thompson seedless; and Alphonse Lavallée, which has a thick, purplish-black skin.

Grapes are available all year round, seasonally depending on variety. Look for plump, firm fruits, avoiding any that are shrivelled or with brown spots. They may sometimes have a faint bloom on the skins, but this is not an indication of quality.

TO USE Rinse; to seed, first halve, then pick out the seed using the point of a small, sharp knife. For juicing and in smoothies; raw as a dessert fruit or snack; in sweet and savoury salads; to serve with cheese.
(see also dried vine fruits, page 236)

Vine leaves

Popular in the Mediterranean and Middle East, the young leaves of the grapevine can be used as a wrapper for meat, vegetable and rice stuffings, such as in Greek dolmades. They can be used fresh, canned or packed in brine. Vine leaves are usually fairly sturdy things and therefore easy to handle.

TO USE When using fresh vine leaves, plunge them into boiling water for a few minutes to soften. When using vine leaves in brine, soak in boiling water for 20 minutes, then rinse and soak in cold water for 20 minutes to remove as much salt as possible.

Exotic fruits

Banana

Most of the bananas found in our supermarkets are large and bright yellow. There are many different varieties, however, including tiny finger and apple bananas and small red bananas with yellowish-pink flesh. They can be eaten raw as a snack or sliced into fruit salads or custard, baked, fried, or mashed and added to cakes, teabreads and muffins.

Bananas start to ripen when they are picked, and can arrive in their destination market when still well short of ripeness. Perfectly ripe specimens are an even yellow all over, whereas those with greenish ends are underripe and will be less sweet and with a crisper texture. As they continue to ripen, the skin will become mottled with brown and the flesh soft and sweet, making them well suited to mashing and adding to cakes and muffins. The degree of preferred ripeness is a personal matter: some can't abide anything less than full softness and sweetness, while others like the starchier texture and moderate sweetness of the unripe fruit.

TO USE Peel. In smoothies; raw as a dessert fruit or snack; in cooked desserts; in salads; in baking.

Green banana

Not to be confused with unripe bananas that have yet to turn yellow, green bananas are used in African, Caribbean and South American cooking as a vegetable, in much the same way as plantains: boiled, fried, steamed, grilled or cooked in stews and curries. Green bananas have a tough, vibrantly green skin, with firm, starchy flesh. They can be cooked in their skins and then peeled, or they can be peeled before cooking.

Banana leaves are large, firm, dark and glossy and are widely used in the tropics to wrap foods for steaming or baking, or lining pots to prevent foods catching and burning.

TO USE To peel green bananas, cut off each end, then slit the skin lengthways and remove in sections. In savoury dishes.

Plantain

Plantains are popular in Caribbean, South American and African cooking. They look like large bananas with thick, tough skins that vary from green to yellow, and with black specks according to ripeness. Although they do taste slightly of banana, the taste is much less sweet. Plantains are always cooked for use as a savoury ingredient, usually sliced, fried and served either as a snack, appetiser or accompaniment in place of rice or potatoes. When cooked, the flesh is much firmer and more starchy than a banana, and similar to potato in texture. They can also be baked, boiled, grilled, steamed, mashed, or dried and ground into flour. Never make the mistake of buying plantains when you want bananas; the two are completely different.

TO USE Slice unpeeled and fry. Cooked as a snack, appetiser or to serve with savoury dishes.

Kiwi fruit

Also called Chinese gooseberries, kiwi fruits are small and oval in shape, sometimes slightly flattened, with a thin, dull brown, hairy skin enclosing soft, bright green flesh studded with tiny black seeds. They are most often eaten raw added to fruit salads or used to decorate cakes, pastries, tarts and other desserts. Kiwi fruits contain an enzyme that prevents gelatine from setting, so do not use in jellies. Most of those sold outside their native New Zealand are somewhat underripe, and much more tart than the ripe fruit.

When buying, choose firm, unblemished fruits that give slightly when gently squeezed.

TO USE Halve and eat using a small spoon, or peel and slice using a sharp knife. For juicing and smoothies; raw as a dessert fruit or snack; in ices and salads.

Star fruit

Native to Indonesia, the tropical star fruit is also known as a carambola. Bright yellow with a waxy-looking skin, the fruit is oval in shape with sharp, ridged edges, making it resemble a star when cut crossways. The flesh is bland but juicy. Eat raw in slices, either on its own or added to fruit salads. In China and India, the unripe fruit is used as a vegetable.

Look for firm, unblemished star fruits and store in the fridge for up to a week.

TO USE Trim off the brown edge of each ridge, then slice the flesh. Raw as a dessert fruit or snack; in salads.

Dragon fruit

Also known as pitahaya, this striking fruit comes from a cactus native to Central America. Dragon fruit is about 10cm (4in) long and oval in shape. The skin may be a vibrant reddish-pink, peach or yellow, and almost scale-like. Inside, the juicy flesh is deep pink or pale, usually white, and studded with tiny black seeds throughout; it has a mild, slightly sweet taste. Eat raw, peeled, either on its own or in fruit salads.

The ripe fruit should give slightly when gently squeezed and should be eaten as soon as possible, within a couple of days of purchase.

TO USE Peel. Raw as a dessert fruit or snack; in salads.

Mango

When mangoes are at their best, they are arguably the finest of all exotic fruits. Grown throughout the tropics, they come in many different varieties. They might be large or small; green, orange, yellow or red; and round, oval or kidney-shaped. The texture varies too, from smooth, soft and buttery to slightly fibrous. Mango is usually eaten raw, on its own, in salsas, fruit salads, tarts and desserts such as pavlova, or in smoothies, sorbets, ices and mousses.

Colour is not a good indication of ripeness. Instead, choose fruits that give slightly when squeezed gently and have a sweet aroma, and avoid any that are wrinkled or very soft (although these may be usable for juicing). Unripe mangoes will ripen at home in a warm place.

TO USE Preparation, see page 227. Serve sliced or cubed. For juicing and smoothies; as a dessert fruit; cooked in desserts; in salads or ices.
(see also dried mango, page 236)

Papaya

Also known as paw-paw, papayas are native to Central America but are grown throughout the tropics. They have a distinctive pear shape and thin, shiny skin that ripens from green to yellow or orange. Ripe papayas will give slightly when gently squeezed. The flesh inside is a peachy-orange colour with a mass of shiny black seeds in the centre. Papaya is smooth and buttery in texture. The flesh has a mild, sweet and slightly scented flavour that is improved with a squeeze of lime juice. Eat on its own or in fruit salads, desserts or smoothies. In Thailand, large, green, unripe papayas are used to make chilli-hot salads.

TO USE Preparation, see page 227. Serve sliced or cubed. For juicing and smoothies; raw as a dessert fruit or snack; in salads or ices.

Guava

Native to Central America and the West Indies, guavas are now grown throughout the tropics. They vary in size, shape and colour and can be round or pear-shaped, with pale yellow to almost red skins and creamy or bright pink flesh with a sweet–sour aromatic flavour. Eat raw, add to fruit salads or purée to make a sauce. Alternatively, cook in crumbles, poach, stuff and bake like apples, or make into jams, jellies and fruit cheeses.

Feijoa is a South American fruit that is related to the guava. It has a tough, red-green skin surrounding a sweet, pineapple–strawberry-scented flesh containing small hard seeds. Use in the same way as guavas.

TO USE Preparation as for papaya, see page 227. Serve sliced or cubed. For juicing and smoothies; raw as a dessert fruit or snack; in cooked desserts; in salads or ices; in preserves.

Preparing mango

1 Slice off the fruit to one side of the stone in the centre. Repeat on the other side.

2 Cut parallel lines into the flesh of one slice, almost to the skin. Cut another set of lines to cut the flesh into squares.

3 Press on the skin side to turn the fruit inside out, so that the flesh is thrust outwards. Cut off the chunks as close as possible to the skin. Repeat with the other half.

Preparing papaya

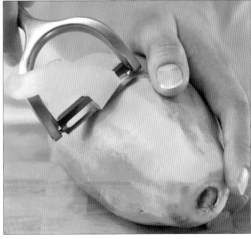

1 To eat whole, use a sharp knife to halve the fruit lengthways and a teaspoon to scoop out the shiny black seeds and fibres.

2 If using in a salad, peel the fruit using a swivel-headed vegetable peeler, then gently cut in half using a sharp knife. Remove the seeds using a teaspoon and slice the flesh, or cut into cubes.

Pineapple

While pineapples can vary greatly in size, all are oval and have a knobbly orange or golden skin topped with a plume of leaves. The yellow flesh has an astringent but sweet flavour and a juicy, fibrous texture. Serve in rings, chunks or wedges, on its own, in fruit salads or ices, or cooked in cakes and desserts. Pineapple is used in savoury dishes too, such as curries and with gammon. Fresh pineapple contains the enzyme, bromelain, which makes it impossible for gelatine to set, so do not use it in jellies. Canned pineapple, however, will not affect the setting of gelatine.

Choose pineapples that feel heavy for their size, with fresh, stiff green leaves. Ripe pineapples have a sweet aroma, and a leaf in the centre should pull out easily. Avoid any that are blemished or bruised.

TO USE Preparation, see page 229. Serve sliced or in chunks. For juicing and smoothies; raw as a dessert fruit or snack; in cakes and cooked desserts; in salads or ices; with savouries.
(see also dried pineapple, page 236, and crystallised fruit, page 237)

Durian

Notorious for their foul smell, which has been likened by many to sewage, this large South-east Asian fruit is oval in shape with a dark-green, spiky shell. Inside is a pale, creamy flesh with a delicious flavour. It can be scooped from the skin and eaten raw, or used to make jams, jellies and sweets. In Indonesia, the unripe fruit is cooked like a vegetable, and the edible seeds roasted.

TO USE Cut the fruit along the segmented joints using a sharp, heavy knife (and protecting your hands from the spines); prise open to reveal the flesh. As a dessert fruit; in preserves.

Kiwano

Also known as horned melon, horned cucumber and jelly melon, kiwanos are native to Africa. They are small and oval in shape with a thick, spiky orange skin. Inside, the flesh is a rich green colour with a gelatinous texture, encasing large, flat, edible seeds. The flavour is very mild and reminiscent of cucumber and lime. The flesh is eaten raw, and is also used for decoration.

TO USE To prepare, halve the fruit then scoop out the flesh using a teaspoon. Raw as a dessert fruit or snack; for decoration.

Preparing pineapple

1 Cut off the base and crown of the pineapple, and stand the fruit on a chopping board.

2 Using a medium-sized knife, peel away a section of skin going just deep enough to remove all or most of the hard, inedible 'eyes' on the skin. Repeat all the way around.

3 Use a small knife to cut out any remaining traces of the eyes.

4 You can buy special tools for coring pineapples, but a 7.5cm (3in) biscuit cutter or an apple corer works just as well. Cut the peeled pineapple into slices about 1cm (½in) thick.

5 Place the biscuit cutter directly over the core and press down firmly to remove the core. If using an apple corer, cut out the core in pieces, as it will be too wide to remove in one piece.

Pomegranate

Native to Iran, the pomegranate has been esteemed since ancient times and played a part in myth and religion. It is about the size of an orange and has a hard, orange-red-blushed skin with a crown-shaped calyx on top. Inside is a mass of edible seeds (each one surrounded by vibrant pink-red translucent flesh) nestling in a web of bitter white pith. The seeds can be separated and used to decorate both sweet and savoury dishes. The juice can be obtained by gently crushing the seeds in a sieve, then used to flavour Middle Eastern-style soups, sauces and stews.

Choose fruits that feel heavy for their size with hard, undamaged skins, and store in the fridge for up to a week.

TO USE Preparation, see page 231. For juicing; as a dessert fruit; in salads and ices; in savouries; for decoration.

Passion fruit

Native to South America, this tropical vine fruit is dark purple and wrinkled when ripe, but smooth and green when unripe. Inside the leathery, inedible skin lies a scented yellow flesh, tart and gelatinous, encasing edible black seeds. Use the flesh to decorate desserts or to flavour drinks and ices.

Granadilla is a large, smooth-skinned orange variety of passion fruit that has a less fragrant flavour but can be used in the same way as passion fruit.

TO USE To remove the flesh, halve the fruit and scoop out flesh and seeds with a teaspoon; to extract the juice, press the seeds in a sieve (see page 231). In smoothies, salads and desserts; in ices; as a decoration; as a flavouring.

Persimmon

Resembling a large, orange tomato with a brown calyx, persimmons have sweet, smooth, honeyed flesh. Add to fruit salads, or purée and use in smoothies, ices and mousses.

Choose ripe persimmons, which are soft and swollen-looking, as underripe fruits are bitter and acidic.

Sharon fruit is a seedless variety of persimmon that was developed in Israel. It has tender flesh and edible skin. The flavour is not astringent and the fruit can be enjoyed while still quite firm.

TO USE Slice open and scoop out the flesh. In smoothies; raw as a dessert fruit or snack; in salads; as a purée; in ices.

Preparing pomegranate

1 Cut off the base of the pomegranate, trying not to cut into the cells that contain the seeds. Make four shallow cuts into the skin using a small, sharp knife. Break the pomegranate in half, then into quarters.

2 Bend the skin of each quarter backwards to push the seeds out into a bowl. Remove any seeds left behind using a teaspoon. Remove any of the bitter pith that remains on the seeds.

Preparing passion fruit

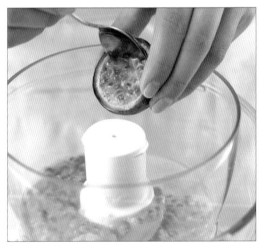

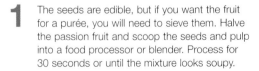

1 The seeds are edible, but if you want the fruit for a purée, you will need to sieve them. Halve the passion fruit and scoop the seeds and pulp into a food processor or blender. Process for 30 seconds or until the mixture looks soupy.

2 Pour into a sieve over a bowl, and press down hard on the pulp with the back of a spoon to release the juice.

Physalis

Also known as the Cape gooseberry, this fruit is believed to be native to South America. It obtained its alternative name after coming into vogue with early settlers in South Africa, who cultivated them there. The small, round, orange fruits are encased in an attractive papery brown husk rather like a Chinese lantern. With a sweet but tangy flavour, they are most often eaten raw – either dipped in chocolate as petits fours or used as a decoration for cakes and desserts. They may also be cooked to make jam.

TO USE Peel back the papery husk. As a dessert fruit, petit four or decoration; in preserves.

Mangosteen

The mangosteen is native to Malaysia and Indonesia, but this apple-shaped tropical fruit is now found throughout South-east Asia. It has a thick, red-brown rind and is topped with chunky leaves and a thick stem. Inside nestles the fruit's creamy-white flesh. It is divided into five or six chunky segments and has an intense but subtle flavour that is simultaneously sweet, sharp, and fragrant. Mangosteen is eaten raw or cooked in preserves.

Look for fruits that give slightly when gently squeezed, and avoid any that are hard or dry-looking.

TO USE Cut the shell through the centre and remove the top part to reveal the fruit. Be careful when cutting open, as juice from the rind will stain. As a dessert fruit; in preserves.

Rambutan

Native to Malaysia and related to the lychee, rambutans are larger oval fruits with a thick brownish-red skin covered with soft, hairy spines. Inside, the translucent, whitish flesh is similar to lychee with the same sweet, fragrant flavour and a long, shiny, inedible stone in the centre. The skin peels off easily and the flesh can be eaten as a snack, or added to fruit salads.

TO USE Peel. Raw as a dessert fruit or snack; in salads.

Lychee

Native to China, these small, oval fruits have a thin, brittle, knobbly skin that varies from pinkish-brown to red. Inside, the flesh is translucent white with a shiny brown stone in the centre. Lychees have a sweet and juicy flesh with a distinctive scented taste reminiscent of Muscat grapes. Lychees are eaten raw as a snack or added to fruit salads. They can also be poached in syrup for serving chilled.

Choose fruits with pink-tinged or red-tinged skins and avoid any that are shrivelled or look dry.

TO USE Peel, halve and remove the stone. Raw as a dessert fruit or snack; in salads; poached.

Longan

Native to China and South-east Asia, longans are related to the lychee. They are small and round, with a brittle, brown skin that has a matt, slightly rough texture. Inside, the flesh is similar to a lychee: translucent white and juicy, with a sweet, fragrant flavour. Enclosed in the flesh lies a large, inedible black stone which gives the fruit its alternative name: dragon's eye.

TO USE Peel, halve and remove the stone. Raw as a dessert fruit or snack; in salads; poached.

Ackee

Related to the lychee, the bright red, pear-shaped ackee is usually eaten as a vegetable, most commonly in the traditional Jamaican dish saltfish and ackee. Inside the fruit are three inedible black seeds surrounded by pale yellow flesh, which has a slightly sweet, lemony flavour.

When buying fresh, ackee must be absolutely ripe, because parts of the unripe fruit are toxic. The fresh fruit is not widely available outside the Caribbean, however, so most cooks will need to use canned ackee, which needs only minimal cooking. Ackee has very little flavour of its own, which is the reason for pairing it with pungent saltfish, but its yielding texture is very appealing.

Prickly pear

Also known as cactus pear and Indian fig, the prickly pear is not a pear at all but the fruit of a cactus native to Central America and the southern United States. The prickly pear has greenish skin covered in sharp spines. The flesh inside is orange-pink and studded with seeds. It has a soft, juicy texture and scented flavour. The flesh is sliced or cut into chunks and eaten as a snack with a squeeze of lime or lemon juice. Prickly pears may also be cooked in sauces, jams and jellies, or puréed.

TO USE Peel: be careful of the spiny skin when preparing; wear rubber gloves and scrub off the prickles, then slice off each end, slit the skin and peel off; slice or cut into chunks. As a snack; in salads; in sauces and preserves.

Custard apple

There are many varieties of this heart-shaped tropical fruit. They have a greenish skin that browns as it ripens. The flavour is sweet and mellow, the flesh soft, creamy, and studded with inedible black seeds. Halve and scoop out the flesh as a snack, or add to fruit salads or ice cream.

Ripe custard apples will give slightly when gently squeezed.

Cherimoya is related to the custard apple and widely available. They are heart-shaped, with pale green skin and a flattened, almost scale-like pattern. The soft, custard-like flesh has a flavour similar to that of pineapple.

Soursop is related to the custard apple. It is larger, with a dark green prickly skin, white flesh and a tangy flavour.

TO USE Cut in half and scoop out the flesh, removing the seeds. As a snack; in salads and ices.

Date

Grown on palm trees, sweet and sticky fresh dates are a staple in North Africa and the Middle East. The small oval fruits have a thin, slightly papery skin and a long, hard stone in the centre. Dates have a very high sugar content. They can be eaten as a snack, or slit open to remove the stone, then filled with cream cheese, marzipan or walnut halves and served as petits fours. Their taste is like that of no other fruit, and much better when they're fresh than in the more commonly available dried version.

Dates can be used in savoury dishes such as spicy North African tagines, fruity stuffings for roast meats such as lamb and pork, canapés such as dates wrapped in bacon or stuffed with blue cheese, and salads such as carrot or cheese.

Look for plump, glossy fruits with a rich brown colour. Paler dates will be less ripe and have a less sweet and sticky taste and texture.

TO USE Slit open and remove the stone. Raw as a dessert fruit or snack; filled as petits fours; in salads and stews.
(see also dried dates, page 236)

Other exotic fruits

Sapodilla

Native to South America, the oval sapodilla is about the size of a plum. It has rough, brown skin and pale, golden flesh. The scented flesh tastes of bananas and pears. Look for ripe fruits with slightly wrinkled skins that give slightly when squeezed. Green-tinged underripe fruits taste unpleasant, but can be ripened at room temperature.

TO USE Peel, remove the stone and slice or cut into chunks. Raw as a dessert fruit or snack; in salads.

Snake fruit

Also known as salak fruit, snake fruit grows on a palm native to Indonesia and Malaysia. The small, fig-shaped fruits have a round base and pinched neck. The skin is thin, hard, glossy and brown, scaled like snakeskin. Inside are four segments of creamy-white flesh, each with a brown stone. The flesh is crisp, with a sweet–sharp flavour.

TO USE Peel and remove the stones. Raw as a dessert fruit or snack.

Breadfruit

Eaten as a vegetable throughout the Caribbean, Pacific islands and South-east Asia. Breadfruit is round and melon-sized, with a rough green rind that browns as it ripens. The flesh inside is creamy-yellow, and when cooked tastes a little like potatoes.

TO USE Remove the rind, core and seeds; boil, bake or fry as for potatoes. Serve with savoury dishes.

Jackfruit

Related to the breadfruit, jackfruit has rough, spiky green skin and can grow to 30kg (66lb), although usually only smaller fruits are sold. Banana-flavoured flesh surrounds walnut-sized seeds. The flesh has a sweet, bland taste and may be eaten raw, although it is usually cooked. The seeds can be boiled, then dried and made into flour, or candied.

TO USE Remove the peel, cut into slices or chunks, remove the seeds. Raw as a dessert fruit or snack; boiled, roasted or fried to serve with savoury dishes.

Jujubes

Also known as Chinese dates, these small olive-shaped fruits are green when unripe, turning brown, and contain a stone. They have a sweet flavour.

TO USE Peel and remove the stone. Raw as a dessert fruit or snack; stew, in preserves or candied.

Ginup

South American ginups, also known as mamoncillo or Spanish lime, are cherry-sized and have a thin, green skin. The flesh is pink-tinged, sweet and juicy. The seeds can be roasted, peeled and eaten.

TO USE Peel and remove the stone. Raw as a dessert fruit or snack.

Jamaican plum

Also known as hoy or hog plum, golden apple, limbu and mombin, Jamaican plums are actually a relative of the mango. They have soft skin and a large stone. The flesh is yellow, sweet and juicy, with a scented flavour and sharp tang, like that of pineapple or apple.

TO USE Peel and remove the stone. Raw as a dessert fruit or snack; poached; in preserves.

Curuba

Also known as banana passion fruit, banana poka, tumbo and taxo. This is a long, oval fruit containing edible black seeds surrounded by sweet–sharp pulp, similar to the passion fruit. Use as for passion fruit.

TO USE To remove the flesh, halve the fruit and scoop out with a teaspoon; to extract the juice, press the seeds in a sieve. In smoothies, salads and desserts; in ices; as a decoration; as a flavouring.

Babaco

This papaya hybrid is a long, cylindrical, five-sided fruit pointed at one end and rounded at the other. Its thin skin is green when unripe, turning yellow. The flesh is pale orange with a sweet, bland flavour.

TO USE Peel, halve and remove the seeds. Slice and drizzle with lemon juice. As a dessert or snack, sprinkled with sugar and citrus juice; in salads.

Mamey sapote

This is a melon-like fruit from South America. It is large and round, with rough brown skin. The flesh is orange-pink, smooth and juicy. It should give slightly when gently squeezed.

TO USE Halve and seed, scoop the flesh using a melon baller or cut into wedges. For juicing and in smoothies; in desserts and salads; in preserves.

Dried, candied and bottled fruits

Dried fruits

This ancient way of preserving fresh fruit is still widely used. Dried fruits can be eaten as a snack, or used as an ingredient in cakes, desserts and savoury dishes. The drying process intensifies the taste of the fruits' natural sugars, making them sweeter than the fresh fruit.

Vine fruits Sultanas, raisins and currants are all dried grapes, with various tastes and textures. Juicy golden sultanas are made from seedless white grapes and are the moistest and softest of the dried vine fruits, with a mild, sweet taste. Raisins have a stronger flavour and may be pale and tender (made from Muscat grapes) or small and dark. Sultanas and raisins are both good added to cakes, teabreads, scones, drop scones, desserts and mincemeat; in savoury dishes such as rice and couscous; salads such as coleslaw; and fruity sweet-and-sour chutneys. Raisins and sultanas are also good sprinkled over breakfast cereals or added to muesli. Currants are the smallest and darkest of the vine fruits; they have a slightly sharp taste and are most often used for baking.

Prunes These are dried plums; they vary with the types of plums used and the drying process. Ready-to-eat prunes are soft and tender, while drier, harder prunes need to be soaked before using. Agen prunes are particularly esteemed. Soak prunes in fruit juice, wine, tea or brandy to improve the flavour; prunes and Armagnac are a classic combination. With a distinctive, not-too-sweet flavour, prunes can be used in tarts, desserts and cakes, and are also added to savoury dishes such as Moroccan tagines and the Scottish chicken and leek soup called cock-a-leekie. They are an essential ingredient in the savoury hors d'oeuvre, devils on horseback: prunes stuffed with chutney, then wrapped in a strip of bacon and grilled until the bacon is cooked.

Dates Sticky, intensely sweet, and firmer than the fresh version (see page 234), dried dates may be sold loose in packets, or pitted and compressed into a block. They can be eaten as a snack, or chopped and added to cakes, desserts and cereals.

Apricots Dried apricots can vary in colour from deep orange to orange-brown depending on how they have been dried. Ready-to-eat dried apricots are tender and moist and do not require soaking, whereas other dried apricots have a much firmer, more leathery, chewy texture and are best soaked before use. All have an intense, sweet–sharp flavour and are good added to cakes, desserts and compotes. Unsulphured dried apricots are darker in colour and have a more intense flavour. Dried apricots are a classic ingredient of savoury Moroccan tagines and Middle Eastern stews, and are a good addition to stuffings for meat, and chutneys.

Peaches Usually sold in halves, dried peaches are sweet, but lack the intensity of flavour of dried apricots. Eat as a snack, or soak before adding to desserts, compotes, cakes and bakes.

Figs Sold loose or pressed into a block, dried figs are sweet, sticky and golden brown with a tough woody stem that should be snipped off before eating or using. Eat them as a snack or use chopped in cakes, teabreads and desserts, sprinkled over cereal, or whole in fruit compotes.

Apples Usually sold as dried rings. These have a pale, golden colour and an intense sharp–sweet flavour. Eat them as a snack, or cook in compotes, stews or savoury sauces.

Pears Usually sold in halves, dried pears have a subtly sweet flavour that makes them good for eating as snacks. They can also be used in compotes, desserts, cakes and savoury stews.

Cranberries With a much sweeter taste than fresh cranberries, dried cranberries still have the astringent, sour, slightly bitter taste of the fresh berry. They are good in cakes, biscuits, muffins, drop scones, desserts, sprinkled over cereals and muesli, or added to stuffings for meat and poultry.

Cherries Sweet but with a tart bite, dark red dried cherries have a similar texture to raisins, although they are much larger. They make a good addition to cakes, teabreads and biscuits, and can be sprinkled over cereal and muesli.

Blueberries Both sweet and tart, dried blueberries can be added to biscuits, cakes, teabreads, drop scones or fruit salads, or sprinkled over cereal or muesli.

Banana There are two forms: pale golden banana chips, which are crisp and best for snacking or adding to muesli; and longer slices, cut lengthways and dried to a tender, sticky consistency. Tender dried bananas are brown, with a sweet, faintly banana flavour, and are good for snacking or adding to cakes and bakes.

Pineapple With a sweet, fragrant flavour, pale yellow squares of dried pineapple are good used in cakes, bakes and desserts.

Mango Most often sold in strips, these dark orange slices have an intense, sweet–sharp, fragrant flavour and chewy texture. They are good for snacking, and can also be added to chutneys, relishes and fruit compotes.

Candied and glacé fruits

Fruits can be preserved by simmering or steeping them in sugar syrup until the fruit is completely saturated with sugar to make either candied, glacé or crystallised fruits.

Candied peel Available in strips, but more commonly as chopped pieces. The sweet, aromatic peel of citrus fruits such as orange, lemon and citron is used in baking and desserts.

Glacé cherries Used as an ingredient in cakes, bakes and desserts, and also as a decoration. The cherries are exceptionally sweet and sticky, and are usually dyed bright scarlet (and sometimes green and yellow), although you can also find natural-coloured glacé cherries, which are a darker red.

Candied fruit Made by soaking the fruit in sugar syrup of increasing concentration over a period of time, candied fruits are served as a sweetmeat or used in petits fours such as Florentines.

Crystallised fruit Usually the same as candied fruit but with a coating of granular sugar, popular crystallised fruits include pineapple, clementines, apricots, cherries and kumquats. They are usually served as sweetmeats, particularly at Christmas.

Bottled fruits

Fresh fruits can be bottled in sugar syrup, liqueur, or a mixture of spirits and sugar, then sealed in sterilised jars. Popular fruits for bottling include pears, peaches, whole peeled clementines, kumquats, cherries and figs. German *rumtopf* is a classic fruit preserve made with soft summer fruits, rum and sugar. Sweet bottled fruits make an excellent out-of-season dessert when served with cream, crème fraîche or ice cream, alongside cakes and similar desserts, or added to fillings for pies, crumbles and cobblers.

Fruits can also be bottled with sugar, vinegar and salt to make preserves to eat with savouries. In the Middle East and North Africa, whole lemons are preserved with salt, then used to flavour savoury stews and tagines. In India, limes are pickled with salt and spices, and in Italy the classic preserve served with polenta and sausage on Christmas day is *mostarda* (sweet mustard fruit pickle). Pickled plums preserved with vinegar, salt and sugar are a speciality of Central Europe.

Preserves

Fresh fruits can be preserved with sugar in sweet jams, clear jellies, marmalades, fruit curds, butters and cheeses. Soft fruits such as berries and stone fruits are particularly well suited to jams and jellies, whereas citrus fruits are good made into marmalade and fruit curds. Apples and pears, with their high pectin content, are good for adding to fruit cheeses and jellies.

Sweet fruity preserves can be used as a spread on bread, toast, scones and crumpets, as a filling for layer cakes, Swiss rolls and pancakes, or in desserts such as steamed pudding and jam roly-poly. Jams can be used in pastries such as jam tarts and turnovers, and spread over the base of tarts such as Bakewell tart. They can also be used to sandwich biscuits or fill doughnuts. Apricot jam is often strained and warmed, then brushed over fresh fruit tarts as a glaze; strawberry and raspberry jam may be added to rice pudding before serving. Fruit curds are good stirred into crème fraîche or yogurt as a dessert or topping for other desserts. Jellies such as redcurrant and cranberry are good served with meats and poultry.

A combination of fresh and dried fruits can be preserved with sugar and vinegar in chutneys and relishes to serve with cheese and cold meats. Classic fruit chutneys include mango chutney, plum chutney, and apple and sultana chutney.

Vegetables

Roots and tubers

King Edward potato

One of the best known of the maincrop varieties, King Edward is a large potato with a pale skin touched with patches of red, and with a creamy-yellow, floury flesh. It has a good flavour, and can lay claim to the title of most useful all-round potato. It is particularly good for baking.

Red King Edward Virtually identical to the pale King Edward but with a red skin.

TO USE Bake in its skin. Peel, roast or mash, or use in recipes requiring mashed potato, such as fishcakes.

Desirée potato

The pink-skinned Desirée was originally cultivated in the early 1960s in the Netherlands and is a good all-round potato. The cream-coloured flesh is not as dry as many maincrop potatoes and is suitable for most culinary purposes. It holds its shape well, and many people consider it to be the best variety for roasting.

TO USE Peel. Roast, boil, steam or mash, or use cold in salads.

Maris Piper potato

With a thin, pale skin and cream-coloured, floury flesh, Maris Piper is a popular maincrop potato with a good flavour. It keeps its shape well when cooked, and is favoured for chip-making by many chefs, but it is not particularly well suited for use in salads.

TO USE Peel. Boil, steam, mash, sauté, roast or cut into chips and deep-fry.

Jersey Royal potato

Under the Common Agricultural Policy of the European Union, Jersey Royals have a protected designation of origin (PDO), which aims to protect the names of regional foods. This means that only potatoes grown in Jersey may be sold under the name Jersey Royals. These new potatoes are highly regarded not just for their flavour and texture but for their true seasonality: they are at their best between April and June. The potato plants are fertilised with vraic, a seaweed fertiliser collected from the Jersey beaches, which has been used since the 12th century. This is what gives them their distinctively nutty flavour. The small, kidney-shaped potatoes have a papery skin, yellow flesh and a waxy texture.

TO USE Scrub. Boil or steam, then serve with butter and a sprinkling of herbs, or crush and drizzle with olive oil and herbs.

Pink Fir Apple potato

An old English variety, the Pink Fir Apple is a small potato that is long and knobbly with a pink skin and smooth, waxy flesh with a distinctive, almost nutty and creamy flavour. It is one of the very best varieties for potato salad

TO USE Scrub. Boil or steam, then serve tossed in melted butter, or cold in potato salad.

Vivaldi potato

Vivaldi is a fairly new variety of potato, created in the UK and released on to the market in 2006. It was developed to have a lower calorie content and fewer carbohydrates than other potatoes: it has around 33 per cent fewer calories and around 25 per cent fewer carbohydrates. Vivaldi has a smooth yellow skin and pale yellow flesh, and is noted for its fine flavour and firm, creamy texture. This is a versatile potato but is perhaps at its best when boiled or steamed for a salad.

TO USE Scrub. Bake, roast, boil, mash, or steam and serve tossed in melted butter, or cold in salads.

More about potatoes

Native to South America, potatoes were introduced to Europe by Spanish explorers in the late 16th century, although it took almost 200 years for them to gain popularity and become the staple food that they are today.

The starchy tubers, which grow underground, several to a plant, vary widely in shape, size and colour. The skin can range from pale creamy- and yellowy-browns to pink, red and purple, and the surface may be smooth, netted or dotted with deep eyes. In size, potatoes can be tiny or enormous, weighing up to 500g (1lb 2oz), and in shape they can be oval, round, long, knobbly, kidney-shaped, or a combination of these. Potatoes are usually described as being either floury or waxy, which describes their texture when cooked, although there are also all-round potatoes that are midway between the two. Floury potatoes become soft and fluffy when cooked, while waxy potatoes keep their shape and have a much firmer, 'waxier' texture.

Potatoes can be divided into two main groups: new and maincrop. New potatoes, available from late spring, are harvested while still young so that they are small and tender with thin skins and often a slightly sweeter taste and firmer texture. Maincrop potatoes, which are harvested in the autumn and available from cold store all year round, are fully grown, mature potatoes.

How to choose and store potatoes

Look for hard, unblemished potatoes and avoid any that are soft and wrinkled, or with green patches (which can be toxic) or shoots. New potatoes should feel slightly damp and their skins should rub off easily. If you buy potatoes in polythene bags, remove them and put them in a brown paper sack or similar, and store in a cool, dry and dark place, making sure they are not exposed to light. Maincrop potatoes keep well, but new potatoes should be used within a few days of purchase.

Preparing and cooking potatoes

Potatoes should be prepared just before you cook them, because their flesh will discolour once cut or peeled. However, you can peel potatoes and keep them covered in water up to 24 hours ahead.

Most of the nutrients in a potato are stored just beneath the skin, so where possible, cook and eat potatoes with the skin on. New potatoes can be scrubbed, or scraped with a knife. You may need to peel maincrop potatoes if you are planning to boil and mash or roast them, although they can be delicious roasted in their skins. To peel, use a sharp vegetable peeler that removes the skin in a thin, even layer.

Boil, crush, mash, roast, bake, steam, deep-fry or sauté, or add to stews and casseroles, or slice thinly and use in baked dishes such as moussaka and potato dauphinoise.

Boil Peel maincrop potatoes and cut into large chunks. Put in cold salted water, bring to the boil, then cook for 10–20 minutes until tender. Scrub or scrape new potatoes. Put into a pan of boiling water and cook for 15–20 minutes until tender.

Crush Boil new potatoes as above, then drain, return to the pan and allow to steam dry for 1–2 minutes. Crush gently with a potato masher, then drizzle with olive oil and sprinkle with fresh herbs and black pepper.

Mash Boil maincrop potatoes as above, then drain and allow to steam dry. Mash with plenty of butter and milk until smooth, and season.

Roast Parboil prepared potatoes for 5–10 minutes, then drain and allow to steam dry for 1–2 minutes. Shake to roughen the surface. Heat oil, goose fat, duck fat or lard in a roasting tin at 220°C (200°C fan oven) mark 7 until very hot, add the potatoes, turn to coat, then roast, turning once or twice and basting with the fat, for 45 minutes–1 hour until golden.

Bake Choose large potatoes, scrub well and pat dry. Prick with a fork, then bake at 200°C (180°C fan oven) mark 6 for 1–1½ hours until tender. Alternatively, cook in a microwave oven; timing depends on the size of the potato.

Other varieties include

There are many hundreds of potato varieties, although only a small percentage of these are available in shops. If you grow your own, look for other varieties and experiment. The following are widely available:

Anya A small new potato with a long, slightly knobbly shape, pale, yellow-brown, pinkish skin with creamy-white flesh and a waxy texture. Boil, steam or use in potato salads.

Cara A large maincrop potato with a rounded shape and creamy flesh, it is good for boiling and baking.

Charlotte These small potatoes with a creamy-yellow skin and flesh have a firm, waxy texture and a good flavour. Boil or steam, or use cold in salads.

Golden Wonder A large, dark-skinned maincrop potato with a floury texture. Use for roasting and baking.

Sweet potato

Native to South America, the sweet potato is not related to the 'common potato'. It is usually elongated in shape, but there are also rounder varieties; the skin can be brown or red and the flesh can be deep orange or pale yellow. Sweet potatoes have a sweet, chestnut flavour and become tender and creamy when cooked; some may also have a somewhat fibrous texture. They are in season during the autumn and winter; look for smaller, firm potatoes as these will have a better texture.

TO USE Bake in its skin. Peel then boil, mash, roast, fry or add to stews and soups. Can be used to thicken soups.

Jerusalem artichoke

This small knobbly tuber is not a relative of the globe artichoke and is actually related to the sunflower. (The name Jerusalem is a corruption of *girasole*, the French word for sunflower.) Either pale brown or purplish-red, Jerusalem artichokes have firm, creamy white flesh with a distinctive, nutty taste.

In season in winter. Look for firm artichokes with as few knobbles as possible, as this will make peeling easier and produce less waste. If the artichokes are young and very clean, they can be cooked with their skins on, but usually they are peeled before cooking.

TO USE Peel. Boil, mash, sauté, fry or roast and use as an accompaniment. The flesh discolours when exposed to air, so drop the peeled and/or cut artichokes into acidulated water (1 tbsp lemon juice dissolved in 1 litre (1¾ pints) of water) as you prepare them.

Salsify

A member of the dandelion family, this long, tapering root has a brown skin and pale, creamy-white flesh. It can be boiled or sautéed and when cooked has a distinctive flavour not unlike that of Jerusalem artichokes. It is also sometimes known as 'oyster plant' because of its alleged similarity (in flavour only) to oysters. Salsify is in season during the winter. Choose firm, undamaged roots.

TO USE Scrub and peel, then cut the root into lengths. Boil for 20–25 minutes until tender, or parboil and sauté. The flesh discolours when exposed to air, so drop the peeled roots into acidulated water (1 tbsp lemon juice dissolved in 1 litre/1¾ pints of water) as you prepare them.

Parsnip

This large, tapering root vegetable is creamy in colour with a distinctive sweet, earthy flavour and tender texture when cooked. Parsnips are good roasted with meat, served with potatoes and carrots, or added to hearty winter stews. Or they can be made into a smooth, blended soup. They also go well with spices.

Parsnips are in season from autumn into winter, but they are at their best in cold weather, which converts more of their starch to sugar. Choose small, young parsnips, as these will have a better texture, and avoid any specimens with blemishes or shoots. You may want to cut out the core of the parsnip which can be tough and woody.

TO USE Scrub and peel; halve or quarter lengthways according to size, or for a stew, cut into chunks. Boil, steam or roast; to roast, first parboil for a couple of minutes, then toss in hot oil and roast.

Carrot

This sweet root vegetable comes in a variety of shapes and sizes: small and rounded, long, thin and tapering, or large and chunky. Eat raw, cut into batons as a snack or with a dip, grated in salads, or juiced. Add to stews, casseroles and soups, or add grated carrots to savoury dishes such as burgers and meatballs, or sweet dishes such as Indian *halwa*, carrot cake and desserts such as Christmas pudding.

Carrots are available all year round, either in season or from cold store. Look for hard, unblemished specimens with smooth skins. Feathery green tops on young, new-season carrots should be bright and fresh-looking (remove soon after buying as they will draw out the moisture from the root). Some authorities say that carrots should always be peeled if they have not been grown organically.

TO USE Top and tail; scrub or peel, chop, slice or grate. Steam, boil, stir-fry, roast; eat raw; for juicing.

Beetroot

Bright pink-purple beetroot has a sweet and earthy taste. It can be long or rounded, and there is also a golden variety. Early-season beetroots are small, maincrop are larger. Eat raw – grated in salads or juiced – or boil, add to stews and soups, roast or wrap in foil and bake, or use cold in salads. A classic use of beetroot is in the colourful beetroot soup *Bortsch*, which is popular in Eastern Europe and Russia. Grated beetroot can be added to cakes to give a moist texture and is good combined with chocolate.

Beetroot is in season from summer until autumn, and from cold store in winter. Look for small, hard specimens, ideally with their tops still attached, and store in a cool, dark place. **Note** If the leaves are in good condition, they may be washed and used in a salad.

TO USE Twist off the leaves, scrub (being careful not to damage or break the skin). Boil or bake until tender, then peel off the skin when cool enough to handle. To use raw, scrub and peel then grate or juice. **Note** Take care when preparing, as beetroot juice will stain. Prepare the cooked vegetable on a plate rather than a wooden or plastic chopping board.

Turnip

These are hearty, cream-coloured vegetables, sometimes blushed with pink-purple. They are usually round and slightly flattened with wispy roots. Small, young turnips have a distinctive flavour – hot and peppery, slightly sweet – and a crisp texture. Larger maincrop turnips tend to be coarser, with a less refined flavour.

Young turnips are in season from spring into summer, and maincrop the rest of the year. Look for firm, smooth, unblemished specimens and store in a cool, dry place.

TO USE Peel and slice or grate young turnips into salads, or peel larger turnips and dice or cut into small chunks before adding to casseroles and stews. Boil small, young turnips until almost tender, then finish cooking in a little butter.

Swede

Known as rutabaga in the US, this large, sturdy root with a thick, creamy-yellow, purple-tinged skin and orange flesh has an earthy, slightly sweet flavour. Good in hearty stews and soups, or roasted with other root vegetables, swede can also be boiled and mashed and served as an accompaniment. In Scotland, mashed swede is known as 'bashed neeps' and is traditionally served with haggis and 'tatties' (potatoes).

Swede is in season from late autumn until spring. Look for small, unblemished swedes, as larger ones tend to be tough and woody.

TO USE Peel. Boil or steam until tender, and mash with butter, add to stews or soups, or cut into chunks and roast.

Celeriac

This large, knobbly vegetable with a thick, coarse skin is the swollen root of a wild form of the celery plant. The flesh is pale and creamy-white with a distinctive mild, sweet, aniseed flavour. Grate and use raw in salads, or blanch slices or thin strips, then refresh in cold water and toss in vinaigrette. Celeriac is tender and well flavoured when cooked; it can be added to soups, stews and casseroles, mashed with other root vegetables, sliced and baked as a gratin, or added to fritters.

Celeriac is in season from autumn until winter. Look for firm, heavy bulbs that are free from blemishes, but avoid very large bulbs, which may be tough. Store in a cool, dry place.

TO USE Peel with a small, sharp knife; a vegetable peeler will not cut deep enough into the thick skin. Grate or slice to use raw, or cut into chunks and steam, boil, mash or add to stews.

Yam

There are many varieties of this starchy tuber, with origins in Asia, Africa and South America. Yams vary in size and shape. They can grow to more than 2m (6½ft) long, but they are best for cooking when they are much smaller. They are usually cylindrical or sausage-shaped with a dark brown skin that maybe tinged with pink and is often coarse and bark-like. The flesh may be white or yellow. The flavour is bland, not nearly as good as that of sweet potatoes, but it goes well with spicy foods. Throughout West Africa, it is boiled and pounded to make a thick paste known as *foo-foo*, which is served with spicy stews.

When buying, look for hard yams with unblemished, unbroken skins, and store in a cool, dark place.

TO USE Peel. Cook in the same way as potatoes: steam, boil, mash, roast, bake or fry.

Taro

Native to South-east Asia and India, taro is a corm – a thickened underground stem, rather like a bulb – which has been cultivated for millennia. It is usually large and barrel-shaped, with a rough brown skin and white flesh. It is a staple in many warm and tropical regions, including the Pacific islands. Taro must be cooked in order to neutralise compounds that cause serious irritation to the mouth if eaten raw. The cooked flesh has a mealy texture, rather like floury potato.

Look for small taro when buying, and store in a cool, dark place.

TO USE Peel. Boil in the same way as potatoes; it must be well cooked to neutralise the toxins it contains.

Cassava

Native to Central and South America, cassava is also known as manioc. The long, thick, tapering tuber has a tough, dark brown skin and hard white or yellow flesh. Varieties can be divided into two groups: bitter and sweet. The bitter variety contains a natural poison and needs to be processed to make it safe to eat. Widely used in the Caribbean and Africa, cassava is served in the same way as potatoes.

When buying, look for firm roots with a smooth skin.

Cassava products Both sweet and bitter cassava are processed to make cassava flour, cassava meal and tapioca.

TO USE Peel. Boil in the same way as potatoes.

Jicama

Native to Mexico, jicama is also known as Mexican potato and yam bean. With a thin brown skin and crisp, white, juicy flesh, it has a sweet and slightly nutty taste, not unlike that of water chestnuts. Jicama may be quite small or weigh up to 3kg (6½lb). It is popular in Chinese cooking: sliced and stir-fried, or eaten raw in a salad. In Mexico, it is usually served raw in thin slices, dipped in lime juice and sprinkled with chilli.

TO USE Peel. Cook like a potato; slice and eat raw or stir-fry.

Eddo

This is a West Indian, small, tropical, root vegetable from the same family as dasheen. An eddo has a small central bulb surrounded by tuberous growths. Its white flesh can be prepared, cooked and used much like a potato. It even tastes quite like a potato.

TO USE Peel and boil in the same way as potatoes; they must be well cooked to neutralise the toxins that they contain.

Kudzu

A starchy root popular in South-east Asian cooking, the irregularly shaped kudzu is similar to the yam, but the skin is less coarse. Inside, the flesh is white and sweet, tasting rather like beetroot.

When buying, look for very young specimens, as older roots will remain tough when cooked. Kudzu is also dried and ground into flour, which can be used for thickening soups or sauces, or for coating fried foods. The leaves can be used as greens, prepared and steamed or sautéed.

TO USE Peel. Cut into small pieces. Boil until tender.

The onion family

Yellow onion

Also known as Spanish onion, the yellow onion is the largest type. Large and round with pale brown skin and light yellow to greenish flesh, the yellow onion is mild and sweet, and is not too pungent. It is an essential ingredient in Spanish tortilla, and is a good all-rounder, which can be fried, stuffed, cut into rings and roasted. Long, slow cooking results in meltingly tender onions with a particularly mild flavour.

Vidalia is a popular variety, favoured for its mild taste. It is are named after the town of Vidalia, Georgia, USA, where it was first grown in the 1940s. Only onions grown in a defined area around the town may be given the name Vidalia.

TO USE Preparation, see page 253. In tortillas; fried, stuffed or roasted; in a wide range of savoury dishes.

Brown onion

A smaller variety of yellow onion, brown onions have thicker, darker brown skins and a more pungent flavour which makes them unsuitable for using raw (unless you really love a powerful onion taste). They are good all-purpose onions, well suited to chopping or slicing and frying in oil before adding other ingredients for sauces, soups, stocks, stews and other savoury dishes. They impart a good flavour and lose much of their pungency during cooking. They may also be roasted whole, in their skins, and served as a side dish.

TO USE Preparation, see page 253. In a wide range of savoury dishes.

Red onion

With a distinctive dark-red/purple papery skin, red onions vary in shape and size, but all have crisp white flesh tinged with magenta and a very mild flavour. Best suited to eating raw, they can be chopped or sliced and added to salads, salsas, dressings and marinated dishes. When cooked, red onions have an exceptionally mild flavour so they are not so well suited to imparting an onion flavour to dishes such as soups and stews. However, they are good roasted whole and served as a vegetable accompaniment.

TO USE Preparation, see page 253. In salads, salsas, dressings, marinades; roasted whole.

White onion

With a greenish, creamy-white, papery skin and crisp white flesh, white onions have a strong flavour and are generally considered too pungent to eat raw. However, they are excellent for cooking, either fried until tender and then combined with other ingredients to make sauces, soups and stews, or baked whole or stuffed.

TO USE Preparation, see page 253. In a wide range of savoury dishes.

Cipolla

Also called borettane onion, cipolla (the Italian word for onion) is a small onion with pale brown, papery skin and pale yellow flesh. It has a good sweet flavour and is usually peeled and cooked whole to show off its unusual shape. Cipolla is also good caramelised, roasted, bottled or pickled.

TO USE Preparation, see page 253. Roasted, caramelised, bottled and pickled.

Grelot

This small white onion from France has crisp white flesh and good flavour. It can be roasted or cooked whole in braised dishes, and its stalk can be used as a flavouring in soups and stews. If unavailable, shallots make a good substitute.

TO USE Preparation, see page 253. Roasted or cooked whole.

Potato onion

A type of shallot, the potato onion is unusual in that it grows entirely underground. It has a yellow skin and flesh and grows in clumps, with as many as eight small bulbs per clump. Once cultivated to fill the gap between cold-stored and new-season onions, potato onions are less commonly found now. If you do come across them, or grow them yourself, use as you would use brown onions.

TO USE Preparation, see page 253. In a wide range of savoury dishes.

Pickling onion

Also known as pearl onions, these small onions are usually about 2.5cm (1in) in diameter and may have yellow, red or white skins. Yellow and red pickling onions usually have a milder flavour than the white varieties. Generally peeled and used whole, they are ideal for pickling or adding to stews and casseroles such as boeuf bourguignon.

Silverskin onions, sometimes called cocktail onions, are tiny, white-skinned onions with a pungent flavour and are most often used for pickling. These are the traditional pickled onion that is added to a Martini cocktail.

TO USE Preparation, see page 253. For pickling; adding whole to casseroles.

Brown shallot

These small, golden-brown-skinned members of the onion family grow in clusters and have pale flesh and a finer flavour than a regular onion. The main bulb may be made of several smaller bulbs. Peel, chop finely and use in dressings and dishes such as sauces where you want to impart a finer onion flavour without the bulk of onions. Alternatively, roast in their skins, or peel and caramelise.

TO USE Preparation, see page 253. In dressings and sauces; roasted whole or caramelised.

Pink shallot

Strongly flavoured pink shallots have pink-red skins and pink-tinged flesh with a crisp texture. They are a popular ingredient in French cooking, and are best finely chopped or sliced and sautéed for inclusion in dishes such as stews and braises. They may also be cooked whole, caramelised in tarts or braised either on their own or in other dishes.

Echalote gris is another variety of pink-tinged shallot. It has the same crisp texture as pink shallot, but with a milder flavour that makes it well suited to eating raw (in salads and dressings) as well as cooking.

TO USE Slice or finely chop and sauté; cook whole and use in tarts and salads.

Red Thai shallot

Smaller in size than brown shallots, these purplish-red shallots have a very strong but sweet flavour. They are a key ingredient in Thai and South-east Asian cooking, where they are often used in startlingly generous quantities. They may be pounded in curry and spice pastes, sliced finely and used raw in salads, or sliced and fried until brown and crisp, then sprinkled over dishes as a seasoning and garnish. Or they may be pickled, whole, in sweet vinegar.

TO USE Raw in spice pastes and salads; slice and fry until brown and crisp for a garnish; pickle whole.

Banana shallot

The largest variety of shallot, banana shallots have pale brown, papery skin and a tapering, torpedo shape. They can vary in size from 6.5cm (2½in) to about 10cm (4in) long. They have a slightly milder flavour than brown and pink shallots. Banana shallots are good finely chopped and used raw in vinaigrettes or sprinkled over salads, or sautéed at the start of a recipe, as you would sauté onions.

TO USE Slice or finely chop and use raw in salads and dressings; sauté in butter or olive oil.

Garlic

The famously powerful, pungent bulb is covered in a papery skin that can be white, pink or purple-tinged. The bulb is divided into tightly packed cloves that are also covered in papery skin. New-season or wet garlic has a milder, sweeter flavour than the drier bulbs available the rest of the year. Mostly used as a spice or aromatic, garlic can be used raw to flavour dressings and butters, or fried at the beginning of savoury recipes. Whole bulbs can be roasted until the flesh is meltingly tender, mild and sweet.

Choose hard, unwrinkled bulbs with no sign of sprouting, and store in a cool, dark place.

Wild garlic, also known as ramsons, is in fact more closely related to the chive. It has long, pointed green leaves with the distinctive garlicky aroma, and may be sliced and added to salads, used as a herb flavouring – for example, in mashed potato or dressings – or steamed or sautéed as a vegetable.

TO USE Peel off the papery skin from each clove and crush, slice or chop. To roast whole bulbs, slice off the top, drizzle with oil, wrap in foil and roast until tender. Raw in dressings, butters, dips, salsas and marinades. Cooked in a wide range of savoury dishes.

Leek

Long, with a white stem and dark green leaves, leeks have a similar flavour to onions. When cooked, their pungent flavour mellows and sweetens and the leeks become meltingly soft. They can be sliced and sautéed, steamed or boiled to serve as a vegetable. If you are sautéeing the leeks, do not let them brown or they may become slightly bitter. Leeks also make a good addition to soups, stews and casseroles and can be used in tart and pie fillings. Parboil or steam whole leeks, drain well, and bake in a white or cheese sauce, or roast wrapped in Parma ham or finely sliced streaky bacon. Classic leek dishes include the chilled soup, vichyssoise, and the Scottish broth cock-a-leekie.

Leeks are in season from autumn through to spring. Choose those that are smallish and firm, with no yellowing leaves. Larger leeks may have a tough, 'woody' core.

TO USE Cut off the root and trim the tough tops from the leaves; cut through the top leaves lengthways and wash thoroughly to remove any trapped grit or dirt. In soups, casseroles and pies; served with a sauce. Use the green tops for stock.

Spring onion

Also called salad onions, green onions or scallions, these long, slim onions with white bulbs and tender green leaves can be an early-maturing variety of onion or an ordinary onion picked when young. Varying in size from slender to bulbous, spring onions have a mild, sweet flavour and are most often eaten raw in salads or as a garnish, or in quick-cook dishes such as stir-fries. They may also be finely chopped and used rather like chives and added to dishes as a flavouring herb; for example, stirred into mashed potato just before serving.

Buy fresh-looking spring onions, store in a cool place or the fridge and use within a few days. Usually the green part is discarded (except in some Chinese recipes), but there is no reason not to use it as long as it is in good condition and well cleaned of grit.

TO USE Trim off the root and any coarse leaves, then slice or use whole. In salads and stir-fries; as a garnish.

More about onions

The onion family, technically known as *Allium*, includes onions, shallots, garlic, leeks, spring onions and chives (see page 292) and all share the same distinctive flavour. Volatile sulphur compounds contained within their flesh give alliums their pungent taste and aroma, but it is the compound allicin that is released when onions are cut, which causes the eyes to water.

All onion bulbs have a distinct structure, consisting of many layers of pale, crisp, moist flesh underneath the papery outer skin. Shallots are similar, although their flesh contains much less water and cannot be cooked as long without burning. Leeks and spring onions are long and narrow, but also consist of many layers of 'leaf' and, like shallots, contain much less moisture than onions. Garlic, in contrast, although covered with a similar papery skin, is made up of segmented cloves around a central core rather than layers of flesh.

How to buy and and store onions

Look for hard specimens with a dry, papery skin and avoid any that are soft, damaged or sprouting. Try to choose individually rather than buying a large plastic bagful. Store in a cool, dry place, but do not store in the fridge, as this will cause the onions to soften.

Preparing onions and shallots

Onions and shallots are usually peeled before chopping, slicing or grating (unless they are to be roasted in their skins), and can often make the eyes water. There are various recommendations to alleviate this, the most popular and effective being to chop them under running water or chill them for an hour before preparation. Onions and shallots can be sliced in various ways according to the dish you plan to make: crossways to make rings; halved, then sliced to make half rings; chopped coarsely or finely; or grated.

Culinary uses for onions

Onions are one of the most versatile and useful of all vegetables. Few cooks would make a soup, stew, casserole, curry or sauce without first gently frying an onion in butter or oil. However, they are not only good for flavouring. They can also be enjoyed as a vegetable in their own right: sliced into rings and coated, then deep-fried, or boiled or roasted whole in their skins. Shallow-fried onions are a classic accompaniment to many dishes such as steak, and grated raw onion is a good addition to burgers, meatballs and meatloaf. Sautéed and caramelised onions, cooked until sweet and tender, are a classic ingredient in many dishes such as French onion soup, Spanish tortilla and tarts such as the French pissaladière.

Other varieties include

In addition to the more well-known members of the onion family, there are a number of other varieties that grow wild, or are sometimes available commercially.

Ramps Also known as wild leek, ramps are the best known of all the wild onions. They are similar in appearance to spring onions, but with a pungent, garlic–onion aroma and flavour. Use as for spring onions, but if eating raw, use sparingly.

Welsh onion Similar in appearance to spring onions, Welsh onions grow in clusters of bulbs; individual bulbs can be pulled off, leaving the remaining plant growing – hence they are sometimes known as everlasting onions. Widely used in China and Japan, the name Welsh has nothing to do with Wales, but relates to the Germanic word *welsche*, meaning 'foreign'. The flavour of Welsh onion is somewhere between spring onions and leeks. Use in stir-fries in place of spring onions.

Bunching onion Also known as Japanese bunching onions, these are very similar to Welsh onions and can be used in the same way.

Chinese shallot Not technically an onion at all, the Chinese shallot is a wild bulb grown in China and used for pickling – and it is usually exported in pickled form.

Elephant garlic This large variety of garlic has much larger cloves than regular garlic, but a considerably milder flavour.

Solo garlic This variety is made up of a single, large, bulb-shaped clove, rather than several small ones. Though milder than regular garlic, it is good for dishes that would need several smaller cloves for a strong flavour.

Garlic shoots Popular in parts of France, Italy and Spain, and in Chinese cooking, tender garlic shoots can be used in the same way as spring onions and chives. They may also be pickled.

Leafy green vegetables

Savoy cabbage

This dark green, crinkle-leafed winter cabbage has an excellent flavour and tender leaves, and is universally regarded as the best of the green cabbages for cooking.

Choose Savoy cabbages that are heavy, with firmly packed leaves, and store in a cool, dark place.

Note All cabbages contain sulphur compounds, which are similar to those that make mustard and onion so pungent. Cooking neutralises the pungency, but the smell may be off-putting while cooking is in progress.

Other green cabbages Many different varieties of green cabbage are available at different times of the year. They may be long and pointed, round and green, and loose or tight-leafed. They vary in taste from mild and sweet to very strong and more assertively 'cabbagey'. Prepare and cook as for Savoy.

TO USE Shred or cut into wedges. Steam, boil or braise, but do not overcook. Add to soups or wrap whole leaves around stuffing and simmer in a sauce.

Red cabbage

A round, hard cabbage with smooth, shiny, tightly packed leaves, red cabbage is a striking purple-red colour and has a milder, sweeter flavour than green. It is most often braised with apple, vinegar, sultanas and spices to make a sweet-and-sour accompaniment, which is good served with fatty meats such as pork and goose. The addition of vinegar and acidic fruit maintains the cabbage's vibrant red colour, which would be lost if boiled. It can be used in stir-fries or raw in salads such as coleslaw.

Red cabbage is available from late autumn through to spring. Look for heavy, firm cabbages with shiny, unwrinkled, dark-coloured leaves, and store in a cool, dark place.

TO USE Remove any tough or damaged outer leaves; shred finely for salads, or more coarsely to braise.

White cabbage

Similar in shape and appearance to red cabbage, white cabbages have spherical heads with firm, tightly packed, pale green leaves. With a sweet, mild taste and firm texture, white cabbage is good used raw in salads such as coleslaw, boiled or steamed as a vegetable accompaniment and served with butter, or added to soups and hearty winter stews.

White cabbage is available all year round. Look for heavy, firm cabbages with unblemished, unwrinkled leaves and store in a cool, dark place.

TO USE Remove any tough or damaged outer leaves; shred finely for salads, slice more coarsely for steaming, boiling or adding to soups and stews, or cut into wedges for steaming.

Spring greens

This dark green vegetable is an early variety of cabbage with tender, loose-packed leaves; it is harvested before it forms a heart. Boil or steam spring greens briefly to retain their sweet, fresh flavour and serve as an accompaniment topped with a knob of butter.

Spring greens were originally available only in spring but are now available most of the year. Look for fresh-looking heads and avoid any with wilting or flabby leaves. Store in the fridge and use within a few days.

TO USE Wash well and shred. Steam or boil until just tender.

Curly kale

One of the hardiest of the cabbage family, dark green kale, with its frilly leaves, is a good winter standby when other vegetables are out of season. The name is Scottish, and the vegetable is well suited to the harsh growing conditions of the Scottish winter. Curly kale is a sprouting plant without a heart. It has thick stalks and tougher leaves than cabbage but can be enjoyed in the same way, as an accompaniment or added to soups and stews.

Curly kale is available throughout the winter. Choose kale with dark green, fresh-looking leaves and avoid any that are wilted or yellowing. Store in a cool, dark place.

TO USE Wash well; shred or slice. Steam or boil until tender, or parboil for a few minutes, then drain and sauté in butter. Add to soups and stews.

Brussels sprout

These controversial vegetables, loved by many and loathed by many, resemble tiny cabbages that grow around a thick stem. Brussels sprouts have a sweet, nutty flavour with a distinct hint of cabbage.

Sprouts are in season throughout autumn and winter, and at their best during cold weather. Look for small, firm sprouts with tightly wrapped leaves, and avoid any that are yellowing. Store in a cool, dark place or in the fridge.

TO USE Remove from the central stem and trim the base of each sprout; remove any loose or wilted leaves; cut larger ones in half. Steam or boil until just tender and serve with butter, or toss with sweet chestnuts. Alternatively, shred and stir-fry with aromatics and spices.

Broccoli

The most common variety of broccoli available in shops is the tight-headed, dark green or purple-tinged calabrese, which has a neat, round head made up of individual florets growing on separate stalks out of the thick central stem. Broccoli can be steamed or boiled until tender and served as an accompaniment, stir-fried or added to Thai-style broths and curries. Cooked broccoli can be combined with a cheese sauce and baked in the same way as cauliflower cheese, or combined with olive oil, garlic, anchovies and chillies, and tossed with pasta.

Broccoli is in season from summer into autumn. Look for firm stalks and tightly packed, fresh-looking heads, and avoid any that are yellowing, limp or wilted. The small side leaves are a good guide to freshness.

Romanesco is a bright apple-green variety with spiralling florets – it looks like an alien cauliflower and can be treated as you would treat calabrese.

TO USE Wash; trim and peel off any thick skin from the stem; separate into florets and slice thick stalks. Steam, boil or stir-fry.

Purple-sprouting broccoli

Regarded by many as superior to calabrese, this purple-green variety of broccoli grows on shooting, fleshy stems rather than in a tightly packed head. It is most often served as an accompaniment with butter or oil and lemon, or as an appetiser drizzled with hollandaise sauce.

Purple-sprouting broccoli is in season in spring. Look for firm stems and fresh-looking heads and eat within a few days of purchase.

TO USE Wash; trim the stalks, stripping away any thick skin; halve if large. Cook standing upright in water so that the stems are boiled and the heads steamed, until just tender.

Cauliflower

Botanically similar to broccoli, creamy white cauliflower grows in round heads, called curds, ranging from tennis-ball-sized ones to very large specimens. It can be steamed or boiled, then served as an accompaniment or coated in cheese sauce, sprinkled with breadcrumbs and baked until golden. The raw vegetable can also be sliced in salads, or the florets used with dips, or cooked in stir-fries and Thai- and Indian-style curries.

Although the vegetable is available all year round, summer cauliflower has the best, sweetest flavour. Look for a firm white head with no blemishes or dark spots, The leaves (if they are still attached to the head) should be fresh and green. Store in a cool, dark place and use within a few days.

TO USE Trim away the leaves; cut away the woody core; break into florets. Eat raw; steam, boil or cook according to your recipe.

Swiss chard

Although often likened to spinach, Swiss chard has much firmer and slightly wrinkled leaves with thick, fleshy edible stalks and ribs. It has a good flavour, with a stronger, more robust taste than spinach. Serve as an accompaniment, sautéed in butter, coated in creamy sauce and cooked au gratin, or added to thick omelettes such as frittata.

Swiss chard is in season from autumn until spring. Choose fresh-looking chard with bright leaves and firm stalks, and avoid any limp specimens. Store in the fridge and use within a few days.

TO USE Rinse; cut the fleshy stems from the leaves; slice the leaves and stalks. Cook together or separately; the stems will need a minute or two longer, or they can be cooked for 20 minutes or more to reach a luxuriously melting softness. Steam, sauté or cook according to your recipe.

Ruby chard

Also known as rhubarb chard, ruby chard is similar to Swiss chard, except that the fleshy stem and ribs are a deep magenta-red colour. Also look for a golden variety with yellow-orange stems.

Rainbow chard is also sometimes available. It has red, gold, orange, pink and white stalks and green glossy leaves. It tastes the same as ruby chard.

TO USE Rinse; cut the fleshy stems from the leaves; slice the leaves and stalks. Cook together or separately; the stems will need a minute or two longer than the leaves. Eat young leaves raw in salads; steam.

Spinach

With tender, dark green leaves and a distinctive 'iron' flavour, spinach is a versatile vegetable that can be served on its own or added to other dishes. It can be steamed or sautéed in butter or olive oil, cooked gently with tomatoes and garlic, added to soups or curries, used in quiches or cooked with eggs in classic dishes such as eggs florentine and *pizza fiorentina*.

Spinach is available all year round; summer spinach is usually paler with tender leaves; winter spinach is darker and coarser. Only young, tender leaves should be used for eating raw. Look for bright, fresh-looking leaves and avoid any that are wilted or with brown patches. Store in the fridge and use within a few days.

TO USE Rinse and pat dry. Steam or sauté. In soups, salads, chopped in omelettes, quiches, soufflés,

Callaloo

Popular in the West Indies, callaloo is the a name given to a number of different leaves – mostly belonging to varieties of dasheen and eddo, and taro. Callaloo is most often cooked in a soup – also called callaloo – which contains coconut milk, salt pork, okra and spices. If callaloo is unavailable, spinach or Swiss chard can be used instead.

TO USE Rinse and pat dry. Steam or sauté.

Kohlrabi

This tasty vegetable is the swollen root of a member of the cabbage family; only the root is eaten, and not the scant, small leaves attached to it. The root is round, pale green (or sometimes purple), with a tough, thick skin. Inside, the flesh is tender, sweet and juicy. It can be eaten raw, sliced or grated in salads, or cooked – sliced or cut into strips and stir-fried, or cut into larger chunks and braised with tomatoes and spices, or added to hearty vegetable stews.

Kohlrabi is in season during summer, autumn and winter. Look for small bulbs, which are young and tender. Avoid larger bulbs, which may be tough.

TO USE Peel off the tough skin with a knife; slice, chop or grate. Eat raw; stir-fry or braise.

Radish

There are several varieties of this small, turnip-shaped vegetable, which is actually a swollen root of a member of the cabbage family. The two most common varieties are the round and bright red radishes, and the longer, red-and-white ones, known as breakfast radishes. They have a crisp, juicy texture and a peppery taste that can range from mild to moderately pungent. They are usually eaten raw, either with other raw vegetables as crudités or added to salads. Radishes can also be served with butter, which subdues and sweetens their peppery flavour. The leaves, if very fresh, make a delicious addition to a tossed salad. Radishes are not suited to cooking. Look for small, bright, firm radishes with fresh-looking leaves and avoid any that are soft or wilted.

TO USE Trim off the hairy roots and leafy tops; slice or eat whole.
(see also daikon, page 265)

Pak choi

Also known as bok choy and horse's ear, the broad, thick, fleshy white stems gather in a bulbous base and are topped with firm, dark green leaves. Pak choi has a fresh taste, rather like spinach with a mildly peppery finish. It is widely used in Chinese and Asian cooking. Look for firm, unblemished stalks topped with fresh-looking leaves, and avoid any that are limp or wilted. Store in the fridge and use within a few days.

TO USE Wash, trim the bases, then halve or quarter, and steam or quickly braise; slice the stems and leaves and stir-fry or add to Asian-style soups at the last minute.

Choi sum

Also known as Chinese flowering cabbage, choi sum is a cabbage-like Asian leaf with bright green leaves and pale, narrow, fleshy stalks. With a mild flavour, choi sum is good in Asian-style dishes. Choi sum takes particularly well to a classic Chinese vegetable dressing of oyster sauce, soy sauce and sesame oil. Just drain the steamed vegetable, put on a serving platter, and drizzle over the liquids. Look for bright, fresh-looking leaves and avoid any that are wilted, or with limp stalks. Store in the fridge and use within a few days.

TO USE Wash the leaves and pat dry, then slice and steam, stir-fry or add to soups.

Chinese cabbage

Also known as Chinese leaves or Peking cabbage, this long cabbage has pale green leaves with thick, white central ribs. The leaves have a crisp texture and a very mild flavour with faintly peppery overtones. They are good sliced and added to salads, or added to stir-fries and cooked briefly. Look for heavy, fresh-looking specimens and avoid any that are limp or wilting. A Chinese cabbage can be too large to use in a single meal, but it keeps exceptionally well in the vegetable compartment of the fridge for up to five days.

TO USE Slice thickly crossways, cutting off as much as you need; rinse well. In salads or stir-fries.

Chinese broccoli

Also known as Chinese kale, this leafy green vegetable has soft green leaves and stems that can be eaten in the same way as purple-sprouting broccoli. Its white flowers distinguish it from choi sum, which has yellow flowers, and indicate when it is ready to eat: look for fresh-looking specimens with white buds, rather than open flowers, and avoid any that are limp or wilting. The stalks will need 2–3 minutes more cooking than the leaves. Like choi sum, this vegetable is very tasty when dressed with oyster sauce, soy sauce and sesame oil.

TO USE Separate and wash the leaves; steam the stalks, adding the leaves after 2–3 minutes; or slice and stir-fry.

Chinese mustard greens

With long green stalks and dark green leaves, these Asian leaves have a fiery mustard flavour. Very young leaves can be combined with other leaves in salads to give bite, but older leaves are better sliced and added to soups or stir-fries. In China the greens are often preserved by pickling, and this is the form in which they are most often seen in Asian food shops.

Look for bright, fresh-looking leaves and avoid any that look tired or wilted. Store in the fridge and use within a few days.

TO USE Separate and wash the leaves; pat dry and use young leaves whole in salads, or slice and use in soups and stir-fries.

Morning glory

Also known as water convolvulus and water spinach, this long, slender, pointed Asian leaf with a narrow, hollow stem grows in marshy areas and tastes similar to spinach. Popular in Thai and Asian cooking, morning glory can be stir-fried, steamed or added to soups.

Buy fresh-looking leaves and avoid any that are starting to wilt. Store in the fridge and use within two days.

TO USE Separate and wash the leaves; pat dry; use whole or sliced. Steam or stir-fry.

Salad leaves

There are numerous varieties of cultivated and wild leaves that are delicious used in salads.

How to buy and store salad leaves

Look for fresh, springy leaves and avoid any that look limp, yellowing or bruised, or show signs of slimy patches. Store in the vegetable drawer of the fridge and use within three days.

Preparing and using salad leaves

Salad leaves are most often eaten raw, frequently combined with other leaves to make salads and garnishes, or they can be added to sandwich fillings. Serve on their own with a drizzle of dressing, or with other salad ingredients.

To prepare, trim, then tear the leaves into pieces if necessary. Rinse in a bowl of cold water and pat or spin dry. Assemble and dress just before serving.

Some salad leaves can be briefly cooked, such as in the classic French dish of braised lettuce hearts and peas. There are also numerous recipes for chilled lettuce soups, and watercress can be cooked into a creamy soup with potato and milk. Strongly flavoured leaves such as rocket and watercress can be blended to make pesto-like sauces for pasta.

Other varieties include

There is a wide range of lettuce varieties, ranging in colour, taste and texture, such as:

Cos (also known as romaine) has long, crisp green leaves with fleshy green hearts and a mild flavour. It is sold as a whole head.

Little gem (also known as baby cos) is a small, oval lettuce with pale green, crisp leaves and juicy pale stalks. Use the leaves whole, in salads, canapés or as a 'scoop' to hold fillings.

Iceberg has a round shape and a very pale colour. The tightly packed head has a crunchy texture and mild, sweet flavour; the texture is perhaps more important than the flavour. The leaves are usually shredded to use in sandwiches, salads and wraps.

Butterhead is available all year round. The pale green, loose-leafed lettuce has a tender texture and a mild flavour, and is good in salads.

Rocket Called arugula in the US, rocket's dark green serrated leaves have a soft texture and a distinctive peppery flavour. Rocket is good in salads, sandwiches and panini, scattered on pizzas or tarts, or as a garnish. It can also be blended with garlic, Parmesan cheese and pine nuts to make a pesto-style sauce for pasta, risotto or mashed potato.

Watercress This piquant-flavoured vegetable has fleshy stems and small, tender, dark green leaves. Extensively cultivated and available all year, it has a distinctively peppery flavour – excellent in salads, sandwiches, soups and with fish and game.

Chicory Also known as endive and Belgian endive, this pale vegetable has pointed leaves packed into a small, tight, tapering head. Its flavour is distinctively bitter. The whole head can be braised, or coated in a creamy sauce and baked. Use the leaves whole or sliced in salads, or serve whole with a dip.

Radicchio This is a type of chicory with a dark purple-red colour, a bitter flavour, and (usually) a small, round, tightly packed head. Add the leaves whole or thinly sliced to salads. Wedges of radicchio can be brushed with oil and chargrilled or griddled.

Curly endive Also known as frisée. This pale green vegetable has ruffled, curly, spiky leaves with a firm texture. It typically has a milder flavour than endive, with a hint of bitterness. It makes a good addition to salads and sandwiches.

Lollo rosso and lollo biondo The leaves are broad and crinkly; rosso's are dark purplish-red, whereas biondo's are green. Both varieties have a tender texture. The flavour is mild and sweet with a hint of bitterness. Use in salads and sandwich fillings.

Oak leaf Also known as feuille de chêne and red oak leaf. This tender vegetable has bronze, serrated leaves and a mild but distinctive flavour. It is used in salads and often combined with other leaves.

Lamb's lettuce Also known as corn salad and mâche, lamb's lettuce is a cultivated variety of a once-wild plant. The bright green, tender leaves have a mild, sweet flavour. It makes a good addition to mixed-leaf salads; or use as a garnish.

Cress and mustard sprouts These tiny sprouts have pale, thin, tender stems with dark green leaves. Their flavour is mild and faintly peppery. Sold growing in tubs, they can be snipped over salads, as a garnish, or added to sandwich fillings.

As well as the cultivated leaves, there are numerous edible wild leaves, including:

Sorrel has dark green leaves and an intense citrusy flavour. Add to salads in moderation, or shred and stir into creamy sauces for fish.

Nettles can be added to soups or herbal infusions, although only the young, tender leaves are used. Thorough cooking removes the sting.

Orache is also known as mountain spinach. It has red-gold leaves and is used in the same way as spinach (see page 257).

Dandelion leaves have a mild, spinach-like flavour when young and can be added to salads.

Shoots, stems and sprouts

Asparagus

By common consent, asparagus is one of the most distinguished of vegetables – a truly seasonal luxury. It has a subtle but distinctive taste and delicate texture. Asparagus may be served as an appetiser with melted butter, vinaigrette or hollandaise sauce, as a topping for canapés, or as a side dish or garnish. It can also be added to risottos, tarts, stir-fries and quiches.

British asparagus is in season from late spring to early summer, and is at its best when freshly picked. Look for fresh, firm stems and tightly furled heads, and avoid any that are limp or damaged. Try to examine the bases (sometimes wrapped in paper or plastic) for signs of shrivelling or wrinkling. Some recipes call for the stalks to be peeled before cooking, but this is not always necessary.

TO USE Cut or snap off the woody base; if the stalk is thick, peel it with a vegetable peeler. Traditionally, asparagus is cooked in a tall, narrow pan in which it stands upright in boiling water, so the stalks boil while the heads steam.

Globe artichoke

This extraordinary-looking vegetable is the bud of a thistle, and little more than 10 per cent of the bud is edible. But the edible portions are a delicacy. The globe artichoke consists of tough, grey-green leaves surrounding a tender heart and inedible 'choke'. It is usually served whole as an appetiser and can be eaten hot or cold. The eating process is slow and deliberate: each leaf is pulled from the globe and the fleshy end dipped in melted butter or vinaigrette. The fleshy part is then scraped off between the teeth and the remaining leaf discarded. When all the leaves have been removed, the central hairy choke is exposed. This is scooped out and discarded, revealing the tender heart. This is the prize morsel, eaten with more melted butter or vinaigrette.

Globe artichokes are in season from spring until autumn. Look for tightly packed green heads and fresh leaves without dry edges.

TO USE Cut off the stalk and remove the tough outer leaves, then boil for about 35 minutes, or until a leaf pulls out easily. The choke can be removed before serving by gently separating the leaves, then scraping out the choke using a teaspoon.

Cardoon

Related to the globe artichoke, the cardoon has a similar flavour, and is popular in southern Europe. It resembles a very large, long, grey-green head of celery, and the inner stems and heart can be eaten raw or cooked. Cardoon is treated in the same way as celery: sliced and used raw in salads, or boiled, braised or sautéed, and is good served plain with butter, or in a creamy or tomato sauce.

When buying, look for firm, plump and pale stalks, and use as soon as possible, as cardoons do not keep well.

TO USE Remove the outer stalks and leaves, strip out any tough strings as for celery, then slice and use raw, or steam, boil, sauté or braise.

Fennel

Also known as Florence fennel and fennel root, this is a member of the parsley family. It takes the form of creamy-white bulbs, either round and plump or sleek and flattish, with feathery green fronds poking out of the top. Fennel has a crisp, celery-like texture and a fresh, sweet taste with a definite hint of aniseed. It can be sliced thinly in salads, or more thickly for braising or sautéing. Wedges or halved fennel can be blanched and then baked with cream and Parmesan or a creamy sauce, braised in stock, or brushed with oil and seasoning and chargrilled or barbecued. Long, slow cooking mellows the pronounced aniseed flavour, and can win over even those who don't like aniseed.

Fennel is in season during late summer and autumn. Look for small, pale bulbs with fresh-looking feathery leaves and no blemishes or brown marks.

TO USE Trim off the feathery fronds and use as a garnish; rinse the bulb and trim the base; slice, halve, quarter or cut into wedges. Eat raw in salads; sauté, bake, braise, grill or barbecue.

Celery

There are two types of celery: white and green. They are the same variety, but white celery is covered in earth as it grows to blanch the stalks, whereas green celery is exposed to light and tends to have a stronger flavour. It may be used raw in salads or with dips, or boiled, braised or sautéed; the cooked vegetable loses the liveliness of the uncooked form, but gains an almost nutty richness. Celery is a good flavouring ingredient in stocks, soups, stews, casseroles and risottos. It is excellent when stir-fried or sautéed, and the leaves can be used like a herb: chopped and sprinkled over dishes just before serving. It makes a healthy, low-calorie snack.

Choose a celery with thick, firm, unblemished stalks and fresh-looking green leaves. Store in the fridge for a week or more.

TO USE Separate the stalks, wash well, then cut almost through the base of each stalk and pull upwards to remove any tough strings. Eat raw or cooked in a wide range of savoury dishes.

Corn

Also known as sweetcorn or corn on the cob. Corn has bright yellow, juicy kernels surrounding a hard inedible core and is covered in silky fibres and coarse green leaves. It is usually cooked whole, boiled or barbecued, and served as an accompaniment with butter. The kernels can also be sliced off to add to other dishes such as salads and soups.

Corn is in season from late summer into autumn. Buy very fresh cobs and use the same day. The sugars start to turn to starch as soon as the cob is picked, so older cobs will be mealy, rather than juicy and sweet.

Baby corn is eaten whole, either raw with a dip, or sliced or halved in stir-fries and Asian-style soups.

TO USE Remove the leaves and fibres from corn cobs, then boil in unsalted water until tender, or hold upright on a board and slice off the kernels. To barbecue, pull back the leaves, remove the fibres, then slide the leaves back and barbecue until tender.

Bamboo shoot

These conical shoots are cut from the plant when they are about 15cm (6in) long and have brown, overlapping leaves. The flesh inside is a pale, creamy colour and is always cooked before adding to other dishes to destroy the toxins it contains. Sliced bamboo shoot is a popular addition to Asian-style stir-fries and soups, as much for its pleasingly crisp texture as for its mild flavour.

Look for fresh shoots in Asian food stores. If they are unavailable, the canned shoots make a very good substitute: they are nearly indistinguishable from fresh and have the benefit of being ready prepared. Asian restaurants use them as a matter of course, and you should follow their example.

TO USE Shave off the brown leaves, then boil the fresh root to destroy the toxins before slicing and adding to stir-fries and soups.

Lotus root

Lotus root is frequently used in Chinese and Asian cooking. It is an underwater rhizome of the lotus flower and looks like a string of pink-beige sausages – but when it is sliced, a decorative pattern of holes is revealed. The flesh is tender, crunchy and sweet and turns pale pink when cooked. Lotus root is good added to salads, stir-fries and Asian-style braised dishes.

Look for lotus root in Chinese and Asian food stores and choose those that feel heavy for their size.

TO USE Scrub well, then peel; slice into sections and immediately dip into acidulated water (1 tbsp lemon juice dissolved in 1 litre/1¾ pints of water) to prevent discoloration. Boil until just tender, then add to salads, stir-fries or braised dishes.

Palm heart

Also known as hearts of palm and palm cabbage, the palm heart is the bud or terminal shoot of various palms. Palm hearts tend to be expensive, because harvesting in the wild kills the tree, although some cultivated trees such as peach palms grow multiple buds, thereby allowing the palm hearts to be harvested and the tree to continue growing.

The firm, cream-coloured flesh has a mild flavour somewhat reminiscent of asparagus. It is good served in salads, hot in a sauce, or fried. Fresh palm hearts are rarely available, but prepared canned hearts are fairly common.

TO USE Trim fresh palm hearts, then cut into lengths. Cut down the tough outer layers lengthways, then peel away, leaving the tender heart. Boil the hearts in a large pan of salted water until the tip of a knife can be inserted into the centre. Drain and refresh in cold water. In salads; fried or with a sauce.

Daikon

Daikon is a type of radish, and is also known as mooli and Oriental radish. Daikon is much larger than a normal radish, and is a thick, long, white root with a creamy, smooth skin. Eat raw or cooked, grated in salads or as a garnish for Japanese *sashimi*, or sliced and added to Asian-style soups and stir-fries. Pickled daikon is a delicacy in Japan and Korea. With a sweet, mildly peppery taste, it is not dissimilar to turnip in flavour and texture.

Look for daikon in Asian food stores. Choose firm specimens and avoid any that are soft or damaged. If you are grating it, use it as soon as possible in order to retain the crisp, crunchy freshness.

TO USE Peel, then grate or slice. In soups and stir-fries.

Water chestnut

Water chestnut is a small corm (a swollen stem base) that grows to 5cm (2in) in diameter and looks rather like a small bulb with a dark brown skin and creamy white flesh. With a crisp, juicy texture, water chestnuts have a bland, faintly nutty flavour and are good raw or cooked: sliced, diced or used whole in stir-fries or minced for dim sum fillings.

Water chestnuts are popular in Chinese cooking, and are valued as much for their crisp texture as for their flavour. Chinese and Asian food stores sometimes sell them in their fresh form. If those are not available, buy canned ones; these are widely available and require no preparation.

TO USE Peel off the dark skin, then slice, dice or mince the flesh, or use whole in stir-fries.

Bean sprout

There are many varieties of bean sprout. The most common are the crisp white mung bean sprouts used in Chinese and Asian cooking. Use them raw in salads, or toss into stir-fries and Asian-style soups at the end of cooking time.

Other common bean sprouts include alfalfa sprouts, which are good in salads and sandwiches, and aduki, chickpea and lentil sprouts, which can be used in the same way as mung bean sprouts. Buy crisp, pale, fresh-looking sprouts and avoid any that are browning or slimy. Store in the fridge and use within a couple of days.

TO USE Beansprouts require no preparation, although some cooks like to pinch off the wispy brown 'tail' from the thinner end of the sprout; use straight from the packet.

Peas and beans

Pea

To enjoy sweet, tender garden peas at their best, eat them as fresh as possible. The moment they are picked, their sugars start to turn to starch. This process will eventually make them taste bland rather than sweet, and their tender texture will turn chewy and coarse. This is why peas frozen straight after picking are often better than fresh. Peas are usually boiled until just tender, and can be served as an accompaniment with butter, added to risottos, pasta sauces, frittatas or tortillas and salads, or blended in soup. They are also delicious eaten very fresh and straight from the pod, as a snack, a nibble with drinks, or even an informal appetiser,

Peas are in season in summer. Grow your own or look for fresh, crisp pods and use that day.

Petit pois is a small variety of pea with a particularly sweet flavour.

TO USE Pop open the pods and nudge out the peas with your thumb, then eat raw or boil until just tender.

Mangetout

Their French name means 'eat all' – and that's exactly what you should do with these perennially popular pea pods. The green, fleshy, flat pod is sweet and crisp, and the peas inside are tiny. Mangetouts can be eaten raw with a dip or in salads. Their flavour is more developed if cooked, however, and they can be steamed or boiled and served as an accompaniment. Or they can be added to stir-fries, or sliced and added to risottos and soups.

Mangetouts are in season in summer. Look for bright green, fresh-looking pods with small, undefined peas inside. If you pick one up and try to bend it, it should be stiff rather than flexible. Store in the fridge and use within a day or two.

TO USE Top and tail, then serve raw, or briefly steam, boil or stir-fry.

Sugarsnap pea

Also known as sugar peas and snow peas, sugarsnap peas are similar to mangetout and are eaten whole. Bright green in colour, the rounded pods have pointed ends and have larger peas inside than mangetouts. They tend to be slightly sweeter and are well suited to eating raw in salads, as a snack, or as crudités with dips. They are also good steamed, boiled or stir-fried, or sliced and added to risottos and soups.

Sugarsnap peas are in season in summer. Look for bright green, fresh-looking pods. Store in the fridge and use within a day or two.

TO USE Trim the ends, then serve raw, or steam, boil or stir-fry.

Green bean

Also known as French beans, haricots verts, bobby beans and snap beans, these small narrow beans are best eaten when very young and tender. Generally, the thinner the bean, the more delicate in texture and flavour it will be. Steam or boil whole and toss in butter to serve as an accompaniment, or refresh in cold water and add to salads such as salade Niçoise or three-bean salad. Green beans are also good when cut into short lengths and added to chunky vegetable soups. This is especially suitable for bigger, tougher beans.

Green beans are in season in summer. Look for fresh, crisp beans and avoid any that are wilted or browning. Store in the fridge and use within a few days.

TO USE Top and tail and pull out any strings from older beans. Steam or boil; or cut into short lengths and add to soup.

Runner bean

Also known as string beans, these long, flat beans with a rough skin are at their best when still young and tender. Steam or boil and serve as an accompaniment, plain or tossed with butter. Or add them to chunky vegetable soups or Mediterranean-style vegetable stews.

Runner beans are in season in summer. Look for young beans with fresh green skins and a firm texture. If fresh, the bean should snap easily, revealing a moist, juicy pod. Store in the fridge and use within a day or two.

TO USE Top and tail, pulling out any strings on older beans; slice at an angle or use a bean slicer to cut into thin strips. Steam, boil or add to soups and stews.

Yard long bean

This is also known as an asparagus bean, snake bean, Chinese long bean or dow gok. The name yard long bean is something of a boast: it is usually sold (in bunches) at about half that length, around 48cm (19in). It is popular in China, South-east Asia and parts of India, where it is used in stir-fries and vegetable curries. It is a variety of cow pea or black-eyed pea, but it is generally harvested before the beans within the green pods are mature; if allowed to mature, the beans can be dried. Although it is not related to green and runner beans, its flavour is similar to runner beans and it can be used in the same ways: cut into short lengths and steam or boil.

As it is imported from various countries, it may be available at any time of year. Look for firm, slender, bright green beans and avoid any that are browning. Store in the fridge and use within a few days.

TO USE Pull out any strings if necessary, then cut into small pieces. Steam, boil, stir-fry or add to curries.

Okra

Okra is also known as ladies' finger, and in the American south can be referred to as gumbo. Okra is a green, velvety, ridged pod which is at its best at about 7.5cm (3in) long – the size of a lady's finger. It has a stem at one end and tapers to a point at the other. When the flesh is cut open, the pods release a slimy liquid which seeps out into the cooking liquid and gives it its distinctive 'gloopy' texture; this works well in stews such as gumbo. In other dishes such as curries, or as an accompaniment, it may be better just to trim the pod and cook whole.

Okra is in season during the summer, although in some places it is available all year round. Look for firm green pods with no brown marks. Store in the fridge and use within a few days.

TO USE Preparation, see page 269.

Broad bean

Broad beans are an ancient vegetable: archaeologists have discovered their remains in some of the earliest known cooking sites. Large, flat, and pale green, the beans grow inside velvety, cushioned pods. Young beans have a fine sweet flavour and tender texture and can be eaten raw. Older beans may be more strongly flavoured and are better eaten skinned, as their skins can become tough and bitter. Broad beans can be boiled or steamed and served as an accompaniment – either plain, in a white sauce or puréed – or refreshed under cold water and used in salads. They can also be added to soups, risottos and thick omelettes.

Broad beans are in season during the summer. Look for small and young, tender pods. Store in the fridge and use within a day or two. Podded frozen beans are widely available.

TO USE Preparation, see page 269. Steam or boil in unsalted water.

Soya bean

Fresh, young soya beans, with two or three beans per pod, are a delicacy in Japan (where they are called *edamame*). The pods are first rubbed with salt, then left to stand before boiling for 5–10 minutes until tender. They are served in the pod, sometimes drizzled with chilli oil, and eaten as a snack – the pod is popped open to remove the bean, then the husk is discarded.

Look for fresh-looking pods with a good colour and avoid any with brown marks or blemishes. Store in the fridge and use within a day or two. Podded frozen beans are widely available.

TO USE Rinse fresh soya beans. Salt and steam whole.

(see also dried soya beans, page 368)

Preparing broad beans

1 Hold the pod in one hand, with the stem pointing towards you. Insert the tip of a thumbnail between the two halves and open up the pod. Using your thumb, gently push out the beans.

2 For older beans, it is best to remove the skin. Make a shallow nick in the skin of each bean, then squeeze off the skin and discard.

Preparing okra

1 For cooking okra whole, wash and remove any wispy black 'hair' on the pods. Trim the end of the caps, taking care not to pierce the pods.

2 If you want to use the gelatinous liquid inside the pod for thickening a stew, okra should be split. Wash and trim as before, then cut in half lengthways, from tip to cap.

Squashes and gourds

Cucumber

Native to southern Asia, the cucumber has been cultivated since ancient times. There are two main types: one is large, smooth-skinned and straight; the other is small, thicker-skinned and knobbly. You can also find smaller thin-skinned varieties, especially growing in Mediterranean countries. The thicker-skinned variety should be peeled before using and has a sweeter, more distinctive flavour – but the seeds can sometimes be a little too crunchy for some tastes. Slice thinly or thickly for sandwiches and salads, cut into sticks for snacks or crudités to serve with dips. Or grate and stir into yogurt for dips such as Indian raita and Greek tzatziki.

Cucumbers are in season in summer, but because they are often grown under glass, they are widely available all year round. Choose firm specimens and avoid any with blemishes or soft patches. Store in the fridge and use within five days.

TO USE Rinse thin-skinned cucumbers or peel thick-skinned ones; slice, chop or grate.

Courgette

Known in the US by its Italian name, zucchini, courgette is a variety of marrow. Harvested while still young and tender, it may be yellow or green in colour. It is one of the most popular of the summer squashes. Courgettes can be steamed and served as an accompaniment, added to Mediterranean-style stews and Asian-style stir-fries, chargrilled or dipped in batter and deep-fried. They are also very good halved and stuffed, then baked until tender, or grated and sautéed with garlic and capers, then tossed with pasta and Parmesan cheese.

Courgettes are in season from summer into autumn. Look for small, firm, glossy specimens and avoid any that are soft, damaged or blemished. Very fresh courgettes may have fine 'hairs' on the skin which will be removed by washing.

TO USE Wash and trim both ends; slice, cut into batons or grate.
(see also courgette flowers, page 303)

Marrow

The largest of the summer squash, marrows can grow to an enormous size but are best picked while still young, small and tender. They are dark green with creamy-white stripes. Marrows can be steamed, sautéed or braised with tomatoes, blended in soups, or stuffed and baked. They have a mild flavour and are good enhanced with stronger-tasting ingredients such as tomatoes or fragrant herbs such as dill.

Marrows are in season from late summer into autumn. Choose small specimens with clear, unblemished flesh and store in a cool, dark place.

TO USE Peel off the thick skin, halve and scoop out the seeds. Stuff and bake, or cut into chunks to steam or sauté.

Pattypan squash

Also known as a scallop squash, custard marrow or button squash, these small, squat summer squash may be green, yellow or white and resemble little flying saucers with scalloped edges. They range in size from baby pattypans 4cm (1½in) across to fully grown specimens of about 12cm (5in). Similar to courgettes in taste and texture, pattypan squashes are best cooked whole to make the most of their decorative appearance. Steam until just tender, then serve as an accompaniment.

Pattypan squash is in season from summer into autumn. Look for clear, unblemished and undamaged skin. Store in the fridge or a cool, dark place and use within a few days.

TO USE Rinse; trim off the stem. Steam whole or slice off the tops, hollow out, stuff and bake.

Crookneck squash

The crookneck is a small summer squash. Yellow-orange in colour, it has a rounded base with bumpy skin and a curved neck resembling a shepherd's crook. With a mild, sweet flesh, crooknecks can be used in a similar way to courgettes: sliced and steamed, fried, chargrilled, braised with tomatoes, or stuffed and baked.

Crooknecks are in season from summer into autumn. Look for smaller specimens, no larger than 15cm (6in) in size. Store in the fridge or a cool, dark place and use within a few days.

TO USE Wash, then trim the ends and slice, or halve and scoop out the centre to stuff.

Spaghetti squash

Also known as vegetable spaghetti, this large, oval squash may be creamy white or orange-yellow in colour and has a thin, hard skin. Inside, the texture is unusual, with tender, edible seeds and flesh made up of firm, spaghetti-like strands – which can vary from pale to yellow or orange. It can be baked or boiled whole, then cut in half, topped with pasta sauce and eaten as you would spaghetti. Look for firm, unblemished specimens and store in a cool, dark place.

TO USE To cook, prick with a skewer and bake or boil for about 40 minutes until tender when pressed with the skewer. Cut in half, loosen the strands with a fork.

Pumpkin

These yellow or orange winter squash, with their hard, grooved skins, are sometimes known more for their decorative quality than their cooking properties – but they are very good to eat. Popular in the US, the sweet, orange flesh can be steamed or roasted as a vegetable or used to fill the sweet, spicy dessert pumpkin pie. It can also be added to soups or stews, puréed, or used to thicken gravy.

Pumpkin is in season from autumn into winter. Look for firm pumpkins with, unblemished skins. Stored whole in a cool, dry place, they will keep for several weeks or even months providing there is no damage to the skin or around the stalk – check regularly. Larger pumpkins may be sold in wedges; look for pieces with firm flesh and avoid any that look fibrous.

TO USE Peel off the skin and remove the seeds and fibrous mass connecting seeds to flesh; cut the flesh into chunks. Steam or roast as you would potatoes.

Butternut squash

A squash with a rounded base and thick neck, butternut squash range in size from around 15–30cm (6–12in) and may be pear- or club-shaped. The skin is a creamy orange-beige in colour, smooth and quite tough; the flesh is an intense orange colour with a firm texture. Roasting is the best method for bringing out its sweetness, but the flesh can also be chopped, sliced or diced and steamed, stir-fried, braised and added to stews and soups. Butternut squash is also good halved, seeded and baked in its skin, with or without stuffing.

In season from autumn into winter. Look for firm squash with smooth, unblemished skin.

TO USE Peel, halve and scoop out the seeds; cut into chunks or slices. To stuff, leave unpeeled, halve and scoop out the seeds.

Acorn squash

Shaped like a giant acorn, these small winter squash have a thick orange or dark green skin with broadly spaced grooves and sweet orange flesh. The large seed cavity makes them ideal for stuffing. A small acorn squash will feed one person; larger ones can be halved to serve two. The flesh can be roasted, steamed or braised, or added to soups and stews as you would with any other squash.

Acorn squash is in season from autumn into winter. Look for firm, heavy specimens with smooth, unblemished skins. They store well (for weeks or even months) if kept in a cool, dry place, as long as there is no damage to the skin or around the stalk – check regularly.

TO USE Halve lengthways or remove a 'lid', then scoop out the seeds and stuff; or peel and cut the flesh into chunks.

Little gem squash

These small, ball-shaped winter squash have a tough, smooth, green skin, surrounding firm, sweet, pale orange flesh. Like acorn squash, little gem is an ideal size for one person and is equally well suited to stuffing and baking whole. Alternatively, the flesh can be roasted, baked, steamed, braised or added to soups.

The squash is in season from autumn into winter. Look for firm, heavy specimens with smooth, unblemished skins. They store well if kept in a cool, dry place as long as there is no damage to the skin or around the stalk – check regularly.

TO USE Halve lengthways or remove a 'lid', then scoop out the seeds and bake stuffed or unstuffed; or peel and cut the flesh into chunks.

Kabocha squash

This heavy, medium-large round squash has bright green knobbled skin and deep grooves, and is popular in Asian cooking. The pale orange flesh is similar to that of acorn squash and is good baked and mashed with butter, or roasted, steamed, braised or added to soups and stews.

Kabocha is often sold in wedges, but also sold whole. Look for firm, heavy squash with unblemished skins and store in a cool, dry place. Whole squash will keep for several weeks or even months providing there is no damage to the skin or around the stalk – check regularly.

TO USE Cut away the skin, halve and scoop out the seeds; slice the flesh or cut into chunks.

Other winter squash

There are many varieties of winter squash, available in numerous shapes, sizes and colours. They can be prepared and cooked in the same way as pumpkin, butternut and acorn squash. Other interesting types to look for include:

Turban squash A large, round orange-skinned squash rather like a flattened pumpkin, but with a distinctive turban-shaped top. Turban squash have a firm, sweet, deep orange flesh with excellent flavour.

Moschata squash A rounded, flattened squash with gnarled skin and distinct ridges. Moschata is unusual for the brown colour of its skin.

Onion squash A small, bulb-shaped squash with orange skin, onion squash is suitable for stuffing and baking.

Coquina squash Similar in appearance to a butternut squash but with a slightly streaky skin, coquina squash also has a similar taste and texture and can be prepared and cooked in the same way.

Preparing squash

1 Peel with a swivel-handled peeler or a cook's knife. Halve the squash, then use a knife to cut through some of the fibrous mass connecting the seeds with the wall of the central cavity.

2 Scoop out the seeds and fibres with a spoon, then cut the flesh into pieces. For steaming, baking or roasting, cut the chunks fairly large – at least 2.5cm (1in) thick.

1 For cooking squash in the skin, wash the squash, then cut in half or quarters.

2 Use a knife to cut through some of the fibrous mass connecting the seeds with the wall of the central cavity, then use a spoon to scoop out the seeds and fibres.

Bottle gourd

Also known as calabash and dudi, this club-shaped gourd can grow up to 60cm (24in) long and has a bulbous base that narrows towards the neck. Yellow-green in colour, the bottle gourd has a mild, cucumber like taste, and can be cooked in the same way as marrow: peeled, seeded, sliced and steamed; stuffed and baked; braised with tomatoes; or added to flavoursome stews.

Look for firm gourds with no damage or blemishes to the skin. Older gourds have a tough skin and are not suitable for eating.

TO USE Peel off the skin, scoop out the seeds and slice or cut into chunks; or stuff and bake.

Chayote

Also known as christophine, choko, chocho, chow chow and pepinello, this small gourd is shaped like squat, fat pear with pale green, slightly ridged skin. The flesh is pale, firm and mildly flavoured with a single edible stone in the centre. Chayote can be sliced raw into salads, cut into larger slices and steamed or braised, or stuffed and baked in the same way as marrow.

Look for small firm chayotes with unblemished skins. Store in the fridge and use within a week.

TO USE Bake in its skin; peel, slice and eat raw or steam or braise.

Winter melon

Also known as wax gourd, this large, elongated Asian gourd has a dark green skin and pale greenish-white flesh with a mild flavour not unlike that of a courgette. The flesh can be sliced or cut into sticks and stir-fried, steamed, braised with other vegetables, or added to soup.

Large winter melons are usually sold in slices, and once cut should be stored in the fridge and used within a few days. Whole melons will keep much longer and should be stored in a cool, dry place.

TO USE Peel off the thick skin; scoop out the seeds and slice the flesh. Steam, stir-fry or braise.

Kantola

Also known as balsam apple and ucche, this small bitter gourd is oval with a tender, green, knobbly skin and grows to about 5cm (2in) long. The flesh is packed with seeds which are edible when young, but as the gourd ripens and the flesh sweetens, they toughen and become inedible. The flesh has a distinct bitter flavour and can be added to Indian- and South-east Asian-style curries and stir-fries.

Choose firm, bright green gourds, when buying.

TO USE Scrub well to remove any dirt trapped in the knobbly skin; slice and salt or blanch before cooking, to mellow the bitterness.

Luffa

Also known as Chinese okra, silk squash and ribbed luffa, this long, dark green gourd with sharply ridged skin is used in Chinese, South-east Asian and Indian cooking. It has a mild and delicate flavour, and the pale flesh is slightly spongy, with slippery seeds. Luffa can be sliced and cooked briefly in stir-fries and Asian-style soups.

Choose young, firm luffa with unblemished skins. Store in the fridge and use within a few days.

TO USE Wash younger gourds and slice. Older gourds with tougher skins should be peeled first.

Bitter melon

Also known as bitter gourd and bitter cucumber, this pale green or white knobbly vegetable is popular in South-east Asian cooking. The pale flesh has a distinctive bitter taste and readily absorbs other flavours. It is good cooked in stir-fries and curries.

Look for firm, unblemished bitter melons and allow to ripen for a couple of days before using. Once they're ripe, use as soon as possible.

TO USE Peel and slice. Some cooks suggest boiling for several minutes to remove the bitter flavour before adding to soups or stir-fries, but this is a matter of taste.

Mediterranean vegetables

Salad tomato

Also known as round tomatoes, these are a good all-rounder that can be used in salads and all types of cooking. Tomatoes are really a fruit, and like all fruits they get their best flavour when allowed to ripen in the sun. However, they are often picked before truly ripe in order to give them a longer shelf life and protect them from damage during both transport and storage. Although some further ripening takes place off the vine, tomatoes picked unripe are almost always somewhat bland and acidic. They can be improved with seasoning and a pinch of sugar when cooking. It is worth noting that in many places where tomatoes grow naturally (and gloriously) in the summer heat, many home cooks would never consider using them out of season.

TO USE Preparation, see page 279. In salads, salsas; baked, stuffed, roasted, fried; in a wide range of savoury dishes.

Plum tomato

These attractive oval tomatoes have a rich, sweet flavour and contain fewer seeds than salad tomatoes. They are usually preferred for cooking, partly because they contain less water than salad tomatoes and therefore don't take as long to cook out the moisture. But they are also excellent used raw in salads. Popular varieties include Italian Roma and San Marzano. Plum tomatoes are rarely available outside the normal late summer tomato season.

TO USE Preparation, see page 279. In salads, salsas; baked, stuffed, roasted, fried; in a wide range of savoury dishes.

Beefsteak tomato

These large, squat tomatoes are often ridged and range in colour from orange and red to dark red-purple depending on variety. They are a fleshy fruit, with a firm texture and sweet mild flavour. To take advantage of their impressive size, slice in salads or sandwiches; scoop out the centre, stuff and bake; or scoop out the centre and stuff with salad, prawns in mayonnaise, or other cold dishes.

TO USE Preparation, see page 279. In salads, salsas; baked, stuffed, roasted, fried; in a wide range of savoury dishes.

Cherry tomato

Also known as baby tomatoes, cherry tomatoes are the smallest type. Usually about 2cm (³/₄in) in diameter, they may be round, plum- or pear-shaped, and have a much sweeter, more intense flavour than salad tomatoes. Their appealing size makes them good for salads, garnishes and canapés, but they are also good for quick-cook pasta sauces, because they do not require much cooking to achieve a sweet, rich flavour. They can also be threaded on to skewers and briefly barbecued, or stir-fried quickly with garlic as an accompaniment.

TO USE Preparation, see page 279. In salads, salsas; baked, stuffed, roasted, fried; in a wide range of savoury dishes.

Yellow tomato

With a bright yellow skin, these tomatoes may be round, plum- or pear-shaped, large or small, and are the same as red tomatoes in all ways but colour. To make the most of their colour, use raw in salads, salsas, sandwiches and on canapés, or in combination with red tomatoes.

TO USE Preparation, see page 279. In salads, salsas; baked, stuffed, roasted, fried; in a wide range of savoury dishes.

Green tomato

Originally this term was used to describe the tart, unripe tomatoes that were picked to use in chutneys and relishes, but several varieties have been specially developed to have a bright green skin even when ripe. To make the most of their colour, use raw in the same way as yellow tomatoes.

TO USE Preparation, see page 279. In salads, salsas; baked, stuffed, roasted, fried; in a wide range of savoury dishes.

Peeling tomatoes

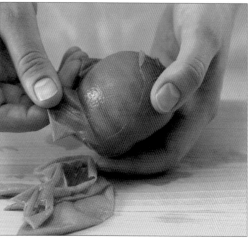

1 Fill a bowl or pan with boiling water. Using a slotted spoon, add the tomato for 15–30 seconds, then remove to a chopping board.

2 Use a small sharp knife to cut out the core in a single cone-shaped piece. Discard. Peel off the skin; it should come away easily.

More about tomatoes

Native to South and Central America, tomatoes are related to the sweet pepper, aubergine and potato. They are technically a fruit, but are eaten as a vegetable, either raw or cooked.

How to buy and store tomatoes

Tomatoes are in season from summer into autumn. Look for firm, unblemished fruits, ideally with fresh green leaves. Tomatoes ripened on the plant will have a better flavour – and you can buy 'vine-ripened' fruits – but you can also ripen slightly green tomatoes at home by placing them in a brown paper bag for a day or two. Never store tomatoes in the fridge, because the cold temperature impairs the flavour and can make the texture mealy. Overripe tomatoes that are too soft for eating raw are excellent for cooking in soups, sauces and stews.

Culinary uses for tomatoes

Incredibly versatile, tomatoes can be eaten raw in salads, either halved, quartered or cut into wedges, sliced in sandwiches, seeded and chopped in salsas and relishes, or juiced. Small varieties are excellent eaten as a snack, with dips, or as a topping for canapés. For cooking, tomatoes are usually best peeled and used in sauces, soups, stews, casseroles and curries, where long, slow cooking will bring out their sweetness and intense flavour. They can also be stuffed and baked in their skins. If you find yourself faced with a glut of tomatoes, preserve them in chutneys and relishes.

Although tomatoes have become the ubiquitous vegetable in kitchens around the world, they are particularly associated with the cooking of the Mediterranean, where they are used in classic dishes such as pasta sauce, ratatouille, pizza, bruschetta, paella, and tomato and mozzarella salad.

Other varieties include

There are countless varieties of tomato ranging from small to large; from uniformly round in shape to plum, oval and ridged; in colour from yellow, orange and green to red, purple and striped.

Yellow pear tomatoes Bright yellow and about the size of a cherry tomato, these distinctive pear-shaped tomatoes can be used in salads, as a garnish, or on canapés.

Pomodorino tomatoes A relatively large, plum-shaped cherry tomato, pomodorino has an intense, sweet flavour.

Sungold tomatoes An orange cherry tomato with a sweet flavour that goes well in salads.

Olives

These small oval fruits vary tremendously in colour, shape and taste. They may be green, brown, purple or black, and their flavour sweet or sharp-tasting, tender and juicy, or dry and firm. Green olives are picked before they are ripe and have a sharper flavour and firmer texture, whereas ripe black olives are tender and sweeter. They may come marinated with herbs and spices, or stuffed with pimiento, anchovy paste, garlic, lemon – literally with dozens of different flavours. If you want the pure taste of the olives in a cooked dish or salad, however, it's best to use unflavoured olives. Olives are often served as a cocktail snack, added to stews, pasta sauces, salads and breads, used to top pizzas or puréed in pastes such as tapenade. For the best flavour, buy olives with the pits still in. Good varieties include Spanish queen olives and Greek Kalamata. Where olives are sold loose, ask to taste before you buy.

TO USE Eat as they are, combine with olive oil and aromatics to marinate, or pit and slice for sauces and stews.

Aubergine

Also known as eggplant and brinjal, aubergines are widely used in both European and Asian cuisines. Shape, size and colour vary greatly according to variety. Aubergines may be large or miniature, bulging and pear-shaped, long and narrow, egg-shaped or round. And they can range in colour from dark purple-black through lilac and cream. The tiny, bitter-tasting green pea aubergines are mainly used in Asian dishes such as Thai green curry, whereas other varieties are good fried, grilled, simmered in stews and curries, or baked with or without stuffing. If you are frying them, you may want to peel them first: the skins can be tough and chewy, especially when exposed to high heat.

Aubergines are in season from summer into autumn. Look for firm, heavy aubergines with glossy skins. Store in the fridge for up to two weeks.

TO USE Rinse and pat dry, then halve, scoop out the centre and stuff; or slice and fry or grill.

Sweet pepper

Known as bell peppers in the US, these fluted capsicums may be green, yellow, orange, red or purple-black. Green peppers are the least ripe and have a fresh, crisp, slightly bitter flavour; yellow, orange and red are sweet and crisp. They can be used raw in salads, salsas and relishes, added to stir-fries, Thai curries, sauces and stews, roasted, or stuffed and baked.

Peppers are in season from summer into autumn. Choose firm, unblemished fruits. **Note** Peppers have tough skin which may turn stringy and chewy when cooked. If you are using the peppers in a cooked dish, you may want to peel them either using heat (see facing page) or with a swivel-headed vegetable peeler.

Sweet baby peppers These small, pointed peppers are ideal for stuffing or roasting and serving as canapés or as part of a selection of antipasti.
Ramiro peppers A long, tapering sweet red pepper, ramiro is sweet and crunchy with a good flavour.

TO USE Halve and remove the seeds and white pith, then stuff and bake; or slice or chop and eat raw or use in a wide range of savoury dishes.

Seeding peppers

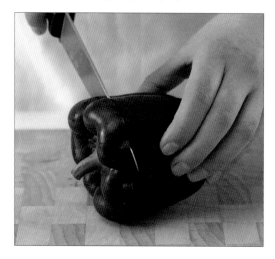

1 Cut around the top of the pepper, leaving the stalk attached to the core.

2 Cut out and discard the core, seeds and white pith. (Alternatively, cut the pepper in half vertically and snap out the white pithy core and seeds then pull away the remaining white membrane.)

Roasting and peeling peppers

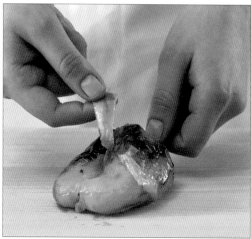

1 Using tongs, hold the pepper over the gas flame on your hob (or put under a preheated grill) until the skin blackens, turning until black all over.

2 Put in a bowl, cover with clingfilm and leave to cool (the steam helps to loosen the skin). Pull off the skin.

Mushrooms and fungi

White mushroom

The most common of the cultivated mushrooms, white mushrooms have creamy white caps, pale gills and a mild flavour, and will vary in size, with closed or open caps, depending on maturity. White mushrooms can be used for many savoury dishes. But if a stronger mushroomy flavour is required, for example in a risotto, they are best combined with other mushrooms such as chestnut or cep (porcini).

Button mushrooms are picked while young and small, before the caps have opened. Add to stews and casseroles such as boeuf bourguignon, Asian-style soups and curries, or prepare à la grecque (in a liquor of water, olive oil, lemon juice, herbs and coriander seeds, and sometimes tomato purée) and serve cold.

TO USE See Using cultivated mushrooms (opposite).

Chestnut mushroom

Similar in appearance to closed-cap white mushrooms, these mushrooms have a pale brown cap with a thick, squat stalk. They also have a slightly firmer, meatier texture and a stronger flavour than white mushrooms, making them a good choice among the supermarket mushrooms. Use in the same way as you would use white mushrooms.

TO USE See Using cultivated mushrooms.

Field mushroom

These large, flat-capped mushrooms, closely related to the common cultivated mushroom, have a pale brown cap and dark brown-black gills. Field mushrooms are good used for most dishes but are particularly suited by their size and shape to stuffing and baking, or drizzling with oil, seasoning and grilling. The colour from their gills will darken creamy sauces and other pale dishes such as cream of mushroom soup and risottos. If you do not want that colour, use white mushrooms.

Flat mushrooms, the cultivated cousin of field mushrooms, are similar in appearance. They have the best flavour of any cultivated mushroom, and are an excellent choice for most dishes, particularly where you want a pronounced mushroomy flavour.

TO USE Preparation, see page 288.

Oyster mushroom

The lovely fan-shaped oyster mushroom is a type of fungus that grows on dead wood (formerly in the wild but now widely cultivated). Its appearance is vaguely similar to that of an oyster shell, with creamy, pink-beige caps and slightly paler gills and stalks. The caps of oyster mushrooms are relatively soft, but much of the stalk may be tough and should be discarded (or set aside and used to flavour soup or stock). They add good flavour to Asian-style dishes such as broths and stir-fries, and are also good when combined with other mushrooms in fillings or dishes such as risottos.

TO USE Preparation, see page 288.

Shiitake mushroom

Widely available in supermarkets, this cultivated Asian mushroom has a distinctive appearance with a round brown cap and a slightly longer, narrower stalk than white mushrooms. Shiitake mushrooms have a distinctive flavour and firm, meaty texture that becomes slippery when cooked. They need slightly longer cooking than white mushrooms, but you should avoid overcooking as this will make them tough. Halve, quarter or slice the caps and sauté or use in Asian-style broths, stir-fries and braised dishes. Shiitake may also be eaten raw or lightly cooked in broth then added to salads.

TO USE Trim off and discard the hard stalks. More tender sections of stalk can be used, and the discarded stalks can add flavour to soup or stock.

Using cultivated mushrooms

Choose mushrooms that look fresh, and avoid any that are withered or slimy. Mushrooms will sweat if stored in plastic, so put in a paper bag, store in the fridge and use within a few days.

TO USE Trim the stalks, and wipe the caps with a damp cloth; unless the skins are thick or discoloured, peeling is inadvisable and unnescessary. Small mushrooms can be cooked whole, halved, or quartered. Larger ones are best sliced or chopped. Or they can be left whole but with the stalk removed, then stuffed and baked or grilled. To cook, sauté in butter or olive oil as an accompaniment or filling for pancakes and omelettes, add to stews, casseroles, curries, soups, risottos and pasta sauces. Add sliced raw mushrooms to salads, marinating them first in vinaigrette if you want to soften them. Small or medium-size mushrooms also make a decadent appetiser when coated in batter, deep-fried, and served with tartare sauce.

Cep

Also known by their Italian name, porcini, these universally treasured wild mushrooms have a distinctive appearance. The fleshy, pale brown cap is relatively small when compared to a chunky, cream-coloured stalk that thickens at the base. They have an intense, nutty flavour, and are good cooked in most ways, sautéed in butter and served on toast or as an omelette filling, in sauces and risottos, or as a stuffing for pasta such as ravioli. As a general rule, very large ceps are likely to have an unwanted spongy texture. They are also more likely to harbour insects, which seem to love ceps (with good reason) more than any other wild mushroom.

Ceps dry well, sliced and left in a warm, dry place for several days. Store in an airtight container and use as for other dried mushrooms (see page 288).

TO USE Clean well and split the stalk to check for insects and maggots. Slice.

Morel

Unlike most wild mushrooms, morels are in season in spring rather than autumn. Their distinctive pale brown pointed caps are full of holes and crevices, rather like a sponge or a coral. The flesh is creamy-white and the stalks short and hollow; insects like the hollows. Never eat morels raw; sauté in butter for about 30 minutes or until tender and add to risottos, fillings or use to top canapés.

Morels are second in expense only to truffles. If you are lucky enough to find them growing in woodland, remember that they dry exceptionally well – indeed, this is how morels are usually sold. Thread on to a piece of string and leave in a warm, dry place until completely dry, then store in an airtight container.

TO USE To prepare, halve lengthways and rinse very well in cold water to remove any debris or insects, then allow to dry on kitchen paper.

Chanterelle

These pretty, wild mushrooms grow in woodland areas throughout Europe; they are usually one of the easiest to find if you go mushroom-hunting. With a distinctive trumpet-shaped cap, the underside may be yellow or orange-tinged, and the flavour is mild and perfumed. Chanterelles are highly regarded and tend to be expensive, although not as expensive as ceps and morels.

Cook whole or sliced, sautéed in butter or in sauces. They may also be dried, or preserved in oil. **Note** If you are picking your own, be careful to avoid the poisonous false chanterelle, which is distinguishable by its well-formed gills.

Girolle is a grey version of the chanterelle. Prepare and cook in the same way.

TO USE Clean well before cooking, carefully brushing free of any debris.

Blewit

There are two types of blewit: the wood blewitt and the field blewit, which grow in circles in woods and fields respectively. Both are strikingly attractive. The wood blewitt has a large, smooth, lilac-blue cap, and on its underside the gills and thick, flaring stalk are lilac too. The field blewit is similar, but paler and slightly grey in colour. Both have a distinctive flavour and tender texture, and must always be cooked. Blewits are suitable for cooking in most mushroom dishes. **Note** Blewits can cause an allergic reaction in some people.

TO USE Preparation, see page 288.

Bay boletus

Related to the cep and with a similar appearance, the bay boletus has a darker brown cap and creamy chestnut stem. Prepare and use in the same way as cep.

Other varieties of boletus There are many varieties of boletus mushroom that are worth looking out for. Edible varieties include the orange-cap boletus, with a rust-red cap and thick white stem, slippery jack, with a chestnut brown cap with a sticky-slimy surface, and the similar, yellow-fleshed granulated boletus. **Note** There are also poisonous varieties of boletus, which have a red specked underside, including *Boletus luridus* and *Boletus satanas*.

TO USE Clean well and split the stalk to check for insects and maggots. Slice.

Horn of plenty

Known as *trompette des morts* in France, the horn of plenty is related to the chanterelle. It is dark brown-black in colour and the stalk grows directly into the frilled, delicate-looking cap of this funnel-shaped fungus, giving it the appearance of a trumpet. The horn of plenty is often available dried. It has a strong flavour and is well suited to cooking in soups, stews and creamy dishes.

TO USE Clean fresh specimens well and trim off the base. Split in half to check there is no debris trapped in the funnel-shaped cap. Slice.

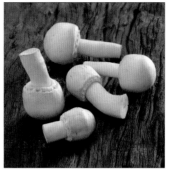

Shimeji

Shimeji is the name of a group of Japanese mushrooms originally found in the wild. All have fairly long, relatively slender stems and a small cap, and they grow in clusters. Some varieties can be cultivated, and they are the ones you are likely to find on sale. Buna-shimeji, shown here, have brown caps and stems. Bunapi-shimeji are a white version. Shimeji are not eaten raw. They can be stir-fried, braised, and added to soups and casseroles. As long as they are not overcooked they retain their pleasingly firm texture.

TO USE Preparation, see page 288.

Straw mushroom

These pale brown mushrooms are widely used in Chinese and Asian cooking and are cultivated on beds of damp straw. They are usually gathered while they are still young and small, although they can grow to quite a large size. They have a dense, bulbous cap, which has an inimitably slippery texture and tender bite when cooked. Straw mushrooms have a very mild flavour, and are valued by Asian cooks for their texture. They are mostly available canned or dried in the West, and are good used in Asian-style soups and braised dishes.

TO USE Preparation, see page 288.

Enokitake

Although the wild varieties of enokitake are found only in Japan, they are now also cultivated elsewhere. Enokitake is a tiny, pin-headed mushroom that grows in clusters on stumps of the enoki (Chinese hackberry) tree. It has a long, pale stem and small, pale-brown cap. With a delicate flavour, enokitake are most often used in Asian-style broths, salads and as a garnish. They need only very brief cooking, so add to your dish at the last moment and do not cook for more than a minute.

TO USE Preparation, see page 288.

Truffle

The truffle is the most highly prized – and expensive – of the edible fungi. Truffles grow underground in certain types of woodland. When the truffles are fully mature and their scent strong, pigs and dogs are used to snuffle them out. White truffles, which are famous for their intense perfume, most famously grow in the Piedmont region of northern Italy but are also found in Croatia. There are several types of black truffle, but the best grows principally in France. The black version is somewhat less expensive than the white. Both have a powerfully rich aroma and flavour, and only a small amount is needed to flavour a dish. Black truffles can be thinly sliced and sautéed, for use in soups, stuffings or terrines and similar dishes; one of the most famous French dishes using them is Tournedos Rossini, a fillet steak topped with a slice of foie gras and sliced black truffle. White truffles, by contrast, are always used raw so their treasured perfume will be released only on making contact with the dish in which they're served. They are usually grated or shaved over dishes such as pasta or risotto.

TO USE Preparation, see page 288.

Giant puffball

Puffballs can grow to be monsters of field and forest, with diameters up to 150cm (5ft) in extreme cases. Most are smaller, however, and those worth eating are young, white and relatively small – less than 7.5cm (3in) in diameter. To check whether a puffball can be eaten you can split it open and look at the interior: it should be white rather than yellow, and show no sign of gills or rotting. Puffballs have a wonderfully firm texture and an aroma that some people compare to that of ceps. They are very versatile and can be cooked in most wild mushroom dishes: sliced and sautéed in butter, used as a filling for omelettes, or added to stews, soups, sauces and risottos.

TO USE Peel thinly if the skin is tough. Slice.

King oyster

This is an imposingly large and muscular variety of the delicate, frilly oyster mushroom. (You would hardly spot the connection in a fully grown king oyster.) Also known as king trumpet mushrooms, they are native to the Mediterranean and have been cultivated since the early 1990s – and cultivated specimens, though by no means a common sight, are far more common than wild. Some come from Asia, but specialist mushroom suppliers in Europe and the US also sell them. King oyster mushrooms have a mild flavour which intensifies greatly with cooking, so they are always cooked. They are prized most highly, however, for their texture, which is firm and silky. King oyster mushrooms need little trimming, since the stalk is just as good to eat as the cap.

TO USE Preparation, see page 288.

More about wild mushrooms and fungi

Although often described separately, mushrooms are a type of fungus, and the term is generally used to describe edible fungi: plants that grow off living, dead and decaying organic matter such as tree stumps. Fungi mostly come into season during autumn, and can be found growing in fields, woods and gardens. They generally have a smoky and much more intense mushroom flavour than cultivated varieties.

How to buy and store mushrooms and fungi

Always choose mushrooms and fungi that look fresh, and avoid any that are withered or slimy. (Although note that there are a few wild varieties that are distinguishable for their sticky, glutinous skins.) Put the mushrooms in a cool, dry place such as a basket, or in a paper bag in the fridge, and use as soon as possible after picking or purchase.

How to prepare and cook mushrooms and fungi

Wild mushrooms and fungi should always be cleaned carefully before cooking. Many varieties may contain bugs or maggots, so are best halved and all cavities checked before slicing and cooking.

Wild mushrooms and fungi have a superior flavour but can usually be cooked in the same way as cultivated mushrooms. With the exception of truffles, which are usually used in minute quantities, mushrooms and fungi can be sliced or chopped and sautéed in butter or added to sauces, stews, soups, risottos and soufflés. Or they can be cooked with eggs and/or cream, used to fill tarts or to top canapés, or as a stuffing for pasta.

Dried mushrooms

Many mushrooms, including ceps, chanterelles and shiitake, are available dried and are excellent for adding to moist dishes such as soups and stews and risottos. The drying process intensifies their flavour, so adding a few dried and reconstituted ceps (porcini) to a risotto made with cultivated mushrooms, for example, will significantly boost the flavour.

To rehydrate dried mushrooms, put in a bowl, pour over boiling water to cover, then leave to soak for 20–30 minutes. Strain the mushrooms, keeping the soaking liquid to one side. Rinse the mushrooms well to remove any debris before adding to your recipe. Strain the soaking liquid through kitchen paper to use in recipes.

Poisonous mushrooms and fungi

Many wild mushrooms and fungi are delicious and well worth gathering from the wild, but this is a potentially dangerous pastime: many are poisonous or hallucinogenic. Furthermore, many common edible species, such as ceps, chanterelles and field mushrooms, have toxic cousins with a similar appearance; this is an added risk for the amateur mushroom gatherer. There are many comprehensive full-colour, illustrated guides and books on mushrooms and fungi, and you should not pick without a copy in your hand. If you cannot be 100 per cent sure about what you are picking, leave it growing in the wild and leave the gathering to experts who will do it safely. You can learn about wild mushrooms by joining a fungus foray organised by a specialist in areas where wild mushrooms can be found. These are fascinating and highly enjoyable.

Other varieties include

Horse mushroom Found growing wild in fields in autumn, this large white fungus closely resembles the field mushroom and can be prepared and cooked in the same way.

Amethyst deceiver In season from late summer until early winter, this small, woodland mushroom is a distinctive lilac colour and can be cooked as for other wild mushrooms.

Chicken-of-the-woods In season from late spring until early autumn, this yellow fungus can be found growing on deciduous trees in a distinctive fan shape. Gather the younger, pale yellow fungus, which is tender and juicy, and avoid older specimens, which will be darker in colour. Blanch in boiling water for a few minutes before slicing and cooking.

Beefsteak fungus Also known as ox-tongue fungus, this large fungus grows on oak and chestnut trees in Europe and parts of the US. Its dark red, mottled flesh gives it a striking resemblance to a piece of meat. To prepare, peel and remove the pores, then slice and salt to remove some of its acidity before cooking.

Honey fungus Growing in clusters on tree trunks and stumps in the same way as Japanese enokitake, these long-stemmed golden mushrooms have a slightly astringent flavour. Always serve cooked.

Hedgehog fungus This sought-after woodland fungus is a pale, beige-cream colour with a thick cap and stem. The young fungus has a slightly peppery flavour that becomes bitter as the fungus matures. Use small specimens whole and slice larger ones.

Dried and bottled vegetables

Traditionally, vegetables were dried or bottled during gluts in the summer to provide variety for the winter months, but they have a useful place in the kitchen even today. They typically have a deeper, mellower flavour than fresh, and provide a storecupboard convenience food which gives you the chance to enjoy the ingredients out of season.

Vegetables are usually dried in a warm place or the sun, or with the use of gentle heat, which intensifies the flavour. Bottled vegetables are usually packed in oil, often with spices and aromatics.

Sun-dried tomato
Usually semi-dried, these tomatoes are sold packed in jars of oil. Drying turns them dark red in colour and gives them a chewy texture and an intense, tangy-sweet flavour. Use the oil for dressings or cooking. Fully dried tomatoes may be sold loose, without oil.

TO USE Snip into pieces. Use in salads, canapés, sandwiches, egg dishes, soups and savouries; on pizza; added to soups, stews and risottos.

Sunblush tomato
Usually found on the deli counter, sunblush tomatoes are partially dried cherry tomatoes. Sunblush have a much shorter shelf life than sun-dried and should be stored in the fridge and used within a week. They are tender and succulent with a sweet flavour, and taste best uncooked.

TO USE In salads, as antipasti; as a topping or garnish for canapés; in risottos.

Oven-roasted mi-cuit tomato
These tomatoes are oven-roasted to give a sweet flavour, and are sold in vacuum packs.

TO USE Serve in the same way as sun-dried and sunblush tomatoes.

Dried aubergine
Slices of chargrilled, sun-dried aubergine make a good addition to vegetable sauces and stews.

TO USE Follow the directions on the pack. Add to sauces or stews.

Sun-dried pepper
Dark red, shrivelled sun-dried peppers are similar in appearance to sun-dried tomatoes. The have an intense flavour and a chewy texture.

TO USE Soak in boiling water for a few minutes until tender. Slice or chop. Add to simmered dishes such as soups and stews.

Dried mushroom
See page 288.

Bottled marinated vegetables
Often sold as antipasti, these well-flavoured vegetables can be used as a short-cut ingredient.

TO USE As antipasti; on toast, crostini, canapés; stirred into pasta, couscous or rice.

Artichoke
Bottled artichoke hearts, sometimes chargrilled before marinating in oil and flavourings, have a good flavour and texture. They make a speedy alternative to preparing fresh artichokes.

TO USE Cut into wedges and use to top canapés or pizzas; in salads, antipasti and pasta. Use the oil for dressings or cooking.

Pepper
Chargrilled peppers, bottled after seeding and peeling, can be found in most supermarkets. Often flavoured with spices and aromatics, they have an intensely sweet, piquant flavour and make a convenient standby for using instead of freshly roasted peppers.

TO USE Cut into strips and use in salads, on pizzas and canapés, in sandwiches and panini, with eggs; add to stews, soups and pasta sauces; blend in dips.

Chilli
Sweet, small, red peppadew hot peppers and sliced green jalapeños are often bottled and are excellent for adding bite to dishes without being overpowering.

TO USE Slice or chop. Add to stews, soups and sauces; on pizzas and in Mexican-style dishes such as quesadillas or burritos.

Mushroom
Wild mushrooms can often be found bottled in oil with spices and aromatics, particularly in regions in which they are grown. Stir into dishes made with cultivated mushrooms to boost flavour and interest.

Herbs and spices

Fresh herbs

Parsley

There are two types of this vivid green herb: flat-leafed and curly. Cooks often prefer to use flat-leafed parsley for Mediterranean dishes. It is robust and easy to grow, and has a full flavour with fresh, grassy undertones. Parsley is one of the most versatile of all fresh herbs, suiting almost any savoury ingredient and compatible with all the European and Europe-derived cuisines. It goes particularly well with fish, ham and vegetables and is good in stuffings for poultry, creamy sauces, and herb butters. It can also be used as a garnish and in bouquet garni and fines herbes (see page 301). The strongly flavoured stalks make a flavoursome addition to stocks and stews.

TO USE Rinse in cold water and pat dry with kitchen paper. Remove the leaves from the stem and use whole, or chop coarsely or finely as required.

Basil

This tender, fragrant herb has an intense aroma that has a natural affinity with tomatoes. Although most often associated with Italian and Mediterranean cooking – and an essential ingredient in pesto – basil is also widely used in Thai cooking. There are numerous varieties, of which the most common is sweet basil, but other varieties include purple-leafed opal basil, lemon basil, which has a distinct lemon scent, cinnamon basil, with a cinnamon scent, and anise-scented Thai basil.

TO USE Tear rather than cut basil leaves: when cut, the edges are likely to turn black. Add to cooked dishes at the last minute, as the flavour diminishes with cooking.

Chive

This herb is a member of the onion family. Slender and hollow-stemmed, chives have a mild oniony flavour that goes especially well with egg and cream dishes, such as omelettes, baked eggs, soufflés and savoury custards. Chive shines forth when combined with potatoes in almost any form, particularly potato salad and the leek-and-potato soup vichyssoise, and is an ideal flavouring for butter, cream cheese, dips and dressings. It is also an essential ingredient in fines herbes (see page 301).

Chinese chives are also known as garlic chives because of their garlicky flavour and aroma. Use as for chives and in stir-fries and Asian-style dishes.

TO USE Rinse in cold water and pat dry with kitchen paper. Hold strands of chives in a bunch and snip over salads and other dishes, either as a flavouring or garnish. Add to cooked dishes at the last minute, as the flavour diminishes with cooking.

Coriander

Known as cilantro in the US, this tender aromatic herb has leaves that are paler, delicate and more rounded than flat-leafed parsley. It has an unmistakeable, almost pungent fragrance. Coriander is used in cuisines throughout the world, from the Mediterranean and Middle East to India and Thailand. It adds a fragrant flavour to salads and salsas, and its flavour remains pronounced when added, just before serving, to Mediterranean stews, Indian curries, North African couscous and tagines, Mexican dishes and Thai stir-fries.

Coriander root is used in Thai cooking and has a stronger flavour than the leaves. It may be chopped and used in spice pastes for curries and stir-fries.

TO USE Rinse in cold water and pat dry with kitchen paper. Remove leaves from the stalks and use whole, or chop coarsely or finely. Scatter over cooked dishes at the last minute, as the flavour diminishes with cooking.
(see also coriander seed, page 312)

Mint

A highly versatile herb, mint is equally suitable for sweet and savoury dishes. There are numerous varieties of mint including spearmint, lemon mint, apple mint, peppermint and pineapple mint, each with their own subtly different flavour. It is an essential ingredient in mint sauce and jelly, tabbouleh and yogurt dips such as tzatziki and raita. Mint can also add its unmistakeable flavour to green salads and rice, as well as couscous salads and sprinkled over Indian and Thai curries, and fragrant Thai stir-fries. Its flavour also goes well with sweet dishes such as fruit salads, and it is an essential ingredient in two famous cocktails: the mojito and the mint julep. With or without alcohol, it adds a refreshing hint of flavour to summer punches and old-fashioned lemonade. Mint tea, a good digestive, is made by infusing fresh or dried leaves in boiling water.

TO USE Rinse in cold water and pat dry with kitchen paper. Tear or chop the leaves, coarsely or finely. Add to cooked dishes at the last minute. Use whole leaves and sprigs for garnishing and infusions.

Dill

Delicate, feathery dill has an anise-scented flavour which has made it a favourite herb in a wide range of national cuisines. It has an affinity with egg, cream, potato and fish dishes, and is a natural pairing for cucumber, courgette and spinach. A popular flavouring in Eastern European and Scandinavian cooking, dill is used to flavour pickled cucumbers, herring and potato salad and other fish dishes, and is often paired with dairy products such as yogurt, cream cheese and feta. Dill is the key flavouring for gravadlax, the classic Scandinavian dry-cured salmon. It is also used as a flavouring for marinades and dressings, and as a garnish.

TO USE Rinse in cold water and pat dry with kitchen paper. Chop finely or coarsely. Add to hot dishes just before serving, as the flavour diminishes with cooking. Use whole sprigs for garnishing.
(see also dill seed, page 317)

Tarragon

This tender-leafed herb has slender, grey-green leaves and a pronounced aniseed flavour. It goes well with chicken and fish, as well as with egg and cream dishes. An ingredient of fines herbes (see page 301), tarragon is also used to flavour Béarnaise and tartare sauce, dressings and mayonnaise. Tarragon leaves can be added to white wine vinegar and left to infuse to make an aromatic vinegar to use in dressings.

French tarragon is far superior to the wild variety, known as Russian tarragon, which has a much coarser and less delicate flavour.

TO USE Rinse in cold water and pat dry with kitchen paper. Remove leaves from the stem and tear or chop, coarsely or finely.

Fennel

Related to dill, with the same feathery, delicate leaves and sweet aniseed flavour, herb fennel comes from a plant that is related to but distinct from vegetable fennel. It is frequently paired with fish, and is particularly popular with oily fish such as sardines and mackerel, where its delicate yet distinctive flavour cuts through the richness of the fish. The fronds are also excellent snipped over salads or hot dishes as a garnish. They can be used to flavour vinegars, dressings and mayonnaise, and go well with cream and egg dishes, such as potato dauphinoise, baked eggs and omelettes.

TO USE Rinse in cold water and pat dry with kitchen paper. Chop finely and add to hot or cold dishes. Use whole or chopped for garnishing.
(see also fennel, page 263 and fennel seed, page 316)

Chervil

Similar in appearance to flat-leafed parsley and coriander, although much more delicate, chervil has a mild aniseed flavour and is good paired with fish, poultry, eggs and cream. It is used in fines herbes (see page 301). Once picked, the herb wilts quickly, so use as soon as possible after picking.

TO USE Rinse in cold water and pat dry with kitchen paper. Snip with scissors. Add to cooked dishes or sprinkle over salads and vegetables.

Angelica

Related to parsley, angelica is a tall plant that is cultivated mainly in Europe. The fresh stalks have a musk-like scent and are frequently chopped and added to desserts made with acidic fruits, such as rhubarb and apple, giving them a muscatel flavour and reducing their acidity. Young angelica leaves can be finely chopped and used to flavour dressings and mayonnaise.

Candied angelica The hollow green stalks of the herb can be cooked in a sugar syrup, then the outer layer peeled to produce a bright green candied confection that is used to decorate cakes and desserts.

TO USE Remove leaves from stalks, rinse and pat dry with kitchen paper. Use stalks whole and snip the leaves with scissors.

Lemon balm

The dull green leaves of lemon balm are pointed and serrated. With a pungent lemony aroma, lemon balm can be used in both sweet and savoury dishes. Pair with any ingredients that go well with lemon, such as fish, chicken and vegetables, or use in fruit salads and other desserts, and drinks such as fruit punches. Lemon balm can be infused in boiling water to make a herbal tea. It is also a good flavouring for sweet creams, syrups and custards.

TO USE Rinse in cold water and pat dry with kitchen paper. Chop the leaves, finely or coarsely, or use whole in punches and infusions.

Borage

This summer herb is valued mostly for its blue-mauve, star-shaped flowers with striking black stamens at their centre. The leaves of the borage plant are soft, quite thick and a dull greyish-green colour. Older leaves are coarse and hairy and therefore not ideal for culinary use, although very small, young leaves can be added to salads, chopped or left whole. Chopped leaves can also be added to mayonnaise. The whole flowers look attractive scattered over savoury or sweet salads. Borage flowers are the traditional decoration used in Pimm's. The flavour of both the flowers and leaves is very mild, rather like cucumber.

TO USE Shred tender young leaves for salads, or gently pull off the flowers to float in drinks or scatter over salads.
(see also edible flowers, page 303)

Comfrey

Comfrey is related to borage (see page 295), with similarly coarse, hairy leaves with a mild cucumber flavour. The delicate bell-shaped flowers (white, yellow or pink) are most often used to decorate salads. Comfrey may also be used to flavour home-made wine, rather like elderflower, and in Bavaria it is used to flavour butter.

TO USE Pick off the flowers, rinse and use whole.
(see also edible flowers, page 303)

Savory

Because it has a pungent, robust, peppery flavour, savory must be used in moderation. Used to excess, it can be overpowering – rather like thyme and rosemary. Traditionally cooked with beans and pulses, it goes well with fresh green and runner beans, as well as dried beans such as flageolet, cannellini and borlotti. Savory is also good in hearty, meaty stews and casseroles, and in chunky, warming soups. There are both winter and summer varieties, which have a similar flavour and can be used in the same way.

TO USE Rinse in cold water and pat dry with kitchen paper. Use whole sprigs in stews and braised dishes, and remove before serving, or strip off the leaves and chop finely.

Sweet cicely

Not commonly available for sale, sweet cicely is usually found growing only in domestic herb gardens. With a sweet, faintly aniseed flavour, the tender, lacy leaves can be used in salads and dressings, but are better suited to desserts such as fruit salads, compotes, fools and pies. It goes well with sharp fruits such as apple, rhubarb and gooseberry.

TO USE Rinse in cold water and pat dry with kitchen paper. Tear or finely chop the leaves.

Lovage

Not so commonly used as it once was, lovage is similar in appearance to celery leaves and has a strong, celery-like flavour. It is good used in robust soups, stews and casseroles and goes particularly well with root vegetables and potatoes. It can also be used in salads, but use sparingly as its flavour can become overpowering. The stems can be chopped and used in the same way as the leaves, and they may also be candied and used in the same way as candied angelica.

TO USE Rinse in cold water and pat dry with kitchen paper. Chop finely or coarsely.

Marjoram

Related to oregano, marjoram has a robust, splendidly fragrant flavour that goes beautifully with tomatoes and Mediterranean-style cooking. There are two types: mild-tasting sweet marjoram and the more strongly flavoured pot marjoram.

Marjoram is a traditional flavouring for tomato sauce. It can also be added to sauces, stews and casseroles, or sprinkled directly on to pizzas. Its flavour complements roast meats; rub over joints or use in stuffing. In Greece, marjoram is a popular flavouring for lamb. Add sprigs of marjoram to oils and wine vinegars and leave to infuse, or finely chop and add to marinades for meat.

TO USE Rinse in cold water and pat dry with kitchen paper. Remove the leaves from the stems and use whole or chopped. Add to hot dishes at the last minute, as the flavour diminishes with cooking.

Oregano

The wild variety of marjoram, oregano is now widely cultivated and available growing in pots. It has a much stronger flavour with a heady and seductive perfume, and can be used (in moderation) in the same ways as marjoram: in sauces, stews and casseroles, as well as with Mediterranean vegetables, roast meats, and meat and game stews. It has a particular affinity with pork. Oregano also goes well with egg and cheese dishes such as tortillas and omelettes, pizza, panini and cheese on toast. Use in moderation, as the flavour can become overpowering.

TO USE Rinse in cold water and pat dry with kitchen paper. Remove the leaves from the stems and use whole or chopped.

Rosemary

A robust herb with spiky leaves and a strong, pungent flavour, rosemary is traditionally used to flavour pork or lamb and other meats such as sausages and rabbit. It is also good used in hearty vegetable and bean stews, but should always be used in moderation, as its flavour can easily become overpowering. Use rosemary to flavour breads such as focaccia, savoury scones and stuffings. It also goes well in sweet dishes such as poached fruit. A sprig of rosemary can be put in a jar of sugar to give it flavour, or simmered in sugar syrup, and then used in cakes, biscuits, fruit salads, sorbets and ices. Rosemary grows well in gardens, and a single bush will be more than enough to supply all your needs.

TO USE Rinse in cold water and pat dry with kitchen paper. Remove the leaves from the woody stalk and chop finely, or use whole sprigs in stews and soups, and remove before serving.

Thyme

Small-leafed thyme has a strong, aromatic flavour which is extremely popular in Mediterranean cooking. Add to slow-cooked stews and casseroles and cook with meat, chicken, game, tomatoes and Mediterranean vegetables. It also goes well with mushrooms, can be used in bouquet garni (see page 301) and makes a good flavouring for strong-tasting pâtés such as game and liver.

There are many varieties of thyme, but the most common are garden thyme and lemon thyme. The latter has a slightly subtler, more lemony flavour that goes well with fish, mild meats such as veal, and egg dishes such as tortillas and frittatas.

TO USE Rinse in cold water and pat dry with kitchen paper. Remove the leaves from the woody stalk and use whole or chop finely, or use whole sprigs in stews and soups, and remove before serving.

Sage

Pale grey-green, velvety sage leaves have a strong, pungent flavour and are best used in moderation – when used appropriately they add a delicious fragrance and subtlety of flavour. Chop and cook with chicken, pork, veal, liver and sausages, or drape a couple of leaves over quail, wrap in bacon and roast. In Italy, sage butter is a standard accompaniment to ravioli and other stuffed pasta. It is also good drizzled over grilled white fish. To make sage butter, fry a few sage leaves in butter for a minute until crisp, then use immediately. The leaves retain their crispness and add visual appeal as well as flavour.

TO USE Rinse in cold water and pat dry with kitchen paper. Pluck off individual leaves and use whole or chop finely.

Bay leaf

The shiny, dark green leaves of the bay laurel usually grow to about 7.5cm (3in) long. The fresh leaves have a strong, inimitable aroma (stronger than that of the more common dried leaves), so only one or two leaves are needed per dish. Bay leaves are a popular addition to robust meat and tomato sauces, stews and casseroles, and can be used to flavour marinades for meat, poultry and fish. Individual leaves can be threaded between ingredients skewered on to kebabs to impart some of their flavour to the meat.

An ingredient in bouquet garni (see page 301), a bay leaf can also add a fragrant flavour to stocks and can be infused in hot milk for dishes such as béchamel sauce. Try them too in sweet dishes, infused in sugar or sugar syrups as for rosemary, and in biscuits, cakes, fruit salads, poached fruit and ices.

TO USE Rinse in cold water and pat dry with kitchen paper. Pluck off one or two individual leaves. Use whole, then remove before serving.

Sassafras

Native to the US, sassafras belongs to the same family as bay. The leaves are most often used dried and crumbled in filé powder – an essential ingredient in Creole cooking – and are also used to thicken soups and stews such as gumbo, where they impart a fragrant, spicy flavour.

The bark, roots and leaves all contain a fragrant oil that is used in soft drinks, confectionery and ices. In the southern states of America, dark red sassafras tea made by boiling the root in water was a popular drink in the past; it also enjoyed some popularity in Britain in the 19th century.

TO USE Crumble the dried leaf in soups and stews.
(see also filé powder, page 323)

Curry leaf

Similar in appearance to bay leaf, this shiny, dark green leaf has a warm, spicy, curry aroma and flavour, and is used in Indian and South-east Asian curries and fruity chutneys. If fresh leaves are unavailable, dried ones make a good alternative.

TO USE Rinse in cold water and pat dry with kitchen paper. Fry in oil with other spices at the beginning of cooking. Whole leaves should be removed from the dish before serving, or the leaf can be crumbled for a stronger flavour.

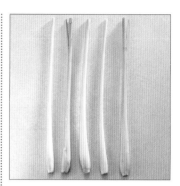

Fenugreek

Also known as methi, fenugreek is related to clover, and the soft leaves have a similar appearance. With a slightly bitter, curried taste, they are used to flavour Indian curries, chutneys, pickles and sauces. The young leaf sprouts can be used in salads, and in India, fenugreek leaves are used as a vegetable in paratha (flatbread) or cooked in the same way as spinach. Fenugreek leaves are also a staple in Yemeni and Ethiopian cooking.

TO USE Wash, pat dry and cook in the same way as spinach.
(see also fenugreek seed, page 314)

Kaffir lime leaf

The leaf of a type of lime, this extravagantly aromatic herb is widely used in Thai and other South-east Asian cuisines. It is dark green and shiny, and has a distinctively citrusy aroma that contributes to the unique taste of Thai dishes such as broths, curries, fishcakes and salads. Store in the fridge, or freeze whole for up to two months. Many cooks who buy lime leaves for Thai food find themselves permanently smitten by their wonderful fragrance, and start using them at every opportunity.

Kaffir lime is a bright green fruit with a knobbly skin that may be grated and used as a flavouring. However, there is very little flesh and juice, which is acid and bitter.

TO USE Tear or shred the leaf to release the flavour. To shred, roll the leaf or leaves tightly and slice thinly.

Lemongrass

Also known as citronella, pale green lemongrass stalks have a strong lemony flavour and are a key aromatic in Thai and South-east Asian cooking. Lemongrass is fibrous and tough, and only a small section of the bulbous end can be used (very finely chopped) in dishes where the herb will be eaten. Store in the fridge for up to two weeks. Dried and powdered lemongrass are also available, but their flavour is a poor substitute for fresh. Use in South-east Asian and Thai stir-fries, curries and soups such as Thai green curry and tom yam soup.

TO USE Crush the fleshy, bulbous base and simmer the whole stalk in broth for soups, curries and braised dishes, then remove before serving. Alternatively, finely chop the fleshy part – about 5cm (2in) – at the end of the stalk, and use in stir-fries, soups and curries.

Drying and freezing herbs

1 To air-dry fresh herbs (apart from basil, mint and tarragon), tie them in small bunches and hang in a warm, well-ventilated place until dry.

2 To freeze herbs, put 1 tsp washed, chopped herbs in each ice cube section. Fill with water. Freeze, then store in bags for three months.

More about herbs

Dried herbs are excellent for adding flavour to cooked dishes, but their fresh counterparts are more lively in flavour and fragrance. Fresh herbs also add visual appeal, especially when left whole or sprinkled on a dish before serving. Buy bunches of fresh herbs from the supermarket or greengrocer and store in the fridge, or buy in pots to grow on a sunny windowsill or in window boxes, or plant a herb garden. All fresh herbs freeze well, and many can be dried (see above).

Fresh versus dried and frozen herbs

In most cases, fresh herbs have a better flavour than dried, but some dry well and make a good or adequate substitute, whereas others lose their flavour and are almost pointless in the kitchen.

As a general rule, tender, soft-leafed, delicately flavoured herbs such as basil, coriander and parsley lose their flavour when dried. They should always be used fresh or frozen from fresh. More robust and strongly flavoured herbs, such as thyme, oregano, curry leaves and dill, dry well and make a good alternative if the fresh herb is unavailable.

For use in salads and garnishes, where the herb is uncooked, only the fresh herb will do. Frozen herbs will not retain their original appearance and texture, so must be added to dishes during cooking.

Using herbs

Fresh herbs get their flavour and aroma from the aromatic oils that are released when they are torn, cut or heated. As a general rule, tender herbs such as basil, coriander and mint are good used raw, added to salads, used as a garnish or stirred into dishes at the last minute, but do not bear long cooking. The more robust herbs such as thyme, rosemary and bay are better used in simmered dishes that allow the flavour of the herb to permeate and mingle with the other ingredients.

Robust herbs can also be used with whole fish such as sardines, trout and mackerel, and with poultry. Stuff the herbs inside before baking, grilling, roasting or steaming, so that the aroma of the herbs permeates the flesh.

Classic herb combinations

Bouquet garni A small bunch of herbs tied together with string or inside a piece of muslin, and an essential flavouring for stocks, soups and stews. The herbs can vary but usually include parsley, thyme and bay leaf; spices such as peppercorns and cloves may also be included. It is removed after cooking.

Fines herbes This classic French combination of finely chopped herbs usually includes chives, chervil, parsley and tarragon, and is good sprinkled over fish, poultry and omelettes.

Edible flowers

Lavender

Pretty purple lavender flowers have an intense aroma which can be used to flavour sugar and sugar syrups for baking, desserts and ices. The flowers can also be infused in boiling water to make tisanes and jellies, or in milk to make custards. Lavender goes well with fruits, particularly strawberry, orange and apple. It can also be used as a decoration for cakes and desserts, and complements lamb. It is also a common ingredient in the Moroccan spice blend ras el hanout (see page 322).

TO USE To make lavender sugar, blend just a few dried flowers with sugar in a food processor, then use in biscuits, shortbread, cakes and desserts. Or simmer fresh or dried flower heads in water, milk or syrup, then leave to infuse before straining and using in ices, jellies and custards. Use fresh flower heads as a garnish.

Pansy

With a mild, sweet–tart flavour, pretty bicoloured pansies make a colourful addition to savoury or fruit salads and look stunning as a decoration for cakes and desserts.

TO USE Pick off flower heads and use a decoration.

Rose Petals

Scented rose petals may be used to make jams and jellies, or for decorating cakes and desserts. They look particularly attractive on desserts and cakes flavoured with rosewater, such as panna cotta or meringues filled with rose-scented cream, but also go well with summer fruits such as strawberries and raspberries. White rose petals look stunning piled up on top of plain white wedding cakes, rather than using sugar flowers, while dark red rose petals look good on chocolate cakes. Rose is a particularly popular flavouring in the Middle East, where desserts and cakes will be flavoured with rosewater or drenched in rose syrups, or served with a spoonful of rose petal jam. Dried rose petals are an ingredient in the Moroccan spice blend ras el hanout (see page 322), which is used to flavour soups, tagines and other savoury dishes.

TO USE Pick unsprayed roses early in the morning after the dew has disappeared. Remove the petals by holding the head firmly and twisting away from the stem. Separate out the petals. Use as they are or brush with egg white, dust with caster sugar to frost and leave to dry before using.
(see also rosewater, page 413)

More about edible flowers

Flowers have been used in cooking for centuries: the Romans used rose, mallow and violet; the Chinese used lily buds; countless dishes from the Middle East and India use rose. Flowers can be used as a flavouring, an ingredient in their own right, or as a garnish or decoration. Whole flowers can be frozen in ice cubes for use in drinks or frozen in 'ice bowls' in which ice creams are served. **Note** Care should be taken that the flowers are edible, and that they have not been sprayed with chemical pesticides or other substances that could be harmful.

Herb flowers

Most herb flowers are edible, scented with the same flavour as the herb, and are excellent in salads or as a garnish. Round, purple-headed chive flowers; the white heads of Chinese chives; tiny white thyme flowers; creamy yellow fennel flowers and purple marjoram flowers – all these are good additions to salads or savoury dishes featuring the herb, such as risottos, soups and stews. Mint and rosemary flowers make a pretty decoration for desserts. Pale pink mint flowers and star-shaped blue-purple borage flowers (see page 295) look dainty floating on top of fruity summer punches.

Herb flowers are not widely available for sale, so you will need home-grown herbs to use their culinary potential. Pick fresh and use immediately.

Other varieties include

There are many varieties of edible flower, including primrose, marigold, mimosa, mallow, clary sage, heartsease and hollyhock. Some of the more commonly used ones are:

Violet An old-fashioned flavouring, violets have a strong taste and are used as the principal ingredient in two classic sweets: Parma violets and violet creams. They can be either purple or white. Crystallised violets for decorating cakes and desserts can be found in most large supermarkets and share the same heady, floral taste. You can also make them yourself: brush the flowers with egg white, dust with caster sugar to frost, and leave to dry before using. Fresh violet petals can also be steeped in boiling water to make a floral infusion, or used to flavour white or red wine vinegar to use for dressings (see page 391).

Chamomile Daisy-like chamomile flowers with a sweet, apple flavour are most often used dried to make a herbal infusion by steeping in boiling water. The infusion is said to have calming properties and the dried flowers can often be found in health-food shops.
Carnation Carnations have a spicy, peppery and slightly clove-like flavour. They are one of the ingredients of the liqueur chartreuse and can be used to decorate sweet and savoury dishes. Pull away the petals from the bitter base and use straight away.
Dandelion Young dandelions have a sweet flavour which becomes bitter as the flower matures. The petals are best known for making dandelion wine and tea, but the petals can also be scattered over rice and salads as a garnish.
Jasmine White jasmine flowers, specifically night-blooming jasmine, are most often used to flavour Jasmine tea. The green tea leaves are layered with heads of jasmine flowers and left to absorb their heady aroma overnight, when the blossoms open.
Elderflower These tiny white flowers grow in clusters, hanging down in umbrella-shaped heads. With a strong, scented aroma, they are most often used to flavour sweet cordials, wine, jellies and jams. They can be simmered with stewed fruits and are commonly paired with sharp-tasting gooseberries. Elderflower is generally found growing wild. Pick off flower heads with open, creamy-white flowers and use immediately. To extract the flavour for cordials, wine and preserves, simmer the flower heads in water until the appropriate flavour has been achieved, then strain and use the liquid as required.
(see also elderberries, page 218)
Courgette flowers The pretty yellow flowers of the courgette plant are popular in Europe, particularly Italy, and a great summer delicacy. Found growing on the end of young courgettes, the flowers can be dipped in a light batter, with or without stuffing, and deep-fried until crisp and golden. Carefully remove the flowers from the courgettes, then open out the petals and remove the pollen stems before stuffing or dipping in batter.
Nasturtium Delicate orange, red and yellow nasturtium flowers have a sweet, slightly peppery flavour and make a pretty addition to savoury salads. Nasturtium buds are pickled and used as a substitute for capers, and the young leaves, which taste similar to watercress, are also edible and can be used sparingly to add flavour to salads. Pick off flower heads and scatter over salads. Tear or slice leaves.

Fresh spices

Turmeric

Fresh turmeric, like ginger, is a rhizome – a thick underground stem. It resembles ginger with papery, pale brown skin, but it is slightly slimmer. When you slice into it, however, you see that you are not dealing with ginger: the flesh is a vibrant orange-yellow, and this is the main attraction of the spice. With a distinctive, slightly bitter and musky flavour, turmeric is used to flavour (and more importantly, colour) curries and chutneys. It is most often found dried and ground, but you may also find the dried root. Turmeric is commonly used in commercial curry pastes and powders, which get their yellow colour from the spice.

TO USE Peel thinly; slice, chop or grate the flesh. **Note** Be careful, as the juice stains.
(see also ground turmeric, page 313)

Ginger

Also known as green ginger, knobbly fresh ginger root has a thin, pale brown skin and juicy, pale yellow flesh. With a warm, faintly peppery, zesty flavour, ginger is favoured in cuisines throughout the world, from Chinese and South-east Asian to African and Indian. It is cooked in curries, braised dishes, spicy stews, stir-fries and chutneys, or used raw in salads, dressings and marinades. Slices of ginger can be steeped in boiling water to make a herbal infusion.

When buying, look for plump, firm, heavy roots with a smooth skin. Wrinkles and softness indicate ginger that's past its fragrant best. Store in a cool, dry place or in the fridge.

TO USE Peel off the thin skin, then slice, chop or grate.
(see also ground ginger, page 319)

Preserved ginger

Pieces of young ginger are often preserved in sugar or syrup. These can be used in cakes and desserts or enjoyed as a sweetmeat.

Crystallised ginger Eaten as a sweet, this confection is made by cooking cubes of ginger in sugar syrup until the flesh is saturated, then rolling them in more sugar to give a crisp and dry coating.

Stem ginger in syrup Sold in jars in most supermarkets, pieces of peeled ginger are cooked and packed in sugar syrup, giving the ginger a smooth, tender texture. Use chopped or sliced in cakes, desserts and ices, or sprinkle over vanilla ice cream.

Dried ginger The dried root may be sold whole or sliced, and should be bruised before using in curries and stews. It is often ground to use as a dried spice.
(see also pickled ginger, page 392)

Galangal

A member of the ginger family, galangal has pale skin ringed with pale brown, and the pink-tinged flesh has an aromatic, peppery flavour. There are two varieties: greater and lesser. Greater galangal resembles ginger root; lesser galangal is smaller, with a more reddish-brown hue, and has a stronger flavour. Widely used in Thai and South-east Asian cooking, the root is peeled, then pounded with other spices to make a paste to flavour curries and braised dishes.

Look for firm, smooth roots in Chinese and Asian food shops and store in the fridge. If you cannot find fresh galangal, ginger may be substituted.

TO USE Peel thinly, then slice, chop, grate or pound in curry pastes.

Horseradish

Cultivated for its long tapering root, horseradish is related to the mustard family and has a potent peppery bite. Best used in moderation, it is most often found in the form of sauce or cream, and is classically served as an accompaniment to roast beef and oily fish such as mackerel and smoked trout. Most horseradish sauces are made by heating the raw ingredient, as horseradish loses its potency when cooked.

TO USE Peel off the yellow-brown skin and grate the white flesh. Once grated, the flesh loses its pungency, so prepare only as much as you need for the recipe.

Wasabi

Fresh wasabi root is rarely found outside Japan. It is related to the horseradish and has bright, apple-green flesh. It is more widely available in two other forms: as pale green powder made from the ground, dried root, and as ready-made wasabi paste. An important condiment in Japan, wasabi is served with sushi and sashimi, and sometimes added to soup. The pretty green colour of wasabi paste belies its peppery potency; only a tiny amount is needed, and an excess can be as painful as a mouthful of chilli sauce.

TO USE Mix powder with an equal volume of water to make a smooth, creamy paste, or use ready-made paste direct from the tube.

Fresh chillies

Bird's eye

Also known as Thai or piquin chillies, these tiny demons are one of the smallest varieties of chilli and are renowned for being fiery-hot. Maturing from green to red in colour, they are rarely more than 1cm (½in) long. Bird's eye chillies are popular not only in Thailand but also in the cooking of Vietnam, Singapore, Malaysia, Indonesia and in the Indian state of Kerala.

TO USE Preparation, see page 308. Handle with care.

Jalapeño

These fat, blunt-ended chillies mature from green to red in colour, growing to between 5cm (2in) and 9cm (3½in) in length. It is usually the green jalapeños that are used in cooking, the red being considered to have an inferior flavour. Named for the city of Jalapa in Mexico, they are extremely popular in the US and are frequently used in Tex-Mex cooking. Jalapeños have a moderate level of chilli heat. They are often used in salsas, served whole – either chargrilled or stuffed with cream cheese and deep-fried – and in the sweet, bright green jalapeño jelly. Sliced, pickled jalapeños sold in jars are a popular addition to quesadillas, burritos, tacos and pizzas.

TO USE Preparation, see page 308.

Scotch bonnet

Similar in appearance to the habanero chilli, the Scotch bonnet from Jamaica is extremely hot – one of the hottest chilli varieties in the world. Either light green, yellow-orange or red in colour, these small, squat, bell-shaped chillies look rather like miniature sweet peppers with characteristic wrinkles in their skin. They have a thin, waxy flesh and are an important ingredient in jerk seasoning (see page 323) and other Caribbean savoury dishes, including hot pepper sauce.

TO USE Preparation, see page 308. Handle with care.

Serrano

This long, slender chilli from Mexico is important in the country's cuisine as a flavouring for sauces and salsas such as guacamole. It is named after the mountain ridges, *serranías*, where the chillies are thought to have originated. Considered to be about five times hotter than jalapeños, Serrano chillies have a sharp, fresh flavour and are usually used while green, before they ripen to red.

TO USE Preparation, see page 308. Handle with care.

Habanero

These short, squat, lantern-shaped chillies are green, maturing to red orange and yellow and are thought to originate from Cuba – their name meaning 'of Havana'. The skin is thin and waxy and the flavour fruity, but the most important point about habaneros is their volcanic heat. They are every bit as hot as Scotch bonnets, and sometimes hotter. Popular in Mexican cooking, they are used in hot sauces.

TO USE Preparation, see page 308. Handle with care.

Poblano

These dark green chillies mature to a dark red, almost black, colour and have a relatively mild flavour. Growing to between 15cm (6in) and 20.5cm (8in) long, they have a broad, squat shape with a pointed end and are popularly used in Mexican cooking. Giving flavour as well as heat, they are a good choice where you don't want too fiery a kick.

TO USE Preparation, see page 308.

Seeding chillies

1 Cut off the cap and slit open lengthways. Using a spoon, scrape out the seeds and the pith (these are the hottest parts of the chilli).

Dicing chillies

1 For diced chilli, cut into thin shreds lengthways, then cut crossways. Wash hands carefully after handling chillies.

More about chillies

Originally native to Central and South America and the West Indies, chillies were cultivated and eaten for thousands of years before they were introduced to the rest of the world by 15th-century explorers.

Belonging to the capsicum family, all chillies have in common a certain spiciness – ranging from mildly spicy to blisteringly hot. This heat comes from the volatile compound capsaicin, which is found more in the chilli's white pith and seeds than in its flesh. The level of heat in a chilli is measured in Scoville heat units, which classify sweet peppers as 0 and the hottest habaneros at 100,000 to 300,000.

There are countless varieties of chilli, each with its own characteristic, shape, size, flavour and degree of heat. Like their relative, the sweet pepper, they turn from green to red as they mature. Their shape varies enormously, from tiny pointed chillies to long, fat ones, slender twisting ones and squat bell-shaped ones. They range in size from barely larger than a pea to something resembling an ordinary sweet pepper.

How to buy and store chillies

Colour and size are no indication of a chilli's heat, so a knowledge of the different varieties is the easiest way to ascertain the probable heat of a chilli. However, strength can vary even on the same plant, so the best way to check the heat of a chilli is to take a tiny piece and taste it.

When it comes to choosing fresh chillies, ascertaining freshness can be difficult, as some varieties are wrinkled even when at their prime. Look for firm, unblemished specimens and avoid any that are bruised, soft, or with loose skins. They store well in in the salad drawer of the fridge.

How to prepare and handle chillies

Most of a chilli's heat resides in the seeds and white pith, so it is usually best to remove these, then finely chop or slice the flesh.

Capsaicin, the substance in chillies that gives them their heat, is not water soluble, so always be sure to scrub your hands well with soap and water immediately after handling or rinse them with milk, as Asian chefs do. Even the tiniest amount of capsaicin can cause severe irritation, so care should be taken to avoid touching any sensitive areas such as eyes, nose or mouth during or after handling chillies. Some people prefer to wear thin rubber gloves when handling chillies to avoid getting the juice on their hands.

Culinary uses for chillies

Chillies are used in cuisines throughout the world – from India, China and South-east Asia to South and Central America, Africa, the Middle East and the Mediterranean. They are added to dishes not only for their heat but also for their flavour. In Thai food in particular, the subtle matching of sweet, hot, salty and sour tastes allows the flavours of fresh chilli to shine through.

They are a popular addition to curries, stews and tagines, and can be used finely chopped, shredded, sliced, whole or pounded to a paste. Chillies can also be added to Italian pasta sauces and Spanish tapas. They are used in varying quantities according to the heat of the chilli and the level of heat required in the dish. In India, you will see large, whole chillies dipped in batter, deep-fried until crisp and golden, and sold as street food; in other parts of the world, small, mild chillies are stuffed and baked or roasted. Chillies can also be chargrilled or used raw in salads, salsas and relishes – and with their bright, fresh colour, they make a popular garnish too, sliced, chopped, cut into strips or made into flowers.

Other varieties include

The featured chillies are some of the most widely seen in recipes or in markets, but you may come across others. Other varieties to look out for are:

Anaheim Growing to about 10cm (4in) long, this slender, blunt-ended chilli is mild and sweet-tasting and may be red or green in colour.

Cayenne These slender, pointed red chillies can grow to between 10cm (4in) and 30.5cm (12in) and are often called finger chillies. Mostly used in hot chilli sauces, they are also dried and ground into cayenne pepper (see page 310).

Cherry These small, round chillies may be red or green and have a sweet flavour and some heat. Good pickled. Their thick skin is usually peeled.

Fresno Developed in the 1950s in Fresno, California, these plump, stubby chillies are mostly used green in the same way as jalapeños, and are good for pickling and sauces.

Mirasol Popular in Mexico, this yellow chilli is used in stews and sauces for its distinctive flavour and the colour it imparts.

Tabasco These chillies may be red or yellow and are mostly grown for Tabasco sauce.

Yellow wax These pale yellow, waxy chillies may be mild or hot and are a popular addition to salads. (see also dried chilli and chilli powders, pages 310–11)

Dried spices

Dried chilli

Whole dried chillies retain all the heat of fresh, but their flavour is more subdued and sometimes slightly more bitter. There are many different types, all with their own characteristics and heat, including mild ancho (dried poblano), fiery dried habanero and chipotle (smoke-dried jalapeño), with its distinctive smoky flavour. They are used throughout the world to add heat to meat and vegetable dishes, sauces, pickles, relishes, salsas and chutneys. Dried chillies are an essential ingredient in the North African spice paste called harissa (see page 322).

TO USE Crumble into dishes, or soak in hot water for 30 minutes before chopping or puréeing.

Crushed dried chillies

Also known as chilli flakes. These are made from whole dried chillies, crushed coarsely to create a spicy mix of seeds and flesh. Used in the same way as chilli powder, crushed dried chillies can add heat to curries, stews, casseroles and sauces. They can also be used as a seasoning, sprinkled over dishes in place of pepper for a more fiery bite. In Thailand, crushed dried chilli is always offered as a condiment at the table for sprinkling.

TO USE Sprinkle over or add to dishes as required.

Cayenne pepper

Made from the tiny cayenne chilli, this fine, brownish-red chilli powder is extremely hot with a potent bite. It is most often used as a seasoning to flavour mild and creamy mornay (cheese) sauces, egg dishes, stews, sauces and devilled dishes. A small pinch is usually all that is required. It is also used to spice up savoury biscuits such as cheese straws and crackers, and can make a good addition to grated cheese before grilling on toast, or to boost barbecue sauces and marinades.

TO USE Sprinkle judiciously.

Chilli powder

Made from finely ground chillies, chilli powder can vary from mild to hot depending on the type of chilli used, so always check the label and the recipe for the type of powder needed. Chilli powder can be used in stews, casseroles, soups, meat and tomato sauces, and chutneys and relishes. Some chilli powder and chilli seasoning contains other herbs and aromatics such as salt, garlic powder, cumin and oregano; these mixes tend to be milder.

TO USE Add to dishes as required.

Paprika

This uses a type of sweet red pepper that is dried and ground. Paprika is an earthy, terracotta red powder and ranges from very mild to very hot; it is also sometimes smoked. It is a key ingredient in Austrian and Hungarian cooking, in particular in goulash, Hungary's national stew, where the spice imparts a rich red colour and smoky flavour. Paprika is also popular in Spanish cooking, where it is often called pimenton and is used in sauces, stews and braised dishes, and as a seasoning, rather like black pepper. It is also a key ingredient in chorizo. It is often sprinkled over pale egg and cheese dishes, and can make a good addition to dressings and marinades.

TO USE Add to dishes as required.

More about dried spices

Many dried spices should be fried before use to remove any harshness of flavour and to enhance their taste. Whole seeds such as coriander and cumin are usually dry-fried (fried without any oil) in a heavy frying pan until they give off a rich aroma, then ground. Ground spices may be fried in oil before adding other ingredients such as vegetables or meat.

Spices tend to lose their flavour and aroma with age, so unless you use up spices very quickly, buy them in small quantities and store in an airtight container in a cool, dark place. Whole spices retain their flavour better than ground, so ideally buy whole spices such as coriander and cumin seeds and grind them as required.

Peppercorn

Peppercorns are the berries of a tropical vine. They may be black, white, or green, depending on how mature they were when they were harvested. Green peppercorns, which are unripe black peppercorns, have the mildest flavour and are usually used whole or crushed in meat pâtés and sauces. Black peppercorns are the most pungent and must be ground or crushed before adding to food in the cooking pot or at the table. White peppercorns – the fully ripe berries that have had the outer skin removed – retain the heat of black pepper but are less fragrant. The French nickname for pepper, le roi des épices (king of spices) conveys a fundamental truth: it is nearly impossible to make any savoury dish taste complete without using peppercorns. The flavour is considerably diminished by prolonged heating, so it is good to taste any long-simmered dish before serving and add more pepper if required.

TO USE Peppercorns do not retain their flavour and aroma well once ground. Crush or grind whole peppercorns as you need them and avoid ready-ground pepper.

Sichuan pepper

These aromatic reddish-brown berries, also known as anise pepper, resemble peppercorns but come from a completely different plant. The pungent, mouth-tingling, slightly citrus flavour of Sichuan pepper is popular in Chinese cooking and goes particularly well with duck and chicken. It is also an essential component of Chinese five-spice powder.

Pink peppercorn This pretty pink berry is not actually a peppercorn but the berry of a South American plant, known locally as pepper tree and Peruvian pepper. Pink peppercorns have a mild flavour and are sometimes included in peppercorn mixtures. On their own, they are a popular seasoning for fish. However, they can cause ill effects, so only use sparingly or as a garnish.

TO USE Grind or crush and add to dishes as required.

Coriander seed

These small, pale brown seeds have a warm, aromatic, slightly citrusy flavour. Widely used in Indian and Middle Eastern cooking, coriander seed is used to flavour stews, casseroles, tagines and curries. It is also a popular ingredient in spice blends such as garam masala (see page 322) and harissa (see page 322) and a common flavouring in sweet and spicy chutneys and relishes. Although most often used in savoury dishes, coriander can also make an interesting addition to sweet dishes such as apple pie. Coriander can be bought already ground, but it quickly loses its aroma. You'll get the best flavour by toasting and grinding the seeds shortly before you want to use them.

TO USE Dry-fry the seeds for about 1 minute until their aroma is released, then crush or grind to a fine powder.

Cumin seed

Small, pointed cumin seeds have a pungent, distinctive aroma. Widely used throughout the world, they are particularly popular in Indian and Middle Eastern dishes, and are also used in the cuisines of South-east Asia and Mexico to flavour savoury dishes such as soups, stews, casseroles, curries, tagines and meat sauces. Cumin is a common ingredient in most curry powders. There are two varieties, black and white; black has a slightly milder, sweeter flavour. Cumin can be bought already ground, but it quickly loses its aroma, so you'll get the best flavour by toasting and grinding the seeds shortly before you want to use them.

TO USE Dry-fry the seeds for about 1 minute until their aroma is released, then crush or grind to a fine powder.

Mustard seed

These tiny round seeds have little smell, but bite into them and you'll discover a fierce, peppery bite. There are three types: white, brown and black. White mustard seed is the largest. It has a pale yellow colour and is most often used for sprouting, in the same way as cress, for use in salads. Brown mustard seeds are slightly less pungent than the potent black seed, and are more widely available. Brown and black seeds are popular in Indian-style curries – fried in oil or ghee, then stirred into dhal (lentils) or used in meat and vegetable curries. Mustard seed is most commonly used as a condiment, crushed or ground and mixed with water or vinegar and other flavourings.

TO USE Fry brown and black seeds in oil or ghee until they pop, then add other ingredients.
(see also mustards, page 403)

Ground turmeric

This bright ochre-yellow spice is ground from the dried turmeric root and has a musky, slightly bitter flavour. It is an essential ingredient in many Indian-style curry powders and dishes and is also a popular ingredient in pickles such as piccalilli, chutneys and relishes. It is also used in some South-east Asian cooking. Used in moderation, ground turmeric adds a rich flavour and colour, and is sometimes used as a cheap alternative to saffron (see page 320). Be careful when using turmeric: its intense colour will stain.

TO USE Add to dishes as required. Sometimes fried with other spices at the beginning of the recipe.
(see also fresh turmeric, page 304)

Fenugreek seed

These small, pale brown, irregularly shaped seeds resemble tiny pebbles and have a wonderful aroma when toasted or dry-fried and ground. A common addition to commercial curry powders, ground fenugreek seeds are used in Indian and Sri Lankan cooking and are a good addition to chutneys and pickles – although they should be used in moderation, as their flavour can become overpowering. The seeds can also be soaked and sprouted in the same way as beans (see page 373) and sprinkled over salads.

TO USE Dry-fry until the aroma is released, then grind.
(see also fenugreek leaf, page 300)

Nigella

Tiny black nigella seeds are fragrant and have a mild and nutty, slightly peppery flavour, a little like cumin. They have been revered since antiquity for their medicinal properties, but their most common use is in Indian and Middle Eastern cooking. The seeds are sometimes sprinkled on naan bread, and are a popular spice in vegetable dishes and dhals (cooked lentils). In the Middle East, nigella seeds are also sprinkled over breads, often combined with sesame seeds. Sometimes referred to as black cumin, and closely resembling onion seed, nigella should not be confused with or substituted for either of these spices.

TO USE Dry-fry for about 1 minute until the aroma is released, then sprinkle over breads or use as required.

Sumac

The sumac bush grows in certain parts of the Mediterranean and throughout the Middle East, but its small red berries are mainly used in Middle Eastern cooking. The whole berries have a sharp, astringent and lemony flavour, and may be used for marinades or to flavour dressings. The ground spice can be rubbed into fish, chicken and meat along with other spices to impart its sharp–sour flavour. Use lemon juice if unavailable.

TO USE Crack whole berries, then soak in water to release the flavour for dressings and marinades. Use the ground spice as a rub.

Asafoetida

Derived from the resin of a tall plant native to Afghanistan and Iran, asafoetida is a popular flavouring in both Indian and Middle Eastern cooking. It goes well with fish and vegetables, and is added to pickles. Although related to the fennel family, asafoetida has a pungent and unpleasant smell when raw (the name means 'foetid gum'). Once cooked, however, the spice takes on a somewhat garlicky taste. The resin itself is extremely hard, so it is often much easier to buy the ground spice, rather than chipping off pieces to grind yourself. Store in a tightly sealed container in a cool, dark place.

TO USE If using the whole spice, chip off the amount required and grind. The ground spice is usually fried with other spices at the beginning of the recipe.

Ajowan

These pale green-brown seeds, related to caraway, are similar to celery seeds in appearance but have a strong flavour and aroma rather like pungent thyme. A popular ingredient in Indian cooking, they are often used in Indian snacks such as Bombay mix, pastries, biscuits and breads such as parathas. If unavailable, thyme makes a good substitute.

TO USE Sprinkle sparingly, whole or crushed, over breads or as required.

Amchoor

Also known as green mango powder, amchoor is made from unripe mangos which have been sun-dried before grinding. The coarse, pale brown powder has a sharp, tart flavour and is used to give a sour edge to dishes in Indian cooking – in much the same way as lemon or lime is used. If amchoor is unavailable, lemon juice can be used as a substitute.

TO USE Crumble the powder well before adding to dishes.

Tamarind

This gloriously gooey stuff is the pulp from the seed pods of the tamarind tree. Sticky, black, sharp-tasting – this a spice with no close relatives in either taste or appearance. Although tamarind is occasionally available in its bulging pale brown pods, it is more often sold in tubs as a concentrate that resembles treacle, or compressed into blocks. Tamarind is used to add a sour edge to Indian and South-east Asian dishes in a similar way to lemon and lime juice – but tamarind has a distinctive flavour of its own. It is also a popular addition to Indian chutneys.

TO USE Dissolve concentrate in a little boiling water, or break up compressed blocks and soak in warm water to extract the juice.

Caraway seed

Caraway seeds are widely used in German, Austrian, Eastern European and Jewish cooking for their distinctively sweet, warm, anise–liquorice flavour. Used in both sweet and savoury dishes, they are a common flavouring for breads, (including rye bread), cakes and biscuits. They are also popularly used in cabbage dishes such as sauerkraut, braised red cabbage, coleslaw, potato dishes, pork and sausages, and stews such as goulash. You can find cheeses, particularly Dutch-style cheeses, flavoured with caraway, and it is the key flavouring in the liqueur kummel. The seeds are also sometimes chewed to sweeten the breath.

TO USE Whole or ground.

Fennel seed

Harvested from the flowers of the fennel plant, these long, grey-green seeds have a mild, sweet aniseed flavour. They are used in Indian curries and as a component of Chinese five-spice powder. Fennel is also a popular flavouring for Mediterranean fish dishes such as bouillabaisse, the classic French fisherman's stew, and grilled oily fish such as sardines and mackerel. It also lends its fragrance successfully to meats such as pork and veal. In parts of the Mediterranean, the seeds are sprinkled over bread dough before baking and added to sweet and savoury biscuits and sweet cakes.

TO USE Dry-fry until the aroma is released, then grind or crush.
(see also fresh fennel, page 294)

Celery seed

These tiny, grey-brown seeds should be used in moderation: they have a distinctive and potent celery flavour, which can overwhelm in excess. The seeds are commonly ground with salt to make celery salt, the classic flavouring for Bloody Mary, but they can also be sprinkled over salads, used to flavour marinades and dressings, sprinkled over bread before baking and used to flavour chutneys and pickles. They are a good complement to both meat and fish.

TO USE Whole or crushed.

Dill seed

The dill plant is closely related to fennel, and the seeds have a similar aniseedy flavour, although they are also reminiscent of caraway. The oval, pale brown seeds are a good flavouring for fish, eggs, potatoes and root vegetables – indeed, for many of the dishes where you would use fresh dill. They are a common flavouring in Scandinavian and Eastern European countries, and the traditional flavouring for pickled cucumbers (dill pickles). They add a fragrant edge to dressings and marinades, and their flavour is brought out, in a calorifically self-indulgent way, by soured cream.

TO USE Whole or crushed.
(see also fresh dill, page 293)

Annatto

These small seeds from a tropical South American tree are widely used in the cooking of that continent. They can be bought whole or ground and are used mostly for their bright orange colour rather than their flavour, which is fairly nondescript. Annatto is used commercially to colour red Leicester cheese and smoked fish.

TO USE Fry the seed in oil to extract its colour, then add the oil to dishes; or use the ground seeds as required.

Anise

The seeds of this plant, also known as aniseed, have a sweet liquorice flavour and are used to flavour various spirits, including French pastis, Greek ouzo and Turkish arak. Anise is most often used to flavour breads, cakes and sweets, including dark red, sugary aniseed balls, but it can also work well in savoury dishes. In India, it is used in spicy curries and, if used subtly, it can go well with fish. In India and Afghanistan, the seeds are chewed after a meal as a digestive and to freshen the breath.

TO USE Whole, crushed or ground.

Star anise

This beautiful, star-shaped spice is the fruit of an evergreen tree and has a distinct aniseed flavour. Popular in Chinese cooking, star anise is an essential ingredient in Chinese five-spice powder. It is available whole or ground, and complements well-flavoured birds such as duck, but it also goes well with chicken, beef and lamb, and with steamed fish. The whole spice can be added to stews, or to syrups for poaching fruits such as pears. A single piece will usually suffice to lend the full fragrance of this seductive spice.

TO USE Whole, broken or ground.

Cinnamon

Brown scrolls of cinnamon are cut from the inner bark of a small evergreen tree native to Sri Lanka. With a warm, sweet and spicy aroma, the ground spice can be used in biscuits, cakes, breads and desserts, or in savoury dishes such as curries and tagines. Add the stick to stews, mulled wine and the poaching syrup for fruit. Cinnamon was an important part of the lucrative spice trade of the 16th–19th centuries. Today, while no longer as valuable, it remains one of the most versatile of all spices.

Cassia is grown on a similar tree and harvested in the same way as cinnamon. Available in strips or ground, it has a coarser, more potent flavour but can be used in the same way, although it is better suited to savoury dishes.

TO USE Add cinnamon whole or ground. When used whole, the stick should be removed before serving.

Ground ginger

The dried, ground form of the fresh root. This pale brown powder retains some of the spicy, gingery taste of the fresh root, but none of its citrusy tang. Generally used to flavour cakes, biscuits and desserts, ground ginger can also be added to savoury dishes such as curries, tagines and other spiced stews and casseroles, as well as chutneys. Grated fresh root ginger can be used instead of the ground spice, but the ground spice cannot be used as a substitute for fresh.

TO USE Add to dishes as required. (see also fresh ginger, page 304)

Nutmeg

Oval brown nutmeg is the seed of an evergreen tree native to South-east Asia. It has a sweet, warm, fragrant flavour that goes particularly well in cakes, bakes, desserts and custards. It is a classic addition to béchamel sauce for lasagne, and is a good complement to spinach dishes. Although it is available ground, nutmeg loses its flavour quickly. You will obtain a much better, more vibrant flavour if you buy the whole nutmeg and grate off a little as and when you need it. Nutmeg graters are sold by some cookware shops, with a design similar to that of a peppermill. A fine grater will do the job just as well.

Mace is the golden, lacy outer covering of nutmeg. It has a similar flavour but is more often used for savoury cooking. It is available in blades or ground.

TO USE Grate whole nutmeg on a fine grater when required.

Cardamom

Widely used in Indian cooking, cardamom pods may be green or black. Inside the hard, papery shell are tiny seeds with a lovely aroma somewhat reminiscent of eucalyptus. Cardamom is an essential ingredient in the sugary, milky Indian tea called *chai*, but it is also good used in rice puddings and as a spice for cakes, poached fruit and other desserts. Cardamom is also used in savoury dishes such as Indian curries and spicy North African stews, and in pickles.

TO USE Split open the pod, remove and crush the seeds, then add to dishes, or crush the whole pod. Add to simmered dishes and remove before serving.

Saffron

Richly coloured amber-red saffron is the dried stigma of a purple-flowering crocus. It has a fragrant, slightly bitter taste and is frequently paired with rice in paella, risotto and pilau. It is also added to some stews such as bouillabaisse and some sweet foods such as saffron buns and Cornish saffron bread. Saffron is the most expensive of all spices, and indeed one of the most expensive foodstuffs of any description. But you need only a few strands to enjoy its flavour. Saffron powder is less expensive but it has an inferior flavour.

TO USE Infuse a few threads in a little boiling water, hot stock or milk for 5 minutes, then stir into stock or add to your dish.

Cloves

The name 'clove' comes from the Latin *clavus*, meaning 'nail', which describes the shape of this small, dark brown spice. It is the dried flower bud of an evergreen tree native to South-east Asia, and has a sweet, pungent flavour that can be used in both sweet and savoury dishes. A classic flavouring for apple dishes, whole cloves may be added to crumbles, pies, tarts and sauces, or the ground spice may be added to cakes and biscuits. Cloves are a classic flavouring for mulled wine and are studded into oranges to make decorations for Christmas. Hams are traditionally studded with cloves before baking, and they are often used with game or for flavouring stocks and poaching liquids.

TO USE Usually used whole, cloves may be left in the dish (for example, baked ham), or removed before serving. The ground spice should be added judiciously. It is just about impossible to grind whole cloves to a really fine powder; if that's what you need, ready-ground cloves may be advisable.

Allspice

This spice belongs to the same family as cloves, and the berries have an aroma reminiscent of cloves, nutmeg and cinnamon – hence the name. Available either whole or ground, allspice is used to flavour biscuits, cakes, milk puddings, fruit pies, Christmas pudding and mulled wine. It is also used in pickling spices, chutneys and relishes, and, in Scandinavia, to flavour certain fish dishes. Allspice can make a good addition to meaty stews, and is a fine complement to baked ham.

TO USE Most often added in its ground form. Whole allspice berries are used for pickling.

Juniper

These small, purple-black berries have a distinctive scent and flavour which is quite unlike that of any other spice. Juniper is often used as a flavouring for game, pork and ham, particularly in casseroles and pâtés, and can also make a good addition to marinades for meats. A few berries can be added to a bag of mulled wine spices. As the flavour of juniper berries can easily become pungent and overpowering, use judiciously. Juniper is most familiar to many people as the key flavouring in gin – which gets its name from *jenever*, the Dutch word for the spice.

TO USE Crush the berries gently using the back of a teaspoon or a pestle to release their aroma, then add to your dish.

Vanilla

Sticky black vanilla pods are the seed case of a type of climbing orchid native to Central America. With its strong, heady aroma, vanilla is one of the most popular flavourings used in sweet cooking – either on its own, or paired with chocolate, coffee or fruits. Interestingly, vanilla is not sweet in itself; we think of it that way because it is used almost exclusively in sweet dishes. The pod can be used to flavour sugar for cakes, biscuits and desserts, or milk or cream for custards, sauces and ice creams. The whole pod can be split and the tiny seeds removed and used in custard or ice cream.

TO USE To flavour sugar, store the whole pod in a jar of sugar and leave for at least two weeks before use. To flavour milk or cream, split the pod, then bring the liquid almost to the boil, add the pod and leave to infuse for about 15 minutes.
(see also vanilla extract, page 413)

Liquorice

The root of a shrub native to Mediterranean regions, liquorice is mainly used commercially to flavour sweets and drinks. Naturally sweet, it has a very strong, bitter-sweet aniseed flavour, and is available either as a woody root with bright yellow flesh, dried and powdered, or as sticks of black extract. It is used in savory dishes in parts of China. Liquorice has many medicinal properties, especially as a cough suppressant, but if excessive amounts are eaten it can have harmful side-effects such as raised blood pressure.

TO USE Chew as a sweet and breath-freshner. In Chinese dishes simmered with meat.

Spice blends

As well as the basic spices, many countries and cuisines have their own specific blends and combinations that are used again and again. Traditionally made from scratch at home, they can now be bought ready-made for adding directly to dishes. Classics include:

Quatre épices

A classic spice mix used in French cooking; the name literally means 'four spices'. It typically contains ground pepper, grated nutmeg, ground cloves and ground cinnamon, and is used in soups, stews, sausages and salamis.

Chinese five-spice powder

A combination of Sichuan peppercorns, cassia, fennel seed, star anise and cloves. This aromatic blend is widely used in Chinese stir-fries and braised dishes, and goes particularly well with duck and meat.

Japanese seven-spice powder

This Japanese spice blend is used as a condiment for sprinkling on dishes such as soups and noodles. Recipes vary, but a classic blend contains two hot spices and five aromatic ones, so a typical seven-spice powder might contain: ground chilli, Sichuan peppercorns, sesame seeds, flax seeds, rape seeds, poppy seeds, dried tangerine or orange peel. The mix frequently includes ground nori seaweed as well.

Garam masala

A classic combination of spices used in Indian cooking, this aromatic spice blend is usually added to dishes towards the end of cooking. Combinations and proportions of spices vary, but a typical garam masala could include coriander, cumin, cardamom and black pepper. Other popular ingredients include cinnamon, cloves and ginger.

Curry powder and paste

Typically, curry powders and pastes are used to flavour Indian-style dishes, but it should be noted that in authentic Indian cooking, spices are always freshly ground and blended for each dish. The curry powders and pastes available in supermarkets tend to be generic blends of spices for the Western cook. Powders are usually described as mild, medium and hot, depending on how much chilli they contain, and would typically include key flavourings such as cumin, coriander and turmeric. There is more variety in jars of paste, but these tend to be created in terms of popular restaurant dishes such as tikka, dopiaza and jalfrezi.

Thai curry pastes

There are numerous classic paste blends used in Thai cooking, made from wet and dry spices, herbs and aromatics, but the most widely available ready-made ones are red and green curry pastes. Others include yellow curry paste, orange curry paste and mussaman curry paste.

Red curry paste typically includes red chillies, cumin seeds, coriander seeds, shallots, garlic, galangal, lemongrass, fresh coriander root, peppercorns and shrimp paste, although there are many variations. **Green curry paste** is similar to red curry paste, and would typically include green chillies and herbs.

Harissa

This spicy red chilli paste is used throughout North Africa but is particularly associated with the cuisines of Tunisia and Morocco. A blend of soaked dried chillies, garlic, cumin, coriander, salt and olive oil, harissa is a lively and versatile mix which can be used in most types of savoury dish.

Rose harissa is a variation made with the addition of rose petals.

Ras el hanout

A complex blend of fragrant dried flower petals and dried spices, ras el hanout comes from Morocco, Tunisia and Algeria. Mixtures may vary, but a typical blend might include cardamom, nutmeg, cloves, ginger and black pepper. Lavender and rose petals are also used in some recipes. Tunisian blends tend to be milder, whereas the Moroccan ones are stronger and more pungent. Ras el hanout adds a warming, spicy, fragrant taste and aroma to tagines and soups.

Dukkah

Recipes vary for this spice mix from Egypt, but a classic dukkah consists of crushed coriander seeds, hazelnuts and sesame seeds, mixed with ground cumin, ground pepper and salt. It is usually served as an accompaniment to bread dipped in olive oil.

Zahtar

A classic blend from the Middle East, this mixture of dried thyme, ground sumac, sesame seeds and salt is sprinkled over dips, vegetables and flatbreads.

Tabil

This Tunisian spice mix is a combination of coriander seeds, caraway seeds, garlic and dried chilli or chilli powder, ground together to make a spicy, aromatic mix to use in tagines and vegetable dishes.

Creole seasoning

Traditional Creole cooking combines French, Caribbean, African or Spanish influences, depending on the region. French–American Indian Creole cooking is particularly associated with Louisiana in the US. Typical dishes such as gumbo and jambalaya consist of rice cooked with spices and local ingredients such as shrimp and okra. Spice mixes vary, but a classic seasoning might include salt, paprika, onion powder, peppercorns, garlic, cayenne pepper, thyme and oregano.

Filé powder is a spicy mix popular in Creole cooking. It is based on ground dried sassafras leaves and is added to gumbo at the end of cooking, contributing to its slightly 'gloopy' texture as well as adding flavour.

Jerk seasoning

This sweet, hot and fragrant spice rub is used in the Caribbean and particularly Jamaica to flavour meat and poultry. Recipes vary, but a typical jerk-seasoning blend would include pepper, salt, sugar, allspice, thyme, nutmeg and cloves.

Piri-piri spice

Of African–Portuguese origin, *piri-piri* is the name given to savoury dishes served with a hot pepper sauce made with the tiny, fiery African bird's eye chillies that go by the same name. *Piri-piri* spice aims to replicate the traditional spicing and flavouring.

Pasta and noodles

Short pasta

Penne

The name *penne* means 'quill', and reflects the shape of this pasta: a short hollow tube with the ends cut on the diagonal, like a quill. Penne lisce are smooth; penne rigate are ridged. Less common varieties of penne include small, slender pennette and pennini, larger pennone, and the half-length mezze penne. They may be made with or without egg and are available plain or flavoured, most commonly with spinach.

TO USE Cook according to the pack instructions. Serve with smooth, chunky or creamy sauces; cold in salads. (Drain, toss with oil, and combine when at room temperature with other salad ingredients.)

Rigatoni

These broad, chunky tubes are ridged on the outside with straight-cut ends and tend to have a slightly chewier texture than other pasta shapes. They may be plain or flavoured and coloured; for example, with spinach, sun-dried tomatoes or herbs. Variations include the stubby, half-length mezzi rigatoni.

Millerighe is a less common shape, a short, stubby version of rigatoni.
Elicoidali resembles a narrow rigatoni, with the ridges spiralling around the tube, rather than straight up and down.

TO USE Cook according to the pack instructions. Serve with ragu, sausages and meat sauces.

Fusilli

The word *fusilli* means 'little spindles', and these short spirals of pasta are a popular shape. They are traditionally made of plain dough, although you will also find fusilli coloured with spinach and tomato (often sold in a packet containing more than one colour).

Eliche, meaning 'spirals' is another spiral-shaped pasta similar to fusilli.
Rotini has a tighter spiral shape than fusilli.

TO USE Cook according to the pack instructions. Serve with creamy sauces such as walnut, or vegetable sauces such as spinach and tomato; in salads; tossed with a sauce and baked.

Farfalle

The Italian word *farfalle* means 'butterflies', which describes this little bow-shaped pasta perfectly. Made of squares of pasta pinched in at the centre, farfalle may have a plain or ridged surface and be made of plain or egg dough. They may be flavoured and coloured. Farfalle have a minor technical problem in being thicker at the centre, where the butterfly's wings meet, and therefore taking slightly longer to cook there than in the thinner wings. But this has not kept farfalle from achieving a large following, especially among children. Farfallone are the larger version.

Strichetti is a regional variation from Emilia-Romagna, and is similar in shape and appearance to farfalle.

TO USE Cook according to the pack instructions. Serve with delicate, creamy sauces; cold in salads. (Drain, toss with oil, and combine when at room temperature with other salad ingredients.)

Conchiglie

This popular, shell-shaped pasta, whose name comes from the Italian for 'seashell', is available with a smooth surface or a ridged shell – conchiglie rigate. They may be made of plain dough or flavoured and coloured with, for example, spinach, tomato or squid ink. The insides of the shell are efficient catchers of sauce.

TO USE Cook according to the pack instructions. Particularly good with meat ragu or cheese sauces, or with vegetable sauces containing broccoli and courgettes.

Trenne

Trenne are cut on the bias at both ends to form a pointed 'quill' shape. The hollow tube is three-sided. Trenne are usually ridged (rigati) on the outside, and this, along with the hollow centre, makes them suitable for serving with a range of sauces, from smooth to chunky. Trennette is a smaller version with the same shape. **Note** This is not to be confused with trenette (see page 330), a thin Lingurian pasta similar to linguine

TO USE Cook according to the pack instructions. Serve with smooth, chunky or creamy sauces; cold in salads. (Drain, toss with oil, and combine when at room temperature with other salad ingredients.)

Maccheroni (short)

Although there is a long variety of maccheroni (see page 332), the short variety is far more common and available in a number of shapes and sizes, with the tubes varying in length and width. The short, curved tubes of maccheroni are frequently sold under the name elbow macaroni. Although good tossed with tomato sauce, they are probably best known baked with a cheese sauce to make what British call macaroni cheese and the Americans call macaroni and cheese.

TO USE Cook according to the pack instructions. Serve with a cheese sauce or smooth tomato sauce, or toss with sauce and bake.

Rotelle

Not a traditional Italian pasta shape, rotelle are shaped like spoked wheels. They are good for holding sauces, and their small size also suits pasta salads. They may be smooth or ridged (rotelle rigate) and are available in a variety of colours and flavours.

Ruote is another wheel-shaped pasta that can be used in the same way as rotelle.

TO USE Cook according to the pack instructions. Serve with cheese, meat ragu or chunky vegetable sauce; cold in salads. (Drain, toss with oil, and combine when at room temperature with other salad ingredients.)

Orecchiette

The name of these curved, flattened rounds means 'little ears' and they are a speciality of Puglia in south-eastern Italy. Traditionally, orecchiette are made by flattening small pieces of pasta with the thumb, which creates the distinctive cup shape. Hand-moulding the pasta produces a thicker, chewier texture than rolled pasta and therefore orecchiette require a slightly longer cooking time. Orecchiette are often served with vegetable sauces; one of the classic ways of serving them is tossed with broccoli, garlic, crushed anchovies and a little chilli.

TO USE Cook according to the pack instructions. Serve with chunky or smooth vegetable sauces, particularly those containing broccoli.

Garganelli

A regional pasta from Emilia-Romagna, these decorative tubes have pointed quill-shaped ends, but are made from rolled, ridged squares of pasta (rather than being a solid tube). They may be made with egg, and are often sold in mixed packs of plain and green spinach garganelli.

TO USE Cook according to the pack instructions. Traditionally served with meat ragu; cold in salads. (Drain, toss with oil, and combine when at room temperature with other salad ingredients.)

Trofie

A regional pasta from Liguria, these short, quite solid pasta shapes are made from flat pieces of pasta, rolled on the work surface to gently twist them; they are usually about 3–4cm (1¼–1½in) long. Like orecchiette, they have a slightly chewier texture than some of the more common varieties of pasta. Traditionally served with pesto, the classic Genoese basil sauce; the original Lingurian recipe includes pesto, green beans and cubes of potato.

TO USE Cook according to the pack instructions. Serve with pesto.

Strozzapreti

This is a regional pasta from Modena in Emilia-Romagna. The word *strozzapreti* is translated as either 'priest stranglers' or 'priest chokers', and explanations as to the origins of this name include the idea that the pasta was so delicious the priests would eat it too quickly, causing them to choke. The short shapes are about 3–4cm (1¼–1½in) long and consist of strips of flattened pasta loosely rolled and twisted between the palms of the hands.

Casareccie is a regional pasta from Sicily, which is also made from flattened strips of pasta loosely rolled and twisted between the hands. They tend to be slightly shorter than strozzapreti.
Gemelli is a similar type of pasta made by twisting two short strands of spaghetti together. The name *gemelli* means 'twins'.

TO USE Cook according to the pack instructions. Serve with meat ragu or tomato sauce.

Long pasta

Spaghetti

Taking its name from the Italian word *spago*, meaning 'string', spaghetti is one of the best-known and most commonly found varieties of long pasta. It consists of long, thin, round strands of pasta that vary in length and thickness. Spaghetti goes well with many types of sauce, but especially tomato-based sauces. Although it is most commonly sold as plain pasta, you can also find coloured and flavoured spaghetti, including spinach and wholewheat.

Spaghettini is a thinner variety of spaghetti that is good with seafood, whereas spaghettoni is thicker.

TO USE Cook according to the pack instructions. Serve with oil-based sauces such as garlic and olive oil, or tomato sauce.

Linguine

The Italian word *linguine* means 'little tongues', and refers to the flattened shape (oval or rectangular in cross-section) of these versatile strands of pasta. Usually made from plain dough, they may vary slightly in width from one manufacturer to another. Linguinette is a narrower variety.

Lingue di passero pasta is similar to linguine, but has narrower strands than both linguine and linguinette. The name means 'sparrows' tongues' in Italian.
Trenette is a flatter, narrower version of linguine, a regional pasta from Liguna. Serve with pasta or seafood sauces.

TO USE Cook according to the pack instructions. Serve with garlic, oil and chilli or a clam sauce.

Fettuccine

These long, ribbon-shaped egg noodles from Rome are a narrower version of tagliatelle and are often sold twisted into similar nests. They go well with smooth sauces and the classic dish *fettuccine all'Alfredo*, where they are served with a creamy Parmesan sauce. Green spinach fettucine is widely available.

Fettuccelle is similar to fettucine, but slightly narrower.

TO USE Cook according to the pack instructions. Serve with smooth vegetable, cream or cheese sauces.

Tagliatelle

A speciality of Bologna, tagliatelle is a popular ribbon-shaped pasta with strands that are about 8–10mm (³/₈–½in) wide, sold coiled into nests. The pasta is made with egg, and may be plain or coloured with spinach. The classic sauce to serve with tagliatelle is ragu, the Bolognese meat sauce.

Taglioline are narrow ribbons of pasta, usually sold coiled into flat rectangular 'nests' that unravel as they cook.
Paglia e fieno, meaning 'straw and hay', consists of fine ribbons of plain and spinach pasta. Because they are extremely thin they are susceptible to overcooking; watch your timer carefully.

TO USE Cook according to the pack instructions. Serve with Bolognese sauce, or other meat or creamy sauces.

Pappardelle

One of the broadest of the ribbon noodles, pappardelle are 2–2.5cm (³/₄–1in) wide; they sometimes have a rippled edge. Made with egg pasta, they are usually plain rather than flavoured and are commonly served with game sauces, the most famous of which is Tuscany's pappardelle alle lepre (with hare sauce). The name comes from the Italian word *pappare*, meaning 'to gobble up'. Anyone who has ever eaten the pasta will understand why it acquired this name.

TO USE Cook according to the pack instructions. Serve with finely chopped or chunky game sauces such as rabbit, hare and boar.

Fusilli col buco

The Italian phrase 'col buco' tells you that this long, corkscrew pasta has a tiny hole through the centre of each strand. It is sold in a U shape, showing how it was hung up to dry, but may be snapped in half to make it easier to fit in the pan when cooking and more manageable to eat. A speciality of Campania in southern Italy, it is usually served with a sauce based on the tomatoes for which the region is famous.

TO USE Cook according to the pack instructions. Serve with a tomato-based sauce.

Bucatini

These long, thin strands of pasta are slightly chunkier than spaghetti and have a hole running through the centre to make a very narrow tube. In Rome, bucatini is traditionally paired with a tomato, bacon and chilli sauce (*all'Amatriciana*) and in Sicily with a fresh sardine sauce. It is also served *alla fra diavolo*, a spicy tomato and shellfish sauce.

Bucatoni is a thicker version of bucatini.
Perciatelli is another name for bucatini.

TO USE Cook according to the pack instructions. Serve with carbonara or spicy tomato sauces.

Maccheroni (long)

These long, thick tubes of pasta are available in varying lengths and thicknesses. They may be made with plain or egg pasta, and may be used whole, like spaghetti, or broken into shorter lengths and used like elbow macaroni.

Maccheroni alla chitarra is also known as tonnarelli. These long strands from Abruzzi are square in section, rather like a square spaghetti.

TO USE Cook according to the pack instructions, either whole or broken into shorter lengths. Serve with smooth vegetable, meat ragu or cream sauces.

Capelli d'angelo

The name of this pasta means 'angel's hair', which enchantingly describes the fine, golden strands. The finest of all the long pastas, it comes in straight strands or, more often, coiled into nests (capelli d'Angelo nidi). Its thinness makes it prone to overcooking; watch the timer carefully.

Capellini and **capelvenere** are similar types of thin pasta.

TO USE Cook according to the pack instructions. Serve in soups or broths, or with smooth, light sauces such as tomato or olive oil and garlic.

Vermicelli

Similar to capelli d'Angelo, vermicelli has very long, thin strands, which are packed into little round nests. Its name means 'little worms' and it may be made of plain or egg dough. It is frequently served with tomato and shellfish sauces. Its thinness makes it prone to overcooking; watch the timer carefully.

Fedelini is a fine pasta similar to vermicelli.

TO USE Cook according to the pack instructions. Serve with clam and tomato sauce or a creamy lemon sauce; add to soups and broths.

Ziti

Similar to maccheroni, ziti is long and hollow, and particularly associated with Naples and southern Italy, where it is the traditional pasta to serve at wedding feasts. It takes its name from the word *zita*, meaning 'fiancée'. It can be broken into lengths or used whole as for maccheroni.

Zitoni are a larger version of ziti.

TO USE Cook according to the pack instructions. Traditionally served with ragu or tuna sauces.

Non-wheat pasta

People with a gluten or wheat intolerance can still enjoy pasta dishes as long as they choose their pasta carefully and look for products labelled wheat and gluten free. An increasing range of non-wheat pasta is available, including:

Corn This golden yellow pasta, is available in a variety of shapes and sizes similar to traditional pasta. Usually sold dried in health-food shops and supermarkets, it is also available coloured with spinach or beetroot. Take care not to overcook as it is likely to turn mushy.

Rice Spaghetti made from 100 per cent rice is pale and susceptible to overcooking, but can be used in the same way as regular spaghetti. Other rice–pasta products may include a certain percentage of corn, quinoa or millet.

Gluten-free pasta In an attempt to get closer to the taste and texture of traditional pasta, some products have been developed using a mix of corn, rice, buckwheat and bean or pea starch. Available in various shapes, such as fusilli.
(see also buckwheat noodles, rice noodles and cellophane noodles, page 343)

Pasta for layering and stuffing

Lasagne

These flat, rectangular sheets of pasta can be made of plain or egg dough, and they may be coloured with spinach. The sheets may be flat or rippled, with straight or ruffled edges, and are designed to be layered with sauce and baked in the oven; a classic lasagne is made with layers of meat ragu sauce and béchamel sauce, although other popular fillings include spinach and ricotta or a chunky vegetable sauce.

TO USE Cook a few sheets of lasagne at a time according to the pack instructions. Layer alternately with ragu or vegetable sauce and béchamel sauce, then bake.

Easy-cook lasagne

A relatively new development, easy-cook lasagne comes in the same plain, egg or verdi options as traditional lasagne, and may be flat or rippled. The sheets are rolled out thinly when made so that they do not need to be pre-cooked, but must be used with plenty of moist sauce to rehydrate them during cooking. The pasta absorbs the liquid and comes out fully cooked when the lasagne itself is cooked. The baking time is usually slightly longer than when using regular lasagne.

TO USE Layer in a dish alternately with ragu or vegetable sauce and béchamel sauce, then bake.

Lasagnette

These strips of pasta with a ruffled edge are used in the same way as lasagne. About 5cm (2in) wide, they are usually layered with sauces, sprinkled with cheese and then baked in the oven.

Festonelle are small squares of lasagnette used in the same way.

TO USE Cook according to the pack instructions. Layer with ricotta, ham and mozzarella, ragu or a chunky vegetable sauce, then bake.

Cannelloni

Usually made from egg pasta, these large, broad tubes are designed to be stuffed, coated in sauce and (optionally) cheese, and then baked. Classic stuffings include ricotta and spinach or meat sauce. Cannelloni can also be made by wrapping cooked lasagne sheets around a filling, then coating in sauce and baking as for the ready-made tubes.

Cannellini are smaller, narrower tubes that can be used in the same way.

TO USE Spoon a ragu or vegetable filling into the tubes and lay in a baking dish, then coat in tomato or béchamel sauce and bake.

Conchiglie giganti

Also known as conchiglioni, these are the giant version of shell-shaped conchiglie. Made of plain, egg or spinach dough, conchiglie giganti are ideal for stuffing with meat or vegetable fillings and baking.

TO USE Cook according to the pack instructions, then stuff each shell with a ragu or vegetable filling, coat in sauce, sprinkle with grated Parmesan cheese and bake.

Lumachoni

These giant 'snails', are large, hollow pasta shapes that can be stuffed and baked in the same way as conchiglie giganti. Similar pasta shapes for stuffing with a tubular shape include chioccioloni, gorzettoni, manicotti and tuffolini.

TO USE Cook according to the pack instructions, then spoon a ragu or vegetable filling into each 'tube', add sauce, sprinkle with grated Parmesan cheese and bake.

Pasta for soup

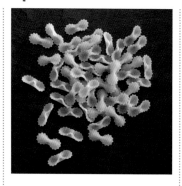

Risoni

Belonging to the category *pastina* (pasta for broth), these tiny, rice-shaped grains of pasta are one of the more popular soup pastas. They are made from plain or egg pasta, and are also referred to as risi.

Semi di melone are similar to risoni, small, flattened pasta shapes that resemble melon seeds.
Orzo is the Italian word for barley, but it is also used to describe a pasta shape slightly larger than risoni, resembling large, fat grains of rice. They are popularly used in Greek cooking, either added to soups such as *avgolemono* or cooked separately and served as an accompaniment to stews.

TO USE Add to soup or broth and cook for a few minutes, or according to the pack instructions.

Farfalline

A tiny version of farfalle, this bow-shaped pasta is good added to minestrone-style soups.

Farfallette are a similar shape and used in the same way.
Funghetti are tiny rounds of pasta are pinched to form a mushroom shape rather than a bow.

TO USE Add to soup or broth and cook for a few minutes, or according to the pack instructions.

Conchigliette

These have the same shape as conchiglie, but they are much smaller. Both size and shape make them an ideal pasta for minestrone-type soups and chunky broths.

Lumachine are another shell-shaped pasta; these 'little snails' are a tiny version of lumachoni.

TO USE Add to soup or broth and cook for a few minutes, or according to the pack instructions.

Tubetti

Little tubes, literally, and a good addition to minestrone-type soups and chunky broths. Tubettini are similar but even smaller, and can be used in the same way.

Occhi di lupo (wolf's eyes) are another kind of small, tube-shaped pasta, slightly larger than tubetti.
Ditalini is available smooth or ridged. These little tubes are similar to tubetti.
Renette is a tiny version of penne.

TO USE Add to soup or broth and cook for a few minutes, or according to the pack instructions.

Stelline

These tiny stars most often find their way into the mouths of young children, and are perfect for babies – no danger of choking. But they can also be added to clear or chunky broths. Sometimes called stellete, which may be somewhat larger (though still never very large).

TO USE Add to soup or broth and cook for a few minutes, or according to the pack instructions.

Quadretti

These are tiny flat squares of pasta, and one of the simplest of all the soup pastas. They make a good addition to light broths.

Quadrettini are similar, but smaller.

TO USE Add to soup or broth and cook for a few minutes, or according to the pack instructions.

Stuffed pasta

Tortelloni

Meaning 'little pies' in Italian, tortelloni are one of the most popular of the stuffed pastas. They may be made of egg or flavoured pasta, which is cut into round discs that are stuffed, then folded in half and twisted. Traditionally, tortelloni were filled with minced meat. Now they are available with a wide variety of fillings, including spinach and ricotta, mozzarella and tomato, and four cheeses.

Tortelli are a larger version.

Tortellini are slightly smaller, and are often sold dried. They are a classic addition to broths, and are served this way as part of the Christmas fare in their home city of Bologna.

TO USE Cook according to the pack instructions. Serve tossed in melted butter or with smooth or cream sauces.

Cappelletti

These 'little hats' resemble a smaller version of tortelloni. Made from either rounds or squares of dough, depending on the region, they are filled, folded in half, then twisted in much the same way as tortelloni. The dough may be plain, flavoured or made with egg. The traditional filling is minced meat and cheese, but many different fillings are now available. Cooked in broth (*brodo*), they are traditionally enjoyed at Christmas and New Year.

TO USE Cook according to the pack instructions. Serve with melted butter or with smooth or cream sauces. Or cook in broth and serve as a soup.

Ravioli

A popular and widely available type of pasta, these stuffed pasta squares with a crimped edge may be made from plain, egg or flavoured dough. Stuffings range from classics such as spinach and ricotta or minced meat, to new ideas such as crab, artichoke or pumpkin. Ravioli can vary in size from small to very large, where just two or three ravioli would make up a portion. Some modern recipes feature 'open ravioli', in which the stuffing is placed on a sheet of pasta but not sealed in with a second sheet.

Rotondi is a large oval ravioli.
Medaglioni is a small round ravioli.

TO USE Cook according to the pack instructions. Serve with melted butter or herb butter, or with cream or tomato sauces.

Other stuffed pastas

As well as the more common varieties of stuffed pasta, you may also find:

Sacchetti

These little 'sacks' of pasta are made from round discs gathered around meat or cheese fillings. Serve with simple vegetable or cream sauces. Sacchettini are a smaller version that may be served with sauce, or in broth.

Caramelle

Shaped like a sweet, with the pasta wrapping twisted at both ends to enclose the filling, these shapes are usually made with egg or flavoured dough and are often filled with a ricotta stuffing. Serve with butter or a simple vegetable or cream sauce.

Agnolotti

These half-moon or sometimes rectangular pasta shapes are a speciality of Piedmont and northern Italy. Similar to ravioli, with a crimped and sometimes serrated edge, agnolotti may be filled with minced meat (beef, pork, veal or a combination) or a vegetable-based filling. Serve tossed in melted butter or with a smooth sauce such as tomato.

Pansotti

A regional speciality of Liguria, these stuffed pasta shapes are made from squares of dough that are folded into a triangle. The traditional filling is a mixture of spinach, chopped egg and Pecorino cheese, and the cooked pansotti are served with a walnut sauce. Serve with melted butter, or with cream or tomato sauces.

Filling ravioli

1 Lay a sheet of dough over a ravioli tray and gently press into the indentations. Place teaspoonfuls of filling into the hollows. Be careful not to overfill the ravioli as the filling may leak out during cooking.

2 Lay a second sheet of pasta on top of the first.

3 Using a circular cutter, cut a row between the lumps of filling in one direction, then cut in the other direction to make squares. Press the edges to seal the dough.

4 Separate the ravioli, dust very lightly with flour, and cover with a clean teatowel until needed. This will help prevent the ravioli drying out while you are preparing more of them.

More about pasta

Pasta-like doughs have been eaten in Italy since Roman times, served with or baked in a sauce. There is, however, some debate over whether they originated in Italy or whether noodles from Asia were introduced and adapted. The simplest pasta is made from a plain dough of durum wheat and water, rolled out flat and then cut into shapes. You will also find pasta *all'uovo*, which has egg added to the dough, and brown pasta *integrale*, which is made with whole wheat and has a slightly coarser texture.

Pasta dough may be flavoured and coloured with (among other things) spinach (*verde*), squid ink (*nero*), sun-dried tomato, herbs or chilli. More unusual flavourings include chocolate, porcini, beetroot and smoked salmon. Pasta verde does not have a distinctive spinach taste and can be served in the same way as plain pasta. However, other flavoured pastas may have a much more pronounced taste and should be served with complementary sauces.

Pasta can be divided into five main categories: long, short, flat, stuffed and *pastina per brodo* (little pasta for soup). Long, short and flat pasta, and tiny pastina, are available dried, and a selection of long, short and flat pasta, such as tagliatelle and lasagne, are sold fresh as well. Stuffed pasta is mainly available fresh, although tortellini are also sold dried.

Buying and storing pasta

Pasta is arguably the world's greatest industrial food product, and one of the few manufactured ingredients that are usually better when made commercially than at home. Furthermore, fresh pasta is not 'better' than dried. It is just different. And most commercial fresh pasta is vastly inferior to dried. Many Italian cooks choose dried pasta over fresh. And the best dried pasta still comes from Italy.

Dried pasta has a long shelf life. Stored in an airtight container in a cool, dry place, it will keep for many months (or even years). Fresh pasta should be stored in the fridge and used within a few days.

Serving pasta and sauces

There are some useful rules about matching certain types of pasta with specific types of sauce. In some regional specialities, however, a particular pasta is always served with the same type of sauce: for example, *fettuccine all'Alfredo* and *trofie con pesto*.

Egg pasta Northern-Italian egg pasta suits northern-style butter and cream sauces that cling to the pasta.
Long, thin shapes Pasta such as spaghetti and vermicelli suit smooth, simple sauces such as garlic and olive oil, as well as tomato sauces and seafood sauces using olive oil.
Chunky, long shapes Pasta such as pappardelle and tagliatelle suit heavier sauces made with game or meat.
Pasta shapes These can be served with smooth or chunky sauces, as the shapes trap the sauce well.
Cheese Often sprinkled over pasta before serving, cheese is not traditionally added to pasta with seafood or a dressing such as olive oil and garlic.

Other varieties include

As well as the more common varieties of pasta, there are many unusual ones:

Arlecchino Strands of brightly coloured tagliatelle made with turmeric, spinach, squid ink and beetroot.
Bigoli Resembling thick spaghetti, this Venetian pasta is made from wholewheat dough and suits smooth sauces.
Chifferini Small curved tubes of pasta resembling short macaroni. They can be used in the same way.
Fiorelli Decorative ruffled rolled tubes of pasta that are good cold in salads or with smooth sauces.
Gnocchi sardi Ridged, shell-shaped pasta from Sardinia. They suit smooth or chunky sauces and can be served as you would conchiglie. The longer gnocchetti sardi have a narrow shape and ridged surface. Usually added to soups.
Pantacce Small flat diamonds of dough with a slightly ruffled edge, these can be baked with sauces, or added to soups.
Maltagliati These flat triangles or diamonds can be used in soups or salads, or baked with sauce.
Radiatori These deeply ridged, semi-tubular shapes resemble little radiators. They suit smooth or chunky sauces and are good used cold in salads.
Various pastina Other shapes that can be added to soups a few minutes before serving include letter-shaped alfabetini, wheel-shaped rotelline, small round fregola, and tiny oval peperini.

Gnocchi

Not actually a type of pasta, but often grouped with it, these little Italian dumplings are usually boiled for a few minutes, then served with butter or a sauce, or they can be coated in sauce and baked. Gnocchi are usually made from mashed potato and flour, rolled into ridged ovals. Other varieties include spinach and ricotta or Parmesan, semolina and pumpkin. Store in a plastic bag in the fridge. Use within a few days.

Cooking pasta

1 Boil the water with about 1 tsp salt per 100g (3½oz) of pasta.

2 When the water has reached a rolling boil, put in all the pasta.

3 Stir well for 30 seconds, to keep the pasta from sticking either to itself or the pan. Once boiling, set the timer for 2 minutes less than the recommended cooking time on the pack and cook uncovered.

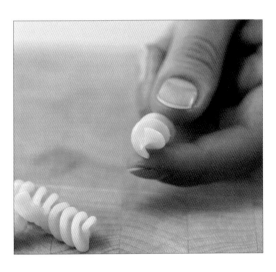

4 Check the pasta when the timer goes off, then every 60 seconds until it is cooked al dente: tender with a little bite at the centre. Scoop out a cup of cooking water (it may be useful for loosening up a thick sauce).

5 Drain the pasta well in a colander. Transfer to a warmed serving bowl, and toss immediately with your chosen sauce.

Noodles

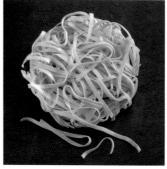

Wheat noodles

Made from a plain wheat dough (just wheat and water), these noodles are popular in China and Japan and are usually sold dried in bundles or folded into portion-sized blocks. They vary in thickness from thin strands to broad flat strips. Wheat noodles can be served in soups or stir-fried with meat, shellfish, chicken or vegetables. Common varieties include long, flat and narrow *udon* noodles and thin, delicate *somen* noodles, also from Japan. Store in a cool, dry place for up to a year.

TO USE Cook in boiling water according to the pack instructions, shaking blocks of noodles with a fork or chopsticks to loosen and separate the strands as they soften. Drain and add to soups or stir-fries.

Egg noodles

Available fresh or dried, these noodles are made with an egg dough and are usually sold in nests or folded into portion-sized blocks. They come in a variety of thicknesses and are used in Chinese and South-east Asian-style soups and stir-fries. Cold noodles can be used in salads. Store fresh noodles in the fridge for up to three days, or dried noodles in a cool, dry place for up to a year.

TO USE Cook in boiling water according to the pack instructions, shaking the strands apart with a fork or chopsticks as they soften. Drain and add to soups or stir-fries. To use cold in salads, refresh under cold water after draining.

Buckwheat noodles

Popular in Japan, these long, flat, narrow noodles are also known as soba. Made from a mixture of wheat and buckwheat, they are pale brown in colour, and have a pleasantly firm texture. Soba noodles made from 100 per cent buckwheat are available and are suitable for a wheat-free diet, as the two plants are not related. Sold dried, in bundles, buckwheat noodles are a popular addition to soups and stir-fries, or they can be dressed in sauce as an accompaniment or used cold in salads. Buy from a good source and store in a cool, dry place for up to a year.

Chasasoba are a type of buckwheat noodle made with green tea, giving them a greenish colour.

TO USE Cook in boiling water according to the pack instructions. Drain, rinse and add to soups or stir-fries. To use cold in salads, refresh under cold water after draining.

Rice noodles

Also called rice stick noodles, these whitish, semi-translucent noodles are available as fine strands or flat strips, ranging in width from broad to narrow. Long flat noodles are usually sold dried and folded into portion-sized blocks, and the fine strands are usually sold in little bundles bound with a strip of paper. They are used in Chinese and South-east Asian-style soups or stir-fries, and cold noodles are good in salads. Very fine rice noodles can be deep-fried until they puff up and turn crisp. Store in a cool, dry place for up to a year.

TO USE Pour over boiling water and leave to stand, or soak according to the pack instructions. Drain and add to soups and stir-fries; deep-fry; refresh under cold water and use in salads.

Cellophane noodles

Also known as glass noodles, these very fine, whitish, semi-translucent noodles are made from mung beans. Always sold dried, they are 'cooked' by soaking rather than boiling, and have a distinctive firm texture. Cellophane noodles are a popular addition to spring roll fillings. They are also good in soups, and can be used cold in salads. Store in a cool, dry place for up to a year.

TO USE Soak in hot or warm water, according to the pack instructions, until tender. Drain and snip into lengths, then add to soups, spring roll fillings or salads.

Other noodles

Less common noodles include:

Bijon A South-east Asian noodle made from corn, bijon can be used in the same way as wheat noodles. Some Chinese rice noodles are also referred to as bijon.

Shirataki Made from a glutinous tuber known as devil's tongue, these noodles are popular in Japan. The starch is pressed into blocks, then sliced into noodles, which are sold packed in liquid either in cans or plastic tubes. They have a slightly greyish colour and rubbery texture and are often added to soups or served in *sukiyaki*, where ingredients are simmered in broth at the table.

Rice and grains

Rice

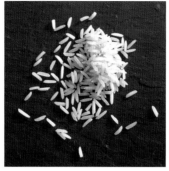

Long-grain rice

These long, narrow grains may be white or brown. Brown rice is covered with its firm husk and contains the rice bran. It has a distinctive nutty flavour and a firm, chewy texture. White rice has been milled to remove the husk. Although tender and more delicately flavoured, it lacks the healthy fibre and many of the nutritional benefits of brown rice. Both grains can be served as an accompaniment to curries and stews, or in place of potatoes. Or they can be used in pilaus and salads, and in stuffings for meat and vegetables.

Converted rice is long-grain white rice that has been parboiled in its husk, then dried before the husk is removed. The process causes some of the nutrients, flavours, husk and bran to move to the white grain, thus boosting its nutritional value. It also hardens the grain's surface, so converted rice is less likely to become sticky when cooked.

TO USE Boil in salted water according to the pack instructions. White rice requires only about 10 minutes; brown rice needs about 25 minutes.

Basmati rice

Generally considered the aristocrat of long-grain rices, basmati is slender and fragrant, with a good flavour and texture. White and brown basmati rices are available. The favoured rice in India, basmati can be served as an accompaniment to curries and other dishes or used in pilaus.

TO USE Rinse the grains well in cold water until the water runs clear, then fry in oil for 1 minute before adding two and a half times its volume of boiling water and a pinch of salt. Cover the pan tightly and simmer for 12 minutes for white rice and 20–25 minutes for brown until all the water has been absorbed, then leave to stand for 5 minutes before fluffing up with a fork and serving.

Thai fragrant rice

Also known as jasmine rice, this tender white rice is widely cultivated in Thailand, where it is highly prized for its fragrance, flavour and tender, slightly sticky texture. Cooked in water or coconut milk, it is served as an accompaniment to Thai and South-east Asian dishes such as stir-fries and curries, but it can also be cooked in milk or coconut milk with spices and sugar to make a scented rice pudding.

TO USE Usually cooked in unsalted water using the absorption method: add double its volume of boiling water; cover the pan tightly and simmer on the lowest heat setting for 12 minutes or until all the water has been absorbed, then leave to stand for 5 minutes before fluffing up with a fork and serving.

Patna rice

A good, all-round long-grain rice from India, this variety comes from the Bihar region and is known locally as parimal rice. It has a good texture with a hint of firmness, and cooks to a dry, fluffy consistency with separate grains. Mild in flavour, patna rice is served as an accompaniment or cooked with spices and herbs in fragrant pilaus. It is also a good choice for salads, or as the base of stuffings for meat and vegetables.

TO USE Boil in salted water until tender, or according to the pack instructions.

Risotto rice

There are three main varieties of the fat, high-starch rice used specifically to make Italian risotto: arborio, carnaroli and vialone nano. The grains are simmered and stirred frequently during cooking to release their starches into the cooking liquid and to produce a rich, creamy-textured risotto. Risotto rice is often cooked with garlic, onions, white wine and stock, then flavoured with Parmesan cheese; other popular additions include mushrooms, spring vegetables such as asparagus, chicken, prawns and herbs. Vialone nano is favoured in Venetian cooking, while arborio rice is preferred in Lombardy and Piedmont.

TO USE Fry the rice in oil for 1–2 minutes until translucent, then add a little white wine and bubble, stirring until nearly absorbed. Stir in a ladleful of hot stock and cook in the same way, stirring and gradually adding more hot stock. Make sure each ladleful is absorbed before adding the next, and continue cooking until the grains are tender but with a slight bite and the risotto is creamy. Cooked risotto is customarily left in the pot for a few minutes before serving.

Paella rice

Sometimes referred to as Valencia rice, after the region of Spain where it is widely grown, paella rice is fat and starchy, and similar to risotto rice. There are three main varieties: bomba, bahia and grano largo. It is usually cooked gently in a large, flat paella pan that has a dimpled base, with additional ingredients including onions, garlic, saffron, tomatoes, stock, sausage, chicken and rabbit and/or shellfish. A traditional paella is not stirred during cooking but shaken from time to time. It is ready when the grains have plumped up and are slightly sticky, and all the liquid has been absorbed.

TO USE Cook gently in a wide, flat pan according to your recipe.

Sushi rice

The short, fat, rounded grains of sushi rice plump up and become sticky and tender when cooked. It is used specifically for making sushi because of the way the grains stick together. Some people find it hard to acquire the knack of cooking sushi rice, which is a skill that Japanese chefs traditionally spend years learning and perfecting.

TO USE Wash the rice well in cold water, then leave to stand for 1 hour. Simmer in an equal volume of boiling water in a covered pan until all the liquid has been absorbed, then fold in a mixture of Japanese rice vinegar, sugar and salt and leave to cool completely before shaping, moulding or rolling with the other sushi ingredients in sheets of nori (dried seaweed).

Glutinous rice

Short, fat-grained glutinous rice is popular in Chinese and South-east Asian cooking and is available in several varieties. It is often referred to as sticky or sweet rice because the grains become sticky when cooked. It may be black or white and is often sweetened and served with fruit as a dessert. An example is the classic Indonesian sweet coconut rice porridge. In Japan, glutinous rice is favoured because it can be eaten easily with chopsticks and is often served as an accompaniment to savoury dishes.

TO USE Glutinous rice is usually cooked by the absorption method, as for sushi rice: wash the rice well in cold water, then leave to stand for 1 hour. Simmer in an equal volume of boiling water in a covered pan until all the liquid has been absorbed.

Wild rice

Not actually a rice, but the grain of a wild marsh grass. Wild rice is native to the Great Lakes region of North America (straddling the US and Canada), and was once a staple of the region's Native American tribes. Now considered something of a gourmet treat due to its high price, wild rice is dark brown-black with a rich, complex, nutty flavour and firm texture. It is often sold in mixes with long-grain or basmati rice. Most wild rice is no longer wild as its high price has led to cultivation in man-made rice paddies. Even when farmed, it is a delightful and luxurious treat.

Red rice is a natural hybrid of wild rice and cultivated white rice. With a red-brown colour and nutty flavour, the grain becomes red with cooking.

TO USE Boil in salted water for 30 minutes, or until tender, or according to the pack instructions.

More about rice

Rice is a veritable playground for adventurous home cooks who love finding new ways to treat basic ingredients. It's one of the most widely cultivated grains, a staple food in many areas of the world, including South America, Africa, India, China and South-east Asia. And, not surprisingly, all those cuisines have contributed something to the vast encyclopedia of international rice cookery. Wherever rice grows in lush green paddy fields, local cooks find good ways to cook it.

This incredibly versatile grain is used in so many ways that only a partial listing is possible. It's served as an accompaniment to curries, stews and Asian-style braised and stir-fried dishes – either cooked plain, with spices or in coconut milk. It can also be used cold to make salads, added to stir-fries and soups, cooked with milk or coconut milk and sugar to make sweet desserts, or used in stuffings for meat and vegetables. You can also cook it with spices, aromatics and herbs to make pilau. Starchy and sticky rices such as risotto, paella and sushi rice are used to make the specific dish they are named after. Long-grain rices are more versatile, and can be used interchangeably, although certain varieties such as basmati are favoured over others for their specific taste and texture.

Rice, like pasta, is the perfect store cupboard standby. Stored in an airtight container in a cool, dry place, it has a shelf life of at least a year.

Preparing and cooking rice

Different rices require different preparation and cooking methods. Some should be rinsed in cold water to remove the outer layer of starch to ensure fluffy, separate grains when cooked. Others, such as risotto rice, are favoured specifically for their starchy qualities and should therefore not be rinsed. Of the several basic methods for cooking long-grain rice, the best is the absorption method:

1 Rinse the grains well in cold water until the water runs clear, to remove any excess starch, then soak in cold water for 30 minutes before draining well.

2 Measure the rice by volume and add twice that volume of boiling water and a pinch of salt. Bring to the boil, then cover and simmer for about 12 minutes, or according to the pack instructions, until all the water has been absorbed.

3 Cover and leave to stand for a few minutes before fluffing up with a fork and serving.

Other varieties include
Pudding rice A short-grain rice with a rounded shape. The grains of pudding rice plump up and become sticky as they cook. Pudding rice is the favourite choice for making sweet milk puddings and can be baked slowly in the oven with milk, sugar and spices until tender.

Java rice A short-grain rice from South-east Asia. Java rice is used for desserts such as rice pudding cooked with coconut milk, sugar and spices. It is highly absorbent and can be used in the same way as pudding rice.

Carolina rice A short-grain rice from the US. Carolina rice can be used for sweet desserts such as rice pudding cooked with milk, sugar and nutmeg, or in savoury stuffings for meat and vegetables.

Surinam rice An unusual long-grain rice from South America, Surinam rice has a good flavour and can be served as for other long-grain rices.

Rice products
As well as rice grains, there are a number of products made using rice:

Ground rice With a slightly gritty texture, this coarse rice flour is used in desserts such as the Lebanese spiced rice pudding *mighlee*, and in biscuits, and is often added to shortbread.

Puffed rice This is made from grains of rice that are heated in steam until they 'puff', rather like popcorn. Puffed rice is a popular cereal and is also used in sweet and savoury snacks.

Rice cakes Made from puffed grains of rice, compressed into rounds or squares, rice cakes make a good alternative to bread for those with gluten-intolerance or an allergy, or for those following a low-calorie diet. Rice cakes may be lightly salted or unsalted, and have a delicate flavour. Flavoured varieties are also available.

Mochi These are firm, round rice cakes from Japan, made from glutinous rice. They can be fried, grilled or boiled briefly and served as an accompaniment.

Flaked rice Made from flattened grains of cooked rice, flaked rice is widely used in China and South-east Asia in both sweet and savoury dishes. It is often used to coat foods before deep-frying.

Rice bran Removed from the rice grain when processing white rice, coarse brown rice bran is used in China and Asia – toasted, then mixed with salt and water and fermented for use in pickles.

Rice flour See page 355.

Rice vinegar See page 391.

Corn

Cornmeal

Cornmeal can be white or yellow, depending on the colour of the corn (maize) from which it is ground; for the cook there is no difference between the two. Much more important is the grade, which may be coarse, medium or fine. Cornmeal is used to make a quick bread that doesn't need yeast, and occasionally cakes, muffins and biscuits. It gives a crisp bite, with a rich flavour and a golden yellow colour. For leavened breads, cakes and baking, cornmeal is usually combined with wheat flour, although unleavened breads such as Mexican tortillas can be made solely with cornmeal. Most cornmeal is ground to remove all the bran and germ (and much of the nutritive value). Stoneground cornmeal has more of the bran and germ, and therefore has a higher nutritional value and coarser texture. It should be refrigerated, tightly sealed, to keep the oil in the germ from becoming rancid. In addition to its uses in baking, cornmeal can be used to coat deep-fried foods, to which it imparts a crunchy crust.

TO USE Cornmeal needs no specific preparation; use as required.

Blue Cornmeal

Ground from blue corn (maize), blue cornmeal is unique to the American south-west. The outer layer of the grain contains a blue pigment (the same one found in red cabbage), which gives the corn and the resulting meal its grey-blue colour. It is used in the same way as yellow cornmeal, but most often to make muffins, tortillas, tortilla chips and *atolé* (a porridge-like dish popular in southern cooking). Blue cornmeal is esteemed by Native Americans, and classic dishes made with it include *chaquegue*, a cornmeal drink, and the wafer-thin cake, *piki*.

TO USE Blue cornmeal needs no specific preparation; use as required.

Polenta

Polenta is a dish made by Italian cooks, traditionally those in the north of the country, by boiling cornmeal (usually fine) in water with salt to make a thick purée rather like porridge. The porridge is served as a staple, in much the same way as other regions use pasta. It is used as an accompaniment, and in some places traditionally served at Christmas with spicy sausage and *mostarda* (mustard fruit pickles). Polenta may be served plain or with cheese stirred through it. It may also be left to cool until firm, then sliced and pan-fried, griddled or baked. Other European countries make their own equivalent of polenta, and the American grits (see facing page) is little different except in name.

TO USE Traditional polenta should be stirred into boiling salted water, then stirred constantly for 45 minutes or until thick and tender. Quick-cook varieties are widely available and can be cooked in only a few minutes. Pre-cooked polenta, sold sealed in plastic, may be regarded as a store cupboard emergency measure.

Grits

Popular in the southern states of the US, hominy grits, often shortened to grits, is the Amercian answer to polenta. They are made from coarsely ground white or yellow maize, boiled in water to make a thin, pale, corn porridge. Grits is usually served as a savoury breakfast food, often as a side dish with eggs and sausage. Bland in itself, it readily picks up flavours from the more flavourful foods with which it is served. Grits may also be flavoured with cheese and baked to make the popular dish cheese grits.

TO USE To make plain grits, boil in water with a pinch of salt according to the pack instructions, or follow your recipe.

Popcorn

Golden popcorn is a type of corn kernel specially bred to give good results in making this popular snack. When the kernels are heated, pressure builds up inside them until it's high enough to break the hull in a fraction of a second. The starch in the interior expands equally rapidly, creating a white, fluffy, irregularly shaped ball. Popcorn is eaten as a snack food, and can be sprinkled with salt, tossed in butter or drizzled with honey, syrup or caramel. In the US, popcorn is often strung together with cranberries to create Christmas strands to hang as decorations. The unpopped kernels are also referred to as popping corn. If eaten without fat or sugar, popcorn is a low-calorie snack.

TO USE Heat a little oil in a pan with enough popcorn kernels to cover the bottom in a single layer. Cover tightly with a lid and cook at moderately high heat until all sounds of popping have stopped.

Hominy

Hominy is made from whole grains of maize which have been processed to remove the tough outer husk and enhance their nutritive value. Developed in Central America, the process has been adapted in Mexico and by Native American tribes in the south-western US. Hominy can be boiled until tender and served as a side dish in place of potatoes or rice. It can also be added to stews, casseroles and soups – often those made with chicken, beef or pork, such as Mexican *pozole* (spicy pork and hominy stew) – or used in breads.

Ground hominy is known as hominy grits, often abbreviated to grits (see left).

TO USE Boil in water until tender, or use according to your recipe.

Wheat

Whole wheat

Also known as wheat berries. These small, golden-brown grains of husked wheat have a chewy texture and a wholesome, nutty taste when cooked. They are good added to soups, stews, casseroles and pilaus, and can be sprinkled over bread before baking. A processed form of whole wheat, resembling small, cream-coloured barley, is also available. This requires no pre-soaking and has a much shorter cooking time.

TO USE Soak overnight in cold water, then boil in salted water for about 1 hour until tender.

Cracked wheat

Cracked wheat is made by crushing uncooked wheat berries. It should not be mistaken for bulgur wheat. Cracked wheat has a nutty flavour and chewy texture similar to whole wheat, and can be served as an accompaniment rather like rice, or used in salads and added to soups, stews and casseroles.

TO USE Boil in salted water until tender.

Bulgur wheat

Bulgur wheat is sometimes referred to as cracked wheat, but it is a completely different product. These pale brown grains are made by cooking, drying and finally crushing wholewheat grains. Bulgur wheat has a pleasantly chewy texture and nutty taste, and is available in various grades, from fine to coarse. Popular in Middle Eastern cooking, bulgur wheat is used in tabbouleh, the classic mint and parsley salad, and several other herb-laden salads. It can also be used in pilaus or as an accompaniment in place of rice.

TO USE Soak in boiling, salted water for 20 minutes or until tender, then drain and use as required.

Wheat flakes

Wheat flakes are made from whole grains of wheat that have been steamed to soften them and then flattened by rollers. They are a popular addition to breakfast cereals such as muesli, and can be sprinkled over loaves of bread before baking or added to the crumble mixture for fruit crumbles. Malted wheat flakes, made from grains that have been allowed briefly to germinate, are also available. These have a darker colour and richer, slightly sweeter, fruitier flavour. Also known as rolled wheat.

TO USE Wheat flakes need no specific preparation; use as required.

Couscous

Usually treated as a grain, pale yellow couscous actually consists of tiny, pasta-like pellets made from moistened, rolled grains of semolina (ground durum wheat, which is also used to make Italian dried pasta). Widely used in Morocco and north Africa, it is served as an accompaniment to wet, spicy stews but is also good when used to make salads or served as an accompaniment instead of rice, pasta or potatoes. Couscous is available in three sizes: fine, medium and giant. The giant variety is known variously as Israeli couscous, pearl couscous and *moghrabieh*. You may also find barley and maize varieties, and flavoured brands.

TO USE Traditionally, the grains are soaked and then steamed in a *couscoussière* (a perforated pot set over a pan of stew). Quick-cook varieties are readily available, and the grains can be soaked in boiling water for just 5 minutes, then stirred with a fork, with the addition of butter or oil and seasoning, to separate the grains.

Semolina

Pale yellow semolina is made from durum wheat, ground either coarsely or finely. It is popularly used to make sweet milk puddings and is added – usually in combination with wheat flour – to cakes, biscuits and some breads. It is the essential ingredient of Italian dried pasta and the North African staple, couscous.

TO USE Semolina needs no specific preparation; use as required.

Wheat bran

The thin, brown, papery outer layer of the wheat grain. Wheat bran is not nutritious, but it provides a valuable source of fibre, which is essential for healthy digestion. Added in small quantities to breads, cereals and some cakes and biscuits, it adds a rich brown colour and wholesome, slightly nutty flavour. A teaspoonful can also be added to breakfast smoothies. Bran contains phytates, which can prevent minerals such as calcium and iron being absorbed into the body, so should not be consumed in excess or routinely added to food. Store in an airtight container in a cool, dry place.

TO USE Wheat bran needs no specific preparation; use in very small quantities.

Wheat germ

Inside a wholewheat grain is the wheat 'germ', the tiny embryo from which the grain will sprout. The wheat germ is removed before the grains are milled to make white flour. However, it is a highly nutritious component of the grain – rich in B vitamins and protein – and can be bought separately to add to breads, breakfast cereals and smoothies. Wheat germ is available, either plain or toasted, from health-food shops and some large supermarkets.

Because it has a high oil content, it has a limited shelf life and should be stored in the fridge in an airtight container for no more than three months.

TO USE Wheat germ needs no specific preparation; use as required.

Gluten

This is a different gluten to the type of protein found in wheat, rye and barley. It is used in Chinese and South-east Asian vegetarian cooking, and is particularly valued by vegetarian Buddhist monks. This chewy substance – also known as seitan – is made from a mixture of wheat flour, salt and water, with the starch rinsed away. It has little or no flavour, and is usually added to highly flavoured braised dishes. It is popular among vegetarians for its resemblance to meat and its protein content.

Gluten is available from Asian food shops. Store it in the fridge and use within a few days once opened.

Konnyaku A gluten product from Japan, konnyaku may be white or brown and has a non-descript flavour and a gelatinous texture. Available in blocks, it can be sliced and added to soups and hotpots. Boil briefly before cooking.

TO USE Slice or cut gluten into pieces and use as required.

Flour

There are numerous types of flour, all made by finely grinding grains to make a fine or medium-fine powder. They may be white or brown, depending on whether the husk and germ have been removed before grinding.

Wheat flour

The most widely used type of flour, wheat flour has a high gluten content, making it ideal for baking breads, cakes and biscuits. It is also used for pastry, pasta, crumbles and batters, to thicken sauces and soups and to coat meat and fish before frying.

White flour By far the most versatile of all wheat flours. White flour can be used for most cooking purposes (apart from bread-making or pasta).
Wholemeal flour Made from wholewheat grains, this flour is pale brown with a slightly coarse texture and a nutty flavour. It is denser than white flour.
Self-raising flour Usually made from white flour with the addition of baking powder. Self-raising flour is used primarily for cakes and biscuits.
Strong bread flour Specifically produced for making bread, strong flour contains high levels of gluten, which improve the elasticity of the dough so that air is trapped inside as it rises. The flour may be white, brown (a mixture of white and wholemeal), wholemeal or Granary (with malted wheat flakes).
Tipo 00 Also known as farina bianca, this fine white Italian flour is used to make pasta.
Chapati flour This fine wholemeal wheat flour, also known as ata, is used to make Indian flatbreads.

Rice flour

Finely ground rice flour is used in Asia to make doughs, dumpling wrappers, cakes and sweets. It is gluten-free and can also be used as a thickener.

Rye flour

This greyish-brown flour is widely used in Russia, Scandinavia and Germany to make dense, dark, rye breads. It has a distinctive, slightly sharp flavour.

Buckwheat flour

This grey-brown flour has a distinctively earthy taste and is traditionally used to make blini and pancakes.

Barley flour

This pale, mildly flavoured flour has a low gluten content and is usually combined with wheat flour to make soft-textured breads.

Millet flour

Pale yellow millet flour has a mild, slightly sweet flavour. Low in gluten, it is best combined with wheat flour to make crumbly breads and cakes.

Spelt flour

Ground from a type of wheat that has been cultivated since the Bronze Age, spelt flour has a slightly nuttier flavour than ordinary wheat flour. Use alone or blend with wheat flour in cakes and breads.

Sorghum flour

Similar to millet flour, and used in the same way.

Potato flour

This fine, white, soft flour is gluten-free and favoured by those on a gluten-free diet for making cakes. It gives a spongy result; best used with other flours.

Chestnut flour

Made from ground sweet chestnuts, this pale, sweet and nutty flour is used in cakes, such as Italian *castagnaccio*, biscuits and bread.

Soya flour

This fine white flour, ground from partially cooked soya beans, is gluten-free with a high protein content. It can be used with other flours to make cakes, biscuits and bread.

Chickpea flour

Also known as gram flour and besan. This pale, creamy yellow flour has a nutty and slightly bitter flavour. It is used to make batter for Indian-style fritters such as pakora, or to thicken savoury sauces.

Cornflour

Pure white, and much finer than wheat flour, cornflour is ground from the white part of the corn kernel. It is used to thicken soups, sauces and gravies, and added in small quantities to desserts such as pavlova to give the meringue a slightly chewy consistency. As a thickener, cornflour is blended with a small amount of cold liquid, then added towards the end of cooking. It is wheat- and gluten-free (although gluten-intolerant people should always check the packaging to ensure there are no traces).

Arrowroot

A white starch powder from the maranta plant, arrowroot becomes clear when dissolved in liquid. It is used as a thickener for desserts and fruit sauces.

Other grains

Oats

Oats are sometimes available as whole grains, which can be added to hearty stews and soups, but they are more widely sold in the form of rolled oats and oatmeal. Pinhead oatmeal is the coarsest grade and is traditionally used in haggis and for making Scottish porridge, although many people now use rolled oats instead. Finer grades of oatmeal are often combined with wheat flour to make breads, cakes such as parkin, biscuits such as oatcakes, pastry and pancakes, or for coating herring and other oily fish before frying. Rolled oats are the main ingredient in flapjacks and can also be added to breads, cakes and biscuits, or used in breakfast cereals such as muesli.

TO USE Oats, oatmeal and rolled oats need no specific preparation; use as required.

Barley

The type of barley most frequently used in the kitchen is pearl barley, where the grains have been husked, steamed and polished. The smooth, creamy-beige grains have a delicate, sweet flavour and a slightly chewy texture. They can be added to soups, salads and stews, or served as an accompaniment. Barley can also be cooked like risotto, and in fact this was one of the grains originally used for that classic Italian dish. The result is more wholesome, somewhat chewier, and less creamy than rice in a risotto. Pot barley, which has less of the husk removed than pearl barley, can be used in he same way but it requires a much longer cooking time. It makes a particularly good alternative to brown rice.

TO USE Add pearl barley to soups and stews, or boil in salted water for 1½–2 hours, until tender. Pot barley should be soaked overnight, then cooked for 2–3 hours.

Quinoa

This South American grain was first eaten and cultivated by the Incas. Pronounced 'keenwa', it is the only grain to contain all eight amino acids and thus to be considered a complete protein. The tiny round grains swell up when cooked and have a mildly nutty taste with quite a firm, slightly slippery texture. Quinoa can be used in pilaus, salads and baked dishes, as well as in stuffings for vegetables. It can also be cooked with fruit juice and dried fruit to make a sweet 'porridge' for breakfast.

TO USE Put the grains in a sieve and rinse thoroughly before using. Simmer in boiling water for 20 minutes, or until tender.

Buckwheat

Unrelated to the cereal wheat, buckwheat's triangular seeds are widely used in Eastern European and Ashkenazi Jewish cooking. Available toasted or plain, with a nutty, wholesome flavour and soft texture when cooked, buckwheat is traditionally cooked into a porridge known as *kasha*, and served as an accompaniment to lamb and beef pot roasts and stews, with onions and brown gravy, or with farfalle in the Jewish dish *kasha varnishkes*. Buckwheat is also used as a filling for a *knish*, the Jewish savoury pastry which is traditionally eaten as a snack food. It is also good for making into stuffings for vegetables.

TO USE If using plain buckwheat, toast in a dry frying pan for a few minutes until it gives off a toasted aroma. Simmer in stock or salted water for 10–20 minutes, until tender.

Spelt

A type of wheat that has been cultivated since the Bronze Age, spelt has slender golden grains. It is often more readily tolerated by those who cannot eat wheat or gluten due to a food intolerance. With a slightly chewy and firm texture, spelt can be cooked and used in the same way as whole wheat, in soups, stews and pilaus.

TO USE Cook as for whole wheat.

Millet

This small, round, mildly flavoured pale-brown grain has been cultivated since prehistoric times. It originated in the Near East and travelled first to China and then to Europe. Although no longer widely eaten, it remains popular in some European countries. Millet can be cooked with milk and sugar into a sweet 'porridge' rather like rice pudding, or added to soups, stews and pilaus.

Millet flakes These can be used in place of millet, or added to muesli or multigrain breads.

TO USE Toast the grains in a dry frying pan for a few minutes before simmering in liquid until tender.

Tapioca

The starchy product tapioca is derived from the vegetable root cassava and consists of small, round, pearly white granules. It is popular in South-east Asia, India and Brazil, where it is generally used to make sweet desserts, cooked with milk and sugar rather like rice pudding. The pearls become extremely soft with cooking.

TO USE Some recipes recommend soaking the grains first, but others simmer tapioca in milk with sugar, and often spices, until tender.

Amaranth

A staple of the Aztecs, amaranth was forbidden by the Spanish conquistadors because the Aztecs revered the grain, believing it had supernatural powers and had made it a part of their religious ceremonies. The grain survived as a weed, however, and is now being eaten once again. It is a small, pale-brown grain with a sticky texture and sweet, mild flavour when cooked. Amaranth can be added to soups and stews, made into a porridge, or ground and used in cakes and breads. In Mexico it is popped (like popping corn) and drenched in honey to make the festival candy *alegria* (meaning happiness) or milled and made into the drink *atole*. In Peru, the grain is brewed to make a beer called *chicha*.

TO USE To cook, simmer in two-and-a-half times its volume of water until tender. To make a porridge, simmer in three times its volume of water.

Sago

Similar to tapioca, sago is a starchy product extracted from a tropical palm. It can be bought as small, round, pearly white granules, as flakes, or ground. It is eaten in South-east Asia, India and Brazil, made into sweet desserts, and cooked with milk and sugar to make a pudding. At one time, the dessert was popular in Britain, but it has fallen out of fashion. When cooked, the pearls become translucent and spongy, and the starch they release is glutinous and thickens the liquid in which they are cooked.

TO USE The grains can be soaked before use or simmered in milk with sugar, and often spices, until tender.

Asian pancakes and wrappers

Made from wheat and rice flours, these thin disks or squares of dough are widely used throughout Asia for wrapping around fillings to make wontons, spring rolls and dumplings for steaming, pan-frying or deep-frying. Some wrappers can be filled and eaten without needing further cooking. They are easy to use, and since they freeze well it may be worth buying a large pack and freezing the wrappers in smaller batches, then pulling out what you need.

Chinese pancakes

Thin Chinese pancakes are made from a wheat dough and traditionally served as an accompaniment to Peking duck or for wrapping around mouthfuls of food. Chinese pancakes are widely available frozen and should be thawed and reheated before serving.

TO USE Thaw if frozen, then interleave the pancakes between sheets of greaseproof paper. Wrap in a tightly sealed foil parcel and steam for 5 minutes or until the pancakes are hot.

Spring roll wrappers

Made from a simple flour-and-water dough, these wafer-thin square sheets come in a variety of sizes both small and large. Traditionally, they are wrapped around a meat, fish or vegetable filling, often with rice noodles, to make a neat finger-shaped parcel. The parcels are then deep-fried until crisp and golden, and served with dipping sauce as a snack or (in China) as part of a dim sum meal. Versions are made all over China and South-east Asia and fillings vary greatly, but common additions include ground pork, prawns, crab, bean sprouts, water chestnuts, spring onions and rice noodles – as well as spices and aromatics.

TO USE Lay a sheet flat on the work surface, spoon some filling across the centre – from one corner to the other – leaving a gap at both ends. Fold one side of the wrapper over the filling, brush the edges of the remaining wrapper with a little cornflour mixed with water to help it stick, then tuck in the two ends of the roll and roll up to make a tight, finger-shaped parcel.

Wonton skins

These wafer-thin sheets are made from an egg-and-flour dough and are usually cut into squares, then dusted in flour and sold in stacks. They are most often filled, for example with minced pork, water chestnut and other flavourings, then squeezed into a purse-shaped wonton and deep-fried, although they may also be boiled, steamed, poached in broth or served in soup. Wonton skins can also be used to make sweet wontons filled with fruit and nuts, or the plain, square skins can be deep-fried on their own and served as a crisp snack with dipping sauces.

Wonton skins are available either fresh – which should be stored in the fridge and used within a week – or frozen.

TO USE There is no specific preparation for wonton skins; use as required. Frozen wonton skins should be fully thawed before separating and using.

Rice papers

Used mainly in Thai and Vietnamese cooking, these pale, semi-translucent, brittle disks usually have a crosshatched pattern formed while they were drying on bamboo mats. They can be bought in a variety of sizes. Made from a paste of rice flour, salt and water, rice papers are bought dried and need to be soaked in water to soften them before wrapping around fillings. In Vietnam they are used to make crystal rolls, a type of 'fresh' spring roll where the softened paper is wrapped around a filling of raw vegetables, herbs and aromatics, then rolled up and eaten. The papers may also be used to make traditional deep-fried spring rolls.

TO USE Fill a large round bowl or dish with about 5cm (2in) of cold water. Slide a rice paper into the bowl and leave for about 20 seconds to soften, then remove from the water and use. If you are frying the rolls, it is important to make sure the papers are completely dry before they go into the hot oil.

Breads

Produced in nearly every cuisine, bread is one of the most common staples, particularly in wheat-growing regions. There is a vast array of different types: leavened or flat, baked or fried, and formed into loaves, rounds, ovals, rings, rolls and a wealth of other shapes.

Leavened breads are often risen with the help of yeast, but bakers may also use a sourdough (or in Italy a *biga*) starter made from a fermented flour-and-water paste, or use baking powder, bicarbonate of soda and cream of tartar. Basic doughs may also be enriched with eggs, milk and butter, as for French brioche, or sweetened with sugar, honey and dried fruit, as for the Italian panettone. Savoury breads may be flavoured with herbs and spices, vegetables (such as sun-dried tomatoes), or cheese. Here is a handful of the more common breads found around the world:

Ciabatta
Originating in Liguria but now found throughout Italy and beyond, ciabatta is a classic Italian bread with a flattish, long-oval shape. It is made with white flour, salt, olive oil and water and traditionally leavened with a sourdough starter. Ciabatta has a chewy texture, and the crust is thin and crisp. It absorbs juices well, and is used in *panzanella*, the Tuscan salad of bread and tomatoes. There are flavoured varieties of ciabatta, including olive and sun-dried tomato.

Focaccia
Also originating in Liguria, but found throughout Italy, focaccia is a soft-textured bread made with olive oil. It may be round or rectangular, and is puffy and flat with a dimpled surface, produced by pressing the uncooked dough with the fingertips. The dimples collect the olive oil that is drizzled over the surface before baking. Focaccia may topped with salt or herbs, onions, cheese or prosciutto.

Grissini
Thought to originate in the Italian city of Turin and now found throughout the country, these long breadsticks are usually made with white flour and olive oil, and can range from almost matchstick-size to the thickness of a finger and about 20cm (8in) long. All are crisp and crunchy, and are usually served with drinks.

Panettone
The traditional Italian Christmas bread, panettone is tall and round. It is made from a slightly sweetened dough enriched with butter, eggs and milk, and studded with dried fruit and flavoured with citrus. The crumb is very tender, and the top is sprinkled with crusty sugar or a syrup.

Baguette
The ubiquitous French loaf. A baguette is a white, stick-shaped bread with a thick, crisp, frequently slashed crust and a soft, tender crumb. It can be split and filled for sandwiches or served as an accompaniment to soups, salads or any other meal. It should be eaten on the day it is bought. A ficelle is a thinner loaf with a similar shape.

Brioche
This popular French breakfast bread is made from a dough enriched with butter, eggs and milk and sweetened with a little sugar. It has a tender yellow crumb and soft crust, and is traditionally cooked in a round, fluted mould and topped with a ball of dough.

Croissant
This rich, crescent-shaped roll from France is made with leavened dough that has been folded and rolled with butter. The result is a pastry with a delicate, flaky and buttery crumb. Although it's usually served for breakfast with butter, jam and coffee, you will also find croissants with savoury fillings. Pain au chocolat is a variation made from similar dough and then wrapped around strips of chocolate to make a rectangular pastry.

Cottage loaf
A traditional English loaf, the cottage loaf is made with white flour and shaped into a round with a large ball of dough pressed on top. The bread has a tender crumb and a firm crust.

Soda bread
The classic Irish bread is made with bicarbonate of soda, buttermilk and either white or wholemeal flour. It is always shaped into a traditional round, slashed on the top into quarters. Similar soda farls, also from Ireland, are made with white flour, and the round is cut into quarters before baking to create the individual farls.

Bagel
To make the traditional Jewish ring-shaped roll, bagel dough is rolled out in a thinnish strip and then formed into a round by bringing the ends together; it can also be shaped into a round and have a hole pressed into the centre. Then it is steamed or boiled before baking. Bagels have a distinctively dense, chewy texture. They may be plain white or

wholegrain, and may be flavoured with poppy seeds, among other things. Usually served filled, especially with smoked salmon and cream cheese.

Challah

The Jewish Sabbath and holiday bread, challah, is made from a plaited enriched dough. It has a tender texture and crust, and a slightly sweet flavour. The most familiar Challah is a plait made from 3, 6 or 12 strands of dough, but it may also be round or crown-shaped for the festival of Rosh Hashanah.

Matzo

Although available all year round, matzo is specifically made and eaten by the Jewish community to celebrate Passover, when leavened bread may not be eaten. The thin, square crackers are made under strict guidelines to be suitable to eat at this time. Matzos have a bland taste and a crisp, hard texture. They are very good as a base for dips and canapés.

Pumpernickel

Square German pumpernickel is dark and dense with a moist texture and slightly sour taste. Sometimes flavoured with caraway, it is usually cut in thin slices and served with cold meats and cheese.

Stollen

Oval-shaped stollen is an enriched, yeast-leavened, fruity Christmas bread from Germany, encasing a log of marzipan in the centre. The earliest references date back to 1474, although this version was plain and made only with oats, flour and water. Ingredients were added over the centuries: butter, then gradually dried fruit, candied peel and the log of marzipan, until it resembled the rich, sweet bread enjoyed today.

Pitta

Widely eaten in the Mediterranean and Middle East, including Egypt, Syria, Israel, Greece and Turkey, these leavened oval flatbreads can be made with white or wholemeal flour. They puff up to create a pocket when baked and can be stuffed with meat and vegetables. They can also be sliced and served with dips such as hummus. Warm shop-bought pitta for a few minutes in the oven to puff up before filling.

Chapati

Widely eaten in central and southern India as an accompaniment, these round flatbreads are made from a simple wholemeal flour-and-water dough cooked on a griddle. They are torn into pieces and used to scoop up dhal (lentil dishes) and curries.

Paratha

Made in a similar way to chapatis, parathas have a richer flavour and a flaky texture due to the ghee that is folded into the dough before griddling.

Naan

Leavened with either yeast or sourdough, this spongy, tear-shaped Indian flatbread is baked against the hot clay walls of a tandoor oven. It has a soft crust, and may be plain, filled (as for Peshwari naan, with nuts and raisins), or flavoured with garlic and spices. It is served with dhal (lentil dishes) and curries.

Tortilla

This flatbread is particularly associated with Mexican cooking but also eaten in much of Latin America. Tortillas may be made of cornmeal or wheat flour. They are usually served wrapped around fillings – in burritos, enchiladas or served as quesadillas. They may also be cut into triangles and deep-fried to make tortilla chips.

Yeast

This microscopic single-celled fungus is used as a leavening agent in breads and griddle cakes. It is a living organism that requires warmth and water to activate it. Sugar is also usually added to feed it. The yeast ferments to produce bubbles of carbon dioxide, which become trapped in bread dough and batters. This makes them rise and gives them their spongy appearance and texture.

Fresh yeast Pale beige-brown with a soft, crumbly texture and a slightly sweet, pungent smell, this type of yeast can be difficult to find, although you may be able to buy it from bakers or health-food shops.

Store fresh yeast in the fridge for up to two weeks, or freeze for up to three months. Dissolve in warm (about 38°C) water or milk with a little sugar, then leave in a warm place for 15 minutes or until it starts to bubble. At that point it can be combined with flour and other ingredients, and left to rise.

Dried yeast Used in the same way as fresh yeast, but easier to find. Dried yeast granules need to be started off in warm liquid with a little sugar before combining with dry ingredients and leaving to rise.

Fast action (easy-blend) dried yeast Developed for home breadmakers and widely available, these fine granules can be combined directly with dry ingredients before stirring in liquid and leaving to rise.

Beans and pulses

Dried beans

Chickpea

These hazelnut-sized peas are also known as chana and garbanzo beans. They are round and creamy-beige in colour with a slightly knobbly surface, and have a rich, nutty flavour and a firm but tender texture. Chickpeas are used throughout the world: in Indian curries, North African stews and Mediterranean casseroles and soups. The cooked beans can be puréed to make Middle Eastern hummus, and the raw, soaked beans can be ground to make falafel. Chickpeas also make a good addition to mixed bean and couscous salads. While the flesh is tender, the skins can be chewy even when fully cooked. Some recipes, especially for hummus, call for skinning the beans before puréeing. You can do this (with difficulty) by rubbing the cooked beans vigorously in a tea towel.

TO USE Soak overnight in cold water. Drain, then boil in fresh, unsalted water for 2 hours or until tender.

Kidney bean

These dark red beans have a pale flesh with a smooth, firm texture and sweetish, slightly earthy flavour. The classic bean to add to Mexican-style chilli con carne, kidney beans are good in any robust, spicy stew or soup, and are perfect for using in mixed bean salads, where their colour adds extra visual appeal.

TO USE Soak overnight in cold water. Drain, boil rapidly in fresh, unsalted water for 10 minutes, then simmer for 1–1½ hours until just tender. **Note** Kidney beans contain toxic substances that can only be removed by boiling rapidly for 10 minutes. They should therefore be added to stews only if they have been pre-boiled.

Cannellini bean

These creamy-white, kidney-shaped beans have a tender, buttery texture and a very mild flavour. A good addition to tomato-based and meat stews, they suit robust flavours with plenty of herbs and aromatics. Cannellini beans can be tossed in a little dressing with salad vegetables such as tomatoes, red onions and cucumber, or in the classic Italian bean salad with tuna fish, *tonno e fagioli*. They are also a good accompaniment instead of rice or potatoes, especially if seasoned with garlic, lemon and parsley.

Soissons, slightly larger than the cannellini, is a dried haricot bean popular in France, particularly in the classic goose (or duck) and sausage stew, cassoulet. It is named after the region near Paris where it was originally grown.

TO USE Soak overnight in cold water. Drain, then boil in fresh, unsalted water for 1½ hours or until tender.

Flageolet bean

Pale green flageolet beans are small, young haricot beans harvested and dried before they are fully ripe. They have a deliciously subtle, fresh flavour and a smooth, buttery texture. Although they go well in robust, tomato-based and meat stews, they can also be served on their own or combined with other beans. Try them in mixed bean salads, with fresh herbs and olive oil, or tossed with garlic and olive oil and served as an accompaniment to roast lamb.

TO USE Soak overnight in cold water. Drain, then boil in fresh, unsalted water for 1–1½ hours until tender.

Butter bean

One of the largest of the dried beans, butter beans are flat and kidney-shaped with a creamy and mild flavour, and a floury texture. This versatile bean is added to vegetable and meat stews, and goes well with strong flavours such as tomatoes and spices. It is also often used in traditional Greek dishes and in recipes from other parts of the Mediterranean. Butter beans taste good in mixed bean and couscous salads, and added to soups.

TO USE Soak overnight in cold water. Drain, then boil in fresh, unsalted water for 1 hour or until tender.

Broad bean

This dried version of the fresh broad bean is pale brown and flat. When bought whole, the skins can be tough, but they are often sold pre-skinned, in which case the beans are usually off-white, thin and 'split'. Popular in Middle Eastern cooking, broad beans are the favoured bean used to make the golden fritter falafel, and for a number of spiced bean purées. They have a distinctive flavour and a tender texture, and can also be added to meat and vegetable stews.

TO USE Soak overnight in cold water. Drain, then boil in fresh, unsalted water for 30–50 minutes until tender.

Borlotti bean

These oval, pinkish-brown beans are streaked with dark red and have a pale, tender and buttery flesh with a slightly sweet, earthy flavour. Popular in Italian cooking, borlotti beans are good used in soups, stews and salads, and feature in the classic pasta and bean soup, *pasta e fagioli*. They lose a bit of their colour when cooked, but retain enough to make them one of the more attractive of the dried beans.

TO USE Soak overnight in cold water. Drain, then boil rapidly in fresh, unsalted water for 10 minutes. Simmer for 1½ hours or until tender. **Note** Borlotti beans contain toxic substances that can only be removed by boiling rapidly for 10 minutes. They should therefore be added to stews only if they have been pre-boiled.

Ful medames

This orange-brown bean from Egypt is eaten throughout the Middle East. It is often cooked in plain dishes, such as a stew with onions, olive oil and spices; this is served with a hard-boiled egg and flatbread as a *mezze*. With a strong, earthy, wholesome flavour, ful medames are also good used in soups, stews and salads, or cooked with spices and aromatics and served with rice.

TO USE Soak overnight in cold water. Drain, then boil in fresh, unsalted water for 2 hours or until tender.

Gunga pea

Also known as Congo peas, pigeon peas, toor dal and red gram, gunga peas are thought to be native to Africa but are widely eaten in India and the Caribbean. The small round peas have a pale brown-beige skin flecked with darker brown and a pale, tender flesh with quite a robust flavour. They are good added to soups, stews and curries, and are the 'pea' in the classic Caribbean dish known as rice and peas.

TO USE Soak overnight in cold water. Drain, then boil in fresh, unsalted water for 45 minutes–1 hour until tender.

Pinto bean

A type of kidney bean that is popular in both Spain and Mexico, pinto beans have a pinky-beige skin with dark orange-red streaks and a tender pale flesh with a nutty flavour. Good used in soups, stews and salads, they were the original bean used to make Mexican refried beans, where the beans are cooked until tender, then fried and roughly mashed with garlic, tomatoes and spices. Pinto beans are also a popular addition to Spanish stews.

TO USE Soak overnight in cold water. Drain, then boil in fresh, unsalted water for 1–1½ hours until tender.

Lima bean

As lima beans are similar in appearance, taste and texture to butter beans, they can be used in the same way. The pale, flat bean is commonly found (though not universally popular) in the US, where it is often added to soups, stews and salads.

TO USE Soak overnight in cold water. Drain, then boil in fresh, unsalted water for 1–1½ hours until tender.

Haricot bean

Known as navy beans in the US, haricot beans are small, oval and creamy-white, and are the classic ingredient in Boston baked beans (cooked with cured pork, tomato and spices). With a mild flavour and smooth, buttery texture, they are good used in robust, well-flavoured soups and stews such as cassoulet, or made into purées flavoured with spices, herbs and aromatics. Haricot beans are also widely used in France, Spain, Portugal and South America.

TO USE Soak overnight in cold water. Drain, then boil in fresh, unsalted water for 1–1½ hours until tender.

Soya bean

These small round beans may be creamy-yellow or black with a pale, tender, smooth flesh. They are very rich in nutrients and are an excellent source of vegetarian protein. The beans themselves have very little flavour, so they are best added to hearty soups and stews that include plenty of vegetables, herbs and spices. As the beans cook, they will absorb the flavours from their tastier companions in the pot.

Black soya beans are usually fermented to make Chinese chilli bean paste (see page 395).

TO USE Soak overnight in cold water. Drain, then boil rapidly in fresh, unsalted water for 15 minutes. Drain again, then boil in fresh, unsalted water for 2 hours or until tender. **Note** Soya beans contain toxic substances that can only be removed by boiling rapidly for 15 minutes. They should therefore be added to stews only if they have been pre-boiled.
(see also soya bean products, page 374)

Black-eyed bean

Also known as black-eyed peas and cow peas, these creamy white beans have a distinctive black mark where the bean was once attached to the pod. With a tender texture and mild flavour, they are good added to soups, stews, curries and salads, and go particularly well with pork and ham. They are popular in Creole and southern American cooking, and are used in the Caribbean and Nigeria to make bean cakes known as *moin-moini*. The cakes are made by soaking and skinning the beans before grinding them with onions and a little stock and mild seasoning, then puréeing and steaming the mixture in cone-shaped pouches made from banana leaves.

TO USE Soak overnight in cold water. Drain, then boil in fresh, unsalted water for 1½ hours or until tender.

Black bean

These small, kidney-shaped beans are used in African, Caribbean and South American cooking and are popular in the southern US. With a distinctive, slightly sweet, earthy flavour, they are good added to soups, stews and salads, and can be cooked with spices to make purées. Black beans are an essential ingredient in the Brazilian *feijoada*, a stew of dried beef, pork and offal.

TO USE Soak overnight in cold water. Drain, then boil rapidly in fresh, unsalted water for 15 minutes. Drain again, then boil in fresh, unsalted water for 1 hour or until tender. **Note** Black beans contain toxic substances that can only be removed by boiling rapidly for 10 minutes. They should therefore be added to stews only if they have been pre-boiled.

Mung bean

Also known as green gram and moong dal, these small beans are widely used in India to make curries. They are available both whole and split. With a tender texture and fresh, slightly sweet flavour, mung beans are also good added to soups, stews and salads. They are also the most popular bean for sprouting (see page 373).

TO USE Mung beans require no soaking and can be boiled in unsalted water for 40 minutes or until tender. If you do soak the beans overnight, the cooking time can be reduced to about 25 minutes.

Aduki bean

These small, dark red beans have a smooth texture and distinctive, slightly sweet flavour. Popular in Japanese cooking, aduki beans are most often used to make sweet dishes: cooked to a purée with sugar and used as a filling for pancakes, wrapped around rice balls to make the Japanese sweet rice cakes known as *ohagi*, or cooked in sweet soups. They may also be used in savoury dishes, added to stews, stir-fries and salads.

TO USE Soak overnight in cold water. Drain, then boil in fresh, unsalted water for 1 hour or until tender.

Green lentil

One of the largest of the lentils, flat grey-green lentils have a mild flavour and soft, slightly 'dry' texture. Green lentils retain their shape well (unless overcooked) and are a good addition to soups and stews, but can also be used to stuff vegetables or added to salads. They go well with pork and gammon, and can be cooked with rice, spices and fried onions in the classic Middle Eastern dish *megadarra*.

TO USE Green lentils require no soaking and can be boiled in unsalted water for 30 minutes or until tender.

Brown lentil

Very similar to green lentils, brown lentils can be used in the same way in soups, stews and rice dishes. Their colour is sadly unexciting, but they have good flavour and a solid skin which holds up well to cooking. The colour can be enlivened by mixing with prettier ingredients, such as peppers, olives, lemon slices or parsley.

TO USE Brown lentils require no soaking and can be boiled in unsalted water for 30 minutes or until tender.

Puy lentil

These small, speckled, dark green gems are the Kings of Lentildom: highly prized for their excellent taste and texture. Grown in France and named after the town of Puy, in the Auvergne, they are often boiled until tender, then cooked briefly with a little stock, fried onion or garlic and fresh herbs, and served as an accompaniment to meats and fish, or tossed in salads. They can also be used in soups and stews in the same way as green and brown lentils. Puy lentils hold their shape better than any other lentil, even when fully cooked.

TO USE Puy lentils require no soaking and can be boiled in unsalted water for 30 minutes or until tender.

Red split lentil

These tiny pink-orange split lentils disintegrate as they cook, producing a thick purée with a slightly dry texture. As they have a mild flavour, red split lentils benefit from the addition of spices and strong flavours. They are used to make spicy Indian dhal – a staple dish in much of India – but they can also be used to thicken soups and casseroles. Red lentils are used in the Middle East to make the spicy fritters known as *kofte*.

TO USE Red lentils require no soaking and can be boiled in unsalted water for 25 minutes or until tender.

Yellow lentil

Also known as chana dal, yellow lentils are slightly larger than red lentils. They disintegrate in the same way when cooked, and can generally be used in exactly the same way to make spicy dhals or to thicken soups and casseroles.

TO USE Yellow lentils require no soaking and can be boiled in unsalted water for 30 minutes or until tender.

Split pea

These dried peas may be green or yellow. Like red and yellow lentils, split peas become soft and floury when cooked, making them ideal for thickening soups and casseroles or for making purées. With a mild flavour, split peas suit spices and robust flavourings. They are popular in Scandinavian and northern European cooking, and are often paired with ham and bacon. Green split peas are traditionally used in the English dish, pease pudding.

TO USE Split peas require no soaking and can be boiled in unsalted water for 45 minutes or until tender.

Canned beans

Although beans and pulses are simple to cook, soaking and lengthy boiling make them impractical to cook when you don't have a lot of time at your disposal. This is why canned beans are such an invaluable store cupboard item. Most types are available ready-cooked in cans and they are relatively inexpensive, although of course they are more expensive than home-cooked beans. They tend to be very soft – certainly softer than home-cooked beans and pulses. This makes them ideal for making purées and dips. But they can also be served as an accompaniment with just brief heating, preferably with added garlic, onion or lemon juice to boost the flavour. When buying, look out for beans canned in water rather than brine, as many varieties can be high in salt.

TO USE Drain and rinse well in cold water before using according to your recipe.

Preparing and cooking beans

1 Pick any grit or small stones from the beans. Put the beans in a bowl or pan and pour over cold water to cover generously. Leave to soak for at least 8 hours, then drain. (If you are in a hurry, pour over boiling water and leave for 1–2 hours.)

2 Put the drained beans in a large pan and add water to cover by at least 5cm (2in). Boil rapidly for 10 minutes. Skim off any scum, and simmer until the beans are tender but not falling apart. Add more water, during cooking if necessary. Drain.

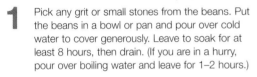

More about beans

Beans, pulses and lentils are the edible seeds of various leguminous plants. Rich in nutrients, they are a good source of vegetarian protein. However, it should be noted that despite being a rich source of protein, most do not constitute a whole protein (containing all eight amino acids) and need to be combined with grains or cereals to make up full protein. They are a good source of fibre, B vitamins, potassium and iron.

Eaten throughout the world for thousands of years, beans, pulses and lentils are used in spicy curries in India and fragrant, spiced dishes and purées throughout the Middle East and North Africa. They are a staple throughout South America, cooked in stews and casseroles or fried and mashed with spices. In the Caribbean they are cooked with rice, and in the US they are enjoyed in the classic dish, Boston baked beans. In Europe they are often served as an accompaniment to meat and fish, or added to rich, hearty stews and soups.

How to buy and store beans

Beans, pulses and lentils have a long shelf life and can be stored in an airtight container in a cool, dark and dry place for many months. However, they tend to become harder with prolonged storage and age and may require much longer cooking to achieve tender results. Buy from stores with a relatively high turnover of stock and use within six to nine months.

How to prepare and cook beans

Always pick through beans, pulses and lentils carefully and remove any tiny stones or grit, then rinse well. Some, such as kidney beans, black beans and borlotti beans require fast boiling for 10 minutes (soya beans need 15 minutes' boiling), to remove any toxins contained in the bean. They should then be drained and boiled in fresh, unsalted water. Others can be brought to the boil and cooked without changing the water.

A pressure cooker is a quick and economical way to cook soaked, dried beans. Cover the beans with plenty of fresh water and bring to pressure. They will take from 5 minutes for cannellini and red kidney beans to 30 minutes for chickpeas. The beans and stock can then be made into a flavoursome soup (but never cook beans in salted stock).

Beans must be cooked without salt, which would toughen the skin and stop the inside from becoming tender. Season when cooked.

Sprouted beans and seeds

Most beans and lentils can be sprouted and then used in soups, stir-fries and salads. With their crisp texture and nutty flavour, sprouted beans are often richer in nutrients than the whole bean. Seeds and some grains can also be sprouted.

You can buy many different varieties of bean sprouts in supermarkets and greengrocers, but you can also – with very little trouble – grow your own at home. Look for fresh-looking sprouts and avoid any with brown patches or that appear slimy. Store in the fridge and use within three days. (Sprouting is an enjoyable kitchen activity for young children.)

Home sprouting

To sprout beans or seeds at home, you can use a specially designed sprouter – usually a square plastic box with three layers – or just a large jar covered with a square of muslin. It will take about three to five days before they are ready to eat. If using a sprouter, follow the directions on the kit, but if using a jam jar, follow the directions below.

1 Rinse a small handful of beans or seeds in cold water, then put in the jar and pour over water to cover. Cover the jar with the square of muslin, secure with a rubber band, and leave in a warm place, out of direct sunlight, until the next day.

2 Drain the beans or seeds by tipping the jar upside down. Rinse, by pouring water through the muslin and tipping upside down to drain again, then put the jar on its side, spreading the beans or seeds out. Leave to sprout in a warm place, out of direct sunlight, rinsing three times a day in cold water to prevent the beans or seeds rotting. Repeat for two to four days until the sprouts have grown to the required size. (If sprouting soya beans or chickpeas, rinse four times a day, rather than three.) Store in the fridge and use within two days.

Popular varieties for sprouting

Mung bean One of the most commonly available types of sprout, mung beans grow thick white shoots, which are fresh and crisp with a slightly nutty flavour. Popular in Chinese and Asian cooking, they can be added to salads, stir-fries or Asian-style soups. Mung bean sprouts only require minimal cooking of 1 minute or less. With cooking, they retain a crisp bite, but become more tender and juicy.

Alfalfa Sprouted from the seeds of a leguminous plant, these fine, pale-green sprouts have a crisp, fresh taste and are most often eaten raw in salads, or combined with other ingredients such as hummus and used to fill sandwiches and wraps.

Chickpea With a nutty flavour and crisp texture, chickpea sprouts are usually added to cooked dishes such as soups and casseroles.

Lentil Only whole lentils can be sprouted, but they will produce white shoots with a mild, peppery flavour and are good added to soups and casseroles.

Aduki bean These small fine sprouts with white shoots are good added to salads for their pretty dark red colour. With a mild, juicy taste and crisp texture, they can also be tossed into stir-fries and cooked briefly.

Soya bean Pale and fleshy with a mild, fresh flavour, soya bean sprouts are good added to stir-fries, soups and braised dishes.

Wheat grass Grown from the sprouted wheat berry (or whole wheat grain), this bright green, lush grass is usually used for juicing. It is believed by some to have medicinal or health-giving properties, and it has a very strong, sweet, grassy flavour and a potent bite. Wheat grass juice should be served in tiny shots and sipped slowly.

Soya bean products

Tofu

Also known as beancurd, soft white tofu is made from the 'milk' obtained from boiled, mashed soya beans. It originated in China, where it is still a major source of protein, and was introduced to Korea and Japan many centuries ago. It is a good source of vegetarian protein and is low in calories; it contains no saturated fat or cholesterol. There are two main types: firm, which can be sliced or cut into cubes and added to soups and stir-fries, deep-fried or used for kebabs; and silken, which is much softer and smoother and is good for mashing or puréeing in sauces, dips and dairy-free ice creams. Tofu has a mild, bland flavour, and it readily absorbs other flavourings: it benefits from strong-tasting marinades, such as soy sauce, ginger, sherry, onion, garlic and chilli. Fresh tofu should be stored in the fridge and used within a few days.

TO USE Drain away the packing liquid. Use silken tofu as required. Rinse firm tofu, pat dry, then slice or cube as required.

Pressed tofu

Sometimes sold as dry or extra-firm tofu, this is made from fresh tofu that has been pressed to extract much of the liquid and to give a firmer texture. Pressed tofu can be sliced or cut into cubes and used in soups, stir-fries and casseroles as for firm tofu, or it can be pan-fried as a 'tofu steak'.

TO USE Slice or cube and use as required.

Fermented tofu

Fermented tofu, a Chinese speciality, takes many months to mature and develop its strong, pungent flavour. Fresh tofu is laid on beds of rice straw to ferment before being dried and marinated in rice wine, salt and spices. It is then packed into jars of brine and left to mature for at least six months. The end result has a powerful smell and piquant bite, and is used in small quantities as a flavouring ingredient in stir-fries and braised dishes. It is also served as a condiment with the rice porridge called *congee*. Two main varieties are available: red fermented tofu and spicy white fermented tofu. Both of them are, to put it very mildly, an acquired taste.

TO USE Cut into cubes and use as required.

Marinated tofu

Ready-marinated tofu is often sold in cubes that have been marinated in soy sauce and Chinese-style spices, which give it a brown outer layer and creamy-white interior. The cubes have quite a firm, chewy texture and are good added to stir-fries, braised dishes, soups and casseroles. Less traditional forms of marinated tofu are also becoming available, including Mediterranean flavourings such as tomato and basil.

Smoked tofu has a distinctive smoky flavour; use in salads, stir-fries or kebabs, paired with robust flavours such as spinach, pumpkin and butternut squash.

TO USE Marinated tofu requires no specific preparation. Use it straight from the pack.

Deep-fried tofu

Crisp and golden deep-fried tofu is available in various forms: as thick blocks, thin sheets, or individual cubes. All are made from fresh firm tofu. The thick blocks are usually grilled and served as 'tofu steaks'; the thin sheets can be split open and filled with vegetables, or sliced or cut into cubes for adding to soups and stir-fries. Cubes of deep-fried tofu can be added to soups, salads, braised dishes and stir-fries. All have a much firmer, chewier texture than fresh tofu.

TO USE Put in a sieve and rinse with boiling water to remove any excess oil, then pat dry before using as required.

Other soya products

Freeze-dried tofu A Japanese speciality, this has a stronger flavour than tofu and a firmer, spongier texture which absorbs other flavours readily. Serve cooked in broth.

Tempeh This is an Indonesian ingredient made from fermented soya beans, it is sold in creamy-yellow blocks and has a knobbly texture and distinctive, slightly nutty flavour. It can be sliced or cubed and used in the same way as tofu.

TVP Sold as chunks or mince, TVP, or textured vegetable protein, is made from 'de-fatted' soya flour (a by-product of processing soya oil). The flour is made into a dough, then steamed to produce a chewy, slightly spongy product with a meat-like texture. It has little natural flavour of its own but is often sold flavoured as either 'beef' or 'chicken'. Dried TVP needs to be re-hydrated in boiling water for 5 minutes before being added to stews, casseroles and sauces using well-flavoured ingredients such as tomatoes, herbs and spices. Frozen TVP mince can be added directly to sauces. TVP products are eaten mostly by those vegetarians who prefer a meat substitute that has a texture similar to meat.

The store cupboard

Dry goods

Salt

Salt (chemical name, sodium chloride) has been used for thousands of years as a flavouring and/or preservative. It is used in cooking and added at the table. Pastry and many sweet recipes such as cakes and scones call for a pinch of salt to bring out the flavour. And it is also used heavily (sometimes too heavily) in most processed foods, from bread and cheese to canned goods, snacks and ready-meals. By drawing the moisture out of fresh ingredients, such as fish and meat, salt can be used to preserve them; they are usually soaked in fresh water to re-hydrate them before use. Aubergine is sometimes lightly salted to draw out any bitter juices. One cooking technique involves baking fish, poultry or meat in a thick salt crust to seal in flavour and moisture. There are several different types of salt available, including coarse or fine sea salt, rock salt obtained from underground deposits, free-running table salt, low-sodium salt aimed at reducing sodium intake, and flavoured salts such as celery salt and garlic salt.

TO USE As a seasoning to taste in cooking or at the table (crush coarse sea salt before sprinkling over food); to flavour cooking water for pasta, rice and potatoes; in pickling and brining solutions for preserves.

Baking powder

This raising agent is used in breads, cakes and batters. The white powder combines an acid ingredient (usually cream of tartar) with an alkali (usually bicarbonate of soda). When liquid is added the chemicals react, creating tiny bubbles of carbon dioxide, which help the bread, cake mixture or batter to rise. Double-action baking powder reacts to heat as well, so rising occurs fully when baked or cooked.

TO USE Combine with dry ingredients such as flour, then sift together to ensure the baking powder is evenly distributed before combining with wet ingredients. Once combined with wet ingredients, bake or cook immediately.

Bicarbonate of soda

Also known as baking soda, this fine white powder is a component of baking powder. On its own, it can be used as a raising agent in cakes, breads and batters that contain an acidic ingredient, for example soda bread or pancakes made with buttermilk. Where no acidic ingredient is present, a chemical acid such as cream of tartar can be added.

TO USE Combine with dry ingredients such as flour, then sift together to ensure the bicarbonate is evenly distributed before combining with wet ingredients. Once combined with wet ingredients, bake or cook immediately.

Cream of tartar

This fine white powder is made from crystallised grape acid, and is a component of baking powder. Its acidic properties, when combined with alkaline bicarbonate of soda and a liquid, act as a raising agent. When the three ingredients react together, they produce tiny bubbles of carbon dioxide, which help the bread dough, cake mixture or batter, to rise.

TO USE Combine with dry ingredients such as flour and bicarbonate of soda, then sift together to ensure the ingredients are evenly mixed before combining with wet ingredients. Once combined with wet ingredients, bake or cook immediately.

Gelatine

Usually made from boiled pig skin or beef bones, this gelling agent is available as thin, clear, brittle leaves or as a powder. Virtually colourless and tasteless, gelatine can be used to set both sweet and savoury dishes. It is used in fruit jellies and mousses, *panna cotta*, chilled cheesecakes, savoury jellies and creamy terrines. Gelatine should not be used with fresh pineapple (although canned pineapple is fine), because fresh pineapple contains an enzyme that will prevent the gelatine from setting. Some recipes call for powdered gelatine and some for sheets of leaf gelatine. The two are essentially interchangeable, as long as you remember that two sheets are the equivalent of 5ml (1 teaspoon) of powdered gelatine.

TO USE Follow the instructions on the pack. As a general rule, soak powdered gelatine in a small amount of water to soften, then warm gently to dissolve. Soak gelatine leaves in water to soften, then add to warm liquid to dissolve.

Vegetarian gelling agents

Gelatine is not suitable for vegetarians and for people with dietary restrictions based on religion, but there are various alternative gelling agents that can be used in its place:

Agar agar Also known as kanten. This is a gelling agent derived from seaweed, and is available as a white powder or threads. It should be dissolved in boiling water and can be used in the same way as gelatine. It doesn't work in all recipes and you may need to use more agar agar to get a firm set.

Carrageen Also known as Irish moss, carrageen is a reddish-purple seaweed that is bleached by the sun to a pale yellow-pink. It can be used as a gelling agent or for thickening sauces, soups and stews. It is a traditional ingredient in Irish cooking and is often cooked in milk, then strained, sweetened, and set as a blancmange-like dessert.

Nuts

Peanut

Also known as groundnuts and monkey nuts. Peanuts are not technically a nut but a pulse – a member of the same family that includes soya beans and green peas. They are native to South America, but are now widely grown in tropical and subtropical climes, including Africa, Australia, South-east Asia, the Americas and the Caribbean. Peanuts grow underground with two 'nuts' in each pale brown, dry, crinkly pod. They are widely used in African cooking, often in stews, and in South-east Asian cooking, for example in Indonesian satay sauce and *gado gado* salad, and sprinkled over Thai dishes such as fried noodles and salads. In the West, they are eaten as a snack or ground into peanut butter, which can be used as a spread or in confectionery and biscuits. Available raw in their shell, peanuts are also sold shelled, salted, roasted or dry roasted.

TO USE Shelled, salted, roasted and dry-roasted peanuts as a snack; shell raw peanuts, then use as they are, or toast in a dry frying pan for a few minutes to bring out the flavour. (see also peanut oil, page 389)

Cashew nut

The tasty, kidney-shaped cashew is native to north-east Brazil but is now grown in most tropical climes, including India, Africa and Australia. It is the seed of a tropical tree that bears bright orange fruits. Always sold shelled, the nut is pale, tender to the bite and sweet and mild in flavour. Cashew nuts are a popular ingredient in stir-fries, Indian curries and salads; their mild flavour is enlivened by saltiness and makes a particularly good partner for poultry. They may also be ground into nut butter to use as a spread. Salted and roasted cashew nuts are often served as a snack.

TO USE Plain nuts can be added to most dishes, or toasted in a dry frying pan for a few minutes to bring out the flavour.

Pistachio nut

Native to western Asia, between Turkey and Afghanistan, pistachio nuts are now grown in other warm climes, including southern Europe and North Africa. The pistachio nut has a smooth, hard shell and papery, purplish skin. Inside, the kernel has pale green flesh and a sweet, distinctive flavour. Pistachio nuts are used widely in both sweet and savoury dishes: good in nut roasts and terrines, rice pilaus and stuffings; chopped and sprinkled over foods as a decoration; used in cakes, biscuits and desserts, or to flavour ice creams. Pistachio nuts are a popular ingredient in Middle Eastern sweetmeats and pastries such as baklava. Pistachio nuts are sold salted and unsalted, and shelled or unshelled, but be sure to buy unsalted nuts for use in sweet dishes.

TO USE Pull apart the hard, split shell to extract the nut. Use as it is, or toast in a dry frying pan for a few minutes to bring out the flavour.

Almond

Most of the world's almonds are grown in California, Spain and Italy, but they can be found in many other countries, from Portugal to Australia. There are two types of almond: bitter and sweet. Bitter almonds contain a chemical that is poisonous when raw; they are mostly processed to produce almond extract and oil. Sweet almonds are harmless, delicious raw, and may be used in sweet and savoury dishes. Almonds are available whole, blanched, split, slivered, flaked and ground. Whole almonds can be used to top cakes and biscuits, added to salads, or toasted and salted as a snack. Slivered almonds, either plain or toasted, are used to decorate cakes, desserts and pastries, and ground almonds are used in cakes, biscuits, marzipan and Indian curries.

TO USE To remove the skin from whole almonds, put the nuts in a bowl and pour over boiling water. Leave to stand for a few minutes, then drain and slip off the skins. This chore may be made somewhat easier by rubbing the nuts in a teatowel. To toast, toss in a dry frying pan for a few minutes until golden.
(see also almond oil, page 389)

Hazelnut

These small, round nuts are native to Europe and are also grown in North America. The hazelnut has a shiny, orange-brown shell, and the creamy-white nut inside is covered in a pale brown skin. With a sweet, distinctive flavour, they are available shelled or unshelled and are mostly used in sweet dishes (although they also make a good addition to stuffings and nut roasts). Whole nuts can be used to top cakes, biscuits, praline and desserts; chopped and ground nuts can be used in cake and biscuit mixtures, pastries and other desserts. Hazelnuts are good when paired with coffee and vanilla, and spectacular when paired with chocolate.

TO USE To peel off the skin from hazelnuts, put the nuts in a bowl and pour over boiling water. Leave to stand for a few minutes, then drain and slip off the skins. This slightly tiresome chore may be made somewhat easier by rubbing the nuts in a teatowel. To toast, toss in a dry frying pan for a few minutes until golden.
(see also hazelnut oil, page 388)

Walnut

There are numerous varieties of walnuts, grown all around the world. The shell is round, pale brown and ridged, while the kernel is deeply wrinkled, with a distinctive, rich, slightly bitter flavour. Served whole in the shell, walnuts make a popular dessert nut for cracking. Shelled walnut halves are used to decorate cakes and biscuits; walnut pieces and ground walnuts are used in cakes, biscuits, pastries and other desserts – they are frequently paired with coffee as a flavouring. Ground walnuts are also used in creamy Italian pasta sauces, and walnut pieces can be used in nut roasts, stuffings and rice pilaus.

Green walnuts are fresh walnuts that have not been dried for keeping. They are moist and juicy with a milky, mild walnut taste and a slight tannic edge. They are excellent with soft cheese, in a salad or a sauce.
Pickled walnut The green nut is sometimes pickled whole to create a tender, quite pungently flavoured accompaniment to serve with cheese and meats, especially as part of a Christmas buffet.

TO USE Serve whole nuts with nutcrackers to break open the shells. For cooking, use halves, pieces or ground walnuts.
(see also walnut oil, page 389)

Pecan nut

By far the greatest source of pecan nuts is the nut's native country, the US, but they are also grown in Israel, Australia and South Africa. Related to the walnut, pecan nuts have a shiny oval shell and a wrinkled appearance similar to walnuts. Their slightly sweet and scented flavour is best suited to sweet dishes, and they are a popular ingredient in cakes, biscuits, pastries, desserts and nut brittle. Their most famous role, however, is in sweet, sticky pecan pie, one of the classic desserts of the southern US. Pecans have a natural affinity with coffee and maple syrup.

TO USE Whole to decorate cakes and biscuits; chopped or ground for cake and biscuit mixtures, tart fillings and desserts.

Macadamia nut

The tender and creamy macadamia nut is most commonly associated with Hawaii, which grows almost 90 per cent of the world's crop. However, it is actually native to Australia, and it is the only Australian edible plant to have widespread international distribution. The red-brown shell is smooth, shiny, and extremely hard to crack. The kernel inside is round and mildly flavoured with an almost buttery taste – not a coincidence, as the nut has a particularly high oil content. Macadamia nuts are eaten as a snack, or used whole, chopped or grated in cakes, biscuits and desserts. They are available raw, roasted in oil or salted, but are almost always the most expensive member of the nut family.

TO USE Whole; chopped coarsely or finely; or grated carefully against a fine grater.

Brazil nut

Grown in Brazil and Amazonian regions, Brazil nuts have a long, dark brown, triangular shell with a slightly rough, puckered surface; the kernel inside is creamy-white with dark brown papery skin. They have a mild and sweet flavour and a crisp texture. Brazil nuts in the shell are a popular dessert nut, and are also eaten as a snack or used in confectionery, often dipped in chocolate. Brazil nuts are a valuable source of the mineral selenium: just one nut will provide a full day's recommended requirement.

TO USE Serve whole nuts with nutcrackers to break open the shells. Shelled nuts need no preparation.

Chestnut

Native to western Asia but flourishing in southern Europe since antiquity, sweet chestnuts – not to be confused with the inedible horse chestnuts – are covered in a shiny brown, leathery skin. They contain far more starch than other nuts and also far less oil, and they are always eaten cooked, either boiled or baked. Heat converts their dense starch into something attractively sweet and tender, if also a little bit dry. Chestnuts are popular in Mediterranean cooking, particularly in cakes, desserts and confectionery. The raw nuts can be roasted over a fire and eaten as a snack; once cooked, they can be tossed with Brussels sprouts and butter, or chopped and used to make a stuffing for Christmas turkey.

Chestnuts are available fresh, or cooked and peeled in cans or in vacuum packs.

Chestnut purée, sold sweetened or unsweetened in cans, is a pale brown purée used mostly in cakes and desserts.

Marrons glacés are candied sweet chestnuts, eaten as a confection.

TO USE Slit fresh chestnut skins, then boil or bake for 20–30 minutes. Cool and peel off the skin. Or, toast over an open fire until blackened, then cool and peel.

Pine nut

Pine nuts, also known as pine kernels, grow in hard seed casings on the cones of pines in Europe, Asia and North America, and contain exceptionally high levels of oil – over 75 per cent in the case of Asian nuts. The oil quickly turns rancid once the casing is removed, so pine nuts must be used up quickly after hulling – and unfortunately, they may already be fairly old by the time you buy them. Pine nuts have perhaps their most famous role in the Genoese pesto sauce (see page 396), but they are also used in the Greek dessert baklava, in cakes and tarts, and as a savoury sprinkling to add crunch and flavour to mixed salads. Pine nuts are often toasted or roasted before use to give them colour and enhance their flavour; this is not necessary, however, when using them for pesto.

TO USE As a snack; in sauces and as a garnish for salads; in sweet dishes. Toast in a dry frying pan for a few minutes to bring out the flavour, if your recipe calls for it.

Coconut

The coconut is the fruit of palm trees that grow throughout tropical regions. Fresh coconuts are large and green, with a leathery skin. In countries where they are grown, they are often sold on the street as a drink; the top will be sliced off and the juice inside drunk, then the soft flesh inside scooped out and eaten. In the West, you will more often find dry, mature coconuts with a hairy, dark brown skin. When the shell is split open, the juice can be drunk or added to soups and curries. The scooped-out flesh can be eaten as a snack or grated, then added to cakes and desserts as well as savoury dishes. It makes a good addition to soups and stews, particularly those from India, Sri Lanka, South-east Asia and the Caribbean.

TO USE To prepare mature coconuts, pierce two holes through the 'eyes' in the top using a hammer and screwdriver and drain out the milk. Using the hammer, crack open at the widest part, then prise out the white flesh using a knife.

(see also coconut products, page 384, coconut oil, page 389)

More about nuts

Most nuts are highly nutritious, rich in unsaturated fats and consequently have a high calorie content. Many, such as peanuts, walnuts and almonds, are pressed for their oil (see pages 388–9). Nuts are also rich in protein, and are often used in vegetarian dishes instead of meat.

How to buy and store nuts

Although some nuts are available fresh, or green, most are dried to extend their shelf life. Nuts in the shell should feel relatively heavy for their size; avoid light nuts, which usually indicate that the kernel will be withered and dry. Also avoid any that are damp or appear mouldy. Due to their high oil content, nuts do not keep particularly well and will turn rancid if not used quickly enough. Buy them in small quantities, store in an airtight container in a cool, dark place, and use within three months.

How to prepare and cook nuts

For hard nuts, you will need to use nutcrackers to crack the hard protective shell, then extract the nut.

Whole nuts can be used for decorating cakes and biscuits. For use in baking and sweet and savoury dishes, nuts are usually chopped, crushed or ground.

Other varieties include

Tiger nut Also known as chufa. Tiger nuts are not really a nut but a small, wrinkled tuber. They have a crisp texture and sweet, slightly almondy flavour, and are mostly eaten in Spain as a snack. Tiger nuts can also be pounded and ground to make a sweet milky drink known as *horchata de chufa,* or used to flavour ices.

Lotus nut Also known as lotus seeds, these small, rounded, light brown seeds have a slightly almondy flavour; they are available dried or canned, from Asian food shops. They may be used whole or pounded in Thai soups and desserts, and in China they are often cooked in a sweet soup to serve at the end of a meal. Lotus seed paste is a popular filling for Chinese pastries and dim sum.

Gingko nut Popular in Chinese and Japanese cooking, the small, cream-coloured gingko nut is usually sold canned or dried. It can be used in sweet and savoury dishes, or eaten as a snack.

Coconut products

Widely used throughout the tropics, coconut is enjoyed in both its whole and processed forms. The processed products are often more convenient than buying fresh coconut and preparing it yourself.

Coconut milk

Creamy coconut milk is not the juice from the centre of the nut but a thick, rich extract made by shredding coconut and soaking it in water, then draining it through muslin. Regular coconut milk is made using twice the volume of water to shredded coconut. Strongly flavoured and sold in cans, coconut milk is used to make soups, curries, coconut rice, Asian-style rice puddings and desserts, and drinks and ices. It is high in saturated fat, but you can find cans of low-fat coconut milk which makes a good substitute for healthier cooking or if you prefer a dish to be less rich.

Coconut cream

Thicker than coconut milk, coconut cream is available in cartons and can be used in the same way: stirred into curries and soups, usually later in cooking, or thinned with water to use as if it were coconut milk. It is made in the same way as coconut milk, but using about half as much water.

Creamed coconut

This thick, creamy paste is sold in cartons and vacuum-sealed sachets. It can be mixed with boiling water, then stirred into curries or into dishes such as soups and rice pudding. To substitute for coconut milk, use 200g (7oz) creamed coconut to 600ml (1 pint) boiling water.

Desiccated coconut

This is made from the dried white flesh of the coconut, and may be sweetened or unsweetened. It is used in confectionery, cakes, biscuits and desserts. Unsweetened desiccated coconut can also be made into a substitute for coconut milk by blending it with the same volume of boiling water in a food processor, then leaving to cool before straining and squeezing through muslin.

Coconut shavings

Dried, toasted shavings of coconut have a sweet flavour and a texture between crisp and chewy. They can be added to cereals and muesli, and make an attractive decoration for cakes and desserts.

Seeds

Poppy seed

These tiny little spheres, blue-black or white, are the innocuous seeds of the opium poppy. The darker variety is more commonly available and has a mild, slightly peppery flavour. Popular in cakes, pastries and biscuits, particularly those from German, Jewish and Eastern European traditions, poppy seeds may be used whole or ground and stirred into cake mixtures and fillings for strudels and other pastries. They may also be sprinkled over breads, bagels and rolls. In India, the white seeds are ground and used to thicken curries and sauces.

TO USE Whole, or grind in a food processor.

Sunflower seed

Looking at these small, pointed, greyish seeds, you would never know that they come from the enormous, bright yellow sunflower. Nutty in flavour and tender but slightly crunchy, sunflower seeds are added to breads and muffins, either mixed into the dough or sprinkled on top before baking. They are also good added to salads and rice pilaus, eaten as a snack, or tossed into muesli.

TO USE Usually sold shelled; if you buy seeds in the black-and-white stripy shells, you will need to split them open using your thumbnails to extract the seeds. Seeds in the shell are more often eaten as a snack.
(see also sunflower oil, page 387)

Pumpkin seed

The dried seeds of the pumpkin are nearly flat, with a dark olive-green skin encasing the pale seed. With a crisp texture and mildly nutty flavour, pumpkin seeds are versatile little things. They're good tossed into salads or rice pilaus, or used in breads and muffins (either sprinkled on top or folded into the dough or batter before baking) – or simply eaten as a snack.

TO USE Often sold shelled; if you buy pumpkin seeds unshelled or pick them straight from the centre of a pumpkin you will need to split open the hard shell to extract the seed. To toast, toss in a dry frying pan for a few minutes until the seeds start to turn brown, then allow to cool.
(see also pumpkin seed oil, page 389)

Tahini

Also known as tahina, this thick, creamy, beige-brown paste is made from ground sesame seeds and is used as an ingredient in Middle Eastern cooking. A darker variety made from unhulled seeds is also available, but has a slightly more bitter flavour. With the same nutty but slightly bitter flavour as sesame seeds, tahini is an essential ingredient in the chickpea purée, hummus, and smoky aubergine purée, *baba gannoush*, and is also used to make sauces for vegetables, meat and fish. Tahini can vary widely in consistency, from a pourable liquid to a very thick paste which needs considerable strength to stir. It is available in jars or plastic tubs and should be stirred or shaken before use, as it may separate when left stationary for long periods. Store in a cool, dark place.

Linseed

Also known as flax seeds. The small, pale brown linseeds are tender yet firm to the bite, and good sprinkled over breads, muffins and rolls, or mixed into the dough or batter before baking. They are frequently combined with other seeds such as sunflower and pumpkin, and are also good sprinkled over salads. Linseeds have considerable nutritional value as a good source of omega-3 essential fatty acids. To get the most out of the healthy oils contained in the seeds, they are best ground. They can then be added to porridge, muesli or smoothies, puréed bean dips such as hummus, nut butters or stirred into soups.

TO USE Grind or use whole.

Sesame seed

Tiny sesame seeds may be white or black, although the white variety is more common. They have a tender but firm texture and distinctive, mildly bitter flavour. Popularly sprinkled on breads, rolls, bagels, pastries and muffins, sesame seeds can also be added to the dough or mixture before baking, or combined with other seeds such as sunflower and pumpkin. They are good toasted and sprinkled over salads, or stirred into creamy chicken dishes. Sesame seeds are pounded and ground for Middle Eastern tahini (see box) and the sweetmeat halwa. And they are used as both an ingredient and a garnish for savoury dishes in China and Japan.

TO USE To toast, toss in a dry frying pan until they start to turn golden and give off a toasted aroma, then leave to cool. Take care not to let them brown too deeply, as this will intensify their bitterness.
(see also sesame oil, page 388)

Oils

Olive oil

Rich, fruity, aromatic, yellow-green olive oil is revered throughout the Mediterranean and Middle East – and indeed everywhere those cuisines have had an influence. There are two grades, with important differences. Extra virgin olive oil is obtained from the first pressing without any application of heat; you'll often see 'cold pressed' on the label. This has the best flavour. Extra virgin is good for making dressings, drizzling over cooked dishes such as risotto, crostini and bruschetta and other appetisers, or served with bread for dipping. Ordinary olive oil (sometimes called 'pure') is made from the solids left over after the first pressing. It is pressed with heat, then refined (purified and stabilised) and blended, sometimes with a small percentage of extra virgin oil. This oil has a milder flavour – good for all-purpose cooking. Oils from different areas will have different flavours: some fruitier, some more peppery, some richer and some more acidic. The best extra virgin oil should not be used for cooking, as heat can mar its flavour, but should be added when the dish is finished so that it just heats through.

TO USE Drizzle over cooked dishes; for pan-frying or sautéing; adding to dressings or bread doughs. It is not suitable for deep-frying or pan-frying at high temperatures.

Sunflower oil

A good all-purpose oil pressed from sunflower seeds, sunflower oil is pale yellow with a very mild flavour. It can be used for frying and deep-frying, or in dressings. Because of its virtual absence of flavour, it is a good choice for heavily spiced or flavoured dishes – for example in Thai and Indian cooking – where a fruitier, more strongly flavoured oil would produce a clash of flavours. Sunflower oil is a good vehicle for aromatics and spices in both cooking and dressings, but it can also be used in more mildly flavoured dishes. It is a good choice if you are making muffins and cakes that call for oil.

TO USE For frying, deep-frying, dressings and baking.

Vegetable oil

This is made from a blend of oils such as rapeseed, safflower, corn oil and soya oil. It may also contain palm oil and coconut oil, both of which are high in saturated fats. With little flavour and a low price, this yellow oil is a good multi-purpose oil, particularly for frying and deep-frying. It generally has a high smoking point so can be heated to high temperatures. Although it can be used for dressings and baking, it is better suited to cooking.

TO USE For frying and deep-frying.

Sesame oil

There are two types of sesame oil, although both have a strong, nutty, sesame flavour. The pale amber oil pressed from untoasted seeds is popular in Middle Eastern and Indian cooking, and can be used for cooking and dressings. The darker oil, made from toasted seeds, has a stronger, more robust flavour and is favoured in Chinese and Japanese cooking – mainly for drizzling over dishes as a flavouring or using with other oils in dressings for salads. It is unsuitable for cooking. Sesame oil has a very strong flavour that can easily overwhelm others, so it should be used in moderation. When buying, be sure to check the label to make sure that the oil is 100 per cent sesame; sesame oil is sometimes blended with cheaper neutral oil to sell at a lower price. The pure oil is vastly superior.

TO USE Pale sesame oil for cooking, flavouring and dressings; toasted sesame oil for flavouring only.

Walnut oil

Originally produced in France, walnut oil can now be found from growers in the US and Australia. This is an expensive oil with a rich, warm, walnut flavour and a lovely golden-amber colour. It is always cold-pressed. Walnut oil is perfect for making dressings, and it is often paired with mild cider or wine vinegars. It can also be used to flavour cakes, biscuits and breads, or drizzled over cooked vegetables and pasta. Use it sparingly or its powerful flavour will dominate other ingredients.

TO USE In dressings; drizzled over vegetables, pasta and other cooked dishes; in baking. It is unsuitable for frying.

Avocado oil

This pale oil, very mild in flavour, is pressed from the large central stone found inside avocados. Valued by some for its high vitamin E content, it is most often used for dressings and for drizzling over crostini, bruschetta and other appetisers. The oil has a high smoking point, so it can also be used for frying, but the high cost makes that an uneconomic option. In dressings it can be used on its own or combined with a more strongly flavoured oil such as olive or walnut.

TO USE For drizzling and dressings.

More about oil

Oil can be defined as fat that remains liquid at room temperature. Pressed and extracted from nuts, seeds, cereals and fruits, oils come in a huge array of different colours, flavours, aromas and cooking properties. When an oil is described as 'virgin', 'extra virgin', and/or 'first pressing' or 'cold pressed', it means that the oil has been extracted by simply crushing or pressing; it should have the finest flavour. Inexpensive oils are usually refined, a process using chemicals, heat and/or filtration to remove impurities and stabilise the oil.

Culinary uses for oils

As a general rule, mildly flavoured oils with a high smoking point are a good choice for deep-frying and cooking, whereas more strongly flavoured oils such as extra virgin olive, walnut and toasted sesame are better for flavouring and making dressings. It should be noted that heating oils repeatedly to a high temperature affects their structure and can transform unsaturated fats into saturated fats.

Other varieties include

Almond oil Pressed from bitter almonds, this pale oil has a mild, fairly sweet flavour and is used for baking and desserts, although not to impart an almond flavour. It is often used to grease tins and moulds for cakes and desserts.

Coconut oil Used in Indian and South-east Asian cooking, this white oil is solid at room temperature. It is extremely high in saturated fat.

Corn oil A good, multi-purpose yellow oil pressed from corn, it is often favoured for deep-frying because of its mild flavour, economical price and high smoking point. A good alternative to sunflower oil, although sometimes at a slightly higher price.

Grapeseed oil Pressed from grape pips. This is pale and mildly flavoured, and is good for dressings and cooking. It can be combined with other, more strongly flavoured oils for dressings. It is relatively expensive for a neutral-tasting oil.

Hazelnut oil With a rich, red-brown colour and a nutty flavour, hazelnut oil is best suited to salad dressings and drizzling, rather than cooking. Use as you would walnut oil.

Hemp oil Pressed from hemp seeds, the oil has a greenish colour and a mild, nutty flavour, and is valued for its high proportion of health-giving essential fatty acids. Available from health-food shops and some supermarkets, it can be used in dressings or for frying and roasting.

Mustard seed oil Popular in Indian cooking, mustard seed oil has a strong flavour that is mellowed by cooking.

Palm oil This thick, ochre-orange oil extracted from the seed of the oil palm is high in saturated fats. It is popular in African and South American cooking.

Peanut oil Also known as groundnut oil, peanut oil has a pale colour and mild flavour and is a very good all-purpose oil, suitable for dressings, frying and deep-frying. It is particularly favoured by Chinese and French cooks.

Plum seed oil Also known as plum oil, this rich, almondy, marzipan-flavoured oil is pressed from the stones of Agen prune plums. It is good used for dressings and in baking.

Poppy seed oil This mild but well-flavoured oil is good for dressings and for drizzling.

Pumpkin seed oil This thick, dark brown oil has a strong pumpkin seed flavour and is good used in dressings. For a milder flavour, combine with another oil such as olive or grapeseed.

Rapeseed oil Also known as canola oil. This yellow oil has a mild, bland flavour, making it a good vehicle for other ingredients and flavours. It can be used for cooking and dressings.

Rice bran oil Extracted from the germ and inner husk of the rice grain, this yellow, mildly flavoured oil is popular in Asian cooking, from India to Japan. Its high smoking point makes it well suited to stir-frying and deep-frying, although it can be used for most cooking methods.

Safflower oil Pressed from the seeds of the safflower, this yellow oil can be used in the same way as sunflower oil for cooking, dressings and baking. Its flavour is slightly more pronounced, however, and is better used with strong flavours, such as garlic, tomatoes and spices, or in tangy mustard dressings.

Soya oil This is a good multi-purpose oil extracted from soya beans. It is mild-flavoured and is well suited to deep-frying because it has a high smoking point.

Flavoured oils Commercially flavoured oils are sold for making dressings and drizzling, and are made by infusing aromatics and other flavourings in the oil for several weeks or months. Popular flavourings include chilli, garlic and lemon. Chilli oil is much used in Thai and South-east Asian cooking, and also served as a condiment for drizzling over cooked dishes such as soups and stir-fries. The base oil may be anything from cheap sunflower oil to expensive extra virgin olive oil. Look closely at the label to see what you are buying – and decide whether it's worth the money being asked for it.

Vinegars

Malt vinegar

This potent vinegar is made from unhopped beer. It has a highly acidic, fairly harsh taste and is popular (not surprisingly) in the UK and other beer-making regions in Europe. This is not a subtle flavour that you long to find in a salad dressing. But it is an excellent choice for pickling vegetables such as onions, and for making preserves such as chutneys, relishes and ketchup. It's also good for strongly flavoured sauces such as mint sauce. Malt vinegar is also, perhaps most famously, the classic condiment served with fish and chips. Malt vinegar may be distilled (clear), or coloured with caramel, when it is known as brown malt vinegar. Pickling vinegar is malt vinegar that is flavoured with spices and manufactured specifically for making pickles. When you are looking for the brown vinegar, make sure it is labelled 'malt vinegar' and not 'non-brewed condiment', which is an imitation of grossly inferior quality.

TO USE In preserves, or sprinkled over fish and chips.

Wine vinegar

Wine vinegar, a store cupboard essential, may be made from red or white wine, and varies enormously in quality and flavour. Basic wine vinegar is made in vast quantities and should offer sound quality at a very reasonable price. More specialised vinegars from smaller producers can have greater individuality, especially when identified by the origin (for example, Champagne) or the grape variety (for example, Cabernet Sauvignon). The finest wine vinegars have traditionally been those produced around Orléans in the Loire Valley in France. Wine vinegar is a popular choice for dressings, marinades and mayonnaise, and is used in classic sauces such as Béarnaise. A little wine vinegar can be added to stews and soups to impart an acidic accent, and a tiny bit can be used in the deglazing liquid for pan juices from roasts and sautés. Buying tip: sometimes the most interesting vinegars are sold by wine merchants, as many good wineries put their discarded wine to good purpose.

TO USE Add to dressings and sauces, soups and stews.

Balsamic vinegar

This dark, almost black, syrupy vinegar is made from grape juice, and is particularly associated with the town of Modena in northern Italy. Traditional balsamic vinegar is aged in wooden casks for a minimum of 12 years and sometimes much longer. Needless to say, it is very expensive. This kind of vinegar will say 'Condimento Tradizionale Balsamico' on the label. Cheaper versions are usually labelled 'Balsamic Vinegar of Modena'. They do not have to be aged and get their sweetness from brown sugar or caramel. Although nothing like true balsamic vinegar, their sweet, rich flavour goes well on dressings, drizzled over vegetables, or served with olive oil and bread for dipping. A splash or two of balsamic vinegar can be stirred into fresh tomato sauces and rich meat stews, and a small amount of vinegar goes well with fresh strawberries tossed with a little sugar.

A clear 'white' balsamic vinegar made from white grape juice and white wine vinegar is also available and good for using on pale salads such as mozzarella and prawn.

TO USE Drizzle over or add to dishes.

More about vinegar

Used for thousands of years as a flavouring, preservative and for its medicinal properties, vinegar is produced from alcohol – mainly wine, beer or cider. A special bacterium (*Acetobacter*) is introduced into the liquid and converts the alcohol into acid, which causes the liquid to lose its original flavour and become sour with that distinctively sharp vinegar tang. The term 'vinegar' comes from the French *vin aigre*, meaning 'sour wine', although of course vinegar is produced from a wide variety of other brewed grains and fruits such as rice wine and coconut toddy.

Culinary uses for vinegar

Vinegar is an exceptionally versatile foodstuff. It is widely used in pickles and preserves such as chutneys. It is used to flavour marinades, dressings and some sauces, stews and braised dishes. It is a classic addition when cooking red cabbage, because it helps to retain the vibrant red colour of the vegetable. Vinegar is often combined with sugar to produce a sweet–sharp flavour, and is used in this way in chutneys and relishes, Chinese-style sweet-and-sour dishes, and some pickles such as Japanese pickled ginger, sweet dill pickles and Italian mustard fruit pickles.

Other varieties include

Cider vinegar Made from fermented apple juice. Cider vinegar is clear, with a golden colour and quite a strong and pungent acidic flavour. It is best used in pickles, chutneys and relishes, especially apple and pear pickles.

Sherry vinegar This is aged in the same type of oak barrel used for fermenting and ageing the fortified wine sherry. This golden-brown or brick-red vinegar has a smooth, rounded flavour of sometimes remarkable intensity. Like balsamic vinegar, Vinaigre de Jerez is protected by a Denomination of Origin and may be aged for decades. It works well in dressings and as a last-minute addition to soups.

Champagne vinegar A type of wine vinegar made from the grape varieties used to make Champagne (generally Chardonnay and Pinot Noir), this has a light colour and a delicate flavour.

Rice vinegar Made from rice wine, this vinegar is popular in Chinese and Japanese cooking. Rice vinegar may range in colour from a clear, pale yellow to a dark brown or even black. In general, rice vinegars tend to be milder than European-style vinegars, although Chinese vinegars are sharper and more pungent, and Japanese vinegars mellower and slightly sweeter. In Japan, rice vinegar is combined with sugar and salt and stirred into sushi rice, or used to make pickles such as *gari* (ginger) and umeboshi (plums). In China, rice vinegar may be added to sweet-and-sour and hot-and-sour dishes. In South-east Asia it is often used in dipping sauces. When using rice vinegar in hot dishes, add at the end of cooking, as heating will affect its flavour. And when buying – especially black vinegars – be prepared to spend more for better quality.

Coconut vinegar Popular in the Philippines, this pale, cloudy vinegar is made from the fermented sap of the coconut palm and has a particularly sharp flavour. It is used in the same way as rice vinegar for making dipping sauces, pickles and as a flavouring for cooked dishes.

Sweet Moscatel vinegar This sweet, mild and smoothly flavoured vinegar made from sweet Spanish wine can be used in dressings and marinades to give a full, fruity flavour, rather like balsamic vinegar.

Sweet Pedro Ximénez vinegar This high-quality, aged balsamic-style vinegar is a type of sherry vinegar made from Pedro Ximénez grapes. Sometimes aged for 15, 25 or 30 years, it has an excellent sweet, mellow flavour and is good used in the same way as balsamic vinegar in dressings, sauces and some sweet dishes. Very expensive at its best.

Flavoured vinegars

Fruit vinegar Usually, fruit vinegar is made with red or white wine vinegar, in which fruit is steeped for several weeks to impart its flavour. The fruit is strained off before use. Popular fruit vinegars include raspberry, strawberry and pear. They are usually used to make light, fruity dressings, or drizzled into the pan juices from meats to make glazes, sauces and gravy.

Herb vinegar Made in the same way as fruit vinegars, by infusing herbs in wine vinegar. Popular herb vinegars include tarragon (the best and most versatile), thyme and rosemary. They can be used for dressings, or savoury sauces.

Spice vinegar Spices such as coriander seeds, cinnamon, chilli and ginger, as well as garlic, can be left to infuse in wine vinegar, malt vinegar, cider vinegar or rice vinegar, then used as you would the unflavoured vinegar. Spiced wine vinegars are good for dressings; spiced malt and cider vinegars are ideal for pickling vegetables; chilli rice vinegar can be served as a condiment.

Pickles

Preserved lemon

Lemons packed into jars and preserved with salt are widely used in Middle Eastern and North African cooking. They have a distinctively salty, sharp citrus flavour and impart a fragrant aroma to dishes such as tagines and stews.

TO USE Only the peel is used, so slice away the peel and discard the centre of the lemon, then chop finely and add to dishes as required.

Caper

Pickled in brine, salt or a mixture of salt and vinegar, capers are widely used as a flavouring in the Mediterranean, including Spain, Italy, Greece and France. The tiny, green-brown buds have a distinctive salty–sour flavour, and can be added to salads, sprinkled over tarts and pizzas, and added to pasta sauces. Capers can also be chopped and added to dressings and sauces such as sauce tartare. Some French and Italian food shops sell capers preserved in dry salt. These have a very good flavour and require no refrigeration, but they do need 30 minutes of soaking in water before using in the same way as ordinary capers.

Caper berries are the larger, fat, teardrop-shaped fruit of the caper bush, still attached to the stem. They make an attractive garnish for salads and other dishes.

TO USE Scoop out the quantity of capers required, making sure the remaining capers remain covered with their brine or vinegar. Rinse capers that have been preserved in brine before adding to dishes or chopping.

Pickled ginger

Also known as *gari* or *sushoga*, these pale pink slivers of pickled ginger are a speciality of Japan and have become famous worldwide alongside the explosive increase in sushi consumption. Preserved in rice vinegar, salt and water, pickled ginger has a sweet, sharp, zesty flavour and a pronounced, enjoyable peppery bite. It is the classic accompaniment to sushi and sashimi.

Pickled ginger is available in jars and vacuum-packed sachets. Once opened, it can be stored in the fridge in a sealed jar for up to six months.

TO USE Spoon out the pickled ginger and drain, then arrange on the plate with sushi or sashimi.

More about pickles

Cooks all over the world have been preserving fruits, vegetables and eggs in solutions of salt, vinegar and sugar for thousands of years. Before refrigeration and sterilisation, this was a crucial method for keeping food safe and appetising for longer periods. Today, pickles continue to form a key part of many cuisines – served alongside countless savoury foods. Often associated with cold northern European countries, pickles are also popular throughout the Middle East and South-east Asia.

How to buy and store pickles

Although pickles have a long shelf life, most are best stored in the fridge once opened and used within a few months. Make sure that the pickling solution covers the pickles completely.

How to prepare pickles, and their culinary uses

Most pickles require little or no preparation and need only to be drained from their pickling solution before they are served. Very salty pickles such as capers, however, are often rinsed before use.

Generally, European-style pickles are served to accompany savoury foods such as cheese and cold meats or as a snack to serve with drinks. Asian pickles are served with Asian-style dishes – for example, pickled ginger (*gari*) with sushi, and mixed vegetable pickles with Japanese rice dishes such as *origiri* (rice balls) and in a bento box (a single-portion packed meal). Some pickles are used as an ingredient in other dishes: for example, chopped cornichons can be added to mayonnaise or tuna salad, and capers are an ingredient in sauce tartare. Capers can also be cooked with butter to serve with skate, added to pasta sauces, scattered over pizzas or used to garnish canapés.

Other varieties include

There are many different varieties of pickles from around the world. Some of the more common are:

Pickled cucumbers Popular in both Eastern European and Ashkenazi Jewish cuisine. There are countless varieties, generally knobbly with a dull, yellow-green colour: they may be large gherkins, bread-and-butter pickles or dill pickles, which are usually larger than a thumb, or baby cornichons, about the size of a little finger. Pickled cucumbers may be salty or pickled in sweet vinegar and are frequently flavoured with dill and mustard seeds.

With a tender but slightly crisp bite, pickled cucumbers can be served to complement cold meats and cheeses. They are also good sliced and added to sandwiches and burgers. Finely chopped, they add flavour to mayonnaise, tartare-style sauces and tuna salad. Baby cornichons can make a good addition to a platter of crudités, as a snack or to serve with cocktails.

Pickled cabbage Two of the best-known forms of pickled cabbage are German sauerkraut, made from finely shredded fermented cabbage and a popular accompaniment to sausages and other savoury foods, and Korean *kimchee*, a dish of fermented salted cabbage spiced with chilli and garlic, served with savoury dishes.

Pickled root vegetables These can be found throughout the kitchens of Europe, the Middle East and Asia. In Europe, you will find pickled beetroot, turnip and carrots served as an accompaniment to savoury dishes and salads; similarly, in the Middle East, pickled turnips are a delicacy, often served as part of a mezze selection.

Pickled onions Popular in the UK, there are numerous types of pickled onions – from tiny pearly white onions pickled in clear vinegar to spicy pickled shallots and robustly flavoured small pickled onions. Tiny white pickled silverskins are also referred to as cocktail onions and are most often used to make the Gibson cocktail (which is a martini in every way apart from its garnish). Larger pickled onions and shallots may be preserved with a variety of spices and flavourings, and are a classic accompaniment to cold meats and cheeses.

Umeboshi One of the best known of Japanese pickles, these pale, brownish-pink shrivelled plums (a variety of plum known as ume) are preserved in a salt solution and have a salty-sharp flavour. They are served at the end of meals to aid digestion, but may also be chopped and added to rice porridge and other savoury dishes. They are a classic addition to a bento box, with a single umeboshi placed in the centre of the rice.

Asian pickles In China and Japan, vegetables such as cucumbers, radish and other root vegetables are salted and pickled and served with rice as an accompaniment. In China, the bland rice porridge *congee* is usually served with pickled vegetables.

Italian mustard fruit pickles Known as mostarda di Cremona in Italy, this Christmas delicacy is made from fruits preserved in a mustard-flavoured syrup. The flavour is sweet yet peppery to the point of fieriness, and the pickle is traditionally served with boiled pork sausage (cotechino) and polenta.

Pickled eggs See page 65.

Pastes and purées

Tomato paste

Also known as tomato purée (especially in the UK), tomato paste is made by cooking whole tomatoes until most of their water has evaporated. Tomato purée can be used to enhance the flavour of sauces, soups, stews, dressings and other savoury dishes. It often contains nothing but tomatoes, but may be flavoured with other ingredients such as herbs. Sun-dried tomato paste is a blend of sun-dried tomatoes, olive oil and seasonings, and has a sweet and rich flavour.

Tomato paste is available in cans, jars and tubes; sun-dried tomato paste is generally sold in jars and tubes. Tubes of paste keep well in the fridge, but cans and jars need to be used up quickly once opened. Check the advice on the label for storage times.

TO USE Stir into sauces, soups, stews and dressings. Use tomato paste in moderation, as the flavour is strong and can easily become overpowering.

Garlic purée

A convenience product, garlic purée is made from crushed garlic, often with oil and added salt. It is available in tubes and sometimes in jars. It saves the fiddly preparation of fresh garlic and can be used in any recipe that calls for crushed garlic. Its flavour, however, is not as good as fresh. The few extra seconds needed to crush or chop fresh garlic may be a good investment of your time.

Once opened, store in the fridge.

TO USE In place of fresh, crushed garlic to flavour dressings, or in cooked dishes. For most cooked dishes, fry briefly in oil before adding other ingredients. One teaspoon is equal to a clove of garlic.

Chilli paste

This is usually sold in small jars, and can range from mild to quite fiery, depending on the variety of chilli used. The paste is made from crushed fresh, or soaked dried, chillies and can be used to add heat to sauces, soups, stews, curries and other savoury dishes. Some pastes contain nothing more than chillies, while other brands also contain crushed spices and other flavourings, such as ginger and garlic; these are a convenient way to add not just heat but extra flavour to a dish. If you have never used a particular brand before, add just a little and check the dish for chilli heat.

Once opened, store in the fridge.

TO USE Stir into dressings, sauces, soups, stews and curries; combine with soy sauce and toss into stir-fries. Use in moderation, as the flavour can be fiery hot.
(see also harissa, page 322)

Red bean paste

Red bean paste is usually made from crushed aduki beans, sweetened with sugar and cooked down to form a thick paste with a sweet flavour and smooth, slightly mealy texture not unlike sweet chestnut purée (see page 383). The dark red-brown paste is popular in Japan and China, where it is used in sweet dishes and desserts such as pancakes, rice balls, cakes and steamed buns.

TO USE Spread thinly over pancakes, or put a dollop in the centre of dough or rice and press around the paste to enclose.
(see also aduki bean, page 369)

Chilli bean paste

This spicy, thick and slightly chunky dark brown paste is a speciality of the Sichuan region of China. It is made from fermented black beans (soya beans), chopped chilli and garlic, and various seasonings. Chilli bean paste has a distinctive and very pungent taste, and is used (sparingly) in stir-fries and braised dishes to add both flavour and heat. The paste is also used in Korean cooking.

Available in cans and jars; store in the fridge once opened.

TO USE Chilli bean paste should always be heated to mellow its flavour. Toss in stir-fries or stir into braised dishes and simmer.

Passata

Usually available bottled or in cartons, this red, pulpy liquid is made by briefly cooking tomatoes and then straining them (passata here means 'passed through a sieve'). Passata is widely used in Italian cooking. It may be smooth or slightly chunky, and is a great addition to sauces, minestrone-style soups and stews in place of chopped tomatoes. Use it in dishes where you require an intense tomato flavour without the bulk, texture or pips of chopped tomatoes. Similar Italian products include *polpa* and *sugocasa*, both of which are made from crushed tomatoes.

TO USE For sauces and many other dishes, gently sauté onions or garlic first, then pour in the passata. Add seasoning and simmer as you would chopped tomatoes.

Pesto

The classic Italian basil sauce from Genoa is a coarse-textured purée traditionally made from fresh basil leaves, garlic, pine nuts, grated Parmesan cheese and extra virgin olive oil. Usually tossed with freshly cooked pasta or gnocchi, pesto can also be used to flavour dressings, smeared on to the base of savoury tarts, stirred into rice or risotto, or added to soups and sauces. It is available both fresh and in jars; the fresh variety has a much subtler, more delicate and refined flavour, although both are good. Commercial pesto is often made with a neutral oil such as sunflower oil, which will not give the same fragrance as olive oil, and sometimes walnuts are used instead of pine nuts. In Genoa, an annual World Pesto Championship is held where competitors gather from all over the world to make the world's best pesto.

The origiinal basil pesto has been joined by numerous variants. These include dark red sun-dried tomato pesto and 'modern' herb and nut combinations such as coriander and hazelnut, and walnut and rocket.

Pistou is a similar basil sauce from Provence. The name in both French and Italian means pestle, which is traditionally used (with a mortar, of course) to pound the ingredients.

TO USE Spoon straight from the jar and use as required.

Anchovy paste

Also known as anchovy relish and Gentleman's Relish, this is a smooth brown paste made from ground anchovies combined with spices, vinegar and water. It has a very strong, salty flavour and is usually spread thinly on hot, buttered toast. It is served as a delicacy for afternoon tea, and is also good spread on toast to dip into boiled eggs, or spread on little toasts topped with halved quail's eggs as canapés.

TO USE Spread directly on to buttered toast; use in moderation.

Olive paste

There are several classic olive pastes – including tapenade from France and *pasta di olive* from Italy – but all are based on olives pounded with olive oil. Tapenade combines the olives with capers, herbs and olive oil, and sometimes with garlic and anchovies as well. It is often served as a dip with crudités or quail's eggs. Or it can be used in more elaborate creations: spread thinly on toast or Italian-style crostini and then with further toppings such as cherry tomatoes and oregano, halved quail's eggs and a drizzle of olive oil, bite-size strips of grilled lemon-and-garlic-marinated chicken. *Pasta di olive* is made only from olives and olive oil, and may be spread on the base of pizzas, toast or crostini, or stirred into sauces and dressings as a flavouring.

Tartufata is a spread made of mushrooms, truffles and olives. Use in the same way as olive paste and tapenade or toss with pasta.

TO USE Spoon directly from the jar and use as required.

Sauces and condiments

Tomato ketchup

This bright red, highly flavoured sauce with a sweet–sour taste is made from tomatoes, sugar, vinegar, salt and other flavourings. The juice is extracted from the tomatoes and then cooked to reduce to a thick, barely pourable consistency. Ketchup is a popular condiment served with chips, sausages, burgers and countless other savoury dishes. However, it can also be used to flavour sauces such as marie rose. It is a barely-kept secret that many professional chefs keep ketchup on hand for adding tomato flavour, extra spice, and a nicely balanced sweet–sour taste to sauces, stews and soups.

TO USE Serve as a condiment; in moderation to flavour sauces and dressings; in Thai recipes.

Mushroom ketchup

Originally produced in the UK, this dark brown liquid is made from mushrooms, vinegar and seasonings. It is robust, salty, and fairly pungent in flavour, and is excellent for splashing into meaty stews, soups and sauces to add depth of flavour.

TO USE Stir into stews, soups and sauces – use judiciously, as it is strong stuff.

Worcestershire sauce

This famous sauce is spicy, robust, and very complex in flavour. It is a dark brown liquid containing a wealth of ingredients including tamarind, soy sauce, anchovies, garlic and vinegar – but the original recipe, owned by Lea & Perrins, is a carefully guarded secret. Worcestershire sauce adds bite, spice and flavour to meaty stews, soups and sauces, and can also add vigour to more simple tomato sauces. It has a natural affinity with cheese and is good drizzled on to cheese on toast. It is also a classic addition to tomato juice, and is indispensable in a Bloody Mary.

TO USE Stir into stews, soups and sauces, drizzle on to cheese on toast, or splash into tomato juice or Bloody Mary – use judiciously.

Anchovy essence

Salty and quite pungent, anchovy essence is a brown sauce made from cured anchovies and seasonings. Its distinctive and powerfully fishy flavour is used to boost the flavour of fish soups, stews and braised dishes, or of sauces to be served with fish. If Thai fish sauce (see page 400) is unavailable, a splash of anchovy essence can be used instead.

TO USE Stir into dishes to taste; use in moderation. Do not add any salt to the dish before you have added the anchovy essence, then taste before adjusting the seasoning.

Chilli sauce

There are numerous chilli sauces from around the world, including Tabasco from Louisiana, sweet chilli sauce from Thailand, Caribbean hot-pepper sauce and Israeli *zhug*. Most are made by steeping chillies in vinegar, often with other spices and flavourings, and may be fiery, mild, sweet or salty. All are used for seasoning, splashing on food as a condiment, or as a dipping sauce either alone or with other flavours. Spicy hot-pepper sauces are used for seasoning, in marinades and as a condiment. Fiery Tabasco is used similarly and is usually the sauce of choice for tomato juice and a Bloody Mary. Chinese chilli sauces tend to be hot and salty. Sweet chilli sauce is a fairly thick, translucent, bright orange-red condiment most often used as a dipping sauce in Thai and South-east Asian cooking. If you have never used a particular brand before, add just a little and check the dish for chilli heat.

TO USE For seasoning savoury dishes, marinades, dressings and sauces. Sweet chilli sauce can be used for dipping.

Soy sauce

This is an essential ingredient in China, Japan and South-east Asia, and there are numerous varieties: each country has its own specialities. Soy sauce is fermented from soya beans, roasted grains, water and salt, or sometimes just from soya beans without the grain. The ingredients and manufacturing method produce striking differences in flavour. Soy sauce can be divided into two main types: light and dark. Light soy sauce is a thin, light brown liquid with a salty, beany fragrance. Dark soy sauce is matured for longer and is often sweetened with caramel, producing a slightly thicker, sweeter and darker liquid with a stronger, less salty, more rounded flavour.

Common types of soy sauce include Japanese shoyu (a matured dark sauce with a rounded flavour); Japanese tamari (which is dark with a strong but not too salty flavour and is usually made without wheat); Indonesian kecap asin (light) and kecap manis (dark) and Vietnamese nuoc tuong.

TO USE Toss with noodles or splash into stir-fries; use to flavour and season soups and braised dishes; as a dipping sauce. Use dark soy sauce judiciously as it adds colour and can make dishes look dingy.

Hoisin sauce

A thick brown sauce from China, made from fermented soya beans, sugar, salt, garlic and spices. Hoisin has a sweet, salty and slightly spicy flavour. It can be used to flavour marinades, and is good splashed into stir-fries or served as a dipping sauce with crispy deep-fried snacks. It is perhaps best known for its role as the classic accompaniment to Peking duck and pancakes, and is often used in marinades for Chinese-style duck dishes. It can be found in most supermarkets and Chinese food stores.

TO USE Serve as a dipping sauce; add to marinades and stir-fries.

Oyster sauce

This thick, dark brown Chinese sauce is made from fermented soya beans, oyster juice, salt and caramel. It has a seductive and surprisingly mellow flavour, and is a popular addition to sauces, soups and braised dishes; common pairings include fish, shellfish, chicken, beef and tofu. It is often drizzled over the top of cooked dishes. In Chinese cooking, plainly steamed or stir-fried greens are often sauced with a fragrant 'dressing' of oyster sauce, sesame oil and soy sauce. There are different levels of quality in oyster sauce; as a general rule, the more expensive versions are better.

TO USE Add to sauces, soups and braised dishes towards the end of cooking, as prolonged heat affects its flavour; drizzle over dishes just before serving.

Plum sauce

Traditionally served with Peking duck, Chinese plum sauce is made from plums, vinegar, salt and sugar. It has a fairly thick consistency and a sweet, salty and fruity flavour. Plum sauce is also served as a dipping sauce with crispy deep-fried snacks, such as spring rolls.

TO USE Serve with Peking duck; as a dipping sauce.

Yellow bean sauce

Not yellow exactly, but yellowish-brown in colour, this popular Chinese sauce is made from crushed and fermented white soya beans flavoured with salt, sugar and spices. Although thick, like black bean sauce, yellow bean sauce is less salty and pungent. It can be used in the same way: in stir-fries, and braised and steamed dishes. It also makes a good addition to marinades.

TO USE Add the sauce to stir-fried, steamed and braised dishes; in marinades. Cooking improves the flavour, and distributes it throughout the dish, so never use cold.

Black bean sauce

This salty Chinese concoction is made by mixing salted and fermented black soya beans with soy sauce, sugar and spices. It has quite a strong and utterly distinctive taste. Black bean sauce is a popular flavouring for steamed, braised and stir-fried dishes. Often used with other strong flavourings and aromatics such as garlic, chilli and green peppers, black bean sauce goes well in both meat and vegetable dishes. **Note** This product is manufactured for use mainly in the West; in China, cooks crush the fermented beans in the wok rather than using a ready-made sauce.

TO USE Add the sauce to steamed, braised and stir-fried dishes. Cooking is required to mellow and bring out its flavour, and to distribute it throughout the dish, so never use cold.

Fish sauce

This surprisingly versatile sauce is used throughout South-east Asia, and different countries have their own versions. All of them are pungent and salty; they may be clear or golden. Thai fish sauce (*nam pla*) is usually made from salted, fermented fish, while Vietnamese *nuoc mam* is more often made from salted, fermented shrimp. Fish sauce is used in soups, stir-fries, curries and braised dishes as a seasoning ingredient – not just with fish but also with vegetables and meat. It has a pungent, sometimes unpleasant and even shocking aroma. Do not be deterred. Once it's added to hot food, the smell disappears and the effect on flavour is invariably delicious. Use sparingly, and not just in South-east Asian dishes. Fish sauce is a good marinade ingredient for fish, meat or poultry, and just a drop or two adds a nice lift to soup or gravy.

TO USE Add towards the end of cooking as a seasoning ingredient.

Chutneys and relishes

Although not strictly an ingredient in their own right, these tangy fruit and vegetable pickles – preserved with vinegar, salt, sugar and spices, and usually characterised by a distinctive sweet–sour flavour – are a staple in many storecupboards. They can be used as an additional ingredient in sandwiches or cheese on toast and added to canapé fillings and crostini toppings, or be served as a condiment alongside cold meats, meat pies and cheeses. Some, such as mango chutney, go particularly well with Indian food and are served as an accompaniment to poppadums.

The original chutneys came from India and were known as *chatni*. Introduced to the British kitchen during colonial times, those spicy, sour relishes were made with spices and herbs. Today, chutneys made in Britain tend to be sweet and mild, and are simmered for a long time to achieve a preserve with a soft, melting texture. They are usually matured for at least one month after making to allow the flavours to blend and deepen. Relishes, in contrast, are usually cooked more quickly so that the fruits and vegetables retain more of their shape and bite. As a result, chutneys are often mellower, with a more rounded flavour, whereas relishes tend to be more fresh-tasting.

How to store chutneys and relishes

Chutneys and relishes usually have a long shelf life; once opened most are best stored in the fridge and used within a few months.

Varieties include

Mango chutney Made from unripe mangoes, this sweet, mildly spiced chutney is a legacy of the original Indian chutneys. It has a soft, slightly sticky texture and sweet–sour flavour, and is popularly served with Indian food – as an accompaniment to curries or poppadums, along with other fresh relishes. It also makes a tasty chutney for serving with cold meats, cheeses and meat pies, and is a good addition to cheese on toast. Mango chutney is sometimes used as an ingredient; for example, added to the spiced fish and rice dish, kedgeree – another legacy of the Raj.

Piccalilli This bright yellow relish is a chunky, crunchy pickle spiced with ginger, chilli and mustard and usually made from onions and cauliflower. It has quite a strong flavour and peppery bite and is a favourite in the UK served with cold meats, pies and cheeses, and frequently used in sandwiches. **Note** The American version uses different vegetables and is usually green rather than yellow.

Sweet pickle This popular British relish is served with cheese, cold meats and pies, as well as being the traditional choice to accompany a ploughman's lunch. Dark brown in colour, sweet pickle combines diced root vegetables such as swede and carrot with onion, cauliflower and gherkin in a sweet–sour sauce of tomato, apple, date and spices. It has a tart, piquant flavour without being hot. Branston pickle is the most popular sweet pickle in the UK.

Green tomato chutney A classic chutney made from the last of the summer's unripened tomatoes. Green tomato chutney has a tangy flavour and usually also includes apples, onions and spices. It is a good accompaniment to cheeses and cold meats.

Corn relish A tangy, mild relish with a sweet–sour flavour. Bright yellow corn relish consists mostly of juicy corn kernels, with flecks of red pepper mixed through. It is a classic for serving with barbecued meats such as burgers and sausages, and is also good served with cold meats and cheeses or in sandwiches.

Tomato relish There are countless variations of this classic dark red relish, ranging from sweet, tangy, fresh-tasting tomato relishes to fiery ones spiked with chilli. It is a classic accompaniment to barbecued meats such as burgers and sausages, but can also be served with pies, cold meats and cheeses, and is a good addition to sandwiches.

Sweet onion chutney Finely sliced onion is cooked until tender and sweet. This type of chutney is usually fairly mild (unlike pickled onions), with a tangy, sweet–sour note and a rounded, fruity flavour. It goes particularly well with sausages and cheese, and makes a good addition to cheese on toast, spread on top or underneath the cheese.

Mustards

English mustard

This strong mustard is bright yellow. It is made from hulled mustard seeds, finely ground, and often with a little flour and turmeric added. The mustard is available as a fine powder as well as in ready-made form. It may be used as a condiment – mixed to a smooth paste with a little water – or added as a flavouring to stews and cheese sauces. English mustard is more pungent than most, so use sparingly as a condiment. There is an old saying that the Colman family (manufacturers of the first commercially successful mustard brand) made their fortune from what people left on their plates.

TO USE As a condiment: mix to a smooth paste with a little water and leave to stand for 10–15 minutes to allow the flavour to develop. To flavour dishes: stir in towards the end of cooking, because its flavour will diminish with prolonged heating.

Wholegrain mustard

Unlike smooth English and Dijon mustards, wholegrain mustards are made from a mixture of crushed and ground mustard seeds, usually mixed with vinegar and spices to create a tangy mustard with a distinctive texture and a certain bite. Meaux mustard from France, often sold in a grey stoneware jar, is one of the best-known wholegrain mustards. It is good served with cold meats, pies and sausages, but also makes a good addition to dressings and sauces. Add to marinades or use in dishes such as honey-mustard chicken. Remember that the mustard has a bit of crunch, and should not be used where you want a perfectly smooth consistency.

TO USE As a condiment; as a flavouring in dressings, marinades and sauces.

Dijon mustard

Dijon mustard is a paler, slightly duller yellow colour than English mustard. It is made from husked black or brown seeds blended with white wine or verjuice (the sour juice from unripe grapes) and spices. One of the best known of the French mustards, it has a smooth texture and salty, sharp taste with a definite bite and a slightly bitter tang. It is only moderately hot. Dijon mustard can be served as a condiment with meats, including steak and cooked sausages, or used as a flavouring for dressings, sauces and marinades. If you don't want the grainy texture of wholegrain, Dijon is a particularly good and flavourful mustard.

TO USE As a condiment; to flavour dressings, sauces and marinades; stir into cooked dishes such as cheese sauce towards the end of cooking time. Store in the fridge once opened, otherwise it will oxidise and turn brown.

More about mustard

Used mainly as a condiment, mustard is made from ground mustard seeds and may be mild or peppery-hot, smooth or grainy. It is available either as powder for mixing into a paste with water, or ready-made, blended with vinegar or wine and other flavourings. Mustard seeds come from three different plants related to the cabbage family: white (pale tan or yellow seeds) and black, which are both native to Europe; and brown, which is native to Asia. Individual mustards tend to use different combinations of these seeds, either crushed or ground to a fine powder.

When the crushed or ground seeds are mixed with water, chemical reactions cause volatile compounds in the mustard to become more pungent, sharp and peppery. This enhanced flavour peaks about 10–15 minutes after the mustard has been mixed with water; after that, the pungency fades. The addition of an acidic ingredient such as vinegar, wine or verjuice (unripe grape juice) preserves the flavour, so all ready-made mustards are a blend of seeds with vinegar or wine and sometimes other flavourings, to produce a mustard with a sharp, peppery and pungent flavour.

The pungency of mustard depends principally on which seeds and preparation method are used to make it. Mustards made with black mustard seeds tend to be hotter, but the choice of liquid also affects the strength of the mustard. Hotter water and liquids will result in a milder mustard, whereas mixing ground or crushed mustard seeds with cold liquids will give a more potent result.

How to buy and store mustards

Mustard has a long shelf life, but should always be stored in a glass or earthenware jar and tightly covered with a non-corrosive lid. Once opened, store in the fridge and use within a few months.

Culinary uses for mustards

As well as being served with cold meats, sausages and cheeses, mustard can be added to dressings, mayonnaise, creamy sauces and mashed potato. It adds flavour when spread on bread for sandwiches, or on cheese on toast, and can be added to marinades for meat, or used as a spice rub to flavour meats before roasting or grilling. Mustard also makes a good addition to cheese or creamy savoury fillings for pastries and pies.

Smooth and grainy mustards can be used in the same way.

Other varieties include

American mustard Created in 1904 by George T. French and sold as salad cream mustard, American mustard is made from ground white mustard seeds, vinegar and sugar, and coloured yellow with turmeric. It has a smooth texture and an extremely mild, slightly sweet flavour. It is the classic condiment served on hot dogs, and as it has very little heat it is often added liberally, rather like a sauce or relish.

German mustard Ranging in colour from yellow to brown, there are a number of different German mustards. All are smooth, with a sweet–sour flavour. The most common varieties are of medium strength, but you will also find more pungent varieties, as well as milder ones such as Bavarian mustard. All are served with the wide variety of German sausages.

Bordeaux mustard The ubiquitous 'French mustard', Bordeaux mustard is made from a mixture of brown and black seeds combined with vinegar, sugar and herbs to produce a dark brown mustard with a mild, fragrant flavour. It goes well with cold meats and sausages.

Flavoured mustards Herb mustards, especially tarragon, are probably the most popular of the flavoured mustards. They are generally smooth, with a pale to dark green colour, and a fragrant, usually mild and sweet taste. They can be served as accompaniments or used as a flavouring for dressings and mayonnaise. Mustards spiked with chilli and horseradish are also popular, and needless to say they have a more peppery, fiery flavour. Honey mustards are sweeter, with a rounded flavour. Provençal mustard is a classic flavoured mustard, blended with garlic and red peppers.

Irish mustard This is a wholegrain mustard, often blended with whiskey and sometimes flavoured with honey.

Chinese mustard Used as a condiment in Chinese and Chinese–American cooking, this very strong mustard is made from brown mustard-seed powder blended with cold water. It is served as a condiment with egg rolls (similar to spring rolls) and is also used in some cooked dishes such as spicy stir-fried chicken and cod braised in mustard sauce.

Wines, beers and spirits

Wine

It's remarkable how often a glass of wine turns out to be the cook's best friend. Whether red, white or rosé, this is an exceptionally useful and versatile product in the kitchen. Wine can be used in both sweet and savoury dishes, and as a cooking medium, a principal flavouring, or in small quantities as a seasoning. A splash of wine used to deglaze the pan juices of a pan-fried or roast dish adds flavour and body to sauces and gravy. Red or white wine can be used as a marinade and in sauces and casseroles: red is generally best for red meat and game, white for risottos, fish and veal dishes; either goes well with chicken. White, red or rosé wine can be used to poach fruits with sugar or make jellies or punches. Sweet wines are good splashed over fruit salads to give body and flavour. Red wine is used to make warm spiced drinks – mulled wine, glögg (Scandinavia) or gluhwein (Germany). When buying wine for cooking, you do not need to spend a lot of money but do choose wines you would be willing to drink: very cheap wine can be unpleasantly sharp or simply too insubstantial to make a real contribution to your dish. Young and fruity wines are generally better than older wines.

TO USE In sweet and savoury dishes as required. Boiling will cause most of the alcohol to evaporate in cooked dishes; for mulled wine, heat gently.

Non-grape wines and rice mirin

As well as grape wines, there are various non-grape wines that can be used in cooking. In South-east Asia, China and Japan, rice wine is used as a flavouring in savoury dishes such as stir-fries, braised dishes and teriyaki sauce. Saké is the best-known rice wine, although it is actually brewed rather than fermented like wine (and should properly be called rice beer). It is served either cold or warm. Mirin is a popular variant of saké used solely for cooking; it has a light, sweetish flavour.

Fruit wines such as strawberry, elderflower and ginger tend to be sweet and fragrant and are best added to desserts such as fruit salads, rather than to savoury dishes.

TO USE Add rice wines to Asian-style stir-fries, braised dishes and teriyaki sauce. Splash fruit and spice wines over fresh fruit salads.

Fortified wine

Stronger than ordinary grape wines, fortified wines are produced by adding brandy to wine during or after its fermentation process. Popular varieties used in cooking include sherry, Marsala, vermouth and port. Sherry is a useful alternative to rice wine in Chinese-style cooking, and adds a robust flavour to gravy, sauces and desserts such as trifle. Marsala is the classic ingredient in the Italian dessert zabaglione, and also adds richness to pan-fried meat dishes and gravy. Dry vermouth can be used in almost any dish where you would normally use dry white wine; it is particularly good in risottos and fish dishes. Its herbal flavours add more complexity than ordinary white wine, and some cooks use it regularly. Sweeter styles of vermouth can be splashed on to fruit salads. Port adds a full-bodied flavour to syrups for poaching fruits, and to mulled wine, sauces and gravy.

TO USE In desserts or savoury dishes such as sauces and gravy, stir-fries, meat stews and risottos.

Beer

Although not nearly so versatile an ingredient as wine, beer is still a useful one to have on hand. Most beer is brewed from malted barley flavoured with hops, although it may also be brewed from other cereals and grains such as wheat, maize and rice. There are numerous types of beer, from richly flavoured ales to dark, heavy porters and stouts, light, fizzy continental-style lagers, and pale, cloudy wheat beers with a rich fruity flavour. All can be added to meaty stews and hotpots to give a robust flavour. The lighter beers can be used to make Yorkshire pudding and batter for deep-fried fish, and in dishes such as Welsh rarebit. If you want to use beer in a recipe, but don't know which would be best, a good general rule is to use beer made in the place where the recipe comes from.

TO USE Add to stews and casseroles in place of part of the cooking liquid or stock; stir into batters or cheese sauce for Welsh rarebit.

Cider

Cider is nothing more than fermented apple juice, and it can be sweet or dry or something in between the two extremes. Both are good used in stews and casseroles, and the sweetness level can be put to good and surprisingly versatile use – especially if there is something acidic in the dish which will balance out the sweetness. Cider goes particularly well in pork dishes containing apple, and makes a good addition to gravy for roast pork. It can be used in place of wine in marinades for meat and fish, though if the cider is for fish it should always be a dry one. Sweet ciders are also suitable for poaching fruits or in fruity punches, and can be mulled with spices, in the same way as mulled wine.

TO USE Add to marinades, stews, casseroles, gravy, desserts and punches.

Spirits

The key words to remember when using spirits are: 'a little goes a long way'. These distilled drinks come in a wide variety of flavours and have a high alcohol content, typically between 37 and 43 per cent but sometimes much more. Vodka, gin, whisky, brandy and rum are perhaps the most frequently used in cooking, as well as mixed into cocktails. Spirits can add flavour and body to sweet and savoury dishes. For example, vodka can be used to flavour tomato sauce for pasta and brandy is often used in marinades for beef casseroles. Calvados, the French apple brandy, is delicious with cream as a sauce for pork. Brandy, rum and whisky are all popular flavourings for cakes and puddings. The flavours of rum and chocolate are particularly compatible.

Liqueurs are alcoholic beverages flavoured with fruit, herbs, spices, nuts, flowers, cream, coffee or chocolate and bottled with additional sugar. Sweet and sticky, and often with an intense flavour, they are useful to add to desserts and ices, and for mixing in cocktails.

TO USE In cocktails; add spirits in small quantities to savouries and desserts.

Sugar

Brown sugar

Brown sugar can be refined or unrefined. Both contain a proportion of molasses, a by-product of sugar manufacture which adds colour and flavour. The difference lies in how the molasses gets there. Unrefined brown sugar is made only from sugar cane, and contains the original molasses that has not been removed completely. Refined brown sugar is made from refined white sugar – either from sugar cane or sugar beet – that has molasses added to it.

There are three main types of brown sugar: muscovado, dark soft brown, and light soft brown. All have fine granules and a moist texture. Muscovado has the darkest colour and a strong flavour of molasses; dark soft brown sugar is slightly paler and less strongly flavoured (although still with a definite molasses kick). Light soft brown sugar is sand-coloured with a milder, more honeyed flavour. All can be used in biscuits and cakes, particularly in rich fruit cakes and dark, sticky gingerbreads, as well as desserts and chutneys.

TO USE For baking, desserts and chutneys.

Demerara sugar

This coarse, large-grained golden sugar has a slightly moist texture. Made from unrefined – or raw – cane sugar, it contains a small amount of molasses, which gives it its colour and slightly honeyed flavour. Demerara can be used for sweetening tea and coffee, sprinkling over cakes and biscuits to decorate, and for some cakes, biscuits and desserts – particularly where a slightly crunchy texture is required, such as flapjacks.

TO USE To sweeten hot drinks; in cakes, biscuits and desserts; sprinkle over cakes and biscuits to decorate.

Preserving sugar

This specialised white sugar has been developed for use in jams, conserves, jellies and marmalades. Made from sugar cane and sugar beet, it is coarser than granulated sugar. The coarse crystals dissolve slowly and create less scum than granulated sugar on top of the pan, resulting in a clearer preserve. Some types of preserving sugar contain pectin to ensure the jam or jelly achieves a good set. This type of preserving sugar is a good choice when making preserves with fruits that have a low pectin content, such as strawberries.

TO USE In jams, conserves, jellies and marmalades.

Granulated sugar

Granulated sugar has coarser grains than caster sugar and is not so well suited to general baking and dessert making. The grains may be white or golden and made from sugar cane or sugar beet. It is the classic choice for sweetening tea and coffee, and for dissolving in warm liquids such as syrups, mulled wine and cider. Granulated sugar is also good for sprinkling over cakes and biscuits as a decoration, either before or after baking. Some people use it for making jam, jelly and marmalade, although preserving sugar is probably a better choice for the novice jam maker.

TO USE To sweeten hot drinks and other warm liquids such as syrups; sprinkle over cakes and biscuits to decorate.

Caster sugar

This fine crystalline sugar is the most popular choice for baking and desserts. Its small crystals dissolve easily in liquids, and it is the best suited to classic baking techniques of all the sugars. Caster sugar can be beaten with butter (creamed), stirred into melted mixtures or whisked into eggs to make cake batters and biscuit doughs; whisked into egg whites to make meringues; sprinkled over cakes and biscuits to decorate or to frost flower petals; or used as a sweetener for sauces, custards, mousses, pastry and numerous other dishes. Made from sugar cane or sugar beet, caster sugar is usually white, because it has been produced from refined sugar, but you may also find golden caster sugar, which has a subtle, buttery-toffee taste and a darker colour. White and golden caster sugar have the same cooking properties and can be used interchangeably.

TO USE For baking and desserts.

Icing sugar

Made from sugar cane or sugar beet, this finely powdered sugar dissolves instantly in water and is used most often for icings and frostings – either beaten with butter or egg white, or dissolved in liquid. It can also be used in baking – for example, in macaroons or certain types of meringue – for making confections such as fondant creams, or for dusting over cakes, biscuits and desserts as decoration. It is also available as golden icing sugar, which is light beige in colour with a mellow, rounded flavour.

Fondant icing sugar is a powdered sugar with added glucose syrup, used to give a soft finish to cake frostings.

TO USE Sift, then use in icings, frostings, cakes, biscuits and confectionery, or dust over cakes and desserts to decorate.

Honey

Clear

Before there was sugar, there was honey. And this thick, sticky, sweet syrup still occupies a valuable place in the human diet in many parts of the world. Produced by bees from flower nectar, clear honey can vary from pale yellow to deep orange-gold depending on variety. Its runny consistency makes it suitable for drizzling over bread, toast, popcorn and desserts such as honey cake, pancakes and biscuits, or for stirring into yogurt, syrups and hot drinks. It also dissolves easily in liquids, and is therefore good used in dressings and marinades. Clear honey is the best type for spreading (often with mustard) over meats such as chicken and gammon before grilling, baking or roasting.

TO USE Spread on bread, toast, crumpets, and so on; use in desserts, cakes, biscuits, dressings and marinades.

Set

Set honey is clear honey with higher levels of dextrose that has been allowed to crystallise, so it is opaque and pale yellow. It has a firm texture that becomes runnier and creamier as you stir, spread or beat it. Set honey has a good spreading consistency for using on toast, bread, crumpets, toasted muffins and scones. It dissolves well in hot liquids so it can be stirred into drinks, but is not suitable for drizzling (although it can be temporarily softened by brief heating in the jar). It can also be beaten with butter and used in some cakes and biscuits.

TO USE As a spread or stirred into hot drinks as a sweetener. It can also be used in some cakes, biscuits and desserts.

Honeycomb

Usually available cut into squares, honeycomb is clear honey that is still held inside the hexagonal wax cells of the honeycomb, where it has been stored by the bees as a food source. It is best used as a spread on toast, bread, crumpets, toasted muffins and scones and is not well suited to cooking. The fine wax comb can be eaten as well, giving a distinctive texture and taste to the honey.

TO USE As a spread. Scrape a thin, even layer of honey from the comb, and avoid digging into the comb and creating craters, into which the honey will pool.

More about honey

The earliest reference to honey goes back to Egyptian times around 5500BC, and by 1300 BC it was being recorded as a valuable commodity. The sweet, sticky syrup is made by bees from flower nectar and stored in wax honeycombs, ready to feed the growing bee larvae. Most commercial honey is drained from the honeycomb, usually by crushing, draining and straining, but it is sometimes available still in the comb – more usually from independent beekeepers, delis and food shops.

How to store honey

Both set and clear honey have a long shelf life, although clear honey will eventually crystallise to form set honey with a slightly crunchy texture. It is still perfectly safe to eat, but will be less suitable for cooking – although gentle heating will make it liquid again. Store in a sealed jar in a cool, dark place.

Culinary uses for honey

Although honey is technically sweeter than sugar, it tastes less sweet due to the other flavouring substances, such as flower aromas, that it naturally contains. It can be used as a spread on bread, toast, crumpets, muffins and scones, and can also be used as a sweetener and flavouring. Clear honey is used for cooking, drizzling over pancakes and stirring into yogurt, and can flavour ice creams, cheesecakes and other desserts. It is widely used in baking, in breads, cakes and biscuit mixtures, where it gives a moist, sticky, slightly dense result with a distinctive, scented fragrance, or it can be drizzled over the top after baking to produce a sticky glaze. It can also be used to sweeten and flavour hot drinks such as herbal teas, hot toddies, milky drinks and the classic cold remedy made with lemon juice, boiling water and honey. It is the flavouring used in the old English drink, mead.

Honey has a place in savoury cooking too. It is good when used to flavour dressings, and contributes both flavour and stickiness to glazes and marinades for meats such as chicken and gammon. It is often combined with mustard in savoury dishes, and goes well with warm spices such as ginger.

Because heating affects the delicate flavour of honey, there is no point in using an expensive, highly flavoured example for cooking. Save these for serving as a spread, drizzling over yogurt or flavouring uncooked dishes.

Other varieties include

Most honeys are made from clover and other field flowers. But there are also many honeys made from specific types of flower, all of which have their own individual taste and aroma. Colour can range from pale yellow to amber-orange and deep reddish-brown, and texture can vary too, particularly among set honeys, which can range from smooth and creamy to more granular.

Clover honey One of the most commonly available types of honey. Clover honey is pale and thick with a mild flavour. It is good for all general uses, including cooking and sweetening hot drinks. Clear clover honey has usually been heat-treated to keep it from crystallising on keeping.

Heather honey With a reddish-brown colour and scented, quite intense flavour, heather honey sets to have a soft, buttery consistency.

Orange blossom honey This popular honey is produced in orange-growing areas such as Spain and Florida. It is sweet in flavour and amber in colour, with a delicate, perfumed flavour. Good drizzled over yogurt or almond cakes, as a flavouring for ice cream or other creamy desserts, or used as a spread.

Manuka honey Produced in New Zealand. This clear, thick, dark golden honey is made from the nectar of the manuka (tea tree), which is native to New Zealand and Australia. Manuka is highly regarded for its intense flavour. It is good drizzled over yogurt or used to flavour ice cream and other creamy, uncooked desserts, or used as a spread.

Acacia honey This pale, fragrant, clear honey is unusual in that it does not crystallise with age. Delicate in flavour, and best enjoyed either drizzled over desserts or used as a spread.

Lavender honey Mainly produced in Provence in southern France, this thick, dark honey has an intense, perfumed flavour and is good used as a spread, in dressings and drizzled over desserts.

Blended honey Honey from different flowers can be blended and labelled as just 'honey' or 'wild flower honey'. Use these as an all-purpose ingredient, as a spread or in cooking.

Syrups

Golden syrup

This thick, pale amber-gold syrup, a by-product of refining sugar cane, is very sweet and sticky. It can be spread on toast, bread, crumpets and toasted muffins, or drizzled over pancakes and ice cream. It is more commonly added to mixtures for biscuits, cakes such as gingerbread, desserts such as treacle tart and sweet sauces such as butterscotch and chocolate.

TO USE Add to cake and biscuit mixtures; in desserts and sauces; as a spread; drizzled over desserts such as pancakes and ice cream.

Maple syrup

Made by tapping maple trees, draining off their sap, and then boiling the sap in large pans. This sugary red-brown syrup is quite runny, and has a very distinctive flavour. Production of maple syrup is based in north-eastern North America, with 80 per cent of it coming from Canada. Particularly popular in Canada and the US, maple syrup is drizzled over pancakes, waffles and ice cream, and can also be used as a flavouring in cakes, biscuits and desserts. Maple syrup production requires intensive, skilled manual labour, so it is always one of the most expensive of sweet syrups.

Maple sugar is made by boiling the maple sap for a longer time, to evaporate most of the water and make the sugar crystallise. It can be used in baking and sweet sauces.

TO USE Serve maple syrup with pancakes, waffles and ice cream; add to cakes and biscuit mixtures and to desserts.

Corn syrup

Made from cornstarch, this syrup has quite a neutral 'sweet' taste and may be pale or dark; darker syrup has a stronger flavour. Corn syrup is used for drizzling over pancakes, waffles and ice cream. It is also good used in cakes, biscuits and icings, or for sweetening ice creams – although it should be noted that it is not as sweet as cane sugar.

TO USE Serve with pancakes, waffles and ice cream; add to cake and biscuit mixtures; use as a sweetener in desserts.

Date syrup

Also known as palm syrup. This dark, sweet, sticky syrup is not extracted from dates but from the date palm tree itself. Popular in the Middle East, India and South America, date syrup can used as a sweetener in cakes, biscuits, ice creams and desserts, or can be served as a table syrup for drizzling over pancakes or ice cream, or spread on bread. It is also a good addition to chutneys.

TO USE In cake and biscuit mixtures; in desserts; in chutneys; as a table syrup.

Treacle

Treacle is made from refined molasses. It is a thick, black, sticky syrup with a liquorice flavour and a very distinctive, almost bitter undertone. Treacle is used mainly in baking, in recipes such as gingerbread, dark fruit cakes and treacle tart. It is also used to make traditional treacle toffee, and to flavour some savoury recipes such as Boston baked beans. In recipes where a lighter flavour is desired, such as treacle tart, it is often combined with golden syrup.

TO USE Add to cake mixtures, desserts, confectionery, and a few savoury dishes.

Malt extract

Also known as barley syrup, this dark brown syrup is produced by malting (germinating) barley grains, then grinding them, soaking them to extract their natural sugars, and boiling the soaking water to concentrate the sugar. Malt extract has a sweet taste and distinctive 'malty' flavour, most often used in baking to add flavour and a moist texture to breads, cakes and desserts. It can also be stirred into hot milky drinks or cold milkshakes instead of sugar to add sweetness and flavour.

TO USE Add to breads, cakes, desserts and milky drinks.

More about syrups

Commercially available syrups are distinct from home-made sugar and water syrups used for sorbets, poached fruits and other desserts. Syrups are usually derived from grains, fruits and tree or plant saps, and are intensely sweet, sticky liquids that vary in colour from pale yellow to amber, brown and black. They may be clear or opaque and can vary in thickness and consistency from quite thin to thick and viscous.

Culinary uses for syrups

Syrups are usually used as a sweetener in cakes, biscuits, desserts and confectionery; they may replace sugar, or be combined with it. In cakes such as gingerbread, the addition of syrup results in a dense, moist texture that keeps well. In recipes such as flapjacks, where syrup is combined with sugar, butter and oats, the ingredients bake into a soft and bubbling mixture rather like an oaty toffee. Once cooled, the flapjacks will be either chewy, if cooked for a short time, or hard, if cooked for a little longer. Some syrups, particularly fragrant ones such as maple syrup, are good drizzled over ice cream, waffles and pancakes.

Other varieties include

Fruit syrup These are made from a mixture of concentrated sugar syrup and fruit juice, and are available in various flavours: blackcurrant and raspberry are two of the most commonly found. Fruit syrups can be diluted in water to serve as a drink, or used to flavour cakes, desserts and sauces.

Rice syrup Produced from rice grains, this dark syrup is less sweet than sugar and has a miid flavour that is useful as a sweetener in cakes, biscuits and sauces.

Wheat syrup This sweet, mildly flavoured syrup is used as a sweetener in cakes, biscuits, sauces and desserts.

Molasses This thick, dark syrup is a by-product of the sugar-refining industry. Molasses can vary considerably in colour and flavour, depending on whether it is produced from sugar beet or cane sugar. The most common type is black, sticky blackstrap molasses, which is produced from sugar cane. It has a strong and distinctively bitter–sweet flavour, and is good used in rich fruity cakes, gingerbread, chutneys and toffee.

Cane syrup This is a product of the sugar-cane refining process, a sweet, mildly flavoured syrup often served at the table in the US with pancakes and waffles. It is also blended with maple syrup to make a less expensive maple-flavoured syrup.

Pomegranate molasses Also known as pomegranate syrup, this is dark and thick and is made by slowly simmering pomegranate juice to reduce it to a syrup. With its sweet, tart, tangy flavour, pomegranate molasses is popular in Mediterranean cooking. It is good used in both sweet and savoury dishes: in marinades for meat and fish, dressings and bean dishes, or to flavour sorbets, summer drinks and desserts.

Agave nectar Also known as agave syrup. This sweet syrup comes from Mexico, and is produced from the cactus-like agave plant, which also gives us tequila. It may be light or dark, and has a slightly thinner consistency than honey. Agave nectar is used as a sweetener, particularly in commercial products in Mexico, but it can also be used in recipes to sweeten desserts, cakes, biscuits, sauces and drinks. The light syrup has a mild flavour which is best suited to pairing with mild-tasting ingredients. The darker syrup has a more distinctive taste that will carry through to cakes and biscuits, and is good served as a table syrup for drizzling on pancakes, waffles and ice cream. The sugars in agave syrup are absorbed more slowly than other sugars, honeys and syrups, so it makes a good choice for those with a sensitivity to sugary foods.

Artificial sweeteners

People who want to avoid sugars and syrups have access to a number of artificial sweeteners, often promoted because of their low calorie content. Although many are manufactured in tiny tablet form, to be added to tea, coffee and other hot drinks instead of sugar, there are a few available in granular form which can be sprinkled over breakfast cereal and other foods. The two most common artificial sweeteners are saccharin and aspartame.

Saccharin This is a white powder made from coal tar. Saccharin is around 300 times sweeter than sugar and is usually used as a sweetener in tea, coffee and other hot drinks, as well as in the manufacture of soft drinks.

Aspartame Around 180 times sweeter than sugar, this low-calorie alternative to sugar is used commercially to sweeten drinks, desserts and confectionery.

Sweet flavourings and essences

Flavourings and essences are used in sweet recipes such as cakes, biscuits, desserts, ice creams, frostings, sweet sauces, confectionery and drinks. As they have an intense taste that can easily become overpowering, they are usually sold in small bottles and added in minute quantities.

Vanilla extract

A dark brown, intensely flavoured liquid extracted from vanilla pods. Vanilla extract can be used to flavour sweet recipes such as cakes, biscuits, ice creams, desserts, syrups, confectionery and frostings. Vanilla has a natural affinity with chocolate, coffee, nuts and fruits. Vanilla extract is quicker and more convenient to use than vanilla pods (see page 321) and is more appropriate for a variety of uses because it can be stirred directly into mixtures and desserts. Vanilla extract is not itself a sweet flavouring and should always be combined with sugar, syrup or another sweetener. When buying, look for genuine vanilla extract. Vanilla flavouring has a high proportion of artificial flavourings.

TO USE In cakes, biscuits, desserts, sweet sauces, confectionery and frostings. Use in small quantities (a few drops to 1 teaspoon for most recipes).

Rosewater

Made from distilled rose petals or rose oil, this clear, fragrant liquid has a strong floral taste and aroma which makes it a popular flavouring in Middle Eastern desserts and sweets. It can be used to flavour cakes, desserts, syrups and drinks, and has a natural affinity with creamy ingredients and fruity flavours – particularly summer berries. Rosewater is used to flavour Turkish delight and for flavouring whipped cream and creamy desserts such as *panna cotta* and rice pudding.

TO USE In cakes, desserts, syrups and drinks. Use in small quantities (usually between 1 teaspoon and 1 tablespoon).

Orange flower water

Distilled from the flowers of the Seville orange, this colourless liquid has a strong floral flavour and aroma. It is used in Middle Eastern cooking to flavour desserts, cakes, biscuits and syrups.

TO USE In desserts, cakes, biscuits, pastries, syrups. Use sparingly (a few drops to ¼ teaspoon).

Almond extract

Distilled from bitter almonds, and with an intense flavour which is quite different from whole sweet almonds. Its distinctive fragrance is used in the almond liqueur amaretto, and can be used to flavour home-made amaretti biscuits: it tastes similar to the ground apricot stones that are authentically used for those biscuits in Italy. It is also added to cakes, biscuits, desserts and creams.

TO USE In desserts, cakes, biscuits and whipped cream. Use sparingly (a few drops to ½ teaspoon).

Peppermint essence

Distilled from fresh leaves. This strongly flavoured essence can be used to flavour desserts, ice creams, confectionery and drinks. It has a natural affinity with chocolate.

TO USE Good-quality peppermint essence is extremely strong: you will need to add only a few drops to confectionery such as peppermint creams, and to custards for ice cream and other desserts. However, most peppermint essence is weaker, so you will need to add more (¼–1 teaspoon).

Coffee essence

A concentrated flavouring, coffee essence is dark brown and can be used as an alternative to instant coffee or espresso. Use it in cakes, desserts, ice creams, sauces, frostings and confectionery. It often contains chicory to boost its bitter flavour.

TO USE In cakes, biscuits, desserts, sweet sauces, confectionery and frostings – use in small quantities.

Flavoured sugar

Sugar flavoured with spices and aromatics such as vanilla, cinnamon, orange zest and lavender can be used to add sweetness and a subtle flavour to cakes, biscuits and desserts. Vanilla sugar is the variety most commonly available commercially, but all flavoured sugars are easily made at home. Put a vanilla pod or cinnamon stick, a few slivers of dried citrus rind or 1 tablespoon of lavender flowers in a jar of sugar. Leave to infuse for several weeks. Store in an airtight container in a cool, dark place.

TO USE In cakes, biscuits and desserts, as you would caster sugar.

Chocolate

Dark chocolate

Also known as bitter chocolate, this rich, very dark brown chocolate usually contains between 35 and 70 per cent cocoa solids and a relatively small proportion of sugar. (In Europe, regulations state that it must contain at least 35 per cent cocoa solids.) With good melting properties and an intense flavour, dark chocolate is the first choice for cooking and is widely used in cakes, biscuits, desserts, confectionery and decorations.

Couverture is often considered the professional's chocolate. It is of the very highest quality, with a high percentage of cocoa solids, making it ideal for melting, cooking and making handmade chocolates. Couverture should be tempered before use to ensure an even distribution of crystals throughout the chocolate, ensuring a glossy surface and a 'crisp', snappable texture. Tempering consists of melting and working the chocolate while carefully controlling its temperature.

TO USE Eat dark chocolate as it is; add to biscuits, cakes, desserts and confectionery, as chips, chunks or melted. Melt in a heatproof bowl over a pan of gently simmering water. If you are ever tempted to make the classic Mexican dish mole, with a sauce combining chocolate, chillies and numerous other ingredients, dark chocolate is the one to use.

Milk chocolate

This chocolate usually contains between 20 and 40 per cent cocoa solids along with a mixture of cocoa butter, milk or cream, sugar and other flavourings. It is a sweet, mild and creamy chocolate, and is mostly used as an eating chocolate. However, milk chocolate chips and chunks are added to cakes, biscuits and desserts. It is less well suited to melting and flavouring, as it does not provide the same powerful chocolate hit as plain chocolate.

TO USE Eat as it is; add to biscuits, cakes and desserts – usually as chips or chunks.

White chocolate

Made mostly from cocoa butter with the cocoa solids removed. White chocolate is a yellowy-cream confection with a mild, sweet and buttery taste. It is often flavoured with vanilla. Although it is made in the same way as chocolate, its minimal cocoa-solid content means that it has little or no chocolate flavour. It does, however, have the same melt-in-the-mouth texture. White chocolate is available in bars and chips, and is most often used in confectionery, biscuits, cakes and desserts such as mousses, ice cream and cheesecake. It can also be used to make decorations for cakes, biscuits and desserts.

TO USE Eat as it is; add to biscuits, cakes and desserts, as chunks, chips or melted. Melt in a heatproof bowl over a pan of gently simmering water; take care not to overheat or the chocolate may seize (become coarse and grainy).

Cocoa powder

This useful product is made from the dry mass left over when cocoa butter has been removed from cocoa paste. It is a fine, red-brown powder with a bitter but intensely chocolatey flavour. Widely used to flavour cakes, biscuits, confectionery and desserts.

TO USE Sift and combine with a sweetener such as sugar or syrup to flavour cakes, biscuits, desserts, confectionery and drinks.

Drinking chocolate

A combination of cocoa powder and sugar. This red-brown powder has a much milder, sweeter flavour than cocoa and dissolves easily in hot liquids. It is designed to be whisked into hot milk to make hot chocolate. Unsuitable for use as a flavouring for cakes, desserts or confectionery.

TO USE Stir into hot milk until dissolved, then whisk until frothy.

Carob

Carob is produced from the large, dark brown bean of the Mediterranean carob tree. It is sometimes regarded as the 'healthy' alternative to chocolate. It is sweet in flavour and lower in fat than chocolate, and contains no caffeine. These qualities attract many people, and with good reason, but it must be noted that carob has none of the depth of chocolate. It is available as a powder, in bars or as carob chips, and can be used to flavour cakes, biscuits and desserts in the same way as cocoa (although it is sweeter and milder). The powder can also be stirred into hot milk to make a hot drink.

TO USE Eat carob bars as they are; use to flavour cakes, biscuits, desserts – either powdered, in chunks, chips or melted – and in hot drinks.

Coffee

Coffee beans

These hard oval beans with a flat underside are usually roasted and ground for brewing into coffee. If you do your own grinding, make sure that you grind the beans to the correct degree of fineness for the brewing equipment you own. A 'burr' grinder, rather than a bladed mill, is the best way of controlling this. The beans may range in colour from chocolate-brown to black, depending on how long they have been roasted, and may have a faint film of oil on the surface (released from the bean after roasting). Strongly brewed coffee can be used as a flavouring for cakes and desserts. Whole coffee beans may be added to some desserts and cakes, such as ice cream or biscotti, to give flavour and an interesting crunch. Coffee naturally contains caffeine, although decaffeinated beans are also available. Coffee beans are usually sold roasted, but some specialist shops sell green beans for roasting at home.

Chocolate-covered coffee beans are sold as a confection, and can also be used as a decoration for coffee-flavoured cakes, biscuits and desserts.

TO USE Grind roasted beans in a coffee grinder. Brew with hot water in an espresso pot, cafetière, filter pot, Turkish coffee pot or percolator; add to sweet recipes as required.

Ground coffee

Made from whole coffee beans, ground coffee is available in a number of grinds suitable for different brewing pots, such as espresso (very fine), cafetière (medium) and filter (fine–medium). Pre-roasted beans can be bought in sealed tins, or in airtight bags with a one-way valve that allows natural gasses to vent. The beans can also be ground to order in specialist shops and some supermarkets. Some commercial ground beans are described as being suitable for all types of brewing, but it is better to get coffee ground specifically for your brewing method (or grind it at home, which is the best choice of all). Once brewed, the coffee can be enjoyed as a drink. When brewed strongly – for example as espresso – it can also be used as a flavouring in drinks, cakes and desserts. Occasionally, the ground coffee may be added directly to a recipe, for example to make a coffee-flavoured pancake batter; don't use these recipes if you don't like the idea of crunching hard coffee particles between your teeth! Store ground coffee in an airtight container in the fridge, as once coffee beans are ground their flavour quickly deteriorates.

TO USE Brew with hot water in an espresso pot, cafetière, filter pot, Turkish coffee pot or percolator; add to sweet recipes as required.

Instant coffee

Instant coffee – called 'soluble coffee' by those in the industry – is available as freeze-dried granules or powder that dissolve easily in boiling water. Instant coffee is a handy convenience product, and its flavour has none of the rich complexity of freshly brewed coffee, but it is useful for making a 'quick cup of coffee', and for flavouring cakes, biscuits and desserts when you want a strong coffee flavour but with very little liquid.

Camp coffee A type of instant coffee, this liquid is a syrup made from sugar, water, coffee and chicory. It is especially useful as a flavouring for cakes and icings because it has an intense coffee flavour without adding too much liquid.

TO USE Dissolve instant coffee in boiling water according to the instructions on the jar to make a hot drink, or dissolve in a very small amount of boiling water (about twice the volume of powder or granules) to flavour cakes, biscuits and desserts.

More about coffee

Coffee grows only in tropical regions. It is valued (almost worshipped in some quarters) for its berries (or 'cherries'), each of which normally contains two seeds. The seeds are what we refer to as beans; they are flat on one side from having shared the round pod with their other half.

There are two main types of coffee bean, robusta and arabica. Robusta is cheaper and inferior, although it can play a small part in good espresso blends. Arabica is superior in every way. After harvest, the beans are removed from their pulpy casings either by drying and milling or by washing and milling. Wet- and dry-processing create important differences in flavour. Once dried and cleaned, the green beans can be stored for many months without losing their intrinsic qualities. But they can't be used to brew coffee until they have been roasted to give them their characteristic flavour and aroma. There are four main types of roast: light, medium, high and continental. A light roast is suited to milder beans with a delicate flavour. The beans for medium, high and continental roasts are heated for longer, giving a stronger, more bitter flavour and aroma. Continental is the highest roast, and is usually the choice for espresso coffee.

Coffee is a huge industry, and the level of quality – from country to country and region to region – can range from horrible to sublime. Buy from a shop or company that can give advice not just about the country of origin but also about regions, roasting styles and brewing methods.

Brazil The world's largest producer, growing both arabica and robusta. A good cup of typical Brazilian coffee should have a smooth, mild flavour with little bitterness or acidity.

Costa Rica Always arabica, often of excellent quality with a full, rounded flavour and mild acidity.

Indonesia Coffee is grown in Sumatra, Java, and other Indonesian islands; rich and full-flavoured with a low acidity and mellow taste.

Ethiopia The original home of arabica and producer of some excellent beans. The chief growing regions are Harrar and Sidamo (sometimes called Yirgacheffe after its central town).

Kenya The best known of the African coffees. Kenyan tends to be fruity coffee with good acidity. Look for AA beans, the highest quality level.

Colombia The coffee here can be of excellent quality, smooth and strong with fairly low acidity.

Caffeine

All coffee beans naturally contain caffeine, which is a stimulant and diuretic. In decaffeinated coffee, available as beans, ground coffee or instant, the caffeine is removed with steam and solvents before roasting. Decaffeinated coffee can have a good flavour, but brands vary greatly.

How to store coffee

Roasted coffee beans do not have an indefinite shelf life: they are best ground and used within a few days of roasting. If this is not possible, beans and ground coffee should be stored in an airtight container in the fridge. Beans may be frozen for three to six months.

Culinary uses for coffee

Coffee is not just a beverage. It is also widely used as a flavouring in sweet dishes: cakes, biscuits, desserts, custards, sauces, ice creams, frostings and confectionery. It goes particularly well with creamy flavours and with vanilla, nuts and especially chocolate. Classic recipes include coffee and walnut cake, éclairs filled with coffee-flavoured crème pâtissière, and coffee ice cream.

Popular brews

There are numerous ways to serve coffee, including:

Espresso This strong Italian coffee is made by forcing steam through finely ground coffee at very high pressure. It is served black in tiny cups.

Cappuccino Made by pouring frothy steamed milk into espresso to give a fluffy white head. Usually dusted with powdered chocolate.

Caffè latte A tall Italian coffee made with hot milk.

Macchiato Espresso served with a dash of milk and a spot of foam on top.

Turkish coffee A style of coffee enjoyed throughout the Middle East, North Africa and the Balkans. Very finely ground coffee is brewed in a pot, then poured out so that the dregs settle at the bottom of the cup. It is usually served with sugar. The last few mouthfuls, thick and grainy, are left undrunk.

Vietnamese coffee A legacy of the French, called *ca phe sua da* or *café vietnamien*. A small aluminium coffee filter is set on top of a glass containing about 1cm (1/2in) condensed milk and the coffee is allowed to drip in. The result is sweet and creamy.

Iced coffee The simplest way to make iced coffee is to pour a shot of espresso over ice for serving black or with milk. Alternatively, ground coffee can be soaked in cold water for several hours and then filtered, or regular brewed coffee can be chilled. In blended iced coffee, the coffee, ice and milk – and sugar or flavoured syrups – are blended together.

Tea

Black tea

All tea begins with the terminal bud and two leaves of the tea bush, a relative of the camellia. Between bush and cup, the harvested plant must be processed – and black tea is made by a process known as oxidation or fermentation. Its leaves are left to wither, or wilt, for up to 18 hours, then they are pressed between steel rollers to break the cells and start complex transformations of flavour and colour; they are spread out and left to oxidise in cool, humid air and finally dried using high heat. Black tea is the most widely drunk tea: Assam, Ceylon, much of Darjeeling and blends such as English breakfast and lapsang souchong are all black teas. There are many types of black tea, with their individual qualities determined by growing region, quality control in leaf selection, and the details of processing. Quality can range from basic (found in tea bags) to exceptional. Although usually served hot as a drink, black tea can also be used to soak fruit before adding to cakes, or sweetened and chilled to make iced tea.

TO USE Allow about 1 teaspoon tea per person and steep in boiling water for 3–5 minutes to achieve the desired strength. Strain and serve black, or with milk or lemon, and sweetened with sugar; in recipes.

Green tea

Green tea preserves some of the flavour and aroma of the fresh leaves. The leaves may be left to wither for a brief time before being pressed and then quickly dried using dry heat or steam. Green tea is briefly steeped in boiling water to make a lightly flavoured brew with a pale green-yellow colour. Classic varieties include gunpowder green tea and jasmine tea. Specialist teas from China and Japan are increasingly widely available.

Oolong tea This comes somewhere between green tea and black tea. The leaves are withered and rolled to achieve a medium-dark colour and medium strength of flavour. Oolong is associated with China and Taiwan but the style can be made anywhere. It is usually served without milk.

White tea White tea is made from unrolled leaves and buds and young leaves. It contains less caffeine than green tea and is a speciality of the Fujian province in China, although it is also grown in Yunnan, Ceylon and Darjeeling.

TO USE Steep briefly in boiling water and serve without milk.

Tisanes

Often referred to as herbal or fruit teas, tisanes are flavoured infusions made by steeping herbs, fruits and other flavourings (usually, although not always, dried) in boiling water. Popular tisanes include fennel, peppermint, camomile, rosehip and lemon balm. Tisanes are often said to have therapeutic properties such as being calming or invigorating, and they are especially popular with those who like a hot drink after a meal but don't want the caffeine in coffee. Most often served as a hot drink, but cooled tisanes can also be stirred into fruit punches and smoothies.

TO USE Steep in boiling water for 5 minutes or until the flavour has suffused sufficiently. Strain and sweeten with honey or sugar, if you like, or leave to cool and add to smoothies and punches.

More about tea

Tea has been drunk in China for at least 1,500 years, but was only introduced to Europe in the 17th century. It quickly grew in popularity and is now drunk throughout the world. Tea plants are an evergreen shrub related to the camellia, and they grow in warm, moist climes; the world's largest producers are China and India. The flavour of the tea we buy varies greatly according to the type of plant, the conditions in which it is grown, the care taken in harvesting, and the manner in which it is processed after picking. All tea contains the stimulant caffeine and some bitter-tasting tannin; the longer the tea is brewed, the more tannin it will contain.

How to buy and store tea

There are three main grades of tea: leaf tea, which takes the longest to brew; broken leaves; and smaller leaf tea known as 'dust', which is normally blended with other teas and used in tea bags. Tea has a long shelf life but should always be stored in an airtight container in a cool, dark place to preserve as much as possible of its original flavour. This is true even of tea bags.

Culinary uses for tea

Tea is most often enjoyed as a drink, steeped in hot water and then strained to remove the leaves. Black tea may be drunk with or without milk or lemon, and with or without sugar. Lighter teas (especially green tea) are usually drunk without milk. Another alternative is to strain the tea, sweeten and allow it to cool, then serve over ice with lemon. In India, black tea leaves are brewed with milk, sugar and spices to make *chai*, while in Morocco tea leaves are brewed with fresh mint and served very sweet.

In cooking, black tea can be brewed to a higher strength than normal and used to soak dried fruit for cake mixtures. Fragrant blends such as Earl Grey can be used to make syrups for poaching fruit. Powdered green *matcha* tea is used in Japan to make a fragrant, pale green ice cream. Fish and poultry can be smoked over smouldering tea leaves.

How to brew black tea

To make a perfect cup of tea, half-fill a tea pot with boiling water and leave to warm, then pour out and add 1 teaspoon tea leaves per person, plus one for the pot. Using freshly drawn and boiled water, pour over the leaves and leave to steep for 3–5 minutes until the desired strength is achieved. Strain into tea cups and serve with milk or lemon, and sugar, if you like.

Other varieties include

Earl Grey This light and fragrant brew is made from black China tea scented with oil of bergamot, giving it its distinctively citrus-like aroma. It is best served black, with a slice of lemon if you like.

Darjeeling Highly regarded among tea-drinkers, Darjeeling tea is grown in the foothills of the Himalayas and has a light, aromatic flavour. First-flush (early-season) pickings have a more delicate taste; second-flush pickings are fruitier and more developed in flavour. Darjeeling can be drunk black or with a little milk or lemon, hot or iced.

English breakfast tea A blended black tea with a robust, full-bodied yet refreshing and quite mellow flavour. Breakfast tea combinations vary from brand to brand and may include Assam, Keemun, Ceylon and Kenyan teas.

Assam A black Indian tea, dark, malty and rich, with a smooth flavour. Assam is best served with milk.

Keemun A black China tea with a light, nutty and fragrant flavour, Keemun makes a refreshing drink and is good lightly brewed and served black, or left to infuse longer and served with milk.

Nilgiri A black tea from southern India. This fresh, fragrant tea has a slightly fruity, well-rounded flavour and is good served either black or with milk.

Ceylon Grown in Sri Lanka, this black tea is of excellent quality; it has a light, slightly citrusy flavour and may be served black or with milk.

Lapsang souchong This large-leafed black China tea is flavoured by smoking the tea leaves over a pinewood fire. The finest leaves are said to come from the hills in northern Fujian province. Lapsang souchong may be drunk black or with a little milk.

Jasmine tea Made from green tea leaves that have been layered with night-blooming jasmine and left to pick up their scent. Jasmine tea is pale when brewed, yellow-green in colour and with a light, delicate, almost floral flavour. It is always drunk black, and is traditionally unsweetened.

Rooibos Also known as redbush, this fragrant dark red-brown brew isn't actually a tea, but the leaves of a herb grown in the South African Cedarberg Mountains. Dried and fermented naturally in the sun to produce dark mahogany-red leaves, rooibos is caffeine-free and low in tannin. Brewed in hot water in the same way as tea, it is usually served black but can also have milk and/or sugar added. Rooibos can be used instead of tea for recipes such as fruity tea cakes.

Essential recipes

Stocks

Vegetable Stock

You will need 225g (8oz) each onions, celery, leeks and carrots, chopped, 1 bouquet garni (2 bay leaves, a few thyme sprigs and a small bunch parsley), 10 black peppercorns, ½ tsp salt.

Makes 1.2 litres (2 pints)

1 Put all the ingredients in a pan and pour in 1.7 litres (3 pints) cold water. Bring slowly to the boil and skim the surface. Partially cover and simmer gently for 30 minutes. Check and adjust the seasoning. Strain the stock through a muslin-lined sieve and leave to cool.

Meat Stock

You will need 450g (1lb) each meat bones and stewing meat, 1 onion, 2 celery sticks and 1 large carrot, sliced, 1 bouquet garni (2 bay leaves, a few thyme sprigs and a small bunch parsley), 1 tsp black peppercorns, ½ tsp salt.

Makes 900ml (1½ pints)

1 Preheat the oven to 220°C (200°C fan oven) gas 7. Put the meat and bones in a roasting tin and roast for 30–40 minutes, turning now and again, until they are well browned.

2 Put the bones in a large pan with the remaining ingredients and pour in 2 litres (3½ pints) cold water. Bring slowly to the boil and skim the surface. Partially cover and simmer gently for 4–5 hours. Check and adjust the seasoning. Strain the stock through a muslin-lined sieve and cool quickly. If necessary, degrease before using (see page 423).

Chicken Stock

You will need 1.6kg (3½lb) chicken bones, 225g (8oz) each onions and celery, sliced, 150g (5oz) leeks, chopped, 1 bouquet garni (2 bay leaves, a few thyme sprigs and a small bunch parsley), 1 tsp black peppercorns, ½ tsp salt.

Makes 1.2 litres (2 pints)

1 Put all the ingredients in a large pan and pour in 3 litres (5¼ pints) cold water. Bring slowly to the boil and skim the surface. Partially cover and simmer gently for 2 hours. Adjust the seasoning if necessary.

2 Strain the stock through a muslin-lined sieve and cool quickly. If necessary, degrease before using (see page 423).

Fish Stock

You will need 900g (2lb) fish bones and trimmings, washed, 2 carrots, 1 onion and 2 celery sticks, sliced, 1 bouquet garni (2 bay leaves, a few thyme sprigs and a small bunch parsley), 6 white peppercorns, ½ tsp salt.

Makes 900ml (1½ pints)

1 Put all the ingredients in a pan and pour in 900ml (1½ pints) cold water. Bring slowly to the boil and skim the surface. Partially cover and simmer gently for 30 minutes. Check and adjust the seasoning.

2 Strain the stock through a muslin-lined sieve and cool quickly. If necessary, degrease before using (see page 423).

Degreasing Stock

Meat and poultry stock needs to be degreased, fish stock occasionally needs degreasing, but vegetable stock does not. You can mop the fat from the surface using kitchen paper, but the following methods are easier and more effective. There are three main methods that you can use: ladling, pouring and chilling.

Ladling　While the stock is warm, place a ladle on the surface. Press down to allow the fat floating on the surface to trickle over the edge until the ladle is full. Discard the fat, then repeat until all the fat has been removed.

Pouring　For this you need a degreasing jug or a double-pouring gravy boat, which has the spout at the base of the vessel. When you fill the jug or gravy boat with a fatty liquid, the fat rises. When you pour, the stock comes out while the fat stays behind in the jug.

Chilling　This technique works best with stock made from meat, whose fat solidifies when cold. Put the stock in the fridge until the fat becomes solid, then remove the pieces of fat using a slotted spoon.

Freezing Stock

Frozen stock is very useful in the kitchen, but it can use up a lot of freezer space. Save valuable space by concentrating the stock before freezing it. To use, simply reconstitute it to its full volume by adding water.

1 To concentrate the stock, put the clarified, degreased stock in a clean pan and bring to the boil. Bubble to reduce it to about 25 per cent of its volume.

2 Pour the stock into plastic containers, filling to leave a space of 2.5cm (1in) at the top.

3 Put the lid on tightly and freeze as quickly as possible.

Note

Alternatively, to make frozen stock cubes, freeze the reduced stock in an ice cube tray, then put the frozen cubes in a sealable tub. You can take out as many cubes as you need and reseal the tub. If the cubes have a build-up of ice on the surface, just wash it off under the cold tap before adding the cube to the dish.

Sauces

Gravy

A rich gravy is traditionally served with roast meat and poultry. If possible, make the gravy in the roasting tin while the joint (or bird) is resting. This will incorporate the meat juices that have escaped during roasting.

Makes about 300ml (½ pint)

1 Carefully pour (or skim) off the fat from a corner of the roasting tin, leaving the sediment behind. Put the tin on the hob over a medium heat and pour in 300ml (½ pint) vegetable water, or chicken, vegetable or meat stock as appropriate.

2 Stir thoroughly, scraping up the sediment, and boil steadily until the gravy is a rich brown colour.

Variations

Rich Wine Gravy: Deglaze the roasting tin with about 150ml (¼ pint) red or white wine, or 90ml (3fl oz) fortified wine such as sherry or Madeira, and allow to bubble for a minute or two before adding the stock or water. For a sweeter flavour, add 2 tbsp redcurrant jelly with the wine.

Thick Gravy: Sprinkle 1–2 tbsp flour into the roasting tin and cook, stirring, until browned, then gradually stir in the liquid and cook, stirring for 2–3 minutes until smooth and slightly thickened.

Notes

- To impart character, include a little mashed roast garlic (cooked with the bird); a splash of wine (bubble to evaporate the alcohol); or fragrant herbs like thyme, bay and tarragon. A little gravy browning can be added to intensify the flavour and colour.

- Roast duck and turkey both have a stronger flavour than chicken, so they can take a more robust gravy. A spoonful or two of cranberry sauce or redcurrant jelly adds a pleasant fruitiness, while a little orange zest or balsamic vinegar can help to offset the richness of duck. You may prefer to use medium dry sherry or Madeira rather than wine in a duck gravy. Aromatic spices, such as cinnamon sticks or cardamom pods, can be simmered in the gravy to lend flavour then removed before serving.

Béchamel Sauce

You will need 300ml (½ pint) semi-skimmed milk, 1 slice of onion, 6 peppercorns, 1 mace blade, 1 bay leaf, 15g (½ oz) each butter and plain flour, salt and pepper, freshly grated nutmeg.

Makes about 300ml (½ pint)

1 Pour the milk into a pan. Add the onion slice, peppercorns, mace and bay leaf. Bring almost to the boil, remove from the heat, cover and leave to infuse for about 20 minutes. Strain.

2 To make the roux, melt the butter in a pan, stir in the flour and cook, stirring, for 1 minute until cooked but not coloured.

3 Remove from the heat and gradually pour on the milk, whisking constantly. Season lightly with salt, pepper and nutmeg.

4 Return to the heat and cook, stirring constantly, until the sauce is thickened and smooth. Simmer gently for 2 minutes.

Cheese (Mornay) Sauce: Off the heat, stir 50g (2oz) finely grated Gruyère or mature Cheddar cheese and a large pinch of mustard powder or cayenne pepper into the finished sauce. Heat gently to melt the cheese if necessary.

Hollandaise Sauce

You will need 4 tbsp white wine vinegar, 1 mace blade, 1 slice of onion, 1 bay leaf, 6 peppercorns, 150g (5oz) unsalted butter, 3 medium egg yolks, a little lemon juice, salt and white pepper.

Makes about 300ml (½ pint)

1 Put the vinegar, mace, onion, bay leaf and peppercorns in a pan. Bring to the boil and reduce to 1 tbsp. Cut the butter into ten pieces.

2 Put the egg yolks in a heatproof bowl with one piece of butter and a pinch of salt. Beat, then strain in the vinegar. Place over a pan of hot water, making sure it doesn't touch the water. Whisk for 3 minutes until pale and starting to thicken.

3 Add a piece of butter and beat until absorbed. Repeat with the remaining pieces of butter. Season and add lemon juice to taste. Serve.

Béarnaise Sauce

You will need 4 tbsp white wine vinegar, 2 shallots, finely chopped, a few fresh tarragon sprigs, 6 peppercorns, 75g (3oz) unsalted butter at roomtemperature, 2 medium egg yolks, 2 tsp freshly chopped parsley or chervil (optional), salt and white pepper.

Makes about 200ml (7fl oz)

1 Put the vinegar, shallots, tarragon and peppercorns in a pan. Bring to the boil and reduce to 1 tbsp. Cut the butter into ten pieces.

2 Put the egg yolks in a heatproof bowl with one piece of butter and a pinch of salt. Beat, then strain in the vinegar. Place over a pan of hot water. Whisk for 3–4 minutes until pale and starting to thicken.

3 Add a piece of butter and beat until completely absorbed. Repeat with the remaining butter. Season with salt and pepper to taste. Stir in the herbs, if using. Serve.

Bread Sauce

You will need 1 onion, quartered, 4 cloves, 2 bay leaves, 450ml (¾ pint) milk, 175g (6oz) fresh breadcrumbs, 50g (2oz) butter, 200ml (7fl oz) crème fraîche, salt and ground black pepper.

Makes about 750ml (1¼ pints)

1 Stud each onion quarter with a clove, then put in a pan with 1 bay leaf and the milk. Gently heat on the lowest setting for 15 minutes.

2 Remove the pan from the heat and discard the onion quarters, cloves and bay leaf.

3 Stir the breadcrumbs, butter and crème fraîche into the milk. Season with salt and black pepper and serve garnished with a bay leaf. Alternatively, store in the fridge for up to two days.

Simple Tomato Sauce

You will need 2 Spanish onions, chopped, 4 tbsp olive oil, 2 garlic cloves, crushed, 2 x 400g cans chopped plum tomatoes, 2 tbsp torn basil leaves, salt and ground black pepper.

Makes about 750ml (1¼ pints)

1 Gently fry the onions in the oil for 10 minutes or until softened. Add the garlic and cook for a further 10 minutes, stirring occasionally, until very soft.

2 Add the tomatoes and season. Bring to the boil and simmer gently for 30 minutes or until the sauce is thick and pulpy. Add the basil and check the seasoning.

Tomato Ketchup

You will need 2.7kg (6lb) ripe tomatoes, 225g (8oz) sugar, 300ml (½ pint) spiced vinegar (page 429), 1 tbsp tarragon vinegar (optional), pinch of cayenne pepper, 1 tsp paprika, 1 tsp salt.

Makes 1.1 litres (2 pints)

1 Slice the tomatoes and cook over a very low heat for about 45 minutes, stirring frequently, until they cook down to a pulp. Bring to the boil and cook rapidly, stirring frequently, until the pulp thickens.

2 Press the pulp through a nylon or stainless steel sieve, then return to the pan and stir in the remaining ingredients. Simmer gently until the mixture thickens.

3 Pour the ketchup into warm, sterilised bottles. Seal and label, and store in a cool, dark place for up to one year.

Barbecue Sauce

You will need 50g (2oz) butter, 1 large onion, peeled and chopped, 1 tsp tomato purée, 2 tbsp each of wine vinegar and Worcestershire sauce, 2 tsp mustard powder, salt and pepper.

Makes about 300ml (½ pint)

1 Melt the butter in a pan, add the onion and sauté gently for 10 minutes until softened. Stir in the tomato purée and cook, stirring, for 2 minutes.

2 Mix together the wine vinegar, Worcestershire sauce, mustard powder, salt and pepper in a bowl, stir in 150ml (¼ pint) water, then add to the pan. Bring to the boil and let bubble for 10 minutes.

Pesto

You will need 50g (2oz) fresh basil leaves, roughly torn, 1–2 garlic cloves, 25g (1oz) pine nuts, 6 tbsp extra virgin olive oil, 2 tbsp freshly grated Parmesan, salt and ground black pepper, lemon juice to taste (optional).

Makes about 200g (7oz)

1 Put the basil leaves in a food processor with the garlic, pine nuts and 2 tbsp olive oil. Process to a fairly smooth paste.

2 Gradually add the remaining oil and season with salt and pepper.

3 Transfer to a bowl and stir in the Parmesan. Check the seasoning and add a squeeze of lemon juice if you like. Cover with a thin layer of olive oil and seal tightly. Store in the fridge for up to three days.

Flavoured Butter

You will need 125g (4oz) unsalted butter, softened (or allow 25g (1oz) unsalted butter per serving).

Makes 125g (4oz)

1 Put the butter in a bowl and beat in the flavourings (see Variations). Turn out on to clingfilm, shape into a log and wrap tightly. Chill in the fridge for at least 1 hour. (Or freeze for up to 1 month.)

2 Slice the log into pieces about 5mm (¼in) thick and serve.

Variations
Anchovy Butter: Add 6 mashed anchovy fillets.

Herb Butter: Add 2 tbsp finely chopped herbs, a squeeze of lemon juice.

Garlic Butter: Add 1 crushed garlic clove, 2 tsp finely chopped fresh parsley.

Pistou

You will need ¾ tsp sea salt, 6 garlic cloves, chopped, 1 tbsp chopped fresh basil, 150ml (¼ pint) olive oil.

Makes about 150ml (¼ pint)

1 Using a pestle and mortar or a strong bowl and the end of a rolling pin, pound the sea salt and garlic together until smooth.

2 Add the basil and pound until broken down to a paste, then slowly blend in the olive oil.

Dressings

French Dressing

You will need 1 tsp Dijon mustard, pinch of sugar, 1 tbsp red or white wine vinegar, 6 tbsp extra virgin olive oil, salt and ground black pepper.

Makes 100ml (3½fl oz)

1 Put the mustard, sugar and vinegar in a small bowl, and season with salt and pepper. Whisk thoroughly, then gradually whisk in the oil until thoroughly combined.

Balsamic Dressing

You will need 2 tbsp balsamic vinegar, 4 tbsp extra virgin olive oil, salt and ground black pepper.

Makes 6 tbsp

1 Whisk the vinegar and oil in a small bowl. Season with salt and pepper to taste.

2 If not using immediately, whisk briefly before drizzling over salad.

Mayonnaise

You will need 2 egg yolks, 2 tsp lemon juice or white wine vinegar, 1 tsp Dijon mustard, pinch of sugar, 300ml (½ pint) light olive oil, salt and pepper.

Makes 300ml (½ pint)

1 Put all the ingredients except the oil into a food processor and blend briefly until pale and creamy.

2 With the blade motor running, pour in the olive oil through the feeder tube, in a steady stream, until the mayonnaise is thick. Thin to the required consistency, if necessary, with a little hot water.

3 Store the mayonnaise in a screw-topped jar in the fridge for up to 3 days.

Notes
- The ingredients must be at room temperature. If eggs are used straight from the fridge the mayonnaise is likely to curdle.
- To make mayonnaise by hand, mix the egg yolks, mustard, sugar and seasoning in a bowl, then whisk in the oil, drop by drop to begin with, then in a slow, steady stream. Finally add the vinegar or lemon juice.

Variations

Herb Mayonnaise: Fold in 2 tbsp chopped herbs, such as chives, chervil, basil, tarragon or coriander.

Lemon Mayonnaise: Use lemon juice. Add 1 tsp grated lemon zest and an extra 1 tbsp lemon juice at the end.

Aïoli: Put 4 crushed garlic cloves into the processor with 2 egg yolks, 1 tbsp lemon juice and ½ tsp salt; process as in stage 1, until evenly combined. Add 300ml (½ pint) light olive oil, as in step 2.

Garlic and Basil Mayonnaise: Add 1 crushed garlic clove at stage 1. Fold 2 tbsp shredded basil into the mayonnaise at the end.

Thousand Island Dressing: Add 2 tsp tomato purée, 2 tbsp chopped stuffed olives, 2 tsp finely chopped onion, 1 chopped hard-boiled egg and 1 tbsp chopped parsley to the finished mayonnaise.

Tartare Sauce: Add 2 tsp chopped tarragon or chives, 4 tsp each chopped capers, gherkins and parsley, and 2 tbsp lemon juice to the finished mayonnaise.

Blue Cheese Dressing: Put 50g (2oz) diced Gorgonzola cheese into a food processor with 2 tbsp milk, 1 tbsp white wine vinegar, a little pepper and 6 tbsp olive oil. Whiz until smooth.

Flavoured Oils

Herb oil is easy to make. Simply take 4 fresh rosemary or thyme sprigs and tap lightly with a rolling pin to release the flavour. Put them into a jug, add 600ml (1 pint) extra virgin olive oil, cover and leave to infuse in a cool place for several days. Strain into a clean bottle and use as required.

Chilli and garlic oil will spike up any salad. To prepare, put the peeled cloves from a whole head of garlic into a small pan with 300ml (½ pint) mild olive oil and 1 small red chilli, deseeded and very finely chopped. Heat gently for 5–6 minutes until the garlic is golden. Cool, then strain the oil into a clean bottle. Use as required.

Flavoured Vinegars

Like oils, wine vinegars can be flavoured with aromatic herbs, fruits, spices, and even flower petals. It is worth noting that the better wine vinegars, such as Champagne and sherry vinegars, need nothing to enhance their natural flavours. Of the fruit vinegars, raspberry vinegar is the most popular and is available from most good supermarkets. Strawberry, blackberry and peach vinegars are also obtainable.

To make your own herb or spiced vinegar, immerse a few herb sprigs, such as rosemary or thyme, or 1 tbsp coriander seeds, 1 or 2 small red chillies, or 1 or 2 peeled garlic cloves in a bottle of good-quality red or white wine vinegar, or cider vinegar. Leave in a cool, dark place to infuse for 2–3 weeks. Strain and re-bottle, adding a fresh herb sprig if desired.

Pastes

Thai Pastes

Red Curry Paste: Wearing rubber gloves to prevent skin irritation, and using a small sharp knife, halve and deseed 2 long, thin, fresh red chilles and 8 dried chillies, then roughly chop the chillies and 4 kaffir lime leaves. Peel a 2.5cm (1in) piece galangal, trim and discard any woody or shrivelled parts, then chop. Peel and chop 4 shallots and 4 garlic cloves. Peel off and discard any tough outer layers from 2 lemon grass stalks. Trim the ends, then chop. Put these prepared ingredients and 1 tsp each ground black pepper and ground turmeric along with 2 tbsp sunflower oil in a spice grinder or mortar. Grind or pound to form a smooth paste, adding a little water if necessary. Store in a screw-topped jar for up to one month.

Green Curry Paste: Wearing rubber gloves to prevent skin irritation, deseed 4 long, thin green chillies and 2–4 small green chillies, then roughly chop. Peel and chop 4 garlic cloves, a 2.5cm (1in) piece fresh root ginger and 1 lemon grass stalk. Chop 6 spring onions, 4 coriander roots and 1 tbsp chopped fresh coriander. Shred 4 kaffir lime leaves. Place all the ingredients in a spice grinder or mortar. Grind or pound to form a smooth paste, adding a little water if necessary. Store in a screw-topped jar for up to one month.

Spice Blends

Curry Powder: Put 1 tbsp each cumin and fenugreek seeds, ½ tsp mustard seeds, 1½ tsp each poppy seeds, black peppercorns and ground ginger, 4 tbsp coriander seeds, ½ tsp hot chilli powder and 2 tbsp ground turmeric into a food processor or grinder. Grind to a fine powder. Store the curry powder in an airtight container and use within one month.

Five-spice Powder: Grind together 1 tbsp fennel seeds, 2 tsp Sichuan pepper and 8 star anise. Stir in ½ tsp ground cloves and 1 tbsp ground cinnamon. Store in an airtight container and use within one month. Use sparingly.

Garam Masala: Grind together 10 green cardamom pods, 1 tbsp black peppercorns and 2 tsp cumin seeds. Store in an airtight container and use within one month.

Indian Pastes

Balti Paste: Put 1 tbsp each fennel seeds and ground allspice, 2–3 roughly chopped garlic cloves, a 1cm (½in) piece fresh root ginger, peeled and roughly chopped, 50g (2oz) garam masala, 25g (1oz) curry powder and 1 tsp salt into a food processor with 8 tbsp water and blend. Divide the paste into three equal portions, then freeze for up to three months.

Harissa: Grill 2 red peppers until softened and charred, cool, then skin, core and remove the seeds. Put 4 deseeded and roughly chopped red chillies in a food processor with 6 peeled garlic cloves, 1 tbsp ground coriander and 1 tbsp caraway seeds. Process to a rough paste, then add the grilled peppers, 2 tsp salt and 4 tbsp olive oil, and whiz until smooth. Put the harissa into a screw-topped jar, cover with a thin layer of olive oil and store in the fridge for up to two weeks.

Korma Paste: Put 3 tbsp ground cinnamon, the seeds from 36 green cardamom pods, 30 cloves, 18 bay leaves, 1 tbsp fennel seeds and 1 tsp salt into a food processor and blend to a powder. Tip the powder into a bowl and add 4 tbsp water, stirring well to make a paste. Divide the paste into three equal portions, then freeze for up to three months.

Madras Paste: Put 1 finely chopped small onion, a 2.5cm (1in) piece fresh root ginger, peeled and finely chopped, 2 crushed garlic cloves, juice of ½ lemon, 1 tbsp each cumin seeds and coriander seeds, 1 tsp cayenne pepper, 2 tsp each ground turmeric and garam masala and 1 tsp salt into a food processor with 2 tbsp water and blend until smooth. Divide into three equal portions, then freeze for up to three months.

Tandoori Paste: Put 24 crushed garlic cloves, a 5cm (2in) piece fresh root ginger, peeled and chopped, 3 tbsp each coriander seeds, cumin seeds, ground fenugreek and paprika, 3 deseeded and chopped red chillies, 3 tsp English mustard, 2 tbsp tomato purée and 1 tsp salt into a food processor with 8 tbsp water and blend to a paste. Divide into three equal portions, then freeze for up to three months.

Pastry

Shortcrust Pastry

This is the most widely used pastry. The proportion of flour to fat is 2:1. The choice of fat is largely a matter of taste – butter gives a rich pastry, but using half white vegetable fat improves the texture.

You will need 225g (8oz) plain flour, plus extra to dust, pinch of salt, 110g (4oz) butter, or half white vegetable fat and half butter, cut into pieces.

Makes 225g (8oz) pastry
Preparation: 10 minutes, plus resting

1 Sift the flour and salt into a bowl, add the fat and mix lightly.

2 Using your fingertips, rub the fat into the flour until the mixture resembles fine breadcrumbs.

3 Sprinkle 3–4 tbsp cold water evenly over the surface and stir with a round-bladed knife until the mixture begins to stick together in large lumps. If the dough seems dry, add a little extra water. With one hand, collect the dough together to form a ball.

4 Knead lightly on a lightly floured surface for a few seconds to form a smooth, firm dough; do not over-work. Wrap in clingfilm and leave to rest in the fridge for 30 minutes before rolling out.

Notes
- To make the pastry in a food processor, put the flour and salt in the processor bowl with the butter. Whiz until the mixture resembles fine crumbs, then add the water. Process briefly, using the pulse button, until the mixture just comes together in a ball. Continue from stage 4.
- Shortcrust pastry can be stored in the fridge for up to 3 days, or frozen for up to 3 months.

Variations
Wholemeal Pastry: Replace half of the white flour with wholemeal flour. A little extra water may be needed to mix the dough.

Nut Pastry: Replace 50g (2oz) of the flour with finely chopped or ground walnuts, hazelnuts or almonds, adding them to the rubbed-in mixture just before the cold water.

Cheese Pastry: Stir in 3–4 tbsp freshly grated Parmesan or 75g (3oz) finely grated Cheddar cheese and a small pinch of mustard powder before adding the water.

Herb Pastry: Stir in 3 tbsp finely chopped herbs, such as parsley, sage, thyme or rosemary, before adding the water.

Olive Pastry: Stir in 4 tbsp finely chopped pitted black olives at step 2.

Poppy Seed Pastry: Add 15g (½oz) poppy seeds before adding the water.

Sweet Shortcrust Pastry

Used for sweet tarts and pies. You will need 125g (4oz) plain flour, pinch of salt, 50g (2oz) unsalted butter, cut into pieces, 2 medium egg yolks, 50g (2oz) caster sugar.

Makes 125g (4oz) pastry

1 Make as for shortcrust pastry above, adding the sugar with the egg yolks at step 2.

Puff Pastry

If you can, make this a day ahead. You will need 450g (1lb) plain flour, pinch of salt, 450g (1lb) butter, chilled, 1 tbsp lemon juice.

Makes 450g (1lb) pastry

1 Sift the flour and salt into a bowl. Dice 50g (2oz) butter. Flatten the rest into a 2cm (¾in) thick slab. Rub the diced butter into the flour. Using a knife, stir in the lemon juice and about 300ml (½ pint) cold water to make a soft elastic dough. Knead on a lightly floured surface until smooth. Cut a cross through half the depth.

2 Open out the 'flaps'. Roll out the dough, keeping the centre four times as thick as the flaps.

3 Put the slab of butter in the centre and fold the flaps over it. Gently roll out to make a rectangle measuring 40.5 x 20.5cm (16 x 8in).

4 Mark off three equal sections from top to bottom. Fold the bottom third of the pastry up over the middle and the top third down. Wrap in clingfilm and chill for 30 minutes (or freeze 5–10 minutes).

5 Repeat the rolling, folding, resting and turning four more times, ensuring the folded edges are to the sides each time. Chill for at least 30 minutes before baking.

Rough Puff Pastry

Rough puff doesn't rise as much as puff pastry but is quicker to make. You will need 450g (1lb) plain flour, pinch of salt, 350g (12oz) butter, 2 tsp lemon juice.

Makes 450g (1lb) pastry

1 Sift the flour and salt into a bowl. Cut the butter into 2cm (¾in) cubes and add to the flour. Mix lightly to coat the butter with flour. Using a knife, stir in the lemon juice and 100ml (3½fl oz) water to make a soft elastic dough.

2 Turn out the dough on to a lightly floured worksurface and knead until smooth. Roll out to a rectangle 30.5 x 10cm (12 x 4in). Mark off three equal sections from top to bottom. Fold the bottom third up over the middle and the top third down. Press the edges with a rolling pin to seal. Wrap in clingfilm and chill for 30 minutes (or freeze for 5–10 minutes).

3 Repeat the rolling, folding, resting and turning five more times, ensuring the folded edges are to the sides. Chill for 30 minutes before baking.

Pasta

Basic Pasta Dough

· ·

You will need 225g (8oz) '00' pasta flour, plus extra to dust, 1 tsp salt, 2 medium eggs, plus 1 egg yolk, beaten, 1 tbsp extra virgin olive oil, 1–2 tbsp cold water.

Makes

1 Sift the flour and salt into a mound on a clean surface. Make a well in the centre and add the eggs, egg yolk, olive oil and 1 tbsp water.

2 Gently beat the eggs together with a fork, then gradually work in the flour, adding a little extra water if needed to form a soft but not sticky dough.

3 Transfer to a lightly floured surface and knead for about 5 minutes until firm, smooth and elastic.

4 Form the dough into a flattish ball, wrap in clingfilm and leave to rest for at least 30 minutes.

Note

To make pasta in a food processor, sift the flour and salt into the bowl and add the eggs, egg yolk, olive oil and 1 tbsp water (together with any flavourings). Whiz until the dough just begins to come together, adding the extra water if necessary to form a soft but not sticky dough. Wrap in clingfilm and rest (as above).

Variations

Flavoured pastas are easy to make. Vegetable purées and flavoured pastes, such as sun-dried tomato and olive, make vibrant coloured pastas – note that some of the colour will be lost during cooking, without detriment to the flavour.

Herb Pasta: Sift the flour and salt into the bowl and stir in 3 tbsp freshly chopped mixed herbs, such as basil, marjoram and parsley. Continue as for the basic pasta dough.

Olive Pasta: Beat the eggs with 2 tbsp black olive paste before adding to the flour. Reduce the water to about 2 tsp.

Sun-dried Tomato Pasta: Beat the eggs with 2 tbsp sun-dried tomato paste before adding to the flour. Reduce the water to about 2 tsp.

Spinach Pasta: Blanch 50g (2oz) spinach leaves in a little boiling water until just wilted. Refresh under cold running water, then drain thoroughly and squeeze out all excess water. Finely chop the spinach and add to the flour. Continue as for the basic pasta dough.

Sweet sauces

Butterscotch Sauce

You will need 50g (2oz) butter, 50g (2oz) golden caster sugar, 75g (3oz) light muscovado sugar, 150g (5oz) golden syrup, 125ml (4fl oz) double cream, a few drops vanilla extract, juice of ½ lemon.

Makes about 450ml (¾ pint)

1 Put the butter, sugars and syrup in a pan and heat gently, stirring, until melted. Cook for 5 minutes, then remove from the heat.

2 Stir in the cream, vanilla and lemon; stir over a low heat for 1–2 minutes. Serve warm or cold.

Chocolate Sauce

You will need 75g (3oz) good-quality dark chocolate, 140ml (4½fl oz) double cream.

Makes 225ml (8fl oz)

1 Put the chocolate in a small heatproof bowl over a pan of gently simmering water. Pour in the cream.

2 Leave the chocolate to stand over the heat for about 10 minutes until completely melted – don't stir while it is melting. Once melted, stir the chocolate and cream together until smooth, then serve immediately.

Apple Sauce

You will need 450g (1lb) cooking apples, such as Bramleys, 2 tbsp sugar, or to taste, 25g (1oz) butter.

Makes about 300g (11oz)

1 Peel, core and slice the apples and put into a pan with 2–3 tbsp water. Cover and cook gently for about 10 minutes, stirring occasionally, until soft and reduced to a pulp.

2 Beat with a wooden spoon until smooth, then pass through a sieve if a smooth sauce is preferred. Stir in sugar to taste, and the butter. Serve warm.

Fresh Vanilla Custard

You will need 600ml (1 pint) whole milk, 1 vanilla pod or 1 tsp vanilla extract, 6 large egg yolks, 2 tbsp golden caster sugar, 2 tbsp cornflour.

Makes 60ml (1 pint)

1 Pour the milk into a pan. Slit the vanilla pod lengthways and scrape out the seeds, adding them to the milk with the pod, or add the vanilla extract. Slowly bring to the boil. Turn off the heat immediately and set aside to infuse for 5 minutes.

2 Put the egg yolks, sugar and cornflour into a bowl and whisk together. Gradually whisk in the warm milk, leaving the vanilla pod behind if using.

3 Rinse the pan and pour the mixture back in. Heat gently, whisking or stirring constantly for 2–3 minutes until the custard thickens – it should just coat the back of a wooden spoon in a thin layer. Serve immediately or cover the surface closely with a round of wet greaseproof paper, then cover with clingfilm and chill until needed.

Caramel Sauce

You will need 50g (2oz) golden caster sugar, 150ml (¼ pint) double cream.

Makes 150ml (¼ pint)

1 Melt the sugar in a small heavy-based pan over a low heat until liquid and golden in colour. Increase the heat to medium and cook to a rich, dark caramel.

2 Immediately take off the heat and pour in the cream in a slow steady stream, taking care as the hot caramel will cause the cream to boil up in the pan.

3 Stir over a gentle heat until the caramel has melted and the sauce is smooth. Serve hot or cold.

Brandy Butter

You will need 150g (5oz) unsalted butter, at room temperature, 150g (5oz) golden icing sugar, sifted, 3 tbsp brandy.

Makes 300g (11oz)

1 Put the butter into a bowl and whisk to soften. Gradually whisk in the icing sugar, pouring in the brandy just before the final addition. Continue whisking until the mixture is pale and fluffy, then spoon into a serving dish.

2 Cover and chill until needed. Remove from the fridge 30 minutes before serving.

Crème Pâtissière

You will need 300ml (½ pint) milk, 1 vanilla pod, split, or 1 tsp vanilla extract, 3 egg yolks, beaten, 50g (2oz) golden caster sugar, 2 tbsp plain flour, 2 tbsp cornflour.

Makes 450ml (¾ pint)

1 Pour the milk into a heavy-based pan. Scrape the vanilla seeds into the milk and add the pod, or add the vanilla extract. Slowly bring to the boil, take off the heat and leave to infuse for 10 minutes. Discard pod.

2 Meanwhile, whisk the egg yolks and sugar together in a bowl until thick and creamy, then whisk in the flour and cornflour until smooth. Gradually whisk in the hot milk, then strain back into the pan.

3 Slowly bring to the boil, whisking constantly. Cook, stirring, for 2–3 minutes until thickened and smooth.

4 Pour into a bowl, cover the surface with a round of wet greaseproof paper and allow to cool. Use as a filling for fruit flans and other pastries.

Sabayon Sauce

You will need 75g (3oz) golden caster sugar, 3 egg yolks, 125ml (4fl oz) double cream, grated zest and juice of 1 lemon.

Makes 300ml (½ pint)

1 Put the sugar and 125ml (4fl oz) water into a small pan over a low heat until dissolved. Increase the heat to high and boil for 7–8 minutes or until the syrup registers 105°C on a sugar thermometer (and looks very syrupy, with large pea-size bubbles).

2 Meanwhile, whisk the egg yolks in a small bowl. Gradually pour on the hot syrup in a thin stream, whisking all the time. Continue to whisk until the mixture is thick, mousse-like and cool.

3 In a separate bowl, whisk the cream until it forms stiff peaks, then add the lemon zest and juice and whip again to soft peaks. Fold the citrus cream into the mousse mixture.

4 Cover and chill in the fridge until required. Whisk well before serving.

Basic breads

Brown Loaf

You will need 300g (11oz) strong plain white flour, sifted, plus extra to dust, 200g (7oz) strong plain wholemeal flour, 15g (½oz) fresh yeast, or 1 tsp ordinary dried yeast, 2 tsp salt, vegetable oil, to oil.

Makes 16 slices
Preparation: 25 minutes, plus sponging and rising
Cooking time: 45–50 minutes, plus cooling

1 Put both flours into a large bowl, make a well in the middle and pour in 325ml (11fl oz) tepid water. Crumble the fresh yeast into the water (if using dried yeast, just sprinkle it over). Draw a little of the flour into the water and yeast, and mix to form a batter. Sprinkle the salt over the remaining dry flour, so that it doesn't come into contact with the yeast. Cover with a clean tea-towel and leave to 'sponge' for 20 minutes.

2 Combine the flour and salt with the batter to make a soft dough and knead for at least 10 minutes until the dough feels smooth and elastic. Shape into a ball, put into an oiled bowl, cover with the tea-towel and leave to rise at warm room temperature until doubled in size, about 2–3 hours.

3 Knock back the dough, knead briefly and shape into a round on a lightly floured baking sheet. Slash the top with a sharp knife and dust with flour. Cover and leave to rise for 45 minutes–1½ hours or until doubled in size and spongy.

4 Bake at 200°C (180°C fan oven) mark 6 for 45–50 minutes or until the loaf sounds hollow when tapped underneath. Transfer to a wire rack and leave to cool.

White Farmhouse Loaf

You will need 575g (1¼lb) strong plain white flour, plus extra to dust, 125g (4oz) strong plain wholemeal flour, 1 tbsp salt, 1 tsp golden caster sugar, 1½ tsp fast-action dried yeast, 25g (1oz) butter, diced, vegetable oil, to oil.

Makes 16 slices
Preparation: 20 minutes, plus rising
Cooking time: 30–35 minutes, plus cooling

1 Sift the white flour into a large bowl and stir in the wholemeal flour, salt, sugar and yeast. Rub in the butter with your fingertips. Make a well in the middle and add about 450ml (¾ pint) warm water. Work to a smooth soft dough, adding a little extra water if necessary.

2 Knead for 10 minutes until smooth, then shape the dough into a ball and put into an oiled bowl. Cover and leave to rise in a warm place for 1–2 hours until doubled in size.

3 Knock back the dough on a lightly floured surface and shape into a large oval loaf. Transfer the dough to a floured baking sheet, cover loosely and leave to rise for a further 30 minutes.

4 Slash the top of the loaf with a sharp knife, dust with flour and bake at 230°C (210°C fan oven) mark 8 for 15 minutes. Lower the oven setting to 200°C (180°C fan oven) mark 6 and bake for a further 15–20 minutes or until the bread is risen and sounds hollow when tapped underneath. Cool on a wire rack.

Soda Bread

You will need 350g (12oz) plain wholemeal flour, 125g (4oz) coarse oatmeal, 2 tsp bicarbonate of soda, 1 tsp salt, 1 tsp thin honey, 300ml (½ pint) buttermilk, 2–3 tbsp milk, vegetable oil, to oil.

Makes 14 slices
Preparation: 15 minutes
Cooking time: 30–35 minutes, plus cooling

1 Combine the flour with the other dry ingredients in a large bowl. Make a well in the middle and gradually beat in the honey, buttermilk and enough milk to form a soft dough.

2 Knead for 5 minutes until smooth. Shape the dough into a 20cm (8in) round and put on a lightly oiled baking sheet.

3 Using a sharp knife, cut a deep cross on top of the dough. Brush with a little milk and bake at 200°C (180°C fan oven) mark 6 for 30–35 minutes until the bread is slightly risen and sounds hollow when tapped underneath. Cool on a wire rack; eat the same day.

Scones

You will need 225g (8oz) self-raising flour, plus extra to dust, pinch of salt, 1 tsp baking powder, 40g (1½oz) butter, diced, plus extra to grease, about 150ml (¼ pint) milk, beaten egg or milk, to glaze, whipped cream, or butter and jam, to serve.

Makes 8 scones
Preparation: 15 minutes
Cooking time: 10 minutes, plus cooling

1 Preheat the oven to 220°C (200°C fan oven) mark 7. Sift the flour, salt and baking powder together and rub in the butter until the mixture resembles fine breadcrumbs. Using a knife, stir in enough milk to give a fairly soft dough.

2 Gently roll or pat out the dough on a lightly floured surface to a 2cm (¾in) thickness and cut out rounds with a 6cm (2½in) plain cutter.

3 Put on a greased baking sheet and brush the tops with beaten egg or milk. Bake for about 10 minutes until golden brown and well risen. Transfer to a wire rack to cool.

4 Serve warm, split and filled with cream, or butter and jam.

Note
To ensure a good rise, avoid heavy handling, and make sure the rolled-out dough is at least 2cm (¾in) thick.

Variations
Wholemeal Scones: Replace half of the white flour with wholemeal flour.

Fruit Scones: Add 50g (2oz) currants, sultanas, raisins or chopped dates (or a mixture) to the dry ingredients.

Cheese and Herb Scones: Sift 1 tsp mustard powder with the dry ingredients. Stir 50g (2oz) finely grated Cheddar cheese into the mixture before adding the milk. After glazing, sprinkle the tops with a little cheese.

Basic cakes and biscuits

Basic Biscuits

The easiest way to make biscuits of consistent thickness is by rolling and then cutting using a biscuit cutter. The dough must be firm enough to roll to a thickness of 3mm (⅛in).

You will need 175g (6oz) unsalted butter, softened, 200g (7oz) golden caster sugar, 350g (12oz) plain flour, 1 medium egg, 2 tsp vanilla bean paste, 2 tbsp golden icing sugar.

Makes 48 biscuits
Preparation: 30 minutes, plus cooling
Cooking time: 12 minutes

1 Preheat the oven to 200°C (180°C fan oven) mark 6. Put the butter, caster sugar, flour, egg and vanilla bean paste into a food processor and whiz to combine. Alternatively, cream the butter and sugar, and then stir in the flour, egg and vanilla.

2 Put the dough on a large sheet of baking parchment. Press the dough gently but firmly with the palm of your hand to flatten it slightly, then put another sheet of baking parchment on top – this will prevent the dough from sticking.

3 Use a rolling pin to roll out the dough to 3mm (⅛in) thick, and then remove the top sheet of baking parchment.

4 Using 6.5cm (2½in) cutters, stamp out biscuits, leaving a 3mm (⅛in) gap between each one.

5 Peel off the trimmings around the shapes, then slide the baking parchment and biscuits on to a flat baking sheet.

6 Re-roll the trimmings between two new sheets of baking parchment, then stamp out shapes as before and slide on to another baking sheet.

7 Bake the biscuits for 10–12 minutes until pale golden. Cool for a few minutes, then transfer to a wire rack to cool completely.

8 Dust the biscuits with sifted icing sugar. Store in an airtight container for up to five days.

Victoria Sandwich Cake

You will need 175g (6oz) butter or margarine, softened, 175g (6oz) caster sugar, plus extra to dredge, 3 medium eggs, beaten, 175g (6oz) self-raising white flour, sifted, 3–4 tbsp jam.

Makes 8 slices
Preparation: 20 minutes, plus cooling
Cooking time: 20 minutes

1 Preheat the oven to 190°C (fan oven 170°C) mark 5. Grease and base line two 18cm (7in) sandwich tins. Beat the butter and sugar together in a bowl until pale and fluffy. Add the eggs, a little at a time, beating well after each addition. Fold in half the flour, using a large metal spoon or plastic-bladed spatula, then fold in the remainder.

2 Divide the mixture evenly between the tins and level the surface with a palette knife. Bake in the centre of the oven for about 20 minutes until well risen and the cakes spring back when lightly pressed in the centre. Loosen the edges of the cakes with a palette knife and leave in the tins for 5 minutes.

3 Turn out, remove the lining paper, invert and leave to cool on a wire rack. Sandwich the cakes together with jam and sprinkle the top with caster sugar.

Fruity Tea Cake

You will need 75g (3oz) dried figs, 75g (3oz) stoned prunes, 150ml (¼ pint) hot Earl Grey tea, 200g (7oz) sultanas, 150g (5oz) dark muscovado sugar, 2 medium eggs, 225g (8oz) self-raising flour, 2 tsp ground mixed spice, vegetable oil to grease.

Makes a 900g (2lb) loaf
Preparation: 30 minutes, plus soaking
Cooking time: 1 hour

1 Chop the figs and prunes, then soak in the tea with the sultanas for 30 minutes.

2 Preheat the oven to 190°C (fan oven 170°C) mark 5. Grease a 900g (2lb) loaf tin and line with greaseproof paper.

3 Beat the sugar and eggs until creamy, then mix in the flour, spice, soaked fruit and tea. Pour into the tin and bake for 1 hour or until a skewer inserted in the centre comes out clean. Cool on a wire rack. Serve sliced, with butter.

White Chocolate Cupcakes

You will need 125g (4oz) butter, softened, 125g (4oz) golden caster sugar, 2 medium eggs, 125g (4oz) self-raising flour, 1 tbsp vanilla extract, 200g (7oz) white chocolate, chopped.

Makes 12 cupcakes
Preparation: 25 minutes
Cooking time: 15–20 minutes

1 Preheat the oven to 190°C (170°C fan oven) mark 5. Line a bun tin or muffin pan with 12 paper cases.

2 Beat the butter, sugar, eggs, flour and vanilla until smooth and creamy. Half-fill the paper cases with the mixture and bake for 15–20 minutes until pale golden, risen and springy to the touch. Transfer to a wire rack to cool.

3 When the cupcakes are cool, melt the chocolate in a heatproof bowl over a pan of gently simmering water. Stir until smooth and leave to cool slightly. Spoon over the cakes and leave to set.

Ultimate Chocolate Brownies

You will need 400g (14oz) plain chocolate with 70% cocoa solids, 200g (7oz) unsalted butter, plus extra to grease, 225g (8oz) light muscovado sugar, 1 tsp vanilla extract, 150g (5oz) pecan nuts, chopped, 25g (1oz) cocoa powder, sifted, plus extra to dust, 75g (3oz) self-raising flour, sifted, 3 large eggs, beaten, ice cream, to serve, optional.

Makes 16 brownies
Preparation: 15 minutes, plus 2 hours cooling
Cooking time: 1 hour 15 minutes

1 Preheat the oven to 170°C (150°C fan oven) mark 3. Grease and base line (use non-stick baking parchment) a 20cm (8in) square, 5cm (2in) deep cake tin. Put the chocolate and butter in a heatproof bowl over a pan of simmering water and stir until melted. Remove from the heat and stir in the sugar, vanilla, pecans, cocoa, flour and eggs.

2 Turn the mixture into the tin and level with the back of a spoon. Bake for about 1 hour 15 minutes or until the centre is set on the surface, but still soft underneath.

3 Leave to cool in the tin for 2 hours. Turn out, dust with cocoa and cut into squares. Serve cold or warm with ice cream.

Pancakes

Plain Pancakes

You will need 125g (4oz) plain flour, pinch of salt, 1 medium egg, 300ml (½ pint) milk, oil and butter to fry.

Makes 8 pancakes
Preparation: 10 minutes, plus standing
Cooking time: about 15 minutes

1 Sift the flour and salt into a bowl, make a well in the middle and whisk in the egg. Work in the milk, then leave to stand for 20 minutes. Heat a frying pan and coat lightly with fat. Coat thinly with batter.

2 Cook for 1½–2 minutes until golden, carefully turning once.

Variations
Buckwheat Crêpes: Replace half of the white flour with buckwheat flour and add an extra egg white.

Orange, Lemon or Lime Crêpes: Add the finely grated zest of 1 lemon, half an orange or 1 lime, with the milk.

Chocolate Crêpes: Replace 15g (½oz) of the flour with sifted cocoa powder.

Drop Scones (Scotch Pancakes)

You will need 125g (4oz) self-raising flour, 2 tbsp caster sugar, 1 medium egg, beaten, 150ml (¼ pint) milk, vegetable oil, to oil, butter, or whipped cream and jam, to serve.

Makes 15–18 pancakes
Preparation: 10 minutes
Cooking time: 12–18 minutes

1 Mix the flour and sugar together in a bowl, make a well in the middle and mix in the egg, with enough milk to make a batter the consistency of thick cream. Heat a heavy frying pan and coat lightly with fat.

2 Drop spoonfuls of batter on to the pan and when bubbles rise to the surface, after 2–3 minutes, turn carefully.

3 Cook for a further 2–3 minutes until golden brown on the other side. Serve warm, with butter or whipped cream and jam.

Fruit sizes

The size of an average kumquat is 5cm (2in) long and 3cm (1¼in) wide.
The size of an average watermelon is 35cm (14in) across.

Kumquat   Longan   Lychee   Japonica   Date   Greengage

Rambutan   Peach   Custard apple   Citron   Ugli Fruit

Grapefruit   Star Fruit   Mango   Dragon Fruit

Pineapple   Ogen   Piel de sapo

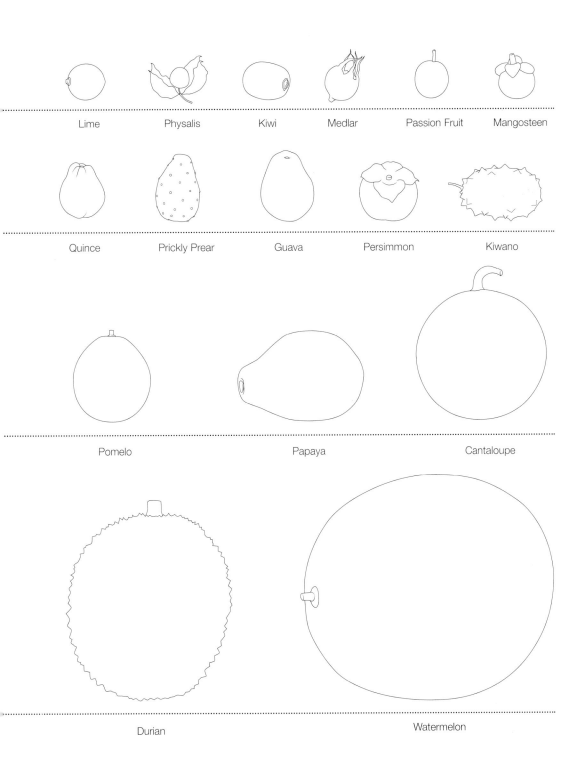

Lime   Physalis   Kiwi   Medlar   Passion Fruit   Mangosteen

Quince   Prickly Prear   Guava   Persimmon   Kiwano

Pomelo   Papaya   Cantaloupe

Durian   Watermelon

Vegetable sizes

The size of an average pattypan squash is 6–8cm (2–3in) across.
The size of an average cardoon is 50cm (20in) in length.

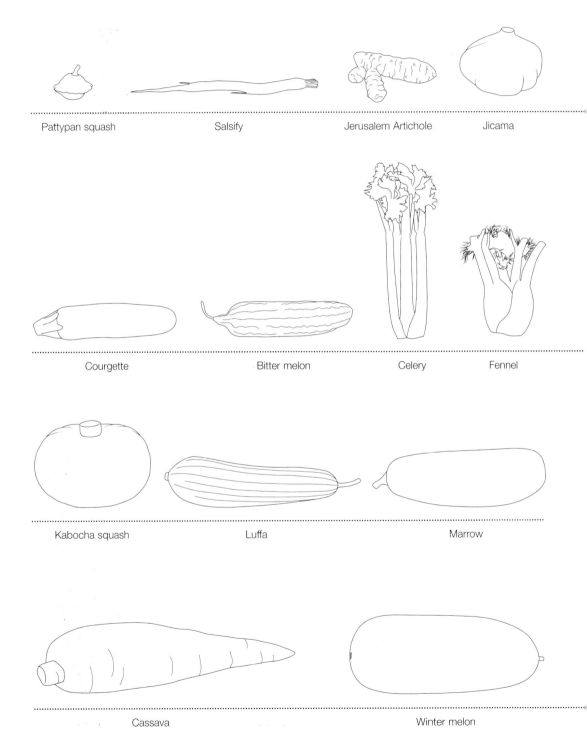

Pattypan squash   Salsify   Jerusalem Artichole   Jicama

Courgette   Bitter melon   Celery   Fennel

Kabocha squash   Luffa   Marrow

Cassava   Winter melon

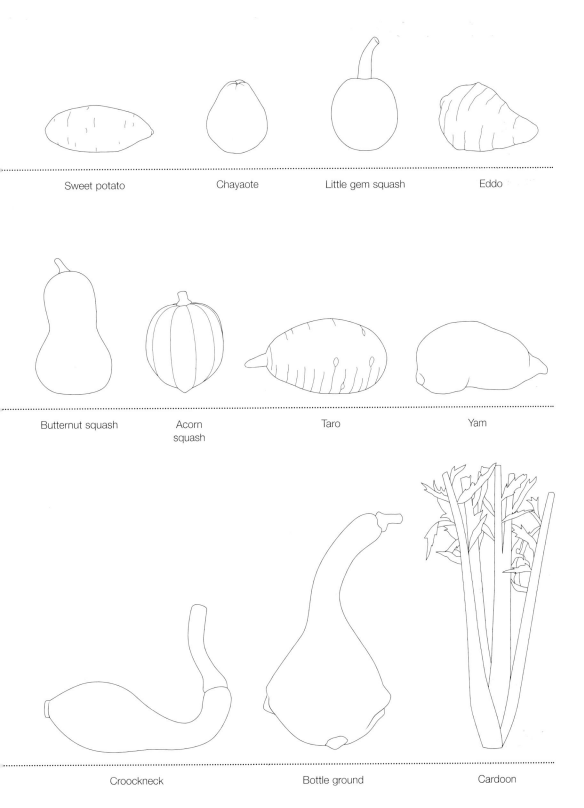

Sweet potato

Chayaote

Little gem squash

Eddo

Butternut squash

Acorn
squash

Taro

Yam

Croockneck

Bottle ground

Cardoon

Glossary

Acidulated water Water to which lemon juice or vinegar has been added in which fruit or vegetables, such as pears or Jerusalem artichokes, are immersed to prevent discolouration.

Al dente Italian term commonly used to describe food, especially pasta and vegetables, which are cooked until tender but still firm to the bite.

Antipasto Italian selection of cold meats, fish, salads etc., served as a starter.

Au gratin Describes a dish that has been coated with sauce, sprinkled with breadcrumbs or cheese and browned under the grill or in the oven. Low-sided gratin dishes are used.

Bain-marie Literally, a water bath, used to keep foods, such as delicate custards and sauces, at a constant low temperature during cooking. On the hob a double saucepan or bowl over a pan of simmering water is used; for oven cooking, the baking dish(es) is placed in a roasting tin containing enough hot water to come halfway up the sides.

Baking blind Pre-baking a pastry case before filling. The pastry case is lined with greaseproof paper and weighted down with dried beans or ceramic baking beans.

Baking powder A raising agent consisting of an acid, usually cream of tartar and an alkali, such as bicarbonate of soda, which react to produce carbon dioxide. This expands during baking and makes cakes and breads rise.

Bard To cover the breast of game birds or poultry, or lean meat with fat to prevent the meat from drying out during roasting.

Baste To spoon the juices and melted fat over meat, poultry, game or vegetables during roasting to keep them moist. The term is also used to describe spooning over a marinade.

Beat To incorporate air into an ingredient or mixture by agitating it vigorously with a spoon, fork, whisk or electric mixer. The technique is also used to soften ingredients.

Béchamel Classic French white sauce, used as the basis for other sauces and savoury dishes.

Beurre manié Equal parts of flour and butter kneaded together to make a paste. Used to thicken soups, stews and casseroles. It is whisked into the hot liquid a little at a time at the end of cooking.

Bind To mix beaten egg or other liquid into a dry mixture to hold it together.

Blanch To immerse food briefly in fast-boiling water to loosen skins, such as peaches or tomatoes, or to remove bitterness, or to destroy enzymes and preserve the colour, flavour and texture of vegetables (especially prior to freezing).

Bone To remove the bones from meat, poultry, game or fish, so that it can be stuffed or simply rolled before cooking.

Bottle To preserve fruit, jams, pickles or other preserves in sterile glass jars.

Bouquet garni Small bunch of herbs – usually a mixture of parsley stems, thyme and a bay leaf – tied in muslin and used to flavour stocks, soups and stews.

Braise To cook meat, poultry, game or vegetables slowly in a small amount of liquid in a pan or casserole with a tight-fitting lid. The food is usually first browned in oil or fat.

Brochette Food cooked on a skewer.

Brûlée A French term, literally meaning 'burnt' used to refer to a dish with a crisp coating of caramelised sugar.

Butterfly To split a food, such as a large prawn or poussin, almost in half and open out flat, so that it will cook more quickly.

Calorie Strictly a kilocalorie, this is used in dietetics to measure the energy value of foods.

Canapé Small appetiser, served with drinks.

Candying Method of preserving fruit or peel by impregnating with sugar.

Caramelise To heat sugar or sugar syrup slowly until it is brown in colour; ie forms a caramel.

Carbonade Rich stew or braise of meat, which includes beer.

Casserole A dish with a tight-fitting lid used for slow-cooking meat, poultry and vegetables, now used to describe food cooked in this way.

Charcuterie French term for cooked pork products, including hams, sausages and terrines.

Chill To cool food in the fridge.

Chine To sever the rib bones from the backbone, close to the spine. This is done to meat joints, such as loin of pork or lamb, to make them easier to carve into chops after cooking.

Clarify To remove sediment or impurities from a liquid. Stock is clarified by heating with egg white, while butter is clarified by melting and skimming. Butter that has been clarified will withstand a higher frying temperature.
To clarify butter heat until melted and all bubbling stops. Take off the heat and let stand until the sediment has sunk to the bottom, then gently pour off the fat, straining it through muslin to remove sediment.

Compote Fresh or dried fruit stewed in sugar syrup. Served hot or cold.

Concassé Diced fresh ingredient,

used as a garnish. The term is most often applied to skinned, deseeded tomatoes.

Coulis A smooth fruit or vegetable purée, thinned if necessary to a pouring consistency.

Court bouillon Aromatic cooking liquid containing wine, vinegar or lemon juice, used for poaching delicate fish, poultry or vegetables.

Consistency Term used to describe the texture of a mixture, eg firm, dropping or soft.

Cream To beat together fat and sugar until the mixture is pale and fluffy, and resembles whipped cream in texture and colour. The method is used in cakes and puddings which contain a high proportion of fat and require the incorporation of a lot of air.

Crêpe French term for a pancake.

Crimp To decorate the edge of a pie, tart or shortbread by pinching it at regular intervals to give a fluted effect.

Croquette Seasoned mixture of cooked potato and fish, meat, poultry or vegetables shaped into a small roll, coated with egg and breadcrumbs and shallow-fried.

Croûte Circle or other shaped piece of fried bread, typically used as a base for serving small game birds.

Croûtons Small pieces of fried or toasted bread, served with soups and salads.

Crudités Raw vegetables, usually cut into slices or sticks, typically served with a dipping sauce as an appetiser.

Crystallise To preserve fruit in sugar syrup.

Curdle To cause sauces or creamed mixtures to separate once the egg is added, usually by overheating or over-beating.

Cure To preserve fish, meat or poultry by smoking, drying or salting.

Daube Braising meat and vegetables with stock, often with wine and herbs added.

Deglaze To heat stock, wine or other liquid with the cooking juices left in the pan after roasting or sautéeing, scraping and stirring vigorously to dissolve the sediment on the bottom of the pan.

Dégorge To draw out moisture from a food, eg salting aubergines to remove bitter juices.

Dice To cut food into small cubes.

Draw To remove the entrails from poultry or game.

Dredge To sprinkle food generously with flour, sugar, icing sugar etc.

Dress To pluck, draw and truss poultry or game. The term is also used to describe tossing a salad in vinaigrette or other dressing.

Dry To preserve food, such as fruit, pasta and pulses by dehydration.

Dust To sprinkle lightly with flour, cornflour, icing sugar etc.

Emulsion A mixture of two liquids, which do not dissolve into one another, such as oil and vinegar. Vigorous shaking or heating will emulsify them, as for a vinaigrette.

En croûte Term used to describe food that is wrapped in pastry before cooking.

En papillote Term used to describe food that is baked in a greaseproof paper or baking parchment parcel and served from the paper.

Enzyme Organic substance in food that causes chemical changes. Enzymes are a complex group. Their action is usually halted during cooking.

Escalope Thin slice of meat, such as pork, veal or turkey, from the top of the leg, usually pan-fried.

Extract Concentrated flavouring, which is used in small quantities, eg yeast extract, vanilla extract.

Ferment Chemical change deliberately or accidentally brought about by fermenting agents, such as yeast or bacteria. Fermentation is utilised for making bread, yogurt, beer and wine.

Fillet Term used to describe boned breasts of birds, boned sides of fish, and the undercut of a loin of beef, lamb, pork or veal.

Flake To separate food, such as cooked fish, into natural pieces.

Flambé Flavouring a dish with alcohol, usually brandy or rum, which is then ignited so that the actual alcohol content is burned off.

Folding in Method of combining a whisked or creamed mixture with other ingredients by cutting and folding so that it retains its lightness. A large metal spoon or plastic-bladed spatula is used.

Frosting To coat leaves and flowers with a fine layer of sugar to use as a decoration. Also an American term for icing cakes.

Fry To cook food in hot fat or oil. There are various methods: shallow-frying in a little fat in a shallow pan; deep-frying where the food is totally immersed in oil; dry-frying in which fatty foods are cooked in a non-stick pan without extra fat; see also Stir-frying.

Galette Cooked savoury or sweet mixture shaped into a round.

Garnish A decoration, usually edible, such as parsley or lemon, which is used to enhance the appearance of a savoury dish.

Glaze A glossy coating given to sweet and savoury dishes to improve their appearance and sometimes flavour. Ingredients for glazes include beaten egg, egg white, milk and syrup.

Gluten A protein constituent of grains, such as wheat and rye, which develops when the flour is missed with water to give the dough elasticity.

Grate To shred hard food, such as cheese and carrots, with a grater or food processor attachment.

Griddle A flat, heavy, metal plate used on the hob for cooking scones or for searing savoury ingredients.

Grind To reduce foods such as coffee beans, nuts and whole spices to small particles using a food mill, pestle and mortar, electric grinder or food processor.

Gut To clean out the entrails from fish.

Hang To suspend meat or game in a cool, dry place for a number of days to tenderise the flesh and develop flavour.

Hull To remove the stalk and calyx from soft fruits, such as strawberries.

Infuse To immerse flavourings, such as aromatic vegetables, herbs, spices and vanilla, in a liquid to impart flavour. Usually the infused liquid is brought to the boil, then left to stand for a while.

Julienne Fine 'matchstick' strips of vegetables or citrus zest, sometimes used as a garnish.

Knead To work dough by pummelling with the heel of the hand.

Knock back To knead a yeast dough for a second time after rising, to ensure an even texture.

Lard To insert small strips of fat or streaky bacon into the flesh of game birds and dry meat before cooking. A special larding needle is used.

Liaison A thickening or binding agent based on a combination of ingredients, such as flour and water, or oil and egg.

Macerate To soften and flavour raw or dried foods by soaking in a liquid, eg soaking fruit in alcohol.

Mandolin A flat wooden or metal frame with adjustable cutting blades for slicing vegetables.

Marinate To soak raw meat, poultry or game – usually in a mixture of oil, wine, vinegar and

flavourings – to soften and impart flavour. The mixture, which is known as a marinade, may also be used to baste the food during cooking.

Medallion Small round piece of meat, usually beef or veal.

Mince To cut food into very fine pieces, using a mincer, food processor or knife.

Mocha Term which has come to mean a blend of chocolate and coffee.

Parboil To boil a vegetable or other food for part of its cooking time before finishing it by another method.

Pare To finely peel the skin or zest from vegetables or fruit.

Pâté A savoury mixture of finely chopped or minced meat, fish and/or vegetables, usually served as a starter with bread or toast.

Patty tin Tray of cup-shaped moulds for cooking small cakes and deep tartlets. Also called a bun tin.

Pectin A naturally occurring substance found in most varieties of fruit and some vegetables, which is necessary for setting jams and jellies. Commercial pectin and sugar with pectin are also available for preserve-making.

Pickle To preserve meat or vegetables in brine or vinegar.

Pith The bitter white skin under the thin zest of citrus fruit.

Pluck To remove the feathers from poultry and game birds.

Poach To cook food gently in liquid at simmering point; the surface should be just trembling.

Pot roast To cook meat in a covered pan with some fat and a little liquid.

Prove To leave bread dough to rise (usually for a second time) after shaping.

Purée To pound, sieve or liquidise vegetables, fish or fruit to a smooth pulp. Purées often form the basis for soups and sauces.

Reduce To fast-boil stock or other liquid in an uncovered pan to evaporate water and concentrate the flavour.

Refresh To cool hot vegetables very quickly by plunging into ice-cold water or holding under cold running water in order to stop the cooking process and preserve the colour.

Render To melt fat slowly to a liquid, either by heating meat trimmings, or to release the fat from fatty meat, such as duck or goose, during roasting.

Rennet An animal-derived enzyme used to coagulate milk in cheese-making. A vegetarian alternative is available.

Roast To cook meat by dry heat in the oven.

Roulade Soufflé or sponge mixture rolled around a savoury or sweet filling.

Roux A mixture of equal quantities of butter (or other fat) and flour cooked together to form the basis of many sauces.

Rub-in Method of incorporating fat into flour by rubbing between the fingertips, used when a short texture is required. Used for pastry, cakes, scones and biscuits.

Salsa Piquant sauce made from chopped fresh vegetables and sometimes fruit.

Sauté To cook food in a small quantity of fat over a high heat, shaking the pan constantly – usually in a sauté pan (a frying pan with straight sides and a wide base).

Scald To pour boiling water over food to clean it, or loosen skin, eg tomatoes. Also used to describe heating milk to just below boiling point.

Score To cut parallel lines in the surface of food, such as fish (or the fat layer on meat), to improve its appearance or help it cook more quickly.

Sear To brown meat quickly in a little hot fat before grilling or roasting.

Seasoned flour Flour mixed with a little salt and pepper, used for dusting meat, fish etc., before frying.

Shred To grate cheese or slice vegetables into very fine pieces or strips.

Sieve To press food through a perforated sieve to obtain a smooth texture.

Sift To shake dry ingredients through a sieve to remove lumps.

Simmer To keep a liquid just below boiling point.

Skim To remove froth, scum or fat from the surface of stock, gravy, stews, jam etc. Use either a skimmer, a spoon or kitchen paper.

Smoke To cure meat, poultry and fish by exposure to wood smoke.

Souse To pickle food, especially fish, in vinegar flavoured with spices.

Steam To cook food in steam, usually in a steamer over rapidly boiling water.

Steep To immerse food in warm or cold liquid to soften it, and sometimes to draw out strong flavours.

Sterilise To destroy bacteria in foods by heating.

Stew To cook food, such as tougher cuts of meat, in flavoured liquid which is kept at simmering point.

Stir-fry To cook small even-sized pieces of food rapidly in a little fat, tossing constantly over a high heat, usually in a wok.

Suet Hard fat of animal origin used in pastry and steamed puddings. A vegetarian alternative is readily available.

Sugar syrup A concentrated solution of sugar in water used to poach fruit and make sorbets, granitas, fruit juices etc.

Sweat To cook chopped or sliced vegetables in a little fat without liquid in a covered pan over a low heat to soften.

Tepid The term used to describe temperature at approximately blood heat, ie 37°C (98.7°F).

Thermometer, Sugar/Fat Used for accurately checking the temperature of boiling sugar syrups, and fat for deep-frying respectively. Dual purpose thermometers are obtainable.

Truss To tie or skewer poultry or game into shape prior to roasting.

Unleavened Flat bread, such as pitta, made without a raising agent.

Vanilla sugar Sugar in which a vanilla pod has been stored to impart its flavour.

Whipping (whisking) Beating air rapidly into a mixture either with a manual or electric whisk. Whipping usually refers to cream.

Zest The thin coloured outer layer of citrus fruit, which can be removed in fine strips with a zester.

Conversion chart

Temperature

°C	Fan oven	Gas mark		°C	Fan oven	Gas mark
110	90	1/4		190	170	5
130	110	1/2		200	180	6
140	120	1		220	200	7
150	130	2		230	210	8
170	150	3		240	220	9
180	160	4				

Liquids

Metric	Imperial		Metric	Imperial
5ml	1tsp		200ml	7fl oz
15ml	1tbsp		250ml	9fl oz
25ml	1fl oz		300ml	1/2 pint
50ml	2fl oz		500ml	18fl oz
100ml	3 1/2 fl oz		600ml	1 pint
125ml	4fl oz		900ml	1 1/2 pints
150ml	5fl oz/1/4 pint		1 litre	1 3/4 pints
175ml	6fl oz			

Measures

Metric	Imperial		Metric	Imperial
5mm	1/4in		10cm	4in
1cm	1/2in		15cm	6in
2cm	3/4in		18cm	7in
2.5cm	1in		20.5cm	8in
3cm	1 1/4in		23cm	9in
4cm	1 1/2in		25.5cm	10in
5cm	2in		28cm	11in
7.5cm	3in		30.5cm	12in

Weights

Metric	Imperial		Metric	Imperial
15g	1/2oz		275g	10oz
25g	1oz		300g	11oz
40g	1 1/2oz		350g	12oz
50g	2oz		375g	13oz
75g	3oz		400g	14oz
100g	3 1/2oz		425g	15oz
125g	4oz		450g	1lb
150g	5oz		550g	1 1/4lb
175g	6oz		700g	1 1/2lb
200g	7oz		900g	2lb
225g	8oz		1.1kg	2 1/2lb
250g	9oz			

Always remember...

- Ovens and grills must be preheated to the specified temperature.
- For fan ovens the temperature should be set to 20°C less.
- Use one set of measurements; do not mix metric and imperial.
- All spoon measures are level.

Index